D1708125

The Illustrated Encyclopedia of British Willow Ware

Connie Rogers

4880 Lower Valley Road, Atglen, PA 19310 USA

Dedication

To my husband Don, who has always encouraged me to pursue my
interests and be my own person.

Library of Congress Cataloging-in-Publication Data

Rogers, Connie.
   Illustrated encyclopedia of British Willow ware / by Connie Rogers.
      p. cm.
   ISBN 0-7643-1932-9
1. Willowware--Collectors and collecting--Great Britain--Catalogs.
2. Pottery--Marks--Catalogs. I. Title.
NK4277 .R64 2004
738.3'7--dc22

2003016032

Copyright © 2004 by Connie Rogers

Designed by Mark David Bowyer
Type set in University Roman Bd BT/Korinna BT/Humanist521 BT

ISBN: 0-7643-1932-9
Printed in China
1 2 3 4

Published by Schiffer Publishing Ltd.
4880 Lower Valley Road
Atglen, PA 19310
Phone: (610) 593-1777; Fax: (610) 593-2002
E-mail: Info@schifferbooks.com
Please visit our web site catalog at **www.schifferbooks.com**
We are always looking for people to write books on new and related
subjects. If you have an idea for a book please contact us at the
above address.

This book may be purchased from the publisher.
Include $3.95 for shipping.
Please try your bookstore first.
You may write for a free catalog.

In Europe, Schiffer books are distributed by
Bushwood Books
6 Marksbury Ave.
Kew Gardens
Surrey TW9 4JF England
Phone: 44 (0)20-8392-8585
Fax: 44 (0)20-8392-9876
E-mail: Bushwd@aol.com
Free postage in the UK. Europe: air mail at cost

Contents

Acknowledgments

First and foremost I want to thank Robert Copeland. His book *Spode's Willow Pattern and other designs after the Chinese* was first published in 1980. It provided the motivation and direction for me to study the willow pattern in earnest. He spoke at the Cincinnati Art Museum in 1984, and I was the most enthusiastic listener in his audience. I first met him at Keele University in Staffordshire in 1990 and have benefited from his expertise since that time. He was a speaker at the International Willow Collectors Convention in Dayton, Ohio, in 1995, and in Richmond, Virginia, in 1999. His friendship over the years has given me encouragement and joy.

Since 1983 Geoffrey Godden has responded to my questions regarding marks I have found on willow. His responses (always by return mail) have not only identified many of the potters using the marks I sent, but he has added other bits of information to guide me. Often his last line is "Sorry to be unhelpful." I think that is a testament to his desire to be helpful to those of us studying British ceramics. He encourages people to write about the subjects they are interested in, thereby learning more.

I am indebted to all those who sent pictures of willow in their collections to be used in this book. Collectors from Australia, Canada, and England have provided photos as well as people from all over the USA. Their names appear in the photo captions. Most of all I want to thank my son, Scot, who took the majority of the pictures. He has been photographing willow pieces at the IWC Conventions for at least twelve years, and he has traveled with me to visit collectors to photograph their willow – to say nothing about his many trips to my house to photograph my collection. Scot and his wife, Nancee, did the proof reading of the text and offered helpful suggestions.

I want to thank Peter Tipthorp, Editor-in-Chief, Tableware International, for permission to use material from *Pottery Gazette* and *Tableware International*. The ads and "Buyer's Notes" provide helpful dating as well as other pertinent information regarding willow pattern production in Britain. My sincere appreciation goes to Wendy Cook, Curator of the Museum of Worcester Porcelain for allowing me to study pattern books of Royal Worcester and Grainger & Co. Others who have given extraordinary help and/or encouragement (in alphabetical order): Dale S. Brouse, Renard Broughton, Frank Davenport, William and Rosemary Dorling at Burgess, Dorling & Leigh, Audrey Dudson, Kay Goodsell at British Ceramic Manufacturers Federation, Stoke-on-Trent, Rodney and Eileen Hampson, the late Margaret Ironside, Kay Kays at the National Museum & Gallery, Cardiff, Henry Kelly, Arnold Kowalsky, Douglas Leishman, Julie McKeown, Carolyn Poole for information on Arklow, Geoffrey Priestman, Andrew Pye, David Quintner, and Jeffrey B. Snyder, my editor at Schiffer Publishing Ltd.

Thank you all for participating in this incredible experience with me!

Connie Rogers, March 2003

Foreword

Much has been written about The Willow Pattern, and, inevitably, much of it is nonsense. The name of the pattern has become synonymous with many blue and white patterns. A visitor to the Spode Showroom in the 1960s, on seeing the Blue Italian pattern on display, remarked to me: "Oh! I see you still make the Willow Pattern!" In September 1817, Josiah Bateman, chief traveler of Wedgwood, commented "all printed China in blue is the same pattern...." And a typical order to the Wedgwood manufactory in June 1824 stated, "It must be blue willow in any pattern."

So, Connie Rogers has attempted, and I believe, succeeded in placing before collectors the most comprehensive catalog of "Willow" patterns ever attempted. Her chapter "The Origin of the Willow Pattern" tries to sort out fact from legend and myth. There may be some who still hold to the belief that Caughley was the first manufactory to produce the Willow Pattern; "It must be so! I've seen it in print!" Connie, and others, have also stated clearly that Caughley did **not** produce THE (standard) Willow Pattern. And this is in print also!

For the large number of eager collectors of The Willow Pattern and other designs after the Chinese, Connie has produced a truly remarkable work, aided by her son, Scot, who has photographed most of the examples. The multitude of examples with the marks (backstamps) provide a most wonderful check-up directory of attributable specimens.

In any "comprehensive" work, as soon as published, more unrecorded examples come to be noticed. This is the great value of such a work as this. May it lead to another, enlarged, edition in the years to come.

Robert Copeland

Introduction

Infinite Variations on a Theme

Being a musician, I feel that this is a fitting subtitle to the book. The Theme and Variations is one of the most popular forms in music, and the willow pattern certainly fits into that format. What other china pattern has inspired so many manufacturers to produce it in variations ranging from ever so slight alterations in blue to widely inventive adaptations in every color combination in the spectrum? I hope you will hear the music in the background as you go through this book. The classical music radio station and CD's have been playing in the room where it was written.

This encyclopedia is offered as a tribute to the hundreds of British potteries that produced the willow pattern. Some of these were part-time potters who built a small pot-work on the farm with a beehive kiln. Others built small potteries or pot-banks with one or two kilns that grew and developed into larger concerns. Many of the partnerships in the nineteenth century changed often as fortunes waxed and waned. The willow pattern may have been one of the very few patterns produced by the small potteries, or it may have been a last-ditch effort to increase sales in a failing business by offering a perennial favorite. Major factories such as Spode and Minton developed the willow pattern and continued to produce it off and on for over 200 years, making some very beautiful wares in pearlware, earthenware, and bone china as well as other bodies developed.

Over 1, 000 color photos are presented to illustrate the wide range of willow pattern produced since c.1790. Close to 1, 000 marks are shown that have been found on the backs of wares decorated with the Standard Willow pattern and its major variants. A separate section has been put together featuring retailers/importers given in alphabetical order. The third major section of the book consists of unattributed wares, illustrating the mark as well as the willow decorated piece on which it was found.

My sources for information for this book include the extensive Bibliography of books and articles; the *Pottery Gazettes,* the people listed in the Acknowledgments, and picture captions; and the wares themselves.

How to Use this Book

In addition to the three main sections of the book described above, the following information can be found in this book:

Origin of the Willow Pattern
New insights into the development of this pattern.

What is Willow?
This chapter gives definitions, descriptions, background information, and illustrations of the twelve main Willow Patterns covered in this encyclopedia.

Table of Manufacturers and Willow Patterns
This table lists all potteries discussed in the book with an overview of the colors and patterns produced. If a pottery or partnership is not listed there, willow from that firm is not illustrated in the book.

Pattern Names for Willow Patterns
This table lists the various names used by the different companies to describe the major Willow Pattern variants. It also gives the source of the name, whether it is the mark, a pattern book, or published information.

Glossary
Terms used in the text are defined and explained in this section.

Appendices
A Shape Index helps locate teapots or bowls if you are interested in seeing examples of specific shapes.

An alphabetical list of retailers/importers illustrated in the book.

An Initial Index is provided as an aid to finding the appropriate pottery in the book when the mark on the piece has only initials, and not a maker's name.

A Word About Marks
Geoffrey Godden has given his kind permission for me to use the numbers he has assigned to marks in his book: *Encyclopaedia of British Pottery and Porcelain Marks.* These numbers will appear as (GG1). In Godden's book the (GG) mark will often consist of initials only with the accompanying statement: "Distinguishing initials found on several printed marks of differing design: name of the individual pattern is often included." One of the purposes of this book is to provide a reference for many of those printed marks that have been found on willow. At times the dates I have given opposite one of Godden's numbered marks will differ from those in his book. This difference reflects new information that he has printed in one of his more recent books such as *Collecting Lustreware, Encyclopaedia of British Porcelain Manufacturers,* or *Godden's Guide to Ironstone.* Other specialist books may also have more current information regarding dating of marks. I only regret that *Staffordshire Potters 1781-1900,* by R. K. Henrywood, Antique Collector's Club, 2003, was not yet in print when I completed my manuscript. He has contributed much information regarding smaller potteries, in particular, through material gleaned from local directories that was not available previously. However, the reader may be able to supplement information in this work by consulting his.

Asterisk
An * after the name of a firm indicates that an entry on that firm is in the book and can be consulted for further information.

The Origin of
the Willow Pattern

The date 1780, Thomas Turner, and the origin of the willow pattern have been unquestionably linked since 1878 when Jewitt published *The Ceramic Art of Great Britain*. Geoffrey Godden, in *Caughley and Worcester Porcelains 1775-1800*, quotes Jewitt who wrote: "In 1780 Mr. Turner introduced the making of the famous 'Willow Pattern' – the first made in England – at Caughley...." Godden discusses this quote in his Appendix II titled "SOME POPULAR MYTHS." It seems that most any reference book on English ceramics will attribute the origin of the willow pattern to Thomas Turner at Caughley.

It became apparent to me how widespread the acceptance of Jewitt's words have become on my first trip to Stoke-on-Trent in the summer of 1990. At that time, there was a "China Service" coach that carried passengers from one pottery to another. A large blue and white version of the willow pattern decorated the timetable and the coach itself. Various elements of the willow pattern were changed appropriate to the Potteries. A bottle kiln replaced the teahouse, and a narrow boat used on the canals replaced the boat. See the entry for Gladstone Pottery for the complete scene.

While riding the China Service coach between the potteries I could not help but listen to the radio which was playing quite loudly. The DJ had some free tickets to give away to the first person calling in with the correct year that the following events had in common:

1) Haydn wrote his symphony in C Major
2) Thomas Turner introduced the willow design
3) Robert Rakes established the first Sunday School
4) The circular saw was invented.
5) The Derby was first run.

A recording of "New Kids on the Block" played while the DJ waited for phone calls to come in. Then the free tickets were given away. The correct year? *1780*, of course!

I appreciate the research of Geoffrey Godden on Caughley, Robert Copeland on Spode, and Geoffrey Priestman on Minton who have put together overwhelming evidence that Thomas Turner did NOT produce the Standard Willow pattern at Caughley. The term "willow" used by Jewitt could have referred to either the Broseley or Mandarin pattern, both of which were introduced at Caughley. Both patterns were based on Chinese originals and were certainly engraved by Thomas Minton. Most Chinoiserie patterns were based on a Chinese original; however, this is the point at which the Willow pattern differs from other English Chinoiserie patterns. There is no one Chinese original from which Standard Willow was copied. Mandarin (also called Willow-Nankin) has many of the elements and a similar overall placement. However, there are many elements in Standard Willow that are not found in Mandarin. How the more complex Standard Willow pattern evolved from the simpler Mandarin pattern is a question that has generated many theories.

Geoffrey Godden gives us food for thought when he says,

The traditional Willow pattern design ... was probably introduced by the Staffordshire potters early in the nineteenth century for the decoration of their earthenwares, which must have under-sold the Caughley porcelains. Perhaps the design was indeed first engraved by Thomas Minton, who is said to have been trained as an engraver at Caughley before he established his own engraving business, and later his own pottery. Minton may well have amended standard Caughley designs or taken parts from several to make a whole new pattern.[1]

Standard Willow pattern 9.5-inch plate transfer-printed in medium blue underglaze on lightweight pearlware. The edge of the rim is indented to make an octagonal shape. There is no foot ring. It is unmarked; however, it may possibly be early Minton. *Author's Collection.* $75-150.

There are actually three important points here: 1) Standard Willow was made on earthenware from the very beginning. It was a pattern used on dinnerware for people who wanted blue and white Oriental-style patterns but could not afford porcelain. (In fact I have not seen any Willow pattern that was made on bone china until the 1870s when it was introduced by Minton, Spode and Wedgwood.) 2) Thomas Minton may, in fact, have been involved in designing the pattern. 3) There was probably more than one Chinese original used to design the Standard Willow pattern.

Robert Copeland writes,

This design was developed by Josiah Spode from an original Chinese pattern, called Mandarin. There is an earlier and more faithful version by Caughley, which Geoffrey Godden calls Willow-Nankin. He stresses, however, that Caughley never made the standard Willow pattern. Certainly Josiah Spode I was the first potter in Staffordshire to copy the Chinese Mandarin design ... It also seems likely that Spode originated the Willow pattern, for those pieces with the coarse engraving and dark colour typical of the 1790s – the earliest Willow pieces – are of Spode manufacture.[2]

Godden and Copeland agree that the Standard Willow pattern probably originated in Staffordshire; however, Copeland goes on to give evidence that the pattern was made by Spode before the nineteenth century. He doesn't mention any involvement by Thomas Minton. Geoffrey Priestman writes that after completing his apprenticeship at Caughley, Thomas Minton spent time in London where he became aware of many Chinese patterns. .

He goes on to say,

Mandarin may well have been combined with another Chinese design to form the famous Standard Willow Pattern, which was introduced on tablewares in the 1790s. Copeland makes a case for its introduction first at the Spode factory in about 1790. This may well be correct, in which case Thomas Minton could have been involved in its original design and engraving.[3]

Chinese Export hand-painted porcelain 9.5-inch plate. Striped Temple pattern is based on the central pattern of this plate. The two borders as well as other elements of Standard Willow pattern are found in this pattern. *Author's Collection.* $150-175.

Chinese Export blue and white patterns in the ten-year period 1970-80, named the pattern "Two Birds." The patterns assembled were separated into categories such as Floral and Landscapes. The more commonly found landscape designs were named and presented at a museum exhibit in 1980 entitled "Hills and Streams." In the exhibit catalog an example of Two Birds is shown dating from 1775-85 that has an inner diaper pattern border and an outer border similar to that found on Two Temples patterns. From 1790-1820 the Two Birds pattern had a honeycomb inner border and a trellis-dagger border as copied at Caughley and Spode.

Chinese Export porcelain 8.75-inch bowl hand-painted underglaze Two Birds pattern. This is the original from which Mandarin (Willow-Nankin) pattern was copied. Elements of Standard Willow pattern are found in this pattern. *Author's Collection.* $150-175.

All three men seem to agree that the development of Standard Willow was based on Mandarin combined with one or more other Chinese patterns. Plate 9 in *Caughley and Worcester Porcelains 1775-1800* by Geoffrey Godden is a photo of fragments of hard-paste Chinese blue and white "Nankin" porcelains. The upper left fragment is an example of a Chinese pattern closely related to the Standard Willow pattern borders. Copeland shows a Chinese porcelain footed bowl, no. 4 p.35, with three men on a bridge: an element of Standard Willow pattern not in Mandarin. It could have happened like that – finding a bridge here and a fence there; however, it seems to me that Priestman is on the right track. I think there was one other pattern combined with Mandarin to form Standard Willow, and I think I have found it!

In comparing the two Chinese patterns shown here with the first photo of an early Standard Willow pattern plate, we see that there are several elements of the Standard Willow pattern that are missing in the Mandarin pattern: the bridge with people on it, the fence, the three columns on the front of the tea house, and the small building(s) to the right behind the tea house. The borders (simple line and trellis-dagger) are not found on Standard Willow. The second Chinese plate has the Standard Willow borders as well as all of these missing elements including the archway at the left side of the bridge.

The Chinese pattern copied by Caughley and Spode (named Mandarin by Spode) is one of the most commonly found patterns on Chinese Export porcelain. Crosby Forbes, curator of the China Trade Museum, Milton, Massachusetts, who collected over 150 different

Striped Temple tureen stand transfer-printed in blue underglaze on pearlware. The central pattern is copied from the Chinese porcelain plate seen above. No mark. *Courtesy Renard Broughton.* NP

The second plate is the only example of this pattern I have seen. It was not one of the 150+ patterns found by Crosby Forbes. I bought it from a dealer in Chinese Export porcelains at the NEC Antiques Fair in Birmingham in 1997. I showed it to Robert Copeland, and he discussed it briefly in the Third Edition of *Spode's Willow Pattern*. We were both quite amazed to see such a plate emerge after all these years. Perhaps a hand-painted pattern as complex as that was not commercially viable to the Chinese potters. I believe that it is entirely possible that elements from this pattern and Two Birds were used to create the Standard Willow pattern.

After making this discovery I have wondered where other examples of this Chinese pattern might be. From conversations with other researchers and collectors, I have come to the conclusion that the pattern was used in the development of two other Chinoiserie patterns. In reading " 'Old Blue' Revisited: Early Chinoiserie Printed Pottery Part II" in the Northern Ceramic Society Newsletter No. 101, March 1996, by Renard Broughton, I noted figure 24 showing an earthenware coffee pot in "Striped Temple" pattern. This is a pattern similar to that on a rare Striped Temple Caughley pattern on a tea canister illustrated in plate 17 of Godden's book. The central pattern is based on the Chinese plate I found. Renard Broughton provided me with a photograph of a tureen stand in Striped Temple on pearlware, also in his possession. It is shown here and can be compared with the pattern on the Chinese plate. The borders used on Standard Willow were not used on Striped Temple; however, the central pattern elements can be seen. In Broughton's article, an example of Chinese Flagbearers pattern is also shown as he points out that pattern was developed from Striped Temple. A platter with Chinese Flagbearers pattern is shown. The ducks and plant life in the water in the foreground can be seen better in the plate than the tureen stand where that part of the pattern was cut off. Those elements, found on both Striped Temple and Chinese Flagbearers are seen on the Chinese plate.

It is interesting to discover that the central pattern on my Chinese plate was used in the development of other English Chinoiserie patterns; however, the connection with the Standard Willow pattern has not been made before. I want to express my thanks to Robert Copeland for seeing, with me, its relationship to the Standard Willow pattern, to Geoffrey Priestman and Frank Davenport for seeing the relationship to Chinese Flagbearers, and to Renard Broughton for bringing it back to Striped Temple – the direct copy of the Chinese central pattern used with Mandarin to form the Standard Willow pattern.

It is somewhat ironic that both Mandarin (Willow-Nankin) and Striped Temple were engraved at Caughley based on Chinese originals; however, it is the combination of those two patterns that formed the Standard Willow pattern, and that didn't happen at Caughley. This discovery gives a little more weight to the consideration that Thomas Minton, trained as an engraver at Caughley, certainly could have worked with Spode to design the willow pattern.

1. Godden, Geoffrey, *Caughley and Worcester Porcelains 1775-1800*, pp. 15-16.
2. Copeland, Robert, *Spode's Willow Pattern and Other Designs After the Chinese*, p. 33.
3. Priestman, Geoffrey, *An Illustrated Guide to Minton Printed Pottery 1796-1836*, p. 4.

Chinese Flagbearers pattern platter transfer-printed in blue underglaze on earthenware. There are 8 indentations on the rim of the platter. This pattern is a little later than Striped Temple and may have developed from it. The pattern is related to the Chinese plate seen above as there are many elements in the pattern the same as, or similar to, its central pattern. There is no mark, but it is generally accepted that it is a Davenport pattern. *Courtesy Renard Broughton.* NP

What is Willow?

There are several basic patterns that Willow collectors are the most interested in collecting. This encyclopedia will consider only those patterns manufactured by British potteries. Unusual variants will not be illustrated unless the maker also produced Standard Willow or Two Temples I or II. Patterns considered willow are as follows: Standard, Two Temples I and II, Mandarin, Booths, Burleigh, John Turner, Worcester, Canton, Border only, and Simplified. These patterns are described and illustrated below.

Standard Willow Pattern

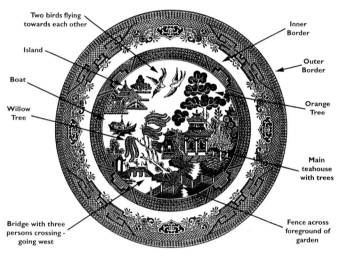

A chart showing a twentieth century example of the Standard Willow pattern. The various motifs of the central pattern are named. *Courtesy Franklin Ladner.*

In the late eighteenth century and early nineteenth century, the word willow was used as a sort of generic term to describe any or all Chinese landscape patterns. The patterns that actually feature a prominent willow tree, however, are the focus of this encyclopedia. The Standard Willow pattern (also referred to as *common, traditional,* and/or *classic willow*) is the most prolific of the designs. The principal features are the willow tree in the center leaning over the bridge with three people on it; the teahouse with three pillars forming the portico; and a large orange (or apple) tree behind it. There is an island on the left and a boat in the lake with a man in it. Two birds are flying towards each other at the top center of the pattern, and a fence crosses the path in the foreground. The two borders of the Standard Willow pattern are also distinctive although both do not always appear on all pieces. The charts above indicate the motifs in the central pattern and two borders.

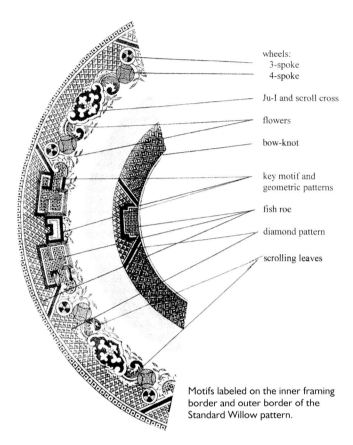

Motifs labeled on the inner framing border and outer border of the Standard Willow pattern.

A further illustration demonstrates the correct matching of the inner and outer borders. In *Willow! Solving the Mystery of our 200-year Love Affair with the Willow Pattern*, 1997, David Richard Quintner gives the following background information regarding the matching of the two borders:

Generally found wrapped around standard Willow Pattern designs, a certain border motif takes its inspiration from Chinese bronzes and their embellishment from early Shang times – or more than 1000 B.C. An important decorative feature on those bronzes is known as **T'ao-t'ieh**: forcefully delineated right-angled shapes whose unabstracted forms are feline or bovine facial masks. As shown in the center example (above), the outer border offers eyes and nose, with the inner border a mouth-shape at the end of a muzzle, the entire effect tiger-like. (The small decorations between the two borders suggests artist and potter did not recognize what they were dealing with.)

This photo shows the way in which the inner and outer borders should be matched with the geometric motifs lined up. Twenty-first century plates and platters are more apt to be appropriately aligned than nineteenth century ones; however, this close-up was taken of a plate made by Goodwins & Harris in the 1830s.

He goes on to say that misalignment or wide separation of the two borders causes the image to slip away. The hand-painted Chinese plate above has three out of four sets of geometric motifs well matched.

Two Temples I

A Copeland/Spode New Stone cup and saucer dated October 1879. The Two Temples I pattern is outlined in gold. The pattern number is 1/1467. There is no space between the central pattern and border. *Author's Collection*. $75-95.

Two Temples II

This 8.50-inch rimmed soup bowl has the Two Temples II pattern. There is no maker's mark; however, the pattern number is 142. The piece has a wide gold band on the outer rim and a series of gold dots on the inner edge of the border. There is a white area between the central pattern and border. *Author's Collection*. $30-40.

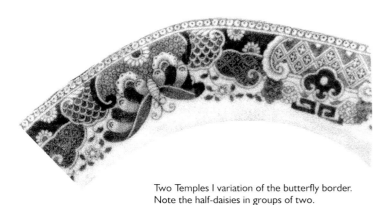

Two Temples I variation of the butterfly border. Note the half-daisies in groups of two.

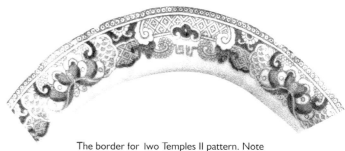

The border for Two Temples II pattern. Note the branches coming out of the single half-daisies at the outer rim.

Known at the Spode factory as Temple, this pattern dates to about 1810. It is closely related to Two Temples II described below. Robert Copeland uses *Two Temples I var. Temple* to describe the Spode pattern; however, willow collectors have simplified the name to Two Temples I. I will use that name in this book. The large building(s) on the left of the pattern appear to be two temples overlapping whereas it is actually one temple in the back, a large gatehouse in the front, and a garden area in between. There is a one-arch bridge with two figures on it. A third figure stands in the doorway, and a fourth is facing the doorway, standing near the clump of rocks by the river. The main feature that distinguishes this pattern from Two Temples II is the position of the willow tree. In Two Temples I, the willow tree is lower than the bridge and next to the fence in the foreground. The willow tree is above the bridge in Two Temples II. The fence in Two Temples I appears to cut off the flow of the water whereas in Two Temples II, there is water on both sides of the fence. The borders of the two patterns are similar; however, this border has a partial daisy shape between the butterfly and the rim as well as several other partial daisies in the area between the butterfly and lattice-work panel. I have not seen Two Temples I produced by potteries other than Copeland/Spode except for wares produced in the early nineteenth century.

The most commonly used name for this pattern is Broseley. Although Godden uses the name Pagoda to describe it, Priestman tells us it was reputedly named by Thomas Minton at Caughley in honor of the adjacent town of Broseley. Evidently the Broseley pattern was introduced in 1782 at Caughley where it was adapted from a Chinese pattern. At Spode, the pattern is known as *Two Temples II Var. Broseley*. The pattern will be referred to in this book as Two Temples II. In the early nineteenth century many different factories used this pattern on bone china tea wares. The left side of this pattern is very similar to Two Temples I; however, the fourth figure beside the rocks is missing. One figure remains in the doorway and two are on the bridge. The willow tree is located above the bridge, and the fence in the foreground crosses the river. The butterfly symbol in the border is closer to the rim. The half-daisy at the rim between the butterfly and lattice-work panel has a small branch extending out from each side. The Two Temples II pattern is quite often seen in reverse. Perhaps this is because the pattern was used on teapots. In some cases the temple side of the pattern would be at the handle, and the bridge at the spout on both sides of the pot. This practice would make it necessary to engrave copper plates with the pattern facing both ways. Two Temples II pattern is found on earthenwares as well as bone china and has been produced in the twentieth century by several different firms.

Mandarin

A plate that measures 10 5/8-inches in diameter has the Mandarin pattern in gray. The impressed date code is for December 1899, and the maker is Copeland. *Courtesy Tim and Kim Allen.* $40-65.

The border for the Mandarin pattern is made up of an outer band of trellis pattern and an inner row of dagger shapes and dots.

The Mandarin pattern is based on "Two Birds, " a very popular Chinese Export pattern. It is probably the pattern engraved by Thomas Minton for Thomas Turner at the Caughley factory c. 1790 that can be considered the original Willow pattern. Geoffrey Godden referred to the pattern as "Willow-Nankin" which described the prominent willow tree and the border found on "Nankin" type wares. By 1795, the pattern was produced at Spode and given the name Mandarin. It resembles the Standard Willow pattern in that it is a right-sided pattern, and the willow tree is central. There is a teahouse and smaller house in back of it with two birds flying above. Another land mass is located at the upper left. The bridge, people, and fence are missing. The pattern has a single border that is a trellis-dagger pattern.

Booths Willow Pattern

An 11-by-14-inch platter in the Booths Willow pattern. The pattern number is A8025 "Real Old Willow". The inner border of diamonds with dots and leaves is gold, as is the outer rim. Booths Mark 7. *Author's Collection.* $140-160.

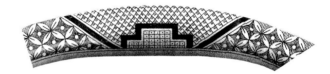

The outer border for the Booths pattern showing the enlarged bow knot pattern taken from the inner border of the Standard Willow pattern.

The Booths willow pattern is a simpler version of Standard Willow. It was named "Real Old Willow" by Booths; however, other companies also made this variant. The island at the upper left is missing, and the willow tree is standing more upright. The willow branches form a simple "X" reminiscent of Spode's Rock pattern. The teahouse is smaller and missing the three columns in front. The fence is up closer to the teahouse, and there is another fence surrounding the land on the left side of the bridge. The outer border of Standard Willow is missing. The inner bowknot border is enlarged and used as the outer border. The inner edge is often decorated with a chevron pattern in gold or brown with dots and/or leaf forms.

Burleigh Willow

This 9-inch Burleigh willow plate is unusual in that it has a pale yellow glaze over the blue pattern. All of the elements of the pattern are present. *Courtesy Nancee Rogers.* $95-125.

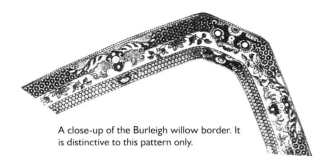

A close-up of the Burleigh willow border. It is distinctive to this pattern only.

Burgess and Leigh developed a variation of the Standard Willow pattern. According to information from the factory it was based on a pattern made by the Dillwyn pottery. It is sometimes called "Dillwyn Willow" in order to differentiate it from the Standard Willow pattern made by the company earlier in its history. The design differs in several ways. The willow tree is more ornate in this pattern, and the apple tree behind the teahouse is missing. The fence has moved to the riverbank, and the bridge has only one arch. There can be five figures in the pattern: three on the bridge, one in the boat, and an optional figure at the lower front of the pattern. He is carrying a long pole with lanterns at either end. On plates and other pieces using a round transfer, his back is seen as he appears to be starting up the path to the teahouse. On platters and other pieces using a rectangular or linear transfer, the figure is coming from the teahouse. There are some pieces in which the fifth figure does not appear at all. The borders are changed from the Standard Willow pattern also. The outer border has panels of honeycomb and large flowers toward the center. Bat-like motifs are prominent. The inner border is made up of bands of honeycomb with floral inserts.

John Turner Pattern

Ten-inch plate by Masons illustrates the John Turner willow variant. The color is a reddish brown. *Courtesy of IWC Convention 1993.* $45-65.

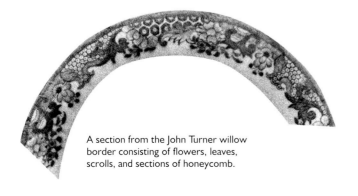

A section from the John Turner willow border consisting of flowers, leaves, scrolls, and sections of honeycomb.

This pattern was developed at the Turner's pottery of Lane End c. 1800-06. It is known as "Turners Willow" and "Two-man Willow" pattern. John Turner senior died in 1787, and his sons William and John were running the pottery until 1806. Willow collectors have used the name **John** Turner for the pattern to avoid any mistaken identification with Thomas Turner at Caughley. The willow tree is on the left side of the pattern, and the one-arch bridge with interesting spots on it is at the lower left of the pattern. There are two men on the bridge. The small buildings and two types of apple trees are on the right hand side. There is an island with a building in the upper left of the pattern, but there are no birds. A line of Catherine wheel scrolls forms the inner border. The outer border has sections of honeycomb alternating with scrolls, leaves, and flowers.

Simeon Shaw, author of *History of the Staffordshire Potteries, 1829,* states that John Turner designed the pattern based on two Chinese originals given to his son William. The problem with that statement is that it is not clear to which "willow pattern" Shaw is referring. Another theory, according to W. L. Little in *Staffordshire Blue* is that William Underwood, an engraver and blue-printer from Worcester designed the pattern at Worcester and brought it with him when he came to work for John Turner in about 1784.

While it is true that the Worcester factory produced the pattern, it did not do so until the twentieth century. Wendy Cook, curator at Worcester Museum, and I spent several days in August 2001 looking through the pattern books and could not find it.

Worcester Willow

Royal Worcester plates showing the central willow pattern. The 7.75-inch plate on the left has the scroll and flower border and is pattern B/389. The 6.75-inch plate on the right has the trellis-dagger border and is pattern B/750. *Author's Collection.* $30-40 each.

Scroll and flower border used with the Worcester center willow pattern.

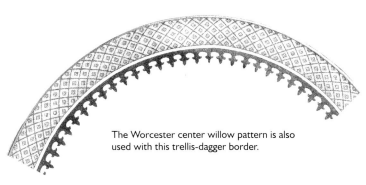

The Worcester center willow pattern is also used with this trellis-dagger border.

There are very few examples of Standard Willow pattern by Worcester. Pattern B446 is known as "Full Willow" in the pattern books; however, it has no willow tree. There are other elements reminiscent of Standard Willow including a pagoda to the right, fence, and boats in the water. There is a one-arch bridge at the upper part of the pattern, but the only figure is standing in the doorway of the pagoda. The pattern is actually closer in form to the Bridgeless Chinoiserie pattern by Davenport, Minton, and others. There are two main border patterns with this central pattern. One has flowers and scrolls, and the other is a trellis-dagger border.

Canton

Canton pattern 9.75-inch rimmed soup bowl in flow blue. Others are simple blue transfer-printed underglaze. Although this piece is marked Masons, its twin is marked Ashworth. *Author's Collection.* $95-125.

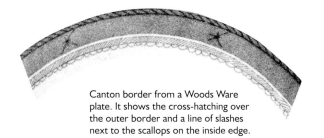

Canton border from a Woods Ware plate. It shows the cross-hatching over the outer border and a line of slashes next to the scallops on the inside edge.

Veryl M. Jensen, who wrote *The First Book of International Willow Ware China* in 1975, states on page 9, "Canton ware from China was the predecessor of Willow pattern dinner ware." It is true that the pattern has a central willow tree, a large temple and/or house, islands, boats, and a bridge; therefore, it is closely related to Standard Willow. Hand-painted Canton may be the most common pattern to come out of China, and it is still coming. Most of the ware we see is heavy with a gray tint and rough, unglazed foot rims. The slight differences due to hand painting are very apparent because the pattern is simpler with broader strokes than other Chinese Export wares. The outer border is blue with a form of cross-hatching over it and scalloped lines or slash marks on the inside edge. Some pieces may have an inner plain blue border as well. English companies such as Ashworth Bros. and Woods & Sons have produced transfer-printed versions of Canton.

Border Only Pattern

This border only pattern is also used as a strip of decoration with different colored background. There is a gold line on either side of the pattern as well as on the handle of this 3-inch jug. The mark states only: WILLOW 8333 in gold. The maker is unknown. *Author's Collection.* $30.

There are two types of border only patterns. Neither has a central pattern. 1) Willow motifs in the border, and 2) Standard Willow border. The first type is illustrated here. Pieces with only a Standard Willow border are usually under trays to hold serving pieces.

Simplified Pattern

These are patterns drawn with simple lines. They can be engraved and transfer-printed or executed with rubber stamp underglaze. The borders vary from one factory to the next and can consist of a simplified motif from the Standard Willow pattern. Decal patterns that leave out the surrounding details are also considered simplified patterns.

An abbreviated border and simple lined pattern decorate this late twentieth century plate by James Broadhurst and Sons Ltd. There is no framing border on this plate. Broadhurst Mark 2. *Courtesy Norma Maurer.* $10-12.

Map showing the Location of Potteries that Produced the Willow Pattern

Map showing the location of potteries that produced the Willow pattern in Britain.

I. Manufacturers listed alphabetically with marks and photographs

Potters are listed alphabetically by surname and/or the name of the pottery. The location(s) and dates of production are given for each entry followed by the marks used by the firm. There will be explanatory comments regarding marks for some of the entries. A brief history is given for each entry followed by a listing of the type of willow manufactured. The photographs and/or reproductions of material from trade magazines will follow with captions giving specific information for each item pictured. An asterisk (*) after the name of a potter indicates there is an entry with more information in the book.

Harvey Adams & Co.

Location: High Street and Sutherland Road, Longton, Staffordshire
Dates: c. 1869-87
Mark:

(GG14) c. 1870-85

Brief History: Formerly Adams & Scrivener. The & Co. in the firm title is Titus Hammersley.
In addition to earthenware, the firm produced a wide range of porcelains including painted, gilded, enameled, jeweled, and with open work on the rim. Harvey Adams was the general Art Director of the company that employed nearly seventy artists, gilders, etc. Most of the china was unmarked, making it difficult to find; however, the pattern books are housed at the Spode factory in Stoke. One of the interesting developments of the company is the invention of the moustache cup. It was a popular item copied by many other firms. In 1887, the firm continued on as Hammersley & Co.*
Type of Willow Manufactured: Standard Willow pattern transfer-printed underglaze in blue on earthenware.

A 9.25-inch plate blue transfer-printed underglaze. The Standard Willow pattern has no undecorated area between borders and central pattern. This is typical of the period. The plate is round with concave rim and single, rounded foot ring. Slight blue-tinted glaze. Three-point stilt marks on the center of the plate. *Author's Collection.* $20-30.

William Adams & Sons

Location: Greengates and Greenfield, Tunstall and Stoke, Staffordshire
Dates: c. 1779-present (2003)
Marks:

Comments Regarding Marks: Marks 1, 2, and 3 are shown in *Adams Ceramics Staffordshire Potters and Pots, 1779-1998* by David A. Furniss, J. Richard Wagner, and Judith Wagner. Mark 1 is figure 7. Mark 2 is shown on page 142, and Mark 3 is figure 70. The ribbon mark was first used by John Meir & Son* in the nineteenth century. Adams used it on Willow from 1896 until the 1940s.
Brief History: Although the Adams family tree can be traced back to 1307, the first master potter was William Adams I of Tunstall. Production began at his Greengates Pottery in 1779. William, his wife, and oldest son died in 1805. The youngest son, Benjamin, continued the pottery until 1820. In 1822 Greengates Pottery was sold to John Meir. Other branches of the family were also potters. The Stoke Group, 1804-1829, under William Adams III, as well as the successor, Adams & Sons at Stoke 1829-1861, produced bone china as well as earthenware. Their display at the Great Exhibition of 1851 in the Crystal Palace, London, included Parian figures. The Stoke Group suffered a setback with Williams Adams IV's declining health in 1847, leaving his brothers to run the potteries. The partnership was dissolved in 1853. William Adams IV and his brother Edward concentrated their energies at Greenfield, leaving the fate of Stoke to brother Thomas. The Stoke firm went into bankruptcy in 1861. Five tons of copper engravings were sold at auction. The Willow pattern plates were among those sold, reportedly to George Jones*.
   William V led the Greenfield pottery through a difficult time, including a fire in 1875. A general recession in the 1880s forced a sale of the Newfield Pottery in 1892. A reorganization of the firm that year involved a name change to W. Adams & Co. The firm was ready for expansion in 1896, when Greengates Pottery became available for purchase from John Meir's son Henry, who did not want to stay in the pottery business. William Adams VI and son W. Anthony Adams led the company through the

Mark 1 (GG19)
c. 1820-40

Mark 2 c. 1917-1960s

Mark 3 c. 1917-1960s

Mark 4 c. 1917-1960s

Mark 5 c. 1891+

Mark 6 (GG30)
c. 1905-17

twentieth century until 1966 when it was purchased by Josiah Wedgwood Ltd. Retaining the Adams name, the company has continued to produce traditional wares as well as new styles. In 1994 Wedgwood closed the Greengates factory but continued to use it as a warehouse.

Type of Willow Manufactured: Underglaze transfer-printed pearlware, earthenware, and ironstone in blue and red. Blue printed Standard Willow pattern is also found with clobbering. Both Meir and Adams copper engraved plates were used, resulting in a number of variations of the Standard Willow pattern. Two Temples II in blue. A polychrome decal based on Two Temples II was used in the early twentieth century. Early pearlware and Two Temples II pattern are very scarce. Ribbon-marked twentieth century dark blue Standard Willow is more commonly found. It was not made after 1965.

Retailer/importer: Fisher, Bruce & Co., Philadelphia*

Standard Willow pattern octagonal-shaped bowl and handled tray transfer-printed in blue underglaze. The red and green clobbering adds another dimension to this lovely set. The full pattern is inside the bowl and on the center of the tray. The bowl is 5.5-inches high and 10-inches wide. The tray including handles is 12.75-inches wide and stands 1.25-inches high. Mark 3. *Courtesy Harry and Jessie Hall.* $375-450.

A flat rimmed pearlware 4-inch plate with 8 lobes. There is a single foot ring. Impressed Mark 1 above. Two Temples II pattern in two shades of blue. *Author's Collection.* NP

The birds on this rimmed soup are different from those on the other Standard Willow pieces by Adams. The bowl measures 7 7/8-inches, and it bears Mark 5. *Courtesy Bill and Joyce Keenan.* $12-18.

An 8-inch ironstone plate with the Standard Willow pattern in dark blue. It is round with a flat rim. The foot ring is recessed. Mark 2. *Author's Collection.* $10-12.

Two Adams ironstone teapots. The one on the left holds 4 cups, and the one on the right holds 6 cups. They are basically the same shape; however, the finial on the smaller teapot stands straight up. Standard Willow. *Courtesy Joette Hightower.* $85-95 and $120-135.

Large red printed teapot with beaded edge on the lid and shoulder. Standard Willow pattern. Plates and other dinnerware pieces in red willow have been found with the same molded edge. Mark 3. *Courtesy IWC Convention 2000.* $175-200.

This vase is wider than it is tall. The height is 5.75-inches, and the width is 6.50. It is Standard Willow in dark blue. Mark 3. The bridge has been expanded to 5 arches with larger stones than on the other Adams pieces – an adjustment made for this wrap-around pattern. *Courtesy Dennis Crosby.* $55-85.

Tea canister with Standard Willow pattern in dark blue. It is unusual to find one that has its lid intact. It stands 5.25-inches tall. Mark 4. *Courtesy Dennis Crosby.* $165-200.

A lithographic polychrome decal based on the Two Temples II pattern decorates this standard shape jug used by Adams. There is a gold line on the top edge and on each side of the handle. Mark 6 with pattern #5863. *Courtesy Paul Kirves and Zeke Jimenez.* $35-55.

William Alsager Adderley

Location: Daisy Bank Pottery, Longton, Staffordshire
Dates: c. 1876-present (2003)
Marks:

Comments Regarding Marks: Marks 1, 2, and 3 were used on bone china and earthenware. Mark 5 varies from GG 55 because it does not have the words "PORCELAINE MODERNE" found on GG 55. OLD WILLOW has been added to the top of the mark when it is used on Standard Willow. Mark 6 is a carryover from the same mark used by Hulse & Adderley* as well as Hulse, Nixon & Adderley*. Only the initials differ. Mark 8 is not a maker's mark but is shown here because the Adderley firm made the blue willow "crockery" used in Miss Cranston's Willow Tea Rooms in Glasgow, Scotland. Some pieces had the Adderley Mark 4 in addition to "MISS CRANSTON'S WILLOW. See *Taking Tea with Mackintosh The Story of Miss Cranston's Tea Rooms* by Perilla Kinchin for more information on the Willow Tea Rooms.

Brief History: Formerly associated with Hulse and Nixon* at Daisy Bank Pottery, beginning in 1876 William A. Adderley took over the business. He continued to produce earthenware and added china to the output. In 1906, the firm became Adderleys Ltd., and the name of Daisy Bank Pottery was changed to Gainsborough Works. In 1947, Adderleys Ltd. was bought by Lawleys Limited. In 1953, Ridgway merged with the Lawley Group, and in 1954, the company was renamed Ridgway, Adderley, Booths & Colcloughs Ltd. By 1955, it was known as Ridgway Potteries Ltd. In 1964, Adderleys became part of Allied English Potteries and later part of the Royal Doulton Group. The Adderley trade name is still used.

Type of Willow Manufactured: Underglaze transfer-printed earthenware and china. Blue, red, and brown in Standard Willow, and blue in Two Temples II. Other colors including blue, brown, red, and black used in the Daisy variant. Lavender over the glaze on bone china with gold trim was used in the Two Temples II pattern. Tableware and ornamental wares were made.

Mark 1 (GG49)
c. 1876-85

Mark 2 (GG49)
c. 1876-85

Mark 3 (GG49)
c. 1891-1905

Mark 4 (GG50)
c. 1906-26

Mark 5 (GG55)
c. 1929-47

Mark 6 c. 1891-1905

Mark 7 (GG57)
c. 1950-62

Mark 8
c. 1903-17

London shape teapot, 5-inches high to the top of the finial. It measures 9-inches from the tip of the spout to the tip of the handle. The shape and size are very close to the Spode* London shape teapot made over 100 years earlier. The tip of the handle extends straight out on the Spode teapot, adding 1/4-inch to the measurement. The handle on the Adderley teapot curves up at the end. Underglaze blue printed Standard Willow. Mark 5. The red willow 8.5-inch soup plate is one of the few pieces of red I have seen. It has single stilt marks on the front and back of the base. The outer border is too large and had to be cut at about 2 o'clock. Mark 4. *Author's Collection.* $95-125 and $15-20.

Six-inch divided relish dish with a handle. Standard Willow pattern with no inner border. *Author's Collection.* $85-100.

Standard Willow pattern covered vegetable transfer-printed in blue underglaze on earthenware. This is a shape used throughout the nineteenth century by many different firms. The base is 4.25.-inches square, and the top measures 8.75-inches. From handle to handle, it is 10-inches. Mark 5. *Author's Collection.* $100-145.

An octagonal-shaped tea set with a Willow sheet pattern in blue. The name of the variant comes from the daisy border. The daisy border has been documented in brown and blue as well as the red shown here. All of the pieces are trimmed in gold. The mark is impressed WAA IVORY, a term used for the earthenware body. *Courtesy Tom and Barbara Allen.* $300+.

Standard Willow pattern blue printed bone china open sugar bowl, 1.75-inches high and 3-inches in diameter. It bears Mark 8 and was used in Miss Cranston's Willow Tea Rooms in Glasgow, Scotland, designed by Charles Rennie Mackintosh. The Hunterian Art Gallery, University of Glasgow, has a Mackintosh Exhibition Gallery. A glass display case there contains an assortment of blue willow dishes made by Adderley for the Willow Tea Rooms. I was fortunate to buy this little bowl while visiting Glasgow in 2000. It has Mark 8. A 4-inch sugar bowl seen on eBay internet auction site had Mark 8 plus Mark 4 above. The London shape teapot shown above was used in the Willow Tea Rooms; however, the pattern is light blue, and the finial is a pink rose bud with green leaves. *Author's Collection.* NP

A compote with the willow sheet pattern in black and the Daisy border in blue. The diameter of the compote is 8.5-inches. The foot and top both have a fluted border. Mark 1. *Courtesy Tom and Barbara Allen.* $150+.

A narrow octagonal 4 cup teapot with dark blue Two Temples II pattern. Note the addition of two small birds above the temple. The angular handle, spout, and finial have gold line trim. The teapot dates from c. 1876-86. *Courtesy Charles and Zeta Hollingsworth.* $100-175.

Standard Willow pattern platter transfer-printed in blue underglaze on earthenware. It measures 11.25-by-14-inches. The birds look particularly acrobatic with their bodies bending upwards displaying their fish tails at the top of the pattern. *Courtesy J and J Cockerill.* $150-225.

Bone china dinner plate, cup and saucer decorated in lavender. Two birds have been added to the Two Temples II pattern. These pieces have gold trim on the wavy edges. Mark 7. *Courtesy IWC Convention 1999.* $35-55.

Henry Alcock & Co. (Ltd.)

Location: Elder Pottery, Cobridge and Clarence Works, Stoke, Staffordshire
Dates: c. 1861-1935
Marks:

Comment Regarding Marks: Both marks contain the pattern name CHING.
Brief History: Henry Alcock's grandfather, John, was the brother of Samuel Alcock.* Henry acquired the Elder Pottery from John and George Alcock who were Samuel Alcock's nephews. In 1910, the pottery moved to Clarence Works, Stoke, and the name was changed to The Henry Alcock Pottery. The company produced earthenwares.
Type of Willow Manufactured: Underglaze transfer-printed blue Mandarin pattern. Full page ads from 1903 to 1910 promoted the "Alcock's Semi China Spiral Shape". Several pieces of blue Mandarin pattern have been found on this shape; however, Alcock's name for the pattern is "CHING".

Mark 1 c. 1900+

c. Mark 2 (GG66)
c. 1910-35

W. H. & J. H. Ainsworth

Location: Stockton Pottery, Stockton-on-Tees, Co. Durham
Dates: c. 1865-1901
Impressed Mark:

(GG61)
c. 1865-1901

Brief History: The pottery was referred to as "Ainsworth's" Pottery or Stockton Pottery. Earthenware was produced beginning in 1840 with wares marked T. AINSWORTH STOCKTON. Another printed mark was used in the form of the impressed mark shown above; however, it had an elaborate ribbon above the castle and anchor with the words "Warranted, Tees Pottery, Stone China." The impressed mark seen here was used throughout the life of the pottery.
Type of Willow Manufactured: Standard Willow and Two Temples II patterns transfer-printed in blue underglaze on earthenware. Dinnerware was made.

Dark blue Mandardin pattern Spiral Shape 10-inch coffee pot. It is shape 46 or 47 shown on the ad for Henry Alcock's Semi China. The pattern is called Ching by Alcock. Mark 1. *Courtesy Charles and Zeta Hollingsworth.* $175-250.

Mandarin pattern creamer in medium blue, called Ching by the Alcock firm. This jug is spiral shaped but more bulbous than the other pieces shown. It is just over 4-inches high at the spout and has gold trim. Mark 2. *Author's Collection.* $20-25.

A 7.50-inch Spiral Shape jug with the same handle as the coffee pot. This dark blue Mandarin jug has a 5-cup capacity. Seven jugs of various heights are shown in the ad. Mark 1. *Author's Collection.* $75-125.

This piece measures 6.75-by-9.75-inches and has a very flat back. There are traces of worn gold in the recesses of the rim. I call it a fish-shaped tray, but I don't really know what it is. *Author's Collection.* $20-45.

Spiral Shape teapot in a light blue Mandarin pattern. A large teapot holding 7 to 8 cups, it is probably number 36 or 37 in the Alcock's ad. Mark 1. *Courtesy IWC Convention 2000.* $175-200.

This full-page ad appeared in the *Pottery Gazette* July 1, 1903. The Alcock firm promoted this new line with ads every month in 1906. Some ads pictured the 7 jug sizes, and others the entire line. January 1, 1910, the ad appeared with the new company title and address: "The Henry Alcock Pottery Ltd., King St. Works, Fenton, Stoke-on-Trent."

Samuel Alcock & Co.

Location: Cobridge China Works, and Hill Pottery, Burslem, Staffordshire
Dates: c. 1826-53
Marks:

June 14, 1843

Comments Regarding Marks: Samuel Alcock marked his wares only with pattern and registration numbers. The Two Temples II pieces do not have pattern numbers.
Brief History: Samuel Alcock, a banker, was not trained through apprenticeship as a potter. His first partnership, 1822-26, was with Ralph Stevenson and Augustus Lloyd Williams. He also had a partnership with Samuel Keeling*. From these he learned the business of running a successful pottery. He hired skilled craftsmen and designers, and his company grew and thrived. By 1840, there were twenty kilns at his combined factories – the same number Minton* had at the time. The factory was running so successfully that it continued after his death in 1848. However, his wife and son filed for bankruptcy in 1859.
Type of Willow Manufactured: Underglaze transfer-printed blue Two Temples II teawares in porcelain with gold trim.

Bone china underglaze transfer-printed blue Two Temples II pattern cup and saucer with gold trim. It is unmarked. Philip Miller dates the set at c. 1830. The tea service above came with this shape cup and saucer, so perhaps it is a shape used with more than one teapot shape. *Author's Collection.* $35-65.

Samuel Alcock bone china teapot, creamer, and covered sugar with underglaze blue printed Two Temples II pattern. It has lavish gold trim. See Miller and Berthoud's *Anthology of British Teapots* plate 1994 for the same teapot shape with registry mark for June 14, 1843. Mark M16. The teapot stands 7.50-inches tall and measures 11-inches from end of handle to top of spout. The sugar with lid stands 6.50-inches high and is almost 6-inches across at the widest part. The creamer is 4 5/8-inches at the spout and 6-inches from tip of spout to edge of handle. *Author's Collection.* NP

The teapot stand is 9 1/8-inches in diameter including handles that have a molded leaf pattern. The stand has 8 lobes on the edge in addition to the handles. It has a single unglazed foot ring. The waste bowl is 6.75-inches across the top and stands 3-inches high. *Author's Collection.* NP.

Bone china underglaze transfer-printed blue Two Temples II pattern teapot, creamer, and covered sugar with gold trim. There is no mark. These ribbed-shaped pieces are pictured on p. 84, plate 26, in Godden's *Encyclopaedia of British Porcelain Manufacturers* as part of a tea service. He attributes the shape to Samuel Alcock, c. 1828-32. These pieces are more thinly potted than the 1843 tea service shown above. *Courtesy Charles and Zeta Hollingsworth.* $250+.

Allerton

Location: Park Works, High Street, Longton, Staffordshire
Dates: c. 1832-1942
Marks:

Brief History: "Est. 1831" appears on the latest marks used by Allerton and refers to the first of three different partnerships that operated the Park Works. Allerton, Brough and Green were in business from 1832 to 1859. In 1860, the firm was titled Charles Allerton & Sons and operated until 1912. Although Charles died in 1863, his four sons carried on the business, dropping out one by one until William was the only one left by 1887, when Charles Bradbury Allerton retired. Taken over by Cauldon Potteries Ltd. in 1912, the name of the firm was changed to Allertons Ltd. and remained until it went out of business in 1942. A significant amount of Standard Willow in earthenware was shipped to the U.S. in the 1920s and 1930s, and sold through retailers such as Sears Roebuck, Butler Brothers, and Maddock and Miller, New York, New York.

Type of Willow Manufactured: Underglaze transfer-printed Standard Willow in blue, red, and in brown with clobbering. Two Temples II was printed in blue. Earthenware tableware was produced. A light blue bone china cup and saucer in Standard Willow with gold trim is shown on Steven Birks' website: www.thepotteries.org.; however, it is the only example on bone china by Allerton I have seen.

Mark 1 c. 1890-1912

Mark 2 (GG86) c. 1890-1912

Mark 3 (GG88) c. 1903-12

Mark 4 (GG93) c. 1929-42

Mark 5 c. 1929-42

This 7.75-inch plate is the earliest example of Allerton transfer-printed blue with Two Temples II pattern. It is very poorly done with a splotchy appearance. Mark 1. *Author's Collection.* $8-10.

A coffee or chocolate pot with a high, short spout. It is 8-inches high. The blue reversed Two Temples II pattern is very clear. The pattern elements are quite large. *Courtesy Charles and Zeta Hollingsworth.* $150-200.

The Standard Willow pattern is transfer-printed in brown underglaze with yellow, green, and rust clobbering. Gold rim and line accents add to the color in the pattern. The flat rim on this 9-inch plate is shaped with 8 wide lobes and 8 narrow ones. The foot ring is recessed. Mark 3. *Author's Collection.* $35-75.

A large teapot with a scalloped edge on the collar and base. The pattern is Standard Willow in cobalt blue underglaze. Mark 3. Dinnerware pieces with this mark are the earliest and have a scalloped rim on the flat ware as well as the hollow ware. *Courtesy IWC Convention.* $275-350.

A child's tea set in Standard Willow pattern. It is transfer-printed in red underglaze. The teapot stands 4.50-inches to the top of the finial and holds 14 oz. The plates are 6.50-inches in diameter. All of the pieces bear Mark 4 except the cups with Mark 5. Mark 5 is often seen on small items such as cups and could have been used earlier than the 1929 date given above. *Author's Collection.* $150-225.

This ad for Allertons Blue Willow appeared in the Butler Brothers, New York, catalog dated November 1932. Larger ads appeared February 1928 and March 1929.

The Sears, Roebuck & Co. 1939 Spring-Summer catalog offers sets and open stock. The fine print makes some fantastic claims as it reads: "The very same ware that Clipper ships brought American women from England two hundred years ago. Applied under the deep glaze, the pattern can't wear off. It portrays the legend of the mandarin's daughter and her lover. Made of best quality English semi porcelain known for the toughness of its texture. Remember, it's the genuine imported English Blue Willow – universally recognized as the finest Willow ware made. Choice of two colors: rich cobalt blue or old rose pink."

Allman, Broughton & Co.

Location: Overhouse Works – Wedgwood Place, Burslem, Staffordshire
Dates: c. 1861-68
Mark:

(GG94)
c. 1861-8

Brief History: A new partnership began April 13, 1861, made up of George Allman, Henry S. Broughton, J. Robinson, and Ralph Lawton. The company manufactured earthenwares. In 1868, the partnership dissolved and the company was known as Robinson, Kirkham & Co.* A year later the old works were torn down and a new, improved factory was built with all the latest advancements in machinery and appliances.

Type of Willow Manufactured: Underglaze transfer-print Standard Willow pattern in blue. Heavy stoneware.

Standard Willow pattern 9.75-inch plate transfer-printed in blue underglaze on heavy ironstone. Three-point stilt marks in the center of the plate. It has a single flat foot ring. *Author's Collection.* $25-35.

Ambassador Ware (See Simpsons (Potters) Ltd.)

Charles Amison (& Co. Ltd.)

Location: Stanley China Works, Wedgwood Street, Longton, Staffordshire
Dates: c. 1889-1962
Mark:

(GGIII) c. 1953-62

Brief History: The partnership of Amison & Lawson began producing china in 1878. Charles Amison was the sole proprietor from 1889 to 1916. After that time the name changed to Charles Amison & Co. In 1930, the company became a limited company. The trade name Stanley China was used from 1906. It became Stanley Bone China in 1949, and Stanley Fine Bone China from 1953. That same year Wedgwood Street was renamed Amison Street. Tea wares, especially in floral patterns, were the main products of the company. From 1951 to 1962, they made a range of floral decorations under the name Staffordshire Floral Bone China. The molds for these were sold to Longton New Art Pottery Co. Ltd. when Amison closed in 1962.
Type of Willow Manufactured: Mandarin pattern with no border in medium blue. Made in the last period of the company's production, printed patterns are often used as a time-saving device when sales begin to drop.

Six-inch plate with medium blue printed Mandarin pattern on bone china. It has a line of gold at the rim. *Author's Collection.* $10-15.

Arklow Pottery

Location: South Quay, Arklow, Co., Wicklow, Ireland
Dates: c. 1890-mid-1970s.
Marks:

Mark 1 c. 1939+

Comments on marks: The Arklow stamp was used only on very good quality dinner services. Pieces marked with a © stamp were made c. 1890-1910 and (D) on the mark dates it from 1910 to 1930-5.
Brief History: Arklow is located on the east coast of Ireland. The pottery produced earthenware goods for table and decoration. It grew to be a major employer in the area. Blue willow was produced early and then revived in the Arklow Classic series. In about 1975, Noritake took over the company and inherited all the Arklow records. The pottery closed in the mid-1980s.
Type of Willow Manufactured: Underglaze transfer-printed blue Standard Willow pattern. Earthenware only. Many pieces have gold trim.

Mark 2 c. 1910-35

Mark 3 c. 1950s

Mark 4 c. 1950s

A 9-inch plate with underglaze transfer-printed blue Standard Willow pattern. It has a gold line around the edge. Mark 1. *IWC Convention 2000.* $10-15.

This blue Standard Willow jug stands 5.75-inches high. It is 3 7/8-inches in diameter. Mark 2. This piece also has a gold line trim. *Courtesy Bill and Joyce Keenan.* $45-65.

Later pieces made at Arklow differ in the following ways: the break in the border pattern, large areas of white, and lack of gold trim. Two forms of the Standard Willow pattern appear on this teapot. It is in reverse on the opposite side so that the teahouse is near the handle looking from either side. Mark 4. *Courtesy Daisy and Tom Eden.* $55-85.

G. L. Ashworth & Bros. (Ltd.)

Location: Broad Street Works, Hanley, Staffordshire
Dates: c. 1862-1968
Marks:

Mark 1 (GG147)
c. 1891+

Comments Concerning Marks: "Real Old Canton" is a pattern name used on some variations of Ashworth's Canton pattern. It is printed underglaze as part of the maker's mark. Hand-painted pattern numbers occur on pieces with over-painting: therefore, it can be assumed that those numbers refer to the decoration rather than the underglaze pattern. An impressed mark: REAL IRONSTONE CHINA under a crown has been found on a Standard Willow pattern bowl and John Turner pattern covered dish by Ashworth.

Mark 2 (GG148)
c. 1891+

Brief History: Francis Morley was in partnership with George L. Ashworth from 1857-1862. Morley had purchased many molds and copper plates from C. J. Mason when he became bankrupt in 1848. When Morley retired, those molds and copper plates were passed on to George L. and Taylor Ashworth who continued to produce Patent Ironstone China. The Mason's crown marks were continued with and without the name "Ashworths". Former Mason's patterns were also produced. By the early twentieth century, the term "Real Ironstone China" came into use both in printed and impressed marks. The company was acquired by John Shaw Goddard in 1883. It was a Limited (Ltd.) company from 1884-1968. In 1968-1973, the name was changed to Mason's Ironstone China Ltd. In 1973, it was acquired by the Wedgwood Group. Remaining archival materials and pattern books are now housed at Wedgwood in Barlaston.

Types of Willow Manufactured: Standard willow is found in underglaze blue as well as brown with clobbering. Two Temples II is found with gold trim. The John Turner variant produced extensively by G. M & C. J. Mason is continued in blue printed wares both with and without over-painting. Two or three versions of the Canton pattern are found in underglaze blue. Finally, there are many variant patterns with a willow tree and other elements of Standard Willow that are sought by Willow collectors. These are often found in many different color treatments. Only one of these variants will be illustrated here.

Retailers/importers: Allan Line*, Hugh C. Edmiston, New York*

Standard Willow pattern 10-inch plate transfer-printed in brown underglaze on earthenware. It is clobbered with rust, green, and cobalt blue. The pattern number for the added colors is 635/9. Mark 1. *Author's Collection.* $85-125.

Standard Willow pattern 6-cup teapot transfer-printed in deep cobalt blue underglaze on earthenware. This round teapot has a flat lid. The cup and saucers that came with this teapot are London shape. Mark 1. *Courtesy Harry and Jessie Hall.* $125-160.

John Turner Willow pattern plates transfer-printed in blue underglaze. The clobbering is not the same. The plate on the left measures 10.50-inches and has Mark 1 with pattern number 4/313/H. It has more green. The plate on the right is 9.50 in diameter. It is marked "Mason's Ironstone China England": a variation of GG143. This mark was carried on by the Ashworth's firm. Different features of the pattern are pulled out with bright colors on the smaller plate; however, there are examples with the coloring and pattern number 4/313/H with the Mason's Ironstone China mark. *Author's Collection.* $95-125. each.

John Turner Willow pattern covered dish transfer-printed in blue underglaze on ironstone. The ornate handles and finial have gold outlining, and there is a gold line at the edge of the lid and dish. The piece measures 12.75-inches from handle to handle. Impressed mark with the words "REAL IRONSTONE CHINA" under a crown. *Courtesy Harry and Jessie Hall.* $150-225.

Four Ashworth teapots are shown here in Canton pattern. Only the teapot at 9 o'clock has Mark 2 for Real Old Canton. It has a serpent handle. The teapots at 12 and 6 o'clock have a larger and more open version of the Canton pattern with Mark 1. An example of that pattern in flow blue on a plate can be seen in the section under G. M & C. J. Mason*. The teapot at 3 o'clock has the same pattern as the other two but is slightly flown. It has an impressed ASHWORTH mark. Some flow blue pieces have gold outlining. *Author's Collection.* $100-175 each.

This 10.50-inch plate shows a variant with elements of the Standard Willow such as the teahouse on the right side, a bridge with figures crossing over the water to a little island. There is a small willow tree and a small boat in the water. An island in the upper left completes the resemblance to the willow pattern. It is blue printed underglaze with shades of red and yellow clobbering. Mark 1 with pattern number 112C. *Author's Collection.* $65-85.

This 10 oz. jug has the same pattern as the plate above except for the colors. It is brown printed underglaze with clobbering in green and shades of yellow. Mark 1. The number 36 is impressed on the base indicating the size. The number corresponds to how many of that article can fit on a board that is carried from one process to another at the factory. The larger the number, the smaller the item. No pattern number is given. *Author's Collection.* $25-55.

GEO. L. ASHWORTH & BROS., LTD.: TWO POPULAR " MASON " PATTERNS.

This picture accompanied an article in *The Pottery Gazette and Glass Trade Review,* April 1, 1920, showing Mason's patterns produced by Ashworth. In the article accompanying the picture the pattern was referred to as "printed Willow". It is the John Turner willow variant.

Atlas China Co., Ltd.

Location: Atlas Works, Wolfe Street, Stoke, Staffordshire
Dates: c. 1906-10.
Mark:

(GG157)
c. 1906-10

Brief History: Formerly Chapman & Sons, Ltd., the company was taken over by Grimwades Ltd.* in 1910. The name was revived 1930-36, and the Atlas mark was used, inserting the name Grimwades.
Type of Willow Manufactured: Mandarin pattern printed in medium blue underglaze on bone china.

A cup and saucer in bone china with underglaze blue printed Mandarin pattern. A line of gold is on the rim of the cup and saucer as well as outlining the cup handle. The same ring handle is seen on a later Grimwades* cup with a decal willow pattern. The pattern number on this cup is 6518. *Author's Collection.* $18-25.

Standard Willow pattern 9.50-inch plate with no inner border. It is transfer-printed in blue underglaze on earthenware. The outer border is too large. There are only three sets of the geometric patterns. The fourth is missing at 12 o'clock. Three single stilt marks are seen on the front of the plate in the center, and it has a single foot ring. This plate was in the first box of willow I ever bought in 1969. I was intrigued with the wonderful Royal Arms mark and Staffordshire name. Mark 1. A small dish not pictured has Mark 3. *Author's Collection.* $20-25.

H. Aynsley & Co.

Location: Commerce Works, Longton, Staffordshire
Dates: c. 1873-1982
Marks:

Mark 1 c. 1891-1932

Brief History: After fifty years in the Chetham* family, the Commerce Works was taken over by H. Aynsley and his managing partner, Oswald Deacon. Evidently, the firm did a large export business. A note in the *Pottery Gazette*, September 1, 1908, described H. Aynsley & Co. as "Manufacturers of General Earthenware suitable for Home, Australian, Canadian, American, Indian, and African Markets." In October 1915, the *Pottery Gazette* described Aynsley's china for children: "More than toy teasets in name. Used by a child in a more realistic way." The company produced "opaque porcelain" ware for steamship companies as well as military and government agencies.

Mark 2 c. 1873-1932

Type of Willow Manufactured: Underglaze blue printed Standard Willow and Mandarin pattern. Tableware and tea sets for children.

Mark 3 (GG179)
c. 1891-1932

Child's tea set in the original box. The pattern is Mandarin in underglaze blue. This is the most commonly found teapot shape in the child sets. A low, round teapot has also been found in child size. Mark 2. *Courtesy IWC Convention 1992.* $125-200.

John Aynsley & Sons

Location: Portland Works, Longton, Staffordshire
Dates: c. 1864-1997
Marks:

Mark I (GG193)
c. 1891+

Mark 2 (GG189)
c. 1875-90

Brief History: After apprenticing at the Minton factory in Stoke, John Aynsley II (grandson of John Aynsley I) worked at several different potteries. He was in partnership with Samuel Bridgwood III* from 1857-65, at Market Place, Longton. The works were demolished to enlarge the market hall. With the compensation received they were able to build a big new factory known as the Portland Works. After Aynsley's death in 1907, the company passed down to his son, then grandson, and on through the generations. In 1933, it became a Limited company. In 1970, it was taken over by Waterford Glass Company Ltd. In 1971, the name was changed to Aynsley China Ltd.; however, the marks did not change from Aynsley. Sydney Works was purchased in 1977, and Alsager Works in 1980. In 1987, a management Group known as Aynsley Group Plc bought Aynsley China Ltd. from Waterford Glass Group. The trade name in use has continued to be Aynsley. The Alsager Works closed in 1996; and the company was taken over by Belleek Pottery in 1997.

Type of Willow Manufactured: Bone china tableware. Standard Willow pattern, blue printed underglaze, and gold overglaze on colored ground. Chinese Willow variant with polychrome enamels overglaze and pattern in gold on colored ground.

Retailer/importer: Rich & Fisher, New York*

Standard Willow pattern demitasse cup and saucer printed in gold overglaze on a blue-green background. The central pattern decorates the cup, and the outer border is on the saucer. Mark 2. *Courtesy Paul Kirves and Zeke Jimenez.* $35-65.

Standard Willow blue-printed 8-inch plate. Note how wide the path is coming from the teahouse compared to that on other plates. There is a gold line at the rim. *Author's Collection.* $8-15.

Chinese Willow variant pattern compote in gold overglaze on bright red background. It is 5-inches across and 2.5-inches high. This pattern is most often seen with black transfer print underglaze and polychrome enamels overglaze. Mark I. *Courtesy Paul Kirves and Zeke Jimenez.* $40-60.

A three-part relish dish that measures 11.50-inches across. The complete Standard Willow pattern is in each section with both framing border and outer border. It is bone china. The irregular edge is decorated with gold, and it has a cobalt blue handle. *Courtesy IWC Convention 1999.* $175-250.

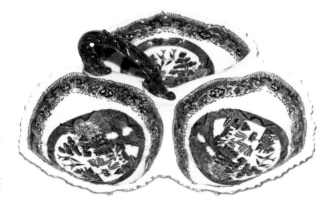

Baker, Bevans & Irwin

Location: Glamorgan Pottery, Swansea, Wales
Dates: c. 1814-38
Marks:

Mark 1 (GG227)

Comments Concerning Marks: Various numbers are found inside the impressed horseshoe. The significance is not known. Mark 2 is the most commonly found printed mark used by the firm. Rarely there will be a blue printed letter S for Swansea incorporated into the Standard Willow pattern. It appears in a box at the right edge of the pattern next to the inner border at 3 o'clock.

Mark 2 (GG226) c. 1813-38

Brief History: The pottery, located next door to the Cambrian Pottery, was conceived and built by George Haynes, manager of the Cambrian Pottery for twenty-one years, after a falling out with Lewis Weston Dillwyn. William Baker, Haynes' son-in-law and assistant at the Cambrian, became one of the partners and manager of the new Glamorgan Pottery. Business partners who had holdings in the iron and copper industry and were interested in investing in the new pottery were William Bevan and his three sons: William Bevan the younger of Morriston, Robert Bevan of Monmouth, and Martin Bevan of Risca. Thomas Irwin, a retired sea captain married to one of William Bevan's daughters, was the sixth partner. George Haynes provided the expertise and energy that guided the pottery, but his name did not appear on the mark. The partnership of Baker, Bevans & Irwin provided the funding to erect the necessary buildings for the manufacture of earthenware.

The Glamorgan Pottery was very successful. In 1812 the number of pieces of earthenware carried on vessels out of the port of Swansea amounted to 50,993. By 1819, the number had almost tripled to a total of 140,280 pieces. The Cambrian was losing ground during that time period while the Glamorgan prospered. Baker died in 1819, but the pottery continued with the same name, and Martin Bevan took control of the company. By December 1829, William Bevan senior, William Bevan junior, and Robert Bevan, co-partners in the Landore Iron Company were bankrupt. George Haynes died in January of 1830, at the age of eighty-five. Business gradually declined until the pottery closed in 1838. In 1839, the Glamorgan Pottery was purchased by Dillwyn. All equipment and molds were transferred to the Cambrian Pottery by Dillwyn.

Type of Willow Manufactured: Transfer-printed underglaze Standard Willow in blue and Two Temples II in pale blue on earthenware.

Standard Willow pattern transfer-printed 9 3/8-inch plate in blue underglaze on earthenware. This plate has 3-point stilt marks on the underside of the base and no foot ring. It has a slightly indented rim. The front gable ends are dark on the small building next to the teahouse. This feature is found on Minton* Standard Willow pattern. The impressed number in Mark 1 is 6. The plate was made in the early years of production. *Courtesy Renard Broughton.* $40-65.

Two Temples II pattern wash basin transfer-printed in blue underglaze on earthenware. A lovely large pattern was engraved especially for this large piece. Mark 2. *Courtesy National Museum & Gallery, Cardiff, Wales.* $200+.

Baker & Chetwynd & Co.

Location: Nile Street, Sylvester Pottery, Burslem, Staffordshire
Dates: c. 1869-75
Mark: Garter

Brief History: There is very little documentation on this partnership. This entry was found in Harrod's directory for Staffordshire in 1870 and also in 1873-4: "Baker & Chetwynd, manufacturers of ironstone china, earthenware, for foreign markets only. Sylvester Pottery, Burslem." By 1876, the name had changed to Charles G. Baker.

Type of Willow Manufactured: Standard Willow pattern transfer-printed in pale blue underglaze on heavy ironstone. No picture is available.

William Baker & Co.

Location: High Street and Fenton Potteries, Fenton, Staffordshire
Dates: c. 1839-1932
Marks:

Mark 1 (GG231) c. 1860-93

Brief History: W. Baker & Co. began business at High Street in 1839. The company later moved to Fenton Potteries. In 1893, Ltd. was added to their style. In the November 1, 1908, issue of the *Pottery Gazette* this information was given for Baker & Co., Ltd., Fenton: "Manufacturers of Granite, printed, and all kinds of earthenware suitable for the Foreign and Colonial markets."

Mark 2. c. 1893-1932

Type of Willow Manufactured: Standard Willow pattern transfer-printed in blue underglaze on earthenware. A plate has been noted with red-orange over-painting signed: "Redecorated by Russell, 1886." The polychrome decal based on Two Temples II was also used.

Mark 3 c. 1893-1932

Mark 4 c. 1893-1932

Cup and saucer decorated with a polychrome decal overglaze based on the Two Temples II central pattern. The pictorial border has 4 sets of a willow scene and 4 sets of elements from the Standard Willow border. The pieces are trimmed in gold. *Courtesy Tim and Kim Allen.* $25-35.

This is the earliest piece of Standard Willow I have found by Baker & Co. It is blue printed underglaze and has Mark 1. The plate measures 7.50-inches. *Author's Collection.* $8-12.

Bakewell Bros., Ltd.

Location: Britannic Works, Hanley, Staffordshire
Dates: c. 1926-43.
Marks:

Brief History: The *Pottery Gazette*, October 1, 1926, printed the following:

Mark 1 (GG236)
c. 1927-43

> Bakewell Bros., Ltd., took over the old factory in Hanley operated by the now defunct firm of Dudson, Wilcox & Till* who manufactured for a long time primarily for the foreign markets. Bakewell intended to produce a full range of general domestic earthenware for the home trade as well ... The "Blue Willow" pattern is also being produced by the firm under review in a complete range of tableware.

Mark 2 (GG236) c. 1931-43

Type of Willow Manufactured: Underglaze blue-printed Standard Willow pattern on earthenware. Polychrome lithographic decal overglaze that is a simplified form of Standard Willow.

Both pieces are blue printed Standard Willow pattern. The 5.25-inch jug bears Mark 2. The platter has Mark 3 and measures 8-by-10 1/8-inches. *Courtesy Dennis Crosby.* $65-85 and $75-125.

Standard Willow pattern plate transfer-printed in blue underglaze on earthenware. The central pattern is squared off to match the indentation for a sauce tureen or bowl that has a square base similar to that of the teapot in the next photograph. The platters made by Bakewell also have this indented angular shape. It has Mark 1. *Author's Collection.* $10-15.

An 8 cup teapot that has a small base and a wide indented collar. The square finial has blue highlights. The teapot is decorated with Standard Willow pattern. The outer border pattern is on the collar and reversed on the lid so that the line of fish roe on the collar meets the fish roe on the lid. Mark 1. *Courtesy Paul Kirves and Jeke Jimenez.* $125-175.

Barker

Location: Lane End (Longton), Staffordshire
Dates: c. 1784-1810
Mark: imp. BARKER

Brief History: John and William Barker were master potters working from 1784-87. John was known to have produced creamware, china glaze, and blue wares. William is known only as a potter. Richard Barker I, also a master potter, worked from 1784 to 1810, at No. 126 Works on the east side of Flint Street. Further partnerships included Richard II, John & James Barker beginning in 1809.

Type of Willow Manufactured: "Barker's Willow" is blue printed underglaze. The pattern varies from the usual Standard Willow pattern in that the third figure on the bridge is turning back. It is not always marked.

A 10.25-inch pearlware plate with no foot ring transfer-printed in blue underglaze in a pattern known as "Barker's Willow". Many elements of the pattern look like they came directly from Standard Willow such as the upper left hand island, the birds, boat, apple tree, and path. Some elements are altered: the third figure is facing the opposite direction from the others, the zig-zag fence is vertical in the pattern rather than horizontal, and there are a few little changes in the teahouse. The borders have similar motifs in different spots with a few not seen in Standard willow. It is an interesting early pattern with a clear engraving. No mark. Author's Collection. $60-100.

Barker Bros. Ltd.

Location: Meir Works, Barker St., Longton, Staffordshire
Dates: c. 1876-1981
Mark:

c. 1891+

Brief History: According to the "Buyer's Notes" in *Pottery Gazette* February 1, 1926, "Barker Bros. Ltd. installed more up-to-date machinery in order to be more competitive in USA market – 'the factory was not originally laid out for bulk production'." In the July 1928 *Pottery Gazette* the following is reported:

> No longer a firm of pottery manufacturers who merely cater for the miscellaneous middle class trade ... there are few factories in the Staffordshire Potteries which have so markedly changed over from one type of trade to another within so short a space of time. And with such conspicuous success.

The product was "exceptional earthenware." The pieces of Standard Willow found by Barker Bros. Ltd. do not represent "exceptional earthenware." Perhaps willow pattern was made prior to 1926. In 1959, the firm was purchased by Alfred Clough Ltd. It closed in 1981, and the works were sold in 1982 to John Tams Ltd.* and demolished.

Type of Willow Manufactured: Standard Willow pattern transfer-printed in blue underglaze. Tableware.

A 10-inch plate decorated with a polychrome decal overglaze. The pattern is a simplified version of Standard Willow. See Burgess Bros.* for the same central decal pattern. The border has elements from the Standard Willow border such as the key motif and bowknots. Mark 2. *Courtesy Louise and Charles Loehr.* $20-35.

This 6-inch plate is not finely printed. The blue is splotchy with uneven color. It also has bits of blue that floated onto the white areas of the front and back of the plate during the transfer process. The inner and outer borders do not match up. The outer border is too small for this plate, and there is an extra section inserted at about 10 o'clock. *Author's Collection.* $4-8.

A fine quality stoneware 9-inch plate with a slight blue cast to the glaze. This results in a very white background for the blue printed Standard Willow pattern. The rim is slightly indented. The border pattern is a bit too large for the plate, causing an overlap of border at about 8 o'clock. It looks almost like a double foot ring because the ball of the plate ends in a ridge just 3/8-inch above the recessed foot ring. *Author's Collection.* $25-35.

Barker & Till

Location: Sytch Pottery, Burslem, Staffordshire
Dates: c. 1846-50
Mark:

c. 1842-50

Brief History: The firm was preceded by Barker, Sutton & Till at Sytch Pottery from 1834-46. Evidently William Barker had two partners until Mr. Sutton left. By 1850, he was in business with his son and moved from Sytch Pottery to Hill Works, Burslem. Thomas Till* remained at the Sytch Pottery and continued in business with his son. The firm produced good quality earthenware.
Type of Willow Manufactured: Standard Willow pattern transfer-printed underglaze in blue. Ironstone tableware.

Gravy boat with the blue Standard Willow pattern in reverse. The outer border of the pattern decorates the inside of the piece. It has a square handle. *Author's Collection.* $20-35.

Barker & Son

Location: Hill Works, Burslem, Staffordshire
Dates: c. 1850-60
Mark:

(GG256a) c. 1850-60

Brief History: William Barker & Son followed Samuel Alcock* at the Hill Works in Burslem. Copper plates were probably kept from William Barker's partnership with Thomas Till* who were in business from 1846-50, at Sytch Pottery in Burslem.
Type of Willow Manufactured: Standard Willow pattern transfer-printed in blue underglaze. Ironstone tableware.

This 9.25-inch plate has the same copper engraving as the Barker & Son plate. It also has an irregular rim. The ridge on the ball of the plate is not as pronounced nor is the recessed foot ring. Three-point stilt marks on the rim of the plate. The border pattern is too large for this plate also. The 3 and 4 spoke wheels are omitted at about 7 o'clock. *Author's Collection.* $20-30.

Samuel Barker & Son (see also Don Pottery*)

Location: Don Pottery, Swinton, Nr. Rotherham, Yorkshire
Dates: c. 1839-93
Mark:

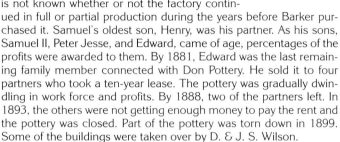

(GG263)
c. 1851-93

Brief History: Samuel Barker purchased the Don Pottery in July 1839. John and William Green, the former owners, had gone bankrupt in 1834. It is not known whether or not the factory continued in full or partial production during the years before Barker purchased it. Samuel's oldest son, Henry, was his partner. As his sons, Samuel II, Peter Jesse, and Edward, came of age, percentages of the profits were awarded to them. By 1881, Edward was the last remaining family member connected with Don Pottery. He sold it to four partners who took a ten-year lease. The pottery was gradually dwindling in work force and profits. By 1888, two of the partners left. In 1893, the others were not getting enough money to pay the rent and the pottery was closed. Part of the pottery was torn down in 1899. Some of the buildings were taken over by D. & J. S. Wilson.

Type of Willow Manufactured: Standard Willow pattern transfer-printed in blue underglaze on earthenware tableware.

Barkers & Kent Ltd.

Location: Foley Pottery, Fenton, Staffordshire
Dates: c. 1889-1941
Mark:

(GG266)
c. 1898-1941

Comments Regarding Marks: The mark above also occurs with the word ENGLAND added. A covered dish shown below has an impressed mark: B&K Ltd.

Brief History: The Foley Pottery is one of the oldest potteries in Fenton. Charles Bourne* used the pottery from 1807-30, for the making of porcelains of excellent quality. Hawley & Co. occupied the pottery for the making of earthenware prior to Barkers & Kent Ltd. Eli Barker, his two sons and James Kent* formed a partnership in 1889. Kent was the traveling partner, but he soon tired of that role and did not remain in business with the Barkers very long. He opened his own pottery in 1897. The firm continued to trade as Barkers & Kent until 1941.

Concerning the products of the company, The *Pottery Gazette,* dated September 1, 1922, makes this report:

> In teaware all the usual stock lines, such as sprig and line, 3 gold lines, celeste and pink banded, etc. are offered, as well as some strictly competitive lines in underglaze printed patterns, amongst which the "Willow" design is prominent. The last mentioned pattern can also be had in colours.

Blue is the only color I have seen in willow by this company.

Type of Willow Manufactured: Standard Willow pattern in blue transfer-printed underglaze on earthenware.

Standard Willow pattern transfer-printed 9.25-inch round plate with concave rim. Three-point stilt marks in the center of the plate and single foot ring. The glaze has a blue tint, giving a very white background for the blue pattern. The border pattern is just a bit too small. An extra three spoke wheel was added at 8:30 o'clock. *Author's Collection.* $30-40.

Standard Willow blue printed pattern 8.75-inch round plate with a concave rim. Three-point stilt marks in the center of the plate, and a single rounded foot ring. The borders are matched up and the correct size for this plate; however, I have a 9.50-inch rimmed soup plate with correct size borders that are not matched. Stray bits of blue underglaze are seen on the back of the plate from lax quality control in the transfer process. *Author's Collection.* $15-20.

An 8.50-inch rounded square covered dish with cobalt blue handles. The full Standard Willow pattern is shown on the lid except for the recessed area on either side of the handle that has been left undecorated. The bottom of the dish has an impressed mark: B & K Ltd. *Courtesy IWC Convention.* $50-100.

T. W. Barlow (& Son), (Ltd.)

Location: Coronation Works, Commerce Street, Longton, Staffordshire
Dates: c. 1856-1940
Mark:

c. 1900-40

Brief History: Thomas Waterhouse Barlow was in partnership with William Cotton at the Coronation Works from 1850 to November 11, 1856. After that Barlow continued on his own until c. 1882, when he took his son into business with him. The name became T. W. Barlow & Son until 1920, when it became a Limited Company. "Coronation Ware" is a twentieth century trademark used on printed marks. The firm produced earthenware.
Type of Willow Manufactured: Standard Willow pattern transfer-printed in blue underglaze on earthenware. It was called "Ye Olde Willow."

Standard Willow pattern 9-inch plate transfer-printed in blue underglaze on earthenware. It has a recessed foot ring. The outer border is badly patched with a cut at 5:30 o'clock and added scrolling leaves and wheels at 10 o'clock. *Author's Collection.* $15-18.

Barratt's of Staffordshire Ltd.

Location: Royal Overhouse Pottery, Burslem, Staffordshire
Dates: c. 1943-1992
Marks:

Mark 1(GG280a)
c. 1945+

Comments Regarding Marks: Marks 1, 2, and 3 all appear on 10 inch plates with the same engraving. Mark 2 is the form of the mark put on ware of any pattern whereas Mark 3 was made especially for willow pattern objects.
Brief History: The company was previously known as Gator Hall & Co.* Barratt's specialized in kitchen and tableware competitively priced. In the late 1980s, the company began producing wares based on late Victorian molds. The shapes are reproduced well. The company has also been a large producer of mugs. In 1994, Barratt's merged with Royal Stafford China*. The firm is now trading as Royal Stafford Tableware.
Type of Willow Manufactured: Blue printed Standard Willow pattern and reversed variation also in blue.

Mark 2 c. 1945+

Mark 3 c. 1945+

Mark 4 c. 1945+

A 9-inch plate in Standard Willow blue printed with beaded edge. The borders are well matched and fitted. Mark 1. *Courtesy Bill and Joyce Keenan.* $15-20.

This 10-inch plate has a shallow fluted rim. The pattern is Standard Willow, but the fish roe has been left off the outer edge of the border. The center pattern and framing border fit into the well and measure 6.15-inches. This leaves all of the side of the well and part of the rim in white. This size and shape plate has been found with both Mark 2 and Mark 3. The 10-inch-plates were also made with smaller pattern and wider expanse of white with WILLOW Mark 1. *Author's Collection.* $12-18 each.

A tip tray advertising dish for Schweppes has a reversed form of the Standard Willow pattern. The bridge has only one arch, and the fence does not cross the path from the teahouse. The key motif and flowers are the most recognizable elements of the Standard border. The dish is 4.75-inches in diameter and bears Mark 4. *Author's Collection.* $10-15.

Batkin, Walker and Broadhurst

Location: Church Street, Lane End, (Longton), Staffordshire
Dates: c. 1840-45
Mark:

Comment regarding mark: Godden's mark 295 has the initials only: B.W.&B. The mark as seen here is shown on p.196 in *Godden's Guide to Ironstone* and is B197 in Kowalsky's *Encyclopedia of Marks*.

(GG295)
c. 1840-45

Brief History: William Batkin, Thomas Henry Walker, and Job Broadhurst were in business until 1845. After the partnership broke up, Thomas Henry Walker* carried on until 1848.
Type of Willow Manufactured: Standard Willow pattern transfer-printed in blue underglaze on earthenware.

Standard Willow pattern 5.5-inch plate transfer-printed in blue underglaze on a light weight earthenware marked Stone China. The concave rim of the plate is uneven, and there is a single foot ring. The border pattern is too small for the plate with an extra section of the geometric motif at 5 and 6 o'clock. *Author's Collection.* $10-20.

Beardmore & Birks

Location: St. Gregory's Works, High St., Longton, Staffordshire
Dates: c.1832-43
Mark:

c. 1832-43

Brief History: The firm succeeded the short-lived partnership of Griffiths, Beardmore & Birks.* Compare the marks of these two firms. The partnership ended with the death of William Birks in April 1843. According to *Jewitt's Ceramic Art of Great Britain 1800-1900*, the various partnerships of this pottery from 1794 through 1874, produced useful ordinary ware primarily for the home trade.
Type of Willow Manufactured: Standard Willow pattern transfer-printed in blue underglaze on lightweight ironstone china.

Standard Willow pattern 10.25-inch plate transfer-printed in blue underglaze on earthenware. It has a concave rim and uneven edge. Three-point stilt marks in the center and a recessed foot ring. The outer border is too small as an extra section has been added at 5 o'clock. It is fine quality lightweight earthenware. *Courtesy Dennis Crosby.* $35-45.

Beardmore & Dawson

Location: Commerce St., Longton, Staffordshire
Dates: c. 1863 (June 10-October 10)
Mark:

1843

Brief History: The partnership between Thomas Beardmore and James Dawson succeeded the firm of Newton and Beardmore; however, it lasted a very brief four months.
Type of Willow Manufactured: Standard Willow pattern transfer-printed in blue underglaze on ironstone.

Standard Willow pattern platter transfer-printed in blue on stoneware. This large platter measures 17.50-by-14-inches. It is a typical mid-nineteenth century ironstone platter with a clear engraving. *Author's Collection.* $95-135.

Frank Beardmore & Co.

Location: Sutherland Pottery, High St., Fenton, Staffordshire
Dates: c. 1903-14
Mark:

(GG307a)
c. 1903-14

Brief History: Thomas Forester, Son & Co.* started producing china and earthenware at the Sutherland works in about 1884. The Frank Beardmore firm followed in 1903, producing earthenware. The term Sutherland Art Ware was used for many of the products. Well-designed tableware and toilet wares were produced. When the company went out of business, many of their patterns and shapes were sought after by other companies.
Type of Willow Manufactured: A unique polychrome version of the Standard Willow pattern was produced by Frank Beardmore. The term BASALTINE WILLOW was used perhaps due to the basalt-like quality of the background glaze on most pieces.

Two vases standing 7 and 10.50-inches high. The colors, painted over a matt blue glaze, are the same as those on the tall jugs in the previous photograph. The white earthenware clay body can be seen inside the vases. *Courtesy Paul Kirves and Zeke Jimenes.* $100-125 and $125-175.

This 6.75-inch teapot has black glazed handle, spout, and parts of the lid. The Standard Willow pattern is over-painted in the same colors as the two vases shown. A teapot has also been found with green glaze in the areas where this one is black. *Courtesy Tim and Kim Allen.* $125-175.

Four jugs with the Standard Willow pattern painted over glaze in many colors. The term "Basaltine" was probably chosen because of the resemblance to black basalt as seen here in the handles and rims of the two taller jugs. The smaller jugs have green glazed handles and borders. The polychrome pattern has a pale green background. *Courtesy Paul Kirves and Zeke Jimenez.* $100-200 each, depending on size.

Isaac & Thomas Bell

Tyneside Pottery M10 Mark with impressed M11 on a Willow pattern plate. No picture available.

Isaac Bell & Galloway and Atkinson

Tyneside Pottery M9 Mark with impressed M54 on Willow pattern plate. No picture available.

J.& M. P. Bell & Co.

Location: The Glasgow Pottery, Glasgow, Scotland
Dates: c. 1842-1928
Marks:

Mark 1 (GG318)
c. 1841-1912

Comments Concerning Marks: The impressed JB bell mark (GG319) can appear with either printed mark. GG 318 gives the initials only. The complete printed mark is shown in *Kovel's New Dictionary of Marks*, #110C.

Brief History: John and Mathew Perston Bell were brothers who decided, in 1841, to build a pottery. John, a lawyer, was the strong partner. Mathew was a shawl manufacturer and had poor health all his life. They hired manager Robert Clough, formerly of Anderston Pottery that was no longer in business. It became the most successful pottery in the history of Scottish ceramic production. All sorts of earthenwares were produced and decorated for the home and foreign markets. Mathew Bell died in 1871, and John died in 1880. The company continued as a limited company under the leadership of the former manager, James Murdoch.

Type of Willow Manufactured: Transfer-printed blue underglaze Standard Willow pattern and Two Temples II. Both patterns were done in light and dark blue. Tableware.

Mark 2 (GG319)
c. 1841-1912

This Standard Willow pattern covered dish is nine-inches square, but measures ten-inches from handle to handle. It has Mark 1. *Courtesy of Elizabeth Lynn.* $85-125.

Footed punch bowl transfer-printed underglaze in Standard Willow pattern. The bowl is 10.25-inches wide and 6.25-inches high. Printed Mark 1. *Courtesy Joyce LaFont.* $200+.

Two Temples II pattern 7 1/8-inch plate transfer-printed in light blue underglaze. Semi China printed Mark 2 is combined with an impressed bell with the initials JB. *Author's Collection.* $12-25.

Belle-Vue Pottery

Location: Humber Bank, Hull, Yorkshire
Dates: c. 1826-41
Marks:

Comment Concerning Marks: Impressed Mark 2 and printed Mark 3 appear on a scalloped edge plate in the York Museum Collection pictured in Figures 31 and 32 in *Yorkshire Potteries* by Oxley Grabham.

Brief History: In 1826 William Bell bought the premises of the former Humber Bank Pottery that had closed in 1806. The works were expanded and given the name Belle-Vue Pottery. Bell offered earthenwares thirty percent cheaper than could be had from Staffordshire Potteries. In the late 1830s, the Hull & Selby Railway Co. built a line along the bank of the Humber River. Bell appealed to the law because the line cut off the pottery from the river. He was not successful in his appeal, and the pottery closed.

Type of Willow Manufactured: Heather Lawrence reports in *Yorkshire Pots and Potteries,* "The pottery also made 'Willow Pattern', one design with two men on the bridge, another with three." I have only seen Standard Willow pattern and not Two Temples II. The blue pattern is very close to gray.

Mark 1
c. 1826-41

Mark 2 c. 1826-41

Mark 3 c. 1826-41

The Two Temples II pattern on this mug is reversed. The mug is 4-inches high and 4-inches in diameter. In 1997, a limited excavation was carried out on the site of the original pottery by Glasgow University Archaeological Research Division (GUARD). A large deposit of shards datable to 1857 and earlier was found, including a handle that matches the one on this mug. Printed Mark 2. *Courtesy of Henry Kelly. Photo by Douglas Leishman.* $100-150.

This jug stands 6.50-inches high. The pale blue Two Temples II pattern is reversed, and it is in linear form. The shape of the jug is from the 1870s. *Courtesy of Henry Kelly. Photo by Douglas Leishman.* $125-175.

Standard Willow pattern jug stands 6 1/8-inches high. It is gray-blue transfer-printed underglaze. A complete squared off central pattern appears on both sides of the jug. Mark 1. *Author's Collection.* $55-85.

Beswick Pottery

Location: Gold Street, Longton, Staffordshire

Dates: c. 1894-present (2003)

Comment Concerning Marks: There are no printed marks on Willow. Impressed shape numbers and impressed MADE IN ENGLAND are found on the ware.

Brief History: The firm of James Wright Beswick was advertising in the *Pottery Gazette* in January 1, 1894. The company occupied the Baltimore Works, Albion Street, Longton. By August of 1896, due to expansion of business, the Britannia Works on High Street were acquired. The present location of the firm on Gold Street was added in 1898. The year 1899 was the end of production at the Baltimore Works and the beginning of full production at Gold Street. Figures and modeled animals became part of Beswick's production before the turn of the century. Beswick died in 1921, leaving the business to his son John. The company under John's direction discontinued the old-fashioned designs and began making cottage ware. The demand for modeled animals continued through the depression and has continued to be a mainstay in production. Initially a private company, Beswick became a private limited company in 1938, and a public limited company in 1957. It became part of the Royal Doulton Group in 1969, keeping the Beswick trade name. The willow series seen below was made beginning in 1938; however, the onset of World War II curtailed production, and few pieces are found.

Type of Willow Manufactured: Mr. Watkin designed pieces modeled in relief. Various elements of the design are used as individual pieces. Light and dark blue on white were made as well as pieces colored with green, orange, brown, and blue on white.

This is the same teapot, shape 511, in light blue with dark blue accent lines, It is photographed from the spout to show the detail of the willow tree surrounding the spout. *Courtesy of Norma and John Gilbert.* $125-250.

A teapot molded into the shape of the teahouse with willow tree on one side, orange tree on the handle side, and birds on the lid. The bright blue makes a striking contrast with the raised areas of the pattern covered with clear glaze over the white background. The teapot stands 6-inches high (without the stand) and measures 9-inches across from spout to handle. It is sitting on the blue teapot stand with the white fence molded in the front. The impressed shape number is 511. *Courtesy of Tim and Kim Allen.* $125-250.

A breakfast set with light blue glaze and dark blue outlines. The teapot is at the back on the right. Facing it is the hot water pot: 7-inches high by 7.50 across from spout to handle. It is impressed 512. It has the molded shape of a small building with bushes and trees on the other side. The creamer and covered sugar are in front left and right of the teapot. The shape numbers are 513 and 514. The two-piece cheese dish, 516, is to the left of the creamer. No. 517, the toast rack, is perhaps the most ingenious shape of the set with the three figures crossing the bridge. The small piece is the pepper from the cruet set – not shown – shape 519. It consists of a boat holding a Mandarin (salt) and the pepper and a mustard of similar shape. *Courtesy of Norma and John Gilbert.* $700+.

T. & J. Bevington & Co.
(Bevington & Co.)

Location: Cambrian Pottery, Swansea, Wales
Dates: c. 1817-1824
Mark:

c. 1817-25

Brief History: In 1817 Lewis Weston Dillwyn leased the Cambrian Pottery to Timothy and John Bevington who formed a partnership with George Haynes senior and junior and John Roby. Dillwyn's 7/10 of the business was turned over to the partners with 3/10 going to the Haynes, 3/10 to John Roby and 1/10 to John Bevington. Thus Timothy and John Bevington each had 2/10. There were some legal problems concerning whether or not the China Works would be operated by the Bevingtons. As it turned out, no china was produced by the partnership and very little earthenware due to the large amount of stock in the warehouse and storerooms from earlier production. The Dillwyn firm had continued to produce china and earthenware even when the demand declined. It was kept in the biscuit or glazed in the white ready for decoration when orders came in. The Bevingtons decorated these wares, many of which were already marked Swansea or Dillwyn & Co. On some pieces the firm added Swansea in red overglaze. A few new transfer-printed patterns were developed and impressed Bevington & Co. In 1821, the partnership was dissolved and known thereafter as T. and J. Bevington. By 1824, the pottery reverted to the Dillwyn* family.

Type of Willow Manufactured: Standard Willow pattern transfer-printed in blue underglaze on earthenware.

Biltons (Ltd.)

Location: London Road, Stoke-on-Trent, Staffordshire
Dates: c. 1901-1999
Mark:

c. 1912-1990

Comment Concerning Marks: All marks found on willow pieces are impressed in several forms but always with the words "Biltons" and "England". Only one is shown here.

Brief History: The company, known as Biltons Ltd. from 1901 to 1912, began by producing mainly teapots. After World War I, novelties, figures, and "fancies" were added to their output. Biltons was closed in 1941, during World War II. Biltons re-opened after the war and became a successful manufacturer of low to mid-priced tableware for many years. In 1986, the company was bought by Coloroll Ceramics and renamed Coloroll Biltons. In 1990, it became part of Staffordshire Tableware Ltd. at the time that company bought out Coloroll. In 1995, there was a management buyout from Staffordshire Tableware Ltd. By 1999, Biltons went into voluntary liquidation.

Type of Willow Manufactured: Blue printed Standard Willow central pattern with variant border. Pink and blue willow with the same Standard Willow variant used by English Ironstone Pottery* and English Ironstone Tableware*.

Standard Willow pattern blue printed plate in underglaze blue. The borders and central pattern are very close together, leaving no white space between. *Courtesy of Jonathan Gray.* $20-25.

This blue printed plate is 9.75-inches in diameter and is coupe shape. The center pattern is Standard Willow, but there have been modifications to the border patterns. The Ju-I motif has moved to middle of the geometric pattern and has a flower in its center. The 3 and 4 spoke wheels are gone. There are more rows of fish roe in a square in both borders, and the bowknot pattern in the inner border has been squared off. It has the impressed mark shown. *Author's Collection.* $8-10.

A plain white teapot with a squared off central Standard Willow pattern on each side. It has an impressed circular mark with Biltons above England. *Author's Collection.* $15-25.

Birks, Rawlins & Co

Location: Vine Pottery, Stoke-on-Trent, Staffordshire
Dates: c. 1900-34
Mark:

(GG379)
c. 1900-15

Brief History: Charles Frederick Goodfellow and Lawrence Arthur Birks, who were brothers-in-law, set up a bone china manufacturing business in 1894 with a friend, Adolphus Rawlins. The firm, known as L. A. Birks & Co., set out to produce fine tableware. More land became available in 1899, and a new factory began production under the name of Birks, Rawlins & Co. William Sidney Rawlins became a new partner and Charles F. Goodfellow left to provide potters clay materials from his Potters Mill in Stoke. The company produced good quality china tableware and novelties including animal and butterfly models. The firm flourished until 1926, when the Great Strike bankrupt a lot of the industry. Birks, Rawlins & Co. closed in 1934.
Type of Willow Manufactured: Standard Willow pattern on bone china tableware in underglaze blue.

Bone china, dark blue printed Standard Willow pattern cup and saucer. Gold trim on the rims of the saucer and cup and on the ring handle. *Author's Collection.* $25-45.

Bishop and Stonier (Ltd.)

Location: Three factories in Hanley, Staffordshire: Waterloo Works, Nelson Place; Stafford Street Works, Miles Bank; and Church Street Works, High Street
Dates: c. 1891-1939
Marks:

Mark 1 (GG386)
c. 1891-1936

Brief History: Various partnerships with Livesley Powell and Frederick Bishop preceeded the firm of Powell, Bishop & Stonier, which was in business from 1878-91. Bishop & Stonier (known as Bisto) produced ironstone, bone china, and earthenware from 1891-1932. By 1926, it was a limited company. George Jones purchased Bishop & Stonier in 1932, but the trade name "Bisto" was used until 1939. Mr. Leslie Bishop, great grandson of founder Frederick Bishop, is still living at the time of this writing.

Mark 2 (GG386)
c. 1891-1936

The company had a very extensive export business. The *Pottery Gazette* dated December 1, 1908, showed a full page ad with this statement: "The sun never sets on Bisto Ware". The "Buyer's Notes" section, dated June 1, 1926, gives this appraisal:

Mark 3 (GG389)
c. 1936-39

... There are probably a round dozen firms in the Staffordshire Potteries of whom it can be said that the old and new in their productions vie with one another continually for favor, and of these B & S Ltd. can be regarded as an apt illustration ... .

Type of Willow Manufactured: Standard Willow pattern blue printed on earthenware toy china, tea and dinnerware, wash sets, and decorative ware. Standard willow in brown printed dinnerware, as well as polychrome and luster variant patterns were also made. A polychrome decal pattern with bright red bridge, boat, and teahouse will be referred to as "Red Bridge" willow variant. The "Goblin" variant that was advertised in the *Pottery Gazette*, February 1, 1928, p. 261, has not been found. The description reads:

One of the newest designs available in china tea and breakfast ware as well as in earthenware dinner ware, is the new "Goblin" pattern which succeeds in presenting in a delicate lace-like form, a modification of the old Chinese "Willow" pattern. Executed in a dove gray as the basis of the design the details being choicely picked-in with enamel colours ... .

Blue printed 7.50-inch plate in the Standard Willow pattern. It is thinly potted with a gold line at the rim. It has the look and feel of bone china; however, it is not translucent. Mark 1. *Author's Collection.* $8-15.

Toothbrush holder from a wash set decorated with the "Red Bridge" willow variant polychrome decal over the glaze. This variant was used by a number of different potteries and is sometimes unmarked. Because of the bright red color used on the bridge, boat, and teahouse I will refer to it as the "Red Bridge" variant. This piece also has the border pattern most often seen with "Red Bridge." The toothbrush holder is trimmed in gold, and could also be used as a vase. Mark 3. *Courtesy IWC Convention 2002.* $65-85.

Child's partial dinner set in light blue Standard Willow. There is a 4.50-inch plate and two sizes of platters: 4-by-5 and 4.25-by-5.50. The gravy or sauceboat is 2-inches high and 4-inches long. The covered vegetable is 2.50-inches high and 5.50 from handle to handle. Mark 2. *Author's Collection.* $300-400 with 4 dinner plates.

Standard Willow central pattern vegetable dish transfer-printed in brown underglaze It is an irregular octagonal shape. The lid and dish both have a brown enamel rim. The molded finial is lined with light brown. Mark 1 with pattern number 3434. *Courtesy IWC Convention 1996.* $75-125.

White pitcher and bowl from a wash set decorated with a polychrome simple willow variant pattern. The willow tree, a bird to the left, and, to the right, a pagoda, boat, and bridge with figures on it are all found on the side of the jug and bowl as well as in smaller motifs on the inside of the rim. Mark 2. *Courtesy Paul Kirves and Zeke Jimenez.* $225-325.

After dinner cup and saucer with gold luster lining in the cup. These pieces have motifs from the same willow variant as the pitcher and bowl above, but the colors are different. There is a black background with white pattern elements. Pattern 4/1266 and Mark 2. *Courtesy Paul Kirves and Zeke Jimenes.* $35-50.

Blackhurst & Tunnicliffe

Location: Hadderidge Pottery, Burslem, Staffordshire
Dates: c. 1877-79
Mark:

(GG 401) c. 1879

Comments concerning the mark: In addition to the printed mark, there is an impressed mark on both pieces shown: STONE WARE in a horseshoe shape with the initials B & T at the bottom. The printed mark also has only initials. B & T could also represent Barker & Till*; however, the quality of these pieces is superior to the plate with the full name of Barker & Till in the mark shown above.
Brief History: There were several partnerships of short duration at the Hadderidge Pottery, beginning in 1859 with Heath & Blackhurst*.

Blackhurst and Bourne ran the works from 1880. Blackhurst & Tunnicliffe had a short span between the other two partnerships beginning July 26, 1877, when Heath & Blackhurst dissolved theirs. Various types of earthenware were produced mainly for the home market.
Type of Willow Manufactured: Lightweight stoneware with bluish tint to the glaze. The underglaze transfer-printed Standard Willow pattern is a medium blue.

Standard Willow pattern platter and small tray transfer-printed in blue underglaze on stoneware. The 11-by-13.5-inch platter has an impressed and printed mark. The 6-by-8-inch tray has the impressed mark only. The small tray is probably meant to hold a sauce tureen. It has a 1/4-inch single foot ring in the same octagonal shape as the tray. The platter has a rounded octagonal shape with additional slight indentations. The border pattern is just a little bit too large as can been seen by the adjustment at 1:30 o'clock. Both pieces are above average quality for mid- to late nineteenth century earthenware. *Author's Collection.* $75-125 and $50-75.

Blair & Co.

Location: Beaconsfield Pottery, Anchor Rd., Longton, Staffordshire
Dates: c. 1879-1930
Marks:

WILLOW
BLAIRS
MADE IN
ENGLAND

Mark 1
c. 1900+

Brief History: The firm operated as Blair & Co. until 1911, when the trade style became Blairs Ltd. In 1923, the name changed to Blairs (Longton) Ltd. and continued until the company went out of business in 1930. In 1895, the partners were William Robert Blair and Thomas Bakewell; however, Mr. Bakewell retired January 1, 1896. Blair & Co. placed an ad in the *Pottery Gazette*, October 1, 1908: "The Largest Makers of the Brilliant Underglaze Printed and Fluted White China." Under "Buyers' Notes" re: Blairs, Ltd. in the *Pottery Gazette*, February 1, 1922, we read, "The tea ware is offered in blue printed 'Willow' etc." In fact, the company had been concentrating on tea ware, toilet ware, and ornamental lines. In the *Pottery Gazette,* May 1, 1924, "Buyers' Notes", pp. 807 and 809, Blairs (Longton) Ltd. is commended for moving strongly into the dinnerware market with a full range of domestic earthenware. Willow is one of three patterns pictured in the article. "The 'Willow' pattern can be had in two blues – light, or matt, and dark cobalt." Another comment made in describing the available patterns: "… the 'Willow' which never seems to lose its popularity."

BLAIRS
CHINA
ENGLAND

Mark 2
(GG405)
c. 1900+

Type of Willow Manufactured: Standard Willow pattern blue printed underglaze on tea ware in fluted shape china as well as on earthenware dinnerware.

Standard Willow pattern sauce dish transfer-printed in blue underglaze on earthenware. It is 4 3/8-inches in diameter. Mark 1. *Author's Collection.* $4-8.

Blyth Porcelain Co., Ltd.

Location: Newtown Pottery, High Street, Longton: renamed Blyth Works, Longton, Staffordshire
Dates: c. 1905-35
Marks:

Mark 1 (GG415)
c. 1905+

Brief History: This company produced china only. An ad in the *Pottery Gazette*, August 1, 1908, states: "The quality of our china makes IT THE BEST VALUE". The company made use of the term "diamond china" as a trademark. An ad in the *Pottery Gazette*, January 1, 1926, makes these claims: "'Diamond China sells at sight'. Quality makes it best value. We have upwards of 30 shapes and several thousand patterns from which to make your selections."
Type of Willow Manufactured: Standard Willow pattern light and dark blue printed on bone china in plain and fluted shapes. Polychrome decal based on Two Temples II pattern has also been found.

Mark 2 (GG414)
c. 1905-35

Bone china fluted shape blue printed Standard Willow pattern in medium blue with gold line trim. The saucer is coupe shaped. The quality is very fine. The cup, especially, is thinly potted. Mark 2. *Author's Collection.* $20-35.

Standard Willow pattern 9-inch serving plate with handles and 7-inch fluted shape plate transfer-printed on bone china. The rim of the plate has a molded pattern near the handles. The engraving of the two pieces is similar: note the fishtail birds and narrow straight path from the teahouse. The pieces were photographed together to illustrate the wide difference in color of blue. Mark 1. *Author's Collection.* $20-40 and $8-15.

Plate, creamer, and covered sugar decorated with a polychrome decal based on the Two Temples II pattern. All pieces have a gold line of added decoration. The quality of the bone china is excellent. Mark 2. *Courtesy IWC Convention 1999.* $10-20 and $35-45.

E. J. D. Bodley

Location: The Old Hill Pottery (1875-92) and Crown Works, (1882-92) Burslem, Staffordshire
Dates: c. 1875-92
Marks:

Mark 1 (GG423)
c. 1870+

Mark 2 c. 1875-92

Comments Concerning Marks: The Royal Arms mark has initials that appear to be E. J. D. Bodley. There is an interruption in the mark due to the vertical impressed mark BODLEY.

Brief History: In 1867 the Old Hill Pottery of Samuel Alcock was divided into two different potteries: one for earthenwares and the other for the manufacture of china. The new firm took over the china factory. In 1867, the partnership was Alcock, Diggory & Co, changing to Bodley & Diggory in 1871, followed by Bodley & Son, and in 1875, by Edwin James Drew Bodley. In 1882, Bodley acquired the Crown Works and continued operating both potteries until 1892, when both were closed. Good quality porcelains were produced by the firm until 1892. During the mid-1880s, Bodley added earthenware to production. Printed and impressed marks were used with the initials of the firm; however, many of the wares were marked with impressed BODLEY.

Type of Willow Manufactured: Two Temples II pattern transfer-printed in blue underglaze with gold trim on bone china, impressed BODLEY. Standard Willow pattern plates transfer-printed in blue and brown on earthenware have been found.

Underglaze transfer-printed blue Standard Willow pattern on 8.75-inch earthenware plate. This round plate has a concave rim and double recessed foot ring. It is a poor example of transfer printing with faint blue smudges in all of the white areas of the pattern. There is a little hole on the face of the plate to the right of the willow branches. The tag on it at the antique mall where I bought it read, "Ugly plate." Mark 2. *Author's Collection.* $20-25.

Trembleuse cup and saucer decorated in Two Temples II pattern with gold trim. The saucer is deeply recessed to hold the cup securely in case the person holding the set "trembles." Fine quality blue printed porcelain with Mark 1. *Author's Collection.* $35-55.

Bo'ness Pottery

Location: Bo'ness, Scotland
Dates: c. 1766-1880s
Mark:

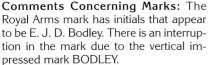

c. 1826-59

Brief History: Located on the south bank of the River Forth, the pottery had several different ownerships until 1826, when it was taken over by James Jamieson. It then traded as J. Jamieson & Co.* Members of the family ran the pottery until 1859, when it was bought by John Marshall. The works were greatly expanded during the Jamieson years. It produced high quality earthenwares, most of which were decorated with transfer prints. J. Marshall & Co. continued production with exports mainly to Canada and Ireland. William McNay* became a partner and was in charge of world travel. However, Marshall died in 1879, and McNay in 1880. The company tried to continue but soon closed.

Type of Willow Manufactured: Blue Standard Willow pattern transfer-printed underglaze.

Standard Willow pattern 10.25-inch plate transfer-printed in blue underglaze on earthenware. It has a deep well and single foot ring. Three-point stilt marks on the rim and a pale blue glaze. The transfer print is identical to the one on the plate by J. and M. P. Bell*; therefore, it seems that both potteries used copper plates from the same engraver. The border pattern is too large as can be seen just past 6 o'clock where the 3 and 4 spoke wheels and part of the scrolling leaf are cut out. *Author's Collection.* $30-40.

Booths

Location: Church Bank Pottery Tunstall, Swan and Soho Potteries (1902-48), Tunstall, Staffordshire
Dates: c. 1868-1980 (Booths Ltd., 1898-1948)
Marks:

Comments Concerning Marks: Marks 5 and 6 are both shown to illustrate two different spellings of the word "Georgian". The mark was used on the light blue version of the pattern on toilet services. The words "Georgian Shape" were not used on other octagonal ware such as the polychrome jug shown with Mark 10 or a light blue printed octagonal 8-inch plate with Mark 7.

Brief History: Thomas Booth & Co., Thomas Booth & Son, and T. G. & F. Booth were former names for the company before it became known as Booths Ltd. in the twentieth century. Charles Bowers, manager at the turn of the century was also a chemist who helped develop scale blue reproductions of old Worcester shapes and patterns. Silicon China was developed at that time which was light in weight and thinly potted. It was very close to porcelain in appearance and claimed by Booths to be "the perfection of English opaque porcelain". The "Buyer's Notes" in the *Pottery Gazette*, pages 911-12, August 1, 1906, discussed the fine quality of Silicon China in connection with the display under exceptionally good light by Booths' representatives Messrs. Green Brothers, 49 Hatton-garden, London. A picture of a Georgian Shape Toilet Service in Willow pattern accompanied the article. It went on to say:

> The majority of us cannot afford a china dinner service, much less a china toilet service, though we admire and appreciate them when we see them. "Silicon China" very closely approximates to fine china.

The June 1, 1915, *Pottery Gazette* announced, "There is also a new line of 'Davenport Willow' which is being supplied on a ware with a stained glaze and remindful of the stone china ware introduced by Spode." In the *Pottery Gazette*, April 1, 1926, the following comment was made under "Buyers' Notes":

> No doubt many of our readers, whenever they come across the name of Booths Ltd., instinctively call to mind the firm's "Real Old Willow" pattern or the "Lowestoft" – two of their best sellers. Excellent patterns these both are, and we notice they are still selling freely ... .

In 1986, I received a full color postcard from California entitled "Hearst Castle Table Setting". Available for sale at the castle, the postcard pictured the dining room with an old oak table set with Booths Real Old Willow. In spite of the elegance of the surroundings and

the china, paper napkins were used. In the center of the table stood a bottle of catsup and a jar of mustard.

In 1948, Booths bought Colclough China Ltd.* The firm was renamed Booths and Colcloughs Ltd. Booths' patterns and trade name were continued. In 1953, Ridgway* merged with Booths and Colcloughs Ltd. In 1955, the name was changed to Ridgway Potteries Ltd. The Booths name continued to appear on back stamps until 1980. The Doulton* Company continued the Booths' Real Old Willow pattern until 1999. The Booths archival material is currently housed at Doulton.

Type of Willow Manufactured: Real Old Willow Patt. No. 9072 from 1908-47; ROW Patt. No. A8025 from 1948-1980; and ROW Patt. No. TC 1126 from 1981-1999, by Royal Doulton: blue underglaze with bowknot outer border and gold or brown chevron pattern inner border with dots and/or leaf forms. The center pattern is found in green with no border on Ribstone, #5304 c. 1930s. It is also found in gold over black or crimson, and on a polychrome lithographic decal. Other patterns: transfer-printed pale blue Willow pattern #7481, with no inner border on octagonal shapes identified as Georgian Shape Willow on wash sets; Scale Willow on a powdered blue ground; and Davenport Willow which is Standard Willow pattern in dark blue with blue stained glaze or clobbered on medium blue. Additional variants not pictured here include "Willow Panel Border" #9041--a willow motif cartouche set in a bowknot border and a linear form of pastel-colored willow with bowknot border.

Retailers/importers: John Barker & Co. Ltd., London*; Gilman Collamore & Co., New York*; Edward B. Dickinson, Inc., New York*; T. Goode & Co., London*; and Tiffany & Co., New York*

Mark 1 c. 1906+

Mark 2 (GG453)
c. 1906+

Mark 3 (GG453)
c. 1906+

Mark 4 c. 1908-47

Mark 5 (GG453)
c. 1906+

Mark 6 (GG453)
c. 1906+

Mark 7 (GG453)
c. 1906+

Mark 8 (GG454)
c. 1948-80

Mark 9 c. 1906+

Mark 10 c. 1922-47

Mark 11 (GG453)
c. 1906+

Mark 13 (GG453)
c. 1915+

Mark 12 (GG455)
c. 1930-48

Mark 14 c. 1906+

Sandwich tray measuring 7"-by-13" in Booths "Real Old Willow" pattern A8025. There is a wide expanse of white because the pattern was elongated to fit the tray. The inner border is decorated in light brown rather than gold. Mark 8. *Author's Collection.* $20-30.

Ceramic business card for sales representative. Toy size dishes have also been found with the same advertising information on the base. Mark 1. *Courtesy Paul Kirves and Zeke Jimenez.* $35-75.

Full color cover for *Pottery Gazette* March 1945 showing dinner plate, Majestic shape teapot, covered dish, and London shape cup and saucer in Booths "Real Old Willow" Pat. No. 9072. Booths "Real Old Willow" was also featured in color on the cover March 1944 with the phrase "Now available for export" and again in September 1947. Evidently Booths' production of this pattern was not curtailed during these later years of World War II restrictions.

Five section hors-d'oeuvre server in 12.50-inch round wooden tray. These sets are also found in oval trays 8-by-12 and 9 x 12 with 5 to 7 sections. Booths "Real Old Willow" with gold trim on rims and inner border. Mark 2. *Author's Collection.* $600-650.

The Booths "Perfecta" tea or coffee pot with "Camel" patented drip-less spout. The little hump can be seen in profile just under the blue border pattern on the spout. It is an opening that catches the drip so that it does not fall on the tablecloth. The drip goes down the opening in the spout and back into the pot. An ad in *Pottery Gazette* July 1, 1926, for the "Camel" claims, "It pays for itself in a few months by the saving in laundry bills". Licenses were granted to manufacturers by the Camel Teapot Co., 49 Hatton, London Gardens. Mark 3. *Courtesy IWC Convention 2000.* $250-350.

Wash set in Georgian Shape Willow. All pieces are octagonal in shape. This pattern varies from "Real Old Willow" in three ways: 1) The color is pale blue. 2) There is no gold trim or inner chevron border with dots and leaves. 3) Though all pieces are marked Willow, the basin and chamber pot have a different Chinoiserie Pattern. Mark 5 above is on the sponge bowl and appears to be a misprint. The basin, pitcher, toothbrush holder, and slop jar all bear Mark 6. *Author's Collection.* $600-1000.

The Booths French press coffee pot for brewing coffee using the "Melior" system. The metal knob on the lid is connected to a steel rod with a metal filter attached. Directions for brewing: Place the ground coffee in the coffee pot and fill with boiling water. The metal filter is placed in the pot and pushed slowly down from top to bottom, thus separating grounds from the coffee beverage. This is an individual Melior coffee pot that stands just 4-inches to the lid. Four different patent numbers appear in the mark for four different countries. Mark 14. *Author's Collection.* $150-250.

Close-up of the Georgian Shape Willow chamber pot with non-willow pattern. It consists of two groups with trees of various kinds and shapes. There is a small pagoda-like building in the center of the trees on the left and a stool in the group of trees on the right side.

Oyster plate with center handle measures 8.50-inches in diameter. Mark 4 is seldom seen on Booths "Real Old Willow". *Courtesy IWC Convention 1994.* $65-100.

FIG. 1.—GEORGIAN TOILET SERVICE.

Pottery Gazette, August 1, 1906. Georgian Toilet Service is pictured on p. 911. The caption on page 912 reads: "We give an illustration (Fig 1) of the Georgian shape toilet service to the familiar Willow pattern decoration. It is supplied in pale blue and with or without gold edge." The article accompanying the photo discusses the quality of their "well-known 'Silicon China' and 'Royal Semi-Porcelain'" which were both produced before that date.

Demitasse cup and saucer with Booths willow pattern in gold on the saucer on a black background. The gold pattern on the cup has elements from the non-willow pattern on the Georgian Shape chamber pot. This pattern has been found with Marks 11 and 12. *Courtesy Paul Kirves and Zeke Jimenes.* $35-75.

Rarely seen Scale Blue Willow pattern in the style of Worcester Scale Blue. The background is a powdered blue ground. A scale pattern was made in the blue under the glaze. The central pattern is Booths willow whereas the four cartouches on the rim of the dish are elements of the non-willow pattern used on the Georgian Shape Willow basin and chamber pot. The dish measures 9-by-11.50-inches and has Mark 9 on the base. *Courtesy of Tim and Kim Allen.* $95-175.

Seven-inch high Mason's shape octagonal pitcher with ornate handle. It is decorated with a polychrome decal overglaze in the Booths willow central pattern. A linear form of the pattern forms a band around the outside near the rim. A few lines of gold enhance the piece. Mark 10. *Courtesy of Tim and Kim Allen.* $175-225.

Booths coffee pot with gold pattern on crimson and black background. The Booths willow central pattern is seen on the crimson while the gold pattern on the black consists of elements from the non-willow pattern on the Georgian Shape chamber pot. The handle and spout have gold line decoration. Booths blue "Real Old Willow" pattern has been seen on this coffee pot shape. Mark 11. *Courtesy of Norma and John Gilbert.* $150-225.

Standard Willow pattern covered vegetable transfer-printed in blue underglaze with blue glaze. Booths name is "Davenport Willow"; however, it is not known whether or not Booths purchased copper plates belonging to Davenport* after that firm went out of business in the late 1880s. There are many differences in the engraving when comparing this pattern to marked Davenport* willow. The most obvious difference is in the height of the trees on either side of the teahouse. The blue glaze on "Davenport Willow" softens the engraving so that there is a slight flow blue effect. The dish measures 8.50-by-10-inches including handles. The scalloped rim is lined in gold. Mark 13. *Courtesy IWC Convention 1999.* $100-175.

Charles Bourne

Location: Foley Pottery, Fenton, Staffordshire
Dates: c. 1817-30
Mark:

c. 1817-30

Comments concerning mark: Many of the porcelains were marked with the initials: CB, sometimes alone, and sometimes as a fraction above the pattern number. These are the only marks Geoffrey Godden mentions; however, Margaret Ironside documented Chinese seal marks on a Charles Bourne tea service in the Broseley or Two Temples II pattern. The various forms of the Chinese seal mark are shown in Newsletters #86 and 89 of the Northern Ceramic Society. There is a very strong possibility that the mark shown here is a Charles Bourne mark.
Brief History: Until 1817, when he began producing bone china at Samuel Spode's former Foley Pottery, Charles Bourne had worked in at least three earthenware factories. The quality of bone china produced at the six-kiln Foley Pottery was very good. Pattern numbers up to 1000 were produced. Mr. Bourne retired from the business in 1830.
Type of Willow Manufactured: Blue transfer-printed Two Temples II pattern underglaze on bone china.

A 7.50-inch plate with single foot ring transfer-printed in the Two Temples II pattern underglaze. The 1.50-inch rim flares upward so that the edge is 1.50-inches high. The rim has a scalloped edge with traces of gold in the recessed areas. *Author's Collection.* $45-75.

Standard Willow pattern grill plate with three sections transfer-printed in medium blue underglaze and clobbered in red, yellow, and green. It is very unusual to see Booths "Davenport Willow" without the blue glaze over the pattern and with colors added over the glaze. Mark 13. *Courtesy Louise and Charles Loehr.* $45-75.

Bourne & Leigh (Ltd.)

Location: Albion and Leighton Potteries, Burslem, Staffordshire
Dates: c. 1892-1941
Mark:

(GG483)
c. 1892-1941

Brief History: Formerly Blackhurst and Bourne, the company produced only earthenwares of a medium quality. In the 1930s, "Leighton Pottery" was added to some of the marks. In 1940, Leighton Pottery Ltd.* succeeded Bourne and Leigh.
Type of Willow Manufactured: Blue, red, and brown transfer-printed underglaze Standard Willow pattern. Table wares.

Standard Willow pattern 10-inch plate transfer-printed in deep cobalt blue underglaze on earthenware. The rim is concave with a molded pattern of double branches at four places. It has a single foot ring and triple stilt marks on the back of the rim. The center pattern is too large to fit into the well of the plate. The inner border extends up onto the rim and partially covers the outer border from 9 o'clock to 1 o'clock. The pattern crowding and a 3-inch row of glaze bubbles at the rim from 2 to 3 o'clock add up to a poorly made plate. *Author's Collection.* $12-15.

Red Standard Willow pattern 9-inch plate. Even though there is no white space between borders, the transfers on this plate fit the size of the plate. The centers of the geometrical shapes are not quite lined up between the two borders. *Author's Collection.* $15-20.

William Bourne & C.

Location: Bell Works, Burslem, Staffordshire
Dates: c. 1804-1818 William Bourne & Co.;
c. 1818-29 William Bourne & Cormie
Mark:

c. 1812-1829

Comments conerning mark: The mark (W. B. & C.) could stand for William Bourne & Co. or William Bourne & Cormie.
Brief History: William Bourne, at the Bell Works, produced great quantities of blue-printed earthenware. Evidently, he made a lot of money. In 1818, he went into a partnership with James Cormie until about 1829.
Type of Willow Manufactured: Standard Willow pattern in blue transfer-printed underglaze on earthenware.

Standard Willow pattern 9.50-inch plate transfer-printed in blue underglaze. Three-point stilt marks just inside the recessed foot ring. The outer border is too small. Additional 3 and 4 spoke wheels were added at 7 o'clock. *Author's Collection.* $20-30.

Bovey Tracey Potteries

Location: Indeo and Heathfield, Bovey Tracey, Devon
Dates: c. 1843-1957
Marks:

Mark 1 (GG498)
c.1843-94

Mark 2 c. 1895-1957

Brief History: There were two main pottery sites in Bovey Tracey in the last half of the eighteenth century; however, the two didn't become truly separate until about 1800. At that time, the works at Heathfield became known as "Folly Pottery". Underglaze transfer-printed pottery was made from c. 1800 until the potteries closed in 1836. The Bovey Heathfield Pottery reopened in 1843 as the Bovey Tracey Pottery Company. The partnerships changed many times. From 1895 to 1957, the company traded as Bovey Pottery Co., Ltd. Pre-Victorian pottery styles influenced their production. The "Buyer's Notes" in *Pottery Gazette* dated September 1, 1928, had this information: "The Bovey Pottery Co., Ltd., Bovey Tracey, Devon ... may be said to shine in the manufacture of all-around, good, useful, cheaper-grade, earthenware. Their productions begin with the cheapest white ware in utilitarian articles, such as bakers, pudding bowls, & jugs, and extend upwards through plain printed dinner ware, such as 'Willow' & 'Pheasant', to attractive styles in lithographs and painted ware."

Type of Willow Manufactured: Standard Willow pattern and Two Temples II pattern transfer-printed underglaze in blue and greenish black from 1800-36, as found on sherds at Indeo and Heathfield sites. I have not seen any examples. From the Bovey Tracey Pottery Co. period to 1957: blue printed Standard Willow pattern.

Standard Willow pattern covered vegetable transfer-printed in blue underglaze on earthenware. It measures 8-inches square and 9.50 from handle to handle. This is a common shape with a domed lid in the late nineteenth century. Mark 1. *Author's Collection.* $85-125.

Standard Willow pattern plates transfer-printed in blue underglaze on earthenware. The 9.50-inch plate on the left has Mark 1, and the 7.50-inch darker blue plate on the right has Mark 2. The larger plate has a concave rim with Three-point stilt marks. It is a heavier clay body than the later plate. Both have single foot rings. *Author's Collection.* $20-25 and $15-20.

Bradleys (see Salisbury Crown China Co.)

E. Brain & Co. Ltd.

Location: Foley China Works, King Street, Fenton, Staffordshire
Dates: c. 1903-63
Mark:

GG540
c. 1913+

Brief History: E. Brain followed Robinson & Son* at the Foley China Works. The date 1850 on the mark may refer to the beginning of Foley China Works as the date is also present on marks from Robinson & Son; however, it does not refer to the establishment of E. Brain and Co. Fine quality porcelain was produced by the company. In 1958, E. Brain & Co. Ltd. took over Coalport China Ltd.*. By 1963, the E. Brain name was no longer associated with the Foley China Works. Old pattern books from the company remain at the Coalport works.
Type of Willow Manufactured: Standard Willow pattern in linear form as a border pattern in polychrome.

Bone china 4.25-inch plate with border only pattern. The polychrome Standard Willow pattern is in linear form with a line of gold on each side of the border. *Author's Collection.* $20-30.

Brameld

Location: Swinton Pottery, Rockingham Works, South Yorkshire
Dates: c. 1806-42
Mark:

c. 1906-42

Comment concerning the mark: The impressed mark appears on earthenwares. It is sometimes accompanied by a + sign and numbers. Significance is unknown.
Brief History: John Brameld and his sons William and Thomas were able to lease the Swinton Pottery in 1806, on their own when the former Leeds partners pulled out. It was doing poorly, and they had to work hard to build it up. Workers came from Leeds Pottery which was temporarily closed. William died in 1813, and Thomas assumed the

running of the works. Two other brothers worked at the pottery. By the time John Brameld died in 1819, the factory was employing 300. Although there was a large export business to Russia, they were unable to pay their bills. They went bankrupt in 1826. The Earl Fitzwilliam agreed to be the mortgagee, and work resumed with restriction of sales to the home market. The works were renamed the Rockingham Works. The Bramelds were not good businessmen, and they were bankrupt again by 1842. The business closed.

Type of Willow Manufactured: Standard Willow pattern transfer-printed in blue underglaze on earthenware. Tableware and toilet ware.

Standard Willow pattern bowl transfer-printed in blue underglaze on pearlware. The 6.25-inch bowl has a flat base and 8-lobed rim. Three-point stilt marks on the rim. It has a large "blob" of blue at 1 o'clock. *Author's Collection.* $25-40.

Sampson Bridgwood & Son

Location: Three Longton locations prior to 1853. Anchor Works, Longton, Staffordshire: 1853-1984.
Dates: c. 1800-1984
Marks:

Mark 1 (GG595) c. 1885

Comments Concerning Marks: Mark 2 differs from GG597 in that it has "Bridgwood" rather than the initials.

Brief History: Sampson Bridgwood's father Samuel Bridgwood I died in 1805. His mother, Kitty, continued the earthenware business under her name. By 1818, the firm was named Kitty Bridgwood & Son. Fragments of an earthenware willow pattern plate from that era with impressed Bridgwood mark were excavated at the Gladstone Pottery Museum site in Longton in the 1970s. In 1822, the firm traded as Sampson Bridgwood and began to produce porcelains. In 1852, construction began for a new factory known as Anchor Works. Sampson took his son Samuel into partnership when they moved into the Anchor Works

Mark 2 (GG597) c. 1910+

Mark 3 (GG594) c. 1891+

in 1853. Sampson and his son died within five months of each other in 1876. The business was carried on by the two daughters and their husbands until 1890, when it was put up for auction. Among the innovations tried at the factory in that period: 1) Use of rubber backstamps which were much quicker than using transfer-printed marks. 2) New shapes in bone china dinner services including the octagonal shape with 'folded' corners. 3) A patent secured in 1885, for their "Process for Producing Copies for Lithography from Photographs and other Designs." The process involved tracing a design to be copied, applying it to lithographic stones or plates and preparing it for lithographic printing. It is possible that the octagonal plate with "folded" corners shown below was decorated using that process as it has a line drawing of the Two Temples II pattern overglaze.

Mark 4 c. 1910+

Mark 5 c. 1910+

After 1890, although the Sampson Bridgwood name was continued, there was no further ownership or management by the Bridgwood family. John Gerrard Aynsley purchased Anchor Works at auction. After his death in 1924, ownership passed to his son Gerrard. A private limited company called Sampson Bridgwood and Son Ltd. was formed in 1921. James Broadhurst & Sons Ltd.* took over in 1965. Bridgwoods was renamed Churchill* Hotelware in 1984.

Type of Willow Manufactured: Underglaze blue transfer-printed Standard Willow pattern on earthenware and porcelain. Overglaze line-drawing print of Two Temples II pattern in blue. Standard Willow Border only pattern in polychrome on bone china colored with a pastel glaze.

Bone china octagonal plate 6.5-inches across with "folded" corners covered with blue enamel. The Two Temples II pattern is line drawn with filled in areas. There is a line of gold around the border pattern. See Color Plate 9 in *Churchill China* by Hampson for a bone china plate in the same shape. Mark 1. *Author's Collection.* $35-55.

Bone china cup and saucer with Border only version of the Standard Willow pattern in polychrome. The border is inside and outside of the cup. The saucer and outside of the cup are decorated in light green. Mark 2. Another piece has been seen in pink with Mark 3. *Courtesy IWC Convention 1998.* $45-65.

Earthenware dish with Two Temples II pattern in dark blue. The central pattern is on the outside and border on the inside. It has a metal rim and handle. *Courtesy IWC Convention 1997.* $85-125.

when it was taken over by Bridgwood and Clarke. Jessie Bridgwood died in 1864, and Clarke worked both potteries for a short time on his own.

Type of Willow Manufactured: Two Temples II pattern in blue transfer-printed underglaze on earthenware.

Mark 1
c. 1820-39

Mark 2 (GG620)
c. 1820-39

Mark 3 (GG620) c. 1820-39

Britannia Pottery Co. Ltd.

(See also Robert Cochran and Cochran & Fleming)

Location: St. Rollox, Glasgow, Scotland
Dates: c. 1920-39
Marks:

Brief History: In the 1850s Robert Cochran, and his brother Andrew, built Britannia Pottery on land next to their glass factory. A twelve-kiln pottery, it was built solely for producing earthenwares for export to North America. In 1920 the pottery was sold to a family of businessmen. At that time the name became Britannia Pottery Co. Ltd. Painted and sponge wares were produced as well as a large output of transfer-printed ware. Many new designs and colors were introduced from 1920. Willow pattern was produced throughout its history.

Type of Willow Manufactured: Underglaze transfer-printed Standard Willow pattern in blue, red, and mulberry. Two Temples II in red underglaze.

Sugar bowl in Standard Willow pattern blue-printed underglaze on bone china. There is a gold line on either side of the border on the base and lid. Mark 5. *Author's Collection.* $15-35.

Bridgwood & Clarke

Location: Churchyard Works, Burslem & Phoenix Works, Tunstall, Staffordshire
Dates: c. 1857-64
Mark: impressed B & C

Brief History: The Churchyard works were located at the house adjoining the one where Josiah Wedgwood was born. Various members of the Wedgwood family occupied the works for many years. It then passed through other tenants until about 1858 when Jesse Bridgwood began to work the factory along with his partner Edward Clarke. Thomas Goodfellow was in business at the Phoenix Works until 1857

Mulberry 9-inch plate with very slight recessed foot ring. Three single stilt marks on the underside of the rim. The outer border pattern is the correct size, but the geometrical motifs are not centered over those in the inner border. The white space between borders helps to show the Standard Willow pattern to advantage. Mark 1. *Author's Collection*. $30-40.

Standard Willow pattern teapot, creamer, and covered sugar transfer-printed in mulberry underglaze on earthenware. The lids are trimmed with the border pattern, but there is no decoration on the teapot spout. Mark 2. *Courtesy Joette Hightower*. $150-225.

Red Standard Willow biscuit jar with rattan handle. The lid has the Two Temples II pattern transfer-printed in red underglaze. This is the only example I have seen of Two Temples II pattern by Britannia Pottery. Mark 3. *Courtesy IWC Convention 1999*. $200-225.

Blue Standard Willow pattern transfer-printed underglaze on 8.50-by-10.75-inch platter. Because it was made in Scotland, perhaps it should be called an ashet. The rim has a wavy edge, and the borders are well matched. Mark 3. *Courtesy Henry Kelly. Photo by Douglas Leishman*. $125-200.

British Anchor Pottery Co. Ltd.

Location: Anchor Road, Longton, Staffordshire
Dates: c. 1884-1982
Marks:

Comments Regarding Marks: More marks are shown here than pieces because the marks changed over the years and many different ones are found on the Standard Willow pattern in blue. Mark 11 is the earliest mark found. It appears on a red 9" plate. The pieces shown represent the colors, patterns, and shapes made by the company.

Brief History: Anchor Road Pottery was previously worked by J. T. Hudden* from 1874-1883. It was an earthenware factory. The *Pottery Gazette* dated July 1, 1899, advertised cobalt Blue Willow. In the August 1, 1908, *Pottery Gazette* British Anchor Pottery Co., Ltd. advertised "The cheapest dinner sets in the Trade". By May 1, 1922, the company had produced 2,640 patterns. The factory closed down for a time during World War II but the company continued in production at the facilities of J. & G. Meakin*. In 1965, the trade name was changed to Hostess Tableware. It became a limited company in 1970, and joined the Alfred Clough Group in 1973. In 1982, the works were closed and sold to Churchill China*.

Type of Willow Manufactured: Standard Willow pattern printed in blue, red, and brown with clobbering. Polychrome decal based on simplified Standard Willow pattern with variant border. Two Temples II pattern printed in blue and brown.

Mark 1 c. 1891+

Mark 2 c. 1891+

Mark 3 (GG622) c. 1891-1913

Mark 4 (GG622) c. 1891-1913

Mark 5 (GG624) c. 1913-40

Mark 6 c. 1891+

Mark 7 (GG625)
c. 1945+

Mark 8 c. 1931+

Standard Willow pattern 9-inch plate transfer-printed in brown underglaze on earthenware with clobbering in cobalt blue, green, and red. This color combination is rarely found by British Anchor Pottery Ltd. The border pattern is so small on this plate that another section with Ju-Is and scroll cross is added at 7 to 8 o'clock. Mark 5. *Courtesy IWC Convention 1999.* $35-65.

Mark 9 c. 1945+

Mark 10 c. 1945+

Mark 11 c. 1884-91

Serving plate with handles in light blue printed Standard Willow pattern. It measures 9.75-inches in diameter and has a single foot ring. There are three single stilt marks on the back of the rim. The detail work on the handles is done in blue. The border pattern is too small and has an insert at about 10 o'clock. Mark 1. *Author's Collection.* $20-35.

Two Temples II blue transfer-printed 7-8 cup teapot in globular shape. The pattern is in reverse on this teapot putting the bridge and willow tree near the spout. Mark 3 shows that the company's name for the pattern is "Broseley". *Author's Collection.* $65-95.

These sugar bowls match the shape of the teapot shown previously; however, they are decorated with the Standard Willow pattern: the left in red, and the right in blue. Mark 4. *Author's Collection.* $15-25 each.

Oversized cup and saucer in brown transfer-printed Two Temples II pattern. The pattern is in linear form on the cup so that the section shown is what is on the back of the teapot seen above. Mark 2. *Courtesy IWC Convention 1993.* $30-45.

Decal decorated serving bowl in simplified Standard Willow pattern. The border pattern is the same as that done by Bakewell Bros.* and Elijah Cotton*; however, this central pattern is larger and missing the blue color. Mark 8 includes the pattern number 3812, and the bowl has the impressed date 1931. *Courtesy Paul Kirves and Zeke Jimenez.* $25-40.

British Art Pottery Co. Ltd.

Location: Rialto Works, Fenton, Staffordshire
Dates: c. 1920-26
Mark:

c. 1920-26

Brief History: This short-lived company is known to have made fine Bone China; however, the willow variant pattern illustrated is earthenware. The *Pottery Gazette* dated March 1, 1926, gave the following information regarding British Art Pottery: "The majority of the patterns supplied in tablewares are available in sets of jugs and a big variety of miscellaneous items. The decorations begin with printed ware such as the 'Willow' ... ." I assume the pattern referred to is Standard Willow pattern although I have not seen any examples of it.
Type of Willow Manufactured: Printed Standard Willow pattern and variant pattern number 638/B, printed in brown with clobbering.

Willow variant plate printed in brown with green, yellow, orange, lavender, cobalt, and light blue clobbering. The 10.25-inch plate also has gold highlights in the pattern and on the rim. It is pattern 638/B. Several elements of the Standard Willow pattern are present including the teahouse, 3 figures on the bridge, and small building at the other side. The birds, orange tree, and small willow tree also appear in this reversed willow variant pattern. *Author's Collection.* $50-65.

British Pottery Co. Ltd.

Location: High Street, Tunstall, Staffordshire
Dates: c. 1920-26
Brief History: This short-lived pottery had a reputation for the most up-to-date equipment for mass production in the potteries. Handling of the wares in every department was minimized. An article in *Pottery Gazette*, June 1, 1922, told of a tour of the pottery with students to show them the mechanical arrangements for the production of teaware. The cups in the photo were decorated with Standard Willow pattern.
Type of Willow Manufactured: Standard Willow pattern transfer-printed underglaze on earthenware, presumably in blue – it is a black and white photo.

Pottery Gazette, June 1, 1922, British Pottery Co. Ltd. illustration of the mass production of tea ware with this mechanical arrangement for the placing of earthenware cups in the tunnel kiln for the glost firing.

James Broadhurst & Sons Ltd.

Location: Crown Pottery, Longton; Portland Pottery, Fenton, Staffordshire
Dates: c. 1847-70; 1870-1984
Marks:

Mark 1 (GG642a)
c. 1961+

Mark 2 (GG642)
c. 1957+

Mark 3 c. 1982+

Mark 4 c. 1982+

Brief History: James Broadhurst I was in various partnerships in Longton from 1847. By 1856, he had taken some or all of his sons in business and traded as James Broadhurst and Sons. James Broadhurst I died in 1858. His widow carried on the business for a time, followed by her son, James Broadhurst II. In *Churchill China*, Rodney Hampson writes that a willow pattern plate is on record in America marked "James Broadhurst/Crown Pottery/Longton". It would have been made c. 1847-70, the years when the firm was at Crown Pottery in Longton. John Aynsley built a new pottery in Fenton in 1870, called Portland Pottery (in honor of Josiah Wedgwood's famous Portland Vase). James Broadhurst II moved in and was able to buy the pottery in 1876. The factory was turned over to his sons, James Broadhurst III and Harry, in 1894. The business was successful in producing competitive type earthenwares for the "ordinary classes" and for export.

In failing health and with no sons to carry on the business, James Broadhurst III went into partnership with Edward Roper in 1922. Roper was able to purchase fifty percent of the business in 1926. The *Pottery Gazette* dated December 1, 1922, devoted a page to touting the wares of James Broadhurst & Sons, Ltd., including a picture of six cups and saucers illustrating the popular border patterns as well as blue printed willow. The "Blue Willow" pattern shown is actually Two Temples II. The article mentions that the factory was one of the first to institute roller printing with an eye to lowering the costs of production. They were also praised for not mixing the production of earthenware and bone china as some of the older factories were doing. Production ceased during World War II from 1939 until 1945, when Edward Roper's son Peter reopened the works. From the 1950s into the 1970s, patterns were developed using rubber stamping. This enabled the firm to increase dinnerware production. In 1964, the company purchased the Anchor Works in Longton of Samuel Bridgwood & Son. In 1979, James Broadhurst & Son bought Sandyford Works, Tunstall, a large modern factory used at first for a warehouse and later as a production unit. In 1984, Broadhursts was renamed Churchill Tableware.

Type of Willow Manufactured: Transfer-printed blue Standard Willow pattern and Two Temples II. Rubber stamped Standard Willow pattern in blue with variant border.

Full page ad in *Tableware International*, 1982. Reissue of Willow pattern by James Broadhurst.

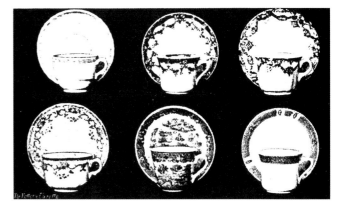

Picture of Two Temples II willow pattern cup and saucer in The *Pottery Gazette*, December 1, 1922.

Simplified Standard Willow central pattern covered vegetable printed in blue. It measures 10.50-inches from handle to handle and is 3.50-inches high. The border pattern is a simplified line drawn border variant pattern. Mark 1. *Courtesy Tim and Kim Allen.* $40-60.

This 9.50-inch plate has the same engraving as that found on Churchill Standard Willow pattern. Distinctive features include four rows of fish roe on the outer border; two different tile decorations in the two doorways to the teahouse; and the placement of the Ju-Is with scroll cross at the top center of the border rather than the geometrical motifs. Marks 3 and 4. *Author's Collection.* $6-8.

Brougham & Mayer

Location: Sandyford Works, Tunstall, Staffordshire
Dates: c. 1853-60
Mark: c. 1853-60

Brief History: James Brougham and John Mayer were partners making earthenware called ironstone or stoneware. The factory had six ovens. The partnership was dissolved in March 1860, and due to retirement, an auction was held the following year of the remaining stock and engravings. Geoffrey Godden writes that the initials B & M could also represent the firm of Booth & Meigh, c. 1828-37. This firm also produced ironstone.

Type of Willow Manufactured: Standard Willow pattern transfer-printed in blue underglaze on earthenware. A platter was seen at Portobello Road market in London in 2002, and the mark was taken from it; however, a photograph of the platter is not available.

Brown & Steventon Ltd.

Location: Royal Pottery, Burslem, Staffordshire
Dates: c. 1900-23
Marks:

Mark 1 (GG654) c. 1920-3

Comment Concerning Mark: The Rd No 414460 on Mark 1 is probably the registration number for the trademark as it has also been seen on pieces with patterns other than Willow.

Brief History: The firm of Brown & Steventon produced only earthenware. The *Pottery Gazette* in reviewing the firm's booth at the British Industries Fair in 1917, wrote: "... a class of ware which are now strongly in demand among the working and lower middle-classes, where many families just now have more money

Mark 2 (GG654) c. 1920-3

than ever before ... firm showed it is in a position to cater to this demand ..." A writer for the *Pottery Gazette*, August 1, 1922, reported: "... We noticed when at the factory recently that the old "Blue Willow" printed pattern, which has long been supplied by the firm in teaware only, is now being engraved so as to be made applicable also to dinnerware and other articles of tableware ..." From 1923, the company traded as John Steventon & Son*.

Type of Willow Manufactured: Underglaze transfer-printed blue Standard Willow pattern on earthenware. Polychrome decal based on Two Temples II overglaze.

Blue transfer-printed 8.75-inch plate in Standard Willow pattern with flat rim and low single foot ring. The border pattern is too large, cutting out part of the border at 9 o'clock. Mark 1. *Author's Collection.* $10-15.

Globular shape teapot with Two Temples II polychrome decal overglaze. This pattern is rarely found on ware by Brown & Steventon. Mark 2. *Courtesy Norma and John Gilbert.* $75-150.

Bone china cup and saucer in Two Temples II pattern in blue underglaze with heavy dark blue areas filled in. A unique border pattern has a band of dark blue with gold lining on each side. The scalloped inner edge and pointed leaf forms give the impression that it is a dagger border. There is no recessed area in the saucer for the cup to sit. The saucer has a single foot ring and is impressed BROWNFIELD. The quality is excellent. *Author's Collection.* $80-100.

William Brownfield (& Son(s))

(GG660) c. 1850-71

Location: Cobridge Works, Cobridge, Staffordshire
Dates: c. 1850-91
Mark:

Comment Concerning Marks: Both earthenware and bone china pieces were marked with impressed BROWNFIELD. The printed mark has only the initials W.B.

Brief History: The Cobridge Works were built in 1808 and occupied by several different partnerships. William Brownfield began in 1836 with Mr. Robinson and Mr. Wood; however, Mr. Robinson died that same year. Mr. Wood and Mr. Brownfield were in business together until Mr. Wood retired in 1850. William Brownfield carried on alone until 1871, when he was joined by his son, William Etches Brownfield, and the firm traded as William Brownfield & Son. Earthenware along with stoneware and Parian were produced from 1850. In 1871, the firm began to produce china. Several buildings were erected for that purpose, and great strides were made in the quality of the ware. By 1876, another son joined the company, and the name changed to William Brownfield & Sons.

Type of Willow Manufactured: Blue and brown transfer-printed underglaze Standard Willow pattern on earthenware and Two Temples II pattern on bone china in blue with gold trim.

Brownhills Pottery Co.

(GG674) c. 1880-91

Location: Brownhills China Works, Tunstall, Staffordshire
Dates: c. 1872-96
Mark:

Brief History: The G. F. Bowers firm occupied the pottery for thirty years before the name was changed to Brownhills Pottery Co. Even though the name suggests that only earthenware was produced, examples of bone china have been noted. Salt Bros. succeeded the Brownhills Pottery Co.

Type of Willow Manufactured: Blue transfer-printed underglaze Two Temples II pattern.

Standard Willow pattern 7.75-inch plate transfer-printed in brown underglaze. It is an eight-lobed plate with concave rim. A blue willow plate has an impressed BROWNFIELD in addition to the printed mark shown above making the attribution certain. The impressed numbers 6/80 in fraction form found on one plate may be a date mark. The borders match up well. *Courtesy Anna Morrison.* $25-35.

Two Temples II blue printed pattern rare breakfast condiment set. It consists of a silver holder with toast racks on each side and egg ring. An oval dish sits in the base, and there are ceramic salt and pepper containers with silver lids. *Courtesy IWC Convention 1994.* $200-275.

Brown-Westhead, Moore & Co.

Location: Cauldon Place & Royal Victoria Works, Shelton, Hanley, Staffordshire
Dates: c. 1862-1904
Mark:

c. 1891-1920

Comment Concerning Marks: This mark may well have been used later when the firm traded as Cauldon Ltd.* as many marks from this firm were continued with "Cauldon" added. I have chosen to use it here to represent the fine quality bone china produced by Brown-Westhead, Moore & Co. Impressed name mark sometimes accompanied with blue printed letter S.

Brief History: The firm produced very fine earthenware and china at the Cauldon Place Works occupied by John Ridgway* from 1830-55. From 1856-8, the firm traded as Ridgway Bates & Co. Thomas Chappell Brown-Westhead joined Bates in 1858, and in 1862, the firm of Brown-Westhead, Moore & Co. was established. When the name was changed to Cauldon Ltd. in 1905, many of the marks continued with the Brown-Westhead Moore & Co. name and/or initials. Some of the prizes awarded the firm can be noted on the reprint from the *Pottery Gazette*, March 1, 1915.

Type of Willow Manufactured: Standard Willow pattern blue printed underglaze on white and blue bodied earthenware as well as bone china.

Retailer/importer: John Mortlock, London*

Tea cup and saucer with scalloped rims lined in gold. The handle is the Old English shape with concave top. Bone china Standard Willow pattern in blue underglaze. Mark shown above. *Courtesy IWC Convention 1999.* $35-45.

Reprint from March 1, 1915, *Pottery Gazette* using both names: Cauldon Ltd. and Brown-Westhead, Moore & Co. Note Grand Prix in Brussels 1910 and Paris 1889.

Standard Willow central pattern blue printed cups and 7-inch plate. A chip on the plate shows a light blue clay body, and the cups have the same background hue. A molded basket-weave rim replaces the outer border pattern. The cups have a molded raised dot pattern on the square handles. The plates and cups are lined in dark blue and gold. Impressed BROWN-WESTHEAD, MOORE & CO. with blue printed S. *Author's Collection.* $10 each.

Burgess Bros.

Location: Carlisle Works, High Street, Longton, Staffordshire
Dates: c. 1922-39
Mark:

(GG708)
c. 1922-39

Brief History: The Carlisle Works were occupied by several different firms in the nineteenth century including the Bridgwoods* and R. H. Plant & Co.* All types of wares including Egyptian black, luster ware, and china had been produced at the works. In the twentieth century Burgess Bros. produced only earthenware. The firm had a relatively short span and closed at the beginning of World War II.

Type of Willow Manufactured: Polychrome decals overglaze in three different willow variant patterns.

This is a 4-inch butter dish insert for a wooden holder. The polychrome decal is based on the Booths Willow pattern. There is no border pattern – just a line of blue on the edge. Mark above. *Author's Collection.* $15-20.

Complete butter dish with wooden holder and 4-inch plate. The pattern is a simplified version of Standard Willow pattern in blue and gold overglaze. Mark above. *Courtesy IWC 2000 Convention.* $35-45.

Ten-inch bread plate in coupe shape decorated with Polychrome decal based on Two Temples II pattern. The sloped rim has a pictorial border. A line of gold serves as the inner border. It has an impressed mark that is similar to the printed mark above without the crown. *Courtesy IWC Convention 2002.* $40-60.

Burgess & Leigh

Location: Central Pottery, Hill Pottery, and Middleport Pottery, Burslem, Staffordshire.
Dates: c. 1851-Present (2003)
Marks:

Mark 1 (GG712) imp. 1883

Comments Regarding Marks: Marks 4, 6, and 7 have been used continuously: The more elaborate Mark 4 on larger items; Mark 6 on smaller pieces; and Mark 7 primarily on cups. "Made in England" without attribution occurs on items such as candlesticks that lack room for a more comprehensive mark. Mark 9 as well as Marks 1 and 2 were used on Standard Willow.

Brief History: Originally established in 1851, the business was known as Hulme & Booth. Retirements in the early 1860s left Mr. Frederick Rathbone Burgess, Mr. William Leigh, and Mr. Frederick Lownds Good who traded as Burgess, Leigh & Co. Mr. Good retired in 1877, and the name was changed to Burgess & Leigh. Through the years five generations of the Leigh family have been involved in the business. The company went into receivership, and was purchased in August 1999, by William and Rosemary Dorling. It was renamed Burgess, Dorling & Leigh.

Central Pottery, the first location of the firm became too small. In 1867, the business took over the earthenware department of Hill Pottery, former home of Samuel Alcock & Co.* Molds and copper plates of some of Samuel Alcock's most popular shapes and patterns were purchased by Burgess & Leigh. After twenty years, due to great expansion in business, it became evident that the company required a more modern facility. Middleport Pottery was built specifically for Burgess & Leigh in 1888 and is an early example of a linear organized factory. Many factories had been built in a grouping around the bottle kilns and, as a result, were not very efficient. In the year 2002, Middleport Pottery, a Grade II listed works, was the only totally intact working Victorian pottery in Stoke-on-Trent.

Transfer-printed patterns have been a staple product throughout the history of the company. The Broseley (Two Temples II) and Standard Willow pattern were produced as early as the 1860s, at Central Pottery. A notebook, "Pressers' Prices" lists a wide variety of objects made in Standard Willow pattern as of November 1872. This list included both tableware and toilet ware. Willow continued to be produced in large quantity when the firm moved to Middleport Pottery. According to "A Descriptive Account of the Potteries of 1893" one of Burgess & Leigh's warehouses was for "Blue Willow." By the time of World War I, production of blue willow had probably slowed or stopped altogether. The company staged a massive campaign in 1924 to introduce their new "Dillwyn" willow pattern. According to the publicity, the pattern was based on a plate made at Dillwyn's factory in Swansea and was purchased by Edmund Leigh in an antique shop. There are no records at the factory, or pictures of the plate, that substantiate this story; however, early patterns have been found that could have been source patterns for "Dillwyn" willow. The pattern is well engraved and has been very popular down through the years. An ad in the March 1, 1962, *Pottery Gazette* states: "BURLEIGH WILLOW Still made by Burgess & Leigh Ltd. Potters. Burslem. England." In fact, Burleigh "Dillwyn" Willow in blue was in continuous production from the time it was introduced in the early 1920s, until the late 1990s.

Mark 2 c. 1891+

Mark 3 (GG722) c. 1920s-30s

Mark 4 (GG723) c. 1920s – present day (2003)

Mark 5 (GG723) dated 1927

Mark 6 (GG223) c. 1920s – present day (2003)

Mark 7 c. 1920s – present day (2003)

Mark 8 (GG223) c. 1931+

Type of Willow Manufactured: Transfer-printed underglaze Standard Willow pattern and Two Temples II in blue. The company lists Broseley Tea Ware in the nineteenth century; however, only teapots have been found. Burgess & Leigh pattern books list patterns 1283-1289 c. 1910, in Broseley (Two Temples II) that are seven different color combinations with gilding used to decorate the Cranborne shape teapot and stand. Only one version is shown in the company archives, and that is #1283 and titled "Willow". It is described as "Printed underglaze golden brown, filled in Baker's green, crimson red, apple and 12's green. Traced and finished in liquid gold. Examples have not been found.

Burleigh "Dillwyn" Willow in "Swansea blue, " from 1920 to late 1990s: Original colors from 1920-24 were Blue with gilding (3052), Briar Green (3053), and Plum (3054). From 1924-c. 1930, available colors were: mulberry, dark blue, light blue, and green dinnerware (patterns 3553-3556), and suiteware in green (3596). Another color was announced by the trade c. 1924: "in that peculiar mixed colour which was in vogue a quarter of a century ago, and which was known at that time as 'Unique'." Judging from the formula, "Unique" may be a gray-blue. All colors except green are also found with enamel colors overglaze. An experimental red plate in the archives at the factory is also clobbered. Examples of "Dillwyn" Willow in red with no gilding or clobbering have been found recently. The Dorlings produced "Dillwyn" Willow in pale blue for a short time in 2000, and some experimental pieces in black, but the pattern was discontinued after that.

Retailers/importers: Lawleys, Stoke-on-Trent*, Mutual Store Ltd., Melbourne* and R. Twinings & Co. Ltd., England*

Mark 9 (GG717)
var. c. 1906-12

Brochure on Burleigh Willow from Burgess & Leigh with sizes, shapes, history, willow legend, and poem. c.1990.

January 1, 1926, ad in *Pottery Gazette* for Burleigh Ware Dillwyn Willow by Burgess & Leigh.

BURLEIGH WILLOW

Burleigh Willow has been in production for over half a century and is based on the Willow Pattern produced at the Cambrian factory of Dillwyn and Company, makers of the famous Swansea ware. This factory flourished from 1764 to 1870. Notable features of Burleigh Willow are the handsome porch to the mansion, the ornate double-decker fence and the rich border design.

THE WILLOW PATTERN STORY

A wealthy mandarin lived with his beautiful daughter Koong-Se in the magnificent mansion in the pattern. The mandarin wished Koong-Se to marry a rich Duke, but she loved Chang, her father's secretary. To prevent his daughter seeing Chang, the mandarin imprisoned Koong-Se in a wing of the house surrounded by water and built a fence across the path. Koong-Se and Chang floated messages to each other across the water and Chang, disguised as a beggar, rescued Koong-Se, while the mandarin entertained the rich Duke. As they fled, Koong-Se and Chang were seen by the mandarin who chased them. Koong-Se can be seen on the bridge carrying her distaff, followed by Chang, with her jewel box, and pursued by the mandarin with a whip. The couple escaped by boat to a house on an island where they lived happily until found by the Duke who killed Chang. Koong-Se set fire to the house and died in the flames. The Gods changed the couple into two doves so that even in death they were not parted.

AN OLD STAFFORDSHIRE SONG

Two pigeons flying high,
Chinese vessels sailing by :
Weeping willows hanging o'er,
Bridge with three men if not four,
Chinese temples, there did stand,
Seem to take up all the land :
Apple trees with apples on,
A pretty fence to end the song.

BURGESS & LEIGH LIMITED
MIDDLEPORT POTTERY, BURSLEM, STAFFORDSHIRE, ENGLAND, ST6 3PE

Pearlware unmarked 9.50-inch rimmed soup bowl in medium blue transfer-printed underglaze. This pattern is a possible forerunner of the "Dillwyn Willow" pattern by Burgess & Leigh. Substitute birds and willow tree for small boats and two small trees as well as a lantern carrier for two figures in front. Change the type of boat and add a path and 3 figures to the bridge and the pattern becomes Burleigh Willow. *Courtesy Nancee Rogers.* $65-85.

Pearlware unmarked 6-inch jug transfer-printed in brown underglaze. The pattern is the same as the pearlware plate on the right in the photo above. Perhaps the most important aspect of this jug is the name John Press and the date 1808. We know that the pattern in question is an early one as it was in use in 1808. *Author's Collection.* $250+.

Pearlware unmarked 9.75-inch blue-printed plate on the right compared to a new 10.5-inch plate produced by Burgess, Dorling & Leigh in black underglaze. The blue plate is another possible ancestor of the "Dillwyn Willow" pattern by Burgess & Leigh. Like the soup plate above, it shares common borders, buildings, and fence arrangement with Burleigh Willow. Substitute birds and willow tree for the large palm trees and replace the two figures in front with the lantern carrier. Change the type of boat, add a path and 3 figures to the bridge, and the pattern is changed to Burleigh Willow. *Author's Collection.* $120-150 and $15.

"Antique" shaped teapot printed in dark blue Two Temples II pattern underglaze. This teapot is pictured on a page with "Antique" shaped teapots in other patterns in an 1893 sales catalog. The page is reprinted in color on page 67 of *Burleigh: The Story of a Pottery* by Julie McKeown. There is no printed mark, but it has a raised pad with Rd. No. that is filled in with glaze and unreadable. *Courtesy Harry and Jessie Hall.* $125-175.

Two examples of nineteenth century Standard Willow pattern blue transfer-printed underglaze. The plate on the right bears Mark 1 and has the impressed date 1883. The piece on the left may possibly have had a lid. It measures 11-inches in diameter and stands 2.75-inches high. The handles have nice blue line decoration along the molded pattern. Mark 2. *Courtesy Nancee Rogers.* $35-45 and $75-100.

Two Cranborne shape teapots and stands in reversed Two Temples II pattern in blue transfer-printed underglaze. The teapot on the right is trimmed in gold. It also has a second willow tree near the teahouse and birds added to the design – both are elements of Standard Willow pattern. This is the pattern most commonly found on the Cranborne teapot that was introduced as part of the "Dillwyn" willow line in the early 1920s. The Cranborne tableware shape dates from c. 1910. The teapot on the left is slightly smaller with a lighter shade of blue and no gold. The smaller teapot and both stands bear Mark 3. The teapot on the right has Mark 4. *Courtesy Nancee Rogers.* $175-250 each.

The pattern on this Cranborne teapot was printed underglaze in mulberry and clobbered overglaze. Julie McKeown, author of *Burleigh, the Story of a Pottery,* found several color combinations listed c. 1910 that were used to decorate Cranborne teapots in Broseley (Two Temples II) pattern; however, none of them had mulberry underglaze. Colors listed were: pink, "K" blue, Imperial blue, Imperial blue flown, golden brown, and apple green – all with enameling over the glaze. The pattern on this teapot has the extra willow tree and birds seen on the teapot on the right above. It has Mark 4 plus the pattern number 3553 – the number c. 1924-30 for Mulberry with and without enameling over glaze. It is good to know that the factory name for the color is, in fact, Mulberry. Pattern numbers are rarely found on Burleighware. *Courtesy Joyce and Bill Keenan.* $250+.

Three Burleigh Willow plates illustrating three color combinations: The top plate is deep blue; the rimmed soup bowl on the lower left is green transfer-printed underglaze. The blue plate on the lower right has a yellow glaze. Mark 4. *Courtesy Nancee Rogers.* $20-25 and $75-100 each.

The Crescent Sandwich Set was advertised in *Pottery Gazette*, December 1, 1928, "in a large range of patterns and colourings as The Success of the Year." The crescent dish measures 8-by-12-inches. The 5.25-inch triangular pieces have Rd. N 733381, and the large dish has Mark 5. Both numbers are from 1927. All pieces have gold trim. *Courtesy Nancee Rogers.* $150-250.

Burleigh "Dillwyn" willow dinner plate transfer-printed in red underglaze and clobbered with rose, green, and yellow. It is trimmed in gold. This gorgeous plate is in the archives at Middleport Factory. *Courtesy William and Rosemary Dorling.* NP

Dinner service of blue printed Burleigh Willow with red and yellow clobbering and gold trim. There are 5 sizes of platters shown in addition to two sauce tureens with ladles, three covered vegetable dishes, and three sizes of plates. Mark 4. *Courtesy IWC 1993 Convention.* $2,000+.

Five Burleigh Ware teapots including two sizes of kettle shape and two sizes of the round shape in Burleigh Willow as well as a teapot in Burgess & Leigh's Pagoda Ware. The last teapot bears Mark 8. The others are marked with Mark 4. Pagoda Ware was introduced with an ad and feature story in *Pottery Gazette* dated April 1, 1931. Tea Wares only were made. The teapot shape was also made with Burleigh "Dillwyn" Willow pattern. *Courtesy Nancee Rogers.* $65-145 each.

Three different shapes of Burleigh Willow coffee pots. The pot in the front is a cocoa jug. All pieces have gold trim and bear Mark 4. *Courtesy Nancee Rogers.* $100-175 each.

The cube shape teapot holds one cup. This shape was used on ships in the Cunard and other lines. Mark 4. *Courtesy Harry and Jessie Hall.* $75-150.

Three examples of Burleigh Willow printed in different shades of mulberry. The plate also is clobbered with red, green, and yellow. Most of the pieces we have found in mulberry come from Canada, New Zealand, and Australia. Perhaps it was a trial color sent to specific markets. *Courtesy Nancee Rogers.* $85-200 each.

Three different toast racks. The one in the center has only the bird motif in front and a tree in the back with the border pattern. It holds 4 pieces of toast. The other two hold just 2 pieces of toast and have areas at the front and back for butter, jam, etc. The one on the left has Mark 7 and the others have Mark 4. *Courtesy Nancee Rogers.* $50-65 for center one. $125-150 each for the others.

Joseph Burn & Co.

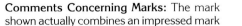

Location: Stepney Bank Pottery, Ouseburn, Newcastle upon Tyne
Dates: c. 1852-60
Marks:

c. 1852-60

Comments Concerning Marks: The mark shown actually combines an impressed mark with the name J BURN & Co. with a printed mark copied from Fell & Co. Mark 4. The only difference in the two marks is the initials. This one has B & Co. Evidently when used alone, the printed mark was used to deceive buyers into thinking the ware was made by Fell & Co.*

Brief History: Joseph Burn followed Thomas Bell & Co. at the Stepney Bank Pottery, originally known as the New Pottery. Printed earthenware of average quality was produced. John Charlton succeeded Joseph Burn at the pottery.

Type of Willow Manufactured: Standard Willow pattern transfer-printed in blue underglaze on earthenware. Willow seems to have been one of the patterns most produced by the firm.

Standard Willow pattern transfer-printed 9.75-inch plate transfer-printed in blue underglaze on earthenware. The plate has a concave rim and wavy edge. The borders are pretty well matched up, but there is a patch at 7 o'clock. The printing quality is average for this period. Printed and impressed mark. *Courtesy J and J Cockerill.* $15-25 as is.

Burn & Woods

Location: Stepney Bank Pottery, Ouseburn, Newcastle upon Tyne
Dates: Unknown
Impressed Mark:

c. nineteenth century

Brief History: I have found no information about this pottery. It is assumed that the partnership may have involved Joseph Burn* (see above). The partnership may have occurred before Joseph Burn began to work on his own.

Type of Willow Manufactured: Standard Willow pattern transfer-printed in dark blue underglaze on earthenware. The plate is finely potted with no foot ring. It has a high gloss quality glaze that is slightly bubbled. The plate is slightly warped and badly cracked.

Standard Willow pattern 9.5-inch plate transfer-printed in blue underglaze on earthenware. This plate is an indented octagonal shape. There is more white space between borders and in the pattern itself, which is more pleasing to the eye. This is the first documented plate with this mark. *Courtesy J and J Cockerill.* NP as is.

Standard Willow pattern transfer-printed 6.5-inch plate transfer-printed in blue underglaze on earthenware. This plate has a concave rim and wavy edge. The printing is blotchy. Impressed mark only. *Courtesy J and J Cockerill.* $6-12.

Burslem Pottery Co. Ltd.

Location: Scotia Works, Burslem, Staffordshire
Dates: c. 1894-1933
Mark:

(GG732)
c. 1894-1933

Brief History: The Scotia Works was originally the parish workhouse of Burslem. It was converted into a manufactory in 1857 by James Vernon*. Several different partnerships operated the works from 1862 until 1894 when it became known as Burslem Pottery Co. Ltd.
Type of Willow Manufactured: Blue transfer-printed Standard Willow pattern underglaze on earthenware.

Blue Standard Willow pattern 10.25-inch plate transfer-printed underglaze. The centers of the geometric parts of the two borders are almost matched up. There is a feeling of space in the pattern with the white area between the borders. *Courtesy Jeff Siptak.* $35-55.

Serving plate known as bread and butter plate or cake plate. It measures 9.75-inches across and has a single foot ring. The dark blue Standard willow pattern is a little crowded, and the geometric design at 10:30 o'clock in the outer border had to be cut to fit. Even so, it has an elegant appearance with a china-like quality to the earthenware and gold trim on the plate and handle decoration. *Author's collection.* $45-55.

William & James Butterfield

Location: Globe Pottery, Tunstall, Staffordshire
Dates: c. 1854-61
Mark:

Brief History: William and James Butterfield were in partnership at Globe Pottery making earthenware. In 1861 the partnership was dissolved, and the firm traded as W. & C. Butterfield.
Type of Willow Manufactured: Two Temples II pattern tableware transfer-printed in red underglaze on earthenware. A large breakfast cup and saucer have been seen with gold trim. The saucer is 8-inches in diameter, and the cup is 4-inches high and 4.5-inches wide. No picture is available.

c. 1854-61

Bursley Ware (see H. J. Wood)

Samuel & John Burton

Location: New Street, Hanley, Staffordshire
Dates: c. 1832-45
Mark:

c. 1832-45

Brief History: James Keeling operated the New Street works until 1831. It was taken over by Samuel & John Burton in 1832. Earthenware was produced. In October of 1833 Samuel Burton married one of the daughters of James Keeling.
Type of Willow Manufactured: Blue transfer-printed Standard Willow pattern underglaze.

Callands Pottery

Location: Landore, Wales
Dates: c.1852-56
Mark: CALLAND & Co.

Brief History: James Hinkley, formerly manager at Cambrian Pottery under Lewis Llewelyn Dillwyn, was the agent for Callands Pottery. Advertising at the outset declared "Earthenware of every variety is manufactured". Unfortunately times were not good for the pottery industry, and it was offered for sale less than a year after it began. A second attempt to sell the pottery was made in 1855. In 1856, it was let for an unrelated purpose. The pottery is best known for the Syria pattern. The willow pattern was also produced. An example is on display at the Swansea Museum.
Type of Willow Manufactured: Standard Willow pattern transfer-printed underglaze in blue on earthenware. No picture is available.

Campbellfield Pottery Co. Ltd.

Location: Springburn Works, Glasgow, Scotland
Dates: c.1881-99
Mark: C. P. Co. Ltd.

Brief History: William Rankine Currie purchased the Springburn Pottery in 1881 forming a limited company with himself as principal shareholder. He had formerly been making redware at the old Campbellfield Works in Gallowgate he had purchased from William Wilson. He was able to produce white ware and stoneware at the new site. A fire at Gallowgate in 1882 damaged that works, and it closed down in 1885. The Springburn Works operated until the company went into voluntary liquidation in 1899.

Type of Willow Manufactured: Standard Willow pattern transfer-printed underglaze in blue on earthenware is seen on page 60 of *Scottish Ceramics* by Henry Kelly. Two Temples II pattern was also produced in polychrome.

Polychrome mug in Two Temples II pattern. The pattern is so large that only part of the temple and some rocks can be seen from this side. *Courtesy Henry Kelly. Photo by Douglas Leishman.* $100-150.

Cardew Design

Location: "Teapottery", Bovey Tracey, Devon
Dates: c. 1991 – present (2003)
Mark:

c. 1991-present (2003)

Brief History: Paul Cardew, B.A. Hons A.T.D. formerly operated "Sunshine Ceramics". In the early 1990s, he formed Cardew Design with partner Peter Kirvan. The firm designs and produces figural teapots including cartoon and literary characters as well as pieces of furniture. Many popular china patterns are used to decorate specific shapes.

Type of Willow Manufactured: Many teapots have Blue Willow decoration. There are other items such as jugs decorated with Standard Willow pattern that have a mark with two birds, CARDEW BLUE, Designed in England, and Made in China.

Small size teapot known as "Afternoon Tea". It comes in 4 and 6 cup sizes. The Willow pattern is in linear form overglaze around the skirt of the tablecloth. The miniature tea set is molded onto the lid, so it all comes up when the lid is removed. *Author's Collection.* $50-60.

Polychrome mug showing the other side of the Two Temples II pattern with the willow tree and two figures on the bridge. *Courtesy Henry Kelly. Photo by Douglas Leishman.* $100-150.

Carlton Ware (see Wiltshaw and Robinson)

John Carr & Son(s)

Location: Low Lights Pottery, North Shields, Northumberland
Dates: c. 1845-1900
Marks:

Mark 1
c. 1854-61+

Mark 2
c. 1854-61+

Comments Regarding Marks: J. C. Bell in *Tyneside Pottery* says that potters often used marks from previous partnerships. For that reason I have placed a + sign after the dates given for the marks above as they may have been used when the name changed to John Carr & Sons. A variety of printed and impressed marks were used separately and in combination. Mark 2 is especially confusing because it contains the word "Staffordshire" which may have been used as a means of attaining better prices. In this instance it is used in combination with a printed mark bearing the word LONDON. This impressed mark may have belonged to a London retailer as it was used by other Tyneside potteries such as Isaac & Thomas Bell and Middlesboro Pottery*. Mark 1 has a 1/2 inch impressed letter C in the crown and ribbon area.

Brief History: John Carr was in business by himself until 1850 when he traded as John Carr & Co. In 1854 the firm was renamed John Carr & Son, and by 1861 it was John Carr & Sons. An image of a willow plate appeared in an ad on page 178 of the February 1, 1882 *Pottery Gazette*. The ad stated "Earthenware Manufacturers for home and Foreign Markets...Dinner, Tea, Toilet, Jug, Teapot, and Miscellaneous Wares."

Type of Willow Manufactured: Transfer-printed Standard Willow pattern underglaze in blue, brown, and black.

Brown transfer-printed Standard Willow pattern 9.25-inch soup plate. Three-point stilt marks on the concave rim. The outer border pattern was cut to fit at just past 6 o'clock. The single foot ring is 1/4-inch wide and flat. Mark 1. *Author's Collection.* $65-85.

Blue printed Standard Willow pattern 9-inch plate warped in the center. Three-point stilt marks on the concave rim and visible on the front. The most noticeable is at 9 o'clock. The single foot ring is flat and 1/2-inch wide. The center of the geometrical pattern in the outer border is not lined up at 12 o'clock as is the inner border. The plate has a pale blue glaze. Mark 2. *Author's Collection.* $30-40.

Cartwright & Edwards, Ltd.

Location: Weston Place, Borough Pottery, and Victoria Works, Longton. Heron Cross Pottery, Fenton, Staffordshire.
Dates: c. 1858-1988
Marks:

Mark 1 c. 1858-91

Mark 2 (GG796)
c. 1891+

Mark 3 c. 1891+

Comment Concerning Marks: Mark 3 appears on a blue willow pudding dish not shown here.

Brief History: Edward Cartwright and Aaron Edwards became partners in 1858 producing earthenware including blue printed wares. They acquired Borough Pottery in 1869 continuing to produce earthenware. Victoria Works was added in 1912 for the production of china. Heron Cross Pottery was acquired at the outbreak of World War I and remodeled for the purpose of producing a class of earthenware that was cheap, attractive, and saleable on a large scale. Their aim was to take over the trade that had previously gone to German and Austrian factories. An article under "Buyer's Notes" in the August 2, 1915, issue of *Pottery Gazette* stated that the firm had always been "up-to-date and go-ahead". The company was purchased by Alfred Clough Ltd. in 1955. They continued to trade as Cartwright & Edwards until 1982 when the name became Cartwright of England. The Alfred Clough Group was purchased by Coloroll in 1988.

Type of Willow Manufactured: Blue transfer-printed underglaze in Standard Willow pattern with standard border and variant border.

Standard Willow pattern 9 1/8-inch plate transfer-printed in blue underglaze on stone china There are slight indentations on the concave rim. Three-point stilt marks in the center with three marks showing on the front. (The brown area in the orange tree is a hole in the plate.) The outer border pattern is badly patched just before and after 6 o'clock. The plate has a single flat foot ring and a bluish tint to the glaze. Mark 1. *Author's Collection.* $15-20.

Cup and saucer with Standard Willow central pattern in blue and variant border pattern with sections of basket weave, curlicues, and flower forms. There is gold trim. Mark 2 has the word Victoria that may refer to Victoria Works where china was produced; however, this set is earthenware. *Author's Collection.* $20-30.

Pottery Gazette, August 2, 1915. "Three useful styles in earthenware tea ware." The willow set is supplied in either dark or matt blue. The shape given for the willow set is "Minton". The pattern is identical to the cup and saucer above; however, the cup shape appears to be different.

Caughley – Salopian Works of Thomas Turner

Location: Nr. Broseley, Shropshire
Dates: c. 1775-99
Marks:

Mark 1 (GG817)
c. 1775-90

Mark 2 (GG815)
c. 1775-90

Brief History: Thomas Turner, a copper plate engraver who learned his trade at Worcester*, built a porcelain factory (Salopian Works) about two miles south of Broseley in Shropshire in the mid-1770s. The first porcelain was produced at the factory in 1775. About eighty percent of the ware was blue printed underglaze. Many patterns were copied from existing Worcester designs and others were based on Chinese porcelain patterns. Floral patterns with gold as well as patterns in gold only were also produced. Thomas Minton* learned the technique of copper plate engraving at Caughley under Thomas Turner. He is particularly associated with the engraving of the earliest printed pattern, known as Full Nankin. He also engraved Broseley, a pattern Minton named in honor of the neighboring town. Both of these patterns were based on Chinese porcelain patterns.

The traditional view that the Willow pattern was developed by Thomas Turner at Caughley may have come from the following quote by Jewitt in *Ceramic Art of Great Britain*: "In 1780 Mr. Turner introduced the making of the Willow Pattern – the first made in England – at Caughley, and about the same time the Broseley Blue Dragon pattern. The Willow is still commonly known in the trade as Broseley pattern." It seems to me that the quote supports the fact that Broseley is the pattern that was developed at Caughley – not the Standard Willow pattern – and it was named by Thomas Minton who engraved it. In 1799 Turner sold the leases to the factory to John Rose, Edward Blakeway and Richard Rose, partners in the nearby Coalport* factory.
Type of Willow Manufactured: Mandarin pattern (Willow-Nankin) and Two Temples II (Pagoda or Broseley) transfer-printed in blue underglaze.

Old Willow Pattern Plate.
CAUGHLEY.

Frontispiece *English China* by Arthur Hayden, 1904. An example of the widespread myth that Thomas Turner introduced the first Willow Pattern. The Standard Willow Pattern shown here was NOT produced at Caughley. See Chapter I: The Origin of the Willow Pattern.

Reproduction of a print taken from an engraving of the Two Temples II pattern named "Broseley" at Caughley. The initials of Thomas Turner, the engraver, are seen at the top right of the pattern below the border. The Coalport China Co. provided this print to the *Pottery Gazette* for use in its article "The Willow Pattern Plate," January 2, 1911, pp. 68-9. The writer of the article (one of the staff) presented this pattern as the original Willow Pattern produced by the Caughley factory.

Two Temples II pattern teapot and matching covered sugar with gold trim. The pattern is transfer-printed in blue underglaze on porcelain with Mark 1. The Chinese shape teapot is seen in plate 329 of *An Anthology of British Teapots.* It is 5.50-inches high, and the covered sugar is 4.50-inches. *Author's Collection.* $500+.

Mandarin pattern cup, saucer, and creamer transfer-printed in blue underglaze with gold trim. The saucer measures 5-inches across and is 1.25-inches high. The cup with Mark 1 has a 2.25-inch opening and is 2.75-inches tall. The creamer has a 3.25-inch opening and is 2.75-inches tall. All pieces are porcelain and have a single foot ring. *Author's Collection.* $250+ for all.

Two Temples II pattern tea bowl and saucer with scalloped edge and gold trim. The saucer has Mark 2 and measures 5.50-inches across and is 1.25-inches high. The tea bowl with Mark 1 is 3 3/8-inches in diameter and 2-inches high. Porcelain with single foot rings. *Author's Collection.* $150+.

Cauldon Ltd.
(Cauldon Potteries Ltd.)

Location: Cauldon Place, Shelton, Hanley, Staffordshire
Dates: c. 1905-1962
Marks:

Comments Regarding Marks: Marks 1 and 7 are found on blue printed Standard Willow pattern table and toilet ware.

Brief History: 1905 was the year that Brown-Westhead, Moore & Co.* became Cauldon Ltd. Some BWM marks were continued with the addition of the word "Cauldon". Another indication of the ties to the former company is noted in this information found in *Pottery Gazette*, April 1, 1915: "Cauldon Ltd. (Brown, Westhead, Moore & Co.) announces a new line of china dinnerware known as the 'Westhead'. Whilst of same high-class body as the more expensive varieties of Cauldon China can be retailed for less." In 1920, the firm was retitled Cauldon Potteries Ltd. The marks incorporate the trade name "Royal Cauldon". *Pottery Gazette*, January 1, 1922, has this description of the company: "Cauldon Potteries Ltd: an amalgamation of Brown-Westhead, Moore & Co., 'Cauldon' Fireproof Ware, 'Cauldon' China, 'Cauldon' Earthenware."

In late 1962, the earthenware division was taken over by Pountney & Co. Ltd.* of Bristol. Cauldon patterns and shapes were produced using Royal Cauldon Mark 7. In 1969, Cauldon Bristol Potteries Ltd. moved to a new factory in Cornwall. The company was bought by A. G. Richardson in 1971. The name Royal Cauldon was adopted by Crown Ducal. In the early 1970s they bought Browns of Ferrybridge in Yorkshire, and when the Cornish factory closed in 1977, it was renamed Cauldon Potteries. In 1983 Cauldon Potteries Limited (Ferrybridge) became part of the Perks Ceramics Group. Meanwhile, from 1958, Cauldon porcelain production was continued by E. Brain & Co.,* a company that bought Coalport.* By 1963 all products were called Coalport. Some of the Cauldon pattern books are kept at the Coalport factory in Fenton.

Type of Willow Manufactured: Underglaze blue transfer-printed Standard Willow and Mandarin (Ching) patterns. Simplified Standard willow in green decal overglaze. Black and white transfers overglaze in Standard Willow pattern with red enameled background.

Retailers/importers: Henry W. King & Co., Ltd.*; Albert Pick*; R. Twining & Co., Ltd.*

CAULDON
ENGLAND

Mark 1 (GG821)
c. 1905-20

ESTD 1774
CAULDON CHINA
ENGLAND

Mark 2 c. 1905-20

Mark 3 c. 1920s

Mark 4 c. 1920s

Mark 5 c. 1905-20

Mark 6 c. 1905-20

Mark 7 (GG824)
c. 1930-50 &
1963-69 at Bristol

A pair of large bone china coffee cups and saucers with Mark 2, showing pattern no. 5726. Dark blue Standard Willow pattern transfer-printed underglaze with gold trim. The handle size seems a bit out of proportion for the large cup. It feels too thin and small to hold the cup easily. *Author's Collection.* $25-35 each.

Octagonal bowl measures 9.25-inches across. Standard Willow pattern printed underglaze in medium blue on earthenware. Mark 3. *Courtesy IWC Convention 2001.* $150-200.

Irish kettle-shaped piece with simplified Standard Willow pattern in black and white on a bright red ground and gold trim. A round vase 8.75-inches wide by 8-inches high has also been seen with this color treatment. Mark 4. *Courtesy IWC Convention 1994.* $250+.

Bone china teapot with Standard Willow pattern in linear form. The outer border is on the shoulder, and it has gold trim. Mark 5. *Courtesy John and Norma Gilbert.* $150-225.

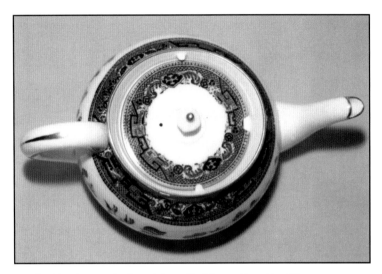

Looking down on the teapot shows the tabs on either side of the opening that extend over the edge of the lid to keep it in place while pouring tea. *Courtesy John and Norma Gilbert.*

Mandarin pattern plate transfer-printed in blue underglaze. Mark 6 shows the name for this pattern at Cauldon is CHING. A number 2 under the name is found on plates and platters. Hollow ware pieces have a number 1. *Courtesy Geraldine Ewaniuk.* $20-25.

Ceramic Art Co. Ltd.

Location: Crown Pottery, Stoke-on-Trent, Staffordshire
Dates: c. 1896-1919
Mark:

c. 1905-19

Brief History: This company is listed in *Kelly's Directory for Staffordshire* for 1896 and 1900 as Art Pottery Manufacturers, located at Howard Pl. Shelton, Hanley. Henrywood provides this information in *Staffordshire Potters 1781-1900*; however, he also reproduces two marks for the company on pages 96 and 97 found on printed wares. The mark on a soup tureen in "Old Chelsea" pattern (p. 97) gives the Crown Pottery, Stoke-on-Trent address with the added words: "Manufrs of Faience direct from factory to purchaser."
Type of Willow Manufactured: Polychrome decal overglaze based on Two Temples II pattern. Standard Willow pattern printed in blue is also found with a simple name mark.

Slop jar with handle decorated in the polychrome decal based on the Two Temples II pattern. There is a border pattern just under the rim. It is 10.5-inches in diameter at the top. *Courtesy IWC Convention 2002.* $75-125.

E. Challinor & Co.

Location: Fenton Potteries, Fenton (1854-62), or Tunstall (1852-54), Staffordshire
Dates: c. 1852-62
Marks:

Mark 1 (GG836)
c. 1853-60

Comments Concerning Marks: Mark 1 definitely pertains to one of the two companies known as E. Challinor & Co. It is found on a twelve-lobed dinner plate with deep well. No photo is available. Mark 2 could have been used by one of these firms or that of Charles Challinor, High St., Tunstall, c. 1848-65 or Edward Challinor, Pinnox Works, Tunstall, c. 1842-60 and other addresses until 1872. Information supplied by Geoffrey Godden.

Mark 2 mid-nineteenth century

Brief History: The Challinor history is complex because there are evidences of Edward Challinor and E. Challinor (& Co.) at several different potteries during the mid-nineteenth century. It is not known how many men we are researching or how they were related to one another. Ironstone wares were shipped to the U.S.A. marked Edward Challinor, E. Challinor & Co., and E. & C. Challinor. These wares include white ironstone, tea leaf decorated white ironstone, and several flow blue patterns on ironstone.

Type of Willow Manufactured: Blue transfer-printed Standard Willow pattern underglaze on earthenware/stoneware.

Standard Willow pattern blue printed 8-inch plate with 12 lobed rim. The outer border is too small. An extra section of wheels was added at 7 o'clock. The plate bears Mark 2; however, it is not known which Challinor firm it represents. *Courtesy Louise and Charles Loehr.* $25-35.

William Chambers Jr.

Location: South Wales Pottery, Llanelly, Wales
Dates: c. 1839-55
Marks:
impressed   CHAMBERS JUNIOR
                      SOUTH WALES
                      POTTERY

c. 1840-55

Comments Concerning Marks: The impressed mark on the first plate shown was not deep enough to reproduce; therefore, it has been typed here.

Brief History: William Chambers Jr. and his father, who was a man of means, moved to Llanelly and began building a pottery in the town in 1839. Dillwyn's* Glamorgan Pottery in Swansea had closed down in 1838, so Chambers was able to hire William Bryant, a potter for twenty-six years at Swansea, as secretary of his new business. Local unskilled workers were hired who were able to learn needed skills from potters moving to Llanelly from the Glamorgan Pottery as well as Staffordshire potters employed by Chambers. Even though the

copper plates and molds were not purchased in the early years of the new pottery, the painted and printed wares produced resembled wares from Dillwyn's factory. William Chambers Jr. was no longer in control of the South Wales Pottery after his father's death in 1855. The pottery continued on under various different partnerships until 1922. Willow pattern was produced during later periods; however, the marks were different, representing the names of the partners.

Type of Willow Produced: Standard Willow pattern transfer-printed underglaze in blue on earthenware known as white ware.

Ten-inch white ware plate with Standard Willow pattern transfer-printed in blue underglaze. The outer border pattern is too small. An extra insert was added at 7 o'clock. The pattern appears well balanced with a good border of white between the two borders. *Courtesy Rita Cohen.* $45-65.

Standard Willow pattern dinner plate transfer-printed in blue underglaze on earthenware. Wares are rarely found from this firm; therefore, another example is shown. This plate has the impressed horseshoe mark above. *Courtesy National Museum & Gallery, Cardiff, Wales.* $45-65.

Jonathan Lowe Chetham

Location: Commerce Street, Longton, Staffordshire
Dates: c. 1841-61
Mark:

(GG877)
c. 1841-62

Brief History: James Chetham and Richard Woolley were partners at the Commerce St. Works from 1796 to 1807 when James Chetham died. His widow, Mrs. Ann Chetham succeeded him in business, and Woolley left the partnership. By 1814 she took her son, Jonathan Lowe Chetham into partnership with her. She died in 1821. John Robinson joined Chetham in 1822, and his son Samuel joined them in 1834, trading as Chetham & Robinson & Son*. John Robinson died in 1840, and his son left the business. Jonathan Lowe Chetham continued on alone until his death in 1861. His sons John, Robert and Frederick carried on after that time. The company produced china and earthenware with printed wares being produced throughout the entire life of the firm.
Type of Willow Manufactured: Standard Willow pattern transfer-printed underglaze in blue on earthenware.

Chetham & Robinson & Son

Location: Commerce Street, Longton, Staffordshire
Dates: c. 1834-40
Mark:

c. 1834-40

Comments Regarding Mark: Script letters are very difficult to read especially when part of the mark is faintly printed. I chose to use the mark from the plate even though a little section is missing because the smaller mark on the tray is lighter in spots. When I decided the initials were C.R.S. I decided to agree with Kowalsky's KAD mark B518 that the initials represent the firm Chetham & Robinson & Son. The other possibility was mentioned in Coysh and Henrywood's *Dictionary I*, p. 188 that CRS may be a retailer for Turner* or Davenport*.
Brief History: The general history was given under Jonathan Lowe Chetham*. John Robinson and his son Samuel became partners with Jonathan after the death of his mother. The partnership ended when John Robinson died and Samuel left the business.
Type of Willow Manufactured: Standard Willow pattern blue printed underglaze. Tableware in earthenware.

Standard Willow pattern 9 1/8-inch plate transfer-printed in blue underglaze on earthenware. The concave rim is slightly lobed with 8 indentations. Three-point stilt marks on the rim with one of each set showing on the top. It has a shallow undercut foot ring, and the glaze is pale blue. Extra wheels are seen in the outer border at about 5 o'clock. *Author's Collection.* $25-30.

Standard Willow pattern blue printed underglaze 10.25-inch plate and 5 1/8-by-7-inch tray. Three-point stilt marks on the flat rim of the plate and the center of the tray. The tray is light in weight and thin whereas the plate is heavier and thicker. The plate has 8 slight indentations on the rim and a shallow recessed foot ring. The back of the tray is flat. Both pieces have a faint blue tint to the glaze. *Author's Collection.* $30-40 each.

Standard Willow pattern blue printed large platter. This photo is a good illustration of the differences in engravings used by a single firm due to larger or smaller size object. Note the number of arches in the bridge as well as the differences in the birds. *Courtesy Andrew Pye.* $175+.

Churchill China

Location: Portland Pottery; Fenton; Anchor Works and Crown Clarence Works, Longton; Sandyford, Tunstall and other locations in Staffordshire

Dates: c. 1974 to present (2003)

Marks:

Mark I printed
c. 1984 –

Mark 2 impressed
c. 1984 –

Mark 3 c. 2000+

Mark 4 c. 1980+

Mark 5 c. 2000+

Comments Regarding Marks 1 and 2: The printed mark is found on flat pieces such as plates and coupe soup bowls. Sometimes the last word in the mark is "proof" rather than "safe". The impressed mark is found on hollow ware and saucers although cups are not marked.

Brief History: The history of Churchill goes back to 1847 when James Broadhurst I first joined a partnership to produce earthenware at Green Dock Works, Longton; however, we begin this history when the name Churchill was first used. In 1974 the Crown Clarence* Works was bought by the James Broadhurst & Sons Ltd.* Group, and Churchill China Ltd. was formed to produce mugs. Sampson Bridgwood & Son* had been purchased in 1965. In 1984, Bridgwoods was re-named Churchill Hotelware, and Broadhursts was renamed Churchill Tableware. The British Anchor Pottery building in Longton was purchased in 1985.

In the "Foreword" to Hampsons' book: *Churchill China*, E. Stephen Roper, Group Chief Executive, writes: "By the middle of 1994 Churchill was Britain's largest family-owned ceramic manufacturer producing over 1.5 million pieces of pottery every week. The two main divisions of Hotelware and Tableware employ around 1, 300 people at five sites throughout Stoke-on-Trent." Churchill has been successful in world-wide marketing of their Tableware. Through Heritage Mint, the Blue Willow pattern has been sold in grocery and variety store promotions in the USA since 1984.

According to Andrew Roper, one of Churchill China's present directors, the Wessex/Royal Wessex brand was introduced in the 1970s, and they registered it as a trademark in the 1980s. Because Heritage Mint has exclusive selling rights for Churchill Willow in the USA, any other Churchill-produced Willow for the USA is printed on their fluted Chelsea shape and marked Wessex or Royal Wessex. The printed pattern is the same on Royal Wessex marked willow as on that marked Churchill.

Type of Willow Manufactured: Standard Willow pattern printed under glaze in blue and red. Blue has been produced since 1984. Less red has been made. Royal Wessex marked blue willow on Chelsea shape has been seen since the mid-1990s, and red since 2001. The engraving used by Churchill is identical to that of James Broadhurst seen in the *Tableware International* ad, 1982.

Promotional leaflet showing blue willow pieces offered in retail stores in the USA through Heritage Mint.

Blue Willow, The Legend...

Once there lived a very wealthy mandarin who had a beautiful daughter named Hong Shee, who fell in love with her father's secretary, a man named Chang. To keep them apart, the father imprisoned his daughter in the palace. One day she escaped, and the two lovers raced over the bridge to a waiting boat. They managed to elude the mandarin, reach the boat, and sail away. A storm developed; the boat foundered; and the couple were lost at sea. It is said that two love birds appeared immediately thereafter—the spirits of Hong Shee and Chang, and live on to this day.

Blue Willow Collectibles...

First offered almost two hundred years ago by a famous English maker of fine china, Blue Willow is still the most popular pattern to ever appear on dinnerware. The popularity of the pattern has not faded with time or life style changes as fads and fashions usually do. Blue Willow is as collectible today as ever and is still made in England and in many other countries around the world.

Promotional leaflet with The Legend and information regarding Churchill willow. Prices appear on opposite side.

Large teapot, holding six to eight cups. Standard Willow pattern blue printed underglaze. *Courtesy Paul Kirves and Zeke Jimenez.* $35-40.

Standard Willow pattern place setting transfer-printed in red underglaze on earthenware. These pieces are Chelsea shape. Mark 5. *Author's Collection.* $30-35 for 4 place settings.

Joseph Clementson

Location: Phoenix Works, Shelton, Staffordshire
Dates: c. 1839-64
Marks:

Mark 1
c. 1839-64

Comments Concerning Marks: Mark 1 has no name or initials; however, the words "Opaque Pearl" occur on other marks attributed to the firm. In addition to the printed mark, the plate is impressed: J CLEMENTSON SHELTON.

Mark 2 (GG910)
c. 1839-64

Brief History: Joseph Clementson's partnership with John Read was dissolved November 28, 1839, and he continued in business on his own. Joseph Clementson purchased the pottery that was known as Phoenix Works during his occupation. Prior to owning his own pottery, Clementson was apprenticed as a printer by John & William Ridgway* of Cauldon Place. Later he worked as a printer's overlooker at Elkin & Knight's* Foley Pottery, Lane End. In order to determine the type of wares to manufacture, Joseph Clementson took a trip to North America. He established a representative first in Canada and later in the USA as well. His son Francis lived for a number of years in Canada and served as Clementson's representative there. The company produced transfer-printed useful ware, flow blue, and white ironstone for the export market.

Type of Willow Manufactured: Underglaze transfer-printed Standard Willow pattern in blue and brown on heavy ironstone. Other colors were also made by Clementson. See Read & Clementson* and Read, Clementson & Anderson*.

Standard Willow pattern coffee pot transfer-printed in blue underglaze on earthenware. This is an example of the fluted Chelsea shape made by Churchill with the Wessex brand name. Mark 4. *Courtesy Charles and Zeta Hollingsworth.* $25-35.

Standard Willow pattern 9.5-inch plate transfer-printed in brown underglaze. Three-point stilt marks under the flat rim of the plate with one of each set showing on the top of the rim. It has a flat single foot ring. The border pattern is too small and not cleanly applied. There is an insert at 6:30 o'clock. The heavy clay body is very white with a clear glaze. Mark 1 plus impressed mark: J CLEMENTSON SHELTON. *Author's Collection.* $30-40.

James & Ralph Clews

Location: Bleak Hill and other locations, Cobridge, Staffordshire
Dates: c. 1813-34
Marks:

Mark 1 (GG918)
c. 1818-34

Brief History: Peter Warburton was potting at Bleak Hill from c. 1802 until his death in January 1813. The Clews brothers took over the works in the fall of 1813. A second factory was rented from William Adams in September 1817, but was not then in good repair. The brothers also worked Andrew Stevenson's former site in Cobridge from 1827-34. The Bleak Hill site, consisting of 1.25 acres near Burslem, was bull-dozed in 1986. Surface finds included biscuit, shell edge, and embossed pieces from the Clews

period as well as pieces impressed W from the Warburtons. Willow pattern shards that were found have a different border and may date to Warburton. Out of the twenty-one boxes of shards recovered, there was very little blue printed ware. For this reason it is assumed that most of the blue printed ware was produced at their second factory site.

A large percentage of the Clews' output was blue printed ware for the export market. The firm produced a fine quality pearlware and stoneware which was not much different in composition. They had a reputation for copying the best selling patterns of other factories. The brothers were not good businessmen. When expanding their business they overvalued their assets and borrowed against the inflated values. The firm was kept afloat by their agent, who also set their prices. In 1827 the firm's retailers in Liverpool and London had to be closed and sold to pay their creditors. By 1832 the Clews were 68,000 pounds in debt with 35,000 pounds of goods (one year's production) not yet sold. A great deal of goods had been sent on consignment, and that resulted in big losses. The Clews were bankrupt in 1834.

Type of Willow Manufactured: Standard Willow and Two Temples II patterns transfer-printed in blue underglaze.
Retailer/importer: China, Glass, and Earthenware House, New York*

Standard Willow pattern 9 5/8-inch plate transfer-printed in blue underglaze on earthenware. It has a concave rim. The borders match up fairly well. Note the birds on this plate have fishtails. Mark 2. *Courtesy Dennis Crosby.* $30-40.

Two Temples II pattern 6.50-inch plate transfer-printed in light blue underglaze on lightweight earthenware. There are slight indentations on the rim. It bears impressed Mark 1 with the number 3 under the mark and the initials G R on either side of the crown. The initials indicate an early (Georgian) date. *Courtesy IWC Convention 1999.* $55-75.

Nine-inch 8-lobed plate printed in light blue Standard Willow pattern. Three-point stilt marks on the back of the rim, and the plate has no foot ring. Mark 1 with the number 11 under the mark. The cup is printed in a darker blue. It is 1 7/8-inches high and 3.25-inches across the top. It has the Stone China Mark 2. *Author's Collection.* $75-95 and $35-45.

This 10-inch Standard Willow pattern plate has a WR monogram at the top center border with the words "Dinners, Drest & Choice. Wines" around the cameo. There is a cartouche with "SHIP TAVERN Water Lane" at the bottom. Evidently the plate came from a service used at Ship Tavern. The plate bears both Marks 1 and 2. *Courtesy Loren Zeller.* $125+.

George Clews & Co., Ltd.

Location: Brownhills Pottery, Tunstall, Staffordshire
Dates: c. 1906-61
Mark:

Brief History: George Clews, whose occupation was listed as "potter's manager," had a seventy-seven year lease on the Brownhills Pottery from the Salt Bros.

c. 1927-61

beginning in 1908. He turned the pottery over to his son Percy and his son's partner, Harry Preece. The two men bought Brownhills Pottery after leasing it for ten years. A third director, Daniel Capper, worked with the other partners and built up a successful pottery business. Early wares included teapots in various different clay bodies. By 1927, colorful hand-painted ware under the glaze was produced. The name Chameleon Ware was used from the beginning of George Clews & Co. It is thought that the term was chosen for the pottery because it changed color in the firing.
Type of Willow Manufactured: Willow variant known as "Chinese" pattern number 65/117 hand-painted underglaze in shades of blue, yellow, and red.

Twelve-inch vase with hand-painted "Chinese" pattern 65/117 showing a temple and willow tree. An interesting simplified willow variant. The other side of the pattern has a rising sun and two banners shown on page 128 of *Chameleon Ware Art Pottery.* *Courtesy Hilary Calvert.* $400-480.

Clifton China
(see Wildblood, Heath & Sons)

Clokie & Co. Ltd.

Location: Castleford Pottery, Yorkshire
Dates: c. 1888-1961
Mark:

Brief History: Clokie & Co. uses 1790 on the mark shown as its date of beginning. That was the year the new fineware pottery and brick and tile kilns were sold to their new owners, David Dunderdale and John Plowes. It was not until 1872 that Hugh McDowell Clokie became a partner in the pottery with John Masterman. After Masterman's death in 1885, Clokie's son, John Thompson, came into the company. He succeeded his father after his death in 1903. The firm continued to trade as Clokie & Co., run by descendents, until it closed in 1961. It became a limited company in 1940. According to a report in *Pottery Gazette*, December 1, 1922, the firm produced "almost everything that a dealer might wish to handle in the way of utilitarian domestic ware." The factory had a number of ways to efficiently produce and distribute their wares, including a railway siding which ran straight into the packing house. The same article reports: "The famous 'Willow' pattern in dark blue is one of the firm's leading specialities. This is always a seller, and it looks well in any room; consequently, there is still a certain glamour about the 'Willow' pattern which never fails to please."
Type of Willow Manufactured: Standard Willow pattern transfer-printed in blue underglaze. Tableware.

(GG925) c. 1940-61

Standard Willow pattern bowl transfer-printed in blue underglaze on earthenware. It is 5-inches across at the top and stands 2.50-inches high. Although Clokie & Co. produced willow for export as well as the home market this is the only piece of willow I have seen. *Author's Collection.* $10-20.

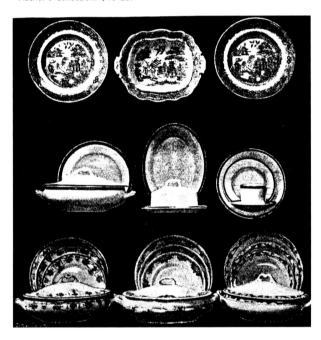

CLOKIE & CO.

Photo accompanying an article in the *Pottery Gazette*, December 1, 1922, showing two plates and the base of a vegetable dish in the Standard Willow pattern on the top row.

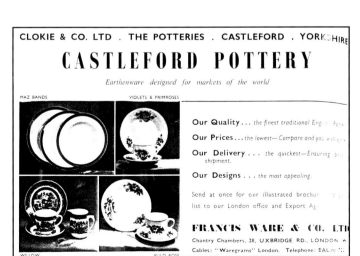

A half-page ad in the *Pottery Gazette*, 1951, showing a Standard Willow pattern cup, saucer, and creamer.

Clyde Pottery Co.

Location: Greenock, Scotland
Dates: c. 1810-1904
Mark:

(GG935) c. 1850-1903

Brief History: James Muir and Alan Ker Junior were two merchants in Greenock who joined with potter James Stevenson to form the Clyde Pottery on the south bank of the River Clyde. With four kilns and housing for the workers, the pottery got off to a fast start producing creamware and pearlware. When Alan Ker Junior died in 1823, the others put it up for sale, but there were no buyers. In 1834, James Muir died. His son Andrew and his brother, also Andrew, bought the pottery and ran it until 1841. Thomas Shirley, an English potter, bought the Clyde Pottery. From 1841 until the death of his son William in 1857, the pottery was known as Thomas Shirley & Co.* A series of partnerships continued to keep Clyde Pottery in business until 1904. The Museum of Scotland in Edinburgh has the only known piece from the first period. There are two known transfer prints from the Muirs period. A great many printed patterns and shapes were developed from the Shirley period.

Type of Willow Manufactured: Standard Willow pattern transfer-printed underglaze in blue. Tableware in earthenware.

Standard Willow pattern 9.25-inch plate blue printed underglaze. Three-point stilt marks in the center of the plate with one of each set showing on the front of the plate. It has a single, 1/4-inch wide flat foot ring and a slightly concave rim. There is an extra set of wheels in the border pattern at 10 o'clock. *Author's Collection.* $35-45.

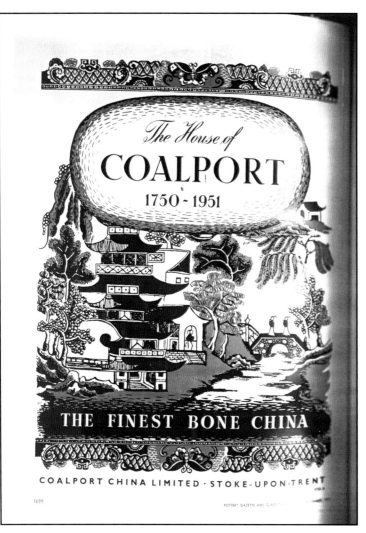

A full page color ad in *Pottery Gazette*, 1951 – the year the company was renamed Coalport China Limited. The pattern in the background is Two Temples II.

Coalport Porcelain Works
(John Rose & Co.)

Mark 1 c. 1810-15

Location: Coalport, Shropshire, and Shelton, Stoke-on-Trent, & Fenton, Staffordshire
Dates: c. 1795-present (2003)
Marks:

Brief History: The Coalport Porcelain Works has been in operation for over 200 years under several different names and ownerships; however, for most of the nineteenth century it was known as John Rose & Co. John Rose founded the company in 1795 after completing his apprenticeship with Thomas Turner at Caughley. His financial backing from Edward Blakeway gave rise to the first title of the company – Rose, Blakeway & Co. A number of circumstances led to the success of the company. Coalport was founded on the northern bank of the River Severn in East Shropshire, where other heavy industry was being developed. Rich clay and coal deposits were nearby. In fact, several potteries sprang up in the area. The eastern branch of the Shropshire canal was completed in 1790, which provided a river/canal link so important for the transporta-

Mark 2 (GG958)
c. 1881-91

Mark 3 (GG959var)
c. 1891-1939

tion of goods. The quality of china produced was superior from the start. It has been often mistaken for Chamberlain Worcester, even in the early days.

By 1797, a London warehouse was opened. Two years later John Rose & Co. took over the Royal Salopian Porcelain Manufactory of Thomas Turner at Caughley*. Wares made at both locations were sold under the name Coalport from 1800 to 1814, after which the Caughley site was closed. In the early nineteenth century the company was often referred to as Coalbrookdale, a place-name better known than the more recently developed Coalport. The name used from 1889 to 1951, was Coalport China Co., and from 1951 to the present day: Coalport China Ltd.

In 1924, the company was bought by Cauldon* Potteries Limited, and in 1926 the factory site and employees were moved to the Cauldon Works in Shelton. George Jones & Sons Ltd.* was purchased in 1936, when Coalport and Cauldon moved to the Crescent Pottery at Stoke-on-Trent. In 1958, E. Brain* bought Coalport, and transferred production to the Foley China Works in Fenton. All products were called Coalport. In July 1967 Coalport became part of the Wedgwood group, retaining the Coalport name on dinnerware patterns. By 1988 tableware production ceased with the Coalport mark, and output became limited to figurines and giftware.

Type of Willow Manufactured: Two Temples I and II, Mandarin (British Nankin), and early variants in blue transfer-printed underglaze. Standard Willow pattern printed underglaze in blue, green, and orange. Two Temples I and II patterns were used very early in the life of the factory c. 1795-1820. Two Temples II was revived in the 1920s; however, Two Temples I and Mandarin were not. Standard Willow pattern was quite late in arriving – c. 1960s. A polychrome variant pattern called "Chinese Willow" was made in the 1980s. It is an underglaze black pattern with shades of green, yellow, red, and blue enameled overglaze. The pattern is a revival of "Chinese Willow" made by Crown Staffordshire* earlier in the twentieth century.

Mark 4 (GG959)
c. 1891-1939

Mark 5 c.1950

Mark 6 (GG962)
c. 1960+

Mark 7 c. 1980+

Porcelain tea bowl transfer-printed underglaze in Two Temples I pattern. There are 12 wide ribs and uneven edge trimmed in gold. Geoffrey Godden dates this unmarked piece 1795-1800. *Author's Collection.* $45-85.

Two different cup shapes with pattern relating to Two Temples I. Both sides of the pattern are shown to illustrate the similarities to Two Temples I. These unmarked porcelain cups date to 1795-1800. *Author's Collection.* $55-125 each.

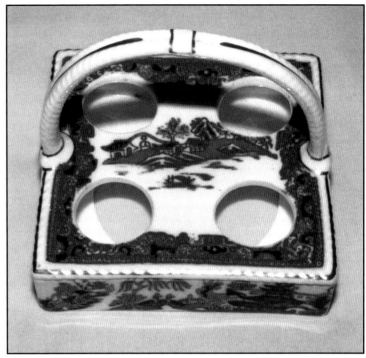

Egg cup stand trimmed in gold with handle. The central Two Temples II reversed pattern is on the sides, and the upper right section of the pattern decorates the middle of the piece. Mark 2. *Courtesy Paul Kirves and Zeke Jimenez.* $150-200.

John Rose Coalport Two Temples II blue printed teapot with gold trim. It is unmarked c. 1805-7. *Anthology of British Teapots* plates 1195-6 show oval prow shape porcelain teapot with domed strainer. Godden's *Coalport & Coalbrookdale Porcelains* plate 44 identifies prow-type teapot by John Rose. *Author's Collection.* $350+.

Covered sugar in Two Temples II reversed pattern transfer-printed in pale blue underglaze on porcelain. It measures 6.75-inches across including the handles and stands 4.50-inches high to the top of the finial. It bears Mark 1. *Author's Collection.* $200+.

Two Temples II pattern transfer-printed in deep cobalt blue in contrast to the pale blue used in the early part of the nineteenth century. The 10.25-inch porcelain plate has gold trim and may have been part of a dinner service. Mark 3. *Author's Collection.* $40-65.

Two different cup and saucer shapes with deep cobalt blue Two Temples II pattern and gold trim. The saucer on each set has the normal pattern whereas the cups have the pattern in reverse. The after dinner coffee cup is 2.50-inches high, and the saucer is 4.50 across. The teacup and saucer have a scalloped rim, and the deep saucer is 6-inches in diameter. The cup has an Old English style handle. It has Mark 4. The other pieces all have Mark 2. *Author's Collection.* $35-45 per set.

Standard Willow central pattern compote stands 5.50-inches high and is 9.50-inches across the top. A small teahouse surrounded by trees four times around the edge is used in lieu of a border pattern. The willow tree and bridge motif decorate the pedestal. The edges of the top and base of the compote are lined with gold. It bears Mark 6. *Courtesy Paul Kirves and Zeke Jimenez.* $100-200.

A 9.50-inch Bicentenary compote "In celebration of 200 years' potting". The 1750 date takes the history of Coalport back to Caughley "established in 1750 by Mr. Browne". A brief history is written on the back of the piece as seen in Mark 5. The pattern on the front of the compote is the original Caughley Willow-Nankin pattern that was renamed Mandarin by Josiah Spode. The following place-names are molded into the border of the plate: Coalport, Broseley, Coalbrookdale, Caughley, Swansea, Nantgarw. The date 1750 is at 9 o'clock, and 1950 is at 3 o'clock. Fish roe line the outer edge of the plate and the foot. The outer rim and inner border are lined with gold, and the mark is printed in gold on the back. The pedestal is 2-inches high. *Author's Collection.* $100+.

Standard Willow pattern 6-inch plate with two different shapes of cups with saucers. The pattern is quite large because there are no borders, and the central pattern fills up the entire space. All pieces have gold trim. The coffee can is 2 1/8-inches high and has an opening of 3 1/8-inches. The pedestal cup is 3-inches high with an opening of 3.50-inches. The narrow, pointed handle is difficult to hold onto. Mark 6. *Author's Collection.* $75-100 for place setting and $25-45 for extra cup and saucer.

Place setting in Chinese Willow pattern enamel decorated overglaze. The dinner plate measures 10.75-inches. This pattern is very brightly colored and prized by collectors. It is not known whether or not complete dinner services were made because it was a very late pattern for Coalport. Mark 7 with colors is unique to this pattern. An extensive range of wares was produced in the pattern by Crown Staffordshire Porcelain Co. Ltd.* *Author's Collection.* $75-125.

Miniature tea set in green Standard Willow pattern with gold trim. Coalport produced these tiny pieces in blue and orange as well. Additional items such as a shoe and bell were also made. Mark 6 has a pattern number of S730 on this set. *Courtesy IWC Convention 1996.* $50+.

the 1850s he and his brother bought land next to their glass works and built Britannia Pottery. The company produced large quantities of white ironstone that was shipped to Canada and the USA. This was their only product until about 1863 when they entered the transferware market at home and abroad. Robert Cochran died in 1869, leaving the business to his oldest son Alexander. (See next entry.)

Mark 3 c. 1846+

Type of Willow Manufactured: Standard Willow pattern transfer-printed underglaze in blue on earthenware.

Standard Willow pattern 8 lobed dish transfer-printed in blue underglaze on earthenware. The borders match at 12 and 6 o'clock, but extra sections are inserted in the sides. Mark 1. *Courtesy Henry Kelly. Photo by Douglas Leishman.* $35-50.

Robert Cochran & Co.

Location: Verreville Pottery (1846-96) and Britannia Pottery (1850s-1918), Glasgow
Dates: c. 1846-1918
Marks:

Mark 1 c. 1846+

Comment Concerning Marks: A light blue willow plate can be seen at the Ulster Folk and Transport Museum at Cultra Manor in Holyrood, Co Down, Northern Ireland. It has an unusual mark with R. C. & Co. Britannia & Verreville Potteries Glasgow c. 1860.
Brief History: Robert Cochran took over the Verreville Pottery and turned it into a commercial success. He was interested in expanding in order to begin export trade; however, the pottery was too old and small. In

Mark 2 c. 1846+

Standard Willow shard from the Verreville Pottery site with Mark 2. It is a lucky find to have a marked shard. *Courtesy Henry Kelly. Photo by Douglas Leishman.*

Cochran & Fleming

Location: Britannia Pottery, St. Rollox, Glasgow
Dates: c. 1896-1920
Mark:

WILLOW
C & F
G

(GG969)
c. 1896+

Comments Concerning Marks: Henry Kelly notes in *Scottish Ceramics*: "... until the advent of the Limited Company, the pottery descriptions become completely useless chronologically. R. COCHRAN & Co.*, COCHRAN & Co., COCHRAN & FLEMING, C. & F. and FLEMING seem to be used with careless abandon, sometimes in combination."

Brief History: There is some overlapping of trade styles between Robert Cochran & Co. and Cochran & Fleming. When Robert Cochran died in August 1869, he had made provisions for his son Alexander to carry on the business in partnership with the manager James Fleming. They continued the pottery for the rest of the nineteenth century, taking Fleming's son Arnold as a partner in 1896. According to Geoffrey Godden, that is the date at which the company became Cochran & Fleming. By 1911 both James Fleming and Alexander Cochran had died, leaving Arnold Fleming as sole proprietor. In 1920 he sold the pottery to a consortium of businessmen who traded as Britannia Pottery to 1939. Transfer-printed earthenware was a large part of the output of the firm.

Type of Willow Manufactured: Standard Willow pattern transfer-printed in blue underglaze on earthenware. Under "Buyers' Notes" in *Pottery Gazette*, January 1, 1906, we read: "Their 'Willow' and 'Pheasant' patterns are stock lines."

Standard Willow pattern 8.75-inch plate with wavy edge. Three single stilt marks at the rim on the underside. The foot ring is recessed. The border is 1.75-inches wide, and the inner border was placed from the well up onto the rim. *Author's Collection.* $20-30.

Cockson & Hardings

Location: Globe Works, Cobridge, Staffordshire
Dates: c. 1856-63
Mark:

c. 1856-63

Comments Concerning Mark: The mark is described in Plate 1158 in Berthod's *Compendium of British Cups* as Cockson & Harding; however, Hardings should be plural. There were two Harding partners together with Cockson to form the title Cockson & Hardings, a firm that produced chinaware.

Brief History: The partnership consisting of Charles Cockson, William Mollart Harding and Joseph Boon Harding produced china. The firm's separate works at Hanley produced earthenware. This partnership was dissolved January 21, 1863, and Charles Cockson carried on alone. Prior to this partnership Cockson was in business with Wingfield Harding, the father of William Mollart and Joseph Boon Harding. That partnership of Harding & Cockson dated from 1834 until 1856 when Harding died.

Type of Willow Manufactured: Pale blue Two Temples II pattern transfer-printed underglaze.

China cup and saucer in pale blue Two Temples II pattern transfer-printed underglaze on porcelain. The shape of the handle does not match the example in Plate 1158 in Berthod's *A Compendium of British Cups* with the mark identified as Cockson & Harding. It is possible the factory, Cockson & Hardings, produced more than one cup handle shape. The mark is on the saucer. *Author's Collection.* $40-70.

H. J. Colclough and Colclough China Ltd.

Location: Vale Works, Goddard Street, Longton, Staffordshire
Dates: c. 1897-1955
Marks:

Brief History: Herbert Joseph Colclough's firm produced china, earthenware and majolica-type wares. His "Royal Vale" China was advertised as Improved Queen's White Ware. The "Buyer's Notes" on page 1883 in *Pottery Gazette* dated December 1, 1930 stated that " 'Willow' and 'Broseley' are well-known printed patterns." Colclough China became a Limited company in 1937 when it succeeded H. J. Colclough. It continued to produce bone china until 1948. Booth purchased Colclough China Ltd. in 1948, and it was renamed Booths and Colcloughs Ltd. A further merger with Ridgway in 1953 resulted in a refiguring of potteries until 1955 when the group became known as Ridgway Potteries Limited.

Type of Willow Manufactured: Standard Willow pattern transfer-printed in underglaze brown on Royal Vale China and blue on bone china. The brown willow example has been clobbered.

Mark 1 (GG989)
c. 1928-37

Mark 2 (GG991) c. 1939+

Standard Willow pattern 6.50-inch plate transfer-printed in brown underglaze on earthenware. Clobbering was added in blue, green, red, and dark blue. There is a gold line around the rim. The shape is square with indented corners. The dark blue clobbering makes it more obvious that an extra section of geometric motifs was added to the outer border at 11 o'clock. Mark 1. *Courtesy IWC Convention 1996.* $15-25.

Bone china cup and saucer with gold-lined scalloped rims. The pedestal cup stands 3-inches high and is 3.25-inches across at the top. The Standard Willow pattern is in linear form around the cup. Mark 2 with number 6652: probably the pattern number. *Author's Collection.* $25-35.

Collingwood Bros.

Location: Crown Pottery, (St. George's Works from 1919), Longton, Staffordshire
Dates: c.1887-1957
Brief History: Charles and Arthur Benjamin Collingwood succeeded Collingwood and Greatbach at Crown Works in 1887. They produced a wide assortment of everyday china tableware. Floral designs were the major part of their production. Blue printed wares were seldom made. The trade name "Royal Coleston" was sometimes used. The company was renamed Collingwood China Ltd. from 1948-57 when it became part of the Keele Street Pottery Group. The works were taken over by Clayton Bone China.

Type of Willow Manufactured: Blue printed underglaze Standard Willow and Two Temples II pattern in toy china for children. *English Toy China* by Doris Lechler, figure #176 shows a partial tea set in pale blue Standard Willow pattern. She notes it is marked Collingwood. Figure #179 is a complete Toy tea set for six in original box with label: Royal Coleston China with a crown and Made in England. The pattern is pale blue Two Temples II. No picture available.

Mark 1 (GG1026)
c. 1946+

Thomas Cone Ltd.

Location: Alma Works, Longton, Staffordshire
Dates: c. 1892-1963
Marks:

Mark 2 (GG1027)
c. 1950+

Brief History: Thomas Cone followed the Middleton & Hudson firm at the Alma Works as the former firm moved to the Delphine Pottery. China had been produced at the works; however, Thomas Cone manufactured earthenware only. An ad in *Pottery Gazette,* November 1, 1908, states: "Alma Works, Longton, Manufacturer of general earthenware (non-crazing) suitable for the home and Colonial markets. Specialty: Semi-porcelain tea and breakfast ware – equal in appearance to Good Class China." Keele Street Pottery Company Ltd.* acquired the Thomas Cone Alma Works sometime between 1947-49 as part of a program of growth through acquisition. The firm continued to trade as Thomas Cone Ltd. after it became part of the Keele St. Pottery Group. In 1950, the name was changed from Keele St. Pottery Group to Staffordshire Potteries Limited*. The parent company acquired land at the Meir airport including hangars and began manufacturing in that location. By 1963, they closed the potteries not located at the Meir site including Thomas Cone.

Type of Willow Manufactured: Standard Willow pattern in blue with trellis-dagger border and Mandarin pattern in blue, pink and green. *Pottery Gazette* carried Thomas Cone Ltd. ads for Willow Pattern starting in 1950. The pattern shown was actually Mandarin.

Thomas Cone Ltd. ad in *Pottery Gazette* January 1953. Willow Pattern shown is the Mandarin pattern. Colors offered include pink, green, and Salopian blue. I have not found examples of green.

A rather crowded version of the Mandarin pattern transfer-printed in dark blue underglaze on a 9-inch plate. There is a wide white space between the central pattern and the trellis-dagger border. This maker has added fish roe at the rim edge of the border. The plate has a low single foot ring. Mark 1. *Author's Collection.* $10-20.

Standard Willow central pattern 6.25-inch plate with trellis-dagger border. The outer half of the plate rim has a molded "bumpy" pattern at the edge just beyond the fish row. Mark 2. *Author's Collection.* $5-10.

Conway Pottery Co. Ltd.

Location: Park Lane, Fenton
Dates: c. 1930-63
Mark:

(GG1032) c. 1945+

Brief History: Conway Pottery Co. Ltd. produced earthenware. Sometime between 1947-49, Keele Street Pottery Company Ltd.* bought the company, and it became part of the Keele St. Pottery Group. At that time, the main product was once-fired white cups. In 1950, the Keele Street Pottery Group changed its name to Staffordshire Potteries Limited*. By 1963, Conway Pottery was closed down. Staffordshire Potteries Limited continued production as one entity, at the Meir site only, with the other companies it had absorbed.

Type of Willow Manufactured: Simple line variation of Standard Willow pattern in blue on earthenware. This pattern was probably produced with a different technique than transfer printing.

Covered box in red Mandarin pattern. It measures 3 7/8-by-3 3/8-inches and is 1.75-inches high. The box was made to hold two small ashtrays, 2.25-by-2.75-inches. Together it is a smoking set. This piece has the trellis-dagger border. I have also seen the set in blue with the Standard Willow pattern in linear form around the outside edge of the box. Mark 1. *Author's Collection.* $20-35.

A saucer that measures 5.75-inches across has simplified variations of the Standard Willow pattern motifs in the center and in linear form around the rim. The pattern is simple line-drawn and may have been produced with rubber stamps underglaze. *Courtesy Geraldine Ewaniuk.* $3-5.

Co-operative Wholesale Society Ltd.,

Location: Windsor Pottery, Longton, Staffordshire
Dates: c. 1922-71
Mark:

Brief History: The Co-operative Wholesale Society Ltd. location at Windsor Pottery produced a wide range of wares in bone china.
Type of Willow Manufactured: Underglaze blue transfer-printed Two Temples II pattern on bone china.

c. 1946-71

Table set for four including coffee pot, creamer, open sugar, and serving plate. Blue printed Two Temples II pattern on bone china with gold trim. Windsor China Mark. *Author's Collection.* $350+.

Co-operative Wholesale Society Ltd.

Location: Crown Clarence Pottery, King Street, Longton, Staffordshire
Dates: c. 1946-late 1960s
Marks:

Brief History: The Crown Clarence Pottery is the site of earthenware manufacturing by the Co-operative Wholesale Society Ltd. The company produced ironstone wares in the 1960s, before Jon Anton acquired it.
Type of Willow Manufactured: Green, pink and blue Standard Willow pattern underglaze on earthenware. The firm made Willow pattern dinner and tea ware.

Mark 1 c. 1946-60s

Mark 2 c. 1946-60s

Mark 3 c. 1946-60s

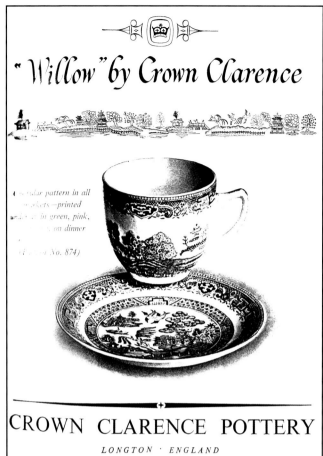

Full page ad in *Pottery Gazette,* July 1953, for "Willow" by Crown Clarence. A Standard Willow (pattern 874) teacup and saucer are pictured. A linear form of the willow pattern adds a unique touch to the ad.

Standard Willow pattern 10-inch plate transfer-printed in green underglaze on earthenware. Mark 1. This is the only piece of willow in over 30 years of collecting that my husband found for me. He bought it at a garage sale for $2.00. *Author's Collection.* $25-35.

A newer ten-inch plate in dark blue printed Standard Willow pattern. The edge is slightly fluted. Plates of this style have Marks 2 and 3. The border patterns are well centered, but the designers chose not to put the geometric motifs at 12, 3, 6, and 9 o'clock. *Author's Collection.* $15-20.

Two Temples I pattern 8.75-inch octagonal-shaped plate transfer-printed in blue underglaze. The scalloped edge has gold trim. The central pattern seems too large for the plate because there is no white separating it from the border in the lower part of the plate. The rim has a molded pattern on either side, almost like handles to hold the plate. The plate is translucent and bears Mark I. *Author's Collection.* $45-65.

Copeland & Garrett

Location: Spode Works, Stoke-on-Trent, Staffordshire
Dates: c. 1833-47
Marks:

Mark I (GG1093)

Brief History: In 1833, William Taylor Copeland was able to purchase the Spode factory, the Spode shares in the London business and a great deal of other property in Stoke including the Fenton Park Colliery. He took Thomas Garrett as his partner, and the firm became Copeland & Garrett. Copeland resided in London and managed the pottery as well as the London business from there while Garrett lived in the potteries and was the on-site partner. Even with the problems created by the potters' strike in 1836, the factory was greatly expanded during their partnership. In 1836, Copeland and Garrett was the second largest pottery in the district with 25 ovens. Only Davenport had more at 30. By 1846, the factory had been enlarged with a new area for the manufacture of porcelain. The modelers and engravers area was modernized for the comfort of the workers.

Mark 2
c. 1838-47

New patterns and shapes were introduced during this period, adding more flamboyant styles. At least six new earthenware bodies were developed including New Blanche seen below. Export expansion came through the Hudson's Bay Company as Copeland & Garrett was the sole supplier of high quality earthenware to North America, Persia, India and many other countries. The partnership was dissolved June 30, 1847. From that time, W. T. Copeland's son Alfred joined him in running the London business and his son William Fowler Mountford Copeland helped with the Stoke manufactory.

Type of Willow Manufactured: Transfer-printed blue underglaze Standard Willow and Two Temples I pattern.

Standard Willow pattern 9-inch plate transfer-printed in blue underglaze on earthenware. It has a concave rim and uneven edge. There is a recessed foot ring that can be seen in the following photo. The writing on the back of the plate in the next photo explains the importance of this particular plate. *Courtesy Robert Copeland.* $200+.

The writing on the plate is as follows: "The impression of this plate was the first one taken off from Mr. George Fourdrinier's New Patent steam press at Mssrs Copeland & Garrett's manufactory by Horton Yates and transferred by Elizabeth Waller in presence of Enoch Rowley foreman of the pottery. 1st Jany 1847"

William T. Copeland (& Sons Ltd.)

Location: Spode Works, Stoke-on-Trent, Staffordshire
Dates: c. 1847-1970
Marks:

Mark 1 (RC232a)
c. 1847-90

Mark 2 (RC231)
c. 1847-90

Mark 3 (RC235)
(GG1073)
c.1850-90

Comments Concerning Marks: In addition to Geoffrey Godden's mark numbers, I am using Robert Copeland's numbers (RC) from his *Spode & Copeland Marks* 2nd edition. It is the most definitive information available on marks for this company. Mark 12 has Rd. No.180288 that is for the mark –not the pattern. In addition to the printed marks shown, the following impressed marks have been found: RC202 (COPELAND), RC204 (COPELAND curved over the letter B) and RC207 (COPELAND curved over a crown.)

Brief History: The company continued to grow and flourish under the guidance of William T. Copeland after his partnership with Thomas Garrett was dissolved in 1847. Copeland was active in local affairs and held many positions of leadership such as Prime Warden of the Goldsmith's Company for two terms and President of the Royal Hospital of Bridewell & Bethlem. In 1866, W. T. Copeland was appointed China and Glass Manufacturer to H.R.H. the Prince of Wales. In 1901, Copelands was appointed Manufacturers of China to H.M. King Edward VII. In 1910, Copelands was appointed Purveyors of China to H.M.

King George V, and in 1938, to H.M. Queen Mary.

Fourdrinier's patent steam printing press was installed in 1847. In 1857, Copelands was the first pottery to install the filter press newly patented by Needham & Kite. Throughout the following 70 years the company continued to improve the facilities and introduce more up-to-date methods of production. In 1923, electrification of the Spode Works came about using Bellis & Morcom marine engine to drive its own alternator. As a result, the Watt beam engine was removed. Use of tunnel kilns of different types improved quantity and quality of the ware. In 1867, Copeland took his four sons: William, Alfred, Edward, and Richard into partnership, and the name was changed to William T. Copeland & Sons. In 1932 the company was incorporated, and it became a limited company.

The development of the parian body, or statuary porcelain, was the greatest contribution of Copelands in the nineteenth century. The exceptional quality of decorative wares continued, and the firm won prizes at International Exhibitions in the mid nineteenth century. The major portion of the output, however, was everyday tableware and toilet ware with five-sixths of the production in earthenware. Many lovely styles and patterns were continued, but as the century wore on, the services were simplified with brief border patterns. Very little of it is of interest to collectors today. In the last quarter of the nineteenth century the chinoiserie patterns from the Spode* period enjoyed a revival of interest.

Type of Willow Manufactured: Standard Willow pattern on earthenware in blue and red. It was produced in several shades of blue on bone china as well as in gold overglaze on blue ground. Standard Willow pattern with Grasshopper border was used on bone china in blue, pink, and turquoise. Mandarin pattern is found on bone china and earthenware underglaze in blue, pink, green, gray, and brown as well as overglaze in gold on crimson ground on bone china. Two Temples I and II patterns were used on various china bodies including stone china. Clobbering on blue printed Two Temples II and gold printed over crimson as well as gold outlining are found with Two Temples I pattern.

Retailers/importers: F. Crook, London*, T. Goode & Co., London* and Tiffany & Co., New York*

Mark 12 (RC266) (GG1076)
Reg.No.180288 c. 1894

Mark 5 (RC240)
c. 1862-91

Mark 6 (RC241)
c. 1891-1920

Mark 7 (RC242)
(GG1077) c. 1904-54

Mark 8 (RC242 var.)
c. 1904-54

Mark 9 impressed date
Oct., 1879

Mark 10 (RC252a)
(GG1074) c. 1883+

Mark 11 (RC262)
c. 1882-94

Mark 13
(RC256) c. 1890

Mark 14 (RC257)
c. 1891+

Mark 15 (RC411)
c. 1892+

Mark 16 (RC259)
(GG1079) c. 1920-57

Three plates with Standard Willow pattern. The 10.25-inch plate in the back has a concave rim with 12 indentations at the edge. Three-point stilt marks. It has a shallow, slightly recessed foot ring. There is damage with a piece of glaze and pattern missing in the rocks at the upper left of the pattern. Mark 4. The 7-inch plate has 8 indentations on the concave rim where there are three single stilt marks. It has a flat bottom. The outer border is too large. The cut occurs at 7 o'clock. The border patterns are well matched on the other two plates. The 7-inch plate has printed Mark 1 and impressed COPELAND. The 9-inch plate has a blue ground with pattern in gold over the glaze. The flat rim is indented in a series of two small scallops followed by a larger one all the way around. The plate is bone china and has an unglazed single flat foot ring. Mark 8. *Author's Collection.* $40-65, $20-30, and $75-150.

Covered sauce tureen on a pedestal in Standard Willow pattern blue printed underglaze on earthenware. This unusual piece stands 8-inches high. The form is one that Robert Copeland had not seen before. He attended the IWC Convention in 1999 where it sold in the auction. It has Mark 12 with impressed date mark for April 1907. *Courtesy Michael Curtner.* $400+.

Wash set consisting of 13.50-inch diameter bowl, large pitcher, smaller pitcher, covered soap dish, and covered toothbrush box. Standard Willow pattern transfer-printed in blue underglaze on earthenware with gold trim. The white sections of the pitchers have molded horizontal ridges and flowers. Impressed mark RC207. *Courtesy IWC Convention 1994.* $900+.

Standard Willow central pattern with Grasshopper border bone china dessert comport in Belinda shape. The pattern is #2140. There is a double line of narrow flutes on the outer surface corresponding to the scallops on the edge. This shape would make it very difficult to get the print transferred successfully. *Courtesy Paul Kirves and Zeke Jimenez.* $200+.

Eight Copeland teapots. Starting with the red one on top and going clockwise: Large Chelsea shape earthenware Red Mandarin pattern teapot with Mark 15. Small bone china Chelsea shape blue Grasshopper Willow pattern #2140, Mark 10. Crichton shape bone china teapot with gold foo dog finial, Standard Willow pattern #1/8669, Mark 6 and Registry pad dated January 1879. Two Temples I pattern in deep cobalt blue on bone china with gold trim, Mark 6. Ohio shape earthenware blue Mandarin pattern teapot with Mark 2. Brown Mandarin pattern Chelsea shape teapot in bone china with Mark 10. Kettle shape blue Mandarin pattern teapot with impressed RC204 indicating B body earthenware. The middle small teapot is Chelsea shape blue Mandarin pattern with an impressed date mark for 1886. *Author's Collection.* $120+ apiece.

Chelsea shape low covered vegetable in red Mandarin pattern on earthenware. Evidently the company calls the color pink, and it looks pink on bone china, but the color is a strong red on earthenware. The mark is impressed COPELAND and dated 1886. *Courtesy IWC Convention 1993.* $85-150.

A group of earthenware blue Mandarin pattern pieces. Serving plate with molded handle pattern has Mark 11. Chelsea shape compote is 8.50-inches across and 2.75-inches high. It is date marked 1909. Chelsea shape gravy has impressed mark RC204 (B body). The little mustard jar is 2-inches high, and the lid adds another-inch. It has Mark 15. *Author's Collection.* $35-50, $85-150, $45-60, $40-50.

A group of bone china Mandarain pattern pieces. Chelsea shape serving plate with Mark 6. A jug that is 5.25-inches high with Mark 3. The jug has been found in other sizes. The small sugar with lid has pattern #1/1908 and Mark 6. The coffee pot that stands 6-inches high to the top of the finial has Mark 3; however, it is not bone china. It has pattern #2/1849, which indicates it is Mandarin pattern on crown body: a white earthenware. Until I tested it for translucency I thought it was bone china. *Author's Collection.* $45-55, $35-50, $20-35, $95-150.

Bone china blue Mandarin pattern eight-inch Cumae vase, as named in the Spode pattern book. The shape of the vase is based on an example of a Lekythos shaped vase excavated at Cumae, an Ionian colony in Italy, northwest of Naples. The excavation took place in 1855. Copeland bought the molds (as well as the copper plate engravings for some of the scenes produced on the vases) from James Duke and nephew who succeeded Samuel Alcock* at the Hill Pottery in Burslem. Robert Copeland owns a bone china vase with a decoration displaying a battle between the Greeks and the Amazons. This is the first example he has seen with Mandarin pattern. It has Mark 3. *Courtesy Paul Kirves and Zeke Jimenez.* $200+.

Two Temples II pattern in round shape on 7.50-inch coffee pot. The pattern is clobbered. The pot is earthenware and bears Mark 14. *Courtesy IWC Convention 1999.* $125-200.

Queen Anne shape jug in blue Mandarin pattern on bone china. The molded pattern in the white area above the trellis-dagger border is like overlapping fish scales. The jug has an applied C handle. The jug is missing the metal lid that would sit in the open grooves on either side of the opening. Mark 10. *Courtesy Paul Kirves and Zeke Jimenez.* $75-150.

A selection of cup shapes made by Copeland in the various willow patterns. The Standard Willow pattern low cup with the saying is Persian shape and is earthenware with Mark 13. Proceeding clockwise, the bone china cup with saying is Regency shape, pat. #8669 and Mark 6. The straight-sided cup with pointed handle is blue Mandarin pattern on earthenware with Mark 15. The pink Mandarin coffee can has pat. #1908 and Mark 6. The low Chelsea shape Mandarin bone china cup has pat. #1327 and Mark 10. The mustache cup is Mandarin in bone china with Mark 3. Darker blue Standard Willow pattern cup has pat. #820 and Mark 7. Two Temples I pattern bone china cup has pat. #1/187 and Mark 3. Bone china bute shape cup has pat. #1327 and Mark 3 as does the little coffee can. The Chelsea shape coffee can has pat. #2140 and Mark 10. *Author's Collection.*

Two Temples II earthenware two-handled mug with "I PINT" written on the front. A mug in this pattern has also been seen with "Imperial Pint" written on it. This piece has Mark 14 with pattern #6805. *Courtesy Harry and Jessie Hall.* $150-200.

Two Temples I pattern place setting in dark cobalt blue with gold outlining the pattern. The plate measures 10-inches. The pieces are stone china. Mark 9 with pattern #1/1467 and impressed date mark for 1879. *Author's Collection.* $125-200.

Two pieces of Two Temples I pattern on bone china in deep cobalt blue with gold trim. The footed dish in the back is the same size and shape as the one in crimson and gold. It has pattern #1/187 and Mark 3. The biscuit jar with lid has Mark 2. *Author's Collection.* $150+ for each.

Cork, Edge & Malkin

Location: Newport Pottery, Burslem, Staffordshire
Dates: c. 1860-70
Mark:

c. 1860-70

Brief History: The partners were Benjamin Cork, Joseph Edge, James Malkin, and William Edge. They succeeded the partnership of Cork & Edge at the Newport Pottery. Ironstone wares including white ironstone for the American market were produced as well as transfer-printed earthenwares. Benjamin Cork retired June 30, 1867; however, the firm continued to trade as Cork, Edge & Malkin until 1870, when the name changed to Edge, Malkin & Co.*

Type of Willow Manufactured: Standard Willow pattern transfer-printed in blue underglaze on earthenware.

This eleven-inch scalloped dish sits on a 3/4-inch foot ring. It is bone china. The Two Temples I pattern is done in gold over a crimson ground. The edges come up over an inch high. Mark 3. *Author's Collection.* $200+.

Standard Willow pattern hot water plate transfer-printed in blue underglaze on earthenware. It measures 10.25-inches in diameter and 2.25-inches deep. *Courtesy Franklin and Charline Ladner.* $85-135.

W. & E. Corn

Mark I c. 1891-1904

Location: Burslem (1864-1904) & Top Bridge Works, Longton (1891-1904), Staffordshire
Dates: c. 1864-1904
Marks:
Brief History: William and Edward Corn traded originally in Burslem and by 1891, were also working out of the Top Bridge Works in Longton. For the first period of production according to Jewitt c.1878, products consisted entirely of white ironstone (granite) exported to the U S and other foreign markets. An ad in the 1890s states: "Manufacturers of plain and embossed White Granite and Ironstone China, printed and enameled earthenware in great variety." Collectors of White Ironstone and Tea Leaf Ironstone in the U.S. find wares marked W. & E. Corn, especially in the Ceres molded pattern. Printed patterns are more rarely found.

Mark 2 c. 1891-1904

Type of Willow Manufactured: Standard Willow pattern transfer-printed underglaze in blue on earthenware and stoneware.

Standard Willow pattern 6-by-8-inch oval bowl transfer-printed underglaze on ironstone. The bowl is a nice quality with a glassy glaze; however, the transfer was not applied well to the rim. Mark 2. *Author's Collection.* $35-45

Coronaware
(see Sampson Hancock & Sons)

Elijah Cotton (Ltd.)

Location: Nelson Pottery, Nelson Road, Hanley, Staffordshire
Dates: c. 1880-1980
Mark:

• BCM / NELSON WARE
MADE IN ENGLAND

c. 1926-81

Brief History: Elijah Cotton rebuilt the Nelson Pottery in 1885 on the site of a pottery that had been built in 1785. Elijah was an energetic man who made a very strong beginning for the new firm. It wasn't long before more space was needed, and he took over the Victoria

Works where Adams and Bromley had been in business. Following Elijah's death in 1895, his oldest son Edward took over the firm. His brother Arthur later joined Edward. By 1928, Elijah Cotton was a limited company. As years went on Arthur's son Nigel became a partner. Nelson Ware became a trade name used by the company in the early twentieth century. A likeness of Lord Nelson appears on some of the marks.

The firm was identified from the beginning as a manufacturer of jugs. The output was remarkable as noted in the ad in *Pottery Gazette*, March 1, 1905 that promised delivery next week even if you needed 30,000 jugs. All sizes and shapes of jugs were made from miniatures with 3 oz. capacity to extra large at 10 pints. Ads for jugs including a blue willow jug with rope handle began in 1899. In looking through *Pottery Gazettes* I found ads for jugs including willow in 1905, 1910 & 1912 for 3 months in a row, 1915, and 1917 every issue for one year. In September 1935, an ad stated: "Elijah Cotton is still the largest manufacturer of jugs in the world." In 1944: "'Cotton' STILL spells Jugs for the export trade." and the September 1953, issue had a page of jugs in color. These later ads did not include the "willow" jug.

Elijah Cotton produced all kinds of earthenware including tea and nursery wares. Under "Buyer's Notes" on p. 1535 in *Pottery Gazette* October 1, 1926, we read the following:

> That they are now manufacturers of a full range of domestic earthenware, as well as being jug specialists is merely the outcome of the amalgamation which took place some years ago of the **Nelson and Wellington Potteries** – next door neighbors. At present – having trouble keeping pace with the demands that are being made upon them – with diffidence, they spoke about new lines. We are glad however to have the firm's permission to mention the fact that they are now producing a full range of articles in the old "Blue Willow", in connection with which they have recently engraved a whole set of copper-plate engravings to enable them to supply dinner, tea and breakfast ware as well as table sundries of every description. A new set of square covered pieces has been modeled, in keeping with the antique character of the design, and we can certainly say, having seen the ware in bulk on the warehouse floor that it is turning out in excellent shape.

Type of Willow Manufactured: Standard Willow pattern underglaze transfer-printed in two shades of blue and a simplified pattern lithographic decal in blue and yellow overglaze. This decal has also been found in green and yellow. I was surprised to discover what an active advertising campaign the company had in the *Pottery Gazette* trade magazine over the years because I have found very little blue willow made by Elijah Cotton. Perhaps it was exported to other parts of the world. A 5 5/8 inch jug was offered on Ebay, an internet auction site, in 2002, from a seller in Nova Scotia. It was the shape shown in the ads, but it didn't have the rope handle.

Sauce dish and creamer in Standard Willow pattern underglaze in dark blue. The creamer is 3-inches high and measures 5.50-inches from spout to handle. It is the closest to a Nelson Ware jug I have found. *Author's Collection.* $15-25.

March 1, 1905.   THE POTTERY GAZETTE.   277
BROUSSON'S AGENCIES, LTD.—continued.

1931.   THE POTTERY GAZETTE AND GLASS TRADE REVIEW   1065

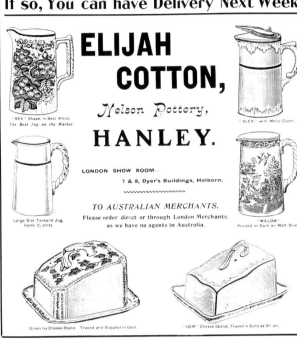

So YOU are in the MARKET for JUGS!

WILL 30,000 SETS SUPPLY YOUR PRESENT NEEDS?

If so, You can have Delivery Next Week.

ELIJAH COTTON,
Nelson Pottery,
HANLEY.

"REX" Shape, in Best White.
The Best Jug on the Market.

"ALEX," with Metal Cover.

Large Size Tankard Jug,
holds 2½ pints.

"WILLOW."
Printed in Dark or Matt Blue.

LONDON SHOW ROOM—
7 & 8, Dyer's Buildings, Holborn.

TO AUSTRALIAN MERCHANTS.
Please order direct or through London Merchants,
as we have no agents in Australia.

Green Ivy Cheese Stand. Traced and Stippled in Gold.

"GEM" Cheese Stand, Traced in Gold as Shown.

Full page ad from March 1, 1905, *Pottery Gazette* features jugs including "Willow" in Dark or Matt Blue.

ELIJAH COTTON
LTD.
NELSON
POTTERY,
HANLEY,
Stoke-on-Trent.

Makers of
NELSON
WARE
in all lines

Full page ad from 1931 showing a simplified willow pattern decal decorated dinner plate and covered vegetable in the middle left.

ELIJAH COTTON LTD.,
HANLEY, Staffs, ENGLAND.

"Willow" pattern, in Dark or Light Blue,
can be supplied in DINNER and TEA WARE,
and Miscellaneous Lines.

Full page ad from April 2, 1928, *Pottery Gazette* with "Willow" pattern plate and teapot offered in Dark or Light Blue.

Blue and yellow decal-decorated simplified Standard Willow pattern 10-inch plate as seen in the previous 1931 ad. The border has bowknots like the inner border of the standard pattern, and there are some yellow geometrical motifs reminiscent of the outer border on Standard Willow pattern. The plate is lined in gold. Pattern #1518 occurs on some pieces. This plate is impressed 8/30 which is probably a date mark. *Courtesy Tim and Kim Allen.* $35-45.

James Couper & Sons

Location: City Pottery, Glasgow, Scotland
Dates: c. 1850-53
Mark:

c. 1850-53

Brief History: The firm of James Couper & Sons produced earthenware at City Pottery from 1850-53. Prior to that time, James Couper and Robert Cochran had purchased the Port Dundas Pottery in Glasgow in 1835. This was not their first partnership. In 1839, they sold the pottery and bought St. Rollox Glass Works. Also in 1835 Couper became a partner with William Murray Jr. and John Fullarton* at the Caledonian Pottery. He left that partnership in 1850 to go to the City Pottery where he was in business until 1853. David Neill made stoneware at City Pottery from 1855-58. After 1858 City Pottery went back to James Couper & Sons and became part of their adjacent glass works where they made Clutha Glass. Marked pieces from the City Pottery are rarely found. Couper's real claim to fame came from his glass making. Pieces are highly prized and fetch huge sums of money.

Type of Willow Manufactured: Pale blue Standard Willow pattern transfer-printed underglaze on earthenware.

Standard Willow pattern pale blue plate transfer-printed underglaze on earthenware. It has a deep well and concave rim. It bears the mark above: the Coat of Arms of the city of Glasgow. *Courtesy Henry Kelly. Photo by Douglas Leishman.* $65-95.

Crown Chelsea (see Thomas Morris)
Crown Devon (see Fielding & Co.)
Crown Dorset (see Staffordshire Fine Ceramics)

Crown Staffordshire Porcelain Co. Ltd.

Location: Minerva Works, Fenton, Staffordshire
Dates: c.1889-1985
Marks:

Mark 1 (GG1152) c. 1930s+

Comments Concerning Marks: All of the five marks shown are varia-tions of Geoffrey Godden's marks 1149 (used on copies of antique porcelains) and 1152; however, the addition of a Rd. No or pattern name to the marks warrant their inclusion here.

Brief History: T. A. & S. Green occupied Minerva Works prior to 1889, the year when the name of the company was changed to Crown Staffordshire Porcelain Co. They continued for some time as proprietors. In 1903 the business became a limited company. Excellent quality porcelains were produced. A specialty of the company was reproduction of Chinese porcelains. The firm also promoted the work of early English porcelain artists such as William Billingsley. In addition to tableware, the company produced figures, animals, and bird models, and miniatures. In 1948, the name was changed to Crown Staffordshire China Co. Ltd.; however, the firm continued to trade as Crown Staffordshire. Semart Importing Company took over in 1964, and in 1973, Crown Staffordshire became part of the Wedgwood* Group. Use of their trade name continued until 1985, when the Coalport* name was adopted. The original pattern books for Crown Staffordshire were moved to the Coalport site in Fenton.

Type of Willow Manufactured: Two Temples II pattern, with added birds, transfer-printed underglaze in blue. Some pieces are clobbered. "Chinese Willow" variant in blue as well as several different polychrome combinations enameled overglaze. This pattern was continued in the 1980s with a Coalport backstamp. See Mark 7 and the last photograph under Coalport*. Crown Staffordshire also did polychrome reproductions of earlier patterns.

Retailers/importers: Henry Birks & Sons Ltd., Winnipeg, * Hugh C. Edmiston, New York*, T. Goode & Co., London, * Hotel McAlpin, New York, * Tiffany & Co. New York*

Mark 2 (GG1149) c. 1911

Mark 3 (GG1149) c. 1906+

CHINESE WILLOW

Mark 4 (GG1152) c. 1930s+

Mark 5 (GG1152) c. 1930s+

Mark 6 (GG1152) c. 1930s+

These Two Temples II pattern pieces have two birds added to the pattern at the top above the small buildings. A small tree usually fills that space in Two Temples II pattern. There is very little of this pattern by Crown Staffordshire. The 9-inch plate is the only clobbered piece I have seen. The 8.25-inch rimmed soup has gold trim but no clobbering. Both pieces are bone china and have a single, unglazed foot ring. Mark 1. *Author's Collection.* $55-85 & 20-35.

Chinese Willow pattern 8-inch plate. This is the normal coloring found on this pattern. It was reissued in the 1980s under the Coalport name after the Crown Staffordshire name was phased out. The plate has Mark 5 with pattern #5351. A serving plate with the same clobbering but with a yellow glaze has #5355. Not all pieces of Chinese Willow have a pattern number. A demitasse cup and saucer matching this 8-inch plate bears Mark 4. *Author's Collection.* $25-35.

A place setting with teapot, sugar, and creamer in a willow variant pattern that is a copy of an antique porcelain pattern. It is transfer-printed in black underglaze and clobbered in bright colors. The plate has Mark 2 with the Rd. No. 589090 dating it to 1911. One of the hollow ware pieces has pat. #10,008. *Courtesy IWC Convention 1999.* NP

A miniature tea set on a tray in Chinese Willow with the same clobbered colors. It has Mark 3, including a little story about the pattern. *Courtesy Joette Hightower.* $100-200.

Modified London shape teapot with creamer and open sugar. The underglaze print is blue rather than black, and the clobbering is more muted on this set. Mark 6 and pattern #F11685. The pattern by Aynsley* has also been found with red background and gold highlighted pattern. *Courtesy Paul Kirves and Zeke Jimenez.* $100-175.

Ten-inch plate with black background. The pattern in gold overglaze is the same variant as in the previous photograph. *Courtesy IWC Convention 1995.* $50-65.

Standard Willow pattern platter transfer-printed in blue underglaze on earthenware. It is 13-by-16 5/8-inches. The border patterns have been trimmed well to match. Mark 2. *Courtesy Geraldine Ewaniuk,* $75-125.

Dale, Deakin & Bailey

Location: Waterloo Works, Longton, Staffordshire
Dates: c. 1826
Marks:

Mark 1 c. 1826

Comments Concerning Marks: The names on Mark 1 were never actually in partnership together at Waterloo Works although it may have been planned. Mark 2 has no names; however, the mark was used by one of the firms mentioned below operating out of Waterloo Works.

Mark 2 c. 1815-63

Brief History: According to the records reported by Rodney Hampson in *Longton Potters 1700-1865*, this partnership did not exist. Batkin, Dale & Deakin were at Waterloo Works from October 30, 1819, to October 7, 1826. William Dale died in 1826, and William Batkin left the business at that time although he retained ownership of the works. Thomas and/or James Deakin were in partnership with Bailey from 1828-32. The works traded as Deakin & Son* from 1832-63. Those dates tell us that Bailey did not join the firm until two years after Dale died. I can only guess that the mark shown was developed while William Dale was still alive and that Bailey may have joined the firm earlier than reported in the records. Earthenware was produced at Waterloo Works.
Type of Willow Manufactured: Standard Willow Pattern underglaze transfer-printed in blue on earthenware. Tableware was made.

Standard Willow pattern 9.75-inch plate transfer-printed in blue underglaze on earthenware. There are 8 slight indentations on the edge of the rim. The flat rim has three-point stilt marks on the underside. There is a slightly recessed foot ring. The outer border pattern is too large. A section with Ju-ls is cut out at 5 o'clock. Mark 1. *Author's Collection.* $25-35.

Davenport

Location: Longport, Staffordshire
Dates: c. 1794-1887
Marks:

Mark 1 (GG1179)
c. 1798-1815

Mark 2 (GG1179a)
c. 1815-60

Mark 3 (GG1183)
c. 1815-30

Mark 4 c. 1820-40

Brief History: John Davenport purchased and enlarged the Unicorn Bank Pottery in 1794. John Brindley had built it beside the canal in Longport in 1773. The pottery began with the production of creamware and pearlware; however, the invention of bone china by Josiah Spode influenced Davenport to begin porcelain manufacture by the late 1790s. In 1801, the manufacture of flint glass was begun at Longport. This is an uncommon practice for a potter; however, glass was produced throughout the life of the company. A large earthenware factory was purchased at Newport about 1810, and was used for the producing much of Davenport's earthenware. Along with Turner, Spode, and Masons, Davenport developed a fine quality stone china. After the Napoleonic War ended in 1815, John Davenport aggressively led his company into the export market. Markets in Europe opened up first, and by 1836, he had an agent in North America. The factory belonging to Robert Williamson & Co. was purchased in 1834.

The name of the firm changed throughout the years. By 1925, it was John Davenport Son & Co. John was retired by sometime early in the 1830s, and his son Henry was manager at Longport. The firm traded for a short time as Henry & William Davenport & Co. William was Henry's youngest brother. From Henry's death in 1835, to

1869, the firm traded as William Davenport & Co. These were successful years for the company. The Davenport firm did a lot of multi-color printing and printing in odd colors as well as the popular blue transfer printing. According to Lockett in a bicentenary lecture in 1994, even with all the varied color printing, there were only 17 different designs used in a 30-year period in the mid-1800s. At one time the factory had 1500 employees which is more than the large Minton* factory employed. Following William's death in 1869, his only son Henry inherited the works. In 1881, it was converted to a private company, and the name became Davenport Ltd. In 1887, the Davenport works were purchased by Thomas Hughes* of the Top Bridge Pottery, Longport.

Type of Willow Manufactured: Standard Willow pattern transfer-printed in blue underglaze on pearlware and earthenware. Two Temples II pattern blue printed underglaze on stone china and bone china. Willow must not have been one of the more popular patterns at Davenport because it is very difficult to find. In *Blue and White Transfer Ware 1780-1840*, p. 28, A. W. Coysh states,

It has recently been stated that John Davenport potted willow pattern services "by the ton." What proof have we of this statement? In nine years of searching the author has only noted a single unmarked willow pattern plate that could be reasonably attributed to Davenport, yet other Davenport pieces are by no means uncommon. Surely, if there had been such a large output, pieces would turn up more frequently? Or has some earlier writer wrongly called "The Chinoiserie Bridgeless Pattern" a willow pattern?

Coysh goes on to lament the inadequate descriptions commonly given for blue and white patterns. Thirty-two years after Coysh wrote those words, we still find that the Chinoiserie Bridgeless Pattern is often called Davenport Willow.

Retailer/importer: Sandbach & Co., Manchester*

Mark 5 (GG1181a) c. 1856

Mark 6 c. 1830-60

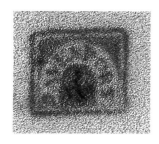

Mark 7 (GG1194)
c. 1830-45 (pale puce)
& c.1870-87 (red)

Mark 8 c. 1830-45

Chinoiserie Bridgeless pattern 9.25-inch plate transfer-printed in blue underglaze. It has no foot ring. This pearlware plate fits inside the plate in the next photo with the same shape and slightly lobed edge. Three single stilt marks on the front of the plate on the rim. This is the earliest blue printed pattern by Davenport and bears impressed Mark 1. The pattern is right-sided with a large teahouse and a smaller one behind as in the willow pattern. The boat seems to be the transportation between the right and left sides as there is no bridge. The fence is on the left side of the water rather than forefront. There are no birds or willow tree. The pattern has no inner border. The similarities to the outer willow border are: Geometrical motifs but with a butterfly in the center; the flower inside the Ju-Is, but without the intersecting scroll cross, and a line of fish roe is at the edge. The 4-spoke wheel is present as are the leaves and flowers at the inner edge of the border. *Author's Collection.* $75-100.

Standard Willow pattern plates transfer-printed in blue underglaze. The 9.50-inch plate has no foot ring. The flat rim has 8 indentations making it slightly lobed. There are 3 single stilt marks on the front of the plate on the rim. The plate is pearlware with impressed Mark 1. The 6 3/8-inch plate is also pearlware, but it has Mark 2 and was made a little later. The rim is concave with 8 lobes at the edge, and it has a recessed foot ring. The color blue is a little darker. I also have a 10-inch plate with impressed Mark 5, dated 1856. It is much heavier earthenware and printed a little darker blue. The concave rim is slightly lobed, and it has a double recessed foot ring. It has 3-point stilt marks on the under side of the rim with a single stilt mark on the top, and the glaze is pale blue. *Author's Collection.* $75-125 and $40-60.

A stone china grouping of pieces in Two Temples II pattern transfer-printed in blue underglaze. The large cup and saucer bear Mark 3 with pattern #142. The rims are scalloped and lined with gold. There is also a row of connected gold dots on both pieces. The 8.25-inch plate on the left has a concave rim with scalloped edge and no gold added. It has a single unglazed foot ring and the rarely found Mark 4. The body is whiter than the cup and saucer that have a bluish-gray tint. The 8 3/8-inch round piece may be the base for a muffin dish. The body is similar to the plate, and the gold decoration matches that of the cup and saucer. It has a single, unglazed foot ring. An impressed B, rosette, and pattern #142 are the only marks. *Author's Collection.* $65-95, $30-45, and $30-45.

Two Temples II pattern water set on bone china in underglaze blue with gold decoration including connected dots. These rarely seen pieces include two water tumblers, a round tray, and pitcher. The blue printing is exceptionally clear and precise, and the quality of the china is excellent. Mark 7 with pattern #6019 dates it near the end of production. There is sadly some damage to the set. *Courtesy IWC Convention 1999.* NP

Two Temples II pattern tray transfer-printed in pale blue underglaze on earthenware. It measures 6.25-by-8 1/8-inches. There is a nice contrast in the printing as darker blue was used to accent parts such as roofs, rocks, the edge of the water, etc. The tray has a wide, flat single foot ring that is unglazed. It has Mark 8, a rare mark. The bone china demitasse cup and saucer are much deeper shades of blue. The gold trim with connecting gold dots is like what we have seen on the stone china pieces. Mark 7 with pattern #3588 dates it to after 1865. *Author's Collection.* $75-150 and $45-75.

Two Temples II blue printed pattern on hydra-shaped jug with serpent handle. The jug stands 5.50-inches high and is trimmed in gold. The stone china body is bluish-gray. Mark 3. *Courtesy Paul Kirves and Zeke Jimenez.* $150-225.

Bone china teapots with Two Temples II pattern transfer-printed in dark blue underglaze. Lavish gold decoration is added to these lovely teapots including the connecting gold dots seen above. The teapot on the left stands 5.5-inches tall to the top of the finial and 6-inches from handle to spout. The teapot on the right is 3.5-inches tall and 7.25-inches from handle to spout. Mark 7 with pattern #3588, after 1865. *Courtesy Loren Zeller.* $150-250 each.

Davies & Co.

Location: Tyne Main Pottery, Sheriff Hill, Newcastle Upon Tyne, Northumberland
Dates: c. 1833-51
Mark:

(GG1201) c. 1833-51

Brief History: The pottery was built in 1831 by Richard Davies & Co., and production was well underway by 1833. The pottery was sold to R. C. Wilson, the managing partner in 1844. The works closed in 1851. The products were white, printed, and luster wares principally for the Norwegian market.
Type of Willow Manufactured: Standard Willow pattern transfer-printed underglaze in blue on earthenware.

Co.'s Commercial Directory of the Merchants Bankers, Professional Gentlemen, Manufacturers and Traders for 1834, lists several Cooksons, most of whom are glass manufacturers (often associated with potteries). There is only one Cockson listed – a china dealer. I have decided to list the firm as Davies, Cookson & Wilson. The impressed marks seen are not deep enough to determine for sure if the letter is c or o.
Type of Willow Manufactured: Standard Willow pattern and Two Temples II transfer-printed underglaze in blue. A small plate with Two Temples II pattern is illustrated in *True Blue* on page 110: Case 13, #4. The maker is listed as Davies, Cookson & Wilson; however, attribution of Mark D9 on page 147 is given as Davies, Cockson & Wilson.

Standard Willow pattern platter in blue printed underglaze. It measures 12.75-by-16.75-inches, and is very light in weight for its size. The indentations on the rim give it an elongated octagonal shape. Three-point stilt marks on the back of the concave rim and three single marks on the top. There is a black impurity in the foreground at the start of the path. Impressed Mark. *Author's Collection.* $75-175.

Standard Willow pattern 9.50-inch plate transfer-printed in blue underglaze on earthenware. It has a concave rim with 8 lobes. Three-point stilt marks on the under side of the rim and 3 single marks on the top. The plate is light in weight with a pale blue glaze and has a recessed foot ring. *Author's Collection.* $95-125.

Davies, Cookson & Wilson

Location: Stepney Bank Pottery, Ouseburn, Newcastle Upon Tyne, Northumberland
Dates: c. 1822-33
Mark:

c. 1822-33

Comments Regarding Mark: This mark consists only of the 3 names of the partners in a circle. A willow plate is known with a number 12 impressed in the center. Mark D9 in *True Blue* also has a number in the center, but I can't make it out.
Brief History: The Stepney Bank Pottery was established c. 1780-90. The partnership of Davies, Cookson & Wilson succeeded John Dryden & Co. c. 1822. There is some question as to the correct spelling of the name of the middle partner. In Geoffrey Godden's revision of *Jewitt's Ceramic Art of Great Britain 1800-1900,* on page 211, the name in the partnership was given as Cookson. In the original, Jewitt spelled the name Coxon. R. C. Bell lists Cookson on page 54 of *Tyneside Pottery.* The 1834 *Pigot and*

Davis

Location: Trent Pottery, Eastwood, Hanley, Staffordshire
Dates: c. 1875-91
Mark: Impressed DAVIS

Brief History: Having been in different partnerships since 1867, by 1875 John Heath Davis carried on the business alone. The first products of the factory were white ironstone exported to the U.S. Later the factory produced dinner, toilet, and tea services for the home and export market.
Type of Willow Manufactured: Standard Willow pattern transfer-printed in blue underglaze on earthenware. No picture available.

Davison & Son Ltd.

Location: Bleak Hill Works, Burslem, Staffordshire
Dates: c. 1898-1952
Marks:

DAVISON & SON C°
ENGLAND

Mark 1 c. 1898+

Brief History: Francis Joseph Emery was sole proprietor of the Bleak Hill Works from 1880 to 94. The Davison firm took over in 1898. Under "Buyer's Notes" in the *Pottery Gazette* dated February 1, 1926, we read that Davison & Son Ltd. Burslem was producing "Medium priced earthenware with leading lines being plain printed or lithographed and gilt patterns." It was further noted that Davison & Sons Ltd. were represented by Mogridge & Underhay 10, Bartlett's-bldgs., Holborn, Longton. In 1952 Davison & Son Ltd. was purchased by Swinnertons Ltd.*

DAVISON & SON LTD
ENGLAND
PAGODA

Mark 2 c. 1898+

Type of Willow Manufactured: Transfer-printed Two Temples II and Standard Willow pattern in blue underglaze. Polychrome decal or lithograph in Two Temples II pattern overglaze.
Retailer/importer: Mogridge and Underhay, Longton, Staffordshire*

Six-cup teapot decorated with polychrome litho based on Two Temples II pattern. The pattern is circular as if it were made for a plate. The border pattern is the same as on the plate shown previously. *Courtesy Tim and Kim Allen.* $75-125.

Two Temples II pattern 9-inch plate transfer-printed in dark blue underglaze on earthenware. It has a large area of white between the central pattern and border. The quality is very ordinary. Mark 1. *Author's Collection.* $12-18.

John Dawson & Co.

Location: South Hylton and Ford Potteries, Sunderland, Durham
Dates: c. 1799-1864
Impressed Mark:

(GG1207) c. 1799-1864

Brief History: Dawson's Pottery, located three miles west of Sunderland, was also known as the Low Ford Pottery. It was opened about 1790, with an output of brown ware and cream-colored ware. John Dawson took over the pottery in 1799, and added tiles to the production. His sons Thomas and John helped him run the pottery. New buildings with new machinery were added in 1836. These improvements and the good supply of Devon clay brought the standard of wares to a very high level. The pottery produced printed and lustered wares with the largest output of any other pottery on Wearside. John Dawson died in 1848, at the age of 88. His sons had preceded him in death, leaving the business to be taken over by his grandsons. They were not trained in the pottery, and it was not well run. The pottery gradually declined until 1864, when it closed. The molds and transfer-printing plates were sold at public auction.
Type of Willow Manufactured: Two Temples II pattern transfer-printed in blue underglaze on earthenware.

Ten-inch dinner plate decorated with polychrome lithographed version of Two Temples II central pattern. The border has a motif of a building with willow tree between sections that contain a geometrical motif. The plate has a line of gold at the rim. *Author's Collection.* $25-40.

Two Temples II pattern 4 1/8-inch plate transfer-printed in blue underglaze on earthenware. There is no border pattern on this small dish with a scalloped edge. *Courtesy J and J Cockerill.* $20-40.

Deakin & Son

c. 1833-41

Location: Waterloo Works (1832-63), and Peel Pottery (1841-63), Longton, Staffordshire
Dates: c. 1832-63
Mark:

Brief History: The firm of Deakin & Son followed the partnership of Deakin & Bailey at Waterloo Works. During the almost 30 years in operation, it was probably a grandfather, father, and son partnership. Peel Pottery on Stafford Street was also occupied by Deakin & Son from 1841. The products included earthenware and stoneware. James Deakin senior and Edwin Deakin were bankrupt in 1863. The Waterloo Works was taken over in 1864, by Lowe & Abberley. Webb & Walters moved into the Peel Pottery.

Type of Willow Manufactured: Standard Willow pattern transfer-printed in blue underglaze on earthenware.

Standard Willow pattern 9-inch plate transfer-printed in blue underglaze. This round plate has a concave rim. *Courtesy Dennis Crosby.* $30-40.

Dillwyn & Co.

Mark 1 (GG3764)
c. 1811-17

Location: Cambrian Pottery, Swansea, Wales
Dates: c. 1811-17
Marks:

Comments Concerning Marks: A plate with Mark 1 also has the written part of the mark impressed.

Brief History: Lewis Weston Dillwyn had been in partnership with George Haynes from June 1802, until March 1810. Haynes left the Cambrian Pottery and used his expertise to establish the Glamorgan Pottery next to the Cam-

Mark 2 (GG3768)
c. 1824-50

brian. In 1811, Lewis Weston Dillwyn took into a limited partnership with him Timothy Bevington and his 25-year old son John. The Bevingtons managed the business with occasional supervision from Dillwyn. In exchange Timothy was given 5/20 and John 2/20 share of the profits. The remaining 13/20 went to Dillwyn. Later Dillwyn purchased 1/20 of Timothy Bevington's holding which resulted in 7/10 for Dillwyn, 2/10 for Timothy Bevington and 1/10 for John Bevington.

Dillwyn & Co. produced dinner, dessert, supper, and tea services in a variety of patterns and shapes both printed and painted. Vases, mantle-piece ornaments and other decorative wares were made. Earthenware was the medium used until Dillwyn added a China Works in 1814-5, in order to begin the production of porcelain. The demand for earthenware had diminished, and he hoped to expand his trade by producing porcelain. The "Swansea willow pattern" developed earlier by George Haynes was continued through this partnership. The pattern is made by other firms and known as "Long Bridge". The Standard Willow pattern was introduced at Swansea in the period of 1811-17. It was used mainly on dinnerware and rarely on tea ware. The pattern was continued to the end of the factory. There were small variations in detail as worn copper plates were replaced during later partnerships. By 1817, Dillwyn was ready to retire so that he could manage the affairs of his wife's father who died that year. The business was leased by the Bevingtons in partnership with George Haynes senior and junior, and John Roby. The company then traded as T. & J. Bevington & Co.*

Type of Willow Manufactured: Standard Willow pattern transfer-printed in blue underglaze on earthenware. Many pieces of "Swansea Willow" are illustrated in Plate XIII in Nance's *The Pottery & Porcelain of Swansea & Nantgarw*; however, this pattern is actually "Long Bridge"[1] Robert Copeland devotes Chapter 12 to "Long Bridge" pattern in *Spode's Willow Pattern*.

Standard Willow pattern 10 1/8-inch plate transfer-printed in blue underglaze. The edge of the plate has 8 indentations, and the rim is concave. It has 3-point stilt marks on the back of the rim with single points on the front. The plate has a recessed foot ring. The outer border pattern is matched to the inner border; however, a bit of transfer is missing at 11 o'clock. Mark 2. *Author's Collection.* $45-65.

1. In *The Leeds Pottery* by Donald Towner, p. 44 he discusses two versions of "Willow Pattern". These are illustrated in Plates 48, i and ii; however, these illustrations are again of "Long Bridge" pattern, dated 1815, and 1820. These are examples of the confusion in the early nineteenth century regarding the identity of the Standard Willow pattern.

J. Dimmock & Co.

Location: Albion Street, Shelton & Stafford Street, Hanley, Staffordshire
Dates: c. 1862-1904
Marks:

Brief History: Formerly Thomas Dimmock & Co.*, John Dimmock continued to produce transfer-printed patterns on earthenware. From 1878, the business was owned by W. D. Cliff. His name appears on most of the marks after that date.
Type of Willow Manufactured: Standard Willow pattern transfer-printed underglaze in blue, red, and brown on earthenware. The most commonly found color on tableware is brown. The blue transfer-printed willow pattern sink is a highly unusual use of the pattern.

Mark I (GG1289)
c. 1862-78

Mark 2 c. 1878-90

Produced by the J. L. Mott Iron Works, New York, and decorated by John Dimmock in the Standard Willow pattern, this sink came from a ship. It measures 14.5-inches across the top. The blue pattern has gold trim as well as gold highlights. The sink is stamped with the date of manufacture: May 1885. The copper plumbing pipes are still attached. The sink bears Mark 3. *Courtesy IWC Convention 1998.* NP

Thomas Dimmock & Co.

Location: Albion St. & Cheapside, Shelton & Tontine St., Hanley, Staffordshire
Dates: c. 1828-59
Marks:

Comments Concerning Marks: GG1300, and impressed monogram sometimes appears with printed Mark 1. The initial D often occurs on marks from this company.
Brief History: In *Jewitt's Ceramic Art of Great Britain 1800-1900*, we read: "The old-established firm of Thomas Dimmock & Co., when John Ward's *History of Stoke-on-Trent* was published in 1843, held three manufactories." One was in Hanley, and the other two in Shelton. Products included blue printed earthenware. The firm was succeeded by J. Dimmock & Co.*
Type of Willow Manufactured: Standard Willow pattern transfer-printed in blue underglaze. Canton pattern with added spear points on the inside of the outer border.

Mark I c. 1828-59

Mark 2 (GG1297)
c. 1828-59

Mark 3 May 1885

Standard Willow pattern pitcher transfer-printed in brown underglaze on earthenware. This is a very heavy pitcher resembling vitrified institutional ware. It stands 7.5-inches high and has Mark 1. *Courtesy IWC Convention 2002.* $100-125.

Standard Willow pattern 10-inch plate transfer-printed in blue underglaze on stone china. It has a concave rim and slightly uneven edge. Three-point stilt marks on the center of the plate with single marks showing on the top. The plate has a cluttered effect because there is no white space between the borders. Mark 1. *Courtesy Dennis Crosby.* $35-45.

Standard Willow pattern 10.75-inch plate with molded basket weave border. It is part of a seafood service that includes a platter with black molded lobster imbedded into it. This plate has black molded forms imbedded into the plate to represent seafood such as shrimps and scallops. The mark is impressed Dimmock. *Courtesy Rita Cohen.* $140-160.

Dixon, Austin & Co.

Location: Garrison Pottery, Sunderland, Durham
Dates: c. 1820-26 and 1827-40
Mark:

(GG3744)
c. 1820-26

Brief History: The Sunderland or Garrison Pottery was founded c. 1807 by Mr. Phillips. It was carried on by Phillips, Dixon and Austin in various partnerships until the works were discontinued in 1865. Printed and colored earthenware was produced in addition to luster decorated items and figures. Dixon, Austin & Co. traded from 1820-26, and is also listed from 1827-40, along with Dixon, Austin, Phillips & Co.

Type of Willow Manufactured: Transfer-printed blue underglaze in Standard Willow and Two Temples II patterns. Standard Willow pattern has been found with the impressed mark Dixon & Co.

Two Temples II central pattern 4.50-inch plate with no border. It is transfer-printed in blue underglaze. The little plate has a scalloped edge. *Courtesy IWC Convention 2000.* $25-30.

Canton pattern 7-inch plate with added dagger border inside the outer border. Parts of the pattern are highlighted with fine yellow lines over the flow blue glaze. Petra Williams shows it in *Flow Blue China II*, page 39, without the yellow highlights. She also pictures a Canton plate to illustrate the pattern. Though we know the pattern as Canton, Thomas Dimmock named it Dagger Border. *Author's Collection.* $25-35.

Dixon, Phillips & Co.

Location: Garrison Pottery, Sunderland, Durham
Dates: c. 1840-65
Mark:

Comments Concerning Mark: The printed garter mark is used in conjunction with a printed name mark: DIXON, PHILLIPS & Co.

Brief History: Dixon, Phillips & Co. was the final partnership in business at the Garrison Pottery. Earthenware of various types continued to be produced.

Type of Willow Manufactured: Standard Willow pattern transfer-printed in blue underglaze on earthenware.

(GG3747) c. 1840-65

Standard Willow pattern small tray transfer-printed in blue underglaze on earthenware. The tray, or small platter, measures 6-by-7-inches. It bears both the printed and impressed name mark. *Courtesy J and J Cockerill.* $30-50.

Two Temples II pattern 8.50-inch plate transfer-printed in blue underglaze. The rim of the plate slants upward toward the edge of the rim. Three-point stilt marks on the underside of the flat rim and three single marks on the top. The plate is light in weight and has no foot ring. It is pearlware with a pale blue glaze. The impressed mark is the smallest of 7 sizes used on Don Pottery. It measures 9/16 of an inch. The largest mark is 1 1/8-inch. The mark was enlarged for use here. *Author's Collection.* $55-75.

Don Pottery (Green & Co.)

Location: Swinton, Nr. Rotherham, York-shire
Dates: c. 1801-39
Mark:

(GG1309) c. 1801-30

Brief History: John Green founded the Don Pottery in 1801, in Swinton, York-shire. His sons John and William Green sold it in 1839, to Samuel Barker & Sons*. The pottery had a small beginning but gradually developed into a two-acre site. It was ideally located near two canals that made it possible to transport goods to the Don and Humber Rivers, and all the way to Liverpool. Later on a railway was built nearby that added further ease in transportation. John Green senior had many partners at the outset of the business who were friends and partners from his previous pottery management work at Leeds Pottery.

His son John was one of the original partners. When John senior died suddenly in 1805, his son William became a partner. Other changes in the partnership occurred at about that same time.

Don Pottery produced high quality creamware and pearlware from the outset due to the experienced workers and management of the company. Creamware was produced until 1820, and pearlware was a staple of the pottery under the Greens. Underglaze black transfer prints with and without on-glaze decorating were produced as well as free hand underglaze decoration.
Type of Willow Manufactured: Standard Willow and Two Temples II patterns transfer-printed in blue underglaze on pearlware. Standard Willow pattern is illustrated in *The Don Pottery 1801-1893* by John D. Griffin.

Doric China Co.

Location: China St., Fenton & High St., Longton, Staffordshire
Dates: c.1924-35
Mark: (GG1323) c. 1926-35

Brief History: The company produced a range of bone china. It was taken over by Royal Albion China* in 1935.
Type of Willow Manufactured: Two Temples II pattern in polychrome lithograph over glaze on bone china tea ware. No picture available.

Doulton & Co. (Ltd.)

Location: Lambeth, London S.E. (1858-1956), & Nile St., Burslem (1882+), Staffordshire
Dates: c. 1858-present (2003)
Marks:

Comments Concerning Marks: Although many of the marks reproduced here are variations of two of the marks found in Godden's *Encyclopedia of British Pottery and Porcelain Marks*, I think it is important to see the variations that occur on the wares. Mark 8 is one of two marks found on bone china dishes. The other has Rd.No.328840, just one number different. The shapes vary from almost round to oval, so the Rd. Nos. relate to the shapes of the pieces and can be dated c. 1898. Pattern numbers occur on very few pieces; however, it has been noted that #2391 (with letters A to D, indicating earthenware) is found on blue patterned pieces with clear glaze. Pieces with colored pattern and/or glazes

Mark 1 (GG1332)
c. 1891-1902

Mark 2 (GG1332)
c. 1891-1902+

other than blue have different pattern numbers. Mark 28, found on the Motoring Willow Pattern is the only mark with designer's initials on a willow pattern piece by Doulton. The initials (C.N. for Charles Noke) are printed on the plate.

Brief History: John Doulton and John Watts were partners from 1815-58. Doulton & Watts produced stoneware bottles, jars and vases of all kinds as well as terra cotta statues, fountains and other architectural pieces. Doulton's second son Henry came into the business in 1835, at the age of 15 and began his apprenticeship working at the potter's wheel. Henry took classes and studied a variety of subjects from chemistry and physics to literature and poetry. He soon became a driving force in the company. In 1846, Henry Doulton began producing sanitary stoneware drainpipes at the Lambeth factory. He not only made a fortune for the company but also made a great contribution to the health of the city of London. In 1858, the name of the company changed to Doulton & Co. By the 1860s Henry Doulton became interested in the nearby Lambeth School of Art and hired many of its students to work at the pottery. Decorative stoneware was produced at Doulton with many individual artists signing their work and becoming famous as designers and decorators of industrial art pottery.

Henry Doulton moved to Stoke-on-Trent in 1877 after buying into the firm of Pinder, Bourne & Co.* He was very critical of the way the factory was run and the quality of the ware. In 1882, he purchased the Nile Street Pottery, Burslem from Pinder, Bourne & Co. Under his direction, the company continued to produce earthenware but the quality of the product was greatly improved. He hired John Slater as head of design and John Bailey as general manager who served the company for 50 years. The production of bone china began in 1884. In 1885, Henry Doulton was awarded the Society of Arts' Albert Medal, and two years later was knighted for his services to art and industry. Charles Noke joined the firm in 1889, as a modeler, and figure making became an important part of the firm's production. Noke also introduced series ware to the production line as he became head of the art department. He retired in 1936. Henry Doulton died in 1897, and the firm, headed by his son Henry Lewis Doulton, became a limited company. The Doulton Co. Ltd. was granted permission to prefix its name with "Royal" by Edward VII in 1901.

During the 1960s and 1970s Royal Doulton made a number of acquisitions including Minton* at whose factory the International Headquarters are located. In 1969, the company purchased the John Beswick Works*. Doulton's char-

acter jugs and figures from "Bunnykins" nursery ware are produced at that location. In 1972, Royal Doulton was bought by Pearson. This merger with Allied English Potteries brought companies such as Royal Crown Derby and Royal Albert* into the group. As a result Royal Doulton became one of the world's leading manufacturers of bone china. The company divided the factories into Fine China Division, Tableware Division and Hotelware Division. In 1984, the company was renamed Royal Doulton Limited. Since 1993, it has been an independent listed company. With declining sales, the company has sought cheaper sites for production such as Indonesia to produce mid-price china. Unfortunately, Royal Doulton has found it necessary to sell off some of its assets. The most recent and far-reaching decision was to sell a large portion of the Minton Museum ceramic collection at auction in April 2002.

Type of Willow Manufactured: Standard Willow pattern in blue, black, brown, and red on earthenware. The ware has clear or flow blue glaze on blue, clear glaze on red and brown with shades of yellow, orange, and red glazes on black. Standard Willow pattern is printed in blue on china and institutional ware. The Willow Pattern Story Series Ware is blue and black printed with some pieces clobbered in polychrome. Real Old Willow Booths pattern was printed in blue from 1981-99, and rust (orange) color in 1989. A polychrome decal based on the Booths pattern with added flowers was produced on bone china. See Parrot & Co.* for an example.

Retailers/importers: Dairy Outfitters Co. Ltd., London, * Gilman Collamore, New York*, Ovington Bros., Brooklyn, New York*, and J. J. Royle, Manchester.*

Mark 3 (GG1332)
c. 1891-1902

Mark 4 (GG1332)
c. 1882-1902

Mark 5 (GG1332)
c. 1891-1902

Mark 6 (GG1329)
c. 1882-91

Mark 7 c. 1973+

Mark 8 (GG1333)
c. 1902+

Mark 9 (GG1333) c. 1902+

Mark 10 (GG1334)
c. 1930+

Mark 11 (GG1334)
c. 1981-1999

Mark 12 (GG1334)
c. 1989+

Mark 13 (GG1334)
c. 1990s

Mark 14 (GG1343)
c. 1891-1902

Mark 15 c. 1882-91

Mark 16 c. 1882-91

Mark 17 c. 1891+

DOULTON'S
WILLOW
MADE IN ENGLAND

Mark 18 c. 1930+

DOULTON'S
WILLOW & ASTER.

Mark 19 c. 1882-91

Chung & Koongshee escape, but are pursued by
the Tipsy Mandarin, whom they elude.

Mark 20 (GG1333) c. 1902+

After travelling many miles they moor their boat
beside an island covered with reeds & there resolved
to settle down & spend their days in peace.

Mark 21 (GG1333) c. 1902+

Here they lived happily.

Mark 22 (GG1333) 8/17

"Koongshee & Chang
live in happiness
& contentment."

Mark 23 (GG1333) c. 1902+

Mark 24 (GG1333) c. 1909-28

Mark 25 (GG1333) c. 1909-28

They purchased a free right to the little island
& having built a house, and from the sale of jewels
obtained all that was necessary. Chang brought the
Island into a high state of cultivation.

Mark 26 (GG1333) April 1929

Chang having achieved a competence by his cultivation
of the land, returned to his literary pursuits and
wrote a book on Agriculture which gained for him
great reputation.

Mark 27 (GG1333) April 1929

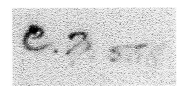

Mark 28 CN566 c. 1912+

Standard Willow pattern border (called Japanese border) used on Arabian
Nights series. The top plate is #7 The Magic Horse, and the bottom plate is
from the Ali Baba series #5 Morgiana pouring oil. Plates in this series are rarely
found. Marks 24 and 25. *Courtesy Nan Rankin.* $200+ each.

Standard Willow central pattern compote with outer border only. It stands 5-inches high and is 8.50-inches across. Most Doulton hollow ware pieces have only the outer border, and the central pattern is larger as a result. Mark 17. *Author's Collection*. $85-125.

Standard Willow pattern 8.75-inch plate and cup. The plate is bone china – rarely found with willow pattern — and the cup is institutional china called Steelite. The plate is trimmed in gold, and has an unglazed single foot ring. It has Mark 8. The cup has ridges at the edges on the underside and might not have had a saucer. Mark 7. *Author's Collection*. $25-40 & $10-15.

Eight earthenware jugs with Standard Willow pattern. All have the border pattern at the top or the bottom except for the front left hand jug with no border. The center front jug and the tall Arno shape jug in the back have Mark 1. The jug with no border has Mark 17, and the rest have Mark 2. The jug at the right front of the Arno jug is Quorn shape, and the one in front of that is octagonal. *Author's Collection*. $100+ each.

Three large jugs in Standard Willow pattern with Mark 1. The tall, slim jug stands 14.5-inches high. The left front Baron shape jug is 9.5-inches high, and the Tavern jug on the right is 7.25-inches high. *Courtesy Joette Hightower, Paul Kirves, and Zeke Jimenez*. $150+ each.

Two Doulton willow coffee pots. The pot on the left is 9-inches tall and has cobalt handle and spout. The border appears at the top and bottom of the pot as well as around the lid. It has Mark 1 with #A2391. The 6.5-inch coffee pot is Cecil shape. It has a pale blue glaze on the spout, usually seen on flow blue items. The lid has a ring finial. It has Mark 2. *Author's Collection*. $200-300 each.

This Standard Willow Pattern teapot has been seen in 2-cup and 4-cup size. It has the verse: "Polly put the kettle on & we'll all take tea." It has Mark 16, a mark that appears on several different Doulton teapots. *Courtesy Jeff Siptak.* $250+.

Two Standard Willow pattern blue printed teapots. The left is oval shaped and stands 5.75-inches tall. Examples of this 4-cup teapot bear Mark 8 and Mark 15 with Made in England added. The Joan shape teapot on the right is 6-inches tall and holds 6 cups. Examples have Mark 1 and Mark 15 with Made in England. *Courtesy Loren Zeller.* $100-175 each.

Extraordinary umbrella stand that is 23.5-inches high and 13-inches wide at the widest part. There are three repeats of the willow pattern in linear form, each one framed with the outer border. Mark 3 has an extra symbol sometimes found on Doulton willow pieces. *Courtesy Loren Zeller.* $1500+.

Ten piece wash set in dark cobalt blue. It is rare to find this many pieces of a set together. All pieces bear Mark 1 except for the 3-part soap dish that has Mark 10. Some pieces have pattern #D2913 marked. *Courtesy IWC Convention.* $2,500+.

Plate 1 in the Willow Pattern Story Series transfer-printed underglaze and clobbered in pastel colors. The green border has not been documented until now. It is reminiscent of a leaded glass window. Mark 20. *Courtesy Charles and Zeta Hollingsworth.* $200+.

Plates 4 and 6 in the Willow Pattern Story Series printed in black on 7 7/8" square-shaped plates. The inner curved section of each plate has a basket weave molded design. These are the first story plates found on this shape. The plates have pattern D4872 and are dated April 1929. The Marks 26 and 27 have Rd No. 731190, c. 1927. *Courtesy Tim and Kim Allen.* $100-150 each.

Plates 1, 3, and 5 in the Willow Pattern Story Series. The blue and white plates are 10.25-inches in diameter. Plate 1 has Mark 20 and is impressed with 25 – the date 1925. Plate 3 has Mark 21 and has impressed 2-28 for 1928. Plate 5 is 9-inches in size and is trimmed in gold. It has a black printed pattern with lavender bird and swirl border. It is one of the few pieces, and the first plate, in all the color combinations found to date, that is bone china. It is date impressed 8-17. Mark 22. *Author's Collection.* $75-150 each.

This 10-inch plate has the same border as the blue and white plates seen above. It is an adaptation of the Standard Willow outer border with 6 cartouches that are miniature scenes from the 6 plates in the series. It is number 5 in the series and is decorated with polychrome enamels over the glaze. The legend on the back, seen in Mark 23, is a little different from the version in Mark 22 on the back of the black and lavender No. 5 plate. *Courtesy Tim and Kim Allen.* $150+.

The Motoring Willow Pattern was introduced by Doulton in 1912; however, this is the first plate known to exist. Louise Irvine has only a rag print shown in her Book: *Royal Doulton Series Ware, Vol. 1.* This photo was sent by email from a woman in England who purchased the plate at a Royal Doulton Convention in London in the late 1990s. It was a surprise to learn that the plate is in color. It has Mark 8 with Mark 28, CN, Charles Noke's initials, plus the number 566. Therefore we know that Charles Noke designed the Motoring Willow Pattern. *Photo and Mark Courtesy Tim and Kim Allen.* $1,200+.

Red Standard Willow pieces by Doulton are not often found. This plate measures 8 1/8-inches and has an impressed number mark 10=82: possibly October 1882. *Courtesy Anna Morrison.* $30-50.

Standard Willow pattern ten-inch bowl printed in brown with sponged light brown in the background. The rim of the bowl has a band of dark brown and a line of gold. The central pattern inside the bowl is framed with the Standard Willow inner border that is usually seen only on flat objects. The bowl is impressed DOULTON and has printed pattern #A669. *Courtesy Ohio Willow Society.* $50-100.

Standard Willow pattern bowl in black underglaze with reddish glaze and gold trim. This bowl measures 10.5-inches from point to point. This glaze color is very rarely seen on Doulton willow. Mark 10. *Courtesy IWC Convention 2001.* $150-250.

A 4.75-inch teapot, stand, covered sugar, and creamer with Holbein (mustard color) glaze and black Standard Willow pattern transfer-printed underglaze. The stand has Mark 1 with pattern #D3382. The teapot and sugar have Mark 15. The creamer has Mark 8. The creamer and sugar also have the stylized "D" found in Mark 3. All the pieces came together as a set, so these marks must have been used during the same period. *Courtesy Loren Zeller.* $300+ for set.

This jam jar with metal lid and handle has a very unique patterned finish to the glaze. The process, with a US Patent number, created a look and feel of tapestry with an uneven surface and vertical ridges all around the sides. The gold decorated blue borders are unusual and too ornate for the piece in my opinion. Mark 4. *Author's Collection.* $150-250.

Standard Willow pattern humidors printed underglaze in brown with a tan colored glaze. This is an unusual color combination. The inner border is used at the top of the pattern around the lip of the opening and on the knob. Mark 1. *Courtesy Paul Kirves and Zeke Jimenez.* $200-250 each.

This eleven-inch covered vegetable dish has Willow & Aster pattern covering most of the surface of the bowl and lid. Branches with flowers are not only in gold on the blue ground border but also printed in blue on the white background. Mark 19. *Courtesy Ohio Willow Society.* $150-250.

Two Lambeth salt-glazed stoneware jugs showing brown and blue glazes. The 9-inch jug bears Mark 14. The Standard Willow outer border was impressed into the top of the tall jug in the mold. Both jugs were dipped in glaze at the top, and the large one was also dipped in brown glaze at the bottom. Motifs from the willow pattern molded onto the sides of the pieces were glazed in blue. Many types of stoneware pieces were decorated in this manner although most have white or clay-colored relief decorations. *Collections of the Author and Harry and Jessie Hall.* $125-175 each.

Large pitcher that measures 10.25-inches high in the Spray pattern. The transfer-printed willow cartouche is 6-inches in diameter. Some of the flower sprays are similar to those on Willow & Aster. This pattern is not often seen. Mark 5. *Courtesy IWC Convention 2001.* $300+.

Standard Willow pattern 8-inch plate with pale blue glaze and Mark 15. It has a slightly recessed foot ring. The 9.5-inch plate is decorated with Willow & Aster pattern on the border. It bears Mark 1 with WILLOW & ASTER. It also has an impressed circular mark with BURSLEM across the top, DOULTON in the middle, and ENGLAND at the bottom. Pattern #9843. The Willow and Aster cartouches are transfer-printed underglaze onto the border covered with dark blue ground. Flowers, aster circles, and outlining are all done in gold. *Author's Collection.* $25-50 and $85-150.

Tureen, creamer, and covered sugar in Booths* "Real Old Willow" by Royal Doulton on Majestic Shape. The company developed the clay body named "English Porcelain" for this pattern. Mark 13. *Courtesy of Tim and Kim Allen.* $200+.

Royal Doulton®
"Real Old Willow"
BOXED GIFTWARE

Brochure for Royal Doulton's "Real Old Willow" giftware shows some of the pieces in Majestic Shape introduced by Booths and continued by Royal Doulton. There is also a picture of new giftware developed by Royal Doulton in "Real Old Willow" pattern.

Dudson

Location: Hope Street, Hanley, Staffordshire
Dates: c. 1800-1898
Brief History: The Hope Street firm was established c. 1800 by Thomas Dudson and has been carried on by the family for approximately 200 years. The earliest extant record book is dated 1819. It shows a wide range of transfer-printed ware was produced in pink, blue-green, and brown as well as blue. Throughout most of the nineteenth century Dudson mixed colors and glazes not only for its own use but also to supply other manufacturers. Factory records from 1834, and 1842-1844, include orders for blue and flow-blue underglaze transfer-printed wares. The clay bodies used ranged from early pearlware to white earthenware, followed by ironstone ware and stone china. Many of the wares produced were unmarked. Dudson also filled special orders for other potters. From 1845, the name of the firm was James Dudson. It became Dudson Bros.* in 1898
Type of Willow Manufactured: An archeological dig on the original factory site uncovered a large quantity of glazed and biscuit shards as well as wasters. Standard Willow pattern and Two Temples II were found in a quantity to indicate that they were staple patterns produced from early to mid-nineteenth century. Rose pink and lavender Standard Willow shards were found in addition to soft, medium blue on pearlware and clear bright blue prints on white earthenware and ironstone ware. Two Temples II teawares were made in medium to light blue on bone china. The pattern was also produced in bright medium blue on pearlware and pale blue on white earthenware. There are a few examples of willow pattern at the Dudson Museum in Hanley including shards in various clay bodies from pearlware to hotelware. No picture is available.

Dudson Bros. (Ltd.)

Location: Hope Street, Hanley (1898-1980), Albert Potteries, Burslem (1947+), and International H. Q.: Scotia Road, Tunstall (present, 2003), Staffordshire
Dates: c. 1898-present (2003)

Mark:

MADE FOR BELLE VUE BY DUDSON BROS HANLEY

c. twentieth century

Brief History: Dudson Bros. was formerly known as James Dudson and J. T. Dudson. It was J. T. Dudson who engineered the change from the production of domestic ware to institutional wares after he took over the business in 1880. He noted the development of the catering industry in hotels and restaurants and decided that it would be advantageous to specialize in that market. By 1891 production of domestic ware ceased. Dudson Bros. was very successful in its new venture. There were problems with restrictions of production during World War I and World War II; however, the factory survived both events through the strength of the family, managers, and work force.

A vigorous expansion began in 1947, as Derek Dudson joined the business. Dudson Bros. acquired the Albert Potteries in Burslem and later the Grindley Hotelware Co. Ltd.* in Tunstall. In 1980, Hope Street Pottery closed and all production moved to Burslem and Tunstall. The firm was instrumental in establishing the British Standard 4034 for Vitrified Hotel Ware. In 1983, further technology resulted in the appearance of Dudson Fine China. It looks like delicate bone china but has the strength of vitrified ware. The only kiln at the Hope Street Pottery has been restored. The factory is a Grade II listed building. It is now open as a museum celebrating over 200 years of the Dudson family business.

Type of Willow Manufactured: Standard Willow pattern transfer-printed underglaze on vitrified ware. A catalog from shortly after World War II shows the Standard Willow pattern as Deco No. 203. In the current Dudson "Service Plates" brochure, a plate is shown in Standard Willow reversed central pattern. It is shown below.

Purchased in 1979, this is the only piece of Standard Willow pattern I have seen by Dudson Bros. It is printed in gray on a vitrified body. The platter measures 11-by-14-inches. It was made for use at the restaurant at Belle Vue, a zoo and entertainment center at Manchester. *Author's Collection.* $35-55.

Willow FLAT PROFILE

Standard Willow reversed central pattern service plate in dark blue illustrated in the 2003 brochure. Only the inner border was used in designing this pattern. According to the brochure, it is available in both Dudson Fine China (Embassy) or Dudson Finest Vitrified (Clubhouse) Hotelware. *Courtesy Alison Morgan, Dudson Museum Administrator.*

Dudson, Wilcox & Till Ltd.

Location: Britannic Works, Hanley, Staffordshire
Dates: c. 1902-26
Mark:

(GG1412)
c. 1902-26

Brief History: The company produced earthenwares primarily for foreign markets. Blue Willow was one of its stock patterns that was continued by Bakewell Bros. Ltd.* when they took over the Britannic Works in 1926.
Type of Willow Manufactured: Standard Willow pattern transfer-printed in dark blue on earthenware.

Standard Willow pattern bowl that is 9 5/8-inches across and 2.75-inches deep. The center pattern framed by the inner border is in the bottom of the bowl with the outer border at the top on the inside. There is no pattern on the outside of the bowl. *Author's Collection.* $35-45.

Standard Willow pattern 4-cup teapot blue printed underglaze. The outer border of the pattern is on the shoulder of the teapot and the edge of the lid. It has the same indented shape seen on the 8-cup teapot by Bakewell Bros. Ltd.* Evidently Bakewell Bros. took over the molds when they took over the pottery in 1926. *Courtesy Charles and Zeta Hollingsworth.* $75-150.

Dunn Bennett & Co. (Ltd.)

Location: Boothen Works, Hanley (1875-1887), Royal Victoria Works, Burslem (1887-1938), Dale Hall Works, Longport, Burslem (1938+), Staffordshire
Dates: c.1875- present (2003)
Marks:

Mark 1 c. 1907+

Mark 2 (GG1423)
c. 1937+

Mark 3 c. 1968+

Brief History: Dunn Bennett & Co. produced earthenware and stoneware at Boothen Works. At the Royal Victoria Works, the firm began producing special ironstone wares for ships, hotels, and restaurants. The company became a limited company in 1907. "Vitreous ironstone" is a term that began to appear in marks. In 1909, the company produced an extremely durable earthenware that was virtually unchippable. (See L. Straus & Sons in Retailers/importers Section for a chipped example of this ware!) In 1968 Dunn Bennett merged with Royal Doulton* and became part of the Hotelware Division producing "Rocklite Vitrified Hotel Ware".
Type of Willow Manufactured: Standard Willow pattern transfer-printed in light and dark blue, on earthenware and vitrified ware as well as red vitrified ware.
Retailers/importers: Baur au Lac, Zurich, * L. Straus & Sons, New York*

Standard Willow pattern in light blue on cheese stand that measures 8.75-inches across. The base is 4 5/8-inches wide, and the piece is 2.25-inches high. It has gold trim on the rim of the dish and the base. The piece is heavy but does not appear highly vitrified. It has Mark 1. *Author's Collection.* $85-150.

Standard Willow pattern small coffee pot. The cylindrical shape and recessed knob on the lid reflect a design made for institutional ware. Mark 2. *Courtesy Joette Hightower.* $65-100.

Standard Willow pattern 7 7/8-inch plate in pink institutional ware. The plate is thick and heavy vitreous ware. Mark 3. *Author's Collection.* $10-15.

Eardley & Hammersley

Location: Church Bank Works, Tunstall, Staffordshire
Dates: d. 1862-66
Marks:

Mark 1 (GG1430)
c. 1862-66

Brief History: The Church Bank Works were built in 1842 by Robert Beswick. He worked the pot-

tery until 1860, when Beech & Hancock took over for two years. Eardley & Hammersley took over in 1862, and were in partnership until 1866. After that Ralph Hammersley* worked the pottery alone. All the firms produced good quality earthenware.

Type of Willow Manufactured: Standard Willow pattern in medium blue transfer-printed underglaze and Two Temples II pattern in pale blue underglaze.

Mark 2 (GG1430)
c. 1862-66

Standard Willow pattern 9-inch plate transfer-printed in blue underglaze on earthenware marked stoneware. It has a concave rim and wavy edge. Three-point stilt marks on the underside of the rim with three single marks on the front. The plate has a single flat foot ring that is .25-inch wide. Mark 1. *Author's Collection.* $20-30.

Two Temples II pattern in pale blue on 8.75-inch plate. It has a 2 5/8-inch emblem printed onto the middle of the pattern with the words: BURNLLE SUNDAY SCHOOL. The date 1866 is in the center. BURNLLE is probably a misprint for BURNLEE, located in the Kirklees area of Yorkshire and now part of Holmfirth, six miles south of Huddersfield. The plate is round with a flat rim that slopes a little upward toward the edge. It has the same stilt marks and foot ring as the Standard Willow pattern plate. It is earthenware marked semi china with a pale blue glaze giving it a china-like appearance. *Author's Collection.* $50-100.

William & Samuel Edge

Location: Market Street, Lane Delph, Staffordshire
Dates: c. 1841-48
Mark:

(GG1436)
c. 1841-48

Brief History: Lane Delph is the early name for the main street area in Fenton. Little is known of this partnership. Stone China on the mark indicates they produced heavy earthenware. I have seen only platters made by William & Samuel Edge.
Type of Willow Manufactured: Standard Willow pattern transfer-printed in blue underglaze on stone china.

Standard Willow pattern platter transfer-printed in blue underglaze on stone china. It measures 12.25-by-15.75-inches. Three-point stilt marks on the back of the rim with single stilt marks on the top. There are slight indentations at the edge of the rim. The border pattern is patched and cut to fit at the lower right and upper left hand corners. It is interesting to note how the path is disconnected by the fence on many of these platters. *Author's Collection.* $125-155.

Edge, Barker & Co.

Location: Fenton and Lane End, Staffordshire
Dates: c. 1835-36
Mark:

(GG1438) c. 1835-36

Brief History: This partnership lasted only two years. It was followed by the firm of Edge, Barker & Barker from 1836-40. First names are not known, so we do not know if the Edge in these partnerships was related to William & Samuel Edge whose partnership began in 1841. From the mark we know that stoneware was produced.
Type of Willow Manufactured: Standard Willow pattern transfer-printed in blue underglaze on stoneware.

Standard Willow pattern platter transfer-printed in blue underglaze on stoneware. It measures 12 3/8-by-15.75. Three-point stilt marks under the rim with three single marks on the top. The edge of the platter is uneven. The outer border has been cut at each corner to ensure the inner and outer borders match on the center of all four sides. The two sections of the path in front of the teahouse are almost round on this platter. *Author's Collection.* $100-125.

Edge, Malkin & Co. (Ltd.)

Location: Newport and Middleport Potteries, Burslem, Staffordshire
Dates: c. 1870-1903
Marks:

Comments Concerning Marks: The standard greyhound mark appears with and without ENGLAND depending on the date. The letter B (Burslem) is not always present. The word WILLOW in the mark appears on wares in the Mandarin pattern as well as on Standard Willow; however, "No. 1" added to the mark seems to refer to Mandarin pattern. Mark 3 (STONEWARE E.M.& Co.) was found on a Standard Willow pattern plate.
Brief History: The partnership succeeded Cork, Edge & Malkin* at both Burslem potteries. Up to 1892, the partners were Joseph Edge, James Malkin, William and John Edge. In the *Pottery Gazette*, September 1, 1899, we read "Registered with a capital of £35,000 in £1 shares to acquire the business now carried on at Burslem by Wm. M. Edge, Wm. S. M. Edge, and Samuel W. Dean." The trade name continued as Edge, Malkin & Co., Ltd. The company produced a large quantity of useful earthenware items including tableware and children's play sets. They exported mainly to North America. In the *Pottery Gazette*, December 1, 1899, an article regarding a fire at the factory stated, "Good came after bad as they replaced it with three floors of long, well-lighted and conveniently fitted warehouse accommodation."
Type of Willow Manufactured: Standard Willow transfer-printed in blue, brown, red and green. Mandarin pattern transfer-printed in blue and red.

Mark 1 (GG1441)
c. 1870-91

Mark 2 (GG1440)
c. 1870-91

Mark 3 (GG1441)
c. 1870-91

Mark 4 (GG1445)
c. 1873-1903

Mark 5
(GG1445)
c. 1873-

Standard Willow pattern platter in blue that measures 10.75-by-13.50-inches. The outer border is cut in three places in order to fit the geometric motifs in the middle of each side. Marks 1 and 2. *Courtesy Louise and Charles Loehr.* $125-175.

Standard Willow pattern mustache cup in blue transfer-printed underglaze on earthenware. These cups are hard to find, and there is often no saucer. Mark 4. *Courtesy IWC Convention 1996.* $100-175.

Standard Willow pattern children's toy dinner set transfer-printed underglaze in blue on earthenware. This large set includes two sizes of covered tureens, several sizes of platters, sauceboats, plates, and serving plates. Mark 4 with ENGLAND. *Courtesy Harry and Jessie Hall.* $850-1,000.

Mandarin pattern syrup pitcher with pewter lid transfer-printed in red underglaze on earthenware. This item has also been seen in blue. Mark 5. *Courtesy Ohio Willow Society.* $150+.

Standard Willow pattern partial children's toy tea set transfer-printed underglaze in brown. The teapot, creamer, sugar, and a cup and saucer are shown. The saucer has Marks 2 and 4 without the letter B. The cup is unmarked. The other pieces have Mark 5 without "No. 1". *Courtesy Anna Morrison.* $100-200.

Edwards & Brown

(GG1458 with Made in England) c. 1910-33

Location: Victoria Works, High Street, Longton, Staffordshire
Dates: c. 1882-1933
Mark:

Brief History: Duchess China was produced by this firm. In 1900, the partners were Joseph Weston Edwards and Richard Bryan. After Bryan retired September 12, 1901, Edwards continued the business on his own under the name of Edwards & Brown.
Type of Willow Manufactured: Standard Willow pattern and Two Temples II pattern printed in light and dark blue on china with gold trim.

Two Temples II pattern cup and saucer printed in dark blue on bone china with gold trim. The verse on the inside of the cup in two lines reads: "Take ye a cuppe o'kindnesse for auld lang syne". *Courtesy IWC Convention 2001.* $40-65.

Elkin, Knight & Co.

Location: The Foley Potteries, Fenton, Staffordshire
Dates: c. 1822-26
Mark:

c. 1822-26

Comments concerning the mark: On page 305 in *Dictionary of Blue & White Vol. 1* by Coysh and Henrywood an impressed eagle mark matching the one above is attributed to Elkin, Knight & Co. It appears on a marked plate from the Rock Cartouche Series by Elkin Knight & Co. The impressed eagle may have been used by other potteries. A plate in the Unattributed Marks section has an impressed eagle together with a printed mark also found on a platter impress marked GOODWINS & HARRIS*.
Brief History: Built by John Smith in the early 1820s, the Foley Potteries were named for the Foley family who owned property in the neighborhood. There were several partnerships at the pottery involving members of the Elkin and Knight families. Elkin, Knight & Co. was succeeded by Elkin, Knight & Bridgwood (also known as Knight, Elkin & Bridgwood) in 1827. Knight, Elkin & Co. has also been documented c. 1835-41. Willow pattern and other blue printed services on earthenware were produced by the successive partnerships.
Type of Willow Manufactured: Standard Willow pattern transfer-printed in blue underglaze on earthenware.

Standard Willow pattern 9.50-inch plate transfer-printed in blue underglaze on earthenware. The concave rim has 8 indentations at the edge. Three-point stilt marks on the underside of the rim. The foot ring is recessed. The outer border has an extension at 5:30 o'clock to make it fit. *Author's Collection.* $20-30.

Elkins & Co.

c. 1822-30

Location: Lane End, Staffordshire
Dates: c. 1822-30
Mark:

Brief History: This firm was one of the earliest of the Elkin family of potters. It was also known as Elkin, Knight and Elkin.
Type of Willow Manufactured: Standard Willow pattern transfer-printed in blue underglaze on earthenware.

Standard Willow pattern 9-inch plate transfer-printed in blue underglaze on earthenware. It has a pale blue glaze and is light in weight. It has a concave rim and uneven edge. *Courtesy Dennis Crosby.* $30-40.

Samuel Elkin

Location: Stafford St. (1856-59) and Mill St. (1860-64), Longton, Staffordshire
Dates: 1856-64
Mark:

(GG1468) c. 1856-64

Brief History: Little is known about the relationship of Samuel Elkin to the other Elkins in the pottery business. The mark shown above is similar to that used by the firm of Elkins & Co.* in the previous entry.
Type of Willow Manufactured: Standard Willow pattern transfer-printed in blue underglaze on earthenware.

Standard Willow pattern 14-by-18-inch platter transfer-printed in blue underglaze on earthenware. Extra three and four spoke wheels were added at the four corners to match the geometrical motifs of the two borders. Note the fishtail birds. *Courtesy Inez Allen and Nan Conlan.* $150-225.

Standard Willow pattern 10.50-inch plate in blue transfer-printed underglaze on earthenware. Three-point stilt marks at the flat foot ring visible on both sides. The rim is concave, and the edge is uneven. It has a pale blue glaze. *Author's Collection.* $30-40.

Ellgreave Pottery Co. Ltd.

Location: Ellgreave Street, Burslem, Staffordshire
Dates: c. 1921-81
Mark:

c. 1926+

Comments Concerning Marks: Impressed ELLGREAVE is found on many teapots and occasionally MARLBORO, the shape name.
Brief History: In 1921, Ellgreave was established as a division of Wood & Sons.* The company produced red-body ware and some earthenware tableware; however, it is best known for its teapots. A full page ad in *Pottery Gazette*, February 1, 1926, stated the following: "The associate firms of Wood & Sons Ltd. Incorporating Trent and New Wharf Potteries, Stanley Pottery, Bursley Ltd., Crown Pottery, Ellgreave Pottery Co. Ltd. – all of Burslem. We need not expound on the Quality and Merits of our Productions – You Know!" In June 1952, the *Pottery Gazette* had an Ellgreave, Burslem ad showing teapots with the statement: "More than 1,500,000 teapots per year."
Type of Willow Manufactured: Variations of Standard Willow pattern under and overglaze in blue and brown on earthenware teapots.

Elkin & Newbon

Location: Stafford Street, Longton, Staffordshire
Dates: c. 1845-56
Mark:

(GG1467) c. 1845-56

Brief History: Samuel Elkin and Thomas Newbon were partners at the Stafford St. pottery that was later used by Samuel Elkin* in 1856-59. Again, the mark illustrates a link to that firm and the firm of Elkins & Co.*
Type of Willow Manufactured: Standard Willow pattern transfer-printed in blue underglaze on earthenware.

A 6-cup teapot with blue decal overglaze based on the Standard Willow pattern. The mark indicates the teapot is ironstone. *Courtesy Paul Kirves and Zeke Jimenez.* $55-85.

Two 6-cup teapots with impressed ELLGREAVE and MARLBORO, the shape name. The teapot on the right is a dark brown color. *Courtesy Paul Kirves and Zeke Jimenez.* $60-115 each.

William Emberton (& Co.)

Location: Highgate Pottery, Brownhills, Tunstall, Staffordshire
Dates: c. 1846-69
Mark:

(GG1485) c. 1851-69

Brief History: The Highgate Pottery was established by George Hood who purchased the land in 1831, and built the factory. William Emberton purchased the pottery in 1846. He had a partnership with Thomas Emberton for about 5 years in which the firm was titled William Emberton & Co. From 1851-69, William Emberton continued on his own account. Production included earthenwares for the home market as well as several Indian markets including Calcutta and Bombay.
Type of Willow Manufactured: Standard Willow pattern transfer-printed in blue and red underglaze on earthenware.

T. I. & J. Emberton

Location: Highgate Pottery, Brownhills, Tunstall, Staffordshire
Dates: c. 1869-82
Mark:

c. 1869-82

Brief History: After the death of William Emberton* the pottery continued under the leadership of his three sons: Thomas, Isaac and James. According to an advertisement in *The Pottery Gazette Diary* of 1882, the firm specialized in lustered, Japanned, printed and enameled earthenwares for the Indian, South American and African markets.
Type of Willow Manufactured: Standard Willow pattern transfer-printed in blue underglaze on earthenware.

Standard Willow pattern 7.75-inch plate transfer-printed in red underglaze. It has a concave rim. The outer border pattern was cut to fit at 2 o'clock. It is difficult to find examples of red willow pattern made in the mid-nineteenth century. *Courtesy Anna Morrison.* $25-35.

Standard Willow pattern 10.50-inch plate transfer-printed in blue underglaze. Three-point stilt marks in the center of the plate just inside the single flat foot ring. The plate has a pale blue glaze. *Courtesy Dennis Crosby.* $30-40.

Empire Porcelain Co. (Ltd.)

Location: Empire Works, Stoke, Staffordshire
Dates: c. 1896-1967 & (1999-2003 in name only)
Marks:

Comment Concerning Marks: Mark 3 has the date on it with number 4 on the left of ENGLAND and 31 on the right. Mark 5 is the form of the mark being used by Steve Cope in producing blue willow c. 2002+.

Brief History: In spite of its name, the Empire Porcelain Co. produced earthenwares. Tableware and other useful wares produced in the early years made use of decal-decoration. In the 1930s, the company experimented with decorative ware and art pottery that have some following with collectors today. In 1958 the company was bought by Qualcast Group. After 1963, it was a limited company. The factory closed in 1967 and the works were demolished. In 1999 Steve Cope of Stoke-on-Trent purchased the company name. After a couple of years he began producing many different items using the Empire Ware back stamp.

Type of Willow Manufactured: Standard Willow and Mandarin patterns transfer-printed in blue underglaze, and willow variants in polychrome decals overglaze including "Red Bridge". Modern accessory items in blue willow include jugs, cheese keeper, vases, and canisters for biscuits, bread and sugar.

Mark 1 (GG1488)
c. 1896-1912

Mark 2 (GG1489)
c. 1912-28

Mark 3 April 1931

Mark 4 c. 1930+

Mark 5 c. 2002+

Mandarin pattern 9-inch plate in dark blue transfer-printed underglaze. The uneven rim is very dark blue with holes cut out at the inner edge of the border. This pattern is also found with a luster band on the rim. Mark 2. *Courtesy Geraldine Ewaniuk.* $25-35.

These 8.5-inch square plates have mirror images of a polychrome willow variant decal in the middle that I call the "Red Bridge" willow variant. The border pattern is missing that is usually seen with the pattern. The rim on the left plate is decorated in a mottled yellow with thin black lines on either side, and the plate on the right has a green border. Mark 3 is dated April 1931. *Courtesy Hugh and Kathy Sykes.* $15-25 each.

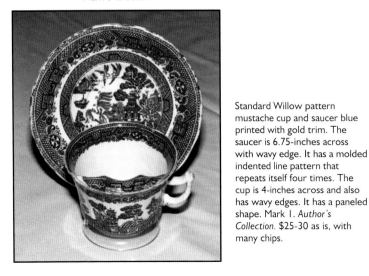

Standard Willow pattern mustache cup and saucer blue printed with gold trim. The saucer is 6.75-inches across with wavy edge. It has a molded indented line pattern that repeats itself four times. The cup is 4-inches across and also has wavy edges. It has a paneled shape. Mark 1. *Author's Collection.* $25-30 as is, with many chips.

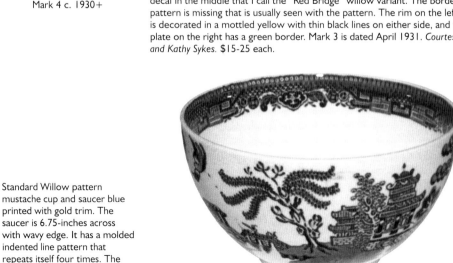

Standard Willow pattern bowl printed in blue. The bowl is 2.25-inch high and 4.50-inches across. It has Mark 4. *Author's Collection.* $8-12.

English Ironstone Pottery Ltd.

Location: Shelton, Staffordshire
Dates: c. 1970-74
Mark:

Old Willow
ENGLISH IRONSTONE POTTERY
COLLEGE ROAD SHELTON
STOKE-ON-TRENT
STAFFORDSHIRE
ENGLAND

c. 1972-74

Comment Concerning Mark: This mark was carried over from Washington Pottery Ltd.* the previous name of this company.

Brief History: In 1970 Washington Pottery Ltd.* was renamed English Ironstone Pottery Ltd. In 1974, the name was changed to English Ironstone Tableware Ltd.*

Type of Willow Manufactured: Variation of the Standard Willow pattern in blue on tableware. A number of elements of the outer border and pattern have been changed as can be seen in this illustration and those of the next entry. The changes are best described by David Richard Quintner in *Willow!* under the heading: "Ready for the 21st Century?"

> The outside border has lost just about all of its chinoiserie elements; the weeping willow tree now dominates the design, and it no longer bars a potential pathway to the bridge and its occupants, who have been spaced equally; the fruit tree that perilously overhung the mansion has been scaled down; the mansion is now higher than the fruit tree and has taken on a more pagoda-like form; the well-trod path aims directly for the mansion's front steps; and the steps no longer face the central pillar; the fence has been given a hinged gate, open for easy egress; the birds are reduced in perspective to a reasonable size; tree varieties are down to four; most small buildings have been eliminated, as has the suggestion of an overhanging rock. So that's how the Willow Pattern looks when ordered by a rational mind! All that remains to muse about is the trio of fungus-like shapes and the wavy rock in the foreground and by the mansion. The question lingers, of course: Do You Like It? Or better, **Does it any longer intrigue you?**[1]

Cup, saucer, and 6.50-inch plate blue printed in the E. I. P. variation of the Standard Willow pattern. The shape of the cup is unchanged from that of Washington Pottery.* *Author's Collection.* $8-12.

1. Quintner, David Richard, *Willow: Solving the Mystery of our 200-year Love Affair with the Willow Pattern*, p. 208.

English Ironstone Tableware

Location: Shelton, Staffordshire
Dates: c. 1974-94
Marks:

Mark 1 c. 1974-94

Mark 2 c. 1974-94

Brief History: This company followed English Ironstone Pottery* producing ironstone-type tableware. Evidently, the company produced a large quantity of wares with a workforce of 430. By mid-1994, it had gone into receivership, and in September 1994, 230 workers were made redundant. Cuts were made to the remaining 200. *Tableware International,* December 1994, reported that Harvergrange Plc. of Edgware purchased the remaining assets. The managing director said that they planned to merge with Grindley Pottery* in Tunstall. English Ironstone Tableware products would continue to be marketed under the E. I. T. brand name. Whether or not new wares were produced, new items were sold through discount stores in the U.S. through 1997-98.

Type of Willow Manufactured: Dark and light blue printed variation of the Standard Willow pattern described under English Ironstone Pottery.*

Mark 3 c. 1974-94

STAFFORDSHIRE
UNDERGLAZE
PRINTING
GENUINE HAND ENGRAVED
DISHWASHER, DETERGENT PROOF
MICRO-WAVE OVEN SAFE
Made English By
Ironstone
Tableware
Limited
England

Mark 4 c. 1974-94

Place setting in light blue with the English Ironstone Pottery* variation of the Standard Willow pattern. The plate has a flat rim and double foot ring. The cup shape has changed. All pieces have impressed Mark 1. Plates in darker blue have printed Mark 4. *Author's Collection.* $10-12.

Six-cup teapot in dark blue in the E.I.P. variation of the Standard Willow pattern. It is a pleasing shape for a teapot to use every day. Hundreds, if not thousands, of these teapots have been sold in the U.S. Marks 2 and 3 have been found on them. *Courtesy Paul Kirves and Zeke Jimenez.* $15-25.

Evans & Glasson

Location: Cambrian Pottery, Swansea
Dates: c. 1850-62
Mark:

(GG1519a) c. 1850-62

Brief History: In 1850 L. Llewelyn Dillwyn turned over the Cambrian Pottery to his commercial manager David Evans and his traveler John Evans Glasson although Dillwyn continued to hold the lease until the pottery closed in 1870. Glasson died in 1852, at the age of 47. David Evans' son D. J. Evans joined the firm in 1855, and took over more of the responsibility as his father gradually retired from the firm. By 1862, David Evans senior had fully retired. The company continued making useful wares in earthenware, but the quality of the wares and the designs deteriorated as the years went on.
Type of Willow Manufactured: Standard Willow pattern transfer-printed in blue underglaze on earthenware.

Standard Willow pattern 9.25-inch plate in light blue transfer-printed underglaze on earthenware. It has a concave rim and wavy edge. The border patterns are not well matched. There is an extra section of border added just after 6 o'clock. *Courtesy IWC Convention 1999.* $30-40.

D. J. Evans & Co.

Location: Cambrian Pottery, Swansea
Dates: c. 1862-70
Mark:

(GG1518) c. 1862-70

Brief History: David John Evans (D. J.) was joined by a younger brother John Josiah in working the Cambrian Pottery after David Evans senior retired from the company. As with the former company, blue and white transfer wares were the main product. Morton Nance tells us that the wares were as a rule thick and clumsy and often the transfers were carelessly applied. The plate shown here is not especially "thick and clumsy", but the quality is not very good, and the glaze is very poor. A better example can be seen at the National Museum and Gallery Cardiff, Wales. Nance mentions that willow is a pattern that was continued from the days of Evans & Glasson right on through the D. J. Evans & Co. period.
Type of Willow Manufactured: Standard Willow pattern transfer-printed underglaze in blue on earthenware.

Standard Willow pattern 9.5/8-inch plate in dark blue transfer-printed underglaze on earthenware. It has a concave rim and wavy edge. Three-point stilt marks straddling the single foot ring. The color is blotchy. The glaze is thin, with a large glaze miss on the left side on the center pattern. The plate is rough to the touch. *Author's Collection.* $15-20.

Thomas Fell & Co. (Ltd.)

Location: St. Peter's Pottery, Newcastle upon Tyne, Northumberland
Dates: c. 1817-90
Marks:

Mark 1
(GG1531+9)
c. 1817-30

Comments Concerning Marks: I have photos of four different size plates with willow pattern: 7 inch, 9.25 inch, 9 5/8 inch and 10 1/8 inch. The engravings are slightly different on each one, and each one has a different mark. One plate has impressed Mark 3 and printed Mark 4. All four marks are shown here but only one plate.

Mark 2 c. 1830-90

Brief History: The St. Peter's Pottery was built by Thomas Bell and Thomas Fell in 1817. Products included white, sponged, printed, and enameled ware for the home and export markets. Fell & Co. was the leading Tyneside firm of its time. In 1869, Fell & Co. became a limited liability company. The shareholders were descendents of the original owners. Under the limited liability company, only the printed wares were marked. T. F. & Co. was the most commonly used mark from that time; however, Fell & Co. continued to be used.

Type of Willow Manufactured: Standard Willow pattern transfer-printed underglaze on earthenware. Various shades of blue were used.

Mark 3 (GG1532)
c. 1830-90

Mark 4 c. 1830-90

Ferrybridge Pottery

Location: South Bank of the River Aire, near Pontefract, Yorkshire
Dates: 1793-1870
Mark:

(GG1540) c. 1801-70

Brief History: From 1793 to 1804, the works were known as Knottingley Pottery. The pottery was built by a consortium of businessmen and traded under various partnerships throughout the years. Ralph Wedgwood, cousin of Josiah Wedgwood in Staffordshire, was hired as a partner in 1798, to bring his expertise as a potter to the new pottery. This partnership failed after 2 1/2 years. Wares during this period were unmarked or marked with impressed "Wedgwood & Co". A "W & Co. Ferrybridge Shape and Pattern Book" was brought back to Staffordshire by Ralph Wedgwood when he left the pottery. This book is now in the Wedgwood Archives in Barlaston. Unmarked wares from the period have been attributed to Ferrybridge from designs found in the book.

Wares produced after 1801, are often marked with initials of the various partnerships either impressed or printed; however, the most commonly found mark from 1801-70, is impressed FERRYBRIDGE. Willow pieces bearing marks from individual partnerships will be found under the name of the partners. This entry is concerned only with the 1801-70, period when the Ferrybridge mark was used even though the pottery continued to operate through much of the twentieth century.

Type of Willow Manufactured: Standard Willow pattern and Two Temples II pattern transfer-printed in blue underglaze on earthenware.

Standard Willow pattern butter tub and stand transfer-printed in blue underglaze on earthenware. The lion finial on the lid is truly remarkable in its detail. The stand is 7.5-by-6-inches, the tub is 6-by-4.75-inches, and the lid measures 5.75-by-4.25-inches. The stand is the only piece of the three that is marked. It has impressed Mark 2. *Courtesy J and J Cockerill.* $200+.

Standard Willow pattern platter transfer-printed underglaze on white earthenware. The platter measures 12 x 16.25-inches. The quality is excellent, and it probably dates to 1840 or earlier. The outer border differs from the Standard Willow border in two main ways: 1) The wheel that usually has three dark spokes has four; and, 2) The mid-section of the geometrical motifs is elongated and has a white area in it. Impressed Mark above. *Author's Collection.* $200-275.

Standard Willow pattern 7-inch plate transfer-printed in medium blue underglaze on lightweight earthenware. The rim is slightly concave with 8 indentations at the edge. It has three single stilt marks in the center. The glaze is very pale blue, giving a white appearance to the clay body. Mark 3. *Author's Collection.* $20-30.

Two Temples II pattern 4.75-inch plate transfer-printed in shades of light blue underglaze on earthenware. The plate has a concave rim with a wavy edge. There is a single foot ring. The pale blue glaze feels uneven on the top and smooth on the back. Impressed Mark above. *Author's Collection.* $35-50.

1964. In 1976, it was bought by a Liverpool company, and in 1982, the company closed. The factory and molds were bought by Caverswall China in 1983, and sold in 1984, to the retailers Thomas Goode & Co.* The factory was demolished in 1987, after being sold again.

Type of Willow Manufactured: Standard Willow pattern in polychrome Lustrine finish; ruby and blue luster backgrounds with willow-type decorations enameled over the glaze; and Standard Willow blue-printed and decal in blue overglaze.

Mark 4 c. 1930+

Mark 5 c. 1979-82

S. Fielding & Co. (Ltd.)

Location: Railway Pottery, Sutherland St., Stoke-on-Trent
Dates: c. 1879-1982
Marks:

Mark 1 (GG1548) c. 1917-30

Comments Concerning Mark: Mark 5 is the last mark used by the company. It was found on a covered bowl with Standard Willow pattern blue decal over glaze.

Brief History: In 1870, Simon Fielding put his life savings into the Railway Works; however, it was not until his son Abraham joined him that production began in earnest in 1879. A period of expansion followed. The first wares produced were majolica, as well as black, brown, and green-glazed ware. It was such a success that the pottery continued to grow and develop. Abraham Fielding introduced a vellum ware that was very successful. The Crown Devon mark began to be used before the turn of the century; however, the name was not changed until 1911, when Railway Pottery became The Devon Pottery. It had become a limited company in 1905.

Lusterware was introduced after World War I. Art Deco tableware, figures, and novelties were produced in the 1920s. Musical tankards and commemorative wares were added in the 1930s. The *Pottery Gazette*, January 1, 1958, had a color photo of ruby luster willow-type designs, featuring decoration #5179 painted in enamel colors over the glaze. S. Fielding & Son Ltd. acquired Shorter and Sons Ltd. in

Mark 2 (GG1551) c. 1930+

Mark 3 (GG1551) var. c. 1930+

Standard Willow pattern 13-inch bowl in polychrome Lustrine finish. It has gold outlining of pattern elements all over the bowl. In addition to the complete willow pattern in the bottom of the bowl, the central pattern appears in linear form on the sides of the bowl. Mark 1. A spectacular piece. *Courtesy Lucile Egger.* $500+.

Standard Willow pattern is printed in circular form in blue on earthenware pitcher that stands 11-inches high to the top of the handle. A round insert with two birds was placed over the willow tree. The outer border pattern circles the jug at the edge of the cobalt wash covering three-inches at the bottom and the area above the shoulder of the jug. Mark 2. *Author's Collection.* $55-95.

A. T. Finney & Sons (Ltd.)

Location: Duchess China Works, Longton, Staffordshire

Dates: c. 1947-1989

Marks:

Mark 1 c. 1947+

Brief History: A. T. Finney was an earthenware manufacturer, Barker Street, Longton in the 1920s. An ad for "Finney's Cups" appeared in the *Pottery Gazette*, July 1, 1926. "Cheap tea sets in stock patterns" were also listed. In January, 1931, the *Pottery Gazette* had an ad for A. T. Finney, Upper Hill Pottery, Longton. This time the ad was for Finney's New Nesting Cups. A. T. Finney took over Blyth Porcelain Co. Ltd.* in 1935. From 1947, the company is listed as a producer of porcelain at Duchess Works. John Tams Ltd.* purchased A.T. Finney in 1989 in order to produce bone china.

Mark 2 c. 1947+

Type of Willow Manufactured: Standard Willow pattern in simplified form in blue on bone china.

Willow variant pattern vase with handles, decorated in colored enamels over the ruby luster background. It stands 7-inches high and is 6.25-inches wide. The opening at the top from front to back is 4-inches. The bulbous section of the vase is molded with raised flutes. Mark 3. *Courtesy John and Norma Gilbert.* $300+.

Standard Willow pattern teapot, creamer, and open sugar decorated with blue decal overglaze. The geometric motifs have been taken out of the border and the inner border left out. The teapot holds four cups. The tea set for two was purchased new in 1988. Mark 1. *Author's Collection.* $55-85.

Willow variant pattern jug decorated in colored enamels over the blue luster background. It stands 6 5/8-inches high and measures 5.75-inches from spout to handle. The body is 4-inches in diameter at the widest part. The bulbous section of the jug is also molded with raised flutes as is the vase above. Blue luster is less often found than the ruby. Mark 4. *Courtesy John and Norma Gilbert.* $400+.

This simplified version of the Standard Willow pattern was illustrated on a plate, cup and saucer on page 204 of the *Pottery Gazette and Glass Trade Review*, February 1967. The description: " 'Willow Pattern' (illustrated), a delightfully modern treatment of this subject and one of ten controlled patterns introduced this year as additions to their proven range." The bridge with three people on it has been scaled down in size and moved up above the left hand branch of the willow tree. The 6-inch plate is an indented, rounded square shape with gold trim. *Author's Collection.* $8-10.

Finsbury China Ltd.

Location: Elsing St., Fenton, Staffordshire
Dates: (1990s+)
Mark: Finsbury China
Fine Bone China
England

Comment Concerning Mark: The mark is inside the thimble.
Brief History: The company was listed in the local telephone directory in November 2001, but correspondence to the company received no response.
Type of Willow Manufactured: Blue decal overglaze with partial willow pattern on bone china.

Thimble with blue decal overglaze with part of the willow pattern. The mark is inside. *Author's Collection.* $3-5.

Flackett, Toft & Robinson

Location: Church Street, Longton, Staffordshire
Dates: c. 1858
Mark:

c. 1858

Comment Concerning Mark: I consulted Geoffrey Godden on this mark because the "&" is between the F and T; however, we agreed that no other firm would fit the initials.
Brief History: From 1853-56, the firm traded as Flackett, Chetham & Toft. It could be any one of three Chethams – John, Frederick, or Robert. Nothing is known of Flackett. The firm of Flackett, Toft & Robinson were only together for a year. After that Toft carried on alone. The factory produced blue printed earthenware.
Type of Willow Manufactured: Standard Willow pattern transfer-printed underglaze in blue on earthenware.

Standard Willow pattern 9.25-inch plate in blue transfer-printed underglaze on earthenware. The plate is round with concave rim. There is no white space between the borders; however, the borders are almost matched. *Courtesy Dennis Crosby.* $20-30.

Fleming

Location: Britannia Pottery, Glasgow, Scotland
Dates: c. 1900-1920
Mark: Impressed   FLEMING
GLASGOW

Brief History: There was an overlapping of trade styles using Cochran & Fleming* and Fleming in the first twenty years of the twentieth century before Britannia Pottery was sold in 1920. From that time to 1939 B. P. Co. Ltd. and Britannia Pottery Co. Ltd.* became the trading styles used.
Type of Willow Manufactured: Standard Willow pattern transfer-printed underglaze in blue on earthenware.

Standard Willow pattern 7.50-inch round plate. The slightly concave rim has a molded edge resembling flattened beads. The outer border pattern, smeared somewhat from placing it on a molded surface, has an insert just above the birds. The plate bears impressed mark FLEMING GLASGOW plus printed Mark 3 under Robert Cochran & Co.* *Author's Collection.* $10-20.

Floyd

Location: Anchor Lane, Lane End, Staffordshire
Dates: c. 1843
Mark:

c. 1843

Brief History: Benjamin Floyd was an earthenware manufacturer known to use his initials B. F. on printed marks. This mark with just the name Floyd could relate to this firm or perhaps James Floyd c. 1845-47 at Stafford St. and Railway Potteries in Longton. James Floyd was known to have produced china in addition to earthenware; however, no marked examples are known.
Type of Willow Manufactured: Standard Willow pattern in blue transfer-printed underglaze on earthenware. A platter and cheese dish are known with this mark.

Standard Willow pattern 9-by-11.50-inch platter transfer-printed in blue underglaze on earthenware. The platter has a wavy edge, three single stilt marks in the center of the platter. The center of the platter dropped some in firing causing it to bow out in the back. As a result there is a large worn area in the center of the back from heavy usage. *Author's Collection.* $35-75.

Ford & Sons (Crownford) Ltd.

Location: Newcastle St., Burslem, Staffordshire
Dates: c. 1938-1960s
Mark:

CROWNFORD CHINA CO. INC
STAFFORDSHIRE · ENGLAND

c. 1938-60s

Brief History: Ford & Sons was established in 1893, at Newcastle St. in Burslem. They operated until 1938, when the company became known as Ford & Sons (Crownford) Ltd. It is not known more specifically when it closed.
Type of Willow Manufactured: Brown printed simplified Burleigh Willow pattern

Wash bowl and pitcher with the basic Burleigh Willow pattern printed in brown. Just the basic pattern was used with no borders or extra elements of the pattern. This has left a lot of white on the pieces. *Courtesy IWC Convention 1999.* $50-100.

Charles Ford

Location: Cannon St., Hanley, Staffordshire
Dates: c. 1871-1925
Marks:

Mark 1 (GG1593)
c. 1874-1904

Mark 2 (GG1594)
c. 1900-25

Brief History: Charles Ford followed Thomas and Charles Ford at the Cannon St. works. Good quality bone china tablewares were produced as well as some ornamental wares. J. A. Robinson and Sons Ltd. bought the business in 1904, and production moved to Alexander China Works, Wolfe St., Stoke about 1912. The firm continued to use the name Charles Ford until about 1925. It became part of Cauldon Potteries Ltd.* sometime in the 1920s.
Type of Willow Manufactured: Standard Willow pattern transfer-printed underglaze in light and dark blue with gold trim on bone china.

Standard Willow pattern 9 7/8-inch plate transfer-printed in light blue with gold trim on bone china. The 3 and 4 spoke wheels have been eliminated at 8 o'clock to make the outer border fit. It has a single unglazed foot ring. Other than Minton*, this is one of the few potteries that made dark gable ends on the two roofs of the small building behind the main teahouse. The gable ends are usually light and/or striped. Impressed Mark 1. *Author's Collection.* $25-35.

Standard Willow pattern creamer and covered sugar in dark blue with gold trim on bone china. The finial on the sugar is a rose. These pieces also have the dark gable ends on the small building. Printed Mark 2. *Author's Collection.* $50-100.

Ford & Challinor

Location: Lion Works, Tunstall, Staffordshire
Dates: c. 1865-80
Mark:

c. 1865-80

Brief History: The partners were Thomas Ford and William Challinor. The firm also traded as Ford Challinor & Co. The factory produced earthenwares including ironstone-type wares.
Type of Willow Manufactured: Standard Willow pattern transfer-printed in blue underglaze on heavy stoneware.

Standard Willow pattern 9.15-inch round plate, cup and saucer transfer-printed in blue underglaze on heavy stoneware. Three-point stilt marks under the concave rim with 3 single marks showing on the top of the plate. A cut was made at 7 o'clock to make the outer border fit. The plate has a rounded single foot ring. It is unusual to find a cup and saucer with the same mark. *Author's Collection.* $40-60 all.

Thomas Forester & Sons (Ltd.)

Location: Phoenix Works, Church St., Longton, Staffordshire
Dates: c. 1883-1959
Mark:

c. 1910-59

Brief History: This firm produced mainly earthenware although china was also a product of the factory. Tea wares are most often found in china. An ad in 1890, showed many different forms of vases produced by the company. From about 1910, the word "Phoenix" became a part of their printed marks. In 1921, fancy goods, earthenware, and china services were made with patterns based on oriental, Persian, and Egyptian art. In the mid-1930s, Art Deco ware was produced, and contemporary patterns followed in the mid-1950s.
Type of Willow Manufactured: Standard Willow pattern transfer-printed in blue on earthenware and polychrome decal of Two Temples II pattern overglaze on bone china.

A 6.75-inch bone china plate with polychrome decal of Two Temples II pattern overglaze. This decal is most often found on earthenware. This plate may have been part of a tea set. *Courtesy IWC Convention 1994.* $15-25.

Forester & Hulme

Location: Sutherland Pottery, Fenton, Staffordshire
Dates: c. 1887-92
Mark:

(GG1611) c. 1887-92

Brief History: Thomas Forester, Son & Co. (not the same person as the previous entry) began at the Sutherland Pottery in 1884, and continued until 1887, when Thomas Forester and Joseph Hulme worked the pottery as partners until 1892. Various kinds of earthenware were produced including ironstone wares.
Type of Willow Manufactured: Standard Willow pattern transfer-printed in blue underglaze on earthenware.

Standard Willow pattern 8.75-inch plate transfer-printed in blue underglaze on earthenware. The plate has a concave rim and recessed foot ring. The geometrical motifs of the two borders are not matched up. *Courtesy Dennis Crosby.* $25-35.

Furnivals (Ltd.)

Mark I (GG1653)
c. 1905-13

Location: Elder Road, Cobridge (1890-1968), and Wedgwood's Mason's Ironstone Works, Hanley (1969+), Staffordshire
Dates: 1890-present (2003)
Marks:

Comments Concerning Marks: The test plate illustrated bears impressed FURNIVAL which dates to the early period of Thomas Furnival & Son(s) c. 1870s; however, the decoration and glaze testing is dated 1908: the Furnivals Ltd. period.

Brief History: Furnivals succeeded Thomas Furnival & Son(s) at Elder Road, Cobridge. It became a limited firm in 1895. Barratts of Staffordshire* took over Furnivals in 1967; however, the factory was closed in 1968. Enoch Wedgwood Ltd.* (Tunstall) purchased the Furnivals Ltd. trade name and some patterns in 1969. This firm was taken over by the Wedgwood Group.

Mark 2 (GG1653)
c. 1905-13

Several Furnivals Ltd. patterns are currently in production in Hanley. Furnivals is known for production of high quality white ironstone wares exported to the U.S. and Canada. The *Pottery Gazette*, October 1, 1908, stated that Furnivals Ltd. produced "All kinds of Earthenware". A notice in *Pottery Gazette* regarding the British Industries Fair 1917: "L72 Furnivals (1913) Ltd. In Toilet ware, the old 'Broseley' pattern, a contemporary of the well-known 'willow' looked exceedingly well on a ewer and basin specially modeled for this class of design." I have not seen an example of Broseley (Two Temples II) pattern by Furnival.
Type of Willow Manufactured: Standard Willow pattern transfer-printed in red and blue underglaze, Two Temples II Toilet Ware and a Border Variant pattern: Hong Kong.

This 10.50 x 13.75-inch platter is decorated with Border only Variant Willow pattern called "Hong Kong". It is one of a set of three sizes of platters. Mark 2. "Engravings by J. Broadhurst" is an interesting addition to the mark. The pattern has been found on plates with Mark 1. *Courtesy IWC Convention 2001.* $150-225.

Gater, Hall & Co.

Location: Furlong Lane Pottery, Burslem (1895-99), New Gordon Pottery, Tunstall (1899-1907), and Royal Overhouse Pottery, Burslem (1907-1943), Staffordshire
Dates: c. 1895-1943
Marks:

Mark I c. 1926-43

Brief History: Thomas Gater & Co. preceded the firm at Furlong Lane Pottery from 1885-94. Then Gater, Hall & Co. traded there until 1899, when they moved to the New Gordon Pottery, Tunstall. Ralph Hammersley & Sons* were at the Overhouse Pottery from 1833 until it was sold to Thomas Gater in 1905. The partnership of Gater, Hall & Co. moved to Royal Overhouse Pottery in 1907, where they continued to produce earthenware of various kinds. Under "Buyer's Notes" in the *Pottery Gazette*, September 1, 1926, p. 1369, we read this announcement: "The dark blue 'Willow' pattern has also been put on the market by Gater, Hall & Co. within the last 6 months, and this is now available not only in dinnerware but in tea ware, breakfast ware, teapots, teapot sets and a full range of suite ware."

Mark 2 (GG1672)
c. 1914-43

Type of Willow Manufactured: Standard Willow pattern transfer-printed underglaze in blue, brown, and black. The blue is both clear and flow blue: plain and with gold trim as well as clobbered in blue, green, red, and yellow. The brown is clobbered in several different color combinations with gold trim. The black transfer has mustard glaze.

Mark 3 c. 1926-43

Standard Willow pattern 10.50-inch test plate half red and half blue. This is one of the few examples of multi-color transfer printing underglaze on willow. Hand written on the back with a dividing line drawn: One side: "Old Glaze 685 Standard" The other side: "New Glaze 685 Standard Cylinder D 1/12/08." The plate is impressed FURNIVAL which dates to the 1870s; however, the handwritten date is the date it was produced using an old blank. *Courtesy Jim Staggs.* NP

Standard Willow pattern 5.15-by-8.50-inch relish transfer-printed in blue underglaze on earthenware. There is no inner border, and the pattern is too large for this dish. The bridge, path, and fence are cut off. Mark 1. *Courtesy Tim and Kim Allen.* $15-25.

Standard Willow pattern teapot and stand transfer-printed in brown underglaze. It has clobbering in shades of gold, rust, and green with gold trim. This is a very distinctive Gater, Hall & Co. shape. The same teapot and stand have been found with flow blue willow pattern. Jugs of various sizes are also found in this shape in flow blue and brown with different shades of clobbering. Mark 2. *Courtesy Harry and Jessie Hall.* $250+.

Standard Willow pattern 9.75-inch flow blue plate and 8-inch brown printed plate. The flow blue plate has a line of gold on both sides of the outer border; however, there is no inner border. It is coupe shape with a single foot ring. Mark 2. The brown printed plate has green, turquoise, rust, and black clobbering as well as gold outlining. The outer border is too large, and a 3-wheel scroll has been cut out at 8 o'clock. This is a rimmed plate with a slightly recessed foot ring. Mark 1. *Author's Collection.* $35-45 each.

Standard Willow pattern jug transfer-printed underglaze with flow blue glaze. It stands 4.75-inches high and holds about a quart. It has Mark 3. *Author's Collection.* $55-75.

Standard Willow pattern octagonal bowl transfer-printed in black underglaze with mustard glaze. The bowl is 7.5-inches wide and 3-inches high. This is the first example seen of this glaze by Gator, Hall & Co. It was purchased in Australia. Mark 3. *Courtesy Kathy and Hugh Sykes.* $125-175.

Gibson & Sons (Ltd.)

Location: Chelsea Pottery (1925-30), Harvey Pottery (closed 1957), Albany Pottery (1884-1965), Burslem, and Howard Pottery, Shelton (1965-78), Staffordshire
Dates: c. 1884-1970s
Marks:

Comment Concerning Marks: Mark 1 is found on Mandarin pattern without the word "Willow".

Brief History: Gibson, Sudlow & Co. traded at the Albany Pottery from 1875-84. Then the title changed to Gibson & Sons with Ltd. added in 1905. The firm has produced earthenware, specializing in teapots since the beginning. There is an ad in *Pottery Gazette* in 1888, for "jet" teapots in nine different shapes. Some prizes that were awarded in the early years: Highest Award Chicago 1893, Grand Prix London 1911, and Grand Prix San Francisco 1915. *Pot-*

Mark 1 (GG1681)
c. 1912+

Mark 2 (GG1690)
c. 1950-55

tery Gazette, February 1, 1912 "Buyer's Notes" describes wares produced including toilet sets, dinnerware, and novelty sets consisting of teapot, stand, sugar basin, cream jug, and hot water jug in matching decoration. One of the largest producers of teapots in the world, the company advertised on the back cover of *Pottery Gazette* for many years, often using the slogan: "Gibson's teapots are Britain's best."

Mark 3 (GG1691)
c. 1950+

A sampling of years with these full-page ads: 1926, 1944, 1951, and 1953. In 1965, the Gibson location moved from Albany Pottery to Howard Pottery, Shelton. Gibson & Sons Ltd. was part of the Howard Pottery Group by 1978.

Type of Willow Manufactured: Standard Willow pattern printed underglaze in blue, green, brown, and red sometimes clobbered overglaze. Mandarin pattern printed underglaze in blue, sometimes clobbered and in dark gray-blue with flow blue glaze. Tea sets with various colored backgrounds decorated with gold silhouette Mandarin pattern. Mandarin pattern in black decal overglaze with added color was also made.

Mandarin pattern tea canister transfer-printed in dark blue-gray with flow blue glaze. It measures 6.50-inches to the top of the finial. Printed Mark 1 does not have the word "Willow". Impressed on the base is GIBSONS ENGLAND and JAPPA which may be the shape name. *Author's Collection.* $75-100.

Standard Willow pattern 8.50-by-13 inch deep platter with lid. It is transfer-printed underglaze in medium blue. Both pieces have the outer willow border on the rim. The lid has two linear versions of the pattern with willow tree pointing to the handle so that the lid is right side up from either side. Mark 1. *Courtesy IWC Convention 2000.* $250-325.

Standard Willow pattern mug transfer-printed in brown underglaze and clobbered with orange, red, green, and cobalt blue. The outer border decorates the rim with a line of fish roe at the edge. Mark 1. *Courtesy of IWC Convention 1997.* $45-65.

Mandarin pattern black decal over the glaze with red, yellow, and blue added. There are gold dots in the trees and the pieces have a platinum rim. Shown are tea plate, cup, saucer, creamer, and open sugar. Mark 2. *Author's Collection.* $20-30.

The teapot at the top right is 8-cup Standard Willow pattern transfer-printed in blue with Mark 1. The other teapots are Mandarin pattern, hold 6 cups, and have Mark 3. The teapots with colored backgrounds have the pattern in gold. Proceeding clockwise is the black teapot with pattern #W 238, pale blue, dark green with pattern #W 240, salmon in the middle, and lastly blue on white with gold trim. Collectors have found open sugar and creamers for some of these colors as well as finding 2-cup size in dark green. The blue Mandarin pattern teapot comes in various sizes and also with clobbering. *Courtesy Joette Hightower.* $55-75 each.

The teapot, covered jug, creamer, and open sugar with gold Mandarin pattern on salmon color background. The covered jug is the hardest piece to find in this set. Mark 3. *Courtesy Kathy and Hugh Sykes.* $100-150.

William Gill & Sons

Location: Providence Pottery, Castleford, Yorkshire
Dates: c. 1880-1929
Comments Concerning Marks: Lawrence shows a Stone China printed mark with the initials W. G. in *Yorkshire Pots and Potteries,* p. 259. It was found on a copper plate engraved with the willow pattern. No examples have been found.
Brief History: In 1858, George Gill, earthenware manufacturer of Castleford, and William Farquhar bought land where they had erected sheds, kilns and buildings for a pottery. Creditors took over in 1862, and William Gill purchased the property in 1863. George Gill remained there until the mid-1870s. William Gill took over the operation of the pottery and traded as William Gill until his son Thomas joined him. Then the name became William Gill & Sons. Even after William died Thomas kept the same name until 1928, when it became William Gill & Sons (Potters) Ltd. Thomas was replaced by William Reginald Gill until 1929.
Type of Willow Manufactured: An ad in *Pottery Gazette,* January 1, 1931 shows a Standard Willow pattern plate; however, I have not seen any willow by this firm.

Pottery Gazette, January 1, 1931, p. 26. Half page ad for earthenware made by William Gill & Sons Potters Ltd. A Standard Willow pattern plate is shown, so evidently the pattern was produced.

Gladstone Pottery

Photograph of the Gladstone Pottery in 1971 before it was established as a museum.

Location: High Street (now Uttoxeter Road), Longton
Dates: c. 1787- Present (2003)
Marks:

Comments Concerning Marks: These marks appear on pieces issued after 1974 when Gladstone Pottery reopened as a museum.
Brief History: The Shelley family purchased lands in Longton, and by 1787, had established a pottery. The business failed by 1789, and was purchased by William Ward. He split the site into two smaller potbanks. The Park Place Works (now Roslyn Works) evolved from one potbank. In 1818 Ward sold the other to John Hendley Sheridan who retained ownership for 40 years. One of his tenants, Thomas Cooper, worked with him to enlarge and modernize the whole factory site. R. Hobson & Co. owned the pottery from

Mark 1 c. 1985+

THE LONDON WILLOW PLATE
Number two in the Series

Mark 2 c. 1985+

1879-1885. It was during this period that the factory became known as the Gladstone Works in honor of the politician W. E. Gladstone who came to Burslem in 1863, to lay the foundation stone of the Wedgwood Memorial Institute. Mayer and Wooley were the owners from 1885-92. The George Proctor period, beginning in 1892 will be reviewed in the next entry.

The bottle ovens fired for the last time in 1960. During the 1960s, when the old pottery factories and bottle ovens were being demolished, there was a group of local people allied with the Trustees of the Cheddleton Flint Mill who were interested in saving part of the traditional landscape of the Potteries. The Gladstone Pottery site was considered the best example of a medium sized typical potbank of the nineteenth century. When the factory was due to be demolished, a local businessman, Derek Johnson of H & R Johnson*, the tile manufacturers, bought the site and turned it over to the Staffordshire Pottery Industry Preservation Trust to be run as a museum. The museum was opened in 1974. The ceremonial final firing of a Staffordshire bottle oven took place at Gladstone Pottery in 1978. In May 1994, ownership of Gladstone Pottery Museum passed to City of Stoke-on-Trent Council.

Type of Willow Manufactured: Souvenir mugs and plates for different cities and towns with elements of the pattern altered to fit the area for which it was produced.

Made for
THE CASTLE MUSEUM
by Gladstone Pottery Museum
Longton, Stoke-on-Trent.

Mark 3 c. 1979+

The
Lincoln Willow

Mark 4 c. 1985+

THE SECRETS OF THE WILLOW PATTERN EXPLAINED

The following are just a few of the key features.

1. The pottery works with bottle-ovens is based on the 200 year old Gladstone Pottery Works, now a unique museum, where this special version of the Willow Pattern was designed and produced.
2. The three figures on the bridge carry a pot & 'saggar' (both associated with the pottery industry) and a coal miner's pick-axe.
3. On the left of the bridge is a coal-mine. Mining is a major local industry, and in Stoke-on-Trent you can actually visit a museum in a mine, at Chatterley Whitfield Mining Museum (open 7 days a week, including Bank Holidays, 10.00am-4.00pm). Telephone (0782) 813337.
4. The boat is a canal barge. Canals played a major part in establishing the City's prosperity and for those interested in canals, a visit to Froghall Wharf is highly recommended, for details on opening time and facilities telephone Ipstones 486.
5. The two Spitfires acknowledge the fact that Reginald Mitchell, their designer, was a local man and a full Spitfire display in his honour can be seen at the City Museum.

The Secrets of the Willow Pattern Explained is a guide to the Stoke-on-Trent willow pattern.

Timetable for the China Service Coach operating in the 1990s between factory sites, museums, visitor centers, and pottery retail shops. The Stoke-on-Trent willow pattern on the timetable and on the side of the coach was designed in 1985 by Peter Brears. It was produced on plates and mugs as shown below.

Nine-inch plate and mug with the Stoke-on-Trent Willow pattern. The mark on the back of the plate states: "The Potteries Willow Plate: This plate was produced to commemorate Stoke-on-Trent's 60th year as a City, the 75th year as a Federation of Six Towns, as well as Gladstone Pottery Museum's 10th year. The design is by Peter Brears. Mark 1. *Courtesy Kathy and Hugh Sykes.* $20-30 each.

London willow pattern 9-inch plate in bone china on the right side is number two in the series. Mark 2. The Lincoln 9-inch plate on the left side is an example of the plates designed for other cities. It is not numbered. Mark 4. The center plate was made in 1979 for the York Castle Museum from a design by H. M. Loadman of Stonegate, York, c. 1900. Local York landmarks replace 10 items in the Standard Willow pattern. Mark 3. The patterns are lithographic transfers. *Author's Collection.* $35-55 each.

THE LONDON
WILLOW PATTERN
PLATE FROM
GLADSTONE
POTTERY MUSEUM

The Gladstone Museum has added a second design to the Willow Series showing famous scenes of London.

Some features of the plate are explained below:-

1. The Tower of London has the tree growing out of it, similar to the original willow design.

2. Saint Paul's is illustrated, its dome is one of the great landmarks in London.

3. Nelson's monument standing on its great column in Trafalgar Square is shown to the left of St. Paul's.

4. The London underground carriages replace the zig zag of the Chinese fencing.

5. On the Tower Bridge there is a thief running away with the Crown Jewels, in hot pursuit a Yeoman of the Guard, and a Guardsman wearing his busby.

6. Big Ben and the Houses of Parliament are shown against Tower Bridge in the design.

7. In front of Buckingham Palace can be seen the Memorial to Queen Victoria.

8. Westminster Abbey which contains the Tomb of Edward the Confessor and where many Kings and Queens of England have been crowned, including William the Conqueror, is shown above the Palace.

9. A Thames barge in full sail is seen floating on the Thames.

10. Two Concordes replace the Birds of the traditional willow pattern and sound a modern note in what is a treatment of historical monuments in an ancient framework of design.

GLADSTONE POTTERY MUSEUM,
UTTOXETER ROAD, LONGTON, STOKE ON TRENT, STAFFS. ST3 0PQ. TEL: (0782) 311378.

This descriptive paper on the 10 elements of the London willow pattern was given with the purchase of the plate at the museum. The series was expanded to include a number of other cities including Oxford, Cambridge, etc. The plates are no longer made.

Gladstone China (George Procter & Co. (Ltd.))

Location: Cobden Works (1892-1940), and Gladstone Pottery (1940-70), Longton, Staffordshire
Dates: c. 1892-1970
Mark:

(GG3173) c. 1924-40

Brief History: The firm was known as George Procter & Co. from 1892 to 1939 even though George Proctor died in

1910. The name was changed to Gladstone China (Longton) Ltd from 1939 to 1952 under the same management. During World War II Gladstone China closed temporarily and the business was combined with the firm of Thomas Poole* which had been granted a government license to continue production. In 1952, after an official merger, the name was changed to Royal Stafford China with most of the production centered at Thomas Poole's factory – the Cobden Works. Gladstone China marks were used until 1970.
Type of Willow Manufactured: Standard Willow pattern in medium blue on bone china.

Standard willow pattern 8.75-inch serving plate in medium blue with gold trim. In this size, the shape is sometimes called a saucer dish. It is molded in a swirl pattern from the foot ring up to the scalloped edge. This serving plate is bone china. *Author's Collection.* $35-55.

Globe Pottery Co. Ltd.

Location: Waterloo Road, Cobridge (1914-34) and Bedford Works, Shelton (1934-64), Staffordshire
Dates: c. 1914-1964
Marks:

Mark 1 (GG1711)
c. 1917-34

Comments Concerning Marks: Mark 1 is the most commonly found mark on willow. Mark 5 was found on a plate, and Mark 6 on a sauce dish. Neither is shown here.
Brief History: Globe Pottery Co. Ltd. was an earthenware factory specializing in tableware. From 1930, vitrified ware was added. The word "vitrified" was added to some marks such as Mark 3 above, but most vitrified wares have the trade name Stanley Hotel Ware. In 1932, Globe Pottery Co. Ltd. bought Ridgways, and production moved to Bedford Works, Shelton. From 1934, Shelton replaced Cobridge in the marks. By 1941

Mark 2 (GG1712)
c. 1930-40

Lawleys Limited had part interest in Globe and Ridgway to make bone china. In 1948, completely owned by Lawleys, a new company was formed: Lawley Group Limited. From 1954 "Co. Ltd." was removed from marks of Globe Pottery. As a part of the Lawley Group, Globe Pottery became a part of Allied English Potteries in 1964.

Mark 3 (GG1713)
c. 1930-40

Type of Willow Manufactured: Standard Willow pattern transfer-printed in blue and pink underglaze. Mandarin pattern blue printed underglaze.

Mark 4 c.1914-34

Mark 5 c.1914-34

Mark 6 (GG1715)
c. 1947-54

Standard Willow pattern soap dish measures 4-by-5-inches. It is vitrified and has Mark 2. *Author's Collection.* $30-35.

Standard Willow pattern 10-inch plate in red and 9-inch plate in blue transfer-printed underglaze on earthenware. The red plate has Mark 3, and the blue plate has Mark 1. The glaze on the blue piece has a nice soft feel to it. *Courtesy Michael Curtner.* $20-25 and 15-20.

Mandarin pattern saucer blue printed underglaze. Globe Pottery's name for this pattern is CHING. Mark 4. This pattern by Globe is rarely seen. *Author's Collection.* $3-5.

Standard Willow pattern 9-by-12-inch platter and gravy boat. This photo shows the interesting shapes in the serving pieces. With patience a collector can put together a set of blue willow dinnerware by Globe Pottery. Mark 1. *Courtesy Michael Curtner.* $85-150 and $55-65.

John & Robert Godwin

Location: Sneyd Green, Cobridge
Dates: c. 1834-64
Brief History: A number of potters with the name of Godwin worked in Staffordshire from the late 18th century. Some were in Cobridge and others in Burslem. John & Robert Godwin produced earthenware of good quality. Not all wares were marked.
Type of Willow Manufactured: Two Temples II pattern transfer-printed underglaze in red on earthenware has been found.

Two Temples II pattern children's tea set transfer-printed in red underglaze on earthenware. Shown are the teapot (4.25-inches), creamer, covered sugar, waste bowl, and two cups with saucers. There is no maker's mark; however, the shapes are documented in *English Toy China* Figure #58 and *Anthology of British Teapots* plate #1908. *Courtesy Anna Morrison.* $500+.

Standard Willow pattern 9.25-by-11.25-inch platter transfer-printed in blue underglaze on earthenware. Three point stilt marks on the back of the rim with single marks on the top. The underside is combed, and Mark 2 is on the rim. It has a pale blue glaze. *Author's Collection.* $55-85.

Thomas & Benjamin Godwin

Location: New Wharf and New Basin Potteries, Burslem, Staffordshire
Dates: c. 1809-34
Marks:

Mark 1
c. 1809-34

Comment Concerning Marks: A mark with the initials T. & B. G in a cartouche with SEMI CHINA is described under 276, p. 102, in *Penny Plain, Two Pence Coloured*, the exhibition catalog at the City Museum & Art Gallery, Stoke-on-Trent, 1994.
Brief History: Thomas Godwin and his son Benjamin manufactured many types of earthenware including fine quality transfer-printed ware. Some wares after 1820, were marked "Stone China". Benjamin died January 15, 1834, thus ending the partnership.

Mark 2
c. 1834-54

Type of Willow Manufactured: Standard Willow pattern transfer-printed in blue underglaze on earthenware.

Thomas Godwin

Location: Canal Works, Navigation Road, Burslem, Staffordshire
Dates: c. 1834-54
Mark:

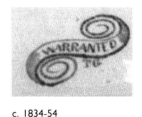

c. 1834-54

Brief History: After his son Benjamin died, Thomas Godwin carried on alone at the Navigation Road Pottery adjoining the New Wharf Pottery. Good quality stone chinaware was produced by the factory.
Type of Willow Manufactured: Standard Willow pattern transfer-printed in blue underglaze on earthenware.

Standard Willow pattern cheese stand transfer-printed in blue underglaze on earthenware. The diameter of the base is 6 5/8-inches, and the top is 9-inches. The stand is 2.25-inches high. The inner border is not used on this piece. *Author's Collection.* $85-145.

Godwin, Rowley & Co.

Location: Market Place, Burslem
Dates: c. 1828-31
Mark:

c. 1828-31

Brief History: William Godwin, Thomas Rowley and others were in partnership at the Market Place Works where a range of earthenware was produced. Transfer-printed patterns were made with a mark: "Staffordshire Stone China".
Type of Willow Manufactured: Standard Willow pattern transfer-printed in blue underglaze on earthenware. No picture available.

J. Goodwin Stoddard & Co.

Location: Foley China Works, King Street, Longton, Staffordshire
Dates: c. 1898-1940
Mark:

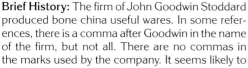

(GG1742)var.
c. 1936-40

Brief History: The firm of John Goodwin Stoddard produced bone china useful wares. In some references, there is a comma after Goodwin in the name of the firm, but not all. There are no commas in the marks used by the company. It seems likely to me that John Goodwin Stoddard may be one person. If so, this entry is out of order alphabetically; however, it is listed under Goodwin in Geoffrey Godden's books. The words "Foley China Works" or "Foley Bone China" were added to marks after 1936.
Type of Willow Manufactured: Standard Willow pattern blue printed on bone china with gold trim.

Standard Willow pattern 9-inch serving plate, cup, and saucer in medium blue with gold trim on bone china. The plate and saucer have a glazed single foot ring. The fluted plate is saucer dish-shaped and often called a bread (and butter) plate for serving sandwiches with tea. The front gables of the small building behind the teahouse are dark as found on Minton* Standard Willow pattern. *Author's Collection.* $30-40 and $20-25 for cup/saucer.

Goodwins & Harris

Location: Crown Works, Lane End, Staffordshire
Dates: c. 1832-37
Mark:

c. 1831-38

Comment Concerning Marks: This printed mark is also found on a plate with an impressed eagle mark shown in the Unattributed Marks section. Impressed GOODWINS & HARRIS (GG1743) appears on the platter shown below in addition to the printed mark.
Brief History: The partnership consisted of John & James Goodwin and Benjamin Harris. In *Longton Potters 1700-*1865, Rodney Hampson lists this partnership as one of the various combinations involving John Goodwin. The Goodwin name is plural in this partnership because there are two of them: John and James. The partnership was dissolved in 1837, and the firm traded as John & James Goodwin for a short time. The pottery had 5 ovens in the mid-1830s.
Type of Willow Manufactured: Standard Willow pattern transfer-printed in blue underglaze on earthenware.

Standard Willow pattern 11-by-13.75-inch platter transfer-printed in blue on earthenware. It bears the printed mark above in addition to impressed GOODWINS & HARRIS and the number 12. It has a combed back in a two-inch band leaving the middle clear where the impressed mark was put. *Author's Collection.* $100-150.

Gordon's Pottery

Location: Prestonpans, Scotland
Dates: c. 1795-1832
Mark: Impressed Crown

Brief History: A Sun Life Insurance policy dated March 29, 1797, was owned by George Gordon of Morrison's Haven near Prestonpans, potter and farmer. This information tells us that George Gordon ran a small pottery, but like many early potters, it was a part-time activity. The family continued in the pottery as well as the farm. In the Jenkins-Gordon court case in 1831, George's sons Robert and George paid Jenkins in kind as well as in cash. Earthenwares were produced including blue printed wares. Marks were not often used; however, impressed Gordon and an impressed crown were used – usually separately, but at least one example has been found with both impressed marks.
Type of Willow Manufactured: Standard Willow pattern transfer-printed in underglaze blue on earthenware.

Standard Willow pattern 13-by-15-inch platter transfer-printed in blue underglaze. The outer border is patched, leaving out a section of Ju-Is with scroll cross at the upper right and lower left corners of the platter. It has an impressed crown mark. *Courtesy of Elizabeth S. Lynn.* $100-175.

William Henry Goss (Ltd.)

Location: Falcon Pottery, Stoke, Staffordshire
Dates: c. 1858-1940
Mark:

(GG1750)
c. 1862+

Brief History: This is a very prestigious firm having produced fine parian ware from the outset. Earthenware and porcelain were also made. Goss perfected the technique for making jeweled porcelain. He also developed an eggshell porcelain as well as an ivory porcelain with the feel of ivory. The company is known for Armorial decorations on china. In 1931, the company was taken over by Cauldon Potteries Ltd.* and renamed Goss China Co. Ltd. The word "England" was not added to the goshawk mark until after about 1935. Production ceased in 1939-40.

Goss China Co. Ltd. was taken over by Coalport* after World War II and by Ridgway* and Adderley* in 1955. The Lawley Group bought the Goss molds and engravings. The Goss trade name became part of the Royal Doulton* Group in 1972. Doulton began producing some of the Goss commemorative porcelains in the 1980s. Many of the original pattern books are owned by Doulton.
Type of Willow Manufactured: Standard Willow Pattern blue printed on earthenware. It is rarely found. Most probably, willow pattern was made after the acquisition by Cauldon Potteries.

Standard Willow pattern 4-inch dish in blue printed underglaze with gold trim. This butter dish fits inside a holder, quite often made of wood. *Courtesy IWC Convention 1995.* $20-30.

Grafton China (see A. B. Jones & Sons (Ltd.))

Grainger & Co.

Location: St. Martin's Gate (New China Works), Worcester
Dates: c. 1805-1902
Marks:

Mark 1 c. 1811-14 and after 1850

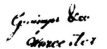

Mark 2 c. 1850+

Brief History: Thomas Grainger (son-in-law of Robert Chamberlain) and John Wood established a porcelain factory in Worcester at St. Martin's Gate sometime between September 1805, and September 1807. Tradition had 1801, as the founding date. In fact "established 1801" was incorporated in Grainger marks from 1890. However, Henry and John Sandon present new information in their book: *Grainger's Worcester Porcelain.* This text and Geoffrey Godden's research that is found in *Encyclopaedia of British Porcelain Manufacturers* have corrected many earlier errors regarding the firm. Thomas Grainger was still apprenticed to Robert Chamberlain in 1803, as recorded in the account books of that firm. In September 1805, Thomas Grainger was granted the rights of a Freeman and Citizen of Worcester. This designation would have been given before he was able to establish a pottery. These two facts move the start of the factory to at least 1805.

Mark 3 c. 1814-37

The first activity at the factory was probably decorating blanks from Coalport* as both Grainger and Wood had been painters at Chamberlain's factory. The first porcelain produced was a hybrid hard paste. Bone china was developed about 1814; however, the first formula used was not very satisfactory. Improvements were made through the years. From the first period, fine tablewares were made in rich patterns such as Japanese style Imari. Tea wares were produced that rivaled those of Coalport, Chamberlain and Barr, Flight and Barr.

Mark 4 (GG1770) c. 1870-89

The factory traded as Grainger, Wood & Co. until the partnership was dissolved March 12, 1811. Thomas Grainger & Co, or Grainger & Co was the trading style from 1811 to 1814, when it became Grainger, Lee & Co. John Lee moved from Worcester in 1837; however, Thomas carried on until his death in 1839. From that time, the company was run by his son George, and traded as Grainger & Co. There is some overlapping of titles and trade names in the account books. In 1889, following the death of George Grainger, the company was bought by Royal Worcester*. Manufacturing continued until 1902 when the works were closed. Molds and designs including pattern books were moved to the Royal Worcester site where many Grainger designs have continued in production.

Mark 5 (GG1771) c. 1902

Mark 6 (GG1771) c. 1898

Type of Willow Manufactured: Two Temples II, called Broseley, pattern # 705 from the First Pattern Series in hybrid hard paste porcelain c. 1812-14, on Broseley shape cup, scalloped cup, and London shape cup documented in the Sandons' *Grainger's Worcester Porcelain.* Later versions of Broseley: # 41, in linear form, in the 1870 pattern book; and pattern # G2/2258, "Best Body Tea Brosely" (misspelled in a pattern book after 1880). "Bamboo" is a variant collected by Willow enthusiasts in rust, gray, black, two shades of blue, and polychrome: all with and without gold trim. None of the pieces I have found of Two Temples II, variation Broseley by Grainger have any pattern numbers indicated. Most Bamboo pieces found have pattern # 1203, but not all are marked.

A linear form of Two Temples II pattern found in 1870 pattern book assigned number 41. *Courtesy Harry Frost, curator Dyson Perrins Museum, November 15, 1983.*

A typical page in a Grainger pattern book. Many pattern numbers are found for the Bamboo pattern in the pattern books depending on the color treatment and gold. This example is pattern #H224 with no gold. The pattern is for tableware and the shape is Baden (the T is missing in the word Table). The print is to be done in Hancock Red. There is a boat in the front right; however, the small willow tree that is usually to the left of the boat is missing in this version. *Courtesy Wendy Cook, curator Dyson Perrins Museum, August 2001.*

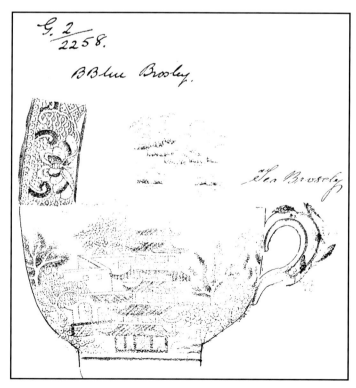

Two Temples II pattern plate and saucer transfer-printed in blue on porcelain. The 7 7/8-inch plate is pale blue with no gold. The rim has a molded pattern of six sets of double rounded lines from edge to center, and the edge is indented. Both pieces have a single unglazed foot ring. The 6.50-inch dark blue saucer has the same molded pattern under the border pattern; however, it is less pronounced. Instead of a white space between the border and main pattern, there is a gold line dividing the two parts of the pattern. I also have a 5.75-inch saucer with the same molding; however, it has extensive gold outlining of the pattern. All pieces have Mark 1. *Author's Collection.* $35-45 and $15-25.

Late pattern book (probably 1880s) pattern G 2/2258. The color is Best Blue and the pattern is Broseley (misspelled in the pattern book). The decoration for cup handle is indicated as well as the border on the inside of the cup (butterfly). *Courtesy Wendy Cook, curator Dyson Perrins Museum, August 2001.*

Two Temples II and Bamboo pattern jugs in the same shape with dark blue pattern on bone china trimmed in gold. The Two Temples II jug is six-inches high with a capacity of 12 oz. and has Mark 4. The Bamboo jug is five-inches high and holds 10 oz. It has Mark 5 with letter H indicating 1898. *Author's Collection.* $45-75 each.

Two Temples II pattern teapot, creamer, and open sugar transfer-printed in dark blue on bone china with gold trim. The pattern is in reverse on this set. Another teapot in this footed shape with kettle style handle has also been seen with Bamboo pattern in gray. Mark 1. *Courtesy Bill and Joyce Keenan.* $200+.

The Bamboo pattern was produced for over 60 years with many different color treatments and pattern numbers. The prominent pagoda appeals to collectors. Round pieces have a boat in the foreground to the right and a small willow tree to the left. The light blue handled plate measures 10.5-inches. It and the polychrome tray, 6.25-by-8-inches, have Mark 3. The 10.5-inch orange printed plate and dark blue cup and saucer have Mark 4. The "Antwerp" shape cup and saucer also have pattern no. 2/1903. All pieces are bone china with gold trim. *Author's Collection.* $25-35, $55-85, $25-35, $15-25.

Two Temples II pattern 6.25-inch pitcher transfer-printed in dark blue on bone china with gold trim. This piece shows the side of the pattern not seen on the teapot, sugar, and creamer. Mark 2. *Courtesy Harry and Jessie Hall.* $65-95.

Bamboo pattern dessert compote that is 4-inches high and 9.25-inches in diameter. The piece has a dark blue pattern with lavish gold outlining and filling in of various pattern elements. Mark 4. *Author's Collection.* $200-275.

Bamboo pattern teapot, creamer, and open sugar in dark blue with gold trim. This set represents the transition from the Grainger factory to Royal Worcester, carrying on some of the same patterns and shapes. The teapot and creamer have Royal Worcester marks dating 1903 while the sugar bowl has Mark 6 with a Reg. No. dated 1896. *Author's Collection.* $100-200.

T. G. Green & Co. (Ltd.)

Location: Church Gresley, Near Burton-on-Trent, Derbyshire
Dates: c. 1864-1987
Marks:

Brief History: Church Gresley was an area in Derbyshire with natural clays and coal suitable for making pottery. There were about 10 potteries producing yellow and red earthenware there in the nineteenth century. The premises that Thomas Goodwin Green purchased from Henry Wileman* in 1864 were built in the 1790s by a Mr. Leedham. Green, who had made his fortune as a builder in Australia, had no experience in the pottery business. He was very determined and through trial and error quickly made a success of the pottery. In the early 1880s, he decided to go into the tableware business, so he built a new modern factory in order to produce white earthenware. He made the bricks, dug the coal, built a lime kiln, and developed a new type of pre-fabricated stressed timber truss to carry the roof over the factory's 50-foot width. All types and colors of earthenware that were stamped, painted, and lined were produced for home and export markets. Stanley and Roger, two of Green's four sons, joined the business. In the mid-1880s it became a limited company. Green appointed his former head clerk, Henry William King, company secretary and later made him his partner. When Thomas Goodwin Green retired, he turned the business over to his son, Roger, and Henry King. The King and Green families continued to control the business until 1964.

Mark 1 (GG1804)
c. 1930s

Mark 2 (GG1804) and Reg. No. 693783 c. 1922+

Mark 3 (GG1798) c. 1892+

Mark 4 (GG1798) c. 1892+

By the 1920s about 700 people were employed by the pottery. The business continued to be self-sufficient as they ground all their materials, made all their own frits and glazes and did all their own color grinding and mixing. The T. G. Green Co. Ltd. had been producing an extensive range of kitchenware, but no one could have anticipated the popularity of their Cornish Ware. This banded ware, primarily blue and white, greatly expanded the firm's output. The factory also took an interest in improved teapots. Green's was one of the suppliers for the CUBE Teapots Company in a wide range of colors and patterns. Green's survived the restrictions of World War II and enjoyed a time of recovery with new machines helping to produce new designs and shapes.

By 1965, the company was in trouble financially and went into voluntary receivership. A London-based firm purchased the business and appointed Patrick Freeman to run it. In 1987 it was bought by Cloverleaf, a part of the Tootal group. In 1991, Tootal was absorbed by Coats Viyella. Green was a tiny part of this huge conglomerate. When the business was put up for sale, Richard Smith and his fellow directors staged a successful management buy-out that re-established Cloverleaf as an independent business. The company continues to produce kitchen and tablewares.

Type of Willow Manufactured: Two Temples II pattern transfer-printed in blue underglaze on earthenware. Standard Willow pattern has been found on a tray impressed Wedgwood with a Green printed mark. Perhaps Green purchased blanks to be decorated that had impressed marks from Wedgwood. A Willow variant pattern was produced named Ming.

Standard Willow pattern 5-by-6.50-inch tray transfer-printed underglaze on earthenware. The color has a gray-green look to it. This piece is a puzzle because it bears printed Mark 1 as well as impressed WEDGWOOD. It is the only piece with Standard Willow pattern I have seen with a T. G. Green mark; however, Wedgwood made a great deal using this color. *Courtesy IWC Convention 1999.* $75-95.

Dutch shape jug with Two Temples II pattern in reverse transfer-printed in blue underglaze on earthenware. The jug is 5-inches high and holds one quart. The outer border of the Standard Willow pattern is used to decorate the top rim, and a different narrow border is used on the inside. The handle decoration consists of flower forms surrounded by small circles. The Two Temples part of the pattern is seen on this side of the jug. The rest of the pattern is on the other side. (See the teapot.) Mark 3. *Author's Collection.* $45-75.

Two Dutch shape jugs in Willow variant patterns that are similar. The larger blue and white jug is "Yang" pattern by Midwinter*. The small jug with black print and clobbering is "Ming" pattern by T. G. Green & Co. Ltd. Both jugs were made in several different sizes. *Author's Collection.* $45-55 and 20-35.

Griffiths, Beardmore & Birks

Location: Flint Street, Lane End, Staffordshire
Dates: c. 1829-31
Mark:

(GG1821) c. 1829-31

Comment Concerning Mark: See Beardmore & Birks* for a similar mark.
Brief History: Thomas Griffiths was in two different partnerships on Stafford Street before 1823 when he became partners with Beardmore at Flint Street. Beardmore & Griffiths were involved in the manufacture of earthenware from 1823-28. Birks joined the firm in 1829. Thomas Griffiths died in 1831. After that, Beardmore & Birks* moved to High St. where the partnership continued.
Type of Willow Manufactured: Standard Willow pattern transfer-printed underglaze in blue on earthenware.

Two Temples II pattern in reverse on a six-cup teapot. It is decorated in the same way as the Dutch jug. This photo shows the bridge, willow tree, and island. The pattern on the other side is the same as on the jug above. The teapot also has the Standard Willow border on the lid and flower pattern on the handle. The inner border from Standard Willow is found on the collar of the teapot. Mark 3. *Courtesy IWC Convention 2001.* $55-85.

Two Temples II pattern transfer-printed in blue on a cube teapot. This teapot also has a wrap-around form of the pattern, but it has the butterfly border usually seen with this pattern. The teapot is 3.50-inches in height and width, and it has a capacity of 3/4 pint. This is a rare item. Mark 2. *Courtesy Jennifer Giblin.* NP

Standard Willow pattern 10.25-inch plate blue printed on earthenware. This 8-lobed plate has a deep well and concave rim. There are three sets of triple stilt marks in the center with one mark from each set showing on the front. It has a pale blue glaze. A chip on the rim at a little past 1 o'clock was glazed over. An extra part of the geometric pattern was inserted at about 6 o'clock. The plate was broken, but it was glued together for the photo. *Author's Collection.* $30-40 if undamaged.

Grimwades Ltd.

Location: Winton, Upper Hanley and Elgin Potteries, Stoke, Staffordshire
Dates: c. 1900-present (2003)
Marks:

Comments Concerning Marks: Marks 3-6 are all variations of Mark 2: GG1832.

Brief History: The Grimwades Bros. business was established in 1885. It began in a small way but grew at a remarkable rate, doubling output every 12 months. An export department was established in 1890, and the large Winton Pottery was built in 1892 to meet the needs of the growing company. In March 1900 there was a merger between the Stoke Pottery of Grimwades Bros., owned by James Plant, and Winton Pottery Co., Ltd., trading under the title of Grimwades Limited. In the same year a lease was purchased for a building in St. Andrew Street, London. This building, known as "Winton House", was the site for the Grimwades Ltd. showrooms. Mr. Leonard L. Grimwade was the first Chairman and Managing Director of the new firm, and James Plant was on the board.

Experiments were carried out for improved methods of kiln firing to save time and money. Climax Rotary Kilns were developed for enamel firing with more efficiency. Nearly half a million souvenirs were produced in 1902, for the Coronation of King Edward VII. Fires at both Stoke and Winton Potteries almost jeopardized the order; however, the company was able to finish production on time. In 1906, Upper Hanley Pottery* was acquired and the following year their facilities were increased again with the purchase of Heron Cross Pottery*, Fenton. By 1913, Atlas China Co. Ltd.* and Rubian Art Pottery* had also been acquired by Grimwades. On April 22, 1913 King George V and Queen Mary made a special visit to the factory. At that time the company employed over 1,000 workers. The term "Royal Winton" was first used in connection with the royal visit; however, there was no official granting of the title. By 1928 "Royal Winton" began to appear regularly in company advertising.

Leonard Grimwade developed a thin printing tissue with a detachable backing, known as "Duplex" paper, which made the lithographic process easier and more profitable to use. A design was printed on the "Duplex" paper that was glued onto the ceramic. After drying, the tissue was removed with a sponge and hot water, leaving the design permanently transferred onto the piece. The Chintz patterns including "Pekin" were produced with this process. Additional embellishments such as gold trim and/or enameling were added to the ware. Grimwades was interested in hygienic pottery and obtained many patents for such items as the "Quick-Cooker" bowl, Fly-less milk bowl and Pie Dish with air vents. The company also produced "Ideal" display stands for use in showrooms.

Leonard L. Grimwade died in a street accident in 1931, and James Plant died later that same year. James Plant Jr. became Managing Director of the company until 1962. His death in 1964 signaled the end of the "golden years" of the firm directed by the Grimwades and Plant families. The Royal Winton name has continued after the busi-

ness was acquired in 1979 by the Howard Pottery Group and later by other firms. The company reissued some popular Chintz patterns from the 1930s. The first in the series of these limited editions was issued in 1997.

Type of Willow Manufactured: Standard Willow pattern transfer-printed underglaze in blue on earthenware. Willow production probably commenced about 1906 when the Upper Hanley Pottery* was acquired as that factory had been producing it earlier. The following statement was found in *Pottery Gazette*, February 1, 1922: ". . a good line is also offered in blue 'Willow' which, in the home trade, is ever in demand." We know that Standard Willow continued in production at least into the 1930s because Mark 4 (1930+) appears on the toast rack shown below. A simplified Standard willow decal in green and yellow was used with a variant border. Polychrome lithograph based on Two Temples II pattern was made from c. 1930-50. Pekin, a variant of Standard Willow pattern motifs with various colored backgrounds and enameling was produced from 1930 on.

Retailers/importers: Henry Birks & Sons, Winnipeg* and Jay Wilfred Co., New York*

Mark 1 (GG1827)
c. 1906+

Mark 2 (GG1832)
c. 1930+

Mark 3 (GG1832
var.) c. 1930+

Mark 4 (GG1832
var.) c. 1930+

Mark 5 (GG1832
var. WINTON
WARE) c. 1930+

Mark 6 (GG1832
var. ROYAL
WINTON)
c. 1930+

Mark 7 (GG1832
var. ROYAL
WINTON)
c. 1930+

Mark 8
c. 1930-36

Mark 9 c. 1951+

Mark 10 (GG1838)
c. 1951+

Mark 11 (GG1838)
c. 1951+

Mark 12 c. 1951+

Mark 13 (GG1835)
c. 1934-50

Mark 14 c. 1926+

The Dinner Ware Showroom, Winton Pottery (Grimwades, Ltd.)

Page from special Grimwades 1913 Catalog produced for the royal visit of King George V and Queen Mary. Note the large selection of toilet sets in addition to dinnerware. Standard Willow pattern pieces are seen on the lower left hand shelf and the second set of pieces on the next row up. This catalog page was reproduced on page 124 of *Royal Winton Porcelain Ceramics Fit for a King* by Eileen Rose Busby and reprinted here by permission of the publisher: The Glass Press, Inc., David E. Richardson, President.

Standard Willow pattern one cup Cube teapot transfer-printed in blue underglaze. Grimwades began supplying the Cube Teapot Co. in 1926. This teapot is impressed CUBE on the base. Mark 14. *Author's Collection.* $65-95.

Standard Willow pattern creamer transfer-printed in blue underglaze on earthenware. It is 4-inches high and 4-inches wide at the base, narrowing to 2.75-inches at the top. Mark 1. *Author's Collection.* $30-45.

Standard Willow pattern 6-inch toast rack blue printed underglaze. This little toast rack holds just 2 pieces of toast. It has the outer willow border around the rim with gold trim at the edge. Small bits of the central pattern appear on the dividers. Mark 4. *Author's Collection.* $75-95.

Octagonal plate, 5-inches across decorated with a simplified Standard willow pattern decal in shades of green and yellow. It has a red line at the edge. A plate like this was pictured in fig. C2 of Veryl Jensen's *First International Book of Willow Ware*. The book was published in 1975, and it took me until 2003 to find a plate for myself. It is part of a sandwich set with rectangular and square serving plates in addition to the individual small plates. The larger pieces have a lot of white background because the center decal is not much larger than this one. Mark 5 with pattern #9541. *Author's Collection.* $45-55.

Two Temples II polychrome lithograph decorated teapot and stand. The teapot is the same shape as one found with Pekin pattern and blue background. The stand has Mark 8. *Courtesy Paul Kirves and Jeke Jimenez.* $125-175 set.

Two Temples II polychrome lithograph decorated pitcher that is part of a wash set. It stands 11-inches high and measures 12-inches from handle to spout. The shape name SAVOY is impressed on the base along with Mark 13. *Author's Collection.* $75-150.

Two Temples II polychrome lithograph decorated footed goblet. This is a form seen more often in glass than ceramic. It stands 5 7/8-inches high and is 3.75-inches wide. Mark 5. *Courtesy Paul Kirves and Jeke Jimenez.* $30-40.

Pekin pattern 8-inch footed blue bowl, 8.5-by-11.75-inch red platter and 9-inch round white bowl The blue bowl is basically octagonal in shape and flared outward with uneven rim. It has a blue iridescent glaze on the base. The red platter and blue bowl have hand-painted background and enameled pattern elements. The white bowl has the polychrome pattern on the inside and outside both. The blue and the white bowl have extensive gold outlining of pattern elements as well as on edges of the pieces. Mark 6 on all three pieces. The blue bowl has pattern #8447 in addition. The white bowl is a very rare item. *Courtesy Loren Zeller.* $400+ each.

Two Temples II polychrome lithograph decorated shaving scuttle. This piece has a pattern #4925/H along with Mark 2. Several other pieces found with this pattern also have this number, even if the mark is different. *Courtesy IWC Convention 2000.* $85-150.

The back of this 9.25-inch bowl has a blue iridescent glaze. This treatment was used on the backs of the early blue Pekin pattern pieces. The front of the bowl has the same pattern as the pieces in the previous picture; however, the rim has the Standard Willow border in black and white with a red line on the rim. Pattern #1/1178 with Mark 6 and impressed date mark 10/28. This is the earliest form of Pekin pattern. *Author's Collection.* $200+.

Blue hand-painted background Pekin pattern rare Duval shape pitcher. Blue iridescent glaze on the base. Note the strong enamel colors over glaze. Mark 6 with impressed DUVAL No. 735028. *Courtesy Tim and Kim Allen.* $200+.

Pekin pattern two sandwich sets with long tray in Orleans shape and side dishes, teapot, and hot water covered jug. One plate is turned over to show the blue iridescent glaze on the back. The hot water jug is the only piece that doesn't have it. There is a lot of gold outlining throughout the pattern elements as well as on the rims of all the pieces. Mark 6 for all pieces except the teapot that has Mark 7 as well as impressed LOTUS – the shape name. *Courtesy Loren Zeller.* $600+.

Teal background after dinner cup and saucer with enameled colors overglaze. The cream soup and saucer have an ivory color background. The pattern is underglaze black and clobbered in shades of red, green, yellow, and orange. All pieces are trimmed in gold. Mark 10. *Courtesy of Tim and Kim Allen.* $95+ each.

At least five different shades of background are seen on this array of 20 small trays and dishes with Pekin pattern marked Royal Winton. None of these pieces has any enameling over the glaze. It is interesting to see the various shapes. *Courtesy Charles and Zeta Hollingsworth.* $45-85 each.

Plum colored creamer with green, yellow, blue, and black enameled overglaze. This is the first documented piece in this color. Tom Allen gave it the name plum. The shape name ELITE is impressed on the base. Mark 7 with pattern #4165. *Courtesy Tim and Kim Allen.* $95+.

Grindley Hotel Ware Co. Ltd.

Location: Globe Pottery, Tunstall, Staffordshire
Dates: c. 1908-79
Mark:

c. 1908-79

Brief History: This firm produced vitrified hotel ware including "Duraline", a special product that became their best ware. In 1979, the company became The Duraline Hotelware Co. Ltd. The W. H. Grindley & Co. firm founded by William Harry Grindley in 1880 did not produce the Standard Willow pattern.
Type of Willow Manufactured: Standard Willow pattern transfer-printed underglaze in blue and Two Temples II pattern in green on vitrified ware.
Retailers/importers: Cook's Restaurant Supplies*, Burley & Co., Chicago*

A grouping of Pekin pattern pieces with green background color including a lamp, covered box, sugar & creamer, and 3 different bowls. All the pattern and color are underglaze. *Courtesy Charles and Zeta Hollingsworth.* Lamp: $175-200; box and creamer/sugar: $90-110 each; bowls: $45-85 each.

Breakfast set for one on a tray in Pekin pattern with black background and gold trim. Pieces include the tea or coffee pot, cup, creamer, open sugar bowl, and toast rack. Mark 10. *Courtesy Charles and Zeta Hollingsworth.* $300+.

Standard Willow pattern 9-inch plate and 5-inch pitcher. The plate has impressed A-11-29 assumed to be a date mark for 1929. These pieces are vitrified hotel ware. *Author's Collection.* $18-25 and $25-35.

William Hackwood

Location: Eastwood, Hanley, Staffordshire
Dates: c. 1827-43
Mark:

Mark 3 c. 1835-36

Comments Concerning Mark: See Samuel Keeling & Co.* below for the same mark with initials S. K. & Co.

(GG1862) c. 1830-40

Mark 2 c. 1835-36

Brief History: There were several different potters named Hackwood in Hanley and Shelton in the nineteenth century. The mark has been attributed to Hackwood because an example was found with the printed mark in combination with impressed Hackwood. Geoffrey Godden lists the following potters, as well as William Hackwood, who could have used the mark: Josiah Hackwood, Upper High Street, Hanley c. 1842-43.
William & Thomas Hackwood, New Hall Pottery, Shelton, 1843-50
Thomas Hackwood, New Hall Pottery, Shelton, 1850-55.

Type of Willow Manufactured: Standard Willow pattern transfer-printed underglaze in blue on earthenware.

Two Temples II pattern 8.75-inch round plate transfer-printed in blue underglaze on heavy ironstone ware. The glaze is very smooth, and the plate gives the appearance of vitrified ware. Three sets of single stilt marks in the center of the plate, and it has a single flat foot ring. Mark 1. *Author's Collection.* $20-30.

Standard Willow pattern 8.75-inch plate transfer-printed in blue underglaze on earthenware. The rim is slightly concave with an irregular edge. Three-point stilt marks on the rim and a single, slightly recessed foot ring. The plate has a pale blue glaze. The pattern can be seen and felt as it is raised from the surface of the plate. The border pattern has an extra set of 3 and 4-spoke wheels at 5 o'clock. *Author's Collection.* $20-30.

Hackwood & Keeling

Location: Market St., Hanley, Staffordshire
Dates: c. 1835-36
Marks:

Brief History: It is not known which of the potters named Hackwood was involved in this partnership. It was a short-lived partnership that produced earthenware.

Type of Willow Manufactured: Standard Willow and Two Temples II patterns transfer-printed in blue underglaze on earthenware.

Mark 1 c. 1835-36

Standard Willow pattern large bowl transfer-printed underglaze in blue on earthenware. The bowl has six large lobes, and the outside is fluted. The full pattern appears on the inside, and a linear form of the central pattern decorates the outside. Mark 3. *Courtesy Louise and Charles Loehr.* $100-150.

Hall & Read

Location: Wellington Works, Burslem; Dresden Works and Victoria Sq., Hanley, Staffordshire
Dates: c. 1882-88
Mark:

c. 1882-88

Comments Concerning Mark: This initial mark of H & R could also relate to Hughes & Robinson, Globe Pottery, Cobridge c. 1888-94.
Brief History: Hall & Read were in partnership at Wellington Works for just one year when they moved to Hanley. The firm produced earthenware and stoneware.
Type of Willow Manufactured: Standard Willow pattern transfer-printed in blue underglaze on stoneware.

Standard Willow pattern platter transfer-printed in blue underglaze on stoneware. The measurements are 14-by-18-inches. The platter was broken in several pieces and repaired with metal staples on the back. *Courtesy Charles Coysh.* $75-150.

Robert Hamilton

Location: Stoke, Staffordshire
Dates: c. 1811-26
Mark:

(GG1901)
c. 1811-26

Brief History: In about 1800, Robert Hamilton went to work for his father-in-law, Thomas Wolfe, an established potter of blue-printed wares in Stoke. The partnership of Wolfe and Hamilton lasted until 1811, when Robert Hamilton set up his own pottery in Stoke, and Wolfe continued at his pottery alone. In *Blue and White Transfer Ware 1780-1840*, Coysh shows two illustrations of printed plates by Robert Hamilton (#47 & 48). He criticizes the quality of the blurred printing and the glaze with impurities and bubbles. The actual transfer work was well done. Hamilton's reputation must not be judged solely on those two examples because the Standard Willow pattern plate in my collection is a lovely piece of pearlware with just a trace of tiny grit on the rim.
Type of Willow Manufactured: Standard Willow pattern transfer-printed underglaze in blue on light weight earthenware.

Standard Willow pattern 9 7/8" plate transfer-printed in blue underglaze on pearlware. There are 8 indentations on the concave rim. Three-point stilt marks on the rim with just one stilt mark of each set showing on the top. There is a slight amount of fine grit in the pale blue glaze that settled into the lower area of the rim. The plate has a flat back. A 3 and 4-spoke wheel are cut out of the border pattern just before 6 o'clock. *Author's Collection.* $40-65.

Ralph Hammersley (& Son)

Location: Church Bank Pottery, Tunstall (1860-83), Black Works, High Street, Tunstall (1885-88), and Over House Pottery, Burslem, (from 1880) Staffordshire
Dates: c. 1859-1905
Marks:

Mark 1 c. 1860-83

Brief History: Ralph Hammersley took over Anthony Shaw's* pottery in Tunstall in about 1859, and continued making ironstone type wares. He had a large export business to the U.S.A., Europe, and the colonial trade. From 1883, the firm traded as Ralph Hammersley & Sons. The company's designs and other effects were sold to various buyers in March 1905.

Mark 2 (GG1912)
c. 1860-83

Type of Willow Manufactured: Standard Willow pattern transfer-printed underglaze in blue on stoneware.

Standard Willow pattern 8 5/8-inch plate transfer-printed in blue underglaze on stoneware. This plate is quite heavy and has a single flat foot ring. The rim is flat. Three sets of single stilt marks on the front and back in the center section. There are some glaze skips on the reverse, and some imperfections on the top. The pattern appears crowded. Mark 1. *Author's Collection.* $20-30.

Standard Willow pattern 9.5-inch plate blue printed stoneware. The rim is concave, and it has a single foot ring. This plate is lighter in weight than the smaller one. The glaze is glassier, and stilt marks are not obvious. There is one glaze skip near the edge on the reverse. The engraving is different from the other plate, and there is more open area in the pattern and more white between the borders. Both plates have a pale blue glaze. Mark 2. *Author's Collection.* $20-30.

gilding pattern as well as the shade of blue used are the same as those seen earlier on the Davenport* water set and teapot.

In 1980 the Alsager Works were purchased by Aynsley China Ltd.* Palissy took over the company's production and trade name when the Hammersley factory closed in 1982. In August 1989, the Aynsley Group bought the trade name and patterns of Hammersley China Ltd. and Palissy Pottery Ltd.* from the Porcelain and Fine China Companies Ltd., owners of Spode Ltd. The Alsager Works were closed in 1996.

Type of Willow Manufactured: Two Temples II transfer-printed underglaze in light and dark blue on bone china.

Retailers/importers: Pitkin & Brook, Chicago*, WINGTON BROTHERS*

Two Temples II pattern teapot, creamer, and open sugar transfer-printed in blue underglaze on bone china. Not an exact match, but close: the teapot has pattern #901, and the creamer and sugar have #930. The teapot also has a retailer/importer mark for WINGTON BROTHERS*. Mark 1. All pieces have the connected dots gilding pattern and the color blue used by Davenport in this pattern. Hammersley & Co. also copied the teapot shape from Davenport. See plates 1305 and 1307 in *An Anthology of British Teapots*. Teapot: *Author's Collection.* Creamer and open sugar: *Paul Kirves and Zeke Jemeniz.* $150-250 set.

Hammersley & Co.

Location: Alsager Pottery, Longton, Staffordshire
Dates: 1887-1989
Marks:

Mark 1
(GG1906)
c. 1912-39

Comment Concerning Marks: Mark 1 appears on the cream and sugar. The teapot has an added mark for retailer/importer WINGTON BROTHERS*. Mark 2 has been seen on light blue printed Two Temples II pattern.

Brief History: George Harris Hammersley had worked in partnership with Harvey Adams & Co.* up to August 4, 1885. He then continued on with Sarah Hammersley who was replaced by Gilbert Hammersley on April 9, 1888. The firm's title changed in about 1887, to Hammersley & Co. as they continued to produce fine quality porcelain. The pattern-number sequences were continued that had been produced by Harvey Adams & Co.* The company records are now preserved at the Spode Works in Stoke. In 1932 to 1974, the name of the firm changed to Hammersley & Co. (Longton) Ltd. In 1970, it was taken over by Copeland-Spode. The name changed in 1974, to Hammersley China Ltd.

In the twentieth century a new pattern number sequence was used, dropping the letter and following a simple sequence of numbers. Hammersley produced reissues of earlier designs and forms from such firms as Davenport, Nantgarw, Ridgway, and Swansea. The Two Temples II tea set illustrated here is an example of that. The

Mark 2 (GG1905)
c. 1912-39

Hampson

Location: Green Dock Works, Longton, Staffordshire
Dates: c. 1854-58
Mark:

c. 1854-58

Brief History: Peter Hampson and J. Broadhurst were in partnership from 1847-49 when Peter Hampson died. Another Peter Hampson continued with Broadhurst until 1854. Peter Hampson was in business alone from 1854-58. He was succeeded by his sons David and John. The factory manufactured earthenware.

Type of Willow Manufactured: Standard Willow pattern transfer-printed underglaze in blue on earthenware. No picture is available.

S. Hancock (& Sons)

Location: Various locations Tunstall; Bridge Pottery, and Gordon Pottery, Stoke, Staffordshire
Dates: 1858-1937
Marks:

Mark 1 c. 1912-37

Brief History: Sampson Hancock worked in several different locations in Tunstall, starting out at the Victoria Pottery. From 1876-81, he was in partnership with Benjamin Hancock, but then continued under his own name until 1891. The title was changed to S. Hancock & Sons in 1891, and the firm moved to Gordon Pottery on Wolfe Street, Stoke the following year. The mainstay of the company was good middle-class dinnerware services in earthenware for the home market as well as production of earthenware, ironstone and granite-type useful wares for export. The pottery may be best known for Morris Ware, an ornamental ware of the Arts and Crafts Movement. It was begun in the early twentieth century with new models and decorative styles added over the years.

In the early 1920s, S. Hancock & Sons, moved to Corona Pottery, Burton-place, Hanley – a much expanded facility. The company added the manufacture of china to their production with several interesting new dinnerware patterns. In January 1923, the *Pottery Gazette* reported the addition of china production under "Buyer's Notes" on page 75. The article went on to discuss the successful history of dinnerware production by the firm and its selection of patterns that would sell and bring regular repeat business.

Mark 2 (GG1935) c. 1912-37

Mark 3 c. 1912-37

Standard Willow pattern teapots transfer-printed in dark blue underglaze. The teapot in the back holds 8 cups, and the smaller one holds 5 cups. The inner border is used on the lid, and the outer border is the normal way around on the pots. The spouts, handles, and finials are all decorated in plain cobalt blue with a gold line trim. Mark 1. *Courtesy Joette Hightower.* $175-225 and $125-175.

Some months ago S. Hancock & Sons went to the trouble of engraving the old "Blue Willow" pattern throughout, and in a second illustration we bring to the notice of our readers a set of pieces in this pattern, which has since been engraved for dinnerware also. It seems worth mentioning that in the case of the last-mentioned the original setting of the 'Willow' pattern has been modified, and a lightening of the design has resulted, giving a very pleasing effect. There is more light and shade in the new treatment of the pattern than is noticeable in certain other makes of "Blue Willow," and the modification seems to us to be a decided improvement.

The lighter effect mentioned came from reversing the outer border of the pattern so that the open area of the border extends to the outside. The "very good 'Blue Willow' design known as the 'Nankin Willow'" was also illustrated and discussed again in the December 1923, *Pottery Gazette* "Buyer's Notes" on page 1943.

Type of Willow Manufactured: Standard Willow pattern transfer-printed underglaze in light and dark blue on earthenware. The outer border is reversed on flat pieces and some hollow ware. Some of the dark blue pieces have a flow blue effect and are higher in price. The word "Willow" appears on some marks, but I have never seen "Nankin Willow" on a mark.

Standard Willow pattern three teapots with the same shape in dark blue underglaze. They range in height from 5 to 6 to 6.75-inches .The spouts and handles are cobalt blue, but the finials were left white with gold line trim. Mark 2. *Courtesy Loren Zeller.* $125-275 each.

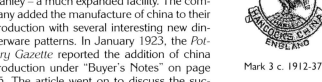

Standard Willow pattern 10.5-inch bowl transfer-printed in light blue underglaze on earthenware. This company often used the outer willow border in reverse with the fish roe towards the inner border and the flowers pointing to the outside. It provides a refreshing change to the pattern. This bowl has wavy edges with gold trim. Mark 1. *Courtesy IWC Convention 2001.* $45-65.

Standard Willow pattern 3-part relish blue printed underglaze with a metal handle. This is the only piece by Hancock I have seen with only little willow motifs used as an outer border. Though not seen often, these large 3-part relish dishes were made by a number of firms such as Copeland, Doulton, Gibson, and Minton in the Willow pattern. A metal handle is unusual. Mark 1. *Courtesy Louise and Charles Loehr.* $125-175.

Standard Willow pattern open sugar, creamer, and demitasse coffee cup and saucer in light blue with reversed outer border. All pieces have a gold line at the edge. These pieces all have Mark 3 with "Hancock's China" on it. This mark wasn't used on the dark blue willow. *Author's Collection.* $30-50 set.

Standard Willow pattern 5.5-inch jug in dark blue with reversed outer border. This Hydra shape jug is usually found in stoneware by firms such as Masons and Davenport. Mark 1. *Courtesy IWC Convention 1993.* $150-200.

S. HANCOCK & SONS.

Photograph of newly engraved pieces of Blue Willow by S. Hancock & Sons in January 1,1923, *Pottery Gazette,* page 77.

Standard Willow pattern light blue teapot on stand with gold trim. The shape matches the teapot on the second row, 4th item on the reprint from *Pottery Gazette* shown below. Mark 3.*Courtesy Loren Zeller.* $175-275 set.

Joseph Harding

Location: Navigation Road, Burslem, Staffordshire
Dates: c. 1850-51
Mark:

(GG1949) c. 1850-51

Brief History: Joseph Harding produced earthenware. He was in business alone for only a short time.
Type of Willow Manufactured: Standard Willow pattern transfer-printed underglaze in blue on earthenware.

Standard Willow pattern 9-inch plate transfer-printed in blue underglaze. The rim is slightly concave, and the edge is 8-lobed. It has a single foot ring. Three-point stilt marks in the center with one mark from each set showing on the front. These can be seen in the pattern 1) in the orange tree, 2) above the fence to the right of the path, and 3) on the willow tree branch at the far left. The plate has a very glassy pale blue glaze. *Author's Collection.* $25-35.

Thomas Harley

Location: Thomas Shelley's Earthenware Works, High Street, Lane End, Staffordshire
Dates: c. 1805-8
Mark:

(GG1951)
c. 1805-8

Comments Concerning Mark: Many wares were unmarked. The impressed "bullet" mark is not often seen, but because it appears with the impressed name mark, it might possibly help in attribution if a piece is found without the name mark. T. Harley is another impressed mark that relates to this firm.
Brief History: The late Thomas Shelley's Works were later known as the Park Works. Thomas Harley had previously been in partnership with John, George, and William Weston. He was in business alone for a short time from 1805-8 producing earthenware. His output included molded wares, luster and printed wares. Harley is known for making

a diamond shaped teapot with swan finial. Some of these had blue printed patterns. Many of the teapots were unmarked, and may have been made by other potters, but it is tempting to attribute them to Harley.
Type of Willow Manufactured: Standard Willow pattern transfer-printed underglaze in blue on earthenware.

Standard Willow pattern dessert plate transfer-printed in blue underglaze on pearlware. This plate has a reticulated edge and bears the mark shown above. *Courtesy Renard Broughton.* $80-135.

Harley & Seckerson or Harley & Co.

Location: Thomas Shelley's Earthenware Works (1808-12) and John Smith's Works (1812-25) Lane End, Staffordshire.
Dates: c. 1808-25
Mark:

HARLEY&Co

c. 1808-25

Brief History: The partnership of Thomas Harley and Peter Seckerson followed the period when Thomas Harley worked alone. The same types of earthenware were produced. The partners made inquiries of china-producing firms regarding china stone and the production of porcelain; however, there is no evidence that it was ever produced.
Type of Willow Manufactured: Standard Willow pattern transfer-printed underglaze in blue on earthenware.

Standard Willow pattern 6-inch plate transfer-printed on pearlware in blue underglaze. The concave rim has 8 indentations at the edge, and it has a recessed foot ring. Three sets of single stilt marks showing on the front and back. A large part of the border pattern was cut out at 8 o'clock. *Author's Collection.* $10-25.

Harris & Goodwin

Location: Flint Street, Lane End (Longton),
Staffordshire
Dates: c. 1834-37
Mark:

c. 1834-37

Comments Concerning the Mark: In the *Northern Ceramic Society Newsletter No. 64*, dated
December 1986, this mark with the initials H and G on either side of
a lion over a crown is attributed to Harris & Goodwin. It was illustrated on a cup in the Two Temples II pattern.

Brief History: The partnership of Benjamin Harris and John Goodwin
produced china. Many of the pieces were unmarked and can only be
attributed through characteristic shapes. This partnership is not to be
confused with the earthenware producing business operated by
Goodwins & Harris*. Both the earthenware partnership and the china
partnership were dissolved the same day: June 6, 1837.

Type of Willow Manufactured: Two Temples II pattern transfer-printed
underglaze in pale blue on china. Tea wares and jugs were produced
with gold trim.

Two Temples II pattern cup and saucer in pale blue transfer-printed
underglaze on china. Both pieces have a wavy edge decorated in gold.
The mark above is on the saucer. *Author's Collection.* $35-50.

Two Temples II pattern jug
transfer-printed in pale blue
underglaze on china. It stands
5-inches high and is trimmed
in gold. There is no mark;
however, the handle shape
seen in Plates 985 and 986 in
Berthoud's *A Cabinet of
Creamers* is attributed to
Harris & Goodwin. *Author's
Collection.* $45-75.

John Harrison

Location: Cliffgate Bank, Stoke-on-Trent,
Staffordshire
Dates: c. 1781-1816
Mark:

c.1781-1816

Comments Concerning Mark: This impressed IH
mark has long been attributed to Joshua Heath, c.
1770-1800; however, many British researchers of blue and white printed wares
have begun to question the attribution. Although Joshua Heath was a potter
during that time, there is no evidence that he used the IH mark. Many early
patterns marked with IH were undoubtedly produced in the 18th century, but
some of the wares appear to be made closer to 1810. R. K. Henrywood in his
Staffordshire Potters, 1781-1900, has suggested the mark may have been used by
John Harrison, a potter at Stoke c. 1781-1816. Unfortunately, other than the
dates and the fact that the initials fit, there is no conclusive evidence that the IH
mark was used by John Harrison. The name is being presented here as a
possible alternative to Joshua Heath. We may never know for sure.

Brief History: John Harrison was an earthenware manufacturer. Blue printed
wares on light weight earthenware were produced. He may have ventured into
porcelain production at the end of this period.

Type of Willow Manufactured: Standard Willow pattern transfer-printed in
blue underglaze on pearlware.

Standard Willow pattern section from supper (or breakfast) set transfer-printed
in medium blue underglaze on pearlware. The line engraving as well as the strap
handle on the domed lid point to a date c. 1800. This is the first supper set
section documented in the willow pattern with this mark. *Courtesy Renard
Broughton.* $250+.

Standard Willow pattern in full on the lower section shown
above with lid. The piece measures approximately 7.5-by-
13.25-inches. Standard Willow pattern plates have also been
found with this mark. *Courtesy Renard Broughton.*

Joseph Heath

Location: Newfield Pottery (1828-41) and High Street, (1845-53) Tunstall, Staffordshire
Dates: c. 1828-41 & 1845-53
Marks:

Brief History: Joseph Heath traded in the earlier period as J. Heath & Co. The firm produced good quality printed earthenwares. Various patterns were made including some American Views. The wares of the second period were heavier ironstone wares. The firm also exported white ironstone wares to the U.S.A.
Type of Willow Manufactured: Standard Willow pattern transfer-printed in blue underglaze with pale blue glaze on earthenware and ironstone.

Mark I c. 1828-41

Mark 2 c. 1845-53

Joshua Heath
(see John Harrison)

Heath & Blackhurst

Location: Hadderidge Pottery, Burslem, Staffordshire
Dates: c. 1859-77
Mark:

(GG1997) c. 1859-77

Brief History: John Heath and Abraham Blackhurst produced earthenware and granite ware. The firm followed the partnership of W. & G. Harding who worked the pottery previously. The partnership was dissolved July 26, 1877. After that time a new partnership of Blackhurst and Tunnicliffe* carried on.
Type of Willow Manufactured: Standard Willow pattern transfer-printed underglaze in blue on earthenware.

Standard Willow pattern 10.25-inch plate transfer-printed in blue underglaze. The plate has a concave rim and wavy edge. The borders are matched up very well, with just one 3-wheel scroll missing at 5 o'clock. It bears the impressed propeller Mark 1. *Courtesy Loren Zeller.* $75-95.

Standard Willow pattern 9 3/8-inches plate transfer-printed in blue underglaze on earthenware. The plate is round with a flat rim and single foot ring. Three-point stilt marks in the center with one from each set showing on the front of the plate. The border patterns are well matched due to a cut made at 8 o'clock. Extra blue streaks in the border may be the result of the cut. The plate has a glassy pale blue glaze. *Author's Collection.* $25-35.

Heathcote China
(see H. M. Williamson & Sons)

Herculaneum

Location: Toxteth Park, Liverpool, Lancashire
Dates: 1796-1840
Mark:

HERCULANEUM

(GG2007) c. 1815

Comments Concerning Mark: The impressed mark shown here was used in several different sizes ranging from 1/16 to 1/8 inch. The smaller the mark, the earlier the date.
Brief History: The classic name of Herculaneum was chosen for a pottery established by Samuel Worthington on the site of a Copper ore plant that went out of business. The buildings and premises were

Standard Willow pattern 10 3/8-inch plate transfer-printed in blue underglaze. This impressive 12-sided plate has 12 ribs on the rim and a flared shape. Three-point stilt marks on the rim and a single foot ring. A bit of the geometric line motif was added in the outer border at 8 o'clock. The plate is ironstone with pale blue glaze. Impressed Mark 2. *Author's Collection.* $75-95.

adapted to the purpose of making pottery. Most of the workmen came from Staffordshire and lived in the housing on the site. Earthenwares of various types were produced in the beginning. Porcelain was added about 1800. Herculaneum was established at a time when most of the eighteenth century potteries in the area were closed or on the decline. It became the largest pottery (and the last) in the Liverpool area. From 1806, when the Herculaneum Company was established the affairs and business concerns were controlled by a Committee of Proprietors.

The wares produced were of a high quality. Although there are a number of marks used by Herculaneum over the years, most of the wares were not marked. Quite often only one or two pieces of a dinner service had a mark. The company developed a large export market. Their close proximity to the nearby Liverpool docks gave Herculaneum a huge advantage over the Staffordshire potteries of the period for exporting their wares. Problems began to develop between management and the Proprietors in the early 1820s. A slow decline followed as investors wanted to put their money into other industries in Liverpool. By 1833, the factory was put up for sale. It was seven more years before it closed.

Type of Willow Manufactured: Standard Willow and Two Temples II pattern transfer-printed underglaze in blue on earthenware and Two Temples II pattern blue printed on porcelain. I know of no other company that produced Two Temples II pattern on earthenware as early as Herculaneum. Plate 153 in *The Illustrated Guide to Liverpool Herculaneum Pottery* shows a covered bowl and stand with Two Temples II pattern on earthenware. The pieces have the impressed mark shown here and are dated c. 1810.

Two Temples II reversed pattern coffee can blue printed on porcelain. This photo shows the temple side of the pattern. The bridge and willow tree are seen in the previous photo. The border is used on the inside of the cup, and it has gold trim. The glaze has an oily feel to it, and the cup is translucent. *Author's Collection.*

Robert Heron (& Son)

Location: Fife or Gallatoun Pottery, Kirkcaldy, Scotland
Dates: c. 1837-1928
Mark:

c. 1837-91

Brief History: The Fife or Gallatoun Pottery was founded in 1790, as a red ware pottery. In 1817, a new pottery was built, but in 1826, the proprietor, Andrew Grey became bankrupt as a result of a general depression in the trade. The pottery and flint mill were sold to John Methven, son of David Methven* owner of Links Pottery at the other end of Kirkcaldy. John died in 1837, and the pottery passed on to his daughter and son-in-law, Mary and Robert Heron. Later, the pottery was run by their son, Robert Methven Heron.

The wares produced by the pottery were printed, painted, sponged and colored earthenwares of the ordinary variety produced by other potteries of the period. In 1882, the firm began producing pots decorated in single colors. Robert Methven Heron brought East European painters back with him from his travels to train the Scots in painting ceramics. The resulting Wemyss Ware became very popular. The wares were decorated with all types of flowers, fruit, birds and landscapes among other things.

Type of Willow Manufactured: Standard Willow pattern transfer-printed in blue underglaze on earthenware.

Standard Willow pattern covered dish transfer-printed underglaze in blue on earthenware. The base of the dish measures 12-by-8.5-inches. The complete pattern with both borders is on the inside with a linear form of the pattern on the outside. Half the pattern appears on each end, and the complete pattern on each side. The size of the mark indicates that it is c. 1815. *Author's Collection.* $250+.

Two Temples II reversed pattern coffee can transfer-printed in blue underglaze on porcelain. The cup stands 2.5-inches high and is 2.25-inches across. It is unmarked. It is attributed to Herculaneum because of the handle shape. See Plates 287 and 288 in *A Compendium of British Cups. Author's Collection.* $50-75.

Standard Willow pattern dish transfer-printed in blue underglaze on earthenware. This is the base of a covered vegetable dish and measures 11.5-by-9.8-inches. *Courtesy Henry Kelly. Photo by Douglas Leishman.* $75-85.

Heron Cross Pottery

c. 1976+

Location: Fenton, Staffordshire
Dates: c. 1976+
Mark:

Brief History: The Heron Cross Pottery was built in 1886 by the Hines Brothers. The pottery was acquired by Cartwright and Edwards* at the beginning of World War I, and reconstructed in order to make cheap earthenware in large quantities. I don't know if the pottery was abandoned, sold or used by Alfred Clough Ltd. when that company purchased Cartwright and Edwards in 1955. The mark above has a date of 1976, the founding date of the Heron Cross Pottery, using this mark of a heron in front of a castle.
The mark was seen on a willow decal-decorated tankard for sale on Ebay, an internet auction site.
Type of Willow Manufactured: Standard Willow pattern decal overglaze in blue on earthenware. No picture available.

Hicks & Meigh

Location: High Street, Shelton, Staffordshire
Dates: c. 1803-22
Mark: square pseudo-Chinese seal

Brief History: Richard Hicks and Job Meigh produced earthenware, stoneware, and china. Richard Hicks was an engraver, apparently apprenticed to Thomas Turner at Caughley prior to his involvement in making pottery in Staffordshire. The china was not marked; however, Geoffrey Godden has been able to attribute some dessert and tea wares to the firm. The shapes are related to stone china shapes that are marked. Margaret Ironside made a study of pseudo-Chinese seal marks and attributes 3 marks to Hicks & Meigh. In The Northern Ceramic Society Newsletter No. 89 page 27 marks No. 20, 21 and 22 are attributed to the firm. The marks were found on three London shape teapots: two of which are in *Anthology of British Teapots*, plates 1297 and 1298. These teapots are decorated in Two Temples II pattern.
Type of Willow Manufactured: Two Temples II pattern transfer-printed in blue underglaze on porcelain. No picture available.

Hicks, Meigh & Johnson

Location: High Street, Shelton, Staffordshire
Dates: c. 1822-35
Mark: Wreath similar to GG2023, but illegible

Brief History: Hicks & Meigh* took Johnson, their traveler, into partnership in 1822. They produced high quality ironstone and earthenware as well as china. It was a large firm employing a staff of 600. The pattern books are lost: however, historians have noted that the pattern numbers went up to 2000. Earthenwares and ironstone wares were marked, but the porcelains were not.
Type of Willow Manufactured: Standard Willow pattern transfer-printed underglaze in blue on ironstone. A large platter was seen on Ebay, an internet auction site. No picture available.

Hilditch & Sons (& Co.)

Location: Church Street, Lane End, Staffordshire
Dates: c. 1819-35
Mark:

c. 1822-30

Comments Concerning Mark: The actual mark is just 3/8 inch square. It is similar to Mark 4 on page 26 of The Northern Ceramic Society Newsletter No. 89. The mark may be that of Hilditch;

however, it appears on a saucer so it is not possible to compare shapes for a more certain attribution.
Brief History: The firm of William Hilditch & Sons was also listed in directories as Hilditch & Co. He was in partnership with Martin preceding and with Hopwood after his partnership with his sons. The firm produced china although attribution is difficult due to the absence of marks. Margaret Ironside's research indicates that occasionally a pseudo-Chinese seal mark was used on porcelain.
Type of Willow Manufactured: Two Temples II transfer-printed in blue underglaze on porcelain.

Two Temples II 7.75-inch saucer transfer-printed in blue underglaze on porcelain. The saucer has a wavy edge and unglazed single foot ring. The indentation for the cup measures 3.75-inches. *Author's Collection.* $15-25.

Hillchurch Pottery

Mark 1 c. 1990+

Mark 2 c. 1990+

Location: Commercial Road, Hanley, Staffordshire
Dates: c. 1990s-present (2003)
Marks:

Brief History: The company produces toy china and decorative wares such as covered boxes.
Type of Willow Manufactured: Standard Willow pattern blue printed earthenware.

Standard Willow pattern toy tea set in blue on earthenware. The shapes are interesting, and each piece has gold trim. Mark 1. The table cloth is hand embroidered in the willow pattern. *Courtesy IWC Convention 1997.* $25-50.

Standard Willow pattern covered boxes printed in blue on earthenware. The approximate sizes are 3-inches round and 2-by 4-inches. Each piece has gold trim. *Author's Collection.* $15-25 each.

T. & J. Hollins

(GG2068)
c. 1789-1809

Location: Far Green, Hanley, Staffordshire
Dates: c.1789-1809
Mark:

Comment Concerning Mark: The impressed name mark was lower case first and later changed to upper case letters.
Brief History: Thomas and John Hollins were nephews of Samuel Hollins, a potter at Vale Pleasant, Shelton. Their brother Richard joined them some time before 1809. The firm then became known as T. J. & R. Hollins. The firm produced creamware as well as many patterns transfer-printed in blue on earthenware. In fact this family of potters (including Samuel Hollins) was among the earliest producers of blue printed wares.
Type of Willow Manufactured: Standard Willow pattern transfer-printed underglaze in blue on earthenware. There are also unmarked examples as well as pieces with workmen's marks in Mandarin pattern that were possibly made by Hollins.

Standard Willow pattern plate transfer-printed in blue underglaze on earthenware. Note the large area of white between the two borders. *Courtesy Rita Cohen.* $75-125.

Hollinshead & Kirkham

Location: Burslem (1870-76), Woodland Pottery (1876-90), and Unicorn Pottery (1890-1956) Tunstall, Staffordshire
Dates: c. 1870-1956.
Marks:

Mark 1 (GG2071)
c. 1891-1900

Mark 2 (GG2071)
c. 1870-91

Comments Concerning Marks: Mark 1 is found on light and dark blue useful wares in Two Temples II pattern transfer-printed underglaze. Marks 1 and 2 are not to be confused with the H & K marks for Hackwood & Keeling, Hanley. The initial marks for Hollinshead & Kirkham include the letter T for Tunstall.
Brief History: The partnership of John Hollinshead and Samuel Kirkham was established in Burslem; however, it moved to Woodland Pottery, Tunstall in 1876. The move was made to Unicorn Pottery in 1890. The firm was listed in the design registration files in 1883, as producing China and Earthenware; however, marked pieces of china have not been found. The firm is known for high quality earthenware production, and exported wares to all parts of the world. The *Pottery Gazette*, May 1, 1926, Buyer's Notes gave this information: "H & K specialize chiefly in dinnerware, toilet ware, and fancies . . . from plain printed or printed and illuminated . . . For flow Canton printed patterns with gilt illumination, they are specially known." In 1956 Johnson Bros. bought the factory.
Type of Willow Manufactured: Standard Willow pattern transfer-printed in blue underglaze and printed on glaze in gold and colored enamels over various color grounds. Two Temples II pattern transfer-printed in two shades of blue and in brown with clobbering..

Mark 3 (GG2072)
c. 1870-1900

Mark 4 (GG2073)
c. 1900-24

Mark 5 (GG2074 var.)
c. 1924-56

Standard Willow pattern 10-inch plate transfer-printed in dark blue underglaze on heavy earthenware. There is a gold line on the edge of the flat rim of the plate. It has a single foot ring. The print is muddy, and the clear glaze is thick and unevenly applied. Mark 3 with impressed H & K TUNSTALL. *Author's Collection.* $10-15.

Standard Willow pattern octagonal plate with on glaze decoration. The center of this very striking plate has a blue ground with the pattern done in gold and enamel colors. The border pattern is gold on gold. The plate measures 9 1/8-inches from point to point and 8 5/8-inches from flat section to flat. Mark 4 with pattern #9980. *Courtesy Tom and Barbara Allen.* $75-150.

Hoods Ltd.

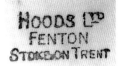

Location: International Works, Fenton, Staffordshire
Dates: c. 1919-60s
Mark:

Comments Concerning Marks: The mark   c. 1919-42
most often seen for this company consists of
three people in conversation, shown from the shoulders up wearing hoods, c. 1919-42. The mark shown here is probably later.
Brief History: Hoods Ltd. produced earthenware including transfer-printed patterns underglaze as well as on-glaze scenic patterns. Fine quality ware is known to have been produced for a hotel in Bermuda. Geoffrey Godden mentions that the firm was still producing wares in the mid-1960s.
Type of Willow Manufactured: Polychrome border pattern consisting of elements of the Standard Willow pattern trimmed in gold.

Standard Willow pattern on a pair of orange vases. The one on the right is turned to show the pattern on the back. The pattern is painted over glaze in black, green, yellow, and gold. Marks 4 and 5 with pattern #9980. *Courtesy Tim and Kim Allen.* $150+ each.

Polychrome border pattern with elements of the Standard Willow pattern decorate this sandwich set on a silver tray. Only one of the small plates is shown in this photo. All pieces are lined in gold. The sandwich tray is 13-inches long with gold line detailing on the handles. *Courtesy Paul Kirves and Zeke Jimenez.* $45-95.

Hope & Carter

Location: Fountain Place, Burslem, Staffordshire
Dates: c. 1862-80
Mark:

Comments Concerning Mark: In addition to the   c. 1862-78
impressed name mark are impressed 180 and a
large letter C. The same impressed marks are found on a dinner plate not shown here.
Brief History: John Hope was formerly in a partnership with Pinder & Bourne* known as Pinder, Bourne & Hope. The partnership of John Hope and John Carter produced earthenware and ironstone ware including white ironstone for the American market. The company was later taken over by Ashworths* who purchased Hope & Carter's pattern and description books. John Hope joined the Ashworths firm that was in a position to supply replacements for Hope & Carter's wares well into the 1880s.
Type of Willow Manufactured: Standard Willow pattern transfer-printed underglaze in blue on heavy ironstone ware.

Two Temples II pattern creamer transfer-printed in brown underglaze with clobbering and gold trim. Mark 2. *Courtesy IWC Convention 1997.* $75-95.

Standard Willow pattern serving plate with handles transfer-printed in blue underglaze on heavy ironstone. The plate measures ten-inches including the embossed pattern handles. The single foot ring is unglazed. The outer border is too small and needed an insert at 9:30 o'clock. *Author's Collection.* $35-45.

Howard Pottery Co. (Ltd.)

Location: Norfolk St., Shelton, Staffordshire
Dates: c. 1925-1970s
Mark:

Mark 1 c. 1925-70s

Brief History: Beginning in 1925 the company made useful wares and ornamental wares such as figures, animal models, lamps, and vases. Alan Luckham joined the firm in 1947. He developed a range of ornamental useful pottery that was decorated with two-tone semi-matt glazes. In the 1970s, the company made oven-to-table ware as well as continuing to make teapot sets and ornamental wares. Brentleigh Ware was the trade name used by the company.

Type of Willow Manufactured: Standard blue printed willow pattern. Medium to dark blue matt glazed pottery with cream-colored willow motifs. The appearance of the ware is that it was produced by wax resist. A pattern was brushed onto the biscuit ware with a sort of wax substance. Then the item was dipped in blue glaze and fired. The glaze did not penetrate the waxed pattern.

Standard Willow pattern motifs resist-painted in ivory with blue semi-matt glaze. Left to right: sugar shaker, biscuit jar, octagonal bowl, and vase. The octagonal bowl has impressed BRENTLEIGH WARE and a number. The vase has impressed 318. The other pieces are not marked. *Courtesy Paul Kirves and Zeke Jimenez.* NP

John Thomas Hudden

Location: Stafford Street, and British Anchor Works, Longton, Staffordshire
Dates: c. 1860-83
Mark:

(GG2105) c. 1860-83

Comments Concerning Mark: Geoffrey Godden states that garter-shaped marks were used by this firm for patterns registered in the 1860s.
Brief History: John Thomas Hudden had a partner named Wathen from 1859-60, but after that he was the sole proprietor. He was at Stafford Street for the entire length of his business, and added the British Anchor Works from 1874 until he went into liquidation in 1883. J. T. Hudden produced printed earthenware.
Type of Willow Manufactured: Standard Willow pattern transfer-printed in blue underglaze in blue on earthenware.

Standard Willow pattern 11-by-13.5-inch platter transfer-printed in blue underglaze on earthenware. Three single stilt marks on the front and back of the platter. The printing is very clear and precise. There is some grit in the glaze on the rim and the underside of the base. *Author's Collection.* $75-100.

Standard Willow partial pattern in blue on the lid of a box measuring 4.25-by-5.25-inches. The outer border is used on the edge of the lid and the lower part of the box. Mark 1 with impressed DUVAL under the printed mark. *Courtesy Paul Kirves and Zeke Jimenez.* $20-40.

William Hudson

Location: Alma Pottery, High Street, and Sutherland Works, Normacot Road Longton, Staffordshire
Dates: c. 1889-1941
Mark:

c. 1912-41

Comments Concerning Mark: This mark is in blue underglaze matching the color of the egg cup. The same mark was used by Hudson & Middleton Ltd.*; however, it is printed in black over the glaze. It is impossible to know for sure whether the two pieces shown were made by the companies indicated because several marks were used by William Hudson and continued after the merger with Middleton. The fact that the mark on the plate is in black over glaze leads me to believe that it was made later and was produced by the partnership of Hudson & Middleton.
Brief History: The trade name for William Hudson was Sutherland China. It was incorporated into the marks of this firm and the succeeding firm of Hudson & Middleton Ltd.* Hudson produced traditional bone china tea ware and dinnerware for the middle market. The wares were decorated with printing, painting and decals.
Type of Willow Manufactured: Standard Willow pattern transfer-printed in blue on bone china.

Standard Willow pattern egg cup transfer-printed in blue on bone china with gold trim. The pattern, in linear form, is not complete on this small object. *Author's Collection.* $12-20.

Hudson & Middleton Ltd.

Location: Sutherland Pottery, Longton, Staffordshire
Dates: c. 1941-present (2003)
Brief History: William Hudson and J. H. Middleton merged their two companies in 1941. Middleton left the Delphine Pottery and joined Hudson at the Sutherland Pottery where production was centered due to wartime regulations. The two firms had produced the same type of mid-priced wares including tea and coffee sets, breakfast sets and other tableware. Production continued retaining some of their individuality at first. Later on other items were added such as mugs, collector cups and specialized giftware. In 1982 the company was taken

over by its parent company, Jesse Shirley & Son Ltd. It continues to trade under its own name.
Type of Willow Manufactured: Standard Willow pattern transfer-printed in blue on bone china.

Standard Willow pattern 6.25" plate transfer-printed in blue on bone china with gold. The plate is square in shape with indented corners. The small building next to the teahouse has been altered and narrowed: probably due to the small size of the plate. The outer border used was intended for use on a small round plate. Many inserts were added on the upper left corner especially. *Author's Collection.* $20-25.

E. Hughes & Co.

Location: Opal China Works, Fenton, Staffordshire
Dates: c. 1889-1940
Marks:

Mark 1
(GG2119)
c. 1914-41

Mark 2
c. 1914-41

Brief History: The firm of Edward Hughes & Co. specialized in tea and breakfast sets as well as pieces decorated with local views and coats of arms. Bone china was produced for the home and export markets. After Hughes' death in 1908, the firm concentrated on tea, coffee, and breakfast services. Ads in the *Pottery Gazette* in 1899, and 1904 illustrated several patterns on cups and saucers including Two Temples II and Mandarin on ribbed shapes. The company closed from 1941-46, during World War II. It reopened with a new title: Hughes (Fenton) Ltd. and closed again in 1953.
Type of Willow Manufactured: Two Temples II and Mandarin patterns transfer-printed in blue underglaze and Two Temples II pattern in gold on glaze with colored enamels.

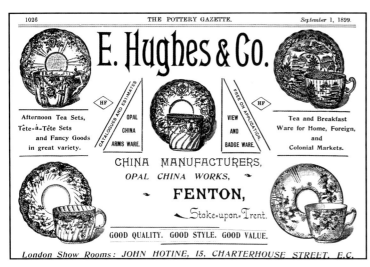

Ad from September 1, 1899, *Pottery Gazette* showing a Two Temples II cup and saucer in the upper right hand corner. The saucer has a wavy edge and the cup is ribbed.

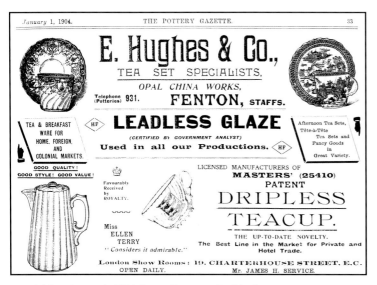

Ad from January 1, 1904, *Pottery Gazette* with a Mandarin pattern cup and saucer in the upper right hand corner. The saucer has a wavy edge, and both pieces have a swirled molding with ribs.

Two Temples II pattern 6-inch plate in bone china decorated with gold on a blue ground and added enamel colors. This 8-sided plate also has a heavy gold line at the edge of the plate and the edge of the center pattern. Mark 2. *Courtesy Tim and Kim Allen.* $35-55.

Two Temples II pattern bone china coffee set on a bright blue ground. The decoration over the glaze includes a lot of red as well as lavish gold application. Mark 1. *Courtesy IWC Convention 2000.* $250+.

Mandarin pattern trio transfer-printed in light blue underglaze on bone china. The plate measures 6.75-inches. The shapes are plain compared to the 1904 version in the ad. Mark 1. *Author's Collection.* $20-30.

Thomas Hughes & Son (Ltd.)

Location: Unicorn Works, Longport, Staffordshire
Dates: c. 1894-1957
Marks:

Mark 1 (GG2122)
c. 1895-1910

Brief History: Thomas Hughes had a pottery at Waterloo Road Burslem from 1866-94. After acquiring the former Davenport Unicorn Pottery in Longport in

1894, he changed locations and took his son into business with him. He retired in 1899. His son Allan continued in business and kept the title of Thomas Hughes & Son. In 1910, it became a limited company. The firm produced earthenware and ironstone wares for the American market. When the firm closed, the Unicorn Works were taken over by Arthur Wood & Son*.

Type of Willow Manufactured: Standard Willow pattern transfer-printed in blue and brown underglaze on earthenware.

Mark 2 (GG2122)
c. 1895-1910

Mark 3 (GG2125)
c. 1935-57

John Hulme & Sons

Location: Harvey Works, Lane End, Staffordshire
Dates: c. 1827-31
Mark:

c. 1827-31

Comments Concerning Mark: This initial mark could pertain to several different potteries; however, Geoffrey Godden suggested to me that John Hulme is a possibility.

Brief History: The Hulme firm occupied the Harvey's Works at Great Charles Street until 1831, when John Hulme died. His son-in-law John Hawley succeeded him. Blue printed earthenware has been documented produced by John Hulme & Sons.

Type of Willow Manufactured: Standard Willow pattern transfer-printed underglaze in blue on earthenware or lightweight stoneware.

Standard Willow pattern plate transfer-printed in blue underglaze on earthenware. Each side of the plate has a molded flower pattern that is trimmed in gold. Mark 1. *Courtesy Louise and Charles Loehr.* $40-60.

Standard Willow pattern 10.25-inch plate transfer-printed in blue underglaze on lightweight stone china. There are eight slight indentations at the edge of the flat rim. Three-point stilt marks in the center of the plate show on the back with single marks on the front. It has a recessed foot ring. There is a half-inch glaze skip just above the lower willow branches on the left. *Author's Collection.* $15-25.

Standard Willow pattern shallow rimmed bowl transfer-printed in brown underglaze on earthenware. As with many bowls, this one has no inner border. Mark 2. *Courtesy Louise and Charles Loehr.* $12-18.

William Hulme

Location: Royal Leighton and Argyle Potteries, Burslem, Staffordshire
Dates: c. 1948-54.
Mark:

(GG2131)
c. 1948-54

Brief History: William Hulme was the proprietor of the Leighton Pottery Ltd.* from 1948-54; however, the pottery operated before that time. See the entry for Leighton Pottery Ltd.* for more information. The advertisement in *Pottery Gazette and Glass Trade Review,* October 1951, claims "Manufacturers of High Class Semi-Porcelain". It is safe to assume that if there is a descriptive word before the word "porcelain" in a mark, the piece is not true porcelain. In this case the mark has "Imperial Porcelain". Judging from the list of overseas agents in the ad, the company had a widespread export business.

Type of Willow Manufactured: Standard Willow pattern printed in blue and pink on thin earthenware. The advertisement states: "Popular favourite. On Cottage and Rex shapes in blue and pink. In sets or open stock." I have seen only the blue.

Full page color advertisement in October 1951 *Pottery Gazette and Glass Trade Review*. It shows an interesting use of motifs from the Willow pattern with a pagoda structure at the top right with a piece of the border pattern. Three small drawings of a bridge with a figure add to the presentation of the Willow pattern pieces.

Standard Willow pattern 9.75-inch plate blue printed on thin earthenware. Three single stilt marks on the back of the flat rim near the edge. The plate has a single foot ring. *Author's Collection.* $12-25.

Hulse & Adderley

Location: Daisy Bank Works, Longton, Staffordshire
Dates: c. 1869-75
Mark:

c. 1869-75

Comments Concerning Mark: The word "England" would not normally appear on a mark prior to 1891. In 2001 a collector purchased a partial set of Willow pattern dishes. The form of the mark was as above; however, three different sets of initials were found on the pieces: W. A. A., H. & A. and H. N. & A. – all with the word "England" added. Evidently the original engravings were used, but the dishes were produced after 1891. The original marks were used adding the word "England".
Brief History: The firm preceding this partnership at Daisy Bank Works was Hulse, Nixon & Adderley*; however, John Nixon died in 1869. Hulse & Adderley continued to work the pottery until 1876 when it was taken over by William Alsager Adderley*. The firm produced earthenware for the most part. China production was added.
Type of Willow Manufactured: Standard Willow pattern transfer-printed in blue underglaze on earthenware.

Standard Willow pattern 8.25-inch plate transfer-printed in blue underglaze on earthenware. With no white space between borders, the pattern gives a very crowded appearance. *Courtesy IWC Convention 2001.* $10-15.

Hulse, Nixon & Adderley

Location: Daisy Bank Works, Longton, Staffordshire
Dates: c, 1853-1868
Mark:

c. 1853-68

Brief History: Richard Booth Hulse, John Nixon and Rupert Adderley were partners until 1857 when Rupert Adderley was succeeded by William Alsager Adderley who may have been his son. The firm

purchased the lease of the Daisy Bank Pottery from C. J. Mason*.
Type of Willow Manufactured: Standard Willow pattern transfer-printed in blue underglaze on earthenware.

Standard Willow pattern handled dish transfer-printed in blue underglaze on earthenware. This dish measures 5.5-by-7.75-inches and would have had a lid. Again we have a crowded pattern with no white space between the two borders. *Courtesy Bill and Joyce Keenan.* $40-60.

Standard Willow pattern tureen transfer-printed underglaze in blue on earthenware. It measures 8-by-10.75-inches. The lid has the outer border, and the inner border was used at the base of the tureen. The pattern is good and clear on this impressive piece. *Courtesy Bill and Joyce Keenan.* $200+.

Industrial Pottery

Location: Grangepans, Bo'ness, Scotland
Dates: c. 1892-94
Mark:

c. 1892-94

Brief History: Known by several different names including the Bo'ness Industrial Co-operative Pottery and Manufacturing Society, Limited, it is usually referred to as the Industrial Pottery. In 1887, the Scottish Wholesale Co-operative Society began discussing the building of a pottery. The Bo'ness site on the banks of the river Forth was chosen the following year, but construction did not begin until 1891. Production began in 1892, but the pottery ran at a loss from the start as it was never able to achieve full production. The ideals of the society were to co-operatively recognize the interests of capital, labor, and trade. Unfortunately the management of the pottery was not successful in working out funding to achieve their goals. The products were utilitarian white earthenware for the low end of the market. Decoration was transfer-printed and painted.
Type of Willow Manufactured: Standard Willow pattern transfer-printed in blue underglaze on earthenware.

Standard Willow pattern 10.5-inch plate transfer-printed in blue underglaze on earthenware. The center pattern is quite small. The edge is scalloped, and the white section of the plate has deep flutes. *Courtesy Henry Kelly. Photo by Douglas Leishman.* $40-60.

James Jamieson & Co.

Location: Bo'ness Pottery, Scotland
Dates: 1826-59
Marks:

Mark 1 c. 1826-59

Comments Concerning Marks: The only difference between the two marks is the placement of the ribbon containing the initials J. J. & Co. Mark 2 has the same placement as the mark shown under Bo'ness Pottery*.
Brief History: Bo'ness was a prosperous port on the south bank of the river Forth. Founded in 1766, the pottery had a long history before it was taken over by James Jamieson in 1826. He died in 1829. His infant son inherited the pottery, which was run by members of the family. The Jamieson period was a very successful one for the pottery. Very good quality printed earthenware was made. Some sponge wares were also produced but not many were marked, so they are not known. Jamieson died in 1859 and the pottery was sold to John Marshall.

Mark 2 c. 1826-59

Type of Willow Manufactured: Standard Willow pattern tableware transfer-printed in blue underglaze on earthenware.

Standard Willow pattern 10.5-inch plate transfer-printed in blue underglaze on earthenware. Mark 1. *Courtesy Henry Kelly. Photo by Douglas Leishman.* $30-50.

H. & R. Johnson (Ltd.)

Location: Crystal Tile Works, Cobridge and Highgate Tile Works, Tunstall, Staffordshire
Dates: 1901-present (2003)
Mark: H. & R. J. ENGLAND TRADE MARK

Brief History: The company has been at the Crystal Tile Works from 1901 to the present and at the Highgate Tile Works from 1916. There have been many mergers and amalgamations over the years. The firm now trades as H. & R. Johnson-Richards Ltd. It has become the largest tile producer incorporating such names as the Campbell Tile Co., T. & R. Boote, and Minton Hollins Ltd.* The company has produced tile exhibits at the Gladstone Pottery Museum*.
Type of Willow Manufactured: Standard Willow pattern blue decal overglaze with abbreviated border pattern.

Johnson Bros. Ltd.

Location: Hanley Pottery (and other Hanley Potteries) and Tunstall, Staffordshire
Dates: 1883-present (2003)
Marks:

Comments Concerning Marks: Marks 1-3 appear in the color of the pattern: i.e. blue mark on blue willow and red mark on red willow. Marks 4 & 5 are dark gray and black. Marks 6 & 7 are green. Mark 5 is a Royal Warrant backstamp. Johnson Bros. first received a Royal Warrant in 1970 and has remained a recipient of this honorary award for consistent quality and customer service. Willow was one of the patterns so honored.
Brief History: The first site of the Johnson Bros. business was at Charles Street, Hanley, a factory established by William Mallor in 1758. Several other potters used the facilities – the last being the J. W. Pankhurst Co. That company went bankrupt in 1882, and went into receivership. The Charles Street pottery was purchased by Alfred, and Frederick George Johnson. The new firm of Johnson Bros. began production in 1883, continuing the white ironstone wares that had previously been made at the factory. There were two more brothers. Robert Lewis joined the partnership in 1888. He became the company's representative in America, and spent most of his life there. Henry James joined the partnership in 1893. He had been apprenticed in 1868 to his uncles James and George Meakin, * master potters of the Eagle Works in Hanley.

The Hanley Pottery was built in 1888. The Alexandra Pottery opened in 1889, followed by the Imperial Pottery in 1891. The Trent Sanitary Works opened in 1896, to manufacture sanitary ware. By the beginning of the twentieth century Johnson Bros. owned 4 tableware factories in Hanley, one in Tunstall and one in Cobridge. Sons of the original partners gradually joined the company, which continues to be run by descendants of the original owners. Semi-porcelain was developed for use on dinnerware such as the flow blue patterns that were produced from about 1891 into the twentieth century. Many printed patterns became popular using single colors as well as combinations of colors. Colored clay bodies were also developed.

Mark 1 (GG2179)
c. 1913+

Mark 2 (GG2179)
c. 1940+

Mark 3 (GG2179)
c. 1940+

Mark 4 (GG2179)
c. 1970+

Mark 5 c. 1970+

Mark 6 c. 1992+

Mark 7 c. 1992+

Mark 8 c. 1999+

Standard Willow pattern 6-inch tile decorated with decal overglaze in blue. The border is a simplified and enlarged version of the Standard inner border. Marked H. & R. Johnson Ltd., Made in England. *Courtesy Nancee Rogers.* $12-20.

Mark 9 c. 1999+

Production slowed during World Wars I and II; however, production quickly gained momentum after each war. Modernization including converting to gas-fired tunnel kilns occurred in the late 1940s. In 1947 a tableware manufacturing plant was purchased in Ontario, Canada to be used as a decorating unit. Ten years later a similar plant was set up in Croydon near Melbourne, Australia. Johnson Bros. twice won the *Queen's Award to Industry* for export achievement – achieving a level of 70% of total sales.

In 1968, Johnson Bros. was acquired by the Wedgwood Group. The Johnson Bros. name continued in use until it was taken over by the Waterford-Wedgwood Group in the early 1980s. Trade names included "Creative Tableware" and "Bull in a China Shop". The Johnson Bros. name was revived in 1991. In 1992 Johnson Bros. was closed, moving all design groups to Barlaston. Tableware continues to be produced and exported to all parts of the world.

Type of Willow Manufactured: Standard Willow pattern transfer-printed in blue and pink on earthenware and ironstone. The factory name for the color is pink; however, it is called red by collectors. Red willow was discontinued in 1965. According to information in Mark 7 above and the "Willow Blue" brochure, willow has been produced since 1940.

Standard Willow pattern bowls transfer-printed in blue underglaze on earthenware. Neither of these shapes is currently being made. The tab-handled bowl has Mark 1, and the square bowl with indented edges has Mark 4. *Author's Collection.* $8-12 each.

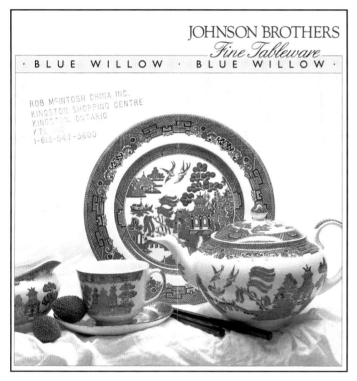

Johnson Bros. brochure distributed by Rob McIntosh China Inc., Kingston, Ontario, Canada, in 1997, showing the then current production pieces in Blue Willow tableware. The teapot (and coffee pot) have no printed mark: just impressed MADE IN ENGLAND.

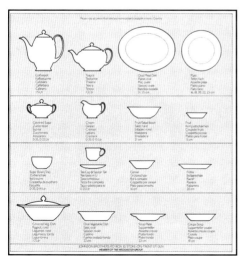

Back of Johnson Bros. 1997 brochure illustrating shapes available in Blue Willow pattern at that time. Of interest are the descriptions of each shape in five different languages. This demonstrates the worldwide availability of Blue Willow tableware.

Standard Willow pattern gravy transfer-printed in red underglaze on earthenware. This double spouted gravy boat has an attached under tray. Mark 1. *Courtesy Daisy and Tom Eden.* $35-55.

Standard Willow pattern pitcher transfer-printed in red underglaze on earthenware. Mark 1. *Courtesy IWC Convention 1993.* $45-65.

New molded pagoda-shaped teapot representing Standard Willow pattern. According to the brochure, the pieces in this "Willow Blue" series are designed in England and hand-painted in the Philippines. I wonder if the Beswick molded ware teapots of the late 1930s were inspiration for this series. *Courtesy Paul Kirves and Zeke Jimenez.* $30-40.

Willow Blue COLLECTABLES

Welcome to the Willow Blue Collectables Club

This collection has been influenced by the oriental love story as depicated on the famous Willow Blue Tableware introduced by Johnson Brothers in 1940.

Originally a family business, Johnson Brothers was founded in 1883 when Frederick and Alfred Johnson, grandsons of a master potter decided to go into business together.

Located in Staffordshire, England, the business soon established a reputation for innovation and practicality.

Today that reputation still remains firm and Johnson Brothers remain committed to the highest standards of craftsmanship.

This hand painted piece has been produced with the above reassurances and has been endorsed by Christopher Johnson a descendant of the original family.

Christopher Johnson

Designed in England, hand painted in the Philippines

JOHNSON BROS
A Member of the
Wedgwood Group

Johnson Bros is a registered trademark of Josiah Wedgwood & Sons Limited, Barlaston, Stoke-on-Trent ST12 9ES

Brochure enclosed with pieces in the "Willow Blue" series including cookie jar, tea sets, shakers, and toast racks. It gives a little background information of the Johnson Brothers firm.

A. B. Jones (& Sons (Ltd.))

Location: Grafton Works (and other addresses) Longton, Staffordshire
Dates: c. 1880-1972
Marks:

Comments Concerning Marks: Mark 1 is green overglaze. Mark 2 is black overglaze. Mark 3 is found in blue underglaze, occasionally with a large number and in black overglaze. Mark 4 is found in blue underglaze, occasionally with a large number and in green overglaze. Mark 5 is found in black overglaze. I don't know the significance of the large numbers. A number 2 can appear on a cup with one mark and on a plate with a different mark. Mark 1 must have been used for a long period of time. Cereal bowls with that mark are identical to bowls with Mark 4.

Brief History: Alfred Bailey Jones was in business by himself at the Eagle Works, Station Square, Longton until 1899. In January 1, 1900 he took his two sons W. B. and A. B. Jones into partnership with him and moved to the Grafton Works, Marlborough Road, Longton. The company produced good quality bone china breakfast, tea, dessert, and dinnerware. The company also produced souvenir and crested ware. A. B. Jones & Sons became a limited company in 1955. Crown House purchased the business in 1966. In 1972 the name was changed to Royal Grafton Bone China Ltd.

Type of Willow Manufactured: Standard Willow pattern transfer-printed in light blue underglaze on bone china. Booths willow pattern hand painted underglaze on earthenware has also been found.

Retailer/importer: Gibson & Patterson Ltd.*, Wellington, New Zealand

Mark 1 (GG2195)
c. 1913+

Mark 2 (GG2196)
c. 1920+

Mark 3 (GG2197)
c. 1930+

Mark 4 (GG2199)
c. 1949+

Mark 5 (GG2199)
c. 1949+

Standard Willow pattern place setting transfer-printed in light blue underglaze on bone china. Note the indented square plate and the linear pattern on the inside of the cup. All pieces are trimmed in gold. The cup has a number 9 handle. Mark 3. *Courtesy Marguerite Smith.* $25-40.

Standard Willow pattern cups with 8-inch plate showing more cup shapes by A. B. Jones & Sons. The ring handle cup is found in two sizes: 3 1/8 and 2 5/8-inches high. The other cup on round foot is 2.5-inches high. All cups have Mark 4, and the plates have Mark 4 or 5. *Author's Collection.* $10-20 each cup and saucer set.

Standard Willow pattern teapot, creamer, and open sugar transfer-printed in blue underglaze on bone china with gold trim. The shapes are lovely but the sugar and creamer are a different shape from the teapot. The four pieces were purchased together along with several tea plates, cups, saucers, and a booklet with the Willow Legend. The second paragraph in the booklet states, "Myott, Son & Co. Ltd. have made a specialty in this line in their well-known 'Royal Grafton' Bone China." Please see the entry for Myott, Son & Co. for more information on a possible connection between these two firms including a mark with the names of both. *Author's Collection.* $200-300.

Standard Willow pattern pair of double egg cups transfer-printed in light blue on bone china. Trimmed in gold. The pattern placement has solved the dilemma of having to decide in which end to put your egg. The pattern on the cup holding the egg will be right side up no matter which end you choose. *Author's Collection.* $20-25 each.

A. E. Jones (& Co.) (see also Palissy Pottery Ltd.)

Location: Palissy Pottery, Longton, Staffordshire
Dates: c. 1905-46
Mark:

ENGLAND

(GG2203)
c. 1908-36

Comments Concerning Mark: This mark was used during the A.E. Jones period and also later by Palissy Pottery Ltd.* Style and pattern are the only guides to assigning the period of the ware.
Brief History: Albert E. Jones produced dinnerware in earthenware and semi-porcelain for the home and export markets. Well-modeled shapes and patterns were introduced in the early twentieth century including some with Chinese and other Oriental influences. In 1930 the name changed to Albert E. Jones Ltd. Toilet services and other miscellaneous useful items were added to production. In 1946 the firm was renamed Palissy Pottery Ltd.*
Type of Willow Manufactured: Polychrome and blue decals based on the Two Temples II pattern on earthenware.

Two cup teapot decorated in a polychrome decal based on the Two Temples II pattern. There is a border made up of willow pattern motifs at the top of the teapot and on the lid. The earthenware teapot has gold trim. *Courtesy Charles Hollingsworth.* $45-75.

Biscuit jar with silver lid and handle decorated with a polychrome decal based on the Two Temples II pattern. The willow motif border appears in full on the side. Small motifs decorate the collar of the biscuit jar. *Courtesy IWC Convention 2000.* $145-95.

Sugar shaker that stands 5.5-inches tall decorated in a polychrome decal based on the Two Temples II pattern. The body shape matches the biscuit jar, and it has a silver lid. *Courtesy IWC Convention 1999.* $35-55.

low" from 1923-34. Jones responded to popular demand and produced wares that appealed to collectors. Unfortunately sales began a decline after 1927, and he was bankrupt by June 1934.

Type of Willow Manufactured: Booths Willow variant in blue and several different polychrome combinations. A. G. Harley Jones' name for the pattern was "Ye Old Chinese Willow". Worcester Willow variant transfer-printed in blue with clobbering and in gold over-glaze on a dark blue ground. A number of Chinoiserie patterns were made in gold on different colored grounds.

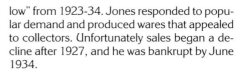

Mark 2
(GG2212)
c. 1923-34

Mark 3
(GG2212)
c. 1923-34

Booths Willow variant pattern identical to "Real Old Willow" transfer-printed in blue underglaze on earthenware. The coffee pot is 7.5-inches tall and has gold trim. Mark 3. *Courtesy Charles and Zeta Hollingsworth.* $75-150.

Pitcher decorated with blue decal based in the Two Temples II pattern. The willow motif border is at the top of the jug, and it has gold trim. *Courtesy Paul Kirves and Zeke Jimenez.* $35-65.

A. G. Harley Jones

Location: Royal Vienna Art Pottery (and other addresses), Fenton, Staffordshire
Dates: c. 1907-34
Marks:

Brief History: This company is listed as having made china as well as earthenware. Production before 1920, centered on ornamental wares. In the early 1920s, earthenwares and crested china were added to help diversify production. A. G. Harley Jones expanded his pottery at this time. All of the willow variants were produced on earthenware. The firm produced a pattern identical to Booths "Real Old Wil-

Mark 1 (GG2208)
c. 1907+

Booths ROW variant pattern 9.75-inch plate in brown underglaze clobbered with yellow, rust, green, and cobalt blue. The wavy edge of this plate is trimmed in gold. Mark 3. This is the first example of this color combination that has surfaced. *Courtesy Charles and Zeta Hollingsworth.* $45-95.

Booths ROW variant pattern vases with blue ground and polychrome pattern overglaze. The two 10.5-inch vases have the willow tree pattern front and back with the birds missing on the back. The 6.25-inch vase shows the teahouse on one side and the willow tree on the other. Mark1. *Courtesy Paul Kirves and Zeke Jimenez.* $100-150 large and $75-100 small.

Polychrome Booths ROW pattern decorated ginger jars on a white background. The jars also have gold trim. The pattern is the same on the two pieces. They are turned to show the entire pattern. The ginger jars are 6.15 and 10-inches tall. Mark 3. *Courtesy Paul Kirves and Zeke Jimenez.* $75-125 and $125-175.

Worcester Willow variant pattern platter transfer-printed underglaze in blue on earthenware with clobbering overglaze. The platter measures 11-by-14.5-inches. Mark 2. The Worcester Willow pattern has also been seen in gold over the glaze on a blue ground with Mark 1. *Author's Collection.* $45-65.

George Jones (& Sons Ltd.)

Location: Trent Pottery and Crescent Pottery, Stoke, Staffordshire
Dates: c. 1861-1951
Marks:

Comments Concerning Marks: Mark 2 is also found with Stoke-on-Trent in place of England. The crescent and initial part of the mark is found impressed as well as printed. I have an 8-inch plate with printed Mark 1 with England at the bottom, impressed Mark 2 and impressed date 5/09.

Brief History: In 1861, George Jones purchased copper engraved plates at an auction of more than 5 tons of copper plates from the bankrupt business of Adams & Sons, Stoke. Many patterns including willow were purchased even though Jones was still looking for a vacant factory in which to set up his pottery business. George Jones was at the Trent Pottery until 1907 producing a wide variety of majolica pieces as well as earthenware and porcelain wares. The business moved to Crescent Pottery in 1907. Tableware, tea ware, dessert services, toilet sets, and decorative pieces were produced with underglaze, overglaze, printed, lithographed, and hand-painted decoration.

Blue-printed wares were produced until the late 1860s, when their popularity had declined. By the 1890s, interest was reawakened and production resumed through the 1930s. The trade

Mark 1 c. 1861-73

Mark 2 (GG2219) c. 1924-51

Mark 3 (GG2219) c. 1924-51

name changed to George Jones & Sons in late 1873. The firm made goods for export as well as the home market as indicated by this quote from *Pottery Gazette*, March 1, 1917: "Great variety of Goods, Useful, and Ornamental, for all markets. Complete Catalogues in English, Spanish, Portuguese, and French on application." And regarding the company's display at the British Industries Fair 1917: "In another corner was the old English blue and white landscape ware, for which there is always a market and of which George Jones & Sons Ltd., are among the best exponents." The blue-printed pattern for which the company is most famous is "Abbey".

Mark 4 (GG2218)
c. 1874-91

Type of Willow Manufactured: Standard Willow pattern transfer-printed in blue underglaze on earthenware. Singan variation of Standard Willow with motifs transfer-printed in blue surrounded by red enamel coloring. In *George Jones Ceramics 1861-1951* Robert Cluett shows a page from a George Jones trade catalog, dated 1924, with a complete line of blue willow dinnerware, yet very little is found.

Standard Willow pattern butter dish insert transfer-printed underglaze in blue. This 4-inch piece is the most commonly found example of blue willow by George Jones. The carved wooden holder is 6-inches across. Mark 2. *Author's Collection.* $45-55.

Standard Willow pattern 8-inch tile transfer-printed underglaze in blue. A little over .25-inch thick, this heavy tile is bigger than a teapot stand. It shows signs of heavy use. The pattern is a little too large for the piece. The inner border covers up the inner edge of the outer border. Mark 1. *Author's Collection.* $40-90.

This butter dish insert is part of a silver breakfast set. The silver tray has a toast rack on either side, a butter dish, and a bell on top. Mark 2. *Courtesy Geoffrey and Eileen Newton.* $125-175.

Standard Willow pattern compote transfer-printed underglaze in blue on earthenware. It is 9-inches in diameter and stands 6-inches high. Mark 2. *Courtesy IWC Convention 1997.* $125-200.

Condiment jar with silver lid in "Singan" pattern. It is 3-inches high. This Willow variant is transfer-printed in blue underglaze. The red enamel is painted around the willow motifs. This type of decoration was popular in the 1920s. *Courtesy Geraldine Ewaniuk.* $55-95.

Standard Willow spirit jugs transfer-printed in blue underglaze on earthenware. Each jug has initials: SW = Scotch Whiskey, B = Brandy, G = Gin, and R = Rum. The jugs are placed in the picture to show the different sides of the pattern. Only one jug is marked with impressed Mark 4. *Courtesy Loren Zeller.* $200+ each.

Jones & Walley

Location: Villa Pottery, Cobridge, Staffordshire
Dates: c. 1841-3
Mark:

c. 1841-3

Comments Concerning Mark: The New Porcelain impressed Mark was seen on the Ebay internet auction site on a Standard Willow pattern drain for a platter

Brief History: This short-lived firm produced various types of earthenware including printed ware and molded jugs. Stock patterns were also produced on ironstone type wares.

Type of Willow Manufactured: Standard Willow pattern transfer-printed in blue underglaze on earthenware. No picture available.

Keele Street Pottery

Location: Keele Street, Tunstall and Meir Airport, Longton, Staffordshire
Dates: c. 1915-67
Mark:

c. 1916-67

Brief History: The firm was established to produce earthenware novelties, figures, children's ware, and tableware for the home market. These kinds of goods had previously been imported from Germany but were not available during World War I. After the war, production continued including export ware. In the late 1940s, the firm began acquiring other pottery businesses. It was renamed the Keele Street Pottery Group. Colorful lithographed wares for the mass market were produced including subjects from children's television programs. The Keele Street Pottery Group moved to the Meir Airport location in 1958.

Type of Willow Manufactured: Polychrome decal based on Two Temples II pattern printed on earthenware in the 1920s.

Advertisement by Keele St. Pottery Co. Ltd. in *Pottery Gazette and Glass Trade Review*, February 1, 1924. The jug at the top right is the same shape as the jug in the following photograph. The lithographic decal based on Two Temples II is seen on the mustard jar below and to the left of the jug.

Dutch shape earthenware pitcher decorated with a polychrome decal based on the Two Temples II pattern. It stands 5.5-inches high and has gold trim. There is no border pattern on this jug – just a small willow motif at the base of the spout. *Author's Collection.* $60-80.

Keeling & Co.

Location: Dale Hall Works, Burslem, Staffordshire
Dates: c. 1886-1936
Marks:

Mark 1
(GG2245)
c. 1912-36

Mark 2
(GG2241)
c. 1886-91

Mark 3
(GG2243)
c. 1886-91

Mark 4
(GG2243)
c. 1886-91

Mark 5
c. 1886-91

Comments Concerning Marks: Marks 3 and 4, with the date 1790, show a potter at work. This is the date the mark was first used at the Dale Hall Works by Bates, Elliott & Co. Other firms used the mark down through the years. "Late Mayers" was added to the mark after the firm of T. J. & J. Mayer, 1843-55. I am including a photograph of Mark 4 engraved on a copper plate along with a Semi China mark in a double square with a diamond and letter 2 (Mark 5). If the Semi China mark is found alone, this documentation can help to give attribution.

Brief History: Keeling & Co. produced a wide range of earthenware including dinnerware, tea ware, kitchenware, toilet ware, and ornamental bowls and vases. Blue printed ware on inexpensive earthenware was popular in the beginning years. "Losol" became the new trademark for the company in 1912. It was described in an article in the *Pottery Gazette*, April 1, 1912, on p. 393:

> The glaze they use contains less than 1 percent of soluble lead and is harmless to the workers. As they found they could work with the "low solubility" glaze, they announce the fact by calling their ware "Losol" a contraction of the words "low solubility."

At the British Industries Fair 1917, Keeling & Co. displayed "Losol" ware fancy articles in the Chinese style. The ware continued to be popular as seen in this comment under Buyer's Notes in *Pottery Gazette* April 1, 1926:

> A feature of the 'Losol' decorations is, perhaps, the combination of enameling with stippled gilding, in association with cobalt as

a base ... Recently, Keeling & Co. have seriously extended the scope of their decorations ...

Type of Willow Manufactured: Two Temples II pattern transfer-printed underglaze in light blue and dark flow blue on earthenware. Standard Willow variant pattern in blue and in brown with clobbering.

Copper plate engraving of Marks 3, 4, and 5. Having the two marks engraved on the same copper plate ties them together as both being marks of Keeling & Co. *Courtesy Ann Dworken.* NP

Two Temples II pattern 8-inch plate transfer-printed underglaze in flow blue on earthenware. It has printed Mark 2 plus impressed B/ L2=02 which is probably a date mark. *Author's Collection.* $15-25.

Reversed Two Temples II pattern 6-cup teapot transfer-printed in blue underglaze on earthenware called semi china. It is a rectangular shape, and has gold trim including a row of gold dots on the shoulder. It bears Mark 5 that probably relates to Keeling & Co. *Courtesy Harry and Jessie Hall.* $125-175.

Two Temples II pattern reversed 12 oz. jug transfer-printed underglaze in flow blue on earthenware. The jug is 4.5-inches high, octagonal in shape, and has a serpent handle with gold trim. It has Mark 3 with the partial pattern name "Broseley" above the figure. *Author's Collection.* $135-175.

Two Teapots transfer-printed in reversed Two Temples II pattern. The pattern is so large that only half of it is seen on one side with the rest of the pattern on the other. By facing the teapots toward each other the full pattern can be seen. Both teapots are octagonal with gold trim and have Mark 4. The light blue printed teapot is 6-cup capacity. *Author's Collection.* $100-150. The flow blue teapot holds 7 or 8 cups. *Courtesy Joette Hightower.* $150-200.

Standard Willow variant pattern 9.75-inch plate transfer-printed in brown with clobbering overglaze. It has Mark I with pattern name Willow and number 5469. When this pattern is found in blue it does not always have the maker's mark. *Author's Collection.* $65-100.

Samuel Keeling & Co.

Location: Market St., Hanley, Staffordshire
Dates: c. 1840-50
Mark:

Comments Concerning Mark: See William Hackwood* above for the same mark without initials.

c. 1840-50

Brief History: This firm specialized in the production of earthenware. Keeling took over the works that had been in the Glass family. In 1850, when Keeling discontinued his business, the works were taken over by J. & G. Meakin*.

Type of Willow Manufactured: Standard Willow pattern transfer-printed underglaze in blue on earthenware.

Standard Willow pattern small tray transfer-printed in blue underglaze on earthenware. At 5.5-by-7.25-inches, it is probably the under tray for a sauce tureen. *Courtesy IWC Convention 1999.* $35-50.

Kensington Pottery Ltd.

Location: Kensington Works, Hanley, and Trubshaw Cross, Burslem, Staffordshire
Dates: c. 1922-62
Brief History: The company started out producing inexpensive earthenware for everyday use, but added ornamental wares from the 1930s. Modern patterns were introduced and new shapes were added. Chintz patterns were introduced in the 1950s. In 1962 Kensington merged with Price Bros. to form a new company: Price Kensington*. Some wares continued to be made using the Kensington Pottery Staffordshire knot mark.
Type of Willow Manufactured: Standard Willow center pattern variant on decal-decorated tableware. It was advertised as pattern # 863A, but I have not seen it.
Retailer/importer: A. S. Newman & Son* London

Advertisement in *Pottery Gazette,* June 1, 1928, page 892. The Kensington Pottery Ltd. Earthenware for all markets including London, Australia, India, Western States, and Greece. Willow Variant lithograph pattern 863A is shown on a plate and covered dish.

James Kent (Ltd.)

Location: Old Foley Pottery, Longton, Staffordshire
Dates: c. 1897-present (2003)
Marks:

Mark I c. 1913+

Comments Concerning Marks: The Globe marks illustrated in Godden have the word LONGTON whereas the marks found on Willow pattern have FENTON. Longton and Fenton are adjacent, and it is my understanding that the factory was actually geographically located in Fenton. J K L in the marks refers to James Kent Longton. Mark 2 has Ltd. added, and Mark 3 has J. KENT.
Brief History: James Kent served his apprenticeship with his brother-in-law John Tams* at Crown Pottery in Longton. In 1889 he entered into a partnership at Foley Pottery, Longton with Eli Barker and his two sons trading as Barkers & Kent*. James Kent left that partnership after a short time due to a falling out with the partners. He bought the Old Foley Pottery in 1897, and began pottery production there on his own. In 1902, he leased and later purchased part of the Baker pottery in Fenton about a mile from Old Foley. It was used as a mill for grinding china stone and flint as well as producing glazes

Mark 2 c. 1913+

for his and other potteries. In 1913, James Kent became a limited company. In the 1930s, James Kent became semi-retired. His son Peter and daughter Ruth were active in running the pottery, and his other son Philip successfully ran the mill. The family was active in the business until it was sold to Bayer UK Ltd. in 1980. Nine years later James Kent pottery went into receivership and was purchased by M. R. Hadida Ltd. It was renamed James Kent (1989) Ltd. and continues to the present day under the same ownership.

Mark 3 before 1913

Standard Willow pattern square shaped teapot transfer-printed in blue underglaze on earthenware. This four-footed teapot is very ornate for medium-priced ware. The spout and handle are on opposite corners of the body. The outer border is used on the lid and edge of the teapot as well as the shoulder with the fish roe side on the straight edges. The central pattern is in linear form around the teapot. Mark 2 with J K L under the crown. *Courtesy Harry and Jessie Hall.* $150-250.

Even though china was produced, the company is better known for its medium-priced earthenware for household use. James Kent produced blue printed ware but gained a reputation for specializing in floral and chintz patterns. Chintz began as low to medium priced ware in the 1920s. Many patterns were still in production in the 1950s. Oven to table ware was introduced in the 1980s, and gift items were reproduced from earlier times. Due to public demand the current owner reintroduced some chintz patterns in 1998. Due to collector interest these are now prestigious wares.

Type of Willow Manufactured: Standard Willow pattern transfer-printed in blue underglaze on earthenware and polychrome chintz-type sheet pattern with motifs from Standard Willow.

Standard Willow pattern 8.75-inch plate transfer-printed in blue underglaze on earthenware. The flat rim has three single stilt marks on the underside. It has a low recessed foot ring. The border pattern is too large, as seen at 11:00 o'clock. The 3 and 4-spoke wheels overlap one of the Ju-Is. Mark 1. *Author's Collection.* $18-25.

Standard Willow sheet pattern in polychrome 9.5-inch tidbit plate with metal center handle. There is a red painted line around the wavy edge of the plate. This pattern has been found unmarked on many items such as biscuit jar, condiment set, and teapot. A plate has been noted with the mark: James Kent Ltd., Fenton, England. This piece has Mark 3. *Courtesy Geoffrey and Eileen Newton.* $45-65.

Standard Willow pattern large coffee can and saucer transfer-printed in blue underglaze on earthenware. These pieces are thinner than the plate seen above. Mark 2. *Author's Collection.* $12-18.

William Kent (Porcelains) Ltd.

Location: Auckland St., Burslem, Staffordshire
Dates: c. 1944-62
Marks:

Brief History: The firm of William Kent produced ornamental earthenwares through 1962. After that the product was limited to electrical porcelains. The Kents of Burslem was a family firm dating back to 1878. "Old Staffordshire Pottery" was produced including figures and flat backs. Presumably it is from those nineteenth century master molds that modern earthenware figures were made by William Kent. A molded initial mark of "w B k" was used on these reproductions.

Type of Willow Manufactured: Standard Willow pattern transfer-printed in blue on animals and coats on Toby Jugs.

Mark 1 c. 1944-62

Mark 2 (GG2272)
c. 1944-62

A pair of cats, 7.25-inches high, decorated all around with the Standard Willow pattern in linear form. Overglaze colors include red bows, green eyes, black and gray on nose and whiskers as well as green and rust on the stands. This is the first pair of cats to be found. Mark 2. *Courtesy Franklin and Charline Ladner.* NP

R. A. Kidston & Co.

Location: Verreville and Anderston Potteries, Glasgow, Scotland
Dates: c.1835-45
Marks:

Comments Concerning Marks: Mark 2 is confusing because it has the words Staffordshire Ware when it was actually made in Scotland. R. A. K. & Co. initials do not fit any Staffordshire potter. It is unusual to find the impressed anchor with this printed mark. The dolphin wrapped around the anchor in Mark 3 was found at the Verreville site and is prior to Cochran. It may have been used in the brief Montgomery period; however, there is a better chance it was used by Kidston.

Mark 1 c. 1835-45

Mark 2 c. 1835-45

Brief History: Robert Alexander Kidston and his brother William were trained in the pottery trade in Stoke on Trent. When R. A. Kidston returned to Glasgow he took over the Anderston Pottery with various different partners. He owned the Anderston Pottery and a glass works when he also took over the Verreville Pottery after it had gone bankrupt under the leadership of Robert Montgomery*. At the Verreville Pottery, Kidston extended the range of wares and the quality of goods produced. Transfer prints in several colors were made. Soft paste porcelain tea wares with violet sprigs have been identified from excavations on the site. The many changes and increased production outstripped public demand, and by 1841, he was bankrupted. It took until 1845 to get the estate settled.

Type of Willow Manufactured: Standard Willow pattern transfer-printed on earthenware in several shades of blue.

Mark 3 c. 1835-45

Standard Willow pattern decorated coat transfer-printed in blue underglaze on earthenware. This Toby Jug stands 6.5-inches tall. The vest is green and knee britches are yellow. The face is flesh colored with a pleasant expression, and hair is gray. The handle and base are white. It has Mark 1 with the number 368. A Toby Jug with rust colored vest has Mark 2. Unmarked jugs from the late nineteenth century of the same form are just 5.5-inches high. The face is white, and the clothing is colored differently. The base and handle are cobalt blue on the older Jugs as well as on some marked "Made in England". *Courtesy Paul Kirves and Zeke Jimenez.* $250-400.

Standard Willow pattern 10.5-inch plate transfer-printed underglaze in blue on earthenware. The concave rim has a wavy edge. Note the fish tail birds are very close together. Mark 3. *Courtesy Henry Kelly. Photo by Douglas Leishman.* $40-60.

Standard Willow pattern 10.5-inch plate transfer-printed underglaze in blue on earthenware. It has a concave rim and 8-lobed edge. Note the fish tail birds are very close together on this plate. The path is rather narrow. It bears Mark 1. A plate with a wider path bears Mark 2. *Courtesy Henry Kelly. Photo by Douglas Leishman.* $40-60.

Kilncraft
(see Staffordshire Potteries Ltd.)

Roy Kirkham & Co. Ltd.

Location: Lascelles St., Tunstall, Staffordshire
Dates: c. 1980-present (2003)
Mark:

c. 1990s

Brief History: The firm produces bone china mugs. A few blue willow mugs were produced in the early 1980s, but sales were low in relation to other patterns available to them.
Type of Willow Manufactured: Standard Willow pattern blue printed on bone china.

Standard Willow pattern platter transfer-printed underglaze in blue on earthenware. It measures 13 7/8-by-17.25-inches. This platter has Mark 2 with the words Staffordshire Ware and an impressed anchor. The initials R.A.K. & Co. represent the maker: Robert A. Kidston. *Courtesy Bill and Joyce Keenan.* $150-250.

Standard Willow pattern bone china mug with blue printed pattern. *Author's Collection.* $8-15.

Knapper & Blackhurst

Location: Boston Works Sandyford, Tunstall (1867-71) and Dale Hall Pottery, Burslem (1882-87), Staffordshire
Dates: c. 1867-71 and 1882-87
Mark:

c. 1882-87

Comments Concerning Mark: The initials K & B could also refer to Knight & Bridgwood, Longton, c. 1884-86.
Brief History: Stephen Knapper and Jabez Blackhurst worked together at Sandyford from 1867-71. After that Blackhurst continued on his own until 1882 when they took over the Dale Hall Pottery from James Edwards & Sons. Stonewares were made during the second period of their partnership and perhaps the first as well.
Type of Willow Manufactured: Standard Willow pattern transfer-printed in blue on stoneware.

Standard Willow pattern 11.25-by-14.25-inch platter transfer-printed in blue underglaze on stone china. This platter has a combed back. The border patterns are well matched. *Author's Collection.* $75-125.

Standard Willow pattern 10.5-inch plate transfer-printed in blue underglaze on stoneware. The plate has a single flat foot ring. Three-point stilt marks on the underside and three single marks on the front of the plate. There are impurities in the glaze. The willow tree has some extra bare branches to the top and left of the tree. *Author's Collection.* $30-40.

Lancaster & Sons (Ltd.)

Location: Dresden Works, Hanley, Staffordshire
Dates: c. 1900-44
Mark:

(GG2320)
c. 1920+

Comment Concerning Mark: All the examples shown bear this mark.
Brief History: This company produced general domestic earthenware and fancies for a wide market. In the 1920s, many popular styles of decoration were introduced including printed patterns. Teapots, jugs, and miscellaneous extra pieces for the table were made for the home and export markets. These notes from the *Pottery Gazette,* February 1, 1941, describe the wares produced:

> After 1918. Range of table accessories with decorations comprised mainly of either monochrome or multicoloured lithographed transfer prints, applied in conjunction with tint grounds. These litho effects –99% of which are controlled by Lancaster – are so good that they are very much akin to the more expensive treatment of printing and enameling.

Lancaster & Sons Ltd. continued full production throughout World War II. In 1944 a new partnership evolved: Lancaster & Sandland Ltd.* See next entry.
Type of Willow Manufactured: Multi-colored lithograph based on the Two Temples II pattern on plain and colored ground. Other multi-colored lithograph willow variant patterns including the "Red Bridge" variant.

J. K. Knight

Location: The Foley Potteries, Fenton, Staffordshire
Dates: c. 1846-53
Mark:

(GG2306)
c. 1846-53

Brief History: John King Knight succeeded the firm of Knight, Elkin & Co. – a firm in which he had been a partner with George Knight and John King Wood Knight. He produced earthenware and stone china.
Type of Willow Manufactured: Standard Willow pattern transfer-printed in blue underglaze on stone china.

Three-inch earthenware tumbler decorated with polychrome lithograph based on Two Temples II pattern. The tumbler is 2.75-inches in diameter. *Author's Collection.* $10-15.

Globular-shaped biscuit jar decorated with polychrome lithograph based on Two Temples II pattern. It is 6-inches high. The blue ground at the top fades to a lighter shade where the pattern was placed. The piece has 3 feet. The silver handle is impressed EPNS. *Author's Collection.* $135-195.

This 4-inch square biscuit jar has a variant pattern lithograph based on Standard Willow. It has 4 black feet, bright blue shoulder, and pale yellow background for the pattern. There is a silver lid and handle. *Courtesy IWC Convention 1994.* $95-135.

Three pitchers of different sizes, all decorated with the "Red Bridge" decal pattern. These are the only pieces by Lancaster I have seen with this pattern. *Courtesy Louise and Charles Loehr.* $235-295.

Lancaster & Sandland Ltd.

Location: Dresden Works, Hanley, Staffordshire
Dates: c. 1944-70
Marks:

Comments Concerning Marks: Mark 3 is found on small pieces from a condiment set in Pagoda pattern with silver luster. Mark 4 is found on incidental pieces with Pagoda pattern with copper luster.
Brief History: Under the new partnership, the firm continued to produce decorative earthenware pieces, adding luster decoration to the range. New lithograph patterns were used by the company, as well as hand painted patterns. Advertising ware, nursery ware, flower pots, and garden pottery were added to the output.
Type of Willow Manufactured: Standard Willow pattern polychrome lithograph and hand painted copper and silver luster ware with willow motifs.

Mark 1 (GG2328)
c. 1949+

Mark 2 c. 1949+

Mark 3
(GG2331)
c. 1955+

Mark 4 (GG2327)
c. 1949+

Standard Willow simplified pattern polychrome lithograph decorated 3 tier tidbit. The pieces are triangular in shape and trimmed in gold. Mark 1. *Courtesy Paul Kirves & Zeke Jimenez.* $55-75.

Standard Willow simplified pattern polychrome lithograph decorated creamer and open sugar. These pieces are each 2-inches high. The creamer is 3.5-inches across and the sugar is 3.25-inches. Both pieces are trimmed in gold. Mark 1. *Courtesy Tim and Kim Allen.* $25-45.

The same shape and size sugar and creamer as the previous photo. The decoration consists of hand-painted motifs of the Standard Willow pattern in blue, red, and copper luster. The pattern is called Pagoda. The silver holder was made by Yeoman Plate. A number of other items including condiment sets (some decorated in silver luster) can be found in Yeoman Plate holders. Mark 2. *Author's Collection.* $45-65.

Thomas Lawrence Ltd.

Location: Trent Bridge Pottery, Stoke; Falcon Works, and Sylvan Works, Longton, Staffordshire
Dates: c. 1888-1964
Marks:

Mark 1 c. 1928+

Comments Concerning Marks: Wares were not marked before 1920. Mark 2 was found on a dresser set decorated with "Red Bridge" Willow variant pattern.

Brief History: The company was founded in Stoke but moved to the Falcon Works in 1897. Thomas Lawrence specialized in toilet ware, vases, jugs, and novelties for the home and export markets. Tableware was not made. In 1938, the name was changed to Thomas Lawrence (Longton) Ltd. During World War II the firm of Shaw & Copestake moved into the Falcon Works with Thomas Lawrence and continued full production. The arrangement worked well, so they continued to do business together using each other's designs and marking them Falcon Ware or SylvaC. By 1957, Thomas Lawrence was an associate of Shaw & Copestake at the Sylvan Works in Longton. In 1961, both companies moved to the new Sylvan works, and by 1964, were fully merged. The Falcon trademark was no longer used.

Mark 2 (GG2342)
c. 1936+

Type of Willow Manufactured: "Red Bridge" Willow variant lithograph decal overglaze on earthenware toilet ware and dresser sets.

Pottery Gazette, September 1, 1928, p. 1356, a one-half page ad for Falcon Ware Toilet Sets. Tower Shape (4240) on the left is the shape used for the "Red Bridge" Willow variant toilet set.

"Red Bridge" Willow variant decorated wash bowl and pitcher in Tower Shape. This is a different border than is usually seen on this pattern. Dresser sets were also decorated with this pattern. *Courtesy IWC Convention 1997.* $175-195.

Leighton Pottery Ltd.

Location: Orme St., Burslem, Staffordshire
Dates: c. 1940-54
Mark:

c. 1940-54

Brief History: In 1940, Leighton Pottery Ltd. became the title of the firm. Bourne & Leigh* had previously traded at Leighton Pottery from the 1930s. Tableware was produced on earthenware. The engravings for the Standard Willow pattern in blue are very similar to those of Bourne & Leigh; however, examples in my collection are different sizes, so it cannot be determined if the companies used the same copper plates.

Type of Willow Manufactured: Standard Willow pattern transfer-printed in blue underglaze on earthenware.

Standard Willow pattern 9 7/8-inch plate transfer-printed in blue underglaze on earthenware. The plate is round with a single foot ring. The borders are well matched and fit the plate exactly. The white area between borders gives a more pleasing effect than the crowded pattern placement by Bourne & Leigh*. *Author's Collection.* $18-22.

Lingard, Webster & Co. (Ltd.)

Location: Swan Bank Pottery, Tunstall, Staffordshire
Dates: c. 1900-present (2003)
Mark:

(GG2375)
c. 1946+

Brief History: This company specializes in the production of teapots using the colored "Rockingham" type of clays found in the North Staffordshire area. The body is disguised by the application of colored slips and glazes so that it is not evident that white earthenware is not used. According to an article under "Buyer's Notes" on page 528 in the *Pottery Gazette,* May 1, 1915, the effects of the combination of colored slips and glazes for decorating teapots are "so pleasingly and harmoniously inter-related as to present effects which grade from the neat and simple to the florid, and even the gorgeous."

Type of Willow Manufactured: Standard Willow pattern molded into the shape of the teapot resulting in an all-over embossed pattern. It is covered with medium blue glaze and gold trim.

Standard Willow pattern molded into the body of the teapot and covered with a medium blue glaze. It has gold accents on the rims, spout, finial, and handle. *Courtesy Tim and Kim Allen.* $75-125.

William Lowe

Location: Sydney Works, High Street, Longton, Staffordshire
Dates: c. 1874-1930
Marks:

Mark 1 c. 1874-91

Comments Concerning Marks: Mark 3 is attributed to William Lowe on the basis of the initials W L in the center and SYDNEY WORKS in the mark. The words in the banner at the top are CHINA AND EARTHENWARE MANUFACTURERS. GG2435 mark with COURT WARE above the crown is found on the "Red Bridge" Willow variant.

Brief History: William Lowe succeeded the partnership of Tams & Lowe* at St. Gregory's Pottery. The name of the pottery was changed to Sydney Works. William Lowe produced useful earthenwares as well as china of an average quality. Examples of blue willow have been found with two different versions of the nineteenth century garter mark as well as Mark 3, with and without ENGLAND, a mark not documented in Godden.

Mark 2 c. 1874-91

Type of Willow Manufactured: Standard Willow pattern transfer-printed in blue underglaze on earthenware. "Red Bridge" willow decal variant with its usual border has also been found. It was produced in the 1920s.

Mark 3 c. 1874-91

Standard Willow pattern 9.5-inch round plate transfer-printed in blue underglaze on earthenware. Three-point stilt marks on the underside of the center of the plate. It has a slightly recessed foot ring. The rim is concave and tilts upward to the edge. The outer border pattern is too small. Additional 3 and 4 spoke wheels were added at 5 o'clock. Mark 1. *Author's Collection.* $20-25.

James Macintyre & Co. (Ltd.)

Location: Washington Works, Burslem, Staffordshire
Dates: c. 1852-1913
Marks:

Mark 1
(GG2824)
c. 1894-1913

Brief History: James Macintyre formed a short-lived partnership with his brother-in-law William Sadler Kennedy but became the sole owner soon after the formation of the company. Production consisted of high-quality utilitarian ware; however, various technical innovations expanded his horizons. In 1863, he patented methods of turning non-circular forms on the lathe. Glazes were developed such as black jet, and were used by firms producing inexpensive teapots. Decorative clay bodies were also developed.

Mark 2
(GG2822)
c. 1867-94

In 1893, the company began to develop ornamental art ware. Harry Barnard was appointed director of that department. The development of Gesso Faience was not a commercial success. William Moorcroft was hired in March 1897. Aurelain Ware, a new shape and decoration, was the first of many innovations developed by Moorcroft. After Barnard left later in 1897, Macintyre encouraged Moorcroft to continue his exploration of underglaze color and slip-trailed decoration. This range was so successful that Moorcroft left in 1913, to establish his own pottery. After that date, the Macintyre firm concentrated on producing electrical porcelain.

Type of Willow Manufactured: Accessory items in Two Temples II reversed pattern transfer-printed underglaze in blue on earthenware. A supplement to the Pottery Gazette in the late 19th century showed a Standard Willow pattern plate with reticulated edge in an ad with other types of wares offered. Examples have not surfaced to date.

Two Temples II reversed pattern 7-inch pot for coffee or hot chocolate. A 7-inch jug matching the shape of this pot with the same handle and pattern arrangement is seen in a Macintyre Catalogue c. 1902. The shape is Lorne and pattern is B 1519. My 7-inch jug has #B1520/1. The Rd. No. 308931 on this pot with Mark 1 is for the year 1897. *Courtesy Louise and Charles Loehr.* $275-325.

Two Temples II reversed pattern biscuit barrel transfer-printed in blue underglaze on earthenware. It has a silver lid and handle. Mark 2. *Courtesy Louise and Charles Loehr.* $175-200.

Charles W. McNay & Sons

Location: Bridgeness Pottery, Bo'ness, Scotland
Dates: c. 1886-1959
Mark:

c. 1888-91

Comment Concerning the Mark: The circle around the initials CW is impressed – not printed.

Brief History: Charles W. McNay, former manager of the Bo'ness Pottery founded the nearby Bridgeness Pottery in 1886, when the former had fallen on hard times. Production was underway by 1888, with 5 kilns and the latest machinery. The factory was successful from the start, employing 200 workers. Charles' brother George was the manager. Materials were purchased from Bo'ness Pottery, and the new firm acquired many former customers from there as well. Transfer-printed patterns on white earthenware were used in the production of tableware. Other means of decorating were added later. Charles died in 1913, leaving his sons Josiah and Charles to run the pottery. After Josiah's death in 1941, Charles was sole owner until the pottery closed in 1959.

Type of Willow Manufactured: Standard Willow pattern transfer-printed in blue underglaze on earthenware.

Standard Willow pattern 9.5-inch soup plate transfer-printed in blue underglaze on earthenware. The printing is a little blotchy with smudges of blue in the white area between the borders. Three-point stilt marks on the back of the rim with single stilt marks on the front. It has a single flat foot ring. *Author's Collection.* $15-20.

Advertisement on page 876 of *Pottery Gazette,* July 1, 1920, listing the types of ware produced and the markets served. Note the name of the firm was retained after the death of Charles W. McNay.

Joseph Machin

Location: Holehouse Works at the end of Waterloo Road, Burslem, Staffordshire
Dates: c. 1802-18
Brief History: The porcelains made by this firm are rarely marked. Philip Miller identifies the teapot in Plate 1363 of *An Anthology of British Teapots* as Machin c. 1810.
Type of Willow Manufactured: The teapot noted above is transfer-printed in blue underglaze in the Two Temples I pattern. No picture available.

Machin & Co.

Location: Holehouse Works at the end of Waterloo Road, Burslem, Staffordshire
Dates: c, 1812-1818 and 1828-30
Brief History: This firm almost certainly relates to Joseph Machin. The & Co. probably refers to Baggaley, at least in the later period. Philip Miller identifies the teapot in Plate 1546 of *An Anthology of British Teapots* as Machin & Co. c. 1820. It bears a pattern number 316
Type of Willow Manufactured: The teapot noted above is transfer-printed in blue underglaze in the Two Temples I pattern. No picture available.

Machin & Potts

Location: Waterloo Pottery, Burslem, Staffordshire
Dates: c. 1834-38
Mark:

c. 1834-38

Brief History: This partnership of William Machin and William Wainwright Potts produced earthenware and china. The firm secured patents for various printing processes including single-color and multi-color printing. The mark shown here relates to the patent for transfer printing by roller, using continuous paper rather than separate copper plates and individual sheets of paper. This type of process would be more commercially viable when used with sheet patterns. It might also have been used in printing common patterns such as willow.
Type of Willow Manufactured: Standard Willow pattern transfer-printed in blue underglaze on earthenware.

Standard Willow pattern 19 3/8-by-15 1/8-inch platter transfer-printed in blue underglaze on earthenware. It is not known if an engraved roller and continuous paper were used to produce such a large platter. The invention is more likely to have been used on dinner plates. *Courtesy Rodney and Eileen Hampson.* $125-175.

Machin & Thomas

Location: Burslem, Staffordshire
Dates: c. 1831-32
Mark:

c. 1831-32

Brief History: William Machin and William Thomas were partners for a short time producing earthenware and china in Burslem. The initials M & T. are thought to have been used by this firm.
Type of Willow Manufactured: Two Temples II pattern transfer-printed in blue underglaze on earthenware.

Two Temples II pattern mug transfer-printed in blue underglaze on earthenware. It measures 3 7/8 high and 3 7/8 wide. It has a wraparound pattern so that the bridge and willow tree are seen on this side and the two temples on the opposite side. *Author's Collection.* $50-100.

John Maddock & Son(s) (Ltd.)

Location: Newcastle St., Burslem, Staffordshire
Dates: c. 1855-1982
Marks:

Comments Concerning Marks: Mark 5 is a combination of a willow mark superimposed on top of the lion and banner mark which is Mark 4.
Brief History: John Maddock & Son succeeded John Maddock who was in business by himself from 1842-55. This large firm produced a wide range of excellent quality earthenware and stoneware with an extensive export market. In 1876, after a trip to America, James Maddock, head of the firm at that time, enlarged the factory and number of employees to over 600. Useful wares rather than ornamental wares were the mainstay of the company. Vitrified hotel ware was added to the range.

By 1896, the firm traded as John Maddock & Sons Ltd. although "Ltd." was not always added to the marks. In the early 1980s, the name was changed to Maddock Hotelware – a division of Royal Stafford China Ltd. In 1985, Maddock was incorporated into Churchill Hotelware Ltd.
Type of Willow Manufactured: Standard Willow pattern transfer-printed in blue on hotel ware; transfer-printed in brown underglaze with clobbering in cobalt, two shades of green, yellow, orange, and reddish brown on vitreous earthenware; polychrome lithographic decal with abbreviated border and gold trim on thin porcelain-type earthenware.

Mark 1 (GG2464)
c. 1896+

Mark 2 (GG2465)
c. 1896+

Mark 3 c. 1896+

Mark 4 (GG2475)
c. 1961+

Mark 5 (GG2475) + willow mark
c. 1961+

Retailers/importers: Burley & Co., Chicago, Illinois*, H. Friedman & Sons, NY*

Standard Willow pattern partial dessert set transfer-printed in brown underglaze with clobbering in cobalt, two shades of green, yellow, orange, reddish brown, and gold trim. There are twelve 9.25-inch plates, two covered jugs, 8-cup teapot, and stand. Mark 1. This colorful willow, dubbed "Royal Willow" by Maddock is rarely seen. *Courtesy Loren Zeller.* $400+.

Standard Willow pattern cup and saucer transfer-printed in blue on heavy hotel ware. The saucer has Mark 2 and the cup has Mark 3. *Author's Collection.* $12-15.

Standard Willow pattern pot transfer-printed in blue on hotel ware. The pot is 2.5-inches high and 3-inches across. Note the molded head used for a handle. This form of handle is occasionally seen on small pieces of Maddock hotel ware. *Courtesy Harry and Jessie Hall.* $30-45.

Standard Willow pattern polychrome decal overglaze on place setting. Note the wear on the small plate because the decoration is overglaze. The borders have been simplified with only the geometrical motifs used from the outer border. The placement forms a square on the small plate and saucer and a six-pointed star on the dinner plate. The clay body is thin like china, but it is not translucent. All pieces are lined with gold. Marks 4 and 5. *Author's Collection.* $75-85.

Type of Willow Manufactured: Standard Willow pattern transfer-printed in light blue underglaze on earthenware. Mandarin pattern transfer-printed in light and dark blue underglaze on earthenware was also produced.

Mandarin pattern trio transfer-printed in light blue underglaze on earthenware. The plate is 7-inches across. Mark 1 with impressed date 12 89 for December 1889. *Author's Collection.* $20-30.

C. T. Maling

Location: Ouseburn Bridge Pottery (1853-59), and A & B Ford Potteries (1859-90), Newcastle upon Tyne
Dates: c. 1853-90
Marks:

Mark 1 (GG2486a)
c. 1859-90

Comments Concerning Marks: In *Tyneside Pottery*, R. C. Bell shows impressed marks C. T. MALING, MALING, and a printed wreath and bell mark found on Standard Willow pattern plates that probably date to c. 1859.

Brief History: Christopher Thompson Maling succeeded his father Robert Maling at the Ouseburn Bridge Pottery in 1853. In 1857, C. T. married Mary Ford, and in 1859, he built Ford (A) Pottery, Ouseburn – named in her honor. It occupied two acres of land and was equipped with the newest machinery and processes. The new factory could produce more in a week than the two-kiln factory of his father could produce in a year. The output consisted of jam pots, jars, and

Mark 2 (GG2487)
c. 1859-90

bottles for potted meats and dairy products. C. T. Maling made enough money to invest £100,000 in building a huge factory (B) a half-mile away on 14 acres in Walker. Factory (B) was the largest and most complete pottery in Britain. All processes used in the converting of raw materials into finished products were carried on in the factory. The flint mill was the largest and best in the country for many years. It ground more than enough flint for use at the pottery, and a great deal was exported. In addition to pots and jars, the firm began to produce tableware, and toilet ware.

C. T. Maling set up a free school at the Ford (A) Pottery before the Education Act of 1870. He also established free soup kitchens. In 1889, C. T. Maling took his three sons, John Ford Maling, Christopher Thompson Maling junior, and Frederick Theodore Maling into partnership, gradually turning over control of the business to them. He retired in 1899. In 1901 C. T. Maling died.

Mandarin pattern 4-cup teapot with infuser transfer-printed in light blue underglaze on earthenware. The edges are trimmed in gold. The infuser is a separate piece that sits in the teapot before putting on the lid. Without the infuser, the lid would sit flat like the one in the next picture. Rd.No.100,732 is on the infuser, dating it to 1888. Mark 1. *Courtesy IWC Convention 2000.* $100-165.

Mandarin pattern 6-cup teapot and stand transfer-printed in dark blue underglaze on earthenware. Both pieces are trimmed in gold. Mark 2. *Courtesy Joette Hightower.* $75-125.

C. T. Maling & Sons (Ltd.)

Location: A and B Ford Potteries, Newcastle upon Tyne
Dates: c. 1890-1963
Marks:

Brief History: This firm succeeded C. T. Maling* and continued to be an outstanding pottery. In 1901 there were 1, 000 men and girls working at the factory. C. T. Maling's sons continued to look out for the welfare of their work force. The workrooms were large and airy with good ventilation. Precautions were taken to lessen the dust. The possibility of lead poisoning was eliminated with the use of fritted lead. The lead was actually converted into glass before being handled providing no danger to workers.

New shapes and designs were introduced as the range of wares expanded to include tea, dinner, dessert, and breakfast services, bedroom wares, and flower pots. "Cetem Ware" was developed as a superior brand of semi-porcelain and advertised as brilliant and durable. At the end of World War I, C. T. Maling & Sons supplied white ware to the British government and lusterware to Canada and Australia. Business lost from the closing of the pottery during the coal strike of 1926, was never built back to its former level. Orders declined for commercial pottery as companies began using glass, plastic and waxed paper cartons for conserves and dairy products. Production of colored ware was prohibited during World War II, and other means of increasing production; however, his death in 1954, brought an end to hopes for the future of ceramic production at the factory. Over time more and more buildings were used for storage in the Hoults' furniture removal business. C. T. Maling & Sons was closed in 1963.

Type of Willow Manufactured: Standard Willow and Two Temples II patterns transfer-printed in blue underglaze on earthenware. Some of the pieces in both patterns have a flow blue effect. Many interesting shapes and forms were made.

Retailer/importer: Ringtons Limited Tea Merchants, Newcastle upon Tyne*

Mark 1 c. 1891+

Mark 2 (GG2489) c. 1908+

Mark 3 (GG2490) c. 1924+

Mark 4 (GG2491) c. 1949-63

Standard Willow pattern vase transfer-printed in light blue underglaze on earthenware. The 7.25-inch vase is sitting in a metal stand. It is interesting to note four arches in the bridge on such a narrow piece. Usually additional arches are put on wide items such as platters. Mark 2. *Courtesy Paul Kirves and Zeke Jimenez.* $20-40.

Standard Willow pattern 5.5-inch vase transfer-printed underglaze on earthenware in flow blue. A narrow band of the outer border was used to decorate the outside of the uneven rim of the vase. Mark 2. *Courtesy IWC Convention 2001.* $25-50.

Standard Willow pattern 4-cup teapot transfer-printed in blue underglaze on earthenware (Cetem Ware). A very large print was used on this teapot so that only a portion of the pattern can be seen. This shape teapot was also decorated with Two Temples II pattern. Mark 2. *Courtesy Charles and Zeta Hollingsworth.* $75-150.

Standard Willow pattern 11-inch grill plate transfer-printed in blue underglaze on earthenware. The inner border is not seen on this plate; however, we do see the complete central pattern and the outer border that is cut to fit the plate. Mark 1. *Courtesy Bill and Joyce Keenan.* $20-35.

Another Standard Willow pattern piece with large transfer print in blue underglaze on Cetem Ware. This hot water pot stands 5.5-inches high with a capacity of 16 oz. Mark 2. *Author's Collection.* $40-85.

Two Temples II reversed pattern transfer-printed rectangular dish in blue underglaze on earthenware. It measures 6.25-by-9.75-inches and the sides are 4-inches high. The linear form of the pattern is repeated several times on the inside and outside of the piece. It may be a planter, but the inside of a planter is usually left undecorated. Mark 3. *Author's Collection.* $125-175.

Standard Willow central pattern transfer-printed bowl in blue underglaze on Cetem Ware. The outer border decorates the outer rim of the bowl. This 9-by-10.75-inch bowl is reminiscent of the shapes of early nineteenth century dessert dishes. Mark 2. *Courtesy IWC Convention 2001.* $55-85.

Two Temples II reversed pattern oval dish transfer-printed underglaze on earthenware in flow blue. The dish measures 11-by-6-inches and is decorated on the inside and outside with border and linear form of the pattern. Mark 3. *Courtesy IWC Convention 1994.* $45-65.

Two Temples II reversed pattern pair of vases transfer-printed underglaze on earthenware in flow blue. The vases are 10-inches high and are photographed to show both sides of the pattern. Mark 3. *Courtesy IWC Convention 2000.* $250-350.

Malkin, Walker & Hulse

Location: British Anchor Pottery, Longton, Staffordshire
Dates: c. 1858-64
Mark:

c. 1858-64

Brief History: The partners were Ralph Malkin, master potter, Thomas Walker, and Joseph Hulse. The Anchor Pottery was probably newly built for the partnership. It was a works that had four ovens. The firm produced transfer-printed earthenware. In 1865, the firm traded as Walker & Bateman. William Bateman may have financed the works for the firm in 1858.
Type of Willow Manufactured: Standard Willow pattern transfer-printed in blue underglaze on stone china.

Standard Willow pattern square serving dish with dome lid transfer-printed in blue underglaze on earthenware. The lid has a lion finial decorated in the same blue dot and white circle pattern as the handles. The dish is 9.5-inches square and 11-inches from handle to handle. The single foot ring is 3/8-inch high, and there are 3 single stilt marks on the inside of the dish. *Author's Collection.* $126-175.

Marple, Turner & Co.

Location: Upper Hanley Pottery, Hanley, Staffordshire
Dates: c. 1851-58
Marks:

Mark 1 c. 1851-58

Comments Concerning Marks: In *Romantic Staffordshire* Ceramics Jeffrey Snyder shows two plates attributed to Marple, Turner & Co., marked with M. T. & Co. in a circular ribbon mark. According to Geoffrey Godden in *Ironstone*, these initials could also relate to Mary Tipper & Co. (c. 1851-60) or to Mellor, Taylor & Co. (c. 1883-1904).

Mark 2 c. 1851-58

Brief History: In *Godden's Guide to Ironstone, Stone & Granite Wares*, a listing is given for Marple, Turner & Co. with the addition of two other firms with the initials M. T. & Co. I note in Godden's *Encyclopeadia of British Pottery and Porcelain Marks* that the marks given for Mellor, Taylor & Co. have the name spelled out. Rodney Hampson states in *Longton Potters 1700-1865,* that no marked pieces are recorded for the firm of Mary Tipper & Co.; therefore, I am listing this company and attributing the marks and plates pictured as Marple, Turner & Co.
Type of Willow Manufactured: Standard Willow pattern transfer-printed in blue underglaze on stone ware.

Standard Willow pattern plates transfer-printed in blue underglaze on earthenware. The 10.5-inch plate on the left has 3-point stilt marks on the underside of the center of the plate and a recessed foot ring. The 9-25-inch plate has single stilt marks on the top of the rim and a single flat foot ring. The engravings are quite different. Note the birds, path, bare branches, and extra branch of the apple tree coming out of the teahouse on the larger plate. Mark 1 on right and Mark 2 on left hand plate. The larger plate has damage. *Author's Collection.* $15-20 right plate.

Jacob Marsh

Location: Lane Delph (1806-18) and Church Street (1819-32), (Boundary Works) Longton, Staffordshire
Dates: c. 1806-32
Marks:

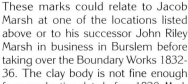

Mark 1 c. 1818-32

Comments Concerning the Marks: These marks could relate to Jacob Marsh at one of the locations listed above or to his successor John Riley Marsh in business in Burslem before taking over the Boundary Works 1832-36. The clay body is not fine enough for a production date before 1820. Mark 2 is attributed to Marsh from information in the *Dictionary of Blue and White Printed Pottery 1780-1880,*

Mark 2 c. 1818-32

p. 239. A Royal Arms Mark with the words OPAQUE CHINA WARRANTED is found on two different items with impressed MARSH. No other known pottery used those words on a Royal Arms Mark.

Brief History: Jacob Marsh was a master potter at Lane Delph before purchasing land in Church Street from Earl Gower in 1818. He built the factory that is currently known as Boundary Works. The date on the pediment is 1819. The firm produced earthenwares although Rodney Hampson in *Longton Potters 1700-*1865, states that marked pieces attributable to the firm in Longton are not known. One or two blue printed patterns other than willow have been found with the impressed mark MARSH.

Type of Willow Manufactured: Standard Willow pattern transfer-printed in blue underglaze on earthenware.

Standard Willow pattern handled dish transfer-printed in blue underglaze on earthenware with pale blue glaze. This "flounder"-shaped dish measures 8.5 by 9.5-inches. The blue on the handle is underglaze. Three-point stilt marks in the center on the back with single stilt marks on the top. The single foot ring stands 1/4-inch high. Mark 1. *Author's Collection.* $55-95.

Standard Willow pattern 7.75-inch plate transfer-printed in blue underglaze on earthenware. It has a double recessed foot ring and 3 single stilt marks on front and back. There are 8 slight indentations on the edge of the concave rim. Fine sand and grit can be felt under the glaze, which is very thin in places on the back. Mark 2. *Courtesy Dennis Crosby.* $20-30.

Miles Mason

Location: Victoria Pottery, Lane Delph and Minerva Works, Fenton, Staffordshire
Dates: c. 1802-13
Marks:

Mark 1
(GG2545)
c. 1807-13

Mark 2 (GG2545)
c. 1807-13

Mark 3 c, 1803-13

Mark 4 (GG2543)
c. 1804-13

Comments Concerning Marks: Although impressed name marks and printed pseudo Chinese seal marks with and without his name were used from the outset, Miles Mason's factory often marked only one piece out of an entire tea service. Therefore, many unmarked pieces are found. Attribution can be made through shape, pattern, and the gold numbers identifying the gilt patterns.

Brief History: The first career of Miles Mason, beginning in the early 1780s, was as a leading Chinaman (dealer in Chinese porcelains) in London. He purchased Chinese export porcelains in bulk at auction and sold them at his retail establishment at 131 Fenchurch St. In the early 1790s, the East India Company discontinued their importation of Chinese porcelains and no longer conducted large auctions for selling the wares. In an effort to secure more stock for sale, Mason entered into partnerships in Liverpool and Staffordshire in order to begin production of porcelains. See Thomas Wolfe* for more information regarding those years.

Miles Mason established his own pottery c. 1800-02, and was in production by 1804, at the latest. It is not known how Mason acquired his expertise in producing porcelain; however, the wares were well-potted from the start in the style of Chinese porcelain. The body in the early years was a hybrid-hard paste porcelain; however, after the move to the Minerva Works, the product became a more standard Staffordshire bone china. A number of blue printed patterns were produced with and without gilt border patterns. In 1813, Miles Mason turned over his factory to his two younger sons George Miles Mason and Charles James Mason*.

Type of Willow Manufactured: Two Temples I and II transfer-printed in blue underglaze on porcelain with and without gilt border decorations.

Two Temples II pattern saucer transfer-printed in light blue underglaze on bone china. The grapevine and gold bands gilt border pattern is #49. Mark 1. *Author's Collection.* $40-65.

Two Temples II reversed pattern teapot in low oval shape transfer-printed in light blue underglaze on bone china with gold border pattern #49. On p. 515 in Godden's *Encyclopaedia of British Porcelain Manufacturers* pieces in this shape and pattern are shown from a tea service donated to the City Museum in Hanley by Mr. And Mrs. Reginald Haggar. Mark 2. *Courtesy Harry and Jessie Hall.* $300+.

Two Temples II reversed pattern cream jug transfer-printed in light blue underglaze on bone china with gilt narrow border of hanging leaves and gold bands #241. This jug is seen in plate 44 of Godden's *Guide to Mason's China and the Ironstone Wares* as a standard shape of the 1803-5 period. Mark 3. *Author's Collection.* $75-150.

Two Temples II reversed pattern sugar basin and lid in low oval shape transfer-printed in light blue underglaze on bone china. The gilt border pattern on this piece is hanging leaf and floret #47. The handles are blue underglaze. Mark 2. *Author's Collection.* $125-200.

Two Temples II reversed pattern oval teapot transfer-printed in medium blue underglaze on porcelain with no gold. This teapot is seen in plate 40 of Godden's *Guide to Mason's China and the Ironstone Wares* c. 1805. Mark 4. *Courtesy Harry and Jessie Hall.* $275+.

Two Temples II pattern tea set in low oval shape transfer-printed in light blue underglaze on bone china. The hollow ware pieces have the pattern in reverse. The gilt narrow border is hanging leaves and gold bands #241. None of the pieces are marked. *Courtesy Louise and Charles Loehr.* $1,400+.

Two Temples I pattern 10-inch plate transfer-printed in medium blue underglaze on porcelain. This plate has an 8-lobed edge and an unglazed foot ring. There are some impurities under the glaze. This size plate has been found with impressed M.MASON, and pseudo Chinese Seal as well as unmarked. Mark 2. *Author's Collection.* $75-150.

G. M. & C. J. Mason

Location: Fenton Stone Works, Lane Delph, Fenton (1813-48), Sampson Bagnall's Works below Minerva Works, Fenton (1825-26), and Daisy Bank Works, Longton (1851-53), Staffordshire
Dates: 1813-48 and 1851-53
Marks:

Mark 1 c. 1820-30

Mark 2 c. 1813+

Mark 3 (GG2530) c. 1820+

Mark 4 c. 1990s

Mark 5 c. 1840s+

Mark 6 (GG145) c. 1891+

Mark 7 c. 1990s

Comments Concerning Marks: The above Patent Ironstone Marks with "England" added relate to the Ashworth period. Because the Ashworth name was not added, the marks appear here.
Brief History: Charles James Mason, the third son of Miles Mason, took out the patent for his "Ironstone China" in 1813, shortly after he and his brother George Miles Mason took over their father's business. This durable ware was fashioned in the style of Chinese porcelain and decorated in blue and white as well as colorful polychrome Chinoiserie designs. "Patent Ironstone China" was first produced at Miles Mason's former factory, the Minerva Works, owned by him until 1816. This non-translucent ware was probably developed in a collaborative effort between the father and sons; however, the patent was taken out in the name of C. J. Mason. Other factories produced similar ironstone clay bodies in the early nineteenth century, but the name "Patent" in the title as well as the quality of the ware and designs set Mason's Patent Ironstone China above the rest in desirability. Charles J. Mason successfully marketed his wares through aggressive advertising coupled with large auctions throughout the country.

George M. Mason took over the administrative side of the partnership. He was also active in helping to establish a mail coach through the potteries as well as a police force. He retired from the partnership in 1826, although he may have continued to give financial support. The title of the firm changed to Charles James Mason & Co from 1829-45. He was a compassionate employer who provided excellent working conditions and a fair wage. He supported the emerging unions; however, he ran into a problem in his own factory when he introduced a new machine to make flat ware to be driven by steam or hand power. It turned out that the machine produced faulty goods and was withdrawn. The gradual mechanization of the factory was thus delayed for a time. From 1845-48, the firm title changed to Charles J. Mason.

By the 1840s, the market was drying up for ironstone ware with Chinoiserie patterns. Vast quantities had been produced, and replacement services were not needed due to the durability of the ware. The firm of Charles J. Mason went bankrupt in 1848; however, the man survived and opened up a new business, also Charles J. Mason, at Daisy Bank. He had an impressive showing at the Exhibition of 1851; however, the wares were probably stock from 1840s, production. Francis Morley, of Ridgway & Morley* (1842-45), and Morley & Co., with partner Samuel Asbury (1845-58), purchased the majority of Mason molds and copper plates. The name MORLEY was added to Mason's basic crown mark on Mason's designs. In 1858, Morley's partnership began with G. L. Ashworth*. Please see the entry for G. L. Ashworth to trace the further history of Mason's Patent Ironstone.

Type of Willow Manufactured: Two Temples I pattern transfer-printed in blue underglaze on ironstone. John Turner variant pattern transfer-printed underglaze in blue, brown, red, and green with some clobbered pieces. Canton pattern was transfer-printed in blue underglaze. Some blue wares were produced in flow blue. A wide range of interesting shapes was produced in table and tea wares in addition to ornamental ware such as vases and temple jars.

Retailers/importers: Crabtree Evelyn, London*, Ringtons Limited Tea Merchants, Newcastle upon Tyne*, and Twinings Ltd., England*

Two Temples I pattern dessert dish transfer-printed in blue underglaze on semi china. It has a single foot ring 1/4-inch high. There is some restoration. The rare Mark 1 appears on this lovely dish. *Courtesy Louise and Charles Loehr.* $200-250.

Two Temples I pattern 6-inch plate transfer-printed in blue on ironstone. This 8-lobed plate has a blue glaze. The single foot ring is unglazed. Mark 2. *Author's Collection.* $45-65.

John Turner willow pattern transfer-printed teapot in blue underglaze, jug in red, and lidded ginger jar in green underglaze on ironstone. This pattern was used extensively by C. J. Mason and later the Ashworth Bros. firm. This teapot shape is rarely found. It stands six-inches high and has Mark 3. Green ginger jars with lids are fairly common, but red pieces are not often seen. Those two pieces have Mark 6. *Courtesy Charles and Zeta Hollingsworth.* $125-200 and $50-75 each.

John Turner willow pattern transfer-printed wash bowl and pitcher in blue on ironstone. The shapes of the two pieces are different from the Hydra jug and octagonal form usually seen on Mason's wash sets. The pitcher stands 9.5-inches to the top of the handle. The bowl is 10.75-by-4.25-inches. Mark 2. *Courtesy Paul Kirves and Zeke Jimenez.* $200-300.

John Turner willow pattern transfer-printed miniature wash bowl and pitcher in blue underglaze with polychrome clobbering. The Hydra shape jug and octagonal bowl are found in sizes ranging from small miniatures to extremely large wash sets; however, most sets are in blue only. The bowl is 3.5-inches wide and 1.25-inches high. The jug is 2.75-inches high. Mark 3. *Courtesy Paul Kirves and Zeke Jimenez.* $250-350.

Blue printed John Turner willow pattern modern Hydra jug with pale clobbering and gold accents. The jug stands 5.15-inches high. It was purchased new in 1990 and was the medium size offered. Several other pieces were offered in this limited series named "Gold Willow". Mark 4. *Author's Collection.* $50-75.

John Turner willow pattern 9.75-inch candlesticks transfer-printed in blue underglaze on ironstone. The Mason firm is one of the few that produced candlesticks in willow pattern. Other shapes are known as well; however, they are hard to find. Mark 3. *Courtesy IWC Convention 2001.* $250+.

John Turner willow pattern footed compote with handles transfer-printed in flow blue on ironstone. The compote measures 8.75-by-11-inches including the handles and stands 5.5-inches high. This piece is a classic Mason's shape. Mark 2. *Author's Collection*. $450+.

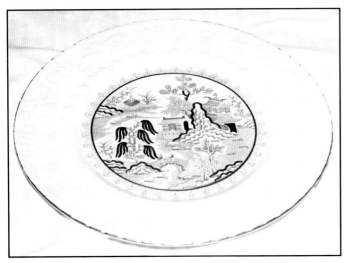

John Turner willow pattern 10-inch plate transfer-printed in green underglaze on ironstone with brown and gold accents overglaze. The central pattern with inner border are printed; however, the outer border is molded into the surface of the plate. This molded border pattern plate has also been seen with the center pattern printed in yellow and in blue. The blue printed center pattern often has the border clobbered with green, yellow, and red. Mark 5. *Courtesy Ohio Willow Society 1997*. $35-75.

John Turner willow pattern tureen, stand, ladle, and lid transfer-printed in red underglaze on ironstone. This large tureen is the same classic Mason's shape as the flow blue compote, and it is rare in red. Mark 6. *Courtesy IWC Convention 1994*. $400+.

Blue printed John Turner willow pattern on earthenware. This cup and saucer give an example of the last adaptation of the pattern to tableware. It was purchased new in the mid-1990s. Mark 7. *Author's Collection*. $10-15.

Canton pattern 9.75 soup plate transfer-printed underglaze in flow blue on ironstone. This version of the Canton pattern was produced by both Masons and Ashworths in blue as well as flow blue. Mark 3. *Author's Collection*. $55-85.

Mayer & Sherratt

Location: Clifton Works, Longton, Staffordshire
Dates: c. 1906-41.
Marks:

Brief History: Mayer & Sherratt produced a fine quality bone china in tableware from 1906, until they closed during the early part of World War II. The company used the trade names "Melba China" and "Melba Bone China" as did the firm Melba China Co. Ltd.*

Type of Willow Manufactured: Standard Willow pattern transfer-printed in blue underglaze on bone china as well as a polychrome decal border pattern similar to the "Red Bridge" willow variant. The patterns have gold trim.

Mark 1 (GG2579)
c. 1921+

Mark 2 (GG2580)
c. 1925-41

Standard Willow pattern pair of plates transfer-printed in blue underglaze on bone china. The scalloped edge plates measure 7.5 and 7.25-inches. The smaller one on the right has a gold line for a middle border. The border pattern was fitted nicely into the scallops on the larger plate. Mark 1. *Author's Collection.* $10-18 each.

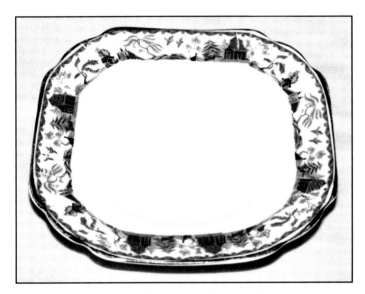

A polychrome decal border pattern decorates this bone china luncheon plate. The pattern is similar to the "Red Bridge" willow variant. Mark 2. *Courtesy IWC Convention 1999.* $8-15.

Alfred Meakin (Ltd.)

Mark 1 c. 1930+

Location: Royal Albert, Victoria & Highgate Works, Tunstall, Staffordshire
Dates: c. 1874-1976
Marks:

Comments Concerning Marks: An additional mark seen is GG2587 with Willow added above the mark. It dates from 1907+

Mark 2 c. 1930+

Brief History: Alfred Meakin was the brother of James and George Meakin.* who ran a large pottery in Hanley. Alfred Meakin died in 1904, and was succeeded by his son Alfred James who lived only four years after that. Robert Johnson, an uncle, bought the company. The Johnson family retained ownership until 1976, when the company merged with Myott, Son & Co.* The Alfred Meakin name was in use until 1976, when the name was changed to Myott-Meakin*.

The factory produced domestic and traditional dinnerware for the middle class market at home and for export; however, the largest part of their production was for export. A great deal of white ironstone was exported to America with

Mark 3 c. 1930+

and without the copper luster tea leaf motif. Children's ware was also made. Alfred Meakin became a limited company in 1897; however, "Ltd." was not used on marks after 1930. At this time the Newfield Pottery was added. The Victoria and Highgate Works was built in 1957. Many new tableware shapes and patterns were introduced at the new factory using on-glaze decals as well as underglaze prints alone and with overglaze enameling. Hotel ware was also made. Alfred Meakin employed 1,000 workers in 1973 and continued to grow.

Type of Willow Manufactured: Standard Willow pattern transfer-printed underglaze in blue, turquoise, and red on earthenware. Standard Willow central pattern with altered border patterns named Manchu. Black printed border pattern with red enameling with the name "Willowette", and polychrome decal based on the Two Temples II pattern.

Mark 4 (GG2590) c. 1930+

Mark 5 c. 1930+

Mark 6 c. 1930+

Mark 7 c. 1941

Mark 8 c. 1930+

Standard Willow pattern 9-by-12-inch platter transfer-printed in red underglaze on earthenware. The 3 and 4 spoke wheels were cut from the outer border in two spots in an attempt to match the geometric motifs of the two borders. Mark 2. *Author's Collection.* $25-55.

Standard Willow pattern 9-inch plate transfer-printed in blue underglaze on earthenware. The plate is coupe-shaped and bears Mark 5. This mark is occasionally found together with Mark 4, which identifies it as Alfred Meakin. *Author's Collection.* $10-15.

Standard Willow pattern covered cheese dish transfer-printed in blue underglaze on earthenware. The pattern is used in linear form around the top of the cover. It is an interesting shape with curved edges on all sides. Mark 2. *Courtesy IWC Convention 1999.* $65-95.

Standard Willow pattern small teapot transfer-printed in underglaze blue on earthenware. The spout was not decorated. Mark 2. *Courtesy Joette Hightower.* $65-95.

Standard Willow central pattern with Manchu border patterns on teapot and matching stand. The central pattern is the same engraving and pattern placement as on the previous teapot; however, this spout is decorated. Mark 6. *Courtesy IWC Convention 2002.* $100-175.

Border pattern transfer-printed creamer in black underglaze with red enamel overglaze and gold trim. Various elements of the Standard Willow pattern are seen in miniature in the border. Mark 8, the Marigold mark, shows the name: "Willowette", and Astoria Shape. *Author's Collection.* $5-15.

Standard Willow pattern condiment set transfer-printed in underglaze blue on earthenware. The under tray has recessed areas to hold the pepper, open salt, and open mustard dishes. Mark 5. *Courtesy IWC Convention 2002.* $95-150.

Standard Willow pattern platter transfer-printed in brown underglaze on earthenware. Willow pattern platters in brown are not often found. This lovely platter measures 14-by-17.75-inches and bears impressed mark: J. & G. MEAKIN. *Courtesy Gerry Hatchitt.* $100-175.

Simplified Standard Willow variant coffee pot printed in green underglaze on earthenware marked ironstone. This pot and a shorter teapot have also been found in blue. This pattern was originally sold through Neiman-Marcus catalogs in the 1970s. Although red was also advertised, it seems to be the color that is found least often. *Author's Collection.* $55-85.

Mug decorated with a polychrome lithograph based on Two Temples II pattern. This is the only piece I have seen made by Meakin in this pattern. Mark 7 has the information that the piece is hotel ware. 1941 may be the date. *Courtesy IWC Convention 1993.* $12-25.

Simplified Standard Willow variant octagonal-shaped bowl printed in blue underglaze on earthenware marked ironstone. This photo shows the enlarged bow-knot border usually found on red, green, and blue pieces of this pattern. *Author's Collection.* $15-30.

J. & G. Meakin (Ltd.)

Location: Market St., Eagle Pottery and Eastwood Pottery, Hanley, Staffordshire
Dates: c. 1851 to present (2003)
Marks:

Mark 1 c. 1851-91

Mark 2 c. 1970+

Brief History: James Meakin Sr. turned over his Cannon Street Pottery to his sons James and George in 1851. He died a year later, and they moved to Market St. where they worked for 7 years. Their business was so successful that they built the Eagle Pottery near the canal on the outskirts of Hanley. It was one of the largest and best-equipped factories in the world. J. & G. Meakin was the largest producer of ironstone in Staffordshire in the latter part of the nineteenth century. The majority of their wares were exported to America and the colonies. White ironstone with molded patterns was popular in the USA. In 1887, J. & G. Meakin purchased the Eastwood Pottery from their brother Charles Meakin. The firm was family owned for 100 years. In 1968 J. & G. Meakin joined Midwinter*, and in 1970 were taken over by the Wedgwood Group. The company continues to produce everyday tableware with their own backstamp.
Type of Willow Manufactured: Standard Willow pattern transfer-printed in brown and blue underglaze on earthenware. Simplified willow pattern printed in green, blue and red on earthenware that is labeled "Dishwasher safe Ironstone".

John Meir

Location: Greengates Pottery from 1822, Tunstall, Staffordshire
Dates: c. 1812-36
Marks:

Mark 1 c. 1812-36

Mark 2 c. 1812-36

Mark 3 c. 1812-30 (+)

Comments Concerning Mark: At the base of the impressed crown mark the letter G is on the left hand side and R on the right — George Rex. The mark could have been used during part of the reign of George III until his death in 1820, and from then until 1830 when George IV died. It would take a short while to discontinue the use of the mark.[1]
Brief History: John Meir was already established in Tunstall when the Greengates Pottery became available. It was purchased from Benjamin Adams in 1822. The firm produced a wide variety of blue printed patterns underglaze. Not all pieces were marked; however, the two impressed marks shown above were used during this period. The stoneware body produced was heavier than the early

pearlware; however, a pale blue glaze was used to whiten the background for the printed patterns.

Type of Willow Manufactured: Standard Willow pattern transfer-printed in light and dark blue underglaze on stoneware.

1. Doreen Otto. "John Meir of Tunstall and the Impressed Crown", Friends of Blue Occasional Paper Number One, Spring 1990, p. 5.

Standard Willow pattern stone china 9.75-inch soup plate transfer-printed in light blue underglaze and 12-paneled handle-less cup and saucer in dark blue. The soup plate has excellent quality clay body and engraving. The shape of the birds, the narrow straight path, and dark gable ends on the small building at the edge of the water are all reminiscent of early Minton*. The flat rim has 8 indentations on the edge and 3-point stilt marks on the under side with single stilt marks on the top. The foot ring is recessed. Impressed Mark 1 and printed Mark 2. The cup and saucer are from the John Meir & Son period and are printed with Mark 3 below. *Author's Collection.* $90-115 and $75-95.

John Meir & Son

Location: Greengates Pottery, Tunstall, Staffordshire
Dates: c. 1837-97.
Marks:

Mark 1 c. 1837-90

Comments Concerning Marks: Mark 3 was continued in use (with a change of initials) by the Adams firm that purchased the factory and its contents in 1897.

Brief History: John Meir took his son Henry into the pottery business with him in 1837. A wide range of good to excellent quality earthenware dinner services were produced in many different patterns and colors transfer-printed underglaze. Henry Meir and his son ran the business from the late 1840s; however, the name continued to be John Meir & Son. By 1897, the Meir family did not want to continue in the pottery business. W. Adams & Son* purchased the factory and its contents. It is possible that Adams produced patterns such as willow from some of the same copper engraved plates that were used by John Meir & Son.

Type of Willow Manufactured: Standard Willow pattern transfer-printed underglaze on earthenware in blue, brown, and red in a wide range of interesting shapes. Two Temples II pattern transfer-printed in pale blue underglaze on earthenware.

Mark 2 c. 1837-90

Mark 3 c. 1837-90

Mark 4 c. 1891-97

Standard Willow pattern 9 7/8-inch plate transfer-printed in blue underglaze on earthenware. There are three-point stilt marks on the underside of the flat rim that has 8 slight indentations on the edge. This plate is later and not quite the same quality as the soup plate above. It bears impressed Mark 3 – a mark attributed to John Meir in "Occasional Paper No. 1 Spring 1990" by Doreen Otto, published by Friends of Blue. *Author's Collection.* $50-70.

Standard Willow pattern cheese stand transfer-printed in blue underglaze on earthenware. The diameter is 8.5-inches at the top and 7-inches at the base. It stands 2-inches high. Mark 3. *Author's Collection.* $75-125.

An exceptional Standard Willow pattern blue-printed tureen with ladle. It measures 12-inches from handle to handle. Mark 3. *Courtesy IWC Convention 1999.* $500+.

Standard Willow pattern large cup and saucer transfer-printed in brown underglaze on earthenware. This shape cup is also found in red and blue willow. A variety of pieces are known with brown Willow pattern made by John Meir & Son. Mark 3. *Author's Collection.* $25-45.

This transfer-printed Standard Willow pattern platter is 11-by-13.75-inches. The mark on this platter is one seldom seen for John Meir & Son. It is Mark 1. *Courtesy Bill and Joyce Keenan.* $95-150.

Two Temples II pattern London shape teapot printed in pale blue underglaze. This is a commemorative teapot with a circle on each side containing the words "FAILSWORTH National Sunday School 1856." Plates were also made with this logo. I understand that Failsworth is located near Manchester. Mark 2. Unfortunately, the teapot was badly cracked when shipped to the owner. *Courtesy Joette Hightower.* NP

Teapot transfer-printed in light blue that is not typical of the willow by John Meir & Son we find. It is an oval fluted shape with a collar and gold trim. This pretty little teapot holds about 4 cups. Mark 4. *Courtesy Paul Kirves and Zeke Jimenez.* $75-125.

Melba China Co. Ltd.

Location: Stafford Street, Longton, Staffordshire
Dates: c. 1948-51
Mark:

(GG2643)
c. 1948-51

Brief History: This firm was in business for a short time at the end of World War II producing bone china tableware. Only pieces bearing the mark above can be attributed to this company because the "Melba" trade name was also used by Mayer & Sherratt*.

Type of Willow Manufactured: Standard Willow pattern transfer-printed in blue underglaze on bone china.

Standard Willow pattern bowl transfer-printed in blue underglaze on bone china. The diameter is 4.75-inches across the top and 3-inches across the base. The bowl has gold trim. *Courtesy Geraldine Ewaniuk.* $10-15.

Standard Willow pattern 7.75-inch plate transfer-printed in dark blue underglaze on stoneware. The plate is quite heavy and has a shiny smooth glaze. Mark 1. *Courtesy Henry Kelly. Photo by Douglas Leishman.* $10-15.

David Methven & Sons

Location: Links Pottery, Kirkcaldy, Scotland
Dates: c. 1847-1928
Marks:

Mark 1 c. 1875-90

Comments Concerning Mark: Mark 2 with the full name was found on a 9.5 inch soup plate.
Brief History: The Links Pottery was started by William Adam, architect, about 1714, as a brick and tile works. Redware was being made by 1805. The pottery was greatly expanded in 1809, to include this new product. In 1827 the property was divided between two brothers. John Methven continued to make redware, and he also bought Fife Pottery located nearby. David Methven took over the pottery in 1847, at which time the production of whiteware began. In 1870, James Methven, a son, took A. R. Young into partnership. By 1892, A. R. Young & Sons were the sole owners; however, the David Methven & Sons name was retained. A new pottery was built in 1897. The pottery closed in 1928.

Mark 2 (GG2653)
c. 1875-90

Mark 3 (GG2651)
c. 1875-90

A standard product was transfer-printed wares of many of the same patterns used by other potteries. Painted wares were a large portion of Methven's output. The firm had a large and varied export market. Sponge ware of fine quality was exported to Asia.
Type of Willow Manufactured: Standard Willow and Two Temples II patterns transfer-printed in blue underglaze on earthenware. Gold outlining of the pattern was sometimes used.

Two Temples II pattern 8.25-inch pitcher transfer-printed in dark blue underglaze on heavy earthenware. The round pattern was probably engraved for a plate. Many details of the pattern are outlined in gold including the border pattern on the outside of the jug. There is no gold on the border pattern on the inside or on the handle. Mark 3. *Author's Collection.* $55-85.

DAVID METHVEN & SONS, KIRKCALDY POTTERY, KIRKCALDY, SCOTLAND
MANUFACTURERS OF EVERY DESCRIPTION OF
EARTHENWARE IN C.C., SPONGED, PRINTED, ENAMELLED, AND GILDED.
FOR ALL HOME, COLONIAL AND FOREIGN MARKETS.
Direct Steamer Kirkcaldy to London and Hull.   Goods for shipment free Glasgow, Leith, Hull, or Liverpool.
PRICES ON APPLICATION.
Representative in England: Mr. W. WORSLEY.
Dublin Show Room: 61 William Street.   Representative: Mr. J. G. MACINTYRE

Advertisement in *Pottery Gazette,* July 1, 1920, p. 876, listing types of wares produced. The prize medal is shown from the Paris Exhibition 1896.

Micklethwaite

Location: Staffordshire
Dates: Unknown
Mark: March 25, 1882

Brief History: There is a website: WWW Tile Image Gallery that shows a tile marked Micklethwaite on the back in the center panel. The style of the back of the tile indicates it was made by T & R. Boote, established in 1842 at Waterloo Pottery, Burslem, Staffordshire. Some firms purchased blanks, decorated them, marked them with a back stamp, and sold them. The caption under the tile notes that the pattern had been made by other tile companies as well. Micklethwaite is on the factory list on the website; however, no information is available.
Type of Willow Manufactured: Standard willow pattern transfer-printed in blue underglaze on a 6 inch dust pressed square tile.

Standard Willow pattern 6-by-6-inch tile transfer-printed in blue underglaze. The dust pressed tile was manufactured by T. & R. Boote, Waterloo Pottery, Burslem, Staffordshire. *Author's Collection.* $15-30.

Middlesbro' Pottery Co.

Location: Near Stockton on Tees, Yorkshire
Dates: c. 1834-52
Mark: c.1834-44

Brief History: The pottery was built in 1834, by Richard Otley, Joseph Taylor, John Davison, and Thomas Garbutt who were the partners of the Middlesbrough Pottery Company. Using clay from south west England, the principal product was white earthenware. Transfer-printed patterns were done in many colors including blue, red, brown, purple, green, and black. Most wares were made for home use although the firm did produce plates with German views that were exported to Germany. From 1844 to 1852, the firm was known as the Middlesbrough Earthenware Company. Isaac Wilson, former manager, took over the works in 1852. The pottery traded under the name of Isaac Wilson & Co. until it closed in 1887.
Type of Willow Manufactured: Standard Willow pattern transfer-printed in blue underglaze on earthenware. Tableware was made, and I have seen quite a few platters over the years.

Standard Willow pattern 14.25-by-18-inch platter transfer-printed in blue underglaze on earthenware. The borders are lined up with the geometric motifs well matched. The rim is flat with slight indentations on the edge. The same engraving has been noted on a shape with concave rim and wavy edge. *Courtesy J and J Cockerill.* $100-175.

W. R. Midwinter (Ltd.)

Location: Albion and Hadderidge Potteries, Burslem, Staffordshire
Dates: c. 1910-87
Marks:

Comments Concerning Marks: Mark 1 is believed to be from the 1920s due to the style of the mark as well as the shape and color of the ware.
Brief History: William Robinson Midwinter had worked at Royal Doulton for 14 years before opening his own pottery in 1910. His first product was Rockingham style teapots. After 4 years, he acquired a larger factory and began producing sanitary ware in addition to tea ware. His wife managed the factory while he served in the Royal Navy during World War I. Upon his return, he acquired neighboring factories and gradually increased output to include moderately priced semi-porcelain dinnerware. Two quotations from the *Pottery Gazette* describe dinnerware production in the 1920s:

> That the firm can offer white and gold stock lines, blue Willow and the like and still be able to supply dignified, hand-decorated patterns suitable of appealing with forcefulness to the buyers of the USA was sufficient proof of their versatility" April 1, 1926, and

> His range of patterns in tableware is certainly both wide and interesting, for whilst it includes such solid productions as "Blue Willow," a line which still meets with a ready sale in some of the principal export markets ... October 1, 1928.

The average number of employees at Midwinter's in the late 1930s was 700; however, the payroll was reduced to a minimum during World War II, and the buildings were used for the war effort. William Midwinter's son Roy returned

Mark 1 c. 1920+

Mark 2 c. 1940+

MIDWINTER ENGLAND

Mark 3 c. 1946+

Mark 4 c. 1946+

Mark 5
(GG2666)
var. c. 1946+

to the pottery after serving in the R.A.F. and was given a thorough training in all areas of the factory before he became Managing Director of the firm. In the 1950s, Roy Midwinter was a driving force behind the development of contemporary style tableware. On a sales trip to Canada he had been disappointed in Midwinter sales. He was inspired by the work of radical new designers in the USA such as Eva Zeisel and Russel Wright. He spent time in California where he found samples of wares to send back to the factory in Staffordshire to study. The launching of Stylecraft was the beginning of a new era for the company, keeping them in the forefront of design and production of dinnerware into the 1960s.

Midwinter purchased A. J. Wilkinson's * Newport Works in 1964 in an effort to compete with larger manufacturers. Unfortunately some of the new styles and shapes were not successful, and the company was taken over in 1968 by J. and G. Meakin*. Two years later the Wedgwood Group absorbed the firms. Midwinter continued to use its own name on marks and designs until the factory closed in 1987.

Type of Willow Manufactured: Standard Willow pattern transfer-printed in red, green, and two shades of blue on semi-porcelain. "YANG" variant in blue underglaze and brown with clobbering. There are no surviving pattern books; however, Steven Jenkins has a "Midwinter Design Directory" in his book *midwinter pottery*. His list for willow: (I have not seen brown.)

> **Hudson Shape (Old Classic)** – (1946+)
> **Willow** – traditional print available in blue or brown.
> **Fashion Shape** – (1955+)
> **Willow** – a color version of the traditional pattern.

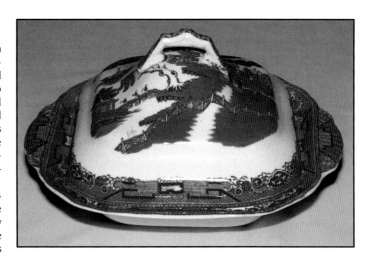

Standard Willow pattern covered vegetable dish transfer-printed in medium blue underglaze on earthenware. The dish is square with rounded corners measuring 8.75-inches in diameter – 10.25-inches including the handles. Mark 1. *Author's Collection.* $75-150.

Standard Willow pattern 6-cup teapot transfer-printed in dark blue underglaze on earthenware. This shape is seen with a group of other pieces illustrating the output pre- and post-war made by Midwinter prior to 1953 when Stylecraft was launched.[1] Mark 2. *Courtesy Paul Kirves and Zeke Jimenez.* $75-125.

Advertisement in *Pottery Gazette*, December 1947, announcing "WILLOW An established favorite".

Standard Willow pattern red printed teapot with a hooked spout. The tip of the spout has some of the border decoration on it. This teapot shape has also been seen in blue with the spout decorated the same way; however, it has no border pattern on the body of the teapot resulting in a larger central pattern. Mark 2. *Courtesy Paul Kirves and Zeke Jimenez.* $75-125.

1. *midwinter pottery a revolution in British tableware* by Steven Jenkins, Colour Plate No. 1, p. 41.

Standard Willow pattern blue printed condiment set with metal central handle. The open dish on the far side would hold the mustard. It has also been suggested that object is an egg bucket. The salt and pepper on this side complete the set. Mark 4. *Courtesy IWC Convention 1996.* $85-135.

Standard Willow pattern blue printed sparrow beak creamer with ornate handle. This little gem stands 3.25-inches high. Mark 2. *Author's Collection.* $15-25.

YANG variant pattern Dutch shaped pitcher transfer-printed in brown underglaze and clobbered with shades of green and brown. This pattern was seen on a blue and white Midwinter jug of the same pattern and shape with a T. G. Green & Co. Ltd.* MING pattern jug. Mark 5 is found on both YANG jugs. *Courtesy Paul Kirves and Zeke Jimenez.* $25-40.

Minton

Location: Stoke, Staffordshire
Dates: c. 1793-present (2003)
Marks:

Brief History: Thomas Minton was apprenticed at age 13 or 14 at Thomas Turner's Caughley porcelain factory and trained to be an engraver. He is closely associated with engraving Full-Nankin and Broseley patterns while there. The former was the first engraved pattern at Caughley, c. 1780, and the latter was named by Minton in honor of the neighboring town of Broseley. After completing his training at Caughley, Thomas Minton joined his brother Arthur, a chinaman in London. Thomas had an opportunity while there to become acquainted with numerous patterns in Chinese export porcelain sold in his brother's shop. He may also have done some engraving while in London. In 1789 he married and moved to Stoke-on-Trent. Minton worked as an independent engraver for Spode and other manufacturers. His success encouraged him to establish his own pottery.

In 1793 in partnership with William Pownall and Joseph Poulson, land was purchased, and a small factory was built. Production began in 1796. The first wares produced were blue printed earthenware Chinoiserie patterns similar to those made at other factories. There was a ready market locally as well as in London through his brother Arthur's retail china business. During the first 30 years, blue printed wares were not marked, and pattern books have not survived.

Creamware and bone china were introduced about 1798. Stoneware, Egyptian black and painted wares were soon added. Bone china was discontinued in 1816, and production resumed in 1824. Table, tea, and dessert wares were the main types of ware produced in the first period. Ornamental porcelains were added after 1824, and gradually other types of wares such as encaustic floor tiles, parian porcelain, pate-sur-pate, and majolica. Minton became a leading Victorian factory. For much of the twentieth century Minton was one of the most important makers of bone china tableware in the world.

The firm traded first as Minton & Poulson. Then the name of Pownall was added. After the death of Poulson in 1808, Minton became sole proprietor. In 1823 Thomas Minton's son Herbert became a joint partner with his father. Herbert had been apprenticed at a young age and had served as traveler and salesman in addition to working in the factory. He was an able businessman with drive and enthusiasm. Under his leadership, the factory gradually evolved from a small pottery, making earthenware and bone china into a world-class manufactory. Thomas Minton died in 1836, and Herbert took John Boyle into partnership that year. That partnership lasted until 1842, when Herbert took his nephews, Michael Daintry Hollins and Colin Minton Campbell into the business. After Herbert died in 1858, Colin

Mark 1 c. 1820-25

Mark 2 (GG2706)
c. 1862-71

Mark 3 (GG2705 & 2706)
c. 1862-71

Mark 4 (GG2707)
with S & England
c. 1891-01

MINTONS

Mark 5 (GG2711)
c. 1873-90

Mark 6 (GG2713)
c. 1873-90

Mark 7 (GG2716)
c. 1912-50

Minton Campbell led the firm until 1885. The firm continued under family control through the rest of the nineteenth century.

Many fine designers worked for Minton through the years. A new factory was built on London Rd. in Stoke in 1953. In 1968, Minton became a member of the Royal Doulton Tableware Group. Production ceased at the Minton Works in 1992. Manufacture of Minton patterns with Minton back stamps has continued at other factories in the group.

Mark 8 (GG2693) var. (imp date 1880)

Type of Willow Manufactured: Standard Willow and Two Temples II patterns transfer-printed in various shades of blue underglaze on earthenware and bone china. Beginning mid-nineteenth century, Standard Willow pattern was printed in orange on bone china, and the dagger border was sometimes used in place of the Standard Willow border in dark blue and gray-blue. Decorative tiles were produced in blue and black. Two Temples II was printed in light blue with clobbering. Both patterns also found in flow blue.

Sales accounts detailed in Geoffrey Priestman's *Minton Printed Pottery 1798-1836*, list Willow pattern supplied by Minton from 1798. Priestman discovered and catalogued over 40 Willow engravings found among the early unmarked copper plates in the Minton archives. Comparison of the engravings and shapes found on unmarked willow with those illustrated in his book will help to identify more of the unmarked wares made in the early nineteenth century.

Retailers/importers: Lawleys Phillips, Regent St.*, Mortlock, Oxford St.*, Phillips, 175-9 Oxford St.*, Regalcy*.

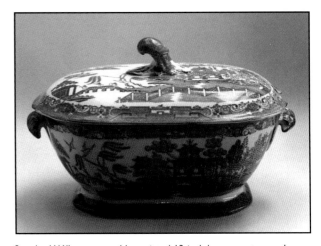

Standard Willow pattern blue printed 13-inch long soup tureen. In *Minton Printed Pottery 1793-1836*, Priestman dates this octagonal shape tureen to c. 1805 considering such features as the "fiddlestick" knobs and handles as well as the shape of the base and lid, which correspond to those on a tureen with another Minton pattern. He traces the prints on the lid and inside to the same engravings on other known Minton pieces. Unmarked *Courtesy Geoffrey Priestman.* $500+.

Standard Willow pattern blue printed dessert dish in a distinctive Minton shape. It measures 9.75-inches wide and dates to c. 1810. The same engraving was used on other dessert dishes in different shapes. The lower rounded lip of this dish is raised in order to function as a handle. It has three single stilt marks on the deep molded foot ring and the inside the rim of the dish. Unmarked. *Courtesy Geoffrey Priestman.* $150+.

Standard Willow pattern 8-inch plate transfer-printed in blue underglaze on pearlware. The octagonal plate has indented corners and a flat back. This is perhaps the earliest form of willow done at Minton c. 1800: the simple birds, dark gable ends of the small building next to the teahouse as well as the narrow path, and the wavy base of the boat. The outer border is also the earlier form with the inner half of the pair of scrolling leaves being lighter than the top half. It is unmarked. *Author's Collection.* $85-150.

Standard Willow pattern blue printed 9.25-inch plate. It is octagonal with slightly indented corners – not quite as angular as the 8-inch plate shown above. The engravings are not the same size but very similar. The plate has a flat back with a small impressed O. *Courtesy Dennis Crosby.* $100-175.

Two Temples II pattern in reverse transfer-printed underglaze on bone china with gold trim. It is the Cottage shape shown in the Minton Shape Book of 1830 and also used on earthenware. The teapot is unmarked, c. 1825. *Courtesy Geoffrey Priestman.* $400+.

Two Temples II reversed blue printed toast water jug. It stands 7.25-inches high and has a capacity of 1.5 pints. The jug has a built-in strainer and a lid that enables the making of toast water and dispensing the liquid while holding back the bits of toast. Toast water was a cure-all liquid popular in the nineteenth century. Mark 1. It has some spout and lid rim chips. *Author's Collection.* $200+.

Two Temples II reversed pattern blue printed octagonal mask jug. It stands 5-inches high and holds almost 1 pint of liquid. The handle has staple repair at the top and bottom. Mark 2 with impressed date mark for 1862. *Author's Collection.* $55-125.

Two Temples II blue printed pair of vases 12.5-inches high. The pattern is a wrap-around pattern, so the two vases are turned to show both sides of the pattern. There is a slight flow blue effect. One of the vases has a hairline. Mark 7. *Courtesy Louise and Charles Loehr.* $275+.

Two Temples II light blue printed pedestal bowl with yellow, dark blue, and green clobbering. The bowl stands 4.5-inches high and is 9-inches across. The outside rim has a molded basket weave pattern. Mark 7. *Courtesy IWC Convention 1999.* $200+.

Two Temples II, left, and Standard Willow pattern jardinières printed in flow blue. The larger one is 7.5-inches high and 9.5-inches wide. The Standard Willow jardinière is 6-inches high and 7.25-inches wide. Each one has the appropriate border pattern around the top. These pieces were made in many different sizes. Another collector has them ranging from 8, 6, 5 1/8 to 4.25 high with the corresponding widths. The right one has Mark 6 with England added, and the left one has Mark 7. *Author's Collection.* $200+.

Standard Willow pattern 10.25-inch plate dark blue printed on Best Body and 6 3/8-inch plate printed in light blue with gold trim on bone china. The heavy plate has a cartouche with crossed keys bearing the numbers 25 – or 52. This plate was probably made to commemorate an anniversary. The engravings on both these plates are based on earlier engravings c. 1815-20 illustrated in *Minton Printed Pottery 1796-1836* by Geoffrey H. Priestman. The shape of the birds is different from the first plate shown above, and the border has light colored outer leaves on the pairs of scrolling leaves; however, the other elements such as the dark gable front have been carried over from the earliest engravings. Marks 3 and 2. *Author's Collection.* $75-100 and $15-20.

Standard Willow pattern child's wash set transfer-printed in blue underglaze on earthenware. The bowl is 8-inches wide and 3.5-inches high. The jug stands 6.75-inches high. There is an interesting use of willow pattern elements in the white space between the borders on the bowl. Mark 2. *Courtesy IWC Convention 2002.* $200+.

Standard Willow pattern transfer-printed on orange underglaze on bone china. This is the only color underglaze other than shades of blue that I have seen on Minton willow. Seen here are a cream soup, creamer, and cup and saucer. Mark 2. *Courtesy Paul Kirves and Zeke Jimenez.* $45-75.

Standard Willow pattern toast rack blue printed on bone china with gold trim. It measures 7.25-by-4.5 and is 2.75-inches high. Mark 5 and date code for 1880. *Courtesy Loren Zeller.* $200+.

Standard Willow pattern 4- and 6-cup teapots transfer-printed in flow blue. The central pattern is quite large with no border pattern used. The handle, spout, and finial on the lid are all enameled in dark blue. Mark 6 with England added. *Courtesy Loren Zeller.* $150-300 each.

Three Standard Willow pattern teapots. The left hand teapot stands 7.25-inches to the top of the handle, holds 30 oz., and has impressed Mark 5. The teapot with white handle, spout, and finial is 4.75-inches high to the top of the finial, holds 24 oz., and has Mark 4. The front teapot is 5.5-inches high to the top of the finial, holds 8 oz., and has Mark 7. *Author's Collection.* $75+ apiece.

Standard Willow central pattern 9.5-inch soup plate with inner and outer dagger borders transfer-printed underglaze in dark blue on Best Body earthenware. The inner border has four cartouches with a contorted vine motif reminiscent of the cartouches used in Chinese Export inner borders. An example of a Chinese soup plate with outer dagger border can be seen fig. 14, p. 97, in *Spode's Willow Pattern.* The inner border has three similar cartouches set in the inner border. Mark 8 with impressed BB and date mark for 1880. *Author's Collection.* $45-95.

A pair of moon vases with Standard Willow pattern blue printed in the center of each. The vases are 6.5-inches high by 6-inches wide and 2-inches deep. Mark 5 plus 1303. *Courtesy Loren Zeller.* $400+ each.

Partial dinner set including 3 sizes of plates, soup tureen with under plate, two covered vegetable dishes, sauce tureen with under plate and ladle, and small platter. The pieces are decorated with Standard Willow central pattern in and a dagger border in dark blue with gold trim. Minton also produced a pale gray-blue with a dagger border. Mark 7. *Courtesy IWC Convention 1993.* $1,000+.

Standard Willow pattern garden seat transfer-printed in blue in 6 panels around the piece. The border pattern was used at the top and bottom of the panels. Plain dark blue enameling separates the panels. This impressive piece stands 20.5-inches tall. *Courtesy IWC Convention 1996.* $800+.

Standard Willow pattern dust pressed square tile transfer-printed in blue underglaze. It measures slightly under 6-inches square. The pattern is identical to that seen earlier with a mark for Micklethwaite. Evidently transfer prints for tiles were available from an engraving service just as prints for dishes were. Note the back of the tile does not have the smooth center panel seen on the tile made by T. & R. Boote. This tile is #M044 on the WWW Tile Image Gallery website and dated pre-1884. *Courtesy IWC Convention 1998.* $20-40.

Minton Hollins & Co.

Location: Patent Tile Works, Stoke, Staffordshire
Dates: c. 1868-1962
Mark:

c. 1868-1928

Brief History: Tile production began in 1830, under Herbert Minton at Mintons China Works. The firm traded as Minton & Hollins and Minton & Co. from 1845-68. In 1868, the partnership dissolved and Colin Minton Campbell took the china works and Michael Daintry Hollins took the tile business. Soon after that the large-scale production of decorative wall tiles began. A new building was erected, and it became a separate factory. The company made high quality decorative and architectural tiles. Later decorated pottery became an important part of their manufacturing output as well.

Type of Willow Manufactured: Standard Willow pattern printed in brown and blue. An all over blue printed pattern is identical to that seen previously with a Micklethwaite* mark. The willow pattern was also used in a cartouche as part of another over-all pattern on blue and brown printed tiles.

Standard Willow pattern in a circle on a brown printed dust pressed square tile. The tile is decorated with another plate behind a vase full of flowers. These features are surrounded by more floral groups. This pattern has also been found on a blue tile. The example seen on the WWW Tile Image Gallery website is #M040 and dated May 1882. *Courtesy IWC Convention 1999.* $20-40.

Robert Montgomery

Location: Verreville Pottery, Glasgow, Scotland
Dates: c. 1830-33
Mark:

c. 1830-33

Brief History: The word Verreville means "glass town". The business began as a glassworks in 1777. John Geddes took over the works in 1802. Under his guidance, transferware was produced on porcelain and earthenware. In 1830, Robert Montgomery took over the pottery, but not the glassworks. He had been a clerk at the pottery under Geddes' management. Montgomery continued to produce the same type of wares begun by Geddes; however, in three years, he was bankrupt. The pottery passed on to Robert A. Kidston* in 1835.

Type of Willow Manufactured: Standard Willow pattern transfer-printed in blue underglaze on earthenware.

Standard Willow pattern 10.5-inch plate transfer-printed in blue underglaze on earthenware. Marked pieces are rarely found due to the short time Montgomery worked the Verreville Pottery. *Courtesy Henry Kelly. Photo by Douglas Leishman.* $35-75.

Samuel Moore & Co.

Location: Wear Pottery, Southwick, Sunderland, Durham
Dates: c. 1803-74
Marks (impressed):

Mark 1 (GG2743)
c. 1803-74

Mark 2 (GG2746)
c. 1803-74

Brief History: The Wear Pottery was founded by Brunton & Co. in 1789. Samuel Moore & Co. took over in 1803. The name continued to be Samuel Moore & Co. after the pottery was acquired by R. T. Wilkinson in 1861. The works closed in 1881. Various types of ordinary earthenware were produced such as white, brown, sponged, and transfer-printed.

Type of Willow Manufactured: Standard Willow pattern transfer-printed in blue underglaze on lightweight and heavier earthenware.

Standard Willow pattern 9 7/8-inch plate transfer-printed in blue underglaze on lightweight earthenware. It has 8 slight indentations on the edge of the flat rim and there is no foot ring. The glaze is worn off much of the back, but it is very shiny on the front with pooling at the edges. Three-point stilt marks on the rim and well-matched borders with a patch at 5 o'clock. *Author's Collection.* $30-40.

Standard Willow pattern 9.25-inch plate transfer-printed in light blue on heavy earthenware. There are 8 slight indentations at the edge of the flat rim. Three-point stilt marks on the back of the rim and single stilt marks on the top. It has a recessed foot ring. There are several lumps and indentations in the glaze. *Author's Collection.* $20-25.

Morley, Fox & Co.

Location: Salopian Works, Fenton, Staffordshire
Dates: c. 1906-44
Mark:

Brief History: Morley, Fox & Co. was a twentieth century manufacturer or earthenware products. According to Buyer's Notes in *Pottery Gazette*, October 1, 1908, the leading lines produced were "TOILETS, JUGS, Tea and Dinner ware, cheese etc." The firm went out of business during World War II.
Type of Willow Manufactured: Toilet sets decorated with a polychrome decal based on Two Temples II pattern.

c. 1906-44

Full page advertisement for Morley, Fox & Co., featuring toilet sets. It is page 1791 in *Pottery Gazette*, December 1, 1922. The set on the left has the same shape jug as the one in the following photo. B4283 is probably the pattern number since there is a different number on the willow decal decorated jug.

A 10.5-inch pitcher decorated with the polychrome decal based on Two Temples II pattern. It is trimmed in gold, and the mark is printed in gold. The matching bowl has not turned up in over 15 years of searching. B582 is probably the pattern number. *Author's Collection.* $75-100.

Thomas Morris

Location: Regent Works, Longton, Staffordshire
Dates: c. 1892-41
Mark:

(GG2781)
c. 1912+

Brief History: Thomas Morris began his business with Arthur John Morris, a partner who took over the firm on his own May 21, 1896. The name continued as Thomas Morris through the years until 1941, when the business ceased. By 1900, Arthur John Morris had acquired partners William Lockett, Charles Frederick Goodfellow, Harry and George Warrilow. From November 1900, the partnership consisted of Arthur John Morris, Samuel Norris, and Harry Davis. Good quality bone china was produced in a wide range of ware. The trade name "Crown Chelsea China" was used from about 1912.
Type of Willow Manufactured: Standard Willow pattern transfer-printed in blue underglaze on bone china with gold trim.

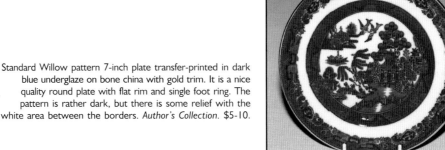

Standard Willow pattern 7-inch plate transfer-printed in dark blue underglaze on bone china with gold trim. It is a nice quality round plate with flat rim and single foot ring. The pattern is rather dark, but there is some relief with the white area between the borders. *Author's Collection.* $5-10.

George Thomas Mountford

Location: Alexander Pottery, Stoke-up-Trent, Staffordshire
Dates: c. 1888-98
Mark:

c. 1888-98

Brief History: An advertisement in 1889, in the *Pottery Gazette* gives the information that the firm produced earthenware, ironstone china, and white granite for the home market as well as for USA. It is certainly not one of the well-known firms in this country for white ironstone; however, we do know that Mountford produced the willow pattern. In 1898 Myott, Son & Co.* took over the Alexander Pottery.
Type of Willow Manufactured: Standard Willow pattern transfer-printed in blue underglaze on earthenware. Tableware.

Standard Willow pattern sauce tureen and under tray transfer-printed in blue underglaze on earthenware. The tray is 5 3/8-by-7-inches. The tureen stands 5-inches high to the top of the finial. The lid is angular in shape with 8 definite sides. The mark is impressed as well as printed, and it has an impressed 90 that is probably a date. *Author's collection.* $75-125 (without ladle).

Murray & Fullarton

Location: Caledonian Pottery, Glasgow, Scotland
Dates: c. 1850-64
Mark:

c. 1850-64

Brief History: The pottery was founded in 1800, near the Forth and Clyde canal in the northern part of Glasgow. It had various different names and owners until 1826, when William Murray and his sons Alexander and William junior, began trading as Murray & Co. In 1835, a clay tobacco pipe works was built next door. William senior ran the clay pipe works even after retiring from the main Caledonian Pottery in 1840. At that time, William junior took two men into partnership: his brother-in-law John Fullarton and James Couper. In 1850 Couper left to pursue his interest in making glass. At this time the partnership became Murray & Fullarton. William Murray junior's son William Fullarton Murray came into the partnership in 1860. William senior died in 1862, and the clay pipe works were sold. Murray junior and Fullarton retired in 1864 which brought an end to their partnership. Early products of Caledonian Pottery included salt-glazed stoneware. Blue and sepia printed wares are known from the Murray & Fullarton partnership.
Type of Willow Manufactured: Standard Willow pattern transfer-printed in blue on earthenware. "Stone China" on a mark in this period does not really indicate a clay body other than the usual earthenware used by the factory.

Standard Willow pattern 10.4-inch plate transfer-printed in blue underglaze on earthenware. This is the first documented piece of willow pattern made by this company. *Courtesy Henry Kelly. Photo by Douglas Leishman.* $15-25.

Myott, Son & Co. (Ltd.)

Location: Alexander Pottery, Stoke (1898-1902), Cobridge (1902-46), and Hanley (1947-76), Staffordshire
Dates: 1898-1976
Marks:

Mark 1 (GG2810)
c. 1900+

Comments Concerning Marks: Mark 1 is a combination of GG2810 with an added banner with the words "Royal Grafton China". Royal Grafton China is the trade name used by A.B. Jones & Sons*. Geoffrey Godden has speculated that perhaps the mark was used on a joint order by the two companies. The two companies may have had some further connection. I purchased a partial tea set of blue willow china by A. B. Jones & Sons that had a worn brochure with it comprised of an 8-page version of "THE LEGEND OF BLUE WILLOW WARE". The following is quoted from page 1 of the brochure under a picture of a willow plate and the title quoted above:

Mark 2 (GG2811)
c. 1907+

The Chinese Love Story that forms the Scheme of a Famous Pottery Decoration: The legend illustrated by the Blue-Willow Ware decoration is centuries old. It originated in China and forms a very pretty love story, so alive with human interest that it never grows old. You may have heard it in whole, or perhaps only in part. In either event you may enjoy having it set before you in complete form so that when next you see a piece of Blue-Willow you will know the story.

MYOTT, SON & Cº
ENGLAND

Mark 3 (GG2811)
var. c. 1907+

Myott, Son & Co. Ltd. have made a specialty in this line in their well-known **"Royal Grafton" Bone China.** The legend is pictured with utmost fidelity to detail, and is a most artistic production.

Look for the stamp under each piece.

The bold print is mine. This brochure and Mark 1 are the only pieces of evidence I have found that there may have been a connection between the two companies (at least in producing the willow pattern). The piece with Mark 1 came from a collector in Canada.

Brief History: Ashley Myott was apprenticed to George Thomas Mountford* at the Alexander Works, Wolfe St., Stoke in 1895. Mr. Mountford died in 1897. At age 19, Ashley Myott took over the business with such success that it was under his control for over 60 years. Myott, Son & Co. produced earthenware and semi-porcelain tableware and toilet ware for the domestic and export market. Decorations included transfer printing, lithographs, colored grounds with gilt and enameling, luster, and hand-painted designs. The *Pottery Gazette*, April 1, 1903, p. 373, stated that the firm made "Bread and butter lines". The *Pottery Gazette*, March 1, 1917, reported on the booth Myott, Son & Co. had at the British Industries Fair in 1917:

> A variant of the old willow design, lithographed on either a luster or plain body looked very well on this ware and proved also equally suitable for toilet sets.

The last two photos shown here illustrate this variant. The *Pottery Gazette*, April 2, 1928, reported on the exhibit at the British Industries Fair of that year for Myott, Son & Co., Alexander Potteries, Hanley (on the site of Brownfields Works, Cobridge – new building):

> ...The exhibit included numerous good printed designs, including samples of "Blue Willow," described as "Ye Olde Willow."

Evidently this design was the willow border variant because Standard Willow pattern has the word "Willow" in the mark.

Type of Willow Manufactured: Standard Willow pattern transfer-printed in different shades of blue underglaze on earthenware with and without gold trim. Border pattern in two shades of blue based on the motifs of Standard Willow pattern with and without gold trim. Blue and polychrome lithographs based on Two Temples II pattern used with blue ground as well as undecorated background with and without gold trim. The word "WILLOW" in the mark appears on Standard Willow pattern only. The words "Ye Olde Willow" appear in marks on the border pattern Standard Willow as well as on some pieces with the lithograph based on Two Temples II pattern.

Mark 4 (GG2811) var. c. 1907+

Mark 5 (GG2811) var. c. 1907+

Mark 6 (GG2811) var. c. 1907+

Mark 7 (GG2811) var. c. 1907+

Standard Willow pattern 9-inch bowl transfer-printed in medium blue underglaze on earthenware. It has a beaded edge on the flat rim. This is one piece out of a dinner set. Mark 5 gives the pattern as "Willow". *Author's Collection.* $25-45.

Border pattern in Standard Willow 10-inch plate in medium blue and 8-inch gravy boat in dark blue. Both pieces have gold line trim. This border pattern is the willow pattern most often associated with Myott by willow collectors. Both pieces have "Ye Olde Willow" in the mark. The plate has Mark 7 and the gravy has Mark 2. *Author's Collection.* $20-25 and $25-40.

This 6-cup teapot is decorated with the polychrome lithograph based on Two Temples II pattern. It has red lines to enhance the spout, finial, handle, and edges of the teapot and lid whereas gold lines are often used in this way. Mark 2 without "Ye Olde Willow". *Courtesy IWC Convention 1999.* $65-100.

Border pattern with Standard Willow pattern in linear form on 6-cup teapot, creamer, and open sugar bowl. Mark 7. *Courtesy Shirley and Jim Hagerty.* $150-200.

Standard Willow pattern 9.25-inch serving plate in medium blue transfer-printed underglaze on earthenware. This is the only piece I have seen marked Myott with such a wide area of white between the borders. It resembles the willow made by A. B. Jones & Sons* and was probably made by that firm with Myott added to the mark. It has Mark 1. *Courtesy Geraldine Ewaniuk.* $35-50.

Blue lithograph pattern based on Two Temples II in a band around the middle of this 14-inch ewer. The top, bottom, and handle are covered with a matching blue ground. There is gold trim on the top. A matching bowl has not been found. Mark 3. *Courtesy Louise and Charles Loehr.* $125-200.

A dresser set decorated with blue lithograph pattern based on Two Temples II central pattern with a pictorial border. The pieces are all trimmed in gold. Myott is one of the few English potteries that used this lithograph in blue. Most companies used the polychrome version. This set has an 8.5-by-14-inch tray, candlesticks, toothbrush holder, hat pin holder, soap dish, powder jar, pin tray, and hair receiver. Mark 6. *Courtesy IWC Convention 1994.* $200+.

Standard Willow pattern teapot transfer-printed in blue underglaze on earthenware that is acid and detergent proof. Coffee pots were also made in this straight-sided shape with large handle and flat finial. Mark 1 includes a bridge like those used in marks by Alfred Meakin before the merger with Myott & Sons. *Courtesy Paul Kirves and Zeke Jimenez.* $45-75.

Standard Willow pattern 6 7/8-inch plate and 10-inch border pattern transfer-printed in blue underglaze on earthenware. Both plates have a ribbed rim and Mark 2. *Author's Collection.* $5-7 and $8-12.

Myott-Meakin Ltd.

Old Willow
MYOTT
MADE IN
STAFFORDSHIRE
ENGLAND
AHANDENGRAVED PATTERN
PERMANENT
UNDERGLAZE COLOURS
ACID AND
DETERGENT PROOF

Mark 1
c. 1974-91

Location: Alexander Pottery, Cobridge, Staffordshire
Dates: c. 1976-1991
Marks:

fine MADE IN
Myott
Meakin *tableware*
ENGLAND

Mark 2
c. 1976-91

Brief History: Myott, Son & Co. Ltd.* merged with Alfred Meakin* in about 1974; however, the name did not change to Myott-Meakin Ltd. until 1976. Trade names were MYOTT and Myott-Meakin. The new company produced tableware, continuing some patterns that were used previously by one or both of the former firms. Marks included terms like "Ironstone" and "Fine tableware". Churchill purchased the company in 1991.
Type of Willow Manufactured: Standard Willow and border pattern using Standard Willow motifs blue printed on earthenware.

Newbon & Beardmore

WARRANTED
FINE CHINA
N. & B.

c. 1858-63

Location: 2 Commerce Street, Longton, Staffordshire
Dates: c. 1858-63
Mark:

Brief History: William Newbon and Thomas Beardmore were producers of ironstone-type wares marked Stone China. The firm succeeded the partnership of Beardmore and Edwards, and was followed by the short-lived partnership of Beardmore & Dawson*. A Standard Willow pattern cheese dish measuring 12 inches in diameter and standing 3 inches high is seen in Plate 21 in *Blue Willow* by Mary Frank Gaston with Mark 40 shown above.
Type of Willow Manufactured: Standard Willow pattern transfer-printed in blue underglaze on stone china. No picture is available.

New Hall

Location: New Hall, Shelton (Hanley), Staffordshire
Dates: c. 1782-1835
Marks:

Mark 1 (GG2875)
c, 1812-35

Mark 2 c. 1800+

Comments Concerning Marks: Mark 1 is occasionally seen on plates transfer-printed in blue underglaze with Two Temples II pattern although no marked examples are shown here. Mark 2 is a pattern number in red confirmed by Philip Miller to be New Hall.

Brief History: A group of Staffordshire potters had acquired the patent rights to manufacture Richard Champion's hard-paste porcelain made of Cornish china clay and china stone. The names of some of these potters were John Turner, Anthony Keeling, Samuel Hollins, John Daniel, and Jacob & Peter Warburton. The name "New Hall" was adopted because the factory site was the New Hall in Shelton (as opposed to the Old Hall). Many interesting shapes were used including silver and globular shaped teapots. Marks were not used in the beginning. In fact pattern numbers may have been used more than factory marks. Early wares had very little decoration apart from gilding. Hand-painted flower patterns were used in addition to transfer printing underglaze. The clay body was changed to bone china in about 1812. At that time there had been about 1050 different patterns – many unmarked. The factory produced about 2300 patterns before it closed.

Type of Willow Manufactured: Two Temples II pattern transfer-printed in light blue underglaze on porcelain with elaborate gold decoration.

Sugar basin with Two Temples II pattern in reverse, transfer-printed in pale blue underglaze on porcelain. It is 4-inches high to the top of the finial and 7-inches wide including the handles. An ornate gold border of leaves and flowers is seen on the lid and sides of the piece, almost blocking out the blue printed pattern. It has Mark 2 in red. Philip Miller identified the shape and red pattern number (which refers to the gilding) as New Hall. *Author's Collection.* $200+.

New Hall Pottery Co. Ltd.

Location: New Hall Works, Hanley, Staffordshire
Dates: c. 1899-1956
Marks:

Mark 1 (GG2871)
c. 1930-51

Mark 2
c. 1930-51

Brief History: The New Hall Works were purchased from Plant and Gilmore in August 1899. The new business was named the New Hall Pottery Co. Specialties in the beginning were toilet ware, tea ware, and jugs. An advertisement appearing in *Pottery Gazette* in 1907 and 1908, listed their products as "Toilet Ware, Jug, Tea Ware, Breakfast Ware, cheese stands, bread trays, butters, steak dishes, teapots, flower pots etc. etc."

Type of Willow Manufactured: Polychrome lithograph based on Standard Willow pattern on earthenware.

Jug decorated with polychrome decal based on Standard Willow pattern. It stands 5 3/8-inches high. Mark 1. A dresser tray with candlestick, ring tree, and various covered round boxes have all been noted with Mark 2 decorated with the same variant pattern. *Courtesy IWC Convention 2002.* $35-55.

Newport Pottery Co. (see also A. J. Wilkinson)

Location: Newport Lane, Burslem, Staffordshire
Dates: c. 1920-64
Mark:

(GG2876)
c. 1920+

Brief History: A. J. Wilkinson's* Royal Staffordshire Pottery took over Newport Pottery in 1920. The pottery was used mainly to produce dinner, tea, and toilet ware with inexpensive decoration on semi-porcelain. Special orders were also made for hotels and restaurants. Clarice Cliff was given her own studio at the pottery in 1926. A comment in the *Pottery Gazette*, March 1, 1928, page 443, noted the Newport Pottery Co. Ltd. was "a very old established business conducted in a pottery that can well boast of historical associations...The home of that once-celebrated firm of Edge, Malkin & Co.*" Production after World War II consisted mainly of advertising ware, figures, vases, and novelties. Newport Pottery was taken over by W. R. Midwinter* in 1964.

Type of Willow Manufactured: Standard willow pattern in various shades of blue and in brown underglaze on earthenware. The brown willow was clobbered in black along with shades of green and brown, and lined in gold. Polychrome decals based on Two Temples II and Standard Willow patterns were also used.

Retailers/importers: Lawleys (Phillips) England*

Low dish with attached under plate decorated with polychrome decal based on Two Temples II pattern. There is gold trim. It has a metal lid and spoon. The mark above without WILLOW and including pattern number 7647 in gold. The pattern number for the polychrome decal based on Standard Willow is 7507. *Courtesy Paul Kirves and Zeke Jimenez.* $25-45.

Standard Willow pattern 7 3/8-inch plate transfer-printed in medium blue underglaze on earthenware with gold trim. The pattern is badly crowded, and the quality of the printing is not very good. Plates printed in darker blue are usually of a better quality. *Author's Collection.* $5-8.

Nicholls & Hallam

Location: Flint Street, Longton, Staffordshire
Dates: c. 1844-45
Mark:

Mark 1 c. 1844-45

Brief History: Thomas Hallam was in partnership with a number of different potters from 1837. He worked alone from 1840-41. Nothing is known of Nicholls. The factory produced earthenware tablewares.
Type of Willow Manufactured: Standard Willow pattern transfer-printed in blue underglaze on earthenware.

Mark 2 c. 1844-45

Standard Willow pattern condiment set, jam pot, and sugar shaker transfer-printed in brown underglaze on earthenware. The pieces have been clobbered and trimmed in gold. All lids are metal as are the holders for the condiment set and jam pot. *Courtesy Harry and Jessie Hall.* $150+.

Standard Willow pattern 9.25-inch plate transfer-printed in blue underglaze on earthenware. There are 8 indentations on the edge of the flat rim. The foot ring is recessed, and it has 3-point stilt marks on the back of the center of the plate. The print is broken in several places on the border and poorly put on. There is some pitting on the top surface. Mark 1. *Author's Collection.* $15-18.

North Staffordshire Pottery Co. Ltd.

Location: Globe Pottery, Cobridge then Cobridge Road, Hanley, Staffordshire
Dates: c. 1940-52
Marks:

Mark 1 c. 1940-52

Comments Concerning Marks: Mark 2 was probably used after 1952 because it has the Ridgways name. It is included here because the two plates in the photo have the same engraving.
Brief History: This firm produced medium priced dinnerware in earthenware. It was acquired by Lawleys Ltd. in 1940 and was taken over by Ridgways in 1952. The name of the pottery was continued on the marks.
Type of Willow Manufactured: Standard Willow pattern transfer-printed in blue, black, and red underglaze on earthenware.

Mark 2 c. 1952+

Standard Willow pattern plate transfer-printed in brown underglaze on heavy earthenware. Dinnerware was made in brown by Old Hall. Mark 1. *Courtesy Kay and John Boob.* $10-20.

Standard Willow pattern plates transfer-printed underglaze on earthenware. The black plate is 9-inches in diameter and bears Mark 1. It has a line of gold between the fish roe and rest of the outer border. The blue plate is just under 8-inches and bears Mark 2. It has the same pattern that was continued after Ridgway Potteries Ltd. took over the factory. *Author's Collection.* $15-20 and $10-15.

Old Hall Earthenware Co. Ltd.

Location: Old Hall Pottery, Hanley, Staffordshire
Dates: c. 1861-86
Marks:

Mark 1 c. 1861-86

Brief History: The Old Hall Earthenware Co. was the first limited liability company in the Staffordshire potteries. It was incorporated in March 1861, and formed by Charles Meigh to succeed Charles Meigh & Son. The firm produced good quality earthenware that sometimes had words like stone china and granite in its marks; however, the product can be considered earthenware.
Type of Willow Manufactured: Standard Willow pattern transfer-printed in blue and brown underglaze on earthenware.

Mark 2 (GG2919) c. 1861-86

Standard Willow pattern cup and saucer transfer-printed in blue underglaze on earthenware. The rounded saucer and cup shape are typical of the period. Mark 1. *Author's Collection.* $15-25.

Standard Willow pattern coffee pot transfer-printed in blue underglaze on heavy earthenware. The pattern is in linear form around the coffee pot. Mark I. *Courtesy Charles and Zeta Hollingsworth.* $100-165.

Old Hall Porcelain Works Ltd.

Location: Old Hall Pottery, Hanley, Staffordshire
Dates: c. 1886-1902
Marks:

Comments Concerning Marks: Mark 3 is included here because it is often used in connection with other marks on Old Hall pieces – especially Mark 2. When it appears alone it can be attributed to Old Hall providing the pattern number and shape are correct for Old Hall.
Brief History: This firm was formerly the Old Hall Earthenware Co.; however, the name was changed, and porcelain was added to its products. Mark 2 had been used by the former company. It was continued with the addition of "England" after 1891.
Type of Willow Manufactured: Mandarin pattern transfer-printed in blue and brown underglaze on earthenware.

Mark 1 c. 1886-1902

Mark 2 (GG2922a)
c. 1891-1902

Mark 3
c. 1886-1902

Mandarin pattern 10-inch plate transfer-printed in light blue underglaze on earthenware with gold trim. In addition to printed Mark 2, it has impressed Mark 2 (GG2919) – the Indian Stone China mark of OHEC and impressed numbers 12/1900. If that is a date, it conflicts with the dates given for the OHEC impressed mark. There are several 7.5-inch plates with the same markings on the back. The plates have a more compressed clay body than the following pieces shown. *Author's Collection.* $18-25.

Mandarin pattern blue printed sauce tureen and brown printed sauce tureen with under plate. The blue tureen has Mark 3. A larger blue tureen in the same low shape with curved sides and edges has both Mark 2 and 3. *Courtesy IWC Convention 2001.* $75-125 blue and $100-150 for brown.

Mandarin pattern large footed tureen transfer-printed in light blue underglaze on earthenware. This shape is not seen as often as the previous one. Mark I. *Courtesy IWC Convention 1996.* $100-175.

Operative Union Pottery

Location: High Street, Burslem, Staffordshire
Dates: c. 1830-50
Mark:
A scroll with tassels at either end with the words:

Operatives
Manufactory
High Street
Burslem

Brief History: The first national union organization was formed in 1831. Membership was open to potters outside the Stoke area as well as Staffordshire potters. It was the National Union of Operative Potters. By 1833, the organization had 8,000 members. Robert Owen inspired a group of potters to start a co-operative pottery in Burslem. But it lasted only 7 months. It was not officially connected with the N.U.O.P. That organization did not survive a strike in 1836-37. The United Branch of Operative Potters organized in 1843. This group kept trade unionism alive; however, the group became more local. The Operative Union Pottery name does not occur in records of the time, so it is not known if the U.B.O.P worked the pottery. By 1868, Whiting, Ford & Co. was running the High Street Pottery. Aside from a small blue printed plate in the Victoria & Albert Museum, a willow pickle dish is the only other marked piece known by this pottery.[1]
Type of Willow Manufactured: Standard Willow partial pattern transfer-printed in blue underglaze on earthenware. No picture available.

1. Hanning, Laurence. "Operatives Manufactory, High Street, Burslem". *The Northern Ceramic Society Newsletter No. 118*, p. 14-15, June 2000.

Palissy Pottery Ltd. (see also A. E. Jones)

Location: Palissy Pottery, Longton, Staffordshire
Dates: c. 1946-88
Marks:

Mark 1
(GG2943)
c. 1946+

Comments Concerning Mark: Mark 1 is a continuation of a mark previously used by A. E. Jones. The plate with Mark 1 relates to the other photos in this section even though it could have been made earlier.
Brief History: Palissy Pottery Ltd. is the new title of A. E. Jones & Co. as of 1946. Palissy had become a well-known trade name, making the change appropriate. By 1946 the production had grown to include many useful accessories and hotel ware. The company was bought by Royal Worcester in 1958, but production continued. By 1965, the Thames River Scene series of engraved underglaze printed patterns were so popular that almost half their exports were of that series. Palissy Pottery Ltd. closed in 1988.
Type of Willow Manufactured: Burleigh Willow central pattern with Standard Willow border patterns transfer-printed in blue and brown underglaze on earthenware. The brown print was clobbered with red, yellow, green, and flow blue.
Retailer/importer: Ringtons Tea*

Mark 2
c. 1946+

The central and inner border pattern are based on Burleigh Dillwyn Willow. It is transfer-printed in brown underglaze on earthenware. The plate has been clobbered in shades of red, yellow, green, and flow blue. It has the Standard Willow outer border. The main differences from Burleigh Willow are on the left side of the pattern where an apple tree emerges from the big rock, and the buildings on the upper left just hang in the air instead of sitting on land surrounded by trees. Mark 1. *Photo from Author's files.* $20-35.

Burleigh Willow central and inner border pattern 9.5-by-12-inch platter transfer-printed in blue underglaze on earthenware. This unmarked platter has the same pattern characteristics including Standard Willow pattern outer border as the marked polychrome plate shown above. It is attributed to Palissy as well. *Author's Collection.* $30-55.

Burleigh Willow central pattern coffee pot transfer-printed in blue underglaze on earthenware. The Standard Willow border is used at the top of the pot whereas the inner border is used on the lid. The coffee pot stands 7.5-inches high and 9-inches across from tip of the spout to the handle. Mark 2. *Author's Collection.* $75-110.

Paragon China Co. Ltd.

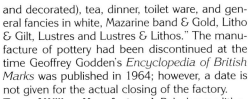

Location: Atlas Works, Longton, Staffordshire
Dates: c. 1919-89
Mark:

(GG2958)
c. 1939-49

Brief History: Begun at Star China Co.* the company was renamed Paragon China Co. in 1919. The Paragon trade name had been in use since about 1903, according to an advertisement in *Pottery Gazette*, December 1, 1908. Between the two World Wars the company was well known for its high quality china tea, coffee, breakfast, and dessert ware. Paragon China Co. received Royal Warrants for its bone china from H.M. Queen Mary, H.M. Queen Elizabeth, and the Queen Mother. These warrants are noted on the marks and help to date the wares. Children's ware was also made. Under Buyer's Notes in *Pottery Gazette,* August 2, 1926, "Paragon China honored by Duchess of York with instructions to equip the nursery of the infant Princess Elizabeth ... similarly equipped the nursery of Princess Mary's household in 1923."

Paragon China became a limited company in 1930. In 1960, it was taken over by Thomas C. Wild & Sons*, and then joined the Allied English Potteries in 1964. Paragon China Co. retained its trade name. The Atlas Works closed in 1987. Paragon was renamed Royal Albert in 1989.
Type of Willow Manufactured: Polychrome variation of Standard Willow pattern on bone china continued from production by Star China Co.*

and decorated), tea, dinner, toilet ware, and general fancies in white, Mazarine band & Gold, Litho & Gilt, Lustres and Lustres & Lithos." The manufacture of pottery had been discontinued at the time Geoffrey Godden's *Encyclopedia of British Marks* was published in 1964; however, a date is not given for the actual closing of the factory.
Type of Willow Manufactured: Polychrome lithograph based on Two Temples II pattern, commonly known among American Willow collectors as "Parrott Willow". This decal pattern, produced by Parrott & Co., was first documented by Veryl Jensen in *The First International Book of Willow Ware*, 1975, and illustrated in Fig. C14. As a result the name "Parrott Willow" has been used in subsequent books about Willow pattern even though many companies used the pattern. Some firms such as Grimwades* actually produced a wider variety of objects decorated with the pattern than Parrott & Co. A Booths Willow variant was also produced by Parrott & Co in blue underglaze. A polychrome decal based on the Booths pattern with additional flowers was also made. Royal Doulton* produced this pattern on bone china.

Mark 2
(GG2972)
c. 1935+

Mark 3 (GG2972)
c. 1935+

Polychrome variation of Standard Willow pattern cup and saucer printed in black with enamel coloring on bone china. The pattern number looks like 98001 and according to the mark, the pattern is a "reproduction of old Chinese". Crown Staffordshire Porcelain Co.* also had a series with this title. *Courtesy IWC Convention 2000.* $50-75.

Parrott & Co. (Ltd.)

Location: Albert Street Pottery, Burslem, Staffordshire
Dates: c. 1921 - c. 1960s
Marks:

Mark 1
(GG2971)
c. 1921+

Brief History: An earthenware manufacturer, little is known about this twentieth century company. The types of wares made were listed in *Pottery Gazette*, February 1, 1926: "Manufacturers of Teapots, teapot stands, hot water jugs (in white

Set of three pitchers decorated with the litho based on Two Temples II pattern. The heights of the jugs are 6.5, 7 1/8, and 7 7/8-inches. This hexagonal shape is rarely seen. Mark 2 without pattern number. *Courtesy Paul Kirves and Zeke Jimenez.* $50-95 each.

Three 8-inch plates are attached to form a tid-bit tray decorated with the litho based on Two Temples II pattern. The glaze is ivory on these plates. Occasionally the glaze on pieces with this pattern is almost mustard color. Mark 3. *Courtesy Daisy and Tom Eden.* $50-75.

Booths Willow central pattern variant plate with polychrome lithograph. Flowers are added to the pattern in the lower left-hand section, and the three figures on the bridge are facing the teahouse. Motifs from the central pattern are used in the border. The plate is indented octagonal in shape. It is part of a dinnerware service. Mark 2 with a pattern number that is difficult to read: 15(87). *Courtesy of Tim and Kim Allen.* $12-20.

Booths Willow central pattern 5.25-inch square plate transfer-printed in blue underglaze on earthenware. A crisscross inner border and basket weave outer border with ochre edge are used on this plate. It is part of a sandwich set. Mark 1 with A5686 above it. *Author's Collection.* $10-18.

Thomas Patterson & Co.

Location: Tyne Pottery (c. 1827-40), and Sheriff Hill Pottery (c. 1839-47), Newcastle upon Tyne, Northumberland
Dates: c. 1827-47
Mark:

c. 1827-47+

Comments Concerning Mark: Impressed PATTERSON in a half circle was also used by George Patterson at Tyne Pottery; however, I am attributing this mark to Thomas Patterson because the same shape platter with the same engraving is seen on page 101 (bottom) of *Tyneside Pottery* by R. C. Bell and tentatively attributed to Thomas Patterson at Sheriff Hill Pottery.

Brief History: Thomas Patterson & Co. was mentioned in directories of 1827, 1827-8, 1828, 1829 and 1837 at Tyne Pottery and in 1847 at Sheriff Hill. Thomas Patterson was also in partnership at Tyne Pottery with Dawson & Codling c. 1833-40. Two other partnerships are known at Sheriff Hill: with C. F. Jackson pre-1840, and with Codling 1840-44. George Patterson, the son of Thomas, is mentioned at Sheriff Hill in directories beginning in 1851. Both Pattersons produced the Standard Willow pattern.

Type of Willow Manufactured: Standard Willow pattern transfer-printed in blue underglaze on thin earthenware with pale blue glaze.

Standard Willow pattern 8-sided platter transfer-printed in blue underglaze on lightweight earthenware with pale blue glaze. The rim has molded bars extending outward at each of the points on the edge with an additional bar in the center of each side and two on each side of the long ends. The platter measures 12-by-15.5-inches, and the molded bars vary from 2.5 to 3-inches apart around the rim. The clay body is thinner and more compact than that found on most mid-nineteenth century platters. *Author's Collection*. $150-225.

Standard Willow pattern chestnut basket and stand transfer-printed in blue underglaze on earthenware. The pieces have impressed PATTERSON; however, I do not have a copy of that mark. Chestnut baskets of this type are usually dated in the first part of the nineteenth century. For that reason, I am including it here. *Courtesy IWC Convention 1996.* $250+.

Pearl Pottery Co. (Ltd.)

Location: Brook Street, Hanley, Staffordshire
Dates: c. 1894-1936
Marks:

Mark 1 c. 1894+

Comments Concerning Mark: Mark 2 is like GG2882 except that the word NEW is not in the mark; therefore this is a mark used by Pearl Pottery Co. – not New Pearl Pottery.
Brief History: The Pearl Pottery was established in 1820 by Ralph Salt. There were several different partnerships during most of the nineteenth century. The firm produced earthenware and white granite for export. According to Jewitt, from about 1892 the pottery was worked by Messrs. Wood and Bennett. The major products at the end of the nineteenth century were dinner, breakfast, tea, and toilet ware. The business was succeeded by the New Pearl Pottery Co. Ltd. at the same location c. 1936-41.

Mark 2
(GG2882) var.
c. 1894+

Type of Willow Manufactured: Standard Willow pattern transfer-printed in blue underglaze on earthenware and "Red Bridge" decal pattern overglaze.

Standard Willow pattern 9-inch plate transfer-printed in dark blue underglaze on average quality earthenware. There are single stilt marks at the rim on the back of the plate. It has a slightly recessed foot ring. The border patterns are well matched. The plate, cup & saucer all bear Mark 1. *Author's Collection.* $15-20.

Ten-inch plate decorated with the "Red Bridge" willow variant decal in reverse overglaze. It has the normal border for this pattern. The plate is well worn and somewhat discolored. Mark 2. *Courtesy Tim and Kim Allen.* $15-20.

George Phillips

Location: Longport, Staffordshire
Dates: c. 1834-47
Mark:

c. 1834-47

Brief History: George Phillips had been in business with Edward Phillips until Edward died. George carried on alone from 1834 until his death in 1847 at age 45. It was a large factory employing between four and five hundred persons. The Phillips firm produced good quality earthenware and stoneware for the home market and export. In 1849, the manufactory was auctioned including 8 ovens, the house, utensils and engravings.

Type of Willow Manufactured: Standard Willow pattern transfer-printed in blue underglaze on earthenware.

Standard Willow pattern sauce tureen with under plate transfer-printed in blue underglaze on earthenware. Wares by Phillips are seldom found, and it is unusual to find an under plate that is marked. The tray measures 7.5-by-5.75-inches. The tureen is 4.5-inches high to the top of the lion finial. The glaze has a rippled feel to it. *Author's Collection.* $150-225.

Standard Willow pattern 10-inch round plate transfer-printed in blue underglaze on earthenware of average quality. The outer border pattern had to be cut at 2 o'clock as it was too large for the plate. In addition to the printed mark, there is a small impressed 8 petal flower. *Courtesy Dennis Crosby.* $25-35.

Pilkington's Tile & Pottery Co. Ltd.

Location: Clifton Junction, Nr. Manchester, Lancashire,
Dates: c. 1893-1964
Mark:

(GG3022)
c. 1897-1904

Brief History: The business was established by four Pilkington brothers who discovered clay while searching for coal seams. William Burton, a young chemist who had worked for Josiah Wedgwood, and his brother Joseph Burton, were responsible for the technical and artistic development of decorative tile production in the early years. William Burton developed a number of different glazes inspired by his interest in ancient glazes. This experimentation led to the making of luster pottery. A number of artists led by Gordon Forsyth designed the art pottery made by the firm. The ornamental earthenware was produced from 1896-1938, and again from 1948-57. The tile business continued until Pilkington's merged with Carter, Stabler and Adams in 1964.

Type of Willow Manufactured: Standard Willow pattern transfer-printed in blue underglaze on 6 inch square tiles.

Standard Willow pattern tiles transfer-printed in blue underglaze. Three tiles have been put together in a wooden frame to form a tray. A tile with this willow pattern is seen on page 102, #94 in *Collecting Victorian Tiles* by Terence A. Lockett. Mark as above, dated in the book as c. 1905. *Author's Collection.* $75-150.

Pinder, Bourne & Co.

Location: Nile Street, Burslem, Staffordshire
Dates: c. 1862-82
Impressed Marks:

Brief History: Thomas Pinder founded the firm in the mid-nineteenth century. In 1851, the style became Pinder, Bourne & Hope. By 1862, the firm was renamed Pinder, Bourne & Co. China had been made for a time previously, but the manufacture of earthenware was more successful. Printed, enameled, and gilt decorated earthenware were made. Other goods included red ware, jet ware, and sanitary ware. The firm had won medals at the London and Paris Exhibitions of 1851, 1855, and 1867. Henry Doulton bought into the firm in 1878; however, the name was not changed until 1882 when Doulton took over fully.

Mark 1 c. 1862-82

Mark 2
(GG3038)
c. 1862-82

Type of Willow Manufactured: Standard Willow pattern transfer-printed in blue, black, and brown underglaze on earthenware as well as Willow & Aster border pattern in blue.

Standard Willow pattern compote transfer-printed in dark brown underglaze on earthenware. It measures 8.5-inches in diameter and stands 5-inches high. This is a very unusual color. Mark 1. *Courtesy IWC Convention 2002.* $75-125.

Willow and Aster border pattern 8-inch teapot stand transfer-printed in blue underglaze on earthenware. There are two circles with Standard Willow pattern and three circles with asters set against a dark cobalt border. This pattern was continued by Doulton & Co.* Mark 2. *Courtesy Paul Kirves and Zeke Jimenez.* $40-75.

R. H. & S. L. Plant (Ltd.)

Location: Tuscan Works, Longton, Staffordshire
Dates: c. 1898-1971
Marks:

Brief History: R. H. Plant established the firm at Carlisle Works, Longton in 1881, with his brother S. L. Plant. In 1898 they moved to the Tuscan Works and renamed the firm R. H. & S. L. Plant. They formed a limited company in 1915. The trademark used was "Tuscan China", and it was used on marks for hotel ware as well as bone china.. A wide range of useful china was produced in many patterns. An article regarding the good quality of "Tuscan" china appeared in *Pottery Gazette*, February 1, 1926:

> …and simple printed patterns such as Worcester 6241…& Roman 3626…to say nothing of the Minton 4178 (Blue Willow, in light or dark blue), are held as stock lines by many of the best houses in the trade.

R. H. & S. L. Plant also made models of birds and butterflies that were hand-painted. The company formed a partnership with Susie Cooper Ltd. in 1958. The Wedgwood Group took over the firm in 1966, and it was renamed Royal Tuscan in 1971.

Type of Willow Manufactured: Standard Willow pattern transfer-printed in light and dark blue underglaze on bone china and hotelware. Mandarin central pattern blue printed on glaze on bone china with a narrow border and gold trim.

Mark 1 (GG3059)
var. c. 1898+

Mark 2 (GG5061)
c. 1907+

Mark 3 (GG3062)
c. 1936+

Mark 4 (GG3064)
c. 1947+

Standard Willow pattern 5.5-inch plate transfer-printed in black underglaze on earthenware. The printing isn't as clear on this plate as on the compote. Mark 1. *Courtesy Bill and Joyce Keenan.* $8-15.

Standard Willow pattern 9.5-inch rimmed soup bowl transfer-printed in blue underglaze on institutional ware. I was surprised to find this piece marked Tuscan China because it is a vitrified clay body and much heavier than other pieces marked Tuscan China by Plant. Mark 3. *Author's Collection.* $15-20.

Standard Willow pattern teapot transfer-printed light blue underglaze on bone china with gold trim. The pattern is in linear form around the teapot. It stands 6.5-inches tall and is 5-inches across. Mark 2 with Made in England. *Courtesy Norma and John Gilbert.* $75-135.

Mandarin pattern cup and saucer blue printed on glaze with gold trim on bone china. This set has a narrow border that is not usually seen with the Mandarin central pattern. The pattern number in gold is D2296. Mark 4. *Author's Collection.* $15-25.

Standard Willow pattern cup and saucer transfer-printed in light blue underglaze on bone china trimmed in gold. The cup has a nice number 9 handle. The saucer is marked with pattern # 4178 in two places – the pattern "Minton 4178" referred to in the *Pottery Gazette* quoted above. Mark 2. A different shape light blue cup and saucer with Mark 1 also has Pattern #4178. *Author's Collection.* $15-22.

Advertisement from *Pottery Gazette*, January 1, 1917, for R. H. & S. L. Plant Tuscan Works listing the various products made by the company.

Standard Willow pattern 10.5-inch plate transfer-printed in blue underglaze on earthenware. This plate has a concave rim and recessed double foot ring. The engraving is the same as on the plate above. Mark 2 with impressed name mark as well. *Author's Collection.* $25-35.

Podmore, Walker & Co.

Location: Well Street (c. 1834-53), Amicable Street (c. 1850-59), and Swan Bank (c. 1853-59), Tunstall, Staffordshire
Dates: c. 1834-59
Marks:

Mark 1 (GG3075)
c. 1834-59

Comments Concerning Marks: Enoch Wedgwood was a partner in this firm, so name marks were used such as Wedgwood & Co as well as the P. W. & Co. marks.

Brief History: Podmore, Walker & Co. produced good quality earthenware including ironstone type ware with a large export market. Over 400 were employed in 1851: 164 men, 133 boys, 60 women and 57 girls. It

Mark 2 (GG3079)
c. 1834-59

was helpful to the firm to have Enoch Wedgwood as a partner. The name Wedgwood & Co. was often used in marks and advertising. The firm was renamed Wedgewood & Co. Ltd. in 1860.

Type of Willow Manufactured: Standard Willow pattern transfer-printed in blue underglaze on earthenware marked Stoneware.

William Pointon (& Co.)

Location: Overhouse Pottery, Burslem, Staffordshire
Dates: c. 1828-54
Mark:

c. 1828-54

Brief History: William Pointon is recorded as a china manufacturer in an 1834 directory; however, no marked examples have been reported. R. K. Henrywood has found references to William Pointon in other directories beginning in 1828 where he is listed as an earthenware manufacturer. In some years, such as 1834, he is listed as producing both earthenware and china. In a letter to me May 2, 2001 Geoffrey Godden stated that the W. P. initials and mark above could be for William Pointon. The dates are correct for the platter shown below.

Type of Willow Manufactured: Standard Willow pattern transfer-printed in blue underglaze on earthenware marked as Stone China.

Standard Willow pattern 10 3/8-inch plate transfer-printed in blue underglaze on earthenware. It has a flat rim with 3-point stilt marks on the back and single stilt marks on the front. There is a flat 1/4-inch wide foot ring. It bears Mark 1. The engraving is exactly the same as that on the following plate with Mark 2. *Author's Collection.* As is: $5.

Standard Willow pattern platter transfer-printed in blue underglaze on earthenware. A plate with the same mark has also been found by a willow collector. *Courtesy Andrew Pye.* $125-175.

Pointon & Co. Ltd.

Location: Norfolk Works, Cauldon Place, Hanley, Staffordshire
Dates: c. 1883-1916
Mark:

(GG3081)
c. 1883-91

Brief History: Both China and earthenware were produced by this firm. Transfer-printed patterns as well as artist-signed hand-painted patterns were used. Useful wares were made including bone china dessert services.

Type of Willow Manufactured: Two Temples II pattern transfer-printed in blue underglaze on bone china. Gold enhancement was sometimes added over glaze.

Two Temples II pattern 8-inch plate transfer-printed in blue underglaze on bone china. The round plate has a flat rim and a high single foot ring. *Author's Collection.* $10-15.

Two Temples II pattern 10-inch plate transfer-printed in blue underglaze on bone china with gold applied over the usual white areas of the pattern. The plate has a scalloped edge. *Courtesy Harry and Jessie Hall.* $25-45.

Thomas Poole

Location: Cobden Works, Longton, Staffordshire
Dates: c. 1880-1952
Mark:

(GG3089)
c. 1929-40 and
(GG3400)
c. 1952

Brief History: Thomas Poole used the trade name "Royal Stafford China". The firm produced a good variety of bone china useful wares. Tea wares were a specialty. The firm introduced the short tea service made up of 21 pieces. An interesting claim was seen in the *Pottery* Gazette, August 1, 1908: "Royal Stafford China: This ware is guaranteed to be produced below the government Standard required to <u>Prevent Lead Poisoning</u>." In 1924, the name was changed to Thomas Poole (Longton) Ltd. The firm merged with Gladstone China Ltd. in 1948. By 1952, the name was changed to "Royal Stafford China". The mark shown above continued to be used.

Type of Willow Manufactured: Standard Willow pattern transfer-printed in blue underglaze on bone china.

Standard Willow pattern serving plate transfer-printed in blue underglaze on bone china. The plate measures 10.25-inches including the handles. It has a fluted area between the round center pattern and the square outer border. There is gold line trim. *Courtesy IWC Convention 2002.* $35-55.

Pountney & Co. (Ltd.)

Location: Temple Back, Victoria Pottery, and the Bristol Pottery, Fishponds, Bristol, Gloucestershire
Dates: c. 1849-1969
Marks:

Mark 1 (GG3112)
c. 1900-23

Mark 2 (GG3113)
c. 1900-25

Comments Concerning Marks: "Established 1750" was used on marks until the publication in 1920 of W. J. Pountney's book *Old Bristol Potteries*, which showed that the Temple Back Pottery's deeds went back to 1683. Marks 1 and 2 seem to have been used interchangeably on pieces in "Mandarin" pattern in flow blue and shades of green.

Brief History: The Temple Back Pottery was set up in 1683 by Edward Ward, a potter from Brislington just outside of Bristol. There were a number of partnerships until 1813 when the name Pountney was first associated with the pottery. John Decimus Pountney went into partnership with Henry Carter. By this time, it was known as the Bristol Pottery. Early wares were unmarked until about 1849 when "P. & Co." or "Pountney & Co." began to be used.

John Decimus Pountney died in 1852, and his widow, Charlotte, carried on for 20 years. The pottery began to have financial troubles during that time. It was sold in 1872, and again in 1878, to two London solicitors: Patrick Johnston and Mr. Rogers who were not interested in reviving the pottery. Mr. Rogers retired in 1883, and Mr. Johnston died in 1884, leaving his nephew Thomas Bertram (T.B.) Johnston in charge. Through the dedication, enthusiasm and expertise of T. B. Johnston, the firm grew and prospered. Shortly after his uncle's death T. B. managed to move the company to Victoria Pottery, built in 1865. It was an improvement over the 200-year-old building they had left, but he wanted to build a new pottery with modern equipment and space.

Mr. Heward Bell, a friend of T. B. Johnston, came into a fortune. He decided to contribute to the building of the new pottery. He joined the Board of Directors in 1900, an 8-acre site was acquired in Fishponds, and work began on the new factory. Johnston led the business until his death in 1938. His son Patrick Bertram Gwinnell Johnston and a nephew Alick S. Newsom became joint managers, and the company continued to thrive. It was an earthenware factory producing dinnerware in many different shapes and with various types of decorations: printing, painting, and lithograph. Sanitary wares and hotel ware were also produced. In the March 1, 1910, edition of *Pottery Gazette*, p. 289, the "Buyer's Notes" had this to say:

> Pountney & Co., Ltd., the Bristol Pottery, Bristol. "Alkalon" China, the distinctive name they give to the special body they now use. It is remarkable for its whiteness and its lightness, qualities in which it closely approximates to china….They have revived the old "Gadroon" shape that was once so popular, …both attractive and useful. The vegetable dishes are deep, oblong and of a useful size. Dinner services in this shape are shown in many decorations of which the "Mandarin" in dark blue is one of the latest and one of the best.

In October 1962, the Royal Cauldon name, pattern books and molds were acquired. The demands of the 1960s proved too much for the old pottery, and it was sold to help pay off debts in 1969. The company became Cauldon Bristol Potteries Ltd. and moved to a site in Cornwall. The move failed, and the company was bankrupt in two years. It was purchased by A. G. Richardson & Co. in 1971.

Type of Willow Manufactured: Standard Willow pattern transfer-printed in blue, green, and red (Gadroon shape) underglaze on earthenware. Worcester Willow pattern called "Mandarin" transfer-printed in flow blue and shades of green, sometimes with clobbering.

Retailer/importer: R. Twining & Co. Ltd., London*

Mark 3 (GG3115)
c. 1922-48

Mark 4 c. 1922-48

Mark 5 c. 1922-48

Worcester Willow pattern called "Mandarin," 9.25-inch plate transfer-printed in gray-green with clobbering of orange-red and gold trim. This plate is Gadroon shape. Mark 1. *Courtesy IWC Convention 2000.* $10-20.

Worcester Willow pattern called "Mandarin" sauce tureen, lid, and tray transfer-printed in flow blue underglaze on Alkalon China. This set illustrates the oblong shape of the serving dishes with Gadroon edge mentioned in the *Pottery Gazette* quoted above. This piece has Mark 1, but similar items have been seen with Mark 2. *Courtesy IWC Convention 1994.* $125-175.

Standard Willow pattern 6.5-inch hot water pot transfer-printed in blue underglaze on earthenware. This pattern seems to have been made later than Mandarin at Pountney. Mark 4. *Courtesy IWC Convention 2001.* $45-70.

Standard Willow pattern 4-cup teapot transfer-printed in blue underglaze on earthenware. This low teapot with flat top and straight sides looks like a 1930s-40s shape. The spout is undecorated, and the finial has the boat from the pattern on the top. Both sides of the teapot have this part of the pattern. The willow tree and bridge section were not used. Mark 3. *Author's Collection.* $45-70.

Pountney & Allies

Location: Temple Back, Bristol Pottery, Bristol, Gloucestershire
Dates: c. 1816-35
Mark:

c. 1816-35

Brief History: The partnership succeeded Carter & Pountney. Subsequently Pountney & Goldney.
Type of Willow Manufactured: Standard Willow pattern transfer-printed in blue underglaze on earthenware. A tureen was seen on the Ebay Internet Auction site. No picture available.

Price Brothers

Location: Crown Works, Top Bridge Works, and Albion Works, Burslem, Staffordshire
Dates: c. 1896-1961
Mark:

c. 1896-1903

Comments Concerning Mark: It is known that Price Brothers used an M & M mark. Known partnerships with initials M & M do not fit the time period. As a result I have chosen to place the mark and photo in this entry.
Brief History: In 1903 the firm moved to Top Bridge and Albion Works and was renamed Price Bros. (Burslem) Ltd. The firm produced earthenware products including wash sets. In 1962 the firm merged with Kensington Potteries Ltd. to form Price & Kensington Potteries Ltd.
Type of Willow Manufactured: Standard Willow pattern transfer-printed in blue underglaze on earthenware.

Standard Willow pattern oval teapot transfer-printed in blue underglaze on earthenware. The pattern is in linear form. The teapot is impressed BRISTOL. *Courtesy Joette Hightower.* $75-115.

Standard Willow pattern wash set transfer-printed in blue underglaze on earthenware. In addition to the basin and large pitcher, there is a smaller pitcher, tumbler, mug, and covered sponge bowl. The numbers 1901 on the mark may not be a date indication, but the set was probably made about that time. *Courtesy Harry and Jessie Hall.* $200+.

Standard Willow central pattern 6 5/8 rimmed cereal bowl transfer-printed in dark blue underglaze on thin earthenware. There are 8 indentations on the edge of the concave rim. The boat and bird motifs are used as a border pattern, and there is a gold line on both sides of the rim. Mark 5 with impressed date 1938. *Author's Collection.* $12-20.

Price & Kensington Potteries Ltd.

Location: Longport, Staffordshire
Dates: c. 1962-present (2003)
Mark:

c. 1962+

Brief History: Continuing the tradition of making teapots, this firm continues to produce teapots that are decorated over glaze with lithos and enamel colors. Many souvenir teapots are made in interesting figural shapes.
Type of Willow Manufactured: Variations of Standard Willow pattern litho or decal overglaze in blue.

Six cup teapot decorated with Willow variant decal overglaze in blue. The decal was supplied to the factory by Mathay Transfers. See below. *Courtesy Paul Kirves and Zeke Jimenez.* $20-30.

A copy of a Matthey Transfer Made in England of pattern No. 6581: WILLOW. This MATTHEYPRINT was Made in U.S.A. and called BLUE WILLOW. These transfers were available to potteries in the U.K. and other parts of the world as well as to amateur ceramics enthusiasts. The decal was copyright dated to 1981 by MATTHEYPRINT.

John & Henry Proctor & Co.

Location: New Town Pottery, High Street, and Heathcote Road, Longton
Dates: c. 1855-84
Mark:

(GG3175)
c. 1857-84

Brief History: This firm succeeded that of Stanley & Lambert* at New Town Pottery. This was a 4-oven works that produced earthenware in cream color, printed, painted, and lustered patterns. In 1861, the business employed 39 men, 13 women, 9 boys and 18 girls. In 1876, J. & H. Proctor moved to Heathcote Road Pottery and continued to produce the same type of earthenwares.
Type of Willow Manufactured: Standard Willow pattern transfer-printed in blue underglaze on earthenware.

Standard Willow pattern tureen transfer-printed in blue underglaze on earthenware. This is a standard form of tureen for the mid-nineteenth century. The ladle may or may not be original to the set. *Courtesy Paul Kirves and Zeke Jimenez.* $225-275.

Samuel Radford (Ltd.)

Location: Newmarket Works, Longton (1877-85), and High Street Fenton (1885-1957), Staffordshire
Dates: c. 1877-1957
Marks:

Mark 1 (GG3184)
var. c. 1880+

Brief History: Radford & Co. succeeded George Copestake Senior at the Newmarket Works, Market Street, Longton. Samuel Radford had been in partnership with Joseph Amison at Chancery Lane, Longton prior to 1877. According to the *Pottery Gazette,* April 1881, Samuel Radford designed all his own patterns. The firm produced bone china tea, breakfast, and dessert services of fine quality. By 1936, the pattern numbers had reached 6500. The company shut down during World War II. T. G. Green* took over the firm's orders. Radford expanded steadily after resuming production when the war ended; however, the firm ceased production in 1957.

Mark 2
(GG3184)
c. 1880+

Type of Willow Manufactured: Standard Willow pattern in blue and brown underglaze on bone china. The brown is often clobbered. Other willow patterns include: Mandarin pattern in blue underglaze on a fluted shape and a polychrome decal based on Two Temples II pattern.

Mark 3
(GG3191)
c. 1928+

RADFORDS

FENTON
MADE IN ENGLAND

Mark 4 (GG3192)
c. 1928+

MANUFACTURER
FENTON

ENGLAND

Mark 5 c. 1928+

Mark 6 (GG3193)
c. 1938-57

Standard Willow round central pattern with square outer border transfer-printed in brown underglaze on bone china. These lovely dishes measure 5, 6, and 7-inches square and have a raised wavy edge. There are 5 colors plus gold trim added over the glaze. Mark 3. *Courtesy Loren Zeller.* $100-175 set of three.

Standard Willow pattern cup and saucer transfer-printed in light blue underglaze on bone china and trimmed in gold. The front gable ends of the small house are dark like those on Minton* Willow pattern. The narrow path and shape of the birds are also reminiscent of Minton's engraving. Mark 5. *Author's Collection.* $15-22.

Standard Willow pattern 8-inch plate transfer-printed in brown underglaze on bone china with clobbering in rust, green, and dark cobalt. This engraving also has the Minton* elements of dark gable ends, narrow path, and shape of the birds. Mark 2 with pattern #1253 – a relatively early pattern number. Some clobbered pieces with this pattern number have later marks from Godden. *Courtesy IWC Convention 1999.* $15-20.

Bone china cup and saucer decorated with polychrome decal based on Two Temples II pattern. This decal is more often used on earthenware. Both pieces have wavy edges trimmed in gold. The set bears Mark 6 with Pattern #4215. If the mark was not used before 1938, this was not a new pattern number when the set was made. Pattern numbers had reached beyond 6500 by 1936. *Courtesy IWC Convention 2001.* $25-40.

Mandarin pattern teapot transfer-printed in medium blue underglaze on bone china. Evidently tea services were made in this fluted shape as I have a serving plate that matches the teapot with the same mark. There is gold trim. Mark 1. *Courtesy Paul Kirves and Zeke Jimenez.* $100-175.

Ratcliffe & Co.

Location: Gold Street Works and Clarence Works, Longton, Staffordshire
Dates: c. 1891-1914
Mark:

(GG3201)
c. 1891-1914

Brief History: The firm was located at Gold Street Works until 1896 when it relocated at Clarence Works in Longton. The *Pottery Gazette*, November 1, 1908, gave this description of the firm: "Ratcliffe & Co., Clarence Works, Longton: Manufacturers of plain and ornamental earthenware suitable for home and foreign markets."
Type of Willow Manufactured: Standard Willow pattern transfer-printed in blue underglaze on earthenware. Very little is found.

Standard Willow central pattern 3-inch butter pat transfer-printed in blue underglaze on earthenware. The entire surface of the butter pat is covered with the central pattern. This is the only piece of willow I have seen with this mark. *Courtesy Charline and Franklin Ladner.* $10-15.

Samuel & John Rathbone

Location: Amicable Street, Tunstall, Staffordshire
Dates: c. 1812-18 and 1823-35
Marks:

Mark 1
c. 1823-35

Mark 2
c. 1823-35

Comments Concerning Marks: Mark 2, the letter R in a sunburst, was attributed to William Ratcliffe in Godden's *Encyclopaedia of British Marks*; however, new information came into his possession. I am using his *Encyclopaedia of British Porcelain Manufacturers* as the source for my attributions.
Brief History: Samuel and John Rathbone were in business from 1812 until 1818 when their oldest brother William joined the firm. The name was changed to W. S. & J. Rathbone in 1818. William died in 1820, but the name continued for three more years. In 1823, Samuel and John resumed trading under their joint names. It is not known whether china was produced during the early years; however, marked blue printed patterns on porcelain can be attributed to the period beginning in 1823. It is certain that earthenware was produced from 1812.
Type of Willow Manufactured: Two Temples II transfer-printed in light blue underglaze on porcelain. Quite often, gold was added to enhance the ware.

Two Temples II pattern covered bowl transfer-printed in medium blue underglaze on porcelain. The bowl has a wavy edge. Both pieces have gold trim, and the knob on the lid is covered with gold. Mark 1. *Courtesy Marian Axley.* $75-150.

Two Temples II pattern cup and saucer transfer-printed in medium blue underglaze on porcelain. It is a London shape cup. Both pieces have a wavy edge trimmed in gold. Mark 2. *Author's Collection.* $35-55.

Two Temples II pattern creamer and covered sugar transfer-printed in light blue underglaze on porcelain. The gold loop and dot pattern is more ornate that just outlining in gold. Mark 2. *Courtesy IWC Convention 1993.* $200+.

Ravensdale Pottery Ltd.

Location: Royal Albert Works, Tunstall, Staffordshire
Dates: c. 1999-present (2003)
Mark:

RAVENSDALE POTTERY LTD.
MADE IN STAFFORDSHIRE ENGLAND
DISHWASHER AND
MICROWAVE SAFE.

c. 1999+

Brief History: The factory was built in 1858, and occupied by a number of different potteries and design businesses. In September 1999, Graham Palmer and Kevin Knapper formed a partnership and moved into the ground floor of the empty building. The firm specializes in oval dishes, steak plates, tableware and special items of cast ware.

Type of Willow Manufactured: Standard Willow variation pattern used by English Ironstone Pottery Ltd.* printed in blue on earthenware that is dishwasher and microwave safe.

Standard Willow variant pattern used by English Ironstone Pottery Ltd.* blue printed platter. It measures 10.25-by-13-inches. *Courtesy IWC Convention 2002.* $10-20.

Type of Willow Manufactured: Standard Willow pattern transfer-printed in green, brown, and black underglaze on lightweight earthenware.

Standard Willow pattern 10.5-inch plate transfer-printed in green underglaze on lightweight earthenware. The plate has 8 indentations on the edge of the flat rim. Three-point stilt marks on back of rim and single stilt marks on front. The plate has a double recessed rim. The 4-spoke wheel was cut from the outer border at 5 o'clock. *Author's Collection.* $45-65.

Standard Willow pattern 10.5-inch plate transfer-printed in two colors underglaze on earthenware. The rim is black; the central pattern and inner border are brown. The shape of the plate is the same as the previous one, and the engraving is the same; however, it is heavier. The outer border has a small cut at 2 o'clock. *Author's Collection.* $40-60.

Read, Clementson & Anderson

Location: High Street, Shelton (Hanley), Staffordshire
Dates: c. 1836
Mark:

(GG3213)
c. 1836

Brief History: Robert Anderson was a dealer in china and earthenwares at Galway, Ireland. He was in a triple partnership with Read and Clementson until the partnership was dissolved September 3, 1836. This was in the middle of the partnership of John Read and Joseph Clementson* (c. 1833-39). Perhaps Anderson had been a partner only in the Irish side of the business.

Read & Clementson

Location: High Street, Shelton (Hanley), Staffordshire
Dates: c. 1833-39
Marks:

Mark I
(GG3212)
c. 1833-39

Brief History: John Read and Joseph Clementson produced good quality printed earthenware in a number of different colors underglaze. Stone china wares included colorful decorations overglaze as well. Tableware of many types was produced for the American market as well as the home market and Irish trade.

Joseph Clementson* went into business by himself at the close of this partnership.

Type of Willow Manufactured: Standard Willow pattern transfer-printed in purple and perhaps other colors underglaze on light-weight earthenware. See Joseph Clementson* for other colors and similar engraving.

Mark 2 (GG3212)
c. 1833-39

Standard Willow pattern 10.5-inch plate transfer-printed in purple underglaze on earthenware. The plate has 8 indentations on the edge of the flat rim. A patch was added to the outer border at 8 o'clock. Mark 1. *Courtesy Jeff Siptak.* $45-65.

Redfern & Drakeford (Ltd.)

Location: Chatfield Works, High Street and Balmoral Works, Boundary Street, Longton, Staffordshire
Dates: c. 1892-1933
Mark:

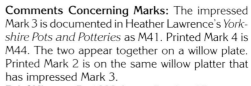

Comments Concerning Marks: Another mark was seen with BALMORAL CHINA ENGLAND in a circle surrounding the lion as seen in this printed mark.

(GG3215) var.
c. 1909-33

Brief History: The firm moved from Chatfield Works to Balmoral Works in 1902. China was produced. The trade name "Balmoral China" often appeared on marks after 1909.

Type of Willow Manufactured: Standard Willow pattern transfer-printed in light blue and polychrome litho based on Two Temples II pattern on bone china.

Standard Willow pattern 2 1/8-inch creamer transfer-printed in light blue underglaze on bone china. This tiny jug is just 2.25-inches from spout to handle, and the opening at the top is 1.25-inches. It has gold trim on the top edge. *Author's Collection.* $15-20.

Reed & Taylor
(see also Swillington Bridge Pottery)

Location: Rock Pottery, Mexborough, Ferrybridge and Swillington Bridge Potteries, Yorkshire
Dates: c. 1830-early 1840s
Marks:

Mark 1 (GG3217)
c. 1833-38

Comments Concerning Marks: The impressed Mark 3 is documented in Heather Lawrence's *Yorkshire Pots and Potteries* as M41. Printed Mark 4 is M44. The two appear together on a willow plate. Printed Mark 2 is on the same willow platter that has impressed Mark 3.

Brief History: By 1833 James Reed and Benjamin Taylor had taken over the Swillington Bridge Pottery*. They had been proprietors of the Mexborough Rock since c. 1830 and Ferrybridge Pottery* since c. 1832. Reed ran the Mexborough works, and Taylor ran the Ferrybridge and Swillington Bridge Potteries. They traded as Reed & Taylor at all three potteries and later as Reed, Taylor & Co. Excavations at Swillington Bridge reveal many products made including creamware, pearlware with blue "grass" edging, and many patterns printed in blue and brown on earthenware. After 1827, ironstone china and opaque granite china were very popular with "Willow Pattern" being very plentiful.

Mark 2 c. 1833-38

Mark 3 (HL41)
c. 1833-38

Swillington Bridge Pottery was owned by William Wilks Jr. who sold it in December 1838. The partnership of Reed & Taylor was dissolved in the early 1840s. Taylor continued on, joined by his son Samuel, at Swillington Bridge trading as "Messrs Taylor" until 1842, and at Ferrybridge until c. 1850. (See Benjamin Taylor & Son* for more information on that partnership.) James Reed continued at Mexborough until his death in 1849.

Type of Willow Manufactured: Standard Willow pattern transfer-printed in blue on earthenware, ironstone china and Opaque China.

Mark 4 (HL44)
c. 1833-38

Standard Willow pattern large platter transfer-printed in blue underglaze on earthenware. There is a nice variety in the shades of blue on this platter. Mark 1. *Courtesy Andrew Pye.* $175-275.

Standard Willow pattern impressive well and tree platter transfer-printed in blue underglaze on Opaque China. It measures 16 1/8-by-20.25-inches. Marks 2 and 3. *Courtesy George Wells.* $225-325.

Regal Pottery Ltd.

Location: Lonpark Industrial Estate, Longton, Staffordshire
Dates: c. 1987-2001
Marks:

Mark 1
c. 1987-2001

Brief History: The company began production in 1987 under the direction of Dave Phillips. Blue willow was one of the first patterns made. Giftware and kitchen ware were very popular in the USA and Australia. The kitchen items included canisters for tea, coffee, sugar, biscuit, pasta, etc., and other items including a kettle, cake stand, and milk jug. Red willow was added, and some items were made in both blue and pink. The company ceased trading in November 2001 in order to develop a new range to be made in English bone china.

Mark 2
c. 1987-2001

Type of Willow Manufactured: Blue and red printed Standard Willow variant pattern used by English Ironstone Pottery Ltd.* on earthenware.

Regal Pottery Co. (Ltd.)

Location: Elder Road, Cobridge, Staffordshire
Dates: c. 1925-31
Mark:

Standard Willow variant pattern 2 piece cheese bell blue printed on earthenware. These were made in red also. Mark 1. *Courtesy IWC Convention 2000.* $20-30.

c. 1925-31

Brief History: The Regal Pottery made earthenware products for the table. Tea ware and dinnerware are known. The trademark used was Regal Ware; however, that trademark was also used by A. G. Richardson.

Type of Willow Manufactured: Standard Willow pattern transfer-printed in blue underglaze on earthenware. The pattern number A3587/P denotes willow pattern.

Standard Willow pattern octagonal plate transfer-printed in blue underglaze on earthenware. This piece measures 8-inches, and the center is recessed. It could be an under plate for a tureen or perhaps a teapot stand. *Courtesy Ohio Willow Society.* $10-20.

Standard Willow variant garlic bread tray red printed on earthenware. It measures 15.75-by-6-inches. The central pattern is used in linear form in two repetitions. Mark 2 states "Pink" Willow; however, it is a nice deep red color. *Author's Collection.* $15-20.

Standard Willow variant kettle-shaped teapot blue printed on earthenware. This pot comes in 12- and 20-cup size. Mark 1. *Courtesy Charles and Zeta Hollingsworth. $25-45.*

William staying at the Bell Works and John going to Cauldon Place with his father. Earthenwares, stone china and porcelain of exceptionally high quality were produced. The firm of John Ridgway & Co. was followed in 1855, by Ridgway, Bates & Co. until 1862, when the Cauldon Place works were taken over by Brown-Westhead, Moore & Co.*

Type of Willow Manufactured: Two Temples II pattern transfer-printed in blue underglaze on porcelain with gold border patterns added.

Two Temples II pattern 6.25-inch teapot stand transfer-printed in blue underglaze on porcelain. The border and edge have gold lines, and there is an elaborate leaf pattern inside the border overlapping the central pattern. The mark shows pattern 2/176. *Author's Collection. $100-125.*

William Reid

Location: Newbigging Pottery, Musselburgh, east of Edinburgh, Scotland
Dates: c. 1801-35
Mark:

c. 1801-35

Brief History: William Reid founded the Newbigging Pottery in 1801. He had previously leased the pottery in West Pans and worked in Bo'ness. After Reid died in 1835, his sons Robert and George carried on the pottery for a number of years. The pottery employed 70 to 80 men and produced earthenware and perhaps stoneware. Many of the early wares were unmarked. An archaeological excavation in December 1980, and January 1981, provided an opportunity to collect shards and ceramic materials for study. Shards were found for printed patterns such as Willow and Two Temples; however, dating is not known as the pottery continued into the twentieth century.

Type of Willow Manufactured: Standard Willow pattern plates have been found with the mark shown above. Coysh & Henrywood refer to a Willow plate and show the mark on page 299 of *The Dictionary of Blue and White Printed Pottery 1780-1880.* No picture is available.

John Ridgway (& Co.)

Location: Cauldon Place, Shelton, Hanley, Staffordshire
Dates: c. 1830-55
Mark:

c. 1830-50

Comment Concerning the Mark: Ridgway porcelains are rarely marked; however fractional pattern numbers were used on tea ware under a 2 until about 1851, when the top number changed to 5.

Brief History: From about 1792 to 1802, Job and George Ridgway worked at the Bell Works in Shelton. When they split up in 1802, Job built the Cauldon Place works at Shelton. His two sons John and William joined the firm and worked at the Bell Works with their uncle as well as at Cauldon Place. In 1830, the two sons separated with

William Ridgway

c. 1830-54

Location: Bell Works, Shelton and Church Works, Hanley, Staffordshire
Dates: c. 1830-54
Mark:

Comment Concerning Mark: It is often difficult to attribute marks that have only the initials. If this mark was indeed used by William Ridgway, it would probably have been at the Bell Works when he was working alone.

Brief History: William Ridgway produced mainly earthenware and ironstone china at the Bell Works during this period. Porcelains were produced earlier when he was in partnership with his brother John at Bell Works; however, more porcelain was produced at Cauldon Place than Bell Works. William Ridgway worked in several locations, and had several different trade styles including W. R. & Co. He took his son Edward John into business with him at Church Works. He was in partnership with Robey in Hanley, and he also had an interest in the firm of Ridgway, Morley, Wear & Co. Morley was his son-in-law. Edward John Ridgway traded first with his father (William Ridgway & Son). From 1835-60, he used the style Ridgway & Abington and later traded under his own name: E. J. Ridgway. The history will be carried further in the next entry of Ridgways*.

Type of Willow Manufactured: Standard Willow pattern transfer-printed in blue underglaze on earthenware and stoneware. A Willow pattern dessert dish is seen in Plate 246 of *Godden's Guide to Iron-stone* on page 315. It has a shield-shaped mark with "Opaque Granite China. W. R. & Co."

Standard Willow pattern blue printed 14.25-by-18-inch platter on good ironstone china. It has clear engraving and well-matched borders. *Author's Collection.* $125-175.

Ridgway & Morley

Location: Shelton, Hanley, Staffordshire
Dates: c. 1842-44
Brief History: The partnership between William Ridgway and Francis Morley succeeded Ridgway, Morley, Wear & Co (mentioned above) on June 24, 1842. Good quality earthenware was produced including ware marked "Improved Granite China" and "Stone Ware". Francis Morley went into business on his own from January 1, 1845.
Type of Willow Manufactured: Standard Willow pattern transfer-printed in blue underglaze on earthenware. A 10-inch plate bearing a Royal Arms mark with R. & M. sold on Ebay Internet Auction in December, 2002. No picture is available.

Ridgways (Ltd.)

Location: Bedford Works, Shelton, Hanley, Staffordshire
Dates: 1879-1983
Marks:

Comments Concerning Marks: As you will notice, the majority of the willow pieces seen here bear Mark 1 which is a combination of GG3310 (registered in 1880) and GG3317 (c. 1927+). Many of these pieces have impressed marks as well, with such dates as 5/06, 11/12, 11/20, 6/22, and 10/24. The impressed mark is put on when the piece is formed, and it can sit on a shelf in storage waiting to be decorated (and printed mark added) for weeks up to years afterward. The sales slip indicates the plate in the first picture, with Mark 1, was purchased in 1918 in Cincinnati, Ohio. This fact as well as the

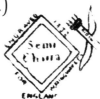

Mark 1 (GG3310 & 3317) c. 1912+

Mark 2 (GG3310 & 3317) c. 1912+

numerous date marks lead me to suggest that the combination of the two marks as seen in Mark 1 above was used before 1927.

Brief History: The Ridgways firm goes back to W. Ridgway & Co.* as indicated in Marks 1-3 above. The date given in the mark, 1832, is usually assumed to be the founding date. The family history is pretty complicated with all the various partnerships and potteries involved. Marks 6 has est. 1792: added to marks c. 1950. That date goes back to the founding of Bell Works by Job and George Ridgway. It was Edward John Ridgway, Job's grandson, who built the Bedford Works in the 1860s.

The Ridgways firm produced very good quality earthenware tableware for the export market. Tea ware, toilet ware, and children's toy china were also produced. Various terms were used by the company to describe the clay bodies used on tableware. "Semi china" was used on willow pattern. Decal patterns, hand-painted, and enameled patterns were also used on semi china.

The firm was renamed Ridgways (Bedford Works) in 1920. In 1929, Cauldon Potteries took over management from John and Edward Ridgway who had led the firm from the early twentieth century. In 1953, Ridgway merged with Booths and Colcloughs operated by the Lawley Group Ltd. From 1955, the firm traded as Ridgway Potteries Ltd. It became part of Allied English Potteries in 1964, and in the 1970s, part of the Royal Doulton Tableware Group. The Ridgways name was phased out about 1983. There were three divisions of Ridgways in the 1970s: Ridgway Bone China, Longton for fancy tableware and teapots; Ridgway Fine Ceramic Tableware, Baddeley Green, Stoke for earthenware tableware; and Ridgway Steelite Hotelware, Hanley for the hotel trade.

Perhaps Ridgways is best known for its 1950s Homemaker pattern designed by Enid Seeney. It was sold exclusively through F. W. Woolworth between 1955 and 1967. It is a black on white pattern featuring a range of 1950s objects including a plant on a stand and a Robin Day chair.

Type of Willow Manufactured: Standard Willow pattern transfer-printed in blue and brown underglaze on earthenware. The brown willow is usually clobbered with shades of orange, green, and cobalt blue with gold outlines on some pattern elements. Two Temples II pattern transfer-printed in blue underglaze on earthenware is also found.

Mark 3 (GG3310 & 3317) c. 1912+

Mark 4 (GG3314) c. 1912+

Mark 5 (GG3317) c. 1912+

Mark 6 (GG3324) var. c. 1950+

Mark 7 c. 1950+

Standard Willow pattern 10-inch plate transfer-printed in blue underglaze on semi china. A booklet titled "The Story of the Willow Pattern Plate" was given to Helen Schwarz, age 15, in 1918, when she purchased the plate from F. W. Woolworth & Co. in Cincinnati, Ohio. Mark 1 and impressed date 1915. *Author's Collection.* $22-32 each.

Standard Willow pattern covered vegetable transfer-printed in blue underglaze on semi china. This is an unusual shape. The lid is 8.75-inches across. The base of the bowl is 5.5-inches and the top is 8-inches in diameter, not including the handles. The bowl has a pattern on the inside as well as the outside. Mark 1. *Author's Collection.* $125-150.

Standard Willow pattern covered jug transfer-printed in blue underglaze on semi china. These jugs are seldom found with lids. I understand the lid could be ordered separately. Mark 1. *Courtesy IWC Convention 1998.* $65-100.

Standard Willow pattern jugs in two different sizes. This is the shape jug seen above with a lid. The larger jug is brown underglaze with shades of orange, green, and cobalt blue clobbered. The handle is also cobalt blue. Some of the elements of the pattern are outlined in gold. It has Mark 2, and the blue jug has Mark 1. Some pieces of "gaudy Ridgway" (as it is sometimes called by collectors) have Mark 3. The pattern number is 3936. *Author's Collection.* $75-125 and $35-65.

Standard Willow pattern wash bowl and pitcher transfer-printed in blue underglaze on semi china. The bowl is decorated with a large circular willow pattern in the middle and a linear form of the pattern on the outside. The pitcher has the full pattern on each side. *Photo from Author's Files.* $200+.

Standard Willow pattern child's tea set for four, transfer-printed in brown underglaze and clobbered in orange, green, cobalt, and gold accents. The handles of the creamer and teapot as well as the spout are enameled in cobalt blue. Many pieces of this set have impressed dates of '24. Mark 5 with pattern #3936. *Courtesy Jeff Siptak.* NP

Standard Willow pattern blue printed dish with attached under plate and lid. The under plate is 6.75-inches across, and the dish is 5-inches wide. It may be a butter dish; however, it seems to be a type of dish used in the early twentieth century, and it has Mark 7 that dates from the 1950s. *Author's Collection.* $85-125.

Two Temples II reversed pattern transfer-printed in blue underglaze on semi china. Tea ware seems to be the main category for this pattern by Ridgways. This is the most common shape found although a short, round creamer is known. After dinner coffee cups are fairly common. Marks I and 7. *Courtesy Joette Hightower.* $75-150 each.

Standard Willow pattern teapot transfer-printed in blue underglaze on earthenware. This shape may have come from the North Staffordshire Pottery* which was taken over by Ridgways in 1952. It has Mark 6. *Courtesy Joette Hightower.* $55-95.

Standard Willow pattern 9-inch plate transfer-printed in blue underglaze on vitrified ware. This section on Ridgways started and ended with a Standard Willow plate although the ceramic material is different. The engraving is very similar considering an inch difference in the sizes of the plates. I think the production occurred about the same time. It has Mark 4. *Author's Collection.* $15-20.

John & Richard Riley

Location: Nile Street (1802-14) and Hill Works (1814-28), Burslem, Staffordshire
Dates: c. 1802-28
Marks:

Mark I (GG3329)
c. 1802-28

Brief History: John & Richard Riley were brothers, one year apart in age. Their firm produced china, earthenware, and stone china. Very little marked china has been found; however, a great deal of blue printed earthenware was made for the home and export markets that is marked. According to records of the firm, they were successful in finding a good formula for iron-stone. A product in 1820, was reported to be the best of many trials. No marked examples of ironstone or stone china have been reported. Both brothers died in 1828.

Type of Willow Manufactured: Standard Willow pattern transfer-printed in blue underglaze on earthenware.

Mark 2 c. 1802-28

Standard Willow pattern 8.5-inch plate transfer-printed in blue underglaze on pearlware. The edge of the flat rim has 8 indentations. The plate has 3-point stilt marks on the back of the rim, and it has a single foot ring. There appears to have been no attempt to line up the geometric motifs in the two borders. Mark 2. *Author's Collection.* $40-65.

Robinson & Son

Location: Foley China Works Longton, Staffordshire
Dates: c. 1881-1903
Mark:

(GG3341)
c. 1881-1903

Brief History: At the outset the partners of this firm were William Robinson and William John Robinson; however, there was a change December 27, 1884. The name continued, but the firm was taken over by Elijah Brain, a cashier, and William Hawker, the pottery manager. These partners were joined later by Alfred Bailey Jones who retired in 1892. The company produced china, and used the trade name "Foley China". The date 1850, in the mark refers to the date claimed for the establishment of the Foley China Works. The firm was succeeded in 1903, by E. Brain & Co. Ltd.*

Type of Willow Manufactured: Mandarin pattern transfer-printed in dark blue underglaze on bone china.

Mandarin pattern teapot and stand transfer-printed in dark blue underglaze on bone china. Both pieces have gold trim. Evidently tea services were made. A serving plate and cup & saucer have turned up, but examples from this maker are not found very often. *Courtesy Joette Hightower.* $100-175.

Robinson, Kirkham & Co.

Location: Overhouse Pottery, Wedgwood's Place (1868-69), and New Wharf Pottery, Burslem (1869-72), Staffordshire
Dates: c. 1868-72
Mark:

c. 1868-69

Comment Concerning Mark: The address on the mark indicates that the piece was made during the period of 1868-69.

Brief History: The partners of this firm were Joseph Robinson, Samuel Kirkham, and John Hollinshead. The product was mainly blue printed earthenware. Wares were shipped to American markets. The partnership dissolved in September 1872. Then for two years Mr. Robinson and Mr. Hollinshead were partners. After that John Hollinshead traded as Hollinshead & Kirkham*.

Type of Willow Manufactured: Standard Willow pattern transfer-printed in blue underglaze on earthenware.

Standard Willow central pattern chestnut basket and under tray transfer-printed in blue underglaze on pearlware. Both pieces have very large cut out border in addition to the large open handles on the basket. This is an outstanding set. Mark 1. *Courtesy IWC Convention 1996.* $300+.

Standard Willow pattern 9.5-inch plate transfer-printed in blue underglaze on earthenware. Three-point stilt marks on the back of the center of the plate with single stilt marks on the front. The wide single foot ring is unglazed. *Author's Collection.* $30-40.

John & George Rogers

Location: Dale Hall, Longport, Staffordshire
Dates: c. 1784-1814+
Impressed Mark:

(GG3367)
c. 1784-1814+

Comments Concerning Mark: This impressed ROGERS mark was carried on by John's son Spencer who was in business until 1842.

Brief History: The brothers may have been in business as early as 1780. In the Bailey's Directory of 1784, the firm was listed as manufacturers of china-glazed blue-painted and cream colored. Later, blue printed earthenware was produced by the firm and by the succeeding firm of John Rogers & Son. John died in 1816, and George died in 1815. The quality of their earthenware was excellent, and it is assumed that a large quantity of it must have been unmarked because there are so few marked examples found. All pieces shown here have the impressed ROGERS mark.

Type of Willow Manufactured: Standard Willow and Two Temples II patterns transfer-printed in blue underglaze on earthenware.

Robinson, Wood & Brownfield

Location: Brownfield's Works, Cobridge, Staffordshire
Dates: c. 1836-41
Mark:

(GG3345)
c. 1836-41

Brief History: The large works built in 1808, and used formerly by Stevenson and R. & J. Clews* was the home of the various partnerships beginning with Noah Robinson, John Wood, and William Brownfield. Noah Robinson died in 1837, and was replaced by John Robinson who may have been his father. The partnership was officially dissolved in 1841. John Robinson had died by this date, but his widow Dorothea succeeded him. The size and history of the Cobridge Works leads to the assumption that a great deal of very fine earthenware was produced by the partnership. It is known that there was a large trade at home and overseas; however, not many wares have been found. This may be due to the short duration of the partnership as well as a strike of the Staffordshire workforce at this time. Dinner and toilet wares were produced in enamel as well as underglaze blue designs. The firm was succeeded by Wood & Brownfield* in 1841.

Type of Willow Manufactured: Standard Willow pattern transfer-printed in blue underglaze on earthenware.

Standard Willow pattern 8.5-by-8-inch sweetmeat dish transfer-printed in blue underglaze on earthenware. The handle is a lovely molded rose with leaves. The dish has a recessed foot ring. It is thought to be rather early as the pattern is extensively line engraved. *Courtesy Renard Broughton.* $75-150 as is.

Standard Willow pattern 9.5-inch plate transfer-printed in blue underglaze on earthenware. The plate has a concave rim. The outer border was too small, and a large section was added between 6 and 7 o'clock. *Courtesy Sue and Robbie Wood.* $25-35.

Roslyn China

Location: Park Place Works, Longport, Staffordshire
Dates: c. 1946-1963
Mark:

c. 1958-63

Brief History: Roslyn China was a trade name used by Reid & Co., in business at Park Place Works from 1913-46. In 1946 the firm was renamed Roslyn China. Some of the marks previously used were continued until 1950. The company specialized in porcelain tableware.

Type of Willow Manufactured: Standard Willow pattern motifs in a border pattern decorated with pastel colors and gold.

Blue printed Standard Willow pattern 5.75-by-8-inch tray and toy china rimmed vegetable dish 3.25-by-4-inches. The tray has no foot ring. There are 3 single stilt marks on the rim. One can be seen just above the birds. None of these pieces marked "ROGERS" has the inner border. *Author's Collection.* $75-100 and $45-65.

Standard Willow pattern 7.5-by-9.5-inch dish with handles transfer-printed in blue underglaze on earthenware. It has a quarter-inch single foot ring and a molded, beaded edge. The print is very clear on this lovely piece. *Author's Collection.* $150-200.

Standard Willow pattern motifs in a border pattern on a plate, cup, and saucer decorated in pastel colors and gold. The plate is 6.25-inches, and the saucer 5.5-inches across. The cup is 2.5-inches high and 3.25-inches wide. The pattern number is 9099, and the name is Golden Willow. *Courtesy Kathy and Hugh Sykes.* $25-40.

Two Temples II reversed pattern toothbrush box and cover transfer-printed in blue underglaze on earthenware. Both pieces have a fish roe border. The butterfly border usually found with this pattern decorates the sides of the box. *Courtesy Reneé Mitchell.* $135-235.

Royal Albert (see Thomas C. Wild)

Royal Albion China Co.

Location: Albion Street, Longton, Staffordshire
Dates: c. 1921-48
Mark:

c. 1930-48

Comment Concerning Mark: Nothing in the mark is readable but the letter M. According to Godden in his *Encyclopaedia of British Porcelain* Manufacturers in the period from 1930-48 the marks feature only the letter M and not the trade name. It is possible that this is a mark used by Royal Albion China Co.
Brief History: A range of porcelain was produced by this firm. They took over Doric China Co. in 1935, and continued to use some marks from that firm as well.
Type of Willow Manufactured: Standard Willow pattern transfer-printed in light blue underglaze on bone china.

Standard Willow pattern 6-inch saucer transfer-printed in light blue underglaze on bone china. The borders are nicely matched up. *Author's Collection.* $3-7.

Royal Stafford China (see Thomas Poole)

Royal Staffordshire Pottery (see A. J. Wilkinson)

Royal Wessex (see Churchill China)

Royal Winton (see Grimwades Ltd.)

Rubian Art Pottery

Location: Park Road, Fenton, Staffordshire
Dates: c. 1906-33
Mark:

c. 1906-13

Brief History: Rubian Art Pottery was established to make ornamental and useful decorative earthenware ranging from flower pots and vases to toilet sets and trinkets. Decorations included majolica-type glazes and decal patterns. The firm was purchased c. 1913, by Grimwades Ltd.* but continued as a separate branch, using its own name. From 1913 to 1933, the firm produced art ware under the Rubay Art Ware trade name. After 1933, to about 1950, Grimwades continued some of the lines, using "Rubian Art" with its own name.
Type of Willow Manufactured: Polychrome "Red Bridge" decal willow variant on black glazed vases and pitchers.

A 6.25-inch pitcher decorated with "Red Bridge" willow variant decal overglaze on black background. Additional flower forms and birds were added to the upper part of the jug. Gold highlights were added to the pattern. This and an 8-inch jug with the same pattern were featured as plates 119 and 120 in *Royal Winton Porcelain* by Busby; however, they were listed under HANDPAINTED. Black vases have also been seen decorated with the "Red Bridge" decal pattern. *Courtesy Tim and Kim Allen.* $125-155.

James Sadler & Sons (Ltd.)

Location: Wellington and Central Potteries, Burslem, Staffordshire
Dates: c. 1882-present (2003)
Marks:

Mark I GG3437)
c. 1947+

Comments Concerning Marks: Some impressed marks were used c. 1937 and earlier; however, most of the teapots found with willow pattern have an embossed mark: SADLER (and) ENGLAND in circular form near the foot ring. Some also have a pattern number and/or printed Mark 1.
Brief History: Sadler is one of the most prolific and best known makers of earthenware teapots in England. The original "Brown Betty" teapot

Mark 2 c. 1958+

was made with red clay and brown (Rockingham) glaze. Although the clay body was changed to white, it is still a stock teapot in their line. The high quality and variety of shapes and decorations were established early in its history. Five-piece sets were produced consisting of teapot, stand, hot-water jug, sugar bowl, and creamer. One of Sadler's leading lines was the Handy Hexagon spoutless (dripless) teapot introduced in 1923. It was made in 6 sizes and countless colors and decorations. The Racing Car Art Deco teapot introduced in the 1940s, is perhaps the most well known of all Sadler (perhaps all British) teapots made in the twentieth century.

In 2000 James Sadler & Sons Ltd. went into receivership as a result of cash flow problems. The company became part of Churchill China (UK) Ltd.* According to the James Sadler website, the great-grandson of the original James Sadler is currently the chairman of the company.

Type of Willow Manufactured: Standard Willow pattern transfer-printed in blue, red, black, and green underglaze as well as gold printed pattern on dark blue and brown overglaze. Products include: teapots, creamers, sugars, jugs, and tea canisters produced on earthenware, and cup and saucer sets blue printed on bone china.

Mark 3 c. 1995+

Mark 4 c. 1926+

Mark 5 c. 1990+

Standard Willow pattern selection of nine different Sadler teapots. There are round 6-cup teapots in blue, blue with gold, and red as well as a 2-cup example in front. The teapot in the middle right hand side holds 8 cups, and the pot in back is a covered hot water jug. The back left 2-cup teapot with kettle handle is from the "Afternoon Tea Collection". The teapot in front of it has a dark blue glaze with small pattern in gold. A Handy Hexagon is seen in front left. The hardest to find are the hot water jug, blue glaze and Hexagon teapots. *Courtesy Paul Kirves and Zeke Jimenez.*

Advertisement in *Pottery Gazette*, June 1, 1928, p. 892, for the Handy Hexagon Spoutless Teapots. This one-half page ad appeared in every issue for the entire year of 1928. It also appeared with the willow-decorated Hexagon in March 1926, May 1931, and January 1, 1944 on the inside front cover.

Standard Willow pattern blue printed round teapot, creamer, and open sugar bowl. This set, the Archive Collection set, and the front teapot in the first picture are the three blue willow teapots that have creamer and sugar bowls to match. *Author's Collection.* $55-95.

Standard Willow pattern selection of nine different blue printed teapots. All have embossed SADLER on the base. The three teapots with trellis-dagger border have Mark 1 also. The five teapots across the middle are 2-cup pots, and the back three plus front teapot hold 6-cups. The teapots at 1:30 and 3:00 o'clock are still available in the "Archive Collection" of Sadler teapots. The teapots at 9:00 and 10:30 o'clock are newer and have Mark 3. *Author's Collection.* Newer teapots: $20-30. Older teapots: $30-50.

Standard Willow pattern black printed 4-cup round teapot with gold trim. Black is a hard to find color. An even more rare color for this teapot is green. A price of $228.50 achieved on an Ebay internet auction in February 2000 attests to this rarity. Mark 1 with pattern #1705 in gold appears on the black teapot. *Courtesy IWC Convention 1996.* $75+.

Brown glazed teapot with motifs from the Standard Willow Pattern in gold. The molded shape of the teapot is trimmed in gold. *Courtesy Tim and Kim Allen.* $55+.

Standard Willow pattern pink printed 6-cup teapot with six-sided collar. Pink willow Sadler teapots are hard to find. Mark 1. *Courtesy Daisy and Tom Eden.* $55+.

Standard Willow pattern jugs trimmed in gold ranging in size from 4.75 to 5.75 to 7-inches in height. Red is the most common color found in these jugs. These are the only two I've seen in blue, and black is found occasionally. The three jugs on the left are turned to show the pattern on the back of the jugs. All bear Mark 1. *Courtesy Paul Kirves and Zeke Jimenez.* $55+ each.

Standard Willow pattern Handy Hexagonal teapots in two sizes and two shades of blue. The embossed mark on the bottom reads: THE HEXAGON PAT. NO. 156051. SADLER, BURSLEM, ENGLAND. A pattern number 2228/E is written in black. A Hexagon teapot has been found with printed Mark 4. These teapots are scarce. *Courtesy Paul Kirves and Zeke Jimenez.* $100+ each.

Standard Willow partial pattern on square teapot with a collar. This is a newer teapot and has the embossed SADLER mark. *Courtesy Charles and Zeta Hollingsworth.* $20-30.

Standard Willow pattern blue printed cup and saucer on bone china. The saucer shows the same linear form of the pattern as found on the cup with additional birds added to the top. The island and boat, usually found at the upper left of the pattern is in the forefront of the saucer. The word "Wellington" in Mark 2 refers to the name of the shape introduced in 1958. *Author's Collection.* $15-20.

St. George's Fine Bone China Ltd.

Location: Bath Street Works, Garth Street, Hanley, Staffordshire
Dates: c. 1990s-2001
Mark:

c. 1990s-2001

Brief History: St. George's Fine Bone China Ltd. was located in the Bath Street Works. The name of the street was changed from Bath St. to Garth St. in the early 1950s; however, the sign on the building retains the name "Bath Street Works". The products of the company were small decorative gift items in bone china. The decorations were decals. Gold trim was sometimes used. The company went bankrupt at the end of 2001.
Type of Willow Manufactured: Blue decal based on Standard Willow pattern on bone china. The decal is the same one used by Sheltonian China*.

Standard Willow pattern decal decorated mint tray in bone china. The tray measures 8.25-by-2.25-inches and is trimmed in gold. The pattern is repeated twice on this piece. Evidently the decal came in one size only. A mug was produced with the decal on each side. *Author's Collection.* $10-15.

Salisbury (Crown) China Co. (Bradleys)

Location: Salisbury Works, Longton, Staffordshire
Dates: c. 1927-61
Mark:

Mark 1
(GG3443)
c. 1927-37

Brief History: This firm was founded by Leslie H. Bradley. Porcelain tableware was produced. In 1949, the word "Crown" was eliminated from the title and marks. Thomas Poole took over the firm in November 1961.
Type of Willow Manufactured: Standard Willow pattern transfer-printed in medium blue underglaze on bone china and a polychrome decal based on Two Temples II pattern.

Mark 2
c. 1927-49

Standard Willow pattern 9-inch serving plate transfer-printed in medium blue underglaze on bone china. The single foot ring is under the edge of the small center pattern. A simple gold line was added to the white space between the two borders. The slightly wavy edge and molded small white handles are lined with gold. Not much willow by this company is found. Mark 1. *Author's Collection.* $25-45.

A bone china serving plate decorated with a polychrome decal based on the Two Temples II pattern. It measures 9.5-inches including the handles. There is a molded pattern at the handles, and the entire piece is lined with gold. Mark 2 with pattern #5946. *Author's Collection.* $25-45.

Salt & Nixon (Ltd.)

Location: Gordon Pottery, Longton, Staffordshire
Dates: c. 1901-34
Marks:

Mark 1 (GG3453)
c. 1901-21

Comment Concerning Marks: The trade names "Saxon China" or "Salon China" were sometimes used on marks.

Brief History: The Gordon Pottery was known as the Jubilee Pottery from 1910 onward. The Salt & Nixon partnership produced good quality bone china. The Buyer's Notes of *Pottery Gazette,* October 1, 1908, touted the firm "for reliable goods in china". Reporting about the British Industries Fair, the *Pottery Gazette,* June 1, 1915, stated on p. 656: "Salt & Nixon…every style of decoration from plain "Willow" upwards…."

Mark 2 (GG3454)
c. 1914-21

Type of Willow Manufactured: Standard Willow pattern transfer-printed in light and dark blue underglaze on bone china with gold trim. Plain and fluted shapes were used.

Standard Willow pattern light blue cup and saucer in fluted shape with Mark 1. Standard Willow pattern dark blue trio in plain shape with Mark 2. The plate has "Made in England" under the chevron instead of alongside it. All pieces are good quality bone china trimmed in gold. *Author's Collection.* $15-20 and $20-25.

Scott

Location: The Southwick Pottery, Sunderland, Durham
Dates: c. 1788-1896
Impressed Marks:

Mark 1 (GG3638)
c. 1838-97

Comments Concerning Mark: The impressed PARIS in Mark 2 is possibly a shape name.

Brief History: Anthony Scott built the Southwick Pottery in 1788, after having a small potwork at Newbottle. Members of the family carried on production at this large pottery until its closing in 1896. Some of the marks found on wares reflect the various partnerships: A Scott & Sons (1829-44), Scott Brothers & Co. (1844-54), A Scott & Son (1872-82), and A. Scott (1882-97). Various types of earthenware were produced from

Mark 2 (GG3638)
var. c. 1838-97

white to brown. Printed and wares that were decorated with luster were produced.

Type of Willow Manufactured: Standard Willow pattern transfer-printed in blue underglaze, and Two Temples II pattern transfer-printed in pale blue underglaze on earthenware.

Standard Willow pattern 9-inch soup plate transfer-printed in blue underglaze on lightweight earthenware. The bowl is 1.75-inches deep. There are 8 indentations on the edge of the concave rim. Three-point stilt marks on the back of the center of the bowl with single stilt marks on the front. It has a recessed foot ring. It is very nice quality and probably dates fairly early in the period. Mark 1. *Author's Collection.* $35-55.

Two Temples II pattern cup and saucer transfer-printed in pale blue underglaze on earthenware. The 6 1/8-inch saucer has 16 panels and a 2.5-inch recessed area for the cup. It has Mark 2. The cup has 12 panels and is not marked. The base of the cup is 1.75-inches across. Even though the cup and saucer were purchased as a set, they may not be. *Author's Collection.* $20-25.

Sewell

Location: St. Anthony's Pottery, Newcastle upon Tyne, Northumberland
Dates: c. 1804-20
Impressed Mark:

(GG3664a)
c. 1804-20

Brief History: Joseph Sewell took over the St. Anthony's Pottery from Foster & Cutter about 1804. He produced creamware, earthenware and luster ware with gold, silver and pink luster. His wares were exported to the continent. Tea services with small teapots, cream jugs and cups and saucers were a specialty of the firm. Joseph Sewell may have retired in 1819; however, the firm is not listed in directories as Sewell & Donkin until 1821.
Type of Willow Manufactured: Standard Willow pattern transfer-printed in blue underglaze on earthenware

Standard Willow pattern 7-inch pickle dish transfer-printed in blue underglaze on earthenware. This is a lovely shell-shaped dish with molded handle. *Courtesy J and J Cockerill.* $75-150.

Standard Willow pattern chestnut basket transfer-printed in blue underglaze on earthenware. It is a wonderfully shaped piece. The raised areas on the molded handles are highlighted with blue enamel. The impressed mark is SEWELL in a curve. *Courtesy Pauline and Keith Reeks.* $150+.

Sewell & Co.

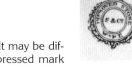

Location: St. Anthony's Pottery, Newcastle upon Tyne, Northumberland
Dates: c. 1853-78
Mark:

(GG3667)
c. 1853-78

Comment Concerning Mark: It may be difficult to read; however, the impressed mark is SEWELL & CO. in an arch.
Brief History: This partnership succeeded Sewell & Donkin, a firm that continued the same type of production as Joseph Sewell began. The willow pattern was produced throughout all three partnerships.
Type of Willow Manufactured: Standard Willow pattern transfer-printed in blue underglaze on earthenware. The engravings used by this firm are a little more crowded in the central pattern than those used by Joseph Sewell.

Standard Willow pattern 9.5-inch plate transfer-printed in blue underglaze on earthenware. There are 12 slight indentations on the edge of the rim. *Courtesy J and J Cockerill.* $15-20 as is.

Sewell & Donkin

Location: St. Anthony's Pottery, Newcastle upon Tyne, Northumberland
Dates: c. 1821-52
Mark: Impressed SEWELL & DONKIN

Brief History: This partnership began after Joseph Sewell retired. A piece has been found with impressed mark SEWELLS & DONKIN from 1819 indicating that Sewell may have retired in 1819 rather than 1821, the accepted date by many authors. Sewell & Donkin were first mentioned in directories in 1821-22.
Type of Willow Manufactured: A Standard Willow pattern large bread plate with impressed mark SEWELL & DONKIN is pictured on p. 108 in Bell's *Tyneside Pottery.*
No picture available.

Anthony Shaw (& Son or & Co.)

Location: High Street, Tunstall & The Mersey Pottery, Burslem, Staffordshire
Dates: c. 1850-1900
Marks:

Mark I (GG3497)
c. 1851-82

Brief History: Anthony Shaw produced earthenware and heavier ironstone ware with names such as Stone China and Opaque Stone China in the marks. The bulk of his goods were exported to America and were little known in Britain. White granite or white ironstone, as it is called in America, was produced in many shapes and embossed patterns in the white and with a copper luster "Tea Leaf" motif. Printed patterns were also produced especially for the American market.

Mark 2 (GG3497)
c. 1851-82

Shaw moved from Tunstall to Burslem in about 1858. The old pottery at High Street Tunstall was taken over by Ralph Hammersley* about 1859. The Burslem works were extensively rebuilt in 1866. In 1882, Anthony's son Edward came into the business, and the name changed to Anthony Shaw & Son. From 1898 to 1900 "& Son" was replaced by "& Co." The business closed in 1900.

Type of Willow Manufactured: Standard Willow pattern transfer-printed in blue, red and brown underglaze on earthenware and ironstone china.

Standard Willow pattern 8.5-inch brown and blue plates transfer-printed underglaze on ironstone. Both plates have single foot rings and 3-point stilt marks on the back of the rim with single stilt marks on the front. The brown plate is round with a flat rim. The blue plate is 12-sided with a molded ridge just inside the rim. The glaze on the blue plate is well worn, and it has Mark 2. The brown plate looks like new. It has Mark 1. *Author's Collection.* $25-35 & 30-40.

Standard Willow pattern blue printed sugar basin and red printed teapot. Both pieces are unmarked. The shape of both is 10-Panel Gothic. The teapot is documented in *Flow Blue and Mulberry Teapot Body Styles,* p. 41, with marked examples. The sugar basin is documented in *Mulberry Ironstone* by Ellen R. Hill, p. T-C-S-#30. Both pieces have a molded leaf pattern on the lid with an indented petal finial. *Author's Collection.* $75-125 & 200+.

Shelley Potteries Ltd.

Location: Foley China Works, Longton, Staffordshire
Dates: c. 1925-1972
Mark:

(GG3510)
c. 1925-40

Brief History: The Shelley family had been operating the china making part of the company as Wileman & Co.* until 1925. Percy Shelley had been in control of the company since 1896, when Joseph Shelley died. There had been a series of art directors for the company including Frederick Rhead. In 1925, the name was changed to Shelleys and then to Shelley Potteries in 1928. The company began an aggressive marketing campaign. Eric Slater, the art director, designed tea ware with Art Deco modernism influences. The Queen Anne shape was one of the best known shapes of the period. Over 170 different patterns were used on the shape. The firm's bone china was of the very finest quality. Children's ware, breakfast, and dessert services were also produced.

The company acquired the adjacent Jackson & Gosling site in 1953, and formed a subsidiary: Shelley Electrical Furnaces Ltd. The name was changed to Shelley China Ltd. in 1965. The next year Allied English Potteries took over Shelley China Ltd. and the subsidiary kiln-making company. In 1972, Shelley became part of the Royal Doulton Tableware Group.

Type of Willow Manufactured: Blue decal based on Two Temples II pattern and red printed pattern with gold trim on bone china.

Seven-inch plate decorated with blue decal based on Two Temples II pattern on bone china. It has gold trim. The pattern number S2085 appears with the mark. *Courtesy Tim and Kim Allen.* $10-20.

Sheltonian China

Location: Islington Works, Longton, Staffordshire
Dates: c. 1990s-present (2003)
Mark:

c. 1990s

Brief History: The company produced decal decorations on bone china.
Type of Willow Manufactured: Blue decal based on Standard Willow pattern toy tea sets on bone china. The decal is the same one as used by St. George's Fine Bone China Ltd.*

Two Temples II pattern cup and saucer transfer-printed in light blue underglaze on earthenware. The cup is London shape, and the pattern on the saucer is reversed. *Courtesy Henry Kelly. Photograph by Douglas Leishman.* $35-45.

Shore & Coggins (Ltd.)

Location: Queen Anne and Edensor Works, Longton, Staffordshire
Dates: c. 1911-64
Marks:

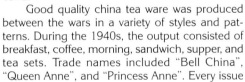

Mark 1
(GG3525)
c. 1930+

Mark 2
c. 1930+

Brief History: J. Shore & Co. was founded in 1887. It is possible that partnership may have also traded under the name of Shore & Coggins. From 1905-10, the firm was titled Shore, Coggins & Holt. From 1911, the company traded as Shore & Coggins. It was purchased in 1918 by T. C. Wild*. Shore & Coggins became a Limited company in 1930. In 1964, it was taken over by the Lawley Group, and merged with Royal Doulton in 1972.

Good quality china tea ware was produced between the wars in a variety of styles and patterns. During the 1940s, the output consisted of breakfast, coffee, morning, sandwich, supper, and tea sets. Trade names included "Bell China", "Queen Anne", and "Princess Anne". Every issue of *Pottery Gazette* in the year 1935, had a full page ad for "Bell China – far and away THE BEST SELLER".
Type of Willow Manufactured: Standard Willow and Mandarin patterns transfer-printed in blue underglaze on bone china with gold trim. The "noted Chelsea Willow pattern" is mentioned on p. 204 of *Miller's Twentieth-Century ceramics*; however, I don't know if "Chelsea" refers to the fluted shape or a variation of the pattern itself.

Standard Willow pattern decal decorated toy tea set for two with 7-inch square tray. All pieces have gold line trim. *Courtesy IWC Convention 1998.* $25-35.

Thomas Shirley & Co.

Location: Clyde Pottery Co., Greenock, Scotland
Dates: c. 1841-57
Mark:

(GG3522)
c. 1841-57

Brief History: Thomas Shirley, an English potter, bought the Clyde Pottery in 1841, in connection with John Milligan who left after a very short time. The firm produced white earthenware with printed patterns. The range of patterns was expanded from the earlier days of the pottery. More forms were also made such as mugs, pitchers and tea ware. Thomas Shirley died in 1850; however, his son William took over the pottery and continued to trade as Thomas Shirley & Co. William was not much of a businessman. With James Farie, he leased the Larne Pottery and spent a great deal of money there turning it into a white ware factory and restoring the house at the pottery. This caused a shortage of cash at the Clyde Pottery. As a result Larne Pottery closed, and Clyde Pottery was purchased by a consortium of businessmen and potters in 1857.
Type of Willow Manufactured: Two Temples II pattern (sometimes reversed) transfer-printed in light blue underglaze on earthenware.

Standard Willow pattern fluted shape cup and saucer transfer-printed in medium blue underglaze on bone china. The border patterns are crowded on the saucer. There is gold trim. Mark 2. *Courtesy Daisy and Tom Eden.* $15-20.

Mandarin pattern serving plate transfer-printed in dark blue underglaze on bone china. The 9-inch plate has molded handles and a molded ridge going from each corner to the indented middle section. The indentations on the edge of the corners soften the square shape of the plate. It is trimmed in gold. Mark 2. *Author's Collection.* $25-45.

Simpsons (Potters) Ltd.

Location: Elder Works, Cobridge, Stafford-shire
Dates: c. 1944-present (2003)
Mark:

(GG3561) c. 1944+

Brief History: Founded as the Soho Pottery* the name was changed to Simpsons in 1944. The firm specialized in toilet ware and tableware of all types using traditional patterns that appealed to the popular market. A contemporary style of dinnerware was begun in the mid-50s. By the mid-70s tableware was no longer produced. Oven to table ware was continued along with fancies. Contract ware is currently made.
Type of Willow Manufactured: Standard Willow pattern transfer-printed in blue underglaze on earthenware.
Retailers: Fondeville & Co., New York* and Henry Morgan & Co., Montreal*

Standard Willow pattern 8-inch plate and demitasse cup and saucer transfer-printed in blue underglaze on earthenware. All pieces have a molded beaded edge. *Author's Collection.* $8-10 & $15-20.

George Fothergill Smith & Co.

Location: The North Shore Pottery, Stockton-on-Tees
Dates: c. 1851-57
Impressed Mark:

(GG3580) c. 1851-57

Brief History: The North Shore Pottery (known as "The Pottery") was owned by James Smith for most of its life: 1845-82. Smith was a brickmaker and builder. He had served an apprenticeship as a cabinetmaker, along with his older brother William who was running the Stafford Pottery, about a mile upstream and across the river. When The Pottery was built, it was operated by the partnership of William Smith Junior & Co. William Smith Junior was the son of William Smith and nephew of James Smith. George Fothergill Smith (son of James) operated The Pottery with others, trading as G. F. S. & Co. from 1851-57. In 1857 his younger brother William joined the company, and they traded as G. & W.S. & Co. until 1867.

Products included good to excellent quality white and colored earthenware useful wares, printed, and sponge decorated. Goods were made for the home market as well as Holland, Germany, Denmark, and some Mediterranean markets.
Type of Willow Manufactured: Standard Willow pattern transfer-printed in blue underglaze on earthenware.

Standard Willow pattern 5.5-by-7.25-inch tray transfer-printed in blue underglaze on earthenware. This may be the under plate for a sauce tureen. As is often the case, the inner border was not used on this little tray. *Author's Collection.* $30-65.

Sampson Smith (Ltd.)

Location: Sutherland Works, Barker St. and other sites, Longton, Staffordshire
Dates: c. 1851-1960
Marks:

SAMPSON SMITH
1851
LONGTON

Mark 1
(GG3584)
c. 1851-90

Comments Concerning Mark: The 1851 date on the impressed mark probably relates to the dissolution of Sampson Smith's partnership with Thomas Cooper on January 16, 1851 after which he began to work on his own.
Brief History: Sampson Smith was one of the most prolific makers of Staffordshire flat-backed

figures, dogs, and other figural objects, working until his death in 1878. The factory continued to make these figures for many years. In 1948, a number of his original molds of figures, dogs, and cottages were found in an unused part of the factory. The production of these pieces was revived; however, the coloring is not as good as on the earlier pieces.

The company also produced china specialties as well as tea and breakfast sets in the nineteenth century although much of the ware was unmarked. It was a large factory employing 200 people in 1861. The firm became a limited company in 1918. Tea ware and breakfast sets continued to be popular in many patterns. The *Pottery Gazette*, October 1, 1915, p. 1094, makes this statement: "Mr. Sampson Smith has some excellent stock lines, including a capital matt and dark blue 'willow'. . . . In existence for some 65 years, 'it is by no means a fossilized concern.'" During World War II production was concentrated with that of Barker Bros.*, the firm's owner. A few stock patterns continued with the Sampson Smith name, and production of fancies and novelties continued.

Mark 2 (GG3586)
c. 1923-30

Mark 3
(GG3587)
c. 1925-30

Type of Willow Manufactured: Standard Willow and Two Temples II patterns transfer-printed in shades of blue underglaze on bone china. I have not found examples with marks dating to 1915. The quote above regarding matt and dark blue willow is related to the two most important compounds of cobaltous oxide used in coloring underglaze prints – the silicate and the aluminate. Cobalt silicates make up the majority of blue colors used underglaze and are generally darker. Cobalt aluminates, used in various formulas that can result in lighter shades of blue, are known as matt blue.

Standard Willow pattern 7 7/8-inch plate transfer-printed in dark blue underglaze on bone china. Examples of willow by Sampson Smith are rarely found. Mark 2. *Author's Collection.* $8-15.

Standard Willow pattern on the coat of Toby jug transfer-printed in blue underglaze on earthenware. The outer border decorates the brim of the hat. This Toby is 7-inches high. Various sizes and color combinations were made in these willow-coated Tobies. Mark 1. *Courtesy Loren Zeller.* $1,200+.

Two Temples II pattern 8.75-inch serving plate transfer-printed in pale blue underglaze on bone china. This is probably an example of the matt blue color by Sampson Smith. The plate has a wavy edge with gold trim. The central pattern sits in the recessed area, and a molded ridge defines the border. Mark 3. *Author's Collection.* $20-30.

William Smith (& Co.)

Location: Stafford Pottery, South Stockton, Stockton-on-Tees, Yorkshire
Dates: c. 1825-55
Marks:

Mark 1 c. 1825-55

Comments Concerning Marks: William Smith used pattern numbers on the stone china marks to denote patterns. No. 14 in Mark 1 is Willow, and No. 13 in Mark 2 is Broseley (Two Temples II). Mark 3 is an impressed mark.

Brief History: William Smith, a Stockton builder founded the Stafford Pottery in July 1825. It was located between Thornaby Road and the River Tees in an area called South Stockton at the time. His partner was John Whalley, a Staffordshire potter. In 1826, they were joined by John Taylor, and the firm traded as William Smith & Co. After a shaky start, George and William Skinner, sons of a Stockton banker were able to assist the company. They became partners in 1829.

Mark 2 c. 1825-55

41
W. S. & Co.'s
WEDGEWOOD

Mark 3 c. 1825-55

The firm specialized in transfer-printed earthenware and stoneware in blue and in multi-color. A large export trade was built up in Belgium, Holland, and Germany. Wedgwood wares were copied for years using marks such as "Wedgwood" and "Wedgewood". Josiah Wedgwood & Sons* were granted an injunction against William Smith & Co. in 1848, prohibiting them from using those names on Stafford Pottery products. In 1855, brothers George and William Skinner took over the pottery and traded as George Skinner & Co.

Type of Willow Manufactured: Standard Willow and Two Temples II pattern transfer-printed underglaze on earthenware and stone ware.

Standard Willow pattern 9.75-inch plate transfer-printed in blue underglaze on stone china. This round plate has a concave rim and single foot ring. Mark 1 and impressed Mark 3. *Courtesy J and J Cockerill.* $30-40.

Two Temples II pattern 8-inch plate transfer-printed in blue underglaze on stone china. There is a nice contrast in the shades of blue in the printing of this plate. It has a scalloped rim. *Courtesy J and J Cockerill.* $30-40.

Soho Pottery (Ltd.)

Location: Tunstall (1901-06) and Elder Works, Cobridge (1906-44), Staffordshire
Dates: c. 1901-44
Marks:

Mark 1 (GG3612)
var. c. 1901-6

Comment Concerning Mark: Mark 3 appears on Standard Willow pattern in blue and the "Red Bridge" variant (without "willow").

Brief History: The Smith & Binnall partnership operated Soho Pottery from 1897-1900. From 1901, the firm traded as Soho Pottery. In *Pottery Gazette*, October 1, 1908, we read "Soho Pottery Ltd., Tunstall: Manufacturers of general earthenware in fine semi-porcelaine." In 1913 the trade name "Solian Ware" was introduced. In the period between World War I and II the pottery became well known for its tableware, toilet ware, and ornamental goods in Solian Ware. The *Pottery Gazette*, February 1, 1935, touts Solian Ware at the British Industries Fair: "'Solian' is more than a mere name in the trade; it represents a 'brand' of ware, in a category which should make it of prime interest to every middle-class pottery dealer." "Ambassador Ware" became a trademark in the 1930s. The firm was renamed Simpsons (Potters)* in 1944.

Type of Willow Manufactured: Standard Willow pattern transfer-printed in blue and brown underglaze on earthenware. Hand painted polychrome Standard Willow pattern overglaze with gold on blue enamel background.

Retailer: A. J. Fondeville, New York*

Mark 2 (GG3613)
var. c. 1906-22

Mark 3 (GG3618)
c. 1930+

Standard Willow pattern bowl transfer-printed in blue underglaze on earthenware. The rimmed bowl measures 9.5-by-7.75-inches and is 2 3/8-inches deep. Mark 1. *Author's Collection.* $25-45.

Standard Willow pattern 13-inch charger hand-painted over the glaze and signed by E. L. Boullenier. The background is blue at the top and green on the lower part. The pattern is done in gold and black. The moon, pathway, and lights in the windows shine brightly with a lighter shade of yellow. Mark 2 with pattern number 5172. *Courtesy Shirley and Jim Hagerty.* $200+.

Spode

Location: Stoke-on-Trent, Staffordshire
Dates: c. 1770-1833 and 1970-present (2003)
Marks:

Mark 1 (RC2a)
(GG3648a) c. 1790-1802

Comments Concerning Marks: In addition to Geoffrey Godden's mark numbers, I am using Robert Copeland's numbers (RC) from his *Spode & Copeland Marks 2ⁿᵈ edition.* It is the most definitive information on marks for this company.
Brief History: Josiah Spode was 6 years old in 1739, when his father died and was buried in a pauper's grave. The next year Josiah was put to work in a pottery. In 1749, he was apprenticed to Thomas Whieldon

Mark 2 (RC31) (GG3648)
c. 1800-20

for five years. At age 21, he was an experienced journeyman potter. He got married and went to work for Turner and Banks in Stoke-upon-Trent. In 1764, he rented their factory and by 1776, had completed the purchase of the factory. The founding date of Josiah Spode's business is traditionally given as 1770.

In 1778, Josiah Spode II was sent to London to open a retail establishment for the company. In 1784, William Copeland III, age 19 went to work for Josiah Spode II in London and began traveling for him. Copeland sold tea on his travels as well as carrying samples of Spode's products, and that provided him with additional income.

An Act was passed in 1784 that repealed the various Duties on Tea that brought the tax down from 119% to 12 1/2%. As a result there was a greater demand for tea and for tea ware. Along with that need, Josiah Spode I saw there was a market for items to match the blue and white Chinese export porcelains. To meet this demand, he perfected the process of transfer printing for underglaze blue patterns on earthenware. Using a little cobalt in the glaze to whiten the appearance of the creamware body, he produced blue printed patterns on pearlware. The Willow Pattern was developed during this period. The following information is printed next to a picture of a Willow Pattern plate at the entrance to the Spode Museum:

> Spode's early patterns were all copied or adapted from Chinese originals. His most famous pattern was produced around 1790 when he took a popular Chinese design, *Mandarin,* and added a bridge with three people and a fence from another Chinese design. The result was the *Willow* pattern, which was to become the most popular underglaze blue pattern of all time. *Willow* pattern is still produced at the Spode factory today.

Josiah Spode I was in the process of developing bone china at the time of his death in 1797. His son Josiah Spode II left London and moved to Stoke to take over the factory. His son William and William Copeland became partners to carry on the London business. Josiah Spode II was producing bone china by 1800. In 1806, The Prince of Wales and the Duke of Clarence visited the Spode factory and appointed Spode "Potter and English Porcelain Manufacturer to H.R.H. the Prince of Wales". In 1813/14, a Stone China body was adopted for use on the replacements for Chinese export porcelain patterns. In 1817, H.M. Queen Charlotte visited the London showroom and ordered some of the newly invented stone china. In 1820 Spode was reappointed to be Potter to H. M. King George IV. Feldspar porcelain was introduced in 1821.

William Copeland died in 1826. His son William Taylor Copeland and Josiah Spode II became partners in the London business. Josiah Spode II died in 1827. Spode III came out of retirement to oversee the

Mark 3 (RC33)
(GG3648)
c. 1810-33

THE SPODE ARCHIVE COLLECTION
'WILLOW'
FIRST INTRODUCED
c 1790
Underglaze print from a hand engraved copper plate

Mark 4 c. 1990+

THE SPODE ARCHIVE COLLECTION
GEORGIAN SERIES
'WILLOW'
FIRST INTRODUCED
c 1790
Reproduced from a hand engraved copper plate

Mark 5 c. 1990+

Mark 6 c. 1990+

Mark 7 c. 1990+

factory, but he died in 1829. In 1833 W. T. Copeland* acquired the Spode factory, the shares in the London business and a great deal of property.

1970 marked the Bicentenary of the founding of the firm by Josiah Spode. At that time the name was changed to Spode Limited, and the next year the company was appointed Manufacturer of China to H. M. Queen Elizabeth II. In 1976 Spode merged with Worcester Royal Porcelain Co. with the title Royal Worcester Spode Ltd. In 1989, the two firms separated though the retail division still operates jointly. In the 1990s, Spode began re-issuing patterns from their Blue Room Collection in groups of six. These patterns are produced in the same way as the original patterns in the early nineteenth century. New copper engravings have been made for plates and other objects in each of the patterns. By 2000 the factory began making miniatures that were received with the same enthusiasm as the other items. The popularity of the new "Blue Room Collection" as well as the continued demand for Blue Italian, a pattern made continuously since 1816 have contributed to the success of Spode at the beginning of the 21st century.

Type of Willow Manufactured: Standard Willow and Mandarin patterns transfer-printed underglaze on earthenware and bone china. Two Temples I and II transfer-printed underglaze on bone china. The "Spode Archive Collection" Standard Willow pattern is found in blue, red, black, green, and lavender. The Two Temples and Mandarin patterns have been produced on earthenware in the "Spode Blue Room Collection Willow Series".

Bottle Oven, Spode Factory, Stoke-on-Trent.   Photo: E. Näiyde, John Hinde Studio

This postcard photo of the Spode factory features a bottle oven that was preserved at the front of the factory as a monument to Spode potters of earlier times. It stands 47-feet high and dates from the end of the eighteenth century. The last bottle oven was fired at Spode in 1960. By 1972 the bricks were getting wet and the structure unstable. Three days before the contractors were to come in and install metal bands to hold it together, the bottle oven collapsed. The inside kiln structure was pulled down later. The foundation ring of bricks has been preserved on the site.

Standard Willow pattern 9.25-inch early indented plate transfer-printed in blue underglaze on pearlware. There is no foot ring, and it has single stilt marks under the rim. Compare the pattern and shape to P609-1 on p. 201 in *Spode transfer-printed Ware 1784-1833*. Mark 1 and top of workman's mark 15 on p. 190 *Spode's Willow Pattern*. This plate is an example of Willow I and dates before 1800. *Courtesy Renard Broughton.* $100-200.

Standard Willow pattern dessert dish transfer-printed in blue underglaze on pearlware. The dish is Devonia shape and measures 9.75-by-7.25-inches at the widest part. The border resembles the c. 1800 octagonal Minton* plate where the inner half of the pair of scrolling leaves are lighter than the top half. The three-spoke wheels in this border have 4 dark spokes rather than 3. Some Minton pieces also have that variation. Mark 1. *Author's Collection.* $125-200.

Standard Willow pattern foot bath with handles transfer-printed in blue underglaze on earthenware. It is 19-inches long, 12.5-inches wide, and 8-inches high. The shape has molded horizontal ridges. A linear form of the pattern was used. Mark 2. *Courtesy Rita Entmacher Cohen* $1,500+.

Mandarin pattern cup and saucer transfer-printed in blue underglaze on pearlware. The saucer is 5.75 across and 1.5-inches high. The cup is 3.75-inches across and 2.75-inches high. It is a rare shape with a little "shelf" inside the cup and the saucer. The wavy edges are trimmed in gold. Both pieces have a quarter-inch single foot ring. The only mark is a double slash in blue on the saucer. Robert Copeland has attributed the set to Spode. *Author's Collection*. $100-150.

Two Temples I pattern basket transfer-printed in blue underglaze on bone china. The owner calls this a bonbon basket. It is 7 7/8-by-7.5-inches and is 4-inches tall. It has gold trim. A section of pattern was added in the forefront with an extra fence and rocks to fill out the space. The pattern on the handle is not usually seen with Two Temples I. Mark 2. *Courtesy Loren Zeller*. $200+.

Mandarin pattern coffee pot, teapot, and stand transfer-printed in blue underglaze on bone china. The coffee pot stands 12-inches high and measures 11-inches from handle to spout. The teapot is 5.5-inches high and 10.5-inches from handle to spout. The teapot stand is 7-by-5.75-inches and has a combed back. All pieces have lavish gold trim. Mark 3. *Courtesy Loren Zeller*. $300+ each.

Two Temples II pattern London shape teapot, cup, and saucer transfer-printed in light blue underglaze on bone china. The china in the teapot is much thicker than that of the delicate cup and saucer. All have Mark 3. The teapot also has impressed B and workmen's mark 20 on p.190 of *Spode's Willow Pattern*. *Author's Collection*. $350+ for all.

Two Temples I pattern teapot transfer-printed in blue underglaze on bone china. This teapot is new oval shape, and has no gold. It is unmarked. *Courtesy Harry and Jessie Hall*. $250+.

Two Temples II pattern child's teapot transfer-printed in pale blue on pearlware. The teapot is just 2.5-inches high. It has a high collar with wavy edge. The border pattern decorates the shoulder of the teapot. Just a part of the pattern is seen. Mark 3. *Courtesy Loren Zeller*. $200+.

Standard Willow pattern place setting in cranberry (red) transfer-printed underglaze on earthenware. All new copper engravings were done for these new pieces from the Spode Blue Room Collection. In addition to red, colors include blue, black, green, and lavender. The cup and saucer have Marks 4 and 5. Mark 7 is on the back of the plate. *Author's Collection.* $25-30, the setting.

Stafford Pottery (see William Smith & Co.)

Staffordshire Fine Ceramics

Location: Williamson St., Tunstall, Staffordshire
Dates: c. 1990s-2001
Mark:

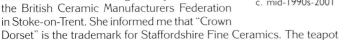

c. mid-1990s-2001

Brief History: This firm was listed in the directories for 2001 according to Kay Goodsell of the British Ceramic Manufacturers Federation in Stoke-on-Trent. She informed me that "Crown Dorset" is the trademark for Staffordshire Fine Ceramics. The teapot was purchased in the mid-1990s.
Type of Willow Manufactured: Standard Willow pattern decal in pink and blue overglaze on earthenware with gold trim.

Standard Willow blue decal pattern decorated 6-cup teapot with a high domed lid. The collar is made to look like a crown. The teapot has gold trim. This style was also made with a red willow decal. *Author's Collection.* $35-45.

Staffordshire Potteries Ltd.

Location: Meir Park, Longton, Staffordshire
Dates: c. 1950-1990
Mark: Embossed mark "KILNCRAFT STL ENGLAND"

Brief History: Charles Griffith Bowers, son of the founder, gained a controlling interest in the Keele Street Pottery*. The firm began taking over a number of other potteries. In 1950, Staffordshire Potteries Ltd. was the name chosen for the entire group. Meir Airport near Longton was the site for most of the production. Later the Sales and Administration departments were also located there. In 1979, the firm acquired Royal Winton and Taunton Vale Industries. Coloroll took over Staffordshire Potteries Ltd. in a hostile bid in 1986. After other takeovers and name changes Biltons* merged with the company in 1990, to form Staffordshire Tableware Ltd.*

Early products included tea ware and beakers; however, dinnerware was added in 1967 when two designers joined the staff. The company made modern style patterns and shapes and catered to the under-25 age bracket. The Kilncraft line was launched in 1972. Mugs and children's ware with cartoon themes were popular.
Type of Willow Manufactured: Standard Willow pattern blue decal decorated kitchen ware and mugs.

Standard Willow pattern blue decal in linear form decorates this 4-inch mug. The embossed mark KILNCRAFT ENGLAND appears in circular form on the base of the mug with the letters STL in the center. *Author's Collection.* $5-10.

Staffordshire Tableware Ltd.

Location: Meir Park, Longton, Staffordshire
Dates: c. 1990-2001
Brief History: Staffordshire Tableware Ltd. was formed by a merger of Biltons* and Staffordshire Potteries Ltd.* in 1990. At this point the firm had a 30% share of the UK dinnerware market for home and export. The products were mugs, chinaware, and dinnerware. Oven-to-tableware was seen in catalogs in 1994; however, the emphasis seemed to be on mugs throughout its history. In 2000, the company went into receivership. In April 2001 all their "intellectual property" was sold to a Romanian Consortium.
Type of Willow Manufactured: A simplified version of Standard Willow pattern dinnerware in blue under the trade name "Royal Norfolk". It was listed for sale in the Argos Catalog, Autumn/Winter 2000.

Listing from *Argos Autumn/Winter 2000 Catalog* for 40 piece set of Royal Norfolk "Willow". The shapes of the pieces are the same as those in "Summerfield Blue" that is a Staffordshire Tableware brand.

Stanley Pottery Ltd.

Location: Edensor Road, Longton, Staffordshire
Dates: c. 1928-31
Marks:

Brief History: The firm was previously known as Colclough & Co.* Some marks were continued using the "Royal Stanley" trade name. Dinnerware made in earthenware was the main product of the company.
Type of Willow Manufactured: Standard Willow pattern transfer-printed in shades of blue underglaze on earthenware.
Retailer/importer: O'Neill-James Company*

Mark 1 c. 1928-31
(Rd. No. c. 1890)

Mark 2
c. 1928-31

Standard Willow pattern 7.75-inch coupe soup bowl transfer-printed in blue underglaze on earthenware. The bowl has a recessed foot ring and three single stilt marks on the outside 1/4- to 1/2-inch down from the edge. Mark 2. *Author's Collection.* $8-15.

Stanley & Lambert

Location: New Town Pottery, Longton, Staffordshire
Dates: c. 1850-54
Mark:

Brief History: Jacob Stanley and Thomas Lambert's partnership ended May 1854. Stanley had owned the pottery from 1847. He continued on alone from 1854-56, at which time it was purchased by John & Henry Procter & Co.* The firm produced earthenware, employing 76 men, 79 women and 49 children.
Type of Willow Manufactured: Standard Willow pattern transfer-printed in blue underglaze on earthenware.

(GG3674)
c. 1850-54

Standard Willow pattern platter transfer-printed in blue underglaze on earthenware. The platter measures 11-by-14-inches. This is a typical mid-nineteenth century Willow Pattern platter; however, the border patterns seem to be too crowded. *Author's Collection.* $65-100.

Star China Co.

Location: St. Gregory's Works & Atlas Works, Longton, Staffordshire
Dates: c. 1900-19
Marks:

Brief History: The company moved from St. Gregory's Works in 1903. At the start the partners were Herbert James Aynsley, John Gerrard Aynsley, and William Illingworth; however, John Aynsley left the company July 9, 1900. Tea ware and other useful items were made in bone china. The *Pottery Gazette* had monthly advertisements for the company in 1908. The following quote is taken from the December 1, 1908, issue:

Dainty! Of Course, it's the Paragon China. Five years ago this beautiful china was introduced to our notice for the first time ... . In over 40 years experience, we had never before seen such PER-FECT CHINA combined with such EXQUISITE

Mark 1
(GG3686)
c. 1913-19

Mark 2
c. 1900-19

SHAPES AND ARTISTIC DESIGNS at such MODERATE PRICES. – Sold over 1,000 tea sets since we introduced them. Manufacturer: STAR CHINA CO., Atlas Works Longton.

In 1919 the company was renamed Paragon China Co. Ltd.*

Type of Willow Manufactured: Standard Willow pattern transfer-printed in medium blue underglaze on bone china. Willow variants in polychrome are also found with mark stating "Reproduction of old Chinese".

Standard Willow pattern demitasse coffee pot transfer-printed in medium blue on bone china. It has gold trim. The pattern is circular as if it were from an engraving to use on a plate. Mark 1. *Courtesy Joette Hightower.* $125-150.

Standard Willow pattern demitasse coffee cup transfer-printed in medium blue on bone china with gold trim. It is a lovely shape that is convenient to use with the large handle and lip that curves outward. Mark 1. *Author's Collection.* $15-20.

A demitasse cup and saucer decorated with willow motifs in simple line drawings colored sparingly with red, green, blue, and gold. The black border has colored accents with gold, and the entire surface of the inside of the cup is gold. Mark 2. *Courtesy IWC Convention 1998.* $20-30.

Standard Willow pattern 2-cup teapot transfer-printed in medium blue on bone china. A linear form of the pattern was used to decorate this little teapot. It has gold trim. Mark 1. *Courtesy Joette Hightower.* $65-100.

Steelite International (see Doulton)
Stepney Pottery
(see Davies, Cookson & Wilson)

Andrew Stevenson

Location: Lower Manufactory, Cobridge, Staffordshire
Dates: c. 1810-36
Comment Concerning Mark: The platter has an impressed name mark.
Brief History: Andrew and his older brother Ralph had a partnership in Glasgow before 1799. Andrew was also in partnership in Cobridge with James Stevenson c. 1806-10. Andrew and Ralph Stevenson had separate potteries after 1810. Ironstone wares were produced; however, the blue printed wares were probably done on earthenware. Both Stevenson firms had a large export trade to North America.
Type of Willow Manufactured: Standard Willow pattern transfer-printed underglaze in blue on earthenware.

Standard Willow pattern platter transfer-printed in blue underglaze on earthenware. The platter measures 13.5-by-16.75-inches and has a combed back. It bears an impressed name mark. *Courtesy Louise and Charles Loehr.* $125-150.

Stevenson, Alcock & Williams

Location: Cobridge, Staffordshire
Dates: c. 1820-26
Mark:

c. 1825

Brief History: Ralph Stevenson, older brother of Andrew, was in partnership with Samuel Alcock* and Augustus Lloyd Williams for a short time. The firm produced marked earthenware in blue printed, polychrome and possibly luster-decorated patterns. Unmarked porcelains were also made. Attribution is made by comparing shapes with marked examples. A characteristic molded edge used by the firm on earthenware has also been found on porcelain pieces.
Type of Willow Manufactured: Canton pattern transfer-printed in dark blue underglaze on earthenware. A lighter blue wash is used to give a contrast in shade.

On the right hand side is a Canton pattern plate transfer-printed in dark blue underglaze on earthenware. A lighter blue wash was used in contrast to the very dark blue used in the main pattern. The border pattern has crosshatches in the middle band with slashes on either side. A dagger border was added on the inside. The bowl on the left is the Chinese original from which the plate was copied. It is unmarked porcelain. *Author's Collection.* The plate has the Stevenson, Alcock & Williams mark. *Courtesy Lucinda and Joe Balmos.* Damaged bowl. $15-25 plate.

Spencer Stevenson & Co. Ltd.

Location: Dresden Works, Longton, Staffordshire
Dates: c. 1948-60
Mark:

(GG3711) c. 1952+

Brief History: The company produced bone china useful wares. The factory name was changed in 1953, to Ensor Works. The trade name Royal Stuart was used on some marks; however, a special mark was used on Willow pattern.
Type of Willow Manufactured: Standard Willow pattern transfer-printed in blue and brown underglaze on bone china.

Standard Willow pattern 10-inch serving plate transfer-printed in pale blue underglaze on bone china. The wavy edge and handles have gold trim. *Courtesy IWC Convention 2001.* $35-55.

Standard Willow pattern breakfast cup and saucer transfer-printed in brown underglaze on bone china. The saucer is 7.75-inches across, and the cup is 5-inches wide across the opening. The saucer has a wavy edge. Both pieces are trimmed in gold. *Courtesy IWC Convention 2001.* $45-75.

John Steventon & Sons Ltd.

Location: Royal Pottery, Burslem, Staffordshire
Dates: c. 1923-36
Comments Concerning Dates: The firm continued on after 1936; however, the product changed to tiles and sanitary wares.
Marks:

Mark 1
c. 1923-36

Comment Concerning Marks: Marks 1 and 2 seem to be used interchangeably on Willow pattern. For instance the teapot shown below is found as often with Mark 1 as with Mark 2

Brief History: The firm was formerly known as Brown & Steventon*. An article in *Pottery Gazette*, March 1, 1926, stated that the firm was well known as a manufacturer of "a good medium-class earthenware for all domestic purposes." A new showroom opened in London that year. Mr. R. J. Steventon or Mr. H. Leese, a traveler to America and Canada for the company, planned to be regularly in attendance at the showroom. Steventon products were decorated in plain prints, enameled patterns, lithos and "a big range of stenciled schemes" in toilet ware. A new pattern "Kato" was shown in the ad. It is Chinese mandarin style (and collected as a willow variant by some). The pattern was made on octagonal shapes and available in plain blue, at lower cost, or with other colors added underglaze. The company also made reproductions of Rogers patterns that had a mark stating: "Reproduction of Rogers 1780". (This refers to the J. and G. Rogers* firm even though it had a probable starting date of 1784.)

Mark 2 (GG3715)
c. 1923-36

Mark 3
c. 1923-36

Type of Willow Manufactured: Standard Willow pattern transfer-printed underglaze in blue, red, and green on earthenware. Polychrome decal in shades of brown, green, and gold has also been found. The same decal in different colors was used by Elijah Cotton*.

Standard Willow pattern teapot transfer-printed in blue underglaze on earthenware. It holds 5 cups and has Mark 1. Another collector has one with Mark 2. Steventon willow in blue is plentiful enough that it is not difficult to complete a set. Mark 2 is the most common. *Courtesy Joette Hightower.* $75-125.

Standard Willow pattern creamer and covered sugar transfer-printed in green underglaze on earthenware. It is more difficult to find green than the other colors – especially in this set. The low, wide shape is distinctive to Steventon. Mark 1. *Courtesy Paul Kirves and Zeke Jimenez.* $55-95.

Standard Willow pattern 8.25-by-11-inch platter transfer-printed in red underglaze on earthenware. This distinctively shaped platter can be found in blue and green willow as well. The Steventon red is a deeper color than that of most manufacturers. Mark 2. *Courtesy Charles and Zeta Hollingsworth.* $75-125.

Polychrome decal of simplified Standard Willow pattern 9-inch plate with center handle of metal. The colors are green and gold with a brown outline that might be underglaze. It has a rust color trim on the wavy edge. The same decal was used in blue and gold by Elijah Cotton* and others during the same time frame. *Courtesy IWC Convention 1998.* $60-75.

Stoddard, J. Goodwin
(see Goodwin)

Joseph Stubbs

Location: Dale Hall, Longport, Staffordshire
Dates: c. 1822-34
Impressed Mark:

(GG3728)
c. 1822-35

Brief History: Joseph Stubbs succeeded Benjamin Stubbs at Dale Hall. Products included transfer-printed wares and lusterwares. The firm had a successful export business in blue printed wares to the American market. Joseph Stubbs retired in 1834, and sold all of his working materials. Stubbs died in 1836.
Type of Willow Manufactured: Standard Willow pattern transfer-printed in blue on pearlware.

Standard Willow pattern 8.5-inch plate transfer-printed in blue underglaze on pearlware. There are 8 slight indentations at the edge of the concave rim. There is no foot ring. The 3-point stilt marks are on the back of the base of the plate with single stilt marks on the front. *Author's Collection.* $40-65.

Sunderland (see Dixon, Austin & Co.)
Sutherland China (see Hudson)

Swansea Pottery

Location: Cambrian Pottery, Swansea, Wales
Partnerships: Coles & Haynes (Haynes & Co.)
Haynes, Dillwyn & Co.
Dates: c. 1783-1802 & 1802-1810
Impressed Mark: SWANSEA

Comments Concerning Mark: A small impressed upper case SWANSEA mark was used by both partnerships above. I have chosen not to guess which one produced the bowl shown below; however, it is almost certainly 1800+.

Brief History: In 1764, William Coles, an iron-master and iron-founder, established the Pottery. In 1775, it was expanded, following the Wedgwood plan. William Coles died c. 1779. The business was carried on by his sons John and Edward. In 1783, the Pottery was offered for sale. By 1789, John Coles and George Haynes were partners. On April 21, 1800, after John Coles died, his executors applied for permission to assign their interest in the leases held in the Corporation to George Haynes. As a result the name of the firm changed in 1801 to George Haynes & Co. William Dillwyn purchased the lease in 1801-02, and the partnership of Haynes, Dillwyn & Co. began.

The wares were very crude in the beginning. Gradually as the facilities became more developed decorated creamware and transfer-printed earthenware were produced.
Type of Willow Manufactured: Standard Willow central pattern and inner framing border with a butterfly motif outer border. Transfer-printed in blue underglaze on earthenware.

Standard Willow pattern bowl with central pattern and inner framing border transfer-printed in blue underglaze on pearlware. The outer border has a butterfly motif. The bowl is 12-inches across and 4.5-inches deep. It is not unusual for different outer borders to appear with Standard Willow central at the turn of the nineteenth century. *Courtesy Rita Entmacher Cohen.* $200+.

The outside of the bowl above showing the tall foot ring and fluted rim. The pattern on the outside of the bowl is not related to Standard Willow pattern at all.

This photo shows the pattern on the opposite side of the bowl. Early nineteenth century bowls were sometimes decorated this way, using different patterns outside than on the inside.

Swillington Bridge Pottery (see also Reed & Taylor)

Location: West bank of the River Aire, south of the road at Swillington Bridge, Yorkshire
Dates: c. 1791-1843
Marks:

Comments Concerning Marks: The printed Mark is M44 in Heather Lawrence's *Yorkshire Pots and Potteries*. It appears here on a plate with M41, an impressed crown mark shown under Reed & Taylor*.

c. 1820-38

Brief History: The pottery was built in 1791, and was run by a number of different partnerships until about 1833, when James Reed and Benjamin Taylor took over. A wide range of wares were produced including creamware painted with enameled colors in many different patterns as well as blue and brown printed pearlware with Chinese and pastoral landscapes. By 1820, ironstone china was produced. It is thought that willow pattern was produced from 1820, as the examples found bear the ironstone marks. The plate in the photo could have been made before or during the Reed & Taylor* partnership.
Type of Willow Manufactured: Standard Willow pattern transfer-printed in blue underglaze on ironstone china.

Standard Willow pattern 9.25-inch plate transfer-printed in blue underglaze on ironstone china. There are slight indentations on the edge of the concave rim. The border pattern used is too large and had to be cut at about 6:30 o'clock. *Courtesy J and J Cockerill.* $30-40.

Swinnertons Ltd.

Location: Vulcan, Washington, and Victoria Potteries, Hanley, Staffordshire
Dates: c. 1906-59
Marks:

Comments Concerning Mark: Mark 4 is assumed to be a mark used by this company. It is related to marks used by Washington Pottery* and has the initial S – Ltd. plus H (for Hanley) under the drawing of the house. The Washington Pottery was acquired by Swinnertons during World War I and sold c. 1953.
Brief History: The company was founded by B. J. Swinnerton with factories in Hanley. The Vulcan Works was the main factory until the Washington Pottery was acquired during World War I when a Mr. W. Bloore joined the firm. In 1911, Swinnertons became a limited company. After B. J. Swinnerton died, Mr. V. G. H. Alcock joined the firm and became chairman. In 1925, the Victoria Pottery was purchased. The Vulcan Pottery was redeveloped in 1952. Davison & Co. Ltd.* was acquired that same year. In 1959, Swinnertons Ltd. was taken over by the Lawley Group, which in turn became a part of Allied English Potteries. The Swinnerton name was no longer used. In 1973 Allied English Potteries merged with Royal Doulton. The few remaining pattern books from Swinnertons (1940s and 1950s) are housed at Royal Doulton. The patterns are listed by number rather than by name.

Swinnertons made good quality earthenware table ware that was moderately priced. The *Pottery Gazette*, April 2, 1923, featured an article telling the success of the company in providing "domestic pottery, in certain specialized branches, suitable for the requirements of the middle classes". The article included the following information regarding the Willow pattern:

Mark 1 (GG3776)
var. c. 1930+

Mark 2 (GG3777)
c. 1930+

Mark 3 (GG3781)
c. 1946+

> The old, and always much-favoured, blue "Willow" pattern is obviously an important factor in the trade of this house – and not merely an addendum to it – for they offer in this pattern a complete range of dinner, tea, and breakfast ware, supported by a big variety of other useful table articles. Particular attention has been paid by

Mark 4 c. 1917-53

Swinnertons, Ltd., to the engraving of their "Willow" pattern, in order to get it true to detail and tradition, whilst in the tint of colour, too, they appear to have been ultra-careful to get the perfect shade. It is patent that the firm has gone to considerable trouble and expense to make their "Willow" pattern JUST RIGHT, and this care and attention is being rewarded in the orders that are daily being received for it.

Type of Willow Manufactured: Standard Willow pattern transfer-printed in blue and red underglaze on earthenware. The ivory "Hampton" body that was used for much red willow was introduced in 1926. The blue willow commonly found has marks dating from 1946 and is named "Old Willow"; however, from the information given above, we learn that blue willow was produced in the 1920s. The "Red Bridge" willow variant and other variant litho patterns were also made.

Standard Willow pattern covered vegetable bowl transfer-printed in blue underglaze on earthenware. This bowl has a very narrow base. The 9-inch lid extends beyond the edge of the bowl. Note the special clarity and openness of the diamond pattern in the outer border, the bow-knot pattern in the inner border, and lid finial. Mark 3. *Author's Collection.* $75-95.

Standard Willow pattern 6-cup teapot transfer-printed in red underglaze on the ivory Hampton body. The lower half of the teapot and the rim of the lid have molded ridges at a slant. Mark 2. *Courtesy Joette Hightower.* $85-150.

Standard Willow pattern oval bowl in red and demitasse cup and saucer in blue. The bowl measures 9.25-by-6.75-inches and has Mark 2. Mark 3 is on the saucer. Neither piece has the inner border. *Author's Collection.* $25-35 and $15-22.

Six piece toilet set decorated in the "Red Bridge" lithographed willow variant pattern. The pattern is reversed on the chamber pot, toothbrush holder, and covered soap dish. It is interesting that the pairs of small birds were placed up high on the pitcher. Mark 1. *Courtesy Paul Kirves and Zeke Jimenez.* $125-225.

Standard Willow pattern 8-inch rimmed bowl transfer-printed in blue underglaze on earthenware. Many collectors seek out these pieces with words on the front. Children's ware is especially prized. Mark 4. *Courtesy Harry and Jessie Hall* $45-65.

John Tams (& Son) (Ltd.)

Location: Crown Pottery, Longton, Staffordshire
Dates: c. 1875-present (2003)
Marks:

Mark 1 (GG3793) c. 1875-1903

Comments Concerning Marks: I have not included photos of Standard Willow pieces with Marks 1, 2 and 5 in order to make room for showing the more unusual "Tams Ware" pieces.

Brief History: John Tams worked the Crown Pottery on his own until 1903, when he was joined by his son. The firm traded as John Tams & Son until 1912, when the name was changed to John Tams Ltd. The company has produced various types of earthenware down through the years. In the beginning, its reputation was established with the high quality of kitchenware, tankards, hospital, and medical ware produced. By 1909, a wide range of use-

Mark 2 c. 1903-12

ful domestic earthenware was developed in addition to ornamental wares including ornamental lusterware known as Celestene Ware. By the 1920s, Willow Ware was one of the company's most popular patterns. It had been widely advertised as one of their specialties from as early as 1908. In 1927, the colored Willow pattern with enamel colors over glaze, known as "Tams Ware" was launched.

Tams continued production through World War II supplying popularly priced dinnerware to home and export markets. After the war, it continued as a family business with an emphasis on tea services, coffee sets, soup sets, cups, and mugs competitively priced. In 1982, Barker Brothers'* works in Longton was acquired and demolished. The Sutherland Works, which opened in 1990, was built on the site. The firm became one of the largest makers of earthenware mugs and tableware.

In 1989, Tams bought A. T. Finney & Sons Ltd.*, maker of Duchess China. Nanrich Pottery, Longton was also acquired. The merging of the two companies formed the beginning of bone china production. Royal Grafton* was purchased in 1992, in order to expand the John Tams Fine Bone China Division. The three factory-warehouse complexes with modern color printing machines and tunnel kilns were successful in producing bone china tableware patterns and mugs for the international market. Almost half of the production was for export. The factory was very efficient with a loss of only 11.5%. Non-saleable items were ground up and sent to a cement factory.

John Tams Ltd. went into receivership in February 2002. As a result Tams Group, Longton, was formed and took over Atlas, Blythe, Crown and Sutherland Works. Production is concentrated on mugs with a third of sales going overseas.

Type of Willow Manufactured: Standard Willow pattern transfer-printed in dark blue underglaze on earthenware. Lighter blue transfer-printed ware is also found with clobbering in pastel colors. It is known as "Nankin Ware". Standard Willow pattern printed in gold overglaze with colors on glossy dark cobalt background. Simplified standard pattern enamel painted overglaze on flat medium blue glaze as well as glossy turquoise glaze and on unglazed ware. This ware is called "Tams Ware".

Mark 3 c. 1912+

Mark 9 c. 1912+

Mark 10 c. 1912+

Mark 11 (GG3796) c. 1913+

Mark 12 c. 1990s

Mark 4 c. 1912+

Mark 5 (GG3795) c. 1903-12

Pottery Gazette, July 1, 1908, p. 737. One-half page ad for John Tams & Son showing a Standard Willow pattern plate.

Mark 6 c. 1912+

Mark 7 c. 1912+

Mark 8 c. 1912+

John Tams Ltd. one-half page ad showing an elaborate bulb pot decorated with Standard Willow pattern with the title "NANKIN WARE". This ad was seen in *Pottery Gazette* for three months in 1915: January, February, and March.

Pottery Gazette, November 1, 1917, p. 1764. One-quarter page ad for TAMS' original WILLOW. The statement: "This pattern is just as popular today as when the original engravings were made 150 years ago." would put the origin of the Willow pattern at the year 1767 – about 25 years too early.

Standard Willow pattern 6.5-inch plate and 4-inch jug transfer-printed in blue underglaze on earthenware. The plate has Mark 6 with the Willow legend on the back. The jug has Mark 3 with WILLOW at the top of the mark. *Author's Collection* $20-25 each.

Standard Willow pattern tea canisters with Tams Nankin Ware Mark 11. The canister on the left is missing its lid, but it is harder to find because of the pastel colors added over glaze. Rarely an ornate vase is found in Nankin Ware. The ware is featured in the second ad seen above from the *Pottery Gazette*. *Courtesy Loren Zeller.* $150+ each.

Standard Willow pattern pedestal bowl with scalloped rim transfer-printed in blue underglaze on earthenware and clobbered overglaze. The bowl is 5-inches high and 9-inches wide. It is an example of the interesting accessory pieces made in Willow pattern by Tams. The bowl can also be found in blue underglaze without the clobbering. Mark 11 Nankin Ware. *Courtesy Hugh and Kathy Sykes.* $200+.

Standard Willow pattern 11.5-by-14-inch platter with shiny deep blue glaze. The pattern is enamel painted over glaze with gold border and gold accents. Vases and a footed bowl have been found in this style, but is more difficult to find than the medium blue non-glossy Tams Ware. This style has Mark 8 with PATENT and the Willow legend. *Courtesy Tim and Kim Allen.* $200+.

"Tams Ware" dresser set including 8.5-by-12.25-inch tray, pair of candlesticks, toothbrush holder, two covered powder jars, and covered box. This is the colored willow ware developed by Tams c. 1927. Most pieces have Mark 4 with pattern number 1350/E. The tray has Mark 7. *Courtesy Paul Kirves and Zeke Jimenez.* $350+.

Simplified Standard Willow pattern overglaze on 8.5-inch octagonal plate with turquoise ground. It has slightly different colored pattern than the other Tams Ware. The border pattern is black printed with colors added. Vases have also been found in this color combination, but rarely. This shape plate was also made on a pedestal with the medium blue flat glaze background. Mark 4. *Courtesy Tim and Kim Allen.* $125-200.

Simplified Standard Willow pattern unglazed 9-inch vase with the pattern enameled onto the unglazed surface. The hand painting is of excellent quality. The inside and bottom of the vase have a shiny glaze. It is perhaps an experimental piece. Mark 4 with pattern #1350/E. *Courtesy Tim and Kim Allen.* NP

"Tams Ware" tall jug and 5 vases in various shapes. The vases range in height from 5 3/8 to 12.75-inches. Most pieces have Mark 4 with pattern number 1350/E. The vase with square top has Mark 9. The tall jug in back and vase with handles in front have Mark 10. *Courtesy Paul Kirves and Zeke Jimenez.* Prices range from $75 up.

Standard Willow pattern 10.75-inch plate blue printed underglaze on earthenware. There are a few minor alterations in this 1990s version of the pattern. The most striking change is in the outer border. A little white space was added to the left hand side of each set of geometric motifs. Mark 12. *Author's Collection.* $8-15.

Tams & Lowe

Location: St. Gregory Works, High Street, Longton, Staffordshire
Dates: c. 1865-74
Mark:

(GG3802) c. 1865-74

Brief History: John Tams and William Lowe were in partnership beginning in 1865 producing earthenware and china. The firm succeeded George Townsend* at St. Gregory Works. Tams and Lowe, manufactured many types of earthenware such as luster and drab wares in addition to printed wares. John Tams* left the firm in 1874, to found his own business at Crown Pottery, also in Longton. William Lowe* continued in business.

Type of Willow Manufactured: Standard Willow pattern transfer-printed in blue underglaze on heavy earthenware.

Standard Willow pattern 10-inch plate transfer-printed in blue underglaze on heavy earthenware. The plate is round with a concave rim. It has a double recessed foot ring and 3-point stilt marks on the base with single stilt marks on the front. Though one-half-inch larger, the plate is the same basic shape as the one by William Lowe*; however, it is a much heavier clay body than that used by Lowe. The engravings are very similar as well. *Author's Collection.* $20-35.

Benjamin Taylor & Son

Location: Ferrybridge, Yorkshire
Dates: c. 1845-50
Marks:

c. 1845-50

Brief History: Benjamin Taylor was in partnership with James Reed at three different Yorkshire potteries. When their partnership was dissolved in the early 1840s, James Reed continued at Mexborough. Benjamin Taylor was at Swillington Bridge Pottery with his son, Samuel, trading as Messrs. Taylor until 1842. They traded at Ferrybridge until 1850 as Benjamin Taylor & Son. Benjamin Taylor was listed as a potter of Swillington in 1942 and as an earthenware manufacturer of Ferrybridge in 1847. He retired to Brotherton, and the pottery was advertised to let in 1850.

Type of Willow Manufactured: Two Temples II pattern transfer-printed in pale blue on earthenware called Semi China.

Two Temples II pattern wash bowl and pitcher transfer-printed in pale blue underglaze on earthenware. The bowl is 14-inches wide and 5-inches high, and the pitcher stands 10-inches high. The pattern is quite large with the butterflies in the border measuring 2.5-by-3.25-inches. Note the complex branches coming out of the half daisies in the border. Both pieces are marked Semi China, and the bowl also has the impressed crown mark with initials BT&SFB – mark #157 in Heather Lawrence's *Yorkshire Pots and Potteries*, attributed to Benjamin Taylor & Son, Ferrybridge. *Author's Collection.* $250+.

G. & S. Taylor

46

Location: Hunslet New Pottery, Yorkshire
Dates: c. 1837-87
Mark:

c. 1837-87

Comments Concerning Mark: Heather Lawrence notes that two pieces of willow pattern have been found with the printed mark shown here (HL 46) in conjunction with the impressed crown mark (HL 157) associated with Ferrybridge* Pottery.

Brief History: The pottery belonging to the Allisons was called Jack Lane Pottery from the 1830s. It was sold by John Allison to George and Samuel Taylor who occupied the adjoining Hunslet New Pottery. The two works were run as one pottery by G. and S. Taylor. It is thought that the Taylors bought biscuitware marked with an impressed crown from Ferrybridge when that pottery ceased production. The printed Ironstone Ware mark was added with the initials G. and S. Taylor.

Type of Willow Manufactured: Standard Willow pattern transfer-printed in blue underglaze on earthenware marked Stoneware. A platter with the printed and impressed marks was sold on the Ebay internet auction in 2003. No picture available.

John Taylor

c. 1851-54

Location: Market Street, Hanley, Staffordshire
Dates: c. 1851-54
Mark:

Brief History: John Taylor worked on his own for a short time. In 1854, the directories give the name of the firm as John Taylor & Sons. The specialty of the firm was silver-luster goods although printed wares were also made.

Type of Willow Manufactured: Standard Willow pattern transfer-printed in blue underglaze on earthenware.

Standard Willow pattern oval covered vegetable dish transfer-printed in blue underglaze on earthenware. It measures 9-by-11-inches and has a lion finial on the lid. The dish has an uneven edge on the rim. The inner border pattern was used to decorate the outside of the dish; however, the full pattern is inside. *Courtesy Bill and Joyce Keenan.* $95-150.

William Taylor

Location: Pearl Pottery, Brook Street, Hanley, Staffordshire
Dates: c. 1860-73
Mark:

c. 1860-73

Brief History: William Taylor began making white granite, colored, and painted earthenware; however, he later concentrated on making white granite-ware (white ironstone) for the American and Canadian markets. "Wheat and Hops" is one of the molded shapes made by this firm.
Type of Willow Manufactured: Standard Willow pattern transfer-printed in blue underglaze on earthenware.

Standard Willow pattern 9 7/8-inch plate transfer-printed in blue underglaze on earthenware. This is a typical round plate of the period with concave rim. The outer border was too large. The cut is at 4:30 o'clock. *Courtesy Dennis Crosby.* $20-35.

Taylor & Kent

Location: Florence Works, Longton, Staffordshire
Dates: c. 1867-1995
Mark:

(GG3808) c. 1900+.

Brief History: From the beginning, the company produced a wide range of moderately priced china useful goods. In the first quarter of the twentieth century, quiet and traditional patterns were produced for the home and export markets. Art-Deco style colors and shapes were introduced from the 1920s. The company discontinued production during World War II, but resumed after the war with a popular Scottish tartan series. The Elizabethan trade name was introduced in 1962, and in 1983, the firm was renamed Elizabethan Fine Bone China. After a merger with Rosina, Queens became the brand name most often used. The company was taken over by the Churchill group in 1995.
Type of Willow Manufactured: Polychrome lithograph based on Two Temples II pattern on bone china.

A 7.25-inch plate decorated with polychrome lithograph based on Two Temples II pattern on bone china. The plate has a red line on the edge of the rim. This pattern is not often seen on bone china. *Author's Collection.* $10-15.

Taylor, Tunnicliffe & Co. (Ltd.)

Location: Broad Street, Shelton and Eastwood Vale, Hanley, Staffordshire
Dates: c. 1867-98
Marks:

Mark 1
(GG3819)
c.1875-91

Brief History: William Tunnicliffe, a potter, went into business with Thomas Taylor who was a tool-maker. Their specialized pottery at Broad Street, Shelton, Hanley served the Birmingham metal industries. The firm manufactured earthenware and porcelain products in association with metal parts. Door fittings, lamp holders, tobacco jars, and photographic developing equipment were produced. They moved to Eastwood Vale in 1876 and built larger facilities there. In addition to porcelain for electrical purposes, the company made a variety of interesting accessory items for the table. Mr. Tunnicliffe retired in 1895, and a private limited company was formed. After 1898 only utilitarian objects were produced.

Type of Willow Manufactured: Standard Willow and Two Temples II patterns transfer-printed in blue and green underglaze on earthenware. The two patterns are often used together in the same piece or set. All the willow pieces I have seen were made with some type of metal part integral to the piece.

Mark 2 (GG3819) c. 1875-91

Mark 3 (GG3819) c. 1875-91

Mark 4 c. 1875-91

Two Temples II pattern salad bowl transfer-printed in blue underglaze on earthenware with a silver rim. The pattern is in linear form around the outside and inside of the bowl with the border at the top. The center of the inside of the bowl has the Standard Willow pattern. See the next photo. Mark 1. *Courtesy Nancy Laska.* $100-175.

Looking into the bowl in the previous picture, we see the Standard Willow central pattern in the base of the bowl surrounded by two repeats of the Two Temples II pattern in linear form.

Standard Willow central pattern butter dish insert transfer-printed in light blue underglaze on earthenware. The border pattern is adapted from the Two Temples II border pattern. I have seen several of these pieces with the same pattern arrangement even though some are printed in dark blue. The holder is made of silver. Mark 1. *Courtesy IWC Convention 1996.* $45-75.

Two Temples II pattern biscuit jar with silver mounting at the top including handle and lid. The glaze or clay body is light blue on this lovely piece. Mark 2. *Courtesy Paul Kirves and Zeke Jimenez.* $150-200.

Two Temples II pattern 6.5-inch humidor transfer-printed in blue underglaze on earthenware. The two handles are decorated with cobalt blue enamel. Mark 3 is on the bottom of the humidor. Mark 4 appears on the underside of the lid: *Courtesy Geraldine Ewaniuk.* $150-200.

John Thomson (& Sons)

Location: Annfield Pottery, East End, Glasgow, Scotland
Dates: 1826-1883
Marks:

Mark 1
c. 1826-60

Comments Concerning Marks: Mark 2 is attributed to John Thomson although there is a slight possibility it could relate to John Tams. Another mark with J.T. initials and Stone Ware in a banner topped with a crown and surrounded by leaves and branches, found on a willow pattern plate, is known to pertain to this pottery.

Mark 2
c. 1826-60

Brief History: John Thomson was just 21 years of age when he founded the Annfield Pottery in 1826. He must have had some capital in addition to his expertise in pottery and a keen business sense as he was quite successful. He brought workers and traditions from Staffordshire in the beginning. It was an earthenware factory that produced table, dessert, and tea services as well as black and brown glazed ware. Garden and fancy flower pots and ornamental vases were also made. Many printed patterns were used, and it may be that copper plates were engraved in Staffordshire.

John Thomson was very active in the Methodist Church. He was also elected Councillor for the First Ward of Glasgow and later served as a magistrate. His income not only came from the pottery but from buying and selling land in the vicinity during the late 1850s and the 1860s. He was married and had six children attain adulthood. Three of his sons went into business with him in the early 1860s. John Thomson died August 21, 1870. His sons carried on the business for a time, but the quality of wares deteriorated after his death.

Type of Willow Manufactured: Standard Willow pattern transfer-printed in various shades of blue underglaze on earthenware.

Rare green printed condiment set on a heart-shaped base. The base is decorated with the Standard Willow central pattern, and the individual pots have Two Temples II pattern. This company produced several varieties of these sets in blue on a circular base with the same pattern arrangement as this one. The owner will probably find a clear glass or white ceramic container to complete the set. This is the only example of green by Taylor, Tunnicliffe & Co. documented. Mark 1. *Courtesy Harry and Jessie Hall.* $125-225.

Standard Willow pattern plate transfer-printed in medium blue underglaze on earthenware. The round plate has a concave rim. Mark 1. *Courtesy Henry Kelly. Photo by Douglas Leishman.* $30-40.

Standard Willow pattern platter transfer-printed in blue underglaze on stoneware. The dimensions are 13.25-by-16.5-inches. It is a typical mid-nineteenth century willow pattern platter with clear printing and a little white space between borders. Mark 2. *Author's Collection.* $75-150.

Thomas Till & Son(s) Ltd.

Location: Sytch Pottery, Burslem, Staffordshire
Dates: c.1850-1928
Marks:

Brief History: Thomas Till had been a partner with Barker and Sutton. After Sutton left, he worked in the firm of Barker & Till* until April 15, 1850. After that he was in business with his son producing many different colors and types of earthenware. Their goods were good middle-class quality. The firm exhibited wares including "pearl white granite" at the 1851 Exhibition. That ware, in many different shapes, was exported to America and known there as "white ironstone". Thomas Till & Son employed at that time 61 men, 34 women, 46 boys and 33 girls. From at least 1869, the name of the firm was changed to Thomas Till & Sons. "Tillson Ware" became a trademark c. 1922.

Type of Willow Manufactured: Standard Willow and Two Temples II patterns transfer-printed in blue underglaze on earthenware. "Chinese Willow" central pattern variant called "Kang-He" was also produced in shades of blue on white or yellow background, and sometimes with red clobbering.

Mark 1 (GG3853)
c. 1850-61

T. TILL & SONS ENGLAND

Mark 2 c. 1891-1928

Mark 3 (GG3860)
c. 1922-28

Two Temples II pattern transfer-printed in dark blue underglaze on earthenware. The pattern is reversed on the cup. The saucer is 5.75-inches across, and the edge is one-inch off the table. Mark 2. *Author's Collection.* $15-22.

Standard Willow pattern 10.25-inch plate transfer-printed in blue underglaze on heavy stoneware. There are 8 indentations on the edge of the flat rim. It has a recessed foot ring. Three-point stilt marks on the base of the plate with single stilt marks on the front. The borders are well matched. Mark 1. *Author's Collection.* $30-40.

Kang-He willow variant in blue underglaze with red clobbering. The center pattern of this 11-inch serving plate is the same as "Chinese Willow" by Crown Staffordshire*. Till & Sons also produced "Kang Border": wares with only the border pattern. Both patterns were done in French green, two different shades of blue, with a yellow background, and other color treatments. Mark 3. *Courtesy IWC Convention 2000.* $75-125.

William Tomlinson & Co.

Location: Ferrybridge Pottery, Yorkshire
Dates: c.1801-04
Mark: Impressed W T & Co

Brief History: William Tomlinson was involved in the partnership that built the Ferrybridge Pottery, which was originally called Knottingly Pottery. For a short time (c. 1801-4) it was called William Tomlinson & Co. before the name was changed to The Ferrybridge Pottery. William Tomlinson took an active role in running the pottery and by 1828 was sole owner of the pottery. He turned over his ownership to his son Edward in 1830 and died 3 years later at the age of 87.
Type of Willow Manufactured: Standard Willow pattern transfer-printed in blue underglaze on earthenware. A mug is pictured with impressed mark W T & Co 3 on p. 13 of *Northern Ceramic Society Newsletter No. 109* (1998) in an article by Renard Broughton. No picture available.

George Townsend

Location: St. Gregory's Works, Gower Street, and Chadwick Street, Longton, Staffordshire.
Dates: c. 1850-65
Marks:

Mark 1 (GG3879)
c. 1850-65

Mark 2 (GG3879)
c. 1850-65

Brief History: George Townsend succeeded Sampson Beardmore at the St. Gregory's Works. He was also working at Gower Street from 1850-53, and Chadwick Street from 1854-1865. He produced china and earthenware, luster, black, and toys. In 1851, he employed 196, and by 1861, he employed 500 workers. He went bankrupt in 1865, and his assignees sold his ware, clay, colors, engraved copper-plates, printing press, etc.
Type of Willow Manufactured: Standard Willow and Two Temples II patterns transfer-printed in blue underglaze on earthenware. The earthenware, glaze and workmanship are the poorest examples I have seen of nineteenth century Willow pattern.

Thomas Till & Sons ad featuring new trade-mark "Tillson Ware". It mentions patterns "New Kang-He and Kang Border in Plain Print and Enamelled". *Pottery Gazette,* January 1, 1923, p. 6.

Standard Willow pattern plates transfer-printed in blue underglaze on earthenware. The 8 7/8-inch plate has a rough blue glaze with lumps on the back. It is warped and doesn't sit evenly on the table. It has a double recessed foot ring with single stilt marks on the base. It has Mark 1. The 7-inch plate is darker blue with a shiny bluish glaze. It has a lump of clay under the pattern and glaze between the teahouse and inner border. It has a single foot ring and single stilt marks on the base: front and back. It has Mark 2. Both plates have tears in the transfer prints. The quality is very poor. *Author's Collection.* $8-10 each.

New patterns illustrated by Thomas Till & Sons. "Kang Border" plate and "Kang He" covered dish are on the right. *Pottery Gazette,* March 1, 1922, p. 383.

John Turner (William & John)

Location: Lane End (Longton), Staffordshire
Dates: 1762-87 & 1787-1803
Mark:

c. 1800

Comments Concerning Mark: Impressed TURNER was used on earthenware at the end of the eighteenth century and into the nineteenth century. No examples are shown here.
Brief History: John Turner was a master potter, making all types of earthenware. He may have been one of the earliest producers of early dark blue printed patterns, but in the absence of printed marks before 1787, the year of his death, we turn to the marked wares of his sons William and John. John Turner may have produced china in addition to earthenware. He was a member of the New Hall Porcelain Co.* from 1781-82. His sons William and John produced some porcelain of two different types. Early New-Hall type wares with early pattern numbers may have been produced by the firm prior to 1800.

In 1800 William and John took out a patent for new types of china and earthenware containing a new ingredient called "Tabberner's Mine Rock" or "Little Mine Rock". The patent for porcelain contained "Cornish Stone", but the patent for earthenware did not. The mark "TURNERS' PATENT" may occur on the earthenware that was the first stone china developed. A bright floral pattern was first used on this ware. Later many lovely similar "Japan" type patterns were produced by the Masons* firm. The 1800 patent porcelain has a very glossy, almost oily feel to it. Not many examples survive to this day. It may have been produced for only a year or two.

The Turners took in partners in 1803; however, by 1806 the firm was bankrupt. The marks Turner, Turner & Co. and Turners' Patent could have been used on wares during this time. John Turner retired and may have joined Thomas Minton* for a time. William Turner was a potter in Fenton 1807-12 and again in Longton from 1824 until 1829,
Type of Willow Manufactured: John Turner two-man willow pattern blue printed underglaze on earthenware. Early Mandarin variant blue printed under glaze on the 1800 patent porcelain.

Mandarin variant pattern tea bowl transfer-printed in blue underglaze on porcelain. This tea bowl was purchased in a dirty state from an outside vendor at the Newark Fair Grounds, in August 1996. The worn gold on the inside of half the bowl had been repainted with a thick yellow substance. I soaked and washed it, and took it to a seminar at Keele University where Geoffrey Godden was identifying porcelains for participants. He asked me several questions: "Where did you get it?" "Why did you buy it?" "Oh, you thought it was interesting, did you?" "Did you pay good money for this?" Then he stopped in mid-sentence and said, "This is a very rare porcelain tea bowl by Turner c. 1800-01 – I would love to see the teapot!" At the end of the session, with my permission, people were allowed to handle the tea bowl to feel the "oily" glaze. The same pattern is seen on a Turner porcelain milk jug in photo 394, p. 733, of Godden's *Encyclopaedia of British Porcelain Manufacturers*. The jug has straight sides, and the tea bowl has 24 flutes. I can understand why Godden would like to see a teapot, but I am pleased to have the little tea bowl. *Author's Collection.* NP

Turpin & Co.

Location: Ouseburn Pottery, Newcastle Upon Tyne, Northumberland
Date: c. 1841
Impressed Mark:

c. 1841

Brief History: Turpin & Co. is mentioned in a directory of 1841. The firm produced transfer-printed earthenware.
Type of Willow Manufactured: Standard Willow and Two Temples II patterns transfer-printed in blue underglaze on earthenware.

John Turner's Two-man Willow pattern 6.25-inch plate transfer-printed in blue underglaze on earthenware. The clay body and glaze both have a bluish cast. There are 8 indentations on the edge of the flat rim. The recessed foot ring is unglazed, and it bears the open crescent mark. *Author's Collection.* $85-125.

Standard Willow pattern 10.25-inch plate transfer-printed in blue underglaze on earthenware. The plate has 3-point stilt marks. The edge of the rim has 8 indentations. *Courtesy Renard Broughton.* $30-40.

Two Temples II central pattern 4 3/8-inch plate transfer-printed in light blue underglaze on earthenware. *Courtesy J and J Cockerill.* $20-35.

Joseph Twigg & Bros.

Location: Newhill Pottery and Kilnhurst Old Pottery, Nr. Swinton, Yorkshire
Dates: c. 1809-84
Marks:

Comments Concerning Marks: Marks 2 and 4 were taken from Heather Lawrences's *Yorkshire Pots and Potteries.* In her book, all four of the marks seen here were definitely used at Kilnhurst Pottery. Mark 2 may possibly have been used at Newhill. Mark 4, with Mark 1, was seen on a large platter that sold on Ebay internet auction.
Brief History: In 1809, Joseph Twigg, a potter of Newhill, bought Wells House in Newhill, converting half of it into a pottery. In 1816, he bought adjoining land. He was in business with his sons Joseph, Benjamin, and John. In 1827, the firm was charged with theft of a recipe for blue printed ware, and the material for it from Messrs Brameld, given to them by James Baguley, china manager at the Swinton Pottery. Joseph Twigg had learned his trade at the Swinton Pottery, and was making similar wares at Newhill. If Swinton recipes were used, it would have been very difficult to distinguish the wares from Swinton products. The Twiggs bought stock from the Don Pottery* sale in 1835. As a result several pieces with Twigg marks are recognizable Don Pottery molds or transfer patterns.

The Twiggs leased the Kilnhurst Pottery in 1839 and ran both potteries as "Joseph Twigg & Bros.". Wares from Newhill were often warehoused at Kilnhurst due to its better location nearer to transportation by canal or railway. Joseph Twigg ran Newhill Pottery until his death c. 1843 when Joseph Jr. took over. He died in the early 1860s. His partner Daniel Matthews tried to run the pottery with a new partner but went bankrupt in 1867. Benjamin Twigg ran the Kilnhurst Pottery that had been purchased by the Twiggs, until his death when John took over. John died in 1877 and was succeeded by his son Daniel who ran the pottery until his retirement in 1884.

Mark 1
(GG39312)
c. 1840-84

TWIGG'S

Mark 2
(GG3910)
c. 1822-84

Mark 3
c. 1840-84

Mark 4
c. 1840-84

The Twiggs were a very successful pottery family that produced a wide variety of earthenware products for export as well as the home market. They produced many popular transfer-printed patterns as well as commemorative ware. Children's ware, molded white earthenware octagonal jugs, sponged, banded, and painted pottery in red and blue were produced as well.
Type of Willow Manufactured: Standard Willow pattern transfer-printed in blue underglaze on earthenware in tableware including many accessory items.

Standard Willow pattern 8.25-inch plate transfer-printed in blue underglaze on earthenware. The plate has a flat foot ring and 3-point stilt marks on the base with single stilt marks on the front. The concave rim tilts upward so that the edge of the plate is 1 1/8-inch from the table. Marks 1 and 3. *Author's Collection.* $25-35.

Standard Willow pattern 8.75-inch cheese stand transfer-printed in blue underglaze on earthenware. This impressive cheese stand is almost 3-inches high. The base is decorated with the outer border upside down. Mark 2. *Courtesy Jayne Steed.* $125-200.

Standard Willow central pattern shell dish transfer-printed in blue underglaze on earthenware. This dish measures 5.5-by-6-inches. It has a molded shell pattern under the printed pattern. Mark 2. *Courtesy Loren Zeller.* $75-150.

Upper Hanley Pottery Co. (Ltd.)

Location: Hanley and Brownfield's Works, Cobridge, Staffordshire
Dates: 1895-1910
Mark:

Brief History: The firm operated at Hanley until 1902 and then moved to Brownfield's Works. Grimwades Ltd.* took over the Upper Hanley Pottery c. 1906.
The firm produced earthenware.
Type of Willow Manufactured: Standard Willow pattern transfer-printed in blue underglaze on earthenware.

U.H.P. C°
ENGLAND

c. 1895-1910

Standard Willow pattern gravy boat transfer-printed in blue underglaze on earthenware. The piece is 9-inches long. There is no border pattern. This and a saucer are the only two pieces of willow pattern I have seen made by this company. *Author's Collection.* $25-30.

James Vernon & Co.

Location: Waterloo Pottery, Burslem, Staffordshire
Dates: c. 1846-75
Mark:

J.VERNON
BURSLEM

c. 1846-75

Brief History: James Vernon established the Waterloo Pottery in about 1846. He produced ordinary earthenware for the South American, West Indian and Mediterranean markets. From about 1875, the trading style changed to James Vernon & Sons and James Vernon junior. J. & G. Vernon took over the works from 1880 to 1889.
Type of Willow Manufactured: Standard Willow pattern transfer-printed in blue underglaze on earthenware.

Standard Willow pattern 10.5-inch plate transfer-printed in blue underglaze on earthenware. There are 8 slight indentations on the edge of the flat rim. The plate has an unglazed recessed foot ring. The glaze is shiny with a fair amount of grit, especially on the back. There is a big cut in the outer border at 5 o'clock. *Author's Collection.* $25-35.

Victoria Porcelain (Fenton) Ltd.

Location: Fenton, Staffordshire
Dates: 1949-57
Mark:

Willow
B
VICTORIA PORCELAIN
FENTON
ENGLAND

c. 1949-57

Brief History: This firm produced earthenware even though the title has the word "porcelain" in it. Most marks have the location of Fenton included. A specific mark was used for their Willow pattern. The firm produced tea ware and dinnerware.
Type of Willow Manufactured: Standard Willow pattern transfer-printed in blue and green underglaze on earthenware.

Standard Willow pattern cream soup with under plate transfer-printed in blue underglaze on earthenware. These sets are hard to find in Willow pattern. It is trimmed in gold. *Courtesy Louise and Charles Loehr.* $40-70.

Standard Willow pattern coffee pot transfer-printed in blue underglaze on earthenware. All of the edges have a gold line added. *Courtesy Joette Hightower.* $55-95.

Standard Willow pattern covered vegetable dish transfer-printed in green underglaze on earthenware. Green willow dinnerware and tea sets were made by this firm. There is no gold trim on the green pieces. *Courtesy IWC Convention 1999.* $65-95.

Wade Ceramics (see Ringtons Ltd.)
H. A. Wain & Sons Ltd.

Location: Melba Works, Longton, Staffordshire
Dates: 1946-present (2003)
Mark:

c. 1951+

Brief History: This firm produced earthenware with a specialty of animal figures. Even though several firms used the trade name "Melba", this is the only firm that used the name written in cursive script. Therefore, I am assuming that the ware shown below was made by H. A Wain & Sons Ltd.
Type of Willow Manufactured: Blue decal overglaze based on Standard Willow pattern on earthenware.

Flour canister with blue decal based on Standard Willow pattern. This looks like a new item. *Courtesy IWC Convention 2002.* $10-15.

Ambrose Walker & Co.

Location: Stafford Pottery, So. Stockton, Stockton-on-Tees, Yorkshire
Dates: c. 1877-90s
Impressed Mark:

243
A.W & Co
SO. STOCKTON

c. 1877-90s

Brief History: Continuing the history of the Stafford Pottery, established by William Smith*, we learn that by 1860, the partnership running the pottery was comprised of George Skinner, Robert Chilton, and John Parrington. Ambrose Walker took Chilton's place, and the firm traded as Skinner, Parrington & Walker until Parrington's death in 1875. The style became Skinner, Walker & Co. until 1877 when Amrose Walker became the sole owner. It was a very large pottery at that time with about 300 employees – twice as large as it had been twenty-five years before. Walker maintained control of the pottery until sometime in the 1890s. By 1905, the firm was re-named "Thornaby Pottery Co. Ltd." Thornaby is the area previously known as South Stockton. The company continued production of earthenware including mocha ware, pink-purple luster and transfer prints with mottos as well as patterns used by other companies.

Type of Willow Manufactured: Standard Willow pattern transfer-printed in blue underglaze on earthenware.

Standard Willow pattern octagonal covered tureen transfer-printed in blue underglaze on stoneware. It is 10-inches across and stands 7-inches high. The full central pattern is seen inside the dish; however, only rectangular fragments of the pattern were used to decorate the outside. *Courtesy Tim and Kim Allen.* $115-165.

Thomas Henry Walker

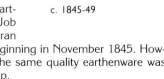

Location: Church Street, Lane End (Longton), Staffordshire
Dates: 1845-49
Mark:

c. 1845-49

Comment Concerning Mark: This is the same style mark used by Batkin, Walker and Broadhurst* c. 1840-45. Only the initials have changed.
Brief History: After serving in a part-nership with William Batkin and Job Broadhurst, Thomas Henry Walker ran the pottery on his own account beginning in November 1845. How-ever, he was bankrupt by 1849. The same quality earthenware was made as in the previous partnership.
Type of Willow Manufactured: Standard Willow pattern transfer-printed in blue underglaze on earthenware marked Warranted Stone China.

Standard Willow pattern platter transfer-printed in blue underglaze on earthenware. The platter measures 12.25-by-15-inches with 8 slight indentations on the edge. The clay body is very white, and it has a smooth glaze. The border pattern was too small, and there are two large patches near the north-west and south-east corners. *Author's Collection.* $95-150.

Thomas Walker

Location: Lion Pottery, Tunstall, Staffordshire
Dates: c. 1845-51
Mark:

c. 1845-51

Comment Concerning Mark: The initials "T W" could refer to other pot-ters; however, a plate is owned by a collector with this printed mark in addition to an impressed "Thos. Walker" (GG3982a).
Brief History: Thomas Walker produced a good quality of earthen-ware with many transfer-printed patterns. The firm also produced undecorated white ironstone for the American market.
Type of Willow Manufactured: Standard Willow pattern transfer-printed in blue underglaze on earthenware and stoneware.

Standard Willow pattern 8 5/8-inch plate transfer-printed in blue underglaze on stoneware. The rim is faceted, and is 12-sided. Three-point stilt marks under the rim with single stilt marks on the top. It has a single 1/8-inch high foot ring. *Author's Collection.* $25-35.

Standard Willow pattern platter transfer-printed in blue underglaze on earthenware. It measures 10.75-by-13.5-inches. There are impurities in the glaze, and it is uneven on the rim. A patch was put in the outer border at 1 o'clock. *Author's Collection.* $65-115.

Walker & Carter

Location: British Anchor Pottery, Longton & Anchor Works, Stoke-on-Trent, Staffordshire
Dates: c. 1865-89
Marks:

Mark 1
c. 1872-89

Comment Concerning Marks: The impressed mark has an anchor in the center. Around the circle: W & C. Stoke-on-Trent.
Brief History: This partnership succeeded that of Thomas Walker and William Bateman at the British Anchor Pottery, Anchor Road, Longton. The pottery had been newly built in 1858, and had four ovens. In about 1872, the firm moved to the Anchor Works in Stoke. Useful items were made in earthenware.
Type of Willow Manufactured: Standard Willow pattern transfer-printed in blue underglaze on earthenware.

Mark 2
c. 1872-89

Standard Willow pattern platter transfer-printed in blue underglaze on earthenware. It measures 13.25-by-16.25 and has a slightly uneven edge, as most of these nineteenth century platters do. Three-point stilt marks on the front with a single stilt mark on the back. There are small patches in the northwest and southeast corners of the outer border. The platter has both marks shown. *Author's Collection.* $95-150.

Wallace & Co.

Location: Newcastle Pottery, Pottery Road, Forth Banks & Pottery Lane, Ouseburn, Newcastle upon Tyne, Northumberland
Dates: c. 1858-86
Impressed Mark:

(GG3984) c. 1858-85

Comments Concerning Mark: This impressed mark may also have been used by the previous firm of James Wallace & Co. c. 1838-58.
Brief History: Prior to 1838, the pottery at Forth Banks was managed by Redhead, Wilson & Co. From 1838-58, James Wallace & Co. were the proprietors. The company traded as Wallace & Co. from

1858, and were earthenware manufacturers. In 1870, the firm moved to Pottery Lane, Ouseburn. By 1885-6, the directories listed Wallace & Co. as producing flower pots, chimney tops and sanitary wares. They appear to have given up making tableware at that time.
Type of Willow Manufactured: Standard Willow pattern transfer-printed in blue underglaze on earthenware.

Standard Willow pattern 10-inch plate transfer-printed in blue underglaze on earthenware. There are 8 slight indentations on the edge of the concave rim. Three-point stilt marks are on the underside of the rim with single stilt marks on the top. The plate has a single foot ring with two additional ridges going outward. It has a pale blue shiny glaze. There is a small patch in the outer rim at 8 o'clock and a major patching problem at 12 o'clock. *Author's Collection.* $25-35.

Edward Walley

Location: Villa Pottery, Cobridge, Staffordshire
Dates: 1845-58
Mark:

(GG3990) c. 1845-58

Comments Concerning Mark: The printed mark (W with the name of the pattern) was a device used by Edward Walley. The impressed mark PEARL WHITE was also used by this firm.
Brief History: Edward Walley had worked previously with Elijah Jones, trading as Jones & Walley*. That partnership was dissolved February 19, 1845, and Edward Walley traded on his own. From 1858-62, the trading style changed to Edward Walley & Son or E. & W. Walley. The firm produced good quality earthenware, lusterware and ironstone ware. Undecorated white ironstone, copper-luster tea leaf ironstone, and transfer-printed wares were exported to America in great quantities.
Type of Willow Manufactured: Standard Willow pattern transfer-printed in purple underglaze on ironstone. Blue-printed wares were probably produced as well since we have seen examples of blue willow by Jones & Walley*.

Standard Willow pattern 10-sided plate transfer-printed in purple on ironstone. This plate shape is documented in the Dieringer's *White Ironstone China Plate Identification Guide 1840-90* on page 28 as "Grape Octagon" 10-sided. Most of these plates had some type of luster decoration: banded or a Tea Leaf variant pattern in the center. The plate has a single foot ring and Three-point stilt marks on the back of the rim with single stilt marks on the front. It bears the printed markas well as impressed PEARL WHITE. *Author's Collection.* $30-40.

Standard Willow pattern 9-inch plate transfer-printed in blue underglaze on earthenware. The plate is very light in weight to be marked "Stone China". The slash mark above the tip of the lion's tail in the mark is a piece of clay. The plate has a recessed foot ring. Eight slight indentations can be felt on the edge of the concave rim. Three-point stilt marks on the underside with single stilt marks on the top. *Author's Collection.* $20-25.

James Warren

Location: Park Place Works, High Street, Longton, Staffordshire
Dates: c. 1843-52
Mark:

c. 1843-52

Comment Concerning Mark: This Stone China mark is described in *Godden's Guide to Ironstone* and assumed to pertain to James Thomas Warren who was listed in most of the directories of the day as a china merchant; however, no marked examples are known in porcelain. The 1851 directory of William White lists Warren as a China and Earthenware manufacturer.
Brief History: James Warren and John Adams were listed as partners in 1841 and resumed partnership again in 1853-65; however, Warren worked alone c. 1843-52. It may have been the father of John Adams who was the original partner. In 1851, Warren employed 35 men, 30 women, 14 boys and 24 girls. Warren and Adams (who had his own business at the time) were reported to have bought bone and stone from John Bourne of Etruria between 1845 and 53.
Type of Willow Manufactured: Standard Willow pattern transfer-printed in blue underglaze on earthenware.

Washington Pottery Ltd.

Location: College Road, Shelton, Staffordshire
Dates: 1946-70
Marks:

c. 1950+

c. 1970-74

Comment Concerning Marks: The house and tree motif was carried on with the new name: English Ironstone Ltd.* from 1970 to 74. Mark 2 seems to be a transition mark; however, it appears on willow that matches that with Mark 1 rather than the pattern used by English Ironstone Ltd.
Brief History: Washington Pottery was founded in 1946. By the early 1950s, an extensive range of patterns were used on tea and coffee sets as well as dinnerware. Techniques used were underglaze printing and painting as well as lithographic patterns, gold stamping and wash bands. The willow pattern in blue was offered with and without gold finishing in 1951. In 1970, the name of the company was changed to English Ironstone Ltd.*
Type of Willow Manufactured: Standard Willow pattern transfer-printed in blue and red underglaze on earthenware with and without gold trim.

Pottery Gazette, March 1, 1951, p. 366. Washington Pottery Limited has a one-page ad picturing pieces from a willow pattern tea set: serving plate, creamer, covered sugar bowl, and teacup with saucer. No mention is made of red. It must have come later.

Standard Willow pattern 9.75-inch dinner plate transfer-printed underglaze in dark blue with red willow demitasse cup and saucer. The cup and saucer are the only pieces I have seen in red The cup and saucer have gold trim. This pattern has a lot of clarity. There is more open space at the inside edge of the outer border, and a wide white space between borders. Plates are found with either of the two marks shown, and the cup and saucer have Mark 1. *Author's Collection.* $8-12 & $15-20.

Standard Willow pattern 6-cup teapot transfer-printed in blue underglaze on earthenware. The teapot has gold trim. Mark 1. *Courtesy Joette Hightower.* $75-115.

J. H. Weatherby & Sons

Location: Falcon Pottery, High Street, Hanley, Staffordshire
Dates: c. 1891-present (2003)
Marks:

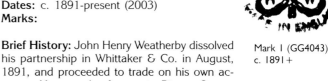

Mark 1 (GG4043)
c. 1891+

Brief History: John Henry Weatherby dissolved his partnership in Whittaker & Co. in August, 1891, and proceeded to trade on his own account. He rented a factory in Pinnox Street, Tunstall, but was only there for a year or two when he purchased the Falcon Pottery. This has always been a family concern. The present managing director is great-grandson of John Henry Weatherby.

The firm began production with printed toilet sets, trinket sets, vases, teapots, tableware, jugs, etc. After World War I the company produced ware for hotels, hospitals, and other institutions. In the 1920s and '30s, experimentation was carried out with matt glazes and Art Deco-style vases. Many new lines in giftware were introduced after World War II. Children's ware came out in the 1960s. The Weatherby firm took over the relief-molded white ironstone wheat designs of A. J. Wilkinson Ltd.* when that firm went out of business in 1970. This ware was exported mainly to North America. Current products are hotel and catering ware, and giftware for the home and export markets.

Mark 2 (GG4044)
c. 1892+

Type of Willow Manufactured: Standard Willow pattern transfer-printed in blue and brown underglaze on earthenware. The brown willow has polychrome clobbering with gold trim. The blue is more commonly found in all types of tableware.

Wathen & Hebb

Location: Foley Works, Longton, Staffordshire
Dates: c. 1854-57
Mark:

WATHEN & HEBB
STAFFORDSHIRE · STONE CHINA

c. 1854-57

Brief History: James Bateman Wathen was in a partnership with John Hebb from 1854 when his partnership with William Fletcher was dissolved. The firm produced transfer-printed earthenware. Later Wathen partnerships are recorded as having produced lusterware as well. The partnership of Wathen & Hebb was dissolved March 28, 1857.
Type of Willow Manufactured: Standard Willow pattern transfer-printed in blue underglaze on earthenware.

Standard Willow pattern 9-inch plate transfer-printed in blue underglaze on earthenware. The plate is not as heavy as the "Stone China" marking might indicate. It has a single flat foot ring with 2-point stilt marks on the front and single stilt marks on the back. The rim is concave, and the edge is uneven. *Author's Collection.* $25-35.

Standard Willow pattern covered cheese keeper transfer-printed in blue underglaze on earthenware. The base is 7.25-by-9.25-inches, and it is 5-inches tall to the top of the handle. The pattern was put on each side with patching at each end. No border patterns were used. The pieces have gold trim. Mark 1. *Author's Collection.* $75-135.

Standard Willow pattern 5.5-inch plate transfer-printed in brown underglaze with clobbering in shades of blue, rust, yellow, and green. There is quite a bit of detail work with the gold in the trees and outer border. Mark 2. *Courtesy Tim and Kim Allen.* $20-30.

Standard Willow pattern 2-handled mug transfer-printed in brown underglaze with clobbering in the same colors as the plate above; however, it does not have as much gold detail. The mug stands 3.25-inches high. This is an unusual item. Mark 2. *Courtesy Jeff Siptak.* $35-65.

Wedgwood & Co. (Ltd.)

Location: Unicorn and Pinnox Pottery, Tunstall, Staffordshire
Dates: c. 1860-1980
Marks:

Mark 1 (GG4055) c. 1835+

Mark 2 c. 1891+

Comment Concerning Marks: Mark 1 was used prior to 1860 by Podmore, Walker & Co.* and continued after the name of the company changed to Wedgwood & Co. Mark 2 can be attributed to Wedgwood & Co. based on the similarity of engravings on the two plates seen in the first photo. The 1835 founding date in the later marks refers to Podmore, Walker & Co. Mark 7 has been used after the take-over by the Wedgwood Group.
Brief History: Podmore, Walker & Co.* was renamed Wedgwood & Co. in 1860. The company manufactured fine quality earthenware

that won the Paris Medal in 1865. Types of ware included printed ware on white and ivory, decorated table, tea, and toilet ware. White granite was also produced (at the Unicorn Works) for the American market as well as flow blue patterns on ironstone. The ware was known as "Imperial Ironstone China" and had an excellent quality clay body and glaze. In the 1870s, the works covered about an acre of ground and provided employment for six or seven hundred people.

In the twentieth century, the company has been known for dinnerware and tea ware in traditional styles. In the *Pottery* Gazette, October 1, 1908, we read: "'Imperial Porcelain', Semi-Porcelain & Decorated & Plain Earthenware to suit all markets." Under "Buyers' Notes" in the *Pottery* Gazette, July 1, 1922, we learn: "…In plain printed dinnerware the old 'Blue Willow' is always in steady demand, " In September 1926, we read: "It will be remembered that the firm in question has, for some years, produced the old 'Willow' pattern in illuminated style, but the latest adaptation of the old 'Indian Tree' design is, we think, to be preferred." P. 1357. I must add – "not by willow collectors!" Art Deco-style shapes were introduced in the 1930s, and contemporary styles came along after World War II designed by David Queensberry of the Queensberry Hunt Partnership.

Confusion continued through the years regarding the two Wedgwood firms. In the *Pottery Gazette*, June 1, 1935, the following statement appeared: "Ware marked Wedgwood and Co. is not made by Josiah Wedgwood & Sons. Wedgwood is the registered trade name of ware." In an effort to end the confusion, Wedgwood & Co. changed its name to Enoch Wedgwood (Tunstall) Ltd. in 1965. Ironically, the company was taken over by the Wedgwood Group in 1980 and renamed Unicorn Pottery.
Type of Willow Manufactured: Standard and Two Temples II patterns transfer-printed in blue underglaze on earthenware. A wide range of tableware and accessory items was made. The Standard Willow pattern was also printed underglaze in red. The "Red Bridge" decal pattern overglaze has been found.

Mark 3 (GG4059) c. 1906+

Mark 4 (GG4061) c. 1908+

Mark 5 (GG4067) var. c. 1956+

Mark 6 c. 1965-80

Mark 7 c. 1980+

Standard Willow pattern plates transfer-printed in blue underglaze on stoneware. The 10 3/8-inch plate on the right was shown in the section on Podmore, Walker & Co.* It has Mark 1. The 7 7/8-inch plate on the left has the same engraving on a smaller scale. It has 12 indentations on the edge of the flat rim and a single foot ring. It has Mark 2. These marks were used previously by Podmore, Walker & Co. and continued when the name changed to Wedgwood & Co. *Author's Collection.* $25-35 and 20-30.

Standard Willow pattern 4-cup teapot and stand transfer-printed in blue on earthenware. This shape teapot was also made with a smaller pattern, leaving a larger amount of white between the border and central pattern. Mark 4. *Courtesy Charles and Zeta Hollingsworth.* $75-125.

Sugar bowl blue printed in Standard Willow pattern with teapot blue printed in Two Temples II reversed pattern. The teapot has gold trim, and the sugar bowl does not. The two pieces are examples of "Primary – No Line" shape as documented on p. 35 in *Flow Blue and Mulberry Teapot Body Styles*. The style features an 8-sided base with an 8-panel bulbous body. The teapot is 7-inches to the top of the finial. Mulberry patterns were made in this shape c. 1845 by Podmore, Walker & Co. Evidently, Wedgwood & Co. used the molds later as this teapot bears Mark 4. The sugar bowl has Mark 3. *Author's Collection.* $150-200 and $35-75.

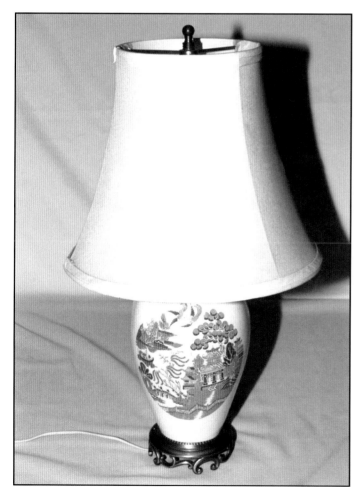

Standard Willow pattern lamp transfer-printed in red underglaze on earthenware. The pattern is circular indicating that dinnerware was probably also made using this engraving; however, this is the only piece of red willow I have seen by Wedgwood & Co. Mark 4. *Author's Collection.* $100-150.

Two Temples II reversed pattern lidded jug transfer-printed in flow blue underglaze on earthenware. It stands 6.75-inches high and has gold trim including gold sponging on the solid blue areas. A replacement brass lid was made for the missing pewter lid. *Author's Collection.* $125-200.

Blue printed dinner plate with reversed variation of the Standard Willow pattern. This simplified version has fewer buildings and trees, adding flower arrangements in the rocks. The teahouse has become a pagoda, and the path is uninterrupted by the fence that has moved to the riverbank. The three figures are crossing a one-arched bridge. This plate is very flat and has Mark 5, notably the only mark used by the company to use the word "Willow". It is also marked 11 53 which may be the production date. *Author's Collection.* $10-15.

Blue printed 4.75-inch tip trays decorated with the same central pattern as seen on the plate above. These little trays are very plentiful and have been found with Marks 6 and 7. *Author's Collection.* $8-15.

"Red Bridge" decal pattern reversed overglaze on 8 3/8-inch plate. The octagonal plate is attached to a silver stand. *Courtesy Tim and Kim Allen.* $35-50.

Josiah Wedgwood (& Sons Ltd.)

Location: Burslem, Etruria and Barlaston, Staffordshire
Dates: c. 1759-present (2003)
Marks:

Mark 1 (GG4075)
c. 1781-1891

Brief History: The Wedgwood family of potters was unique in that the business carried through nine generations. Josiah Wedgwood I was the youngest child of Thomas Wedgwood, a potter at Churchyard Works in Burslem, who died when Josiah was 9 years old. His oldest brother Thomas inherited the pottery that had been founded by their great-grandfather in 1656. After attending school in Newcastle-under-Lyme, at the age of 14, Josiah was apprenticed to his brother Thomas. During his apprenticeship he suffered a severe case of small pox causing permanent damage to his right knee. At the age of 38, his right leg was amputated above the knee and a wooden leg fitted. He recovered well from the operation and lived to the age of 65.

Josiah I worked in partnership with John Harrison and Thomas Alders for two years and then was taken into partnership with Thomas Whieldon, a highly respected potter in Staffordshire. In May 1759, he rented Ivy House and went to work on his own. He moved to Brick House Works at the beginning of 1763, and hired his brother Thomas (who came to be known as "useful" Thomas) as journeyman. By 1766, Thomas became a partner with 1/8 share of the profits. It was during the time at Brick House that the firm produced a creamware tea and coffee service that Queen Charlotte prized. Wedgwood was given permission to the title "Pottery to Her Majesty".

Josiah I purchased a 350 acre estate in 1767, and building began for a modern new factory. The first firings occurred in 1769. The name "Etruria" was chosen to emulate the Etruscan society in central Italy that produced

WEDGWOOD

Mark 2 (GG4091)
c. 1878-91

WEDGWOOD

Mark 3 (GG4094)
c. 1900+

Mark 4 (GG4094)
var. c. 1910+

Mark 5 c. 1891-1950

fine works of art appreciated by people in the 18th century. The earthenware products were marked from the beginning – a practice that soon spread to other potteries of the day. In 1936, the Wedgwood family purchased 382 acres in Barlaston. The foundation stone was laid in 1938, for a new factory that became the most advanced in Britain. Firing was powered by electricity in the Brown Boven tunnel ovens. The production of earthenware was moved to Barlaston in 1940, and Etruria closed June 13, 1950. The policy of acquiring other companies began in 1966. At the present time (2003) some of the major brand names in use by the Wedgwood Group are Adams, Coalport and Mason's Ironstone.

The Wedgwood firm is known for many different types of ware: creamware, black basalt, cane ware, jasper, green glaze, pearlware, bone china, majolica and drab ware. Wedgwood's creamware, known as Queen's Ware from 1765, was a major achievement for Josiah I. The body was whiter than that of his competitors by the addition of Cornish china clay and china stone to it. The shapes were fashioned after silver and porcelain shapes. Wedgwood developed a pearl glaze that he began to use in about 1774 that would whiten his Queen's ware a little more for tea ware. It contained a small bit of cobalt. He experimented with this for about five years before naming it "Pearl White". It was also known as "Pearl Ware" or just "Pearl" Although cream-colored earthenware with a bluish glaze had been made in Staffordshire for many years, it was Josiah Wedgwood I who perfected it. He was reluctant to produce the ware as he considered his Queen's Ware a finer product; however, he submitted to pressure, and very fine blue-painted patterns were made on pearlware.

Josiah I did not want the Wedgwood wares to resemble the tin-glazed continental wares or the Chinoiserie printed patterns of other Staffordshire potteries. Other firms considered pearlware as the perfect medium for transfer printing underglaze the Chinese export porcelain blue and white patterns that were in demand. The Wedgwood firm did not use underglaze blue printing until 10 years after Josiah I's death in 1795. The body was changed somewhat from the pearlware developed earlier for use with blue painted patterns. Botanical subjects were chosen at first, but inevitably chinoiserie designs were produced. The Wedgwood's Willow pattern was based on that of Minton* and was engraved by J. Mollart in 1806; however, the pattern was not produced by Wedgwood until 1818. It has been in and out of production from that time to about the year 2000.

The Wedgwood firm was slow to adopt the production of bone china. The first period was from 1812-22, mainly on tea and dessert ware. Replacement orders were made until 1831. The amount of bone ash in the formula was only about 25% whereas Josiah Spode II used about 50% in his bone china. When bone china was reintroduced in 1878 at Wedgwood, the percentage of bone ash had risen to 47%. Dinnerware and tea ware patterns were designed specifically for use on bone china. Elegance and restraint were the guiding attributes in designing Wedgwood patterns on bone china.

**WEDGWOOD
ETRURIA ENGLAND**

Mark 6 c. 1891-1950

464
15

WILLOW

Mark 7 c. 1891-1950

CHILDREN'S STORIES
A series for young collectors
1971 Edition

The illustration depicts a scene from "The Sandman'—one of 156 fairy tales written by the famous Dane, Hans Christian Andersen who was born in Odense on April 2, 1805 and died just outside Copenhagen on August 4, 1875. The Tales have been translated into 80 languages and they are read today by children all over the world.

Mark 8 (GG4099)
c. 1971

Mark 9 (GG4099)
c. 1940+

Decoration under glaze
Detergent proof

Mark 10 (GG4099)
var. c. 1970s

WEDGWOOD®
Bone China
MADE IN ENGLAND

CHINESE LEGEND©

Mark 11 (GG4098)
c. 1962+

The exception to this is seen in the designs and colors of Fairyland Lustre made from 1915-31 under the supervision of Daisy Makeig-Jones primarily on bone china. Fanciful subjects (often grotesque) portrayed in bright colors underglaze, enamel colors on glaze, painted on luster and gold printing resulted in ware that competed with the production of ornamental bone china wares by the leading porcelain manufacturers: Coalport, Derby, Minton, Spode, and Worcester. Daisy Makeig-Jones was not allowed to sign her creations; however, she did manage to work her DJ monogram into some of her designs.

During the twentieth century an increasing proportion of bone china has been produced by Wedgwood until it has become 75% of their output. In the late 1980s, a pastel color version of the willow pattern named Chinese Legend was produced on bone china for about 10 years.

Type of Willow Manufactured: Standard Willow and Two Temples II patterns transfer-printed underglaze on earthenware and bone china. Two Temples II pattern is found most often on toy china in blue, green, and black. Underglaze colors for Standard Willow pattern include blue, red, brown, green, black, and yellow. Polychrome clobbering as well as on glaze gold patterns are also found. Chinese Legend is a polychrome lithograph on bone china.

Pottery Gazette, July 1, 1944, p. 370. There was a series of advertisements during World War II titled "History of Wedgwood" featuring a different pattern each month. The engraving date of 1806 for the willow pattern is given rather than 1818, the date of first production. The willow illustrated is Queen's Ware on Traditional shapes produced in the twentieth century up to about 1980.

Standard Willow pattern dessert dish and 8 1/8-inch plate transfer-printed in medium blue underglaze on pearlware. The dessert dish is 7-by-10-inches and has a 1/4-inch foot ring. Both pieces have three sets of single stilt marks under the rim. The plate has a concave rim and no foot ring. It is very light in weight and is the earliest piece of willow by Wedgwood I have seen. Mark 1 is on both pieces. The plate also has an impressed 4 and printed letter S. *Author's Collection.* $75-125 and $50-75.

Standard Willow pattern 9-inch plate transfer-printed in blue underglaze on bone china. The outer border has been replaced with a flower and scroll pattern with a white background. There are traces of gold in the border and inside the red line on the edge of the plate. Mark 2 with the impressed name mark. The pattern number is too worn to read. *Author's Collection.* $35-75.

Standard Willow pattern 7-inch plate with Two Temples II pattern toy teapot. Both are blue printed underglaze on Queens Ware. The plate has no foot ring and a slightly concave rim. In addition to printed Mark 5, it has the impressed name mark plus ENGLAND and 4WD, dating it to c. 1924-30. The toy teapot has Mark 6. *Author's Collection.* $8-10 and $55-85.

Standard Willow central pattern octagonal cup, saucer, and small cup transfer-printed in brown underglaze on bone china. The small cup has a simple gold line added and is pattern Y1299. The cup and saucer are clobbered with rust and yellow with a great deal of gold outlining. The pattern number is Y1285. The prefix Y was put on bone china tableware and coffee ware c. 1879-1921. These pieces have Mark 2 and date prior to 1891. Blue printed willow pattern was also used on this octagonal shape in bone china. *Author's Collection.* $65-85 set. $25-40 cup.

Standard Willow pattern 10.5-inch plate printed in gold overglaze on bone china. There is no inner border on this plate – just a line of gold. It is unusual to see the entire pattern printed in gold. A gold willow border pattern in linear form on a cobalt blue ground was also made. Mark 3 with ENGLAND. *Courtesy Harry and Jessie Hall.* $75-135.

Standard Willow central pattern 7-inch octagonal bowl blue printed inside with Fairyland Lustre glaze on bone china. A floral motif border was used on the inside and outside of the bowl. The prefix Z was used on Fairyland Lustre ornamental bowls and vases. There are three pattern numbers listed for willow: Z 5407 and Z 5228 have the name "Willow Fairyland". Z 5228 is listed as "willow". This bowl has #Z 5406, listed as "coral and bronze". Perhaps that describes the color treatment for the outside of the bowl. See next photo. *Courtesy Barbara Stevens.* $1,500+.

Outside of Fairyland Lustre octagonal bowl. The central Standard Willow pattern is almost covered up by the bronze-gold luster glaze. Mark 4 with pattern #Z 5406. *Courtesy Barbara Stevens.*

Standard Willow central pattern 7-inch octagonal bowl in shades of blue, red, black, green, and gold with Fairyland Lustre glaze on bone china. This bowl has the same pattern treatment with a different color scheme as the bowl in the previous two photos. The pattern #Z 5407 is titled "Willow Fairyland". Mark 4. *Courtesy Rita Entmacher Cohen.* $1,500+.

Two Temples II pattern toy cup and saucer transfer-printed in blue underglaze on bone china. The saucer is 3-inches across, and the cup is 1.5-inches high. Mark 1 with impressed date letters that are unreadable. Before 1891. *Author's Collection.* $30-55.

Two Temples II pattern toy dinner set transfer-printed in teal green underglaze on Queens Ware. Two sizes of covered dishes and platters are shown in addition to a dinner plate, soup plate, and a sauceboat with under plate. This is part of a 19 piece set with 6 plates and 6 soups. Mark 6. *Courtesy Rita Entmacher Cohen.* $895.

Standard Willow pattern transfer-printed 8.75-inch plate in brown underglaze on Queens Ware. It has a pierced rim and polychrome clobbering. Impressed name mark with Mark 6 and pattern #C 3984. The prefix C was used for Queen's Ware "fancies" (ornamental pieces) from 1872. *Author's Collection.* $125-175.

Standard Willow pattern wash basin and pitcher transfer-printed in brown underglaze with clobbering on Queen's Ware. The pattern on the outside of the wash basin is Two Temples II. Mark 6 with pattern #B 2463. The prefix B was used on Queen's Ware toilet sets from 1872. *Courtesy Tim and Kim Allen.* $350+.

Standard Willow pattern teapot transfer-printed in brown underglaze on Queen's Ware. The spout, finial, and kettle handle are gold decorated, and much of the pattern is outlined in gold. Mark 5. *Courtesy Harry and Jessie Hall.* $125-175.

Standard Willow pattern wash basin and pitcher transfer-printed in green underglaze on Queen's Ware. The pattern on the outside of the basin is Two Temples II just as it was on the brown printed set. Evidently this is the practice of the company in decorating these sets. The bowl is 16-inches across. This is the only example of green willow I have seen by Wedgwood. Mark 7 is unusual and may indicate that it was a special order of some kind. *Courtesy IWC Convention 2000.* $450+.

Standard Willow pattern foot bath transfer-printed in blue underglaze on Queen's Ware. It is 20-inches long, 14-inches wide, and 8.5-inches high. It is interesting that there are two circular patterns on each side. Perhaps large plate engravings were used rather than going to the time and expense to engrave a special large engraving for this piece. *Courtesy Shirley & Jim Hagerty.* $1,500.+.

Standard Willow pattern 10-inch plate transfer-printed in blue underglaze on Queen's Ware and clobbered in shades of red, yellow, and green. The clobbering is much like that done by William Adams & Sons* with the red outlining. Mark 5 with impressed name mark and 3AJ, dating it to 1907-24. *Author's Collection.* $55-95.

Wedgwood made a series of 6-inch collector plates on Queen's Ware for "young collectors" with lithographed patterns depicting children's stories written by Hans Christian Andersen. The 15-year series began in 1971 with "The Sandman". It has an illustration of the Sandman telling a bedtime story describing the willow pattern that is inside an umbrella. The plate has Mark 8. *Author's Collection.* $40-65.

Standard Willow pattern 6-cup teapot transfer-printed in blue underglaze on Queen's Ware in the Barlaston shape. We don't see willow on this shape very often. Mark 5. *Courtesy Charles and Zeta Hollingsworth.* $75-150.

Standard Willow pattern traditional shape teapots transfer-printed in blue underglaze on Queen's Ware. This shape was made for a number of years in several sizes. The 2-cup teapot has Mark 5, and the 6-cup teapot has Mark 10. *Author's Collection.* $35-55 each.

Standard Willow pattern candlesticks blue printed on Queen's Ware. This was a special promotion item in 1997 along with a mantle clock that could be ordered from the factory. Wedgwood is not producing willow currently (2003) except for such special issues. *Courtesy Paul Kirves and Zeke Jimenez.*

Standard Willow pattern temple jar decorated in pastel shades on bone china. The piece stands 9.5-inches high to the top of the finial. The name of the pattern is Chinese Legend, and the number is R 4781. The prefix R is used on bone china with lithograph or silkscreen decoration. This pattern was issued in the 1980s and made for about 10 years. It was produced on giftware items such as this piece as well as dinnerware. Mark 11. *Author's Collection.* $150-300.

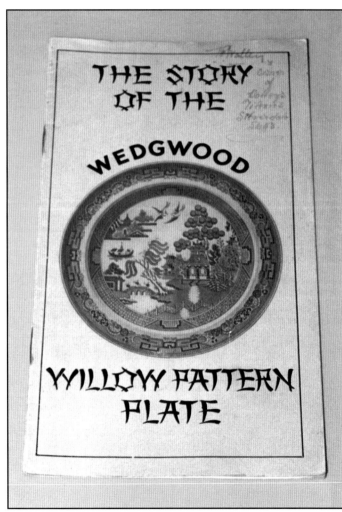

The Story of the Wedgwood Willow Pattern Plate. A small booklet put out by the company. The story by Harry Barnard can also be found on the Wedgwood Museum website. It dates back to the 1920s and is based on the old Etruria location of the factory.

Wedgwood

Josiah Wedgwood & Sons Limited
Barlaston, Stoke-on-Trent, England ST12 9ES
and 32-34 Wigmore Street, London W1H 0HJ
New York Toronto Sydney Melbourne Tokyo Hong Kong Singapore

CHINESE LEGEND
(R4781)
FINE BONE CHINA
Shape Form forme forma Traditional

Sales leaflet from Wedgwood, dated 1988, illustrating some pieces in Chinese Legend pattern, traditional shape. All the shapes of available pieces are drawn on the back. Reflecting the trend toward larger servings, the dinner plate is 10.75-inches in diameter. The pattern was produced for about 10 years.

Wessex Ceramics
(see Churchill China)

George Weston

Location: High Street, Longton, Staffordshire
Dates: c. 1815-29
Mark:

c. 1815-29

Brief History: George, William and John Weston had a partnership with James Hull who left the partnership in 1796, and Thomas Harley who left in 1801. John Weston left in 1804. George and William continued in business together until 1815, when the partnership was dissolved, and George Weston continued on alone. His son may have joined him in the business that went bankrupt in 1829. The works were sold at auction. Products included earthenware, Ironstone china and perhaps china although no marked examples are known.
Type of Willow Manufactured: Standard Willow pattern transfer-printed in blue on earthenware called Ironstone China.

Wetley China (see Sampson Smith)
Joseph White & Co.

Location: Redcross Street and Baptist Mills, Bristol
Dates: c. 1828-90s
Mark:

c. 1828-90s

Brief History: For many generations the White family had been tobacco pipe makers. Joseph White was a potter in Bristol. His son Joseph was apprenticed to John Decimus Pountney, master potter, in 1814, "to be educated as a turner". In 1828, Joseph and his brother James started a potting business of their own. Their specialties were yellow ware and black teapots. In 1840, after a dispute with their father (who was their landlord) they purchased the mills and other premises at Baptist Mills. I have not found evidence that they produced transfer-printed wares. Stoneware glazes were developed that aided in the production of utilitarian jugs and kitchenware. They retired from the business in 1855, and left it to their sons to continue.

Joseph's sons William Daniel and Frederick J. White traveled to Canada. Frederick convinced his father to establish a pottery in Canada. This pottery was established in Crouchville near St. John in the 1860s, and operated until the 1880s. The Bristol pottery continued until the 1890s. The Canadian pottery produced the same type of earthenware as the Bristol pottery although it is known that transfer-printed wares were definitely a part of their output.
Type of Willow Manufactured: Two Temples II pattern transfer-printed in blue underglaze on semi china. The little plate pictured may have been produced at one of the potteries mentioned above.

Two Temples II central pattern 4.75-inch plate transfer-printed in blue underglaze on semi china. Three sets of 3-point stilt marks on the base with no foot ring. The raised flat rim has a rippled edge. *Author's Collection.* $20-40.

Standard Willow pattern 9.75-inch plate transfer-printed in blue underglaze on ironstone china. There are 8 indentations on the edge of the flat rim with Three-point stilt marks on the underside and single marks on the top. The plate has a recessed foot ring and pale blue glaze. *Author's Collection.* $35-45.

Thomas C. Wild (& Sons) (Ltd.)

Location: Royal Albert Crown China Works, High Street, Longton, Staffordshire
Dates: c. 1894-1970
Mark:

(GG4144) c. 1917+

Brief History: Thomas Clark Wild produced good quality bone china tea and dinner wares. His trading style changed to T. C. Wild & Sons c. 1917, for five years and then changed to Thomas C. Wild & Sons. Limited was added from January 1, 1933. The trade name "Royal Albert Crown China" was used from 1905-1935. In 1935, it became "Royal Albert Bone China". T. C. Wild & Sons bought Shore & Coggins* in 1918, and other companies including Paragon China Ltd. in 1960. In 1964, it merged with the Lawley Group to become Allied English Potteries. In 1970, the company was renamed Royal Albert Ltd.

Type of Willow Manufactured: Standard Willow pattern transfer-printed in blue underglaze on bone china and polychrome Booths variant central pattern with border of willow motifs.

Standard Willow pattern cup and saucer transfer-printed in blue underglaze on bone china and trimmed in gold. There is no border pattern on the cup. A gold line substitutes for the inner border on the saucer. These pieces are the only examples of Standard Willow pattern I have seen by this company. *Author's Collection.* $15-25.

A polychrome lithograph based on Booths willow central pattern decorates the saucer. The border pattern is made up of willow pattern motifs in linear form. Two rows of the border pattern were used to decorate the cup. *Courtesy John and Norma Gilbert.* $20-30.

Wildblood, Heath (& Sons Ltd.)

Location: Peel Works, Stafford Street, Longton, Staffordshire
Dates: c. 1887-1927
Mark:

(GG4151) c. 1908+

Brief History: Richard Vernon Wildblood began potting in 1887. From 1889, to 1899, he traded in a partnership as Wildblood & Heath. From 1899 until 1927, the name was changed to Wildblood, Heath & Sons Ltd. The trademark "Clifton China" was used. The firm produced a good quality bone china in useful services. During World War I the firm added novelty ware and fancies to fill the market void left by the withdrawal of German and other imports. By 1921, the firm added such items as fancy vases, crested china, toy tea ware and children's tea sets.

Type of Willow Manufactured: Standard Willow pattern transfer-printed in matt blue and dark blue underglaze on bone china. Sampson Smith* is another company that advertised willow in matt and dark blue. Two of the most important compounds of cobaltous oxide used in coloring underglaze prints are the silicate and the aluminate. Cobalt silicates are most often used and generally cause the blue to be darker. Cobalt aluminates are used in various formulas that can result in lighter (matt) shades of blue. I have not seen willow examples by this firm in dark blue.

Pottery Gazette, January 1, 1923, one-half page ad gives their Specialties as Tea & Breakfast Sets. It also lists Matt Blue Willow and Dark Blue Willow.

Standard Willow pattern place setting transfer-printed in matt blue underglaze on bone china. All pieces have a scalloped edge lined in gold. Round plates were also made, and they are also trimmed in gold. *Courtesy IWC Convention 2002.* $25-45.

Henry Wileman

Location: The Foley Potteries, Fenton, Staffordshire
Dates: c. 1857-64
Mark:

Standard Willow pattern 9-inch plate transfer-printed in blue underglaze on earthenware. Three-point stilt marks on the base with single stilt marks on the top. It has a recessed foot ring and concave rim. The base is bowed out so that it doesn't sit flat. *Author's Collection.* $20-25.

c. 1857-64

Comment Concerning Mark: The platter shown below has an impressed crown mark in addition to the printed mark.
Brief History: The specialties of this company were earthenware, ironstone, china, Egyptian Black, and stoneware. The firm was carried on after 1864 by J. Wileman & Co., followed by J. F. Wileman.*
Type of Willow Manufactured: Standard Willow pattern transfer-printed in blue underglaze on stone china.

Standard Willow pattern platter transfer-printed in blue underglaze on stone china. It measures 9.25-by-11.5-inches and has a combed back. Three-point stilt marks on the back with single stilt marks on the top. *Author's Collection.* $75-125.

J. F. Wileman

Location: The Foley Potteries, Fenton, Stafford-shire
Dates: 1869-92
Impressed Mark:

c. 1869-92

Brief History: James Francis Wileman succeeded the partnership of James and Charles Wileman who traded as J. Wileman & Co. James F. Wileman concentrated on earthenwares: printed, lusters, Egyptian, and shining black as well as cream-colored wares. A large percentage of the ware was exported.
Type of Willow Manufactured: Standard Willow pattern transfer-printed in blue underglaze on earthenware.

A. J. Wilkinson (Ltd.)

Location: Royal Staffordshire Pottery, Burslem, Staffordshire
Dates: c. 1882-1964
Marks:

Mark 1
(GG4170)
c. 1907+

Comments Concerning Marks: Mark 1 is GG4150, and Marks 2-4 are variations of that mark found on various types of Willow pattern.
Brief History: Arthur J. Wilkinson founded the company in 1882, and it was taken over by the Shorter family in 1891. It continued under its own name making tableware, toilet sets, and ornamental ware as well as continuing to produce "Royal Patent Ironstone" continued from their predecessors Wilkinson & Hulme. It became a Limited company in 1896, when the old central Pottery was renamed Royal Staffordshire Pottery. In the twentieth century novelties and fancies including models of birds and figures were produced. In 1920, Newport Pottery was purchased. In the 1920s, new ranges of toilet ware and moderately priced earthenware were introduced. Honeyglaze, an ivory colored glaze was developed in the early 1920s, and used on many of these new ranges. In the *Pottery Gazette*, September 1, 1922, "Buyer's Notes" we read:

Mark 2
(GG4170)
var.
c. 1907+

An outstanding design amongst the newer samples is offered in the form of a very smart lithographed pattern taking the number 7098 – a coloured 'Willow' decoration in which the colour combinations are really first class. As is the case in the majority of the more recent decorations of this house, the pattern can be had throughout in dinnerware, teaware, and a wide variety of table fancies, including a useful nest of scallops from 4 inches to 10 inches in size.

Mark 3
(GG4170) var.
c. 1907+

My first reaction in reading this information is that it is describing the pattern seen in the third photo below; however, the pattern on several pieces I have seen is 9287. I know of no other lithographed polychrome willow pattern by this firm. Perhaps the pattern number was incorrect in the *Pottery Gazette*. The pattern in question was often used with Honeyglaze developed at that time.

Beginning in 1930, Clarice Cliff wares were made. From the early 1950s, and into the 1960s, the firm continued to make Clarice Cliff ware in small quantities in addition to traditional printed decorations, commemoratives, and coronation ware. A. J. Wilkinson was taken over by W. R. Midwinter* in 1964.

Type of Willow Manufactured: Standard Willow pattern transfer-printed in shades of blue and brown underglaze on earthenware The brown willow is clobbered in shades of blue, green, rust, yellow, and black, with gold trim. Polychrome litho based on Standard Willow central pattern and outer border with minimized or missing inner border. This decal was used at Newport Pottery* as well as several U.S. Potteries – most extensively by Edwin M. Knowles, Newell, West Virginia c. 1920s. A lithograph of a cottage scene has a polychrome litho Standard Willow outer border pattern with orange clobbering.

Mark 4 (GG4170)
var. c. 1907+

Mark 5 (GG4176)
c. 1920+

Standard Willow pattern polychrome litho decorated octagonal-shaped pitcher and 6 tumblers. The pitcher is 7-inches high and 5-inches across the spout. The tumblers are 3.5-inches high and 2.75-inches across. Mark 5 with pattern #9287. *Courtesy Hugh and Kathy Sykes.* $150-225.

Octagonal 8.5-inch plate with Standard Willow pattern outer border pattern. It is a litho with orange clobbering overglaze. The central scene features a thatched roof cottage and is unrelated to the willow pattern. This is an example of the surprising ways in which aspects of the willow pattern have been used. Mark 5. *Author's Collection.* $35-55.

Standard Willow pattern 8.5-inch round bowl and 6.25-inch plate transfer-printed in blue underglaze on earthenware. The bowl is a lighter shade of blue with gold trim. It has Mark 1. The plate is a deeper blue with no gold and has Mark 2. I have a similar little blue plate with Mark 3. *Author's Collection.* $25-30 and $5-8.

John Wilkinson

c. 1824-40

Location: Whitehaven Pottery, West Cumberland, Cumbria
Dates: c. 1824-63
Mark:

Comment Concerning Mark: During the time period c. 1824, the initial J was often written as I; therefore I. W. can be interpreted as J. W. By 1840, the initials in the mark were written as J. W.
Brief History: The Whitehaven Pottery was run by Woodnorth, Harrison & Hall from 1800, until John Wilkinson took it over in 1824. The pottery produced earthenware and stone china. There are about a dozen known transfer-printed patterns. Some of the wares were exported. Wilkinson's widow Mary ran the pottery until their son Randle took over, trading as Wilkinson's Pottery Company.
Type of Willow Manufactured: Standard Willow pattern transfer-printed in blue underglaze on stone china. Dinner services were produced.

Standard Willow pattern 8.75-inch plate on 3.5-inch Bakelite stand. The brown printed plate is clobbered in shades of light blue, green, yellow, rust, and black with a gold line on the wavy edge. Mark 1 with pattern #1734. *Courtesy Tim and Kim Allen.* $65-95.

Standard Willow pattern 9 7/8-inch plate transfer-printed in blue underglaze on stone china. There are 8 slight indentations on the edge of the concave rim with 3-point stilt marks under the rim and single stilt marks on top. The plate has a recessed foot ring and pale blue glaze. There is a dark blue area on the border at 4 o'clock where the transfer was cut, and a bit of the inner border is missing there as well. *Author's Collection.* $25-35.

H. M. Williamson & Sons

Location: Bridge Pottery, Longton, Staffordshire
Dates: 1879-41
Marks:

Mark 1
(GG4179)
c. 1879+

Comment Concerning Marks: Mark 1 is impressed. The others are printed.
Brief History: This firm was producing bone china useful wares including tea services in the nineteenth century. Heathcote China was a trade name used by the company. Twentieth century wares included children's china with patterns from nursery rhymes as well as animal subjects. The company was absorbed by E. Brain & Co. Ltd.*
Type of Willow Manufactured: Standard Willow pattern transfer-printed in medium and dark blue on bone china with gold trim.

Mark 2
(GG4180)
c. 1903+

Mark 3 (GG4185)
c. 1928-41

BEST BONE
HEATHCOTE CHINA
MADE IN ENGLAND

Standard Willow pattern 9-inch serving plate transfer-printed in medium blue underglaze on bone china with gold edge. The handle extensions on either side add only 1/4-inch to the diameter. There is a lovely molded leaf-type pattern on the rim by the handles that is 4-inches in depth. It cannot be seen in the photograph. Plates with deeply scalloped edges have also been seen in this shade of blue. Impressed Mark 1. *Author's Collection.* $30-45.

Standard Willow pattern cup and saucer transfer-printed in dark blue underglaze on bone china with gold accents. The wavy edges of both pieces are lined with gold. Quite a large willow motif decorates the inside of the cup. The motto reads: "WE'LL TAK A CVP O' KINDNESS YET FOR DAYS 'O'AVLD LANG SYNE". Mark 2. A Williamson cup and saucer in dark blue on a different shape was seen at the IWC Convention in 1998 with the words: "A PRESENT FROM BALACHULISH". It had Mark 3. *Author's Collection.* $35-55.

Wiltshaw & Robinson

Location: Carlton Works (1890-1987), and Vine Pottery (1990-92), Stoke-on-Trent, Staffordshire
Dates: c. 1890-1992 & 1998-present (2003)
Marks:

Mark 1 (GG4201)
c. 1894+

Brief History: James Frederick Wiltshaw with the Robinson brothers as partners (James Alcock and William Herbert) established the Carlton Works on Copeland Street in Stoke. In the beginning the firm produced ware similar to what was being made at other potteries including transfer-printed ware and flow blue. Management difficulties arose, and James Robinson's nephew Harold Taylor Robinson took over his share. By 1911, James Wiltshaw took over the firm. He hired Horace Wain as designer who began to develop Oriental and Persian designs that achieved interest for the company. The *Pottery Gazette,* May 1, 1915, under "Buyer's Notes", discussed Wiltshaw & Robinson's Oriental patterns and pictured "Three Popular Styles in Oriental Treatment". The following is a quote from that article:

Mark 2 (GG4201)
var. c. 1894+

Mark 3 (GG4204) c. 1925+

A number of the Eastern types of design which they have brought out lately are of uncommon merit. As we write we have in mind, amongst other designs, the No. 2021 decoration, a sort of illuminated 'Willow' pattern, delicately treated in enamels and gold over a background of powder blue. This pattern, like the majority of the firm's newest decorative treatments, is supplied right through in a full range of vases, flowerpots, bulb bowls, &c., &c.

Frederick Cuthbert Wiltshaw took over after his father's death in 1918. He encouraged the company to compete with luster items on the market with a product called "Lustrous". Egyptian themes on ware were popular in the 1920s, and the Oriental patterns were expanded with enamels over various colored luster backgrounds with names such as Rouge Royale, Bleu, Vert, and Noir. Enoch Boulton became the designer in the 1920s.

In 1928, Birks, Rawlins & Co. was purchased in order to expand the output to include china manufacture of tea and dinnerware. Through the years many different designers worked with the firm and the company continued to expand their lines of production. The company was renamed Carlton Ware in 1957. It was taken over by Arthur Wood & Son in 1967 but continued production with their name. In 1987 County Potteries took over, but after an unsuccessful merger with Kent and later purchase, the company closed in 1992. Francis Joseph acquired the name in 1997 along with a few molds. An active Collector's Club has helped promote the new productions. Wares can be seen and purchased from its website market.

Type of Willow Manufactured: Standard Willow and Two Temples II patterns transfer-printed in blue underglaze on earthenware. Standard Willow central pattern enameled with added gold over glaze on white. Worcester willow pattern in flow blue underglaze and printed in gold overglaze on white and on powder blue background with enameling in green, blue, pink, and red. Willow-type chinoiserie patterns (Mikado, New Mikado, Barge, Chinaland and others) enameled overglaze with various color grounds as well as gold on white.

Standard Willow central pattern condiment set transfer-printed in blue underglaze on earthenware. I have a separate salt shaker that matches the one in this set except that it has the Two Temples II central pattern and Standard Willow outer border at the neck just below the lid. It stands 4.5-inches high. All pieces have Mark 3. *Courtesy IWC Convention 2001.* $150-200.

A 6-inch jug and 5.25-inch teapot with flow blue Worcester Willow pattern on earthenware. Both pieces are trimmed in gold. The teapot has reg. #332264 dating it to 1899. Mark 1. *Courtesy Loren Zeller.* $200-250 and $250-300.

Standard Willow central pattern humidor enameled overglaze with gold on white background. This humidor has pattern #2041. Mark 2. *Courtesy IWC Convention 1995.* $250-325.

Worcester Willow pattern wash basin and pitcher printed in gold on powder blue ground and enameled with green, blue, pink, and red. The bowl has the pattern on the outside decorated the same as the pitcher and the complete pattern printed in gold on the white inside surface. The set has pattern #2021 – described above as "a sort of illuminated 'Willow' pattern" in the quote from *Pottery Gazette,* May 1, 1915. Mark 1. *Author's Collection.* $1,500+.

Pottery Gazette, April 1, 1926, p. 580. One-half page advertisement illustrating some of the new Oriental designs enameled on Rouge Royale. These patterns were produced for quite a long time. The *Pottery Gazette*, June 1, 1953, had a cover in color featuring a Carlton Ware jar with Oriental pattern.

Six-inch white ginger jar with a lid. This is also Mikado pattern as in the previous photo; however, it is done all in gold on an off-white background. Mark 3. *Courtesy Geraldine Ewaniuk*. $75-150.

Mikado enameled pattern #4433 on Rouge Royale trimmed in gold. Mikado has a different pattern number on different backgrounds and decorating treatment. This one dates to the late 1930s. The lidded ginger jar stands 7-inches high to the top of the finial. It has an impressed 311 that is an early shape number used for many years. This pattern has several elements of the Standard Willow pattern including teahouse, birds, boat, and bridge. Mikado is used in part on smaller items such as this jar, and the full pattern is put on larger objects. Mark 3. *Author's Collection*. $75-150.

Wilton Ware (see A. G. Harley Jones)

F. Winkle & Co. (Ltd.)

Location: Colonial Pottery, Stoke, Staffordshire
Dates: c. 1890-1931
Impressed Mark:

Brief History: Winkle & Wood were partners at the Pearl Pottery, Hanley. They took over the Colonial Pottery in 1889. In 1890, Wood continued at the Pearl Pottery while Winkle traded at Colonial Pottery as F. Winkle & Co. It became a limited company in 1910. The firm produced good quality earthenware some of which was marked stoneware.

c. 1890-1931

Type of Willow Manufactured: Standard Willow pattern transfer-printed in blue underglaze on earthenware marked stoneware. The pieces found do not have 3 figures on the bridge even though there is space in the pattern. One or no figures on the bridge are seen in the photos below.

Standard Willow pattern 4.25-inch plate transfer-printed in blue underglaze on earthenware marked stoneware. There are no people on the bridge in this pattern. *Courtesy Dennis Crosby.* $10-15.

Thomas Wolfe

Location: "Big Works" in Church Street, Stoke, Staffordshire
Dates: c. 1782-95 and c. 1810-18
Comments Concerning Marks: The wares of Thomas Wolfe were very rarely marked. Attributions are made by associating patterns, shapes and stilt marks to known wares. Four point stilt marks were generally used with one point often missing. This creates a three-point stilt mark in a right angle triangle rather than the usual shape.
Brief History: Thomas Wolfe was son of a potter and had worked with him in Stoke from about 1782-95, producing earthenware. Then he worked at Upper Islington, Liverpool in partnership with Miles Mason and John Lucock where he began producing porcelain. (see Thomas Wolfe & Co.*) He returned to Stoke c. 1800, and formed a partnership with his son-in-law, Robert Hamilton, producing earthenware and bone china. That partnership was dissolved in 1810, and he worked on his own until his death in 1818.

In *Northern Ceramic Society Newsletter No. 84*, December 1991, Trevor Martin has an article on Wolfe blue printed patterns. On page 35, there is a picture of an octagonal Standard Willow pattern plate that may possibly have been made by Thomas Wolfe. The size, shape and color of the print are similar to a known Buddleia pattern plate. It has the four point stilt marks with one missing mark found on Wolfe wares although this feature is not exclusive to Wolfe.
Type of Willow Manufactured: Standard Willow pattern transfer-printed in blue underglaze on earthenware. The distinguishing feature of the engraving is that the path does not stop at the steps of the teahouse. It continues round the left hand side of the building. No picture available.

Thomas Wolfe & Co.

Location: 1-2 Upper Islington, Liverpool
Dates: c. 1795-1800
Brief History: Thomas Wolfe leased a small porcelain manufactory in Liverpool with partners Miles Mason and John Lucock. The purpose of the venture was to supply china in the style of the Chinese Export porcelains that were no longer available. These would be sold in Mason's retail business in London. Lucock was an engraver. Shards found in an excavation of the site in 1968, indicate that blue printed tea wares were the principal product. A few shards indicate that other wares such as tureens and tankards were produced although no known pieces have survived. Blue printed patterns were produced in six main designs according to the shards found. These wares are sometimes referred to as Wolfe-Mason porcelains. The partnership was dissolved in 1800, and Thomas Wolfe returned to Stoke.
Type of Willow Manufactured: By far, the pattern found most often at the site is a version of Two Temples I. It has been named "Shuttered Window".[1] The name comes from a distinguishing feature of two pairs of long windows in the central zigzag wall. The detail is quite intricate with the upper two-thirds showing closer window panes than the lower portion. In other versions of Two Temples I, including Copeland/Spode, there are usually just two windows that are square in shape and generally appear to be open. Geoffrey Godden devotes Chapter Two in *Mason's China and the Ironstone Wares* to the Wolfe-Mason patterns in general and to this pattern in particular. He refers to the pattern as "Pagoda" – the name he used for Two Temples I and II in his early book on Caughley.

Standard Willow pattern 4.25-inch sauce dish transfer-printed in blue underglaze on earthenware. There is just one figure on the bridge in this pattern. I wonder if there are more people on the bridge on the larger pieces made by F. Winkle & Co.? *Courtesy IWC Convention 2001.* $8-12.

1. "Liverpool Porcelains – Thomas Wolfe & Co." by Trevor Markin and Brian Allaker. *Made in Liverpool, Liverpool Pottery & Porcelain 1700-1850*, p.34-36.

Two Temples I variant "Shuttered Window" pattern tea bowl and saucer transfer-printed in blue underglaze on porcelain. The four long windows in the central zigzag wall have darker areas in the top. This set is unmarked but attributed to Thomas Wolfe & Co. *Author's Collection.* $75-150.

Price & Kensington*, producer of novelty teapots, in the 1950s. After acquiring Carlton Ware in 1967, the firm continued production of that company's line of Rouge Royale gold and enamel decorated ware. Carlton Ware was sold in 1987. Anthony Wood is present manager of the company that includes tea ware, crested ware and assorted giftware in its current catalog.

Type of Willow Manufactured: Standard Willow pattern transfer-printed in blue, red, and brown on teapots. Shapes include Antique, Boston, Chatsworth, and Melbourne. Two figures decal in blue by MATTHEYPRINT* is used as well as Standard Willow pattern decal on covered ginger jar trimmed in gold.

Mark 5 (GG4235)
c. 1934+

Mark 6 (GG4237)
c. 1954+

Arthur Wood
(& Sons (Longport) Ltd.)

Location: Bradwell Works, Longport, Staffordshire
Dates: c. 1904-present (2003)
Marks:

Brief History: The firm was founded in 1884, as Capper & Wood and has remained on its original site for well over 100 years. In 1904, trading began as Arthur Wood. The *Pottery Gazette,* July 1, 1926 gave this assessment of the firm under "Buyer's Notes":

> Arthur Wood is one of the oldest established manufacturers of teapots in the potteries, has an interesting and very diversified range of goods – Hygenic (infuser) over 20 years ago, cube, and nondrip "camel." Majority of Mr. Woods teapots are produced in sizes from 60s to 6's, i.e. 11 sizes. The three largest must needs be made with a tab as well as a handle to facilitate lifting.

The *Pottery* Gazette, September 1, 1928, noted the company's change of name.

> Arthur Wood & Sons (Longport) Ltd.: "New name for the old-established business which has been known under the personal name of Mr. Arthur Wood. ... On the ivory body there is no limit to the class of decorations; one can have for the asking: dark blue or matt blue 'Willow' lithograph patterns in borders or all-over treatments etc."

Its specialty had been teapots with new types added to the line down through the years. Fancies were added in the 1920s, including vases, jug sets, and tankards decorated with popular subjects such as sports, London sights etc. Arthur Wood merged with

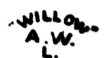

Mark 1 (GG4233)
c. 1904-28

Mark 2 (GG4234)
c. 1928+

Mark 3 c. 1904+

Mark 4 c. 1904+

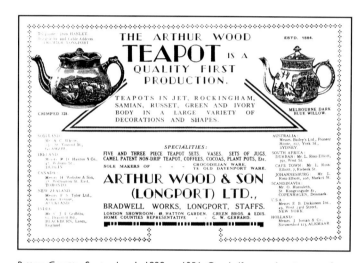

Pottery Gazette, September 1, 1928, p. 1356. One-half page advertisement for the renamed firm of Arthur Wood & Son (Longport) Ltd. showing a Melbourne shape dark blue willow teapot.

Standard Willow pattern Melbourne shape teapot transfer-printed in blue underglaze on earthenware. This 6-cup teapot is illustrated in the ad above and was probably introduced about 1928. It bears Marks 1 and 2 that overlap in dating at 1928. *Courtesy Harry and Jessie Hall.* $125-150.

Standard Willow pattern teapot transfer-printed in blue underglaze on earthenware. In addition to Mark 3, this 6-cup teapot has impressed CHATSWORTH MADE IN ENGLAND. I assume that Chatsworth is the name of the shape. It has a nice domed lid and wide handle. *Author's Collection.* $75-125.

Standard Willow pattern Antique shape teapot transfer-printed in red underglaze on earthenware. A note in *Pottery Gazette*, April 1, 1905, p. 447, states, "Two new shapes: the 'Antique' and the Sydney – pretty pots neatly ornamented." This Antique shape is found in pink and brown with Mark 4 as well as this red example with Mark 6, giving it a production life of about 50 years. It is the most commonly found Arthur Wood teapot although I have not seen it in blue. Items marked "Antique" are generally considered to be anything but; however, in regards to Arthur Wood's teapots, it is one of the oldest shapes made. *Courtesy Charles and Zeta Hollingsworth.* $75-150.

Boston shape teapot with MATTHEYPRINT blue decal pattern. This is a 6-cup teapot and has gold trim. It bears Mark 3 with printed number 5510. *Courtesy Paul Kirves and Zeke Jimenez.* $50-75.

Wood & Brownfield

Location: Clews Works, Cobridge, Staffordshire
Dates: c. 1841-50
Mark:

(GG4242)
c. 1841-50

Comments Concerning Mark: There are several firms that used the initials W. & B. in their mark; however, John Wood & William Brownfield are known to have used this Stone China mark. (See William Brownfield*)

Brief History: The date is uncertain; however, sometime in 1841, the partnership of Robinson, Wood & Brownfield* was dissolved and renamed Wood & Brownfield*. On October 30, 1850, this partnership was dissolved, and William Brownfield continued on his own. Better than average earthenware table services were produced. Jugs were a specialty of the company.

Type of Willow Manufactured: Standard Willow pattern transfer-printed in blue underglaze on earthenware.

Standard Willow pattern 10.25-inch plate transfer-printed in blue underglaze on earthenware. There are 8 slight indentations on the edge of the concave rim. The outer border seems to be the right size; however, the geometric motifs are not quite matched up between the two borders. *Courtesy Dennis Crosby.* $25-35.

Standard Willow pattern 4-cup teapot transfer-printed in blue underglaze on earthenware. This round teapot bears Mark 5. *Courtesy Charles and Zeta Hollingsworth.* $50-85.

Wood, Challinor & Co.

Location: Well Street Pottery, Tunstall, Staffordshire
Dates: c. 1860-64
Mark:

(GG4245) c. 1860-64

Brief History: This firm was in business for only a short time. The product was blue printed earthenware with a Stone Ware mark.
Type of Willow Manufactured: Standard Willow pattern table ware transfer-printed in blue underglaze on earthenware.

Standard Willow pattern 12-inch cheese stand transfer-printed in blue underglaze on earthenware marked stoneware. This large cheese stand is printed with an engraving the size intended for a dinner plate. An added outer border pattern was applied to fill up the space. *Courtesy IWC Convention 1997.* $150-200.

Enoch Wood & Sons

Location: Fountain Place, Burslem
Dates: c. 1818-1846
Impressed Mark:

(GG4260) impressed
c. 1818-46

Brief History: Enoch Wood came from an important potting family. His father, Aaron Wood, master potter born in 1717, was mold maker and designer for Whieldon, Josiah Wedgwood* and the Salt Glaze Potters of Staffordshire. Aaron's older brother Ralph was famous for his figures and Toby Jugs. His younger brother Moses was the first of an unbroken line of seven generations of Master Potters, covering more than two centuries. Enoch was in partnership with his cousin Ralph Wood (one of two sons of Ralph Wood) from 1784 to 1790, but then began working with James Caldwell until 1818. At that time he went into business with his three sons Enoch, Joseph, and Edward. The firm traded as Enoch Wood & Sons until 1846, even though the father died in 1840. A vast amount of fine quality blue printed wares were exported to America by this company. A single shipment to a Philadelphia dealer in 1834, consisted of 262,000 pieces. Chinoiserie patterns, historical patterns with 71 known views of England and perhaps even more American scenes. Romantic patterns were also produced. Colors other than blue were produced such as pink, purple, black, sepia, green, and mulberry. Enoch Wood was also known as a collector of pottery.
Type of Willow Manufactured: Standard Willow pattern transfer-printed in blue underglaze on earthenware marked Granite Ware. Tableware was produced.

Standard Willow pattern pedestal dish with lid transfer-printed in blue underglaze on earthenware. The pieces are octagonal in shape. The base is 6-inches across, and it is 9.25-inches wide at the rim. The covered dish stands 6.5-inches high to the top of the finial. There is a complete central pattern inside the dish as well as on the lid. There are three linear forms of the central pattern on the outside. The inner border decorates the base, and the outer border decorates the rim of the dish and lid. *Author's Collection.* $175-250.

Wood & Sons (Ltd.)

Location: Trent and New Wharf Potteries, and other sites, Burslem, Staffordshire
Dates: c. 1865-present (2003)
Marks:

Comment Concerning Mark: Mark 10 is the most current mark used on willow. It was used in the 1990s to 2002.
Brief History: In 1865 Absolom Wood, a descendant of Moses Wood founded Wood Son & Co. The original factory, called Villa Pottery, was located in Cobridge. Three of Absolom's sons became master potters: Thomas F. (T.F.), William, and Henry J. Wood. In 1877, T. F. and William purchased the site on Navigation Road which they named New Wharf Pottery. Two years later the Trent Pottery, adjacent to New Wharf was purchased. At that time the Villa Pottery was transferred to within the additional site. The site as it is today was made up by the acquisition of land in 1889 by Henry J. Wood. He later traded as H. J. Wood*. By 1910, T. F. Wood was the principal proprietor of Wood & Sons Ltd., a firm that had about 1,000 employees. T. F.'s son Harry became chairman of the firm, and it is T. F.'s descendents that have been involved with the company through the years.

Wood & Sons purchased Ellgreave Pottery in 1921, and merged with H. J. Wood in 1930. The firm purchased Stanley Pottery, including Crown Pottery in 1931. The firm thrived until about 1979, when a major recession began. In 1982, the Yorke family purchased the company with Edmund Yorke as managing director. The firm was renamed Wood & Sons in about 1991. A new board of directors under Edmund Yorke, chairman began managing

Mark 1 (GG4287)
var. c. 1910+

Mark 2
(GG4287) var.
c. 1910+

Mark 3 (GG4287)
c. 1910+

the company in 1993. By January 2002 the directors put the company into Administration. Wood & Sons was purchased in the fall of 2002 by Strathtay-Greenwellies Ltd., a Worcester company with a strong commitment to British manufacturing.

The products of Wood & Sons have included ironstone, semi-porcelain and fine quality earthenware as well as vitrified hotel ware. Dinner, tea, and toilet wares have been the principal wares made to a higher standard than many other companies. Artistic designers who worked for the company include Frederick Rhead and Charlotte Rhead. Undecorated wares were also supplied to outside decorators including Gray's Pottery and Susie Cooper who bought blanks and had shapes made. The Crown Pottery was home for the Susie Cooper Pottery from 1931 to 1958. The *Pottery Gazette,* February 1, 1935, p. 163, illustrates a range of new patterns designed for Wood & Sons by Susie Cooper. The shape name is Wren – a shape also decorated with willow pattern. The Wren shape was made in the white during the Second World War (illustrated *Glass Trade Review May, 1944*, p. 243).

Wood & Sons prospered after World War II with the development of contemporary giftware lines. New shapes and patterns continued to be produced in tableware. The Continental shape was used on several patterns in the 1990s. The teapot, coffee pot, pitcher, creamer, and sauce boat in that shape are the same as the Alpine Domestic Tableware shape list issued by the company in 1982, and can be seen on the willow flyer dated January 12, 1987. All through the twentieth century Wood & Sons has used its willow pattern on a number of different shapes as well as adapting the pattern itself from time to time. Willow was one of the patterns in full dinnerware production at the time the company went into Administration. It was being offered through Mid America Tablewares Inc. in the USA. The pieces purchased at a discount Outlet in Williamsburg, Virginia, were of a superior quality to any other willow currently made on earthenware.

Type of Willow Manufactured: Standard Willow pattern transfer-printed underglaze in blue, red, and brown, also found with clobbering. Booths Willow pattern in blue. "Pekin" pattern based on Booths willow in flow blue, brown, and turquoise underglaze with clobbering. "Hankow" pattern based on Booths central willow pattern in red and lime green underglaze with clobbering. "Gleneagles" pattern that is the blue version of "Hankow" with an added orange diamond border pattern from the Standard Willow inner border. Canton pattern transfer-printed underglaze in blue and pink on dinner and tea ware as well as accessories. Some have clobbering and/or gold trim. "Westover" simple variant cartoon type pattern is included just for fun.

Retailers/importers:
Albert Pick, Chicago*, and Soane & Smith Ltd., London*.

Mark 4 (GG4288)
c. 1917+

Mark 5 (GG4288)
c. 1917+

Mark 6 (GG4288)
c. 1917+

Mark 7 (GG4291)
c. 1931+

Mark 8 (GG4290)
c. 1930+

Mark 9 c. 1920s-30s

Mark 10 c. 1990s-2002

Flyer from Wood & Sons, January 12, 1987, showing pieces available in Blue Willow pattern on Continental Shape. Note that the teapot and jug at the far left have the Booth's variant willow pattern.

Standard Willow pattern 6-cup teapot transfer-printed in blue underglaze on earthenware. This hexagonal shape was used extensively on Woods Willow and other patterns such as Canton. It is trimmed with bits of the inner border. Mark 4. *Courtesy Joette Hightower,* $75-125.

Standard Willow pattern teapot stand for hexagonal teapot shown previously. It measures 5.5-inches from flat side across and 6.1/8-inches across at the points. This piece gives a good close-up view of the Woods willow pattern. Mark 4. *Courtesy IWC Convention 2001.* $75-100.

This 8.5-inch octagonal plate has a simplified Standard Willow pattern with the crossed branches of the willow tree resembling the tree in the Booths Willow pattern. The plate has only one border that has been adapted from elements in the standard borders. Mark 1. *Author's Collection.* $18-25.

Standard Willow pattern 9.5-inch bowl transfer-printed in brown underglaze and clobbered in green, rust, and very dark blue. This is the first piece I've seen in this color combination. Because it has pattern #3620 in addition to Mark 4, other pieces must have been made. *Courtesy Charles and Zeta Hollingsworth.* $35-65.

Booths Willow central pattern was used to decorate these hexagonal jugs. The small jug is 4.5-inches high and holds 16 oz. The larger jug is 5.5-inches high and holds 28 oz. This shape jug is also found with clobbering over brown printed Pekin pattern. Mark 4. *Author's Collection.* $35-55 and $45-75.

A sampling of small blue printed pieces with different pattern treatment. The top row has a butter pat with a small piece of the pattern and coaster or small plate from a child's set with the full central pattern. There are three individual jam dishes in the front with different elements of the pattern. Mark 4. *Courtesy Dale S. Brouse.* $10-15 each.

Standard Willow pattern covered butter dish transfer-printed in blue underglaze on earthenware. The attached under plate is 7-inches across, and the opening is almost 4-inches. Other butter dishes I have seen would have the sides decorated and a simple flat lid across the top. On this set the lid is 2.5-inches high and fits down over the sides. Mark 4. *Courtesy Dale S. Brouse.* $125-165.

This COSY jug was patented by Edmund William Abram in 1921 and produced by Wood & Sons. The name came from its double lid that is said to keep liquids hot for twice as long as an ordinary pot. The patented lid has slits that hold back the "leaves, grounds or pips". The COSY pot, with patented lid and no-drip spout, is also known as the "world's utility jug". It stands 7-inches tall and holds 22 oz. This is another example of the Booths form of the central willow pattern. Mark 5. *Author's Collection.* $100-185.

Booths central willow pattern blue printed teapot in a shape that is seldom seen. The Standard outer border is used. Mark 4. *Courtesy Joette Hightower.* $75-100.

Susie Cooper crayon pattern on a Wren Shape teapot shown with a willow teapot also on Wren Shape. This shape was designed by Susie Cooper while she was at Crown Pottery. Again it is the Booths central willow pattern with Standard willow outer border. Mark 8 on the Susie Cooper teapot and Mark 4 on the willow teapot. *Author's Collection.* $200-275 and $75-125.

The distinctive spouts on hollow ware in Wren shape can be seen on the 30 oz jug, gravy boat, and creamer. Note the 5-inch jug has the Booths central willow pattern and the other pieces have the Standard Willow pattern. Mark 4. *Author's Collection.* $35-45, $30-40, and $25-35.

Pekin pattern 9.75-inch soup plate transfer-printed underglaze in flow blue on earthenware. This central pattern is based on the Booths Willow pattern. It has a bowknot border. Mark 2. *Author's Collection.* $75-125.

Turquoise 10.5-inch plate and 7.25-by-9.5-inch brown bowl in Pekin pattern with clobbering. These two pieces have a bowknot border pattern and bear Mark 2. These are the only color combinations known in this pattern apart from flow blue. The 5.75-inch red plate has a basket weave border pattern with a diamond and * inner border. It is Hankow pattern with Mark 7. The central pattern in all of these pieces is based on Booths Willow pattern. It is the border pattern that determines the name. *Author's Collection.* $18-25, $25-35, and $10-15.

Lime green underglaze 9-inch plate, bowl, covered bowl, cup and saucer with clobbering. These pieces have the basket weave border and inner border matching the red plate in the previous photo. The name is Hankow, and the mark is 7. Red and lime green are the only colors known in Hankow pattern. *Courtesy Charles and Zeta Hollingsworth.* $18-25 each for plate, bowl, and cup/saucer. $25-35 for covered bowl.

Canton pattern teapot, creamer, and covered sugar on hexagonal shape. The pink teapot is the same shape as the blue willow teapot shown in the first photo. The pointed finial on the sugar bowl is very susceptible to damage. Canton pattern does not seem to be very popular with Willow collectors in the U.S.A. It was made in blue with clobbering for special orders. *Author's Collection.* $75-100, $25-35, and $35-45.

Gleneagles is the name given to this underglaze blue pattern with orange diamond inner border and orange edge line. The added orange parts are the only differences in the pattern from Hankow pattern seen above. Mark 3. The cup shape is the same as seen in the Woods & Sons 1987 flyer. *Author's Collection.* $12-18.

Westover pattern hexagonal teapot transfer-printed in blue underglaze and clobbered. D B C "Westover" was found in a pattern book at Wood & Son from the 1920s and 1930s. The significance of DBC remains a mystery. The pattern #2410 is found on some pieces. The pattern is sort of a cartoon take-off of the willow pattern, and some Willow collectors seek it out.

H. J. Wood (Ltd.)

Location: Alexandra Pottery, Burslem, Staffordshire
Dates: c. 1884-1930
Marks:

Mark 1 (GG4266) c. 1891+

Brief History: Henry J. Wood was the brother of Thomas J. Wood, the proprietor of Wood & Sons in the early twentieth century. Although H. J. Wood was independent for many years, the firm merged with Wood & Sons in 1930. H. J. was a good businessman with a creative bent. He saw the value in hiring designers to develop a good-class of ornamental artware. Bursley Ltd. was set up at Crown Pottery to produce it.

Mark 2 c. 1930+

Type of Willow Manufactured: Standard Willow pattern transfer-printed in blue underglaze on earthenware. Simplified willow variant pattern hand-painted in polychrome on pale blue ground with luster glaze. Simplified Booths willow pattern in black with gold trim on crimson ground.

Mark 3 c. 1930+

Canton pattern covered vegetable transfer-printed in pink underglaze on earthenware. The pattern is in linear form and continues around the corner for two full sequences on the lid of the dish. Complete dinner and tea services were made in this pattern in pink and blue as well as accessory items such as vases and lamps. Mark 6. *Author's Collection.* $75-125.

Standard Willow central pattern scalloped dish transfer-printed in blue underglaze on earthenware. It measures 4.75-by-6.5-inches. This is the only piece of blue willow I have seen with an H. J. Wood mark. Mark 1. *Courtesy IWC Convention 1993.* $12-18.

Hand-painted pair of 8-inch vases in polychrome Pagoda pattern on a pale blue ground. There is an iridescent glaze that adds a nice sheen to the vases. Mark 2. *Courtesy IWC Convention 2000.* $200-275.

Red background bottle-shaped vase stands 11.5-inches high. The pattern in black with gold highlights is a simplified Booths pattern. Mark 3. *Courtesy IWC Convention 2001.* $200-250.

S. Woolf

Location: Australian Pottery (1860-87) and Mexborough Pottery (1873-74), Yorkshire
Dates: c. 1860-87
Mark:

c. 1860-1887

Comment Concerning Mark: This is the same printed mark seen earlier under Swillington Bridge; however, it has the initials. S. W. added.
Brief History: Lewis Woolf and his sons, Sydney and Henry worked the Ferrybridge Pottery from about 1856, into the 1880s. In the late 1850s, they also built the Australian Pottery adjacent to the premises. It was so named because a great part of the product was exported to Australia. In 1860, the Australian Pottery was given to Sydney Woolf to run. He became the owner in 1877. He also purchased the Mexborough Pottery in 1873; however, he was forced to mortgage it the following January. Various types of earthenware and ironstone china useful wares were made.
Type of Willow Manufactured: Standard Willow pattern transfer-printed in blue underglaze on earthenware or ironstone china.

Standard Willow pattern 9.75-inch soup plate transfer-printed in blue underglaze on ironstone china. There are 8 indentations on the edge of the concave rim. Three-point stilt marks on the underside of the rim with single stilt marks on the top. There are patches in the outer rim at 6 and 9 o'clock. *Author's Collection.* $35-45.

Worcester Royal Porcelain Co. Ltd.

Location: Severn Street, Worcester
Dates: c. 1862-present (2003)
Marks:

Comments Concerning Marks: The crescent used in marking Worcester may have come from the arms of the Warmstry family on which there were four crescents. The mark from 1862, has consisted of a crown above a circle in which there are four entwined Ws. These Ws represent Worcester, Wignoria, the Latinised form of Worcester, Warmstry, the site of the first factory and Wall for Dr. John Wall of the first period. There is one example of each of the marks used according to numbers assigned the marks by Geoffrey Godden.

Mark 1 (GG4350)
c. 1876-91

All pieces are specifically date marked with the codes of letters, dots and other symbols. Those dates will be given when known in the captions for the objects shown below.

Brief History: The factory was begun in 1751 with the leasing of Warmstry House to Richard Holdship, a glover of the city of Worcester. A document was drawn up entitled "Articles for carrying on the Worcester Tonquin Manufacture, June 1751". Fifteen subscribers signed the twenty-nine articles that formed the agreement. A copy of the document is still owned by The Worcester Royal Porcelain Co. Ltd. Porcelain was produced throughout many different partnerships beginning with the soapstone type body of the Dr. Wall (1st period).

Worcester was known from its beginning in the mid-eighteenth century for its blue and white decorated porcelains. Underglaze painted blue patterns were the principal product, made in abundance. By 1765, patterns were simplified in order to copy them more quickly and increase the output to fulfill the huge demand for these wares. During the same period the transfer printing process was introduced at Worcester. The first use of transfer printing was with on glaze patterns in black. These wares were popular for a considerable length of time. It may have been 1770, or later before underglaze blue printing was used on a large scale. A strike in 1770, of artists whose job was to paint blue decorations by hand influenced the slowness of the factory to adopt underglaze transfer printing in blue. However, the technique gradually developed in quality and quantity.

The Worcester Royal Porcelain Co. Ltd. came into being in 1862, at the end of the partnership of Kerr and Binns. The Articles of Association for the new firm were drawn up June 24, 1862. The main persons involved were Richard William Binns, acting as Art Director; Edward Phillips, in charge of production; and William Litherland, a Liverpool retailer who was also a shareholder.

The company was producing bone china of a very high quality from this period. Many forms of ware were produced including hand-painted ornamental ware with exceptional gilding. Tea and tableware continued to be an important specialty. These were decorated with hand-painted patterns as well as transfer-printed patterns of all colors underglaze. Various types of gilding were used on tea and tableware. Two types of earthenware have been produced: Crown Ware from 1860-1930, and Royal Worcester Vitreous (RWV) from 1870-1930. From 1862, most ware was marked using a series of marks with systems of dating by year.

In 1889 The Worcester Royal Porcelain Co. Ltd. purchased Grainger & Co.* a porcelain manufactory in Worcester. Production continued at the Grainger factory until 1902. Molds, copper plates and pattern books were transferred to the Royal Worcester factory. Many Grainger patterns were continued with Worcester marks. In 1976, the firm merged with Spode to be renamed Royal Worcester Spode Ltd. In 1989, the two firms separated though the retail division continues to operate jointly.

Type of Willow Manufactured: The Worcester Willow pattern was developed about 1875. Even though it has no actual willow tree, it is referred

Mark 2 (GG4354)
c. 1891-1899

Mark 3 (GG4354)
c. 1900+

Mark 4
c. 1870-1930

Mark 5 c. 1923

Mark 6
c. 1870-1930

Mark 7 c. 1886

to in pattern and shape books as "Willow". It was produced in two shades of blue, brown, gray, red, and gold with two different border patterns. The B/446 pattern is known as "Full Willow" and has the scroll and flower border. The same pattern on Crown Ware with number D33 is listed as "The Royal Worcester Willow Pattern". Two Temples II pattern was made on a small scale and was possibly a continuation of the Grainger pattern acquired when Grainger & Co. was purchased in 1889. The John Turner pattern was produced in underglaze blue on Crown Ware in the twentieth century; however, it has not been located in the pattern books. None of the known pieces have a pattern number. Standard Willow pattern was transfer-printed in several different colors underglaze in panels inserted in a diaper pattern border. A Standard Willow variant pattern with just two figures on the bridge and other small alterations in the pattern was also made in underglaze blue on Vitreous Ware with no known pattern numbers.

Comments Concerning Pattern Numbers: A section of examples of willow patterns from Royal Worcester pattern books follows the photographs. Porcelains have prefixes of B, W, C or Z. The B Series dates from August 1876-May 1883, ending with B/1081. The W Series dates from May 1883-1913, ending with W/9999. (There are 22 W pattern books.) The C Series dates from 1913-1928, ending with C/3390. The Z Series dates from 1928. Earthenwares have D or H prefixes. D patterns as well as some W patterns were produced on Crown Ware. Worcester used the term Crown Ware as early as the 1860s, to describe their earthenware body; however, D pattern numbers are from the 1920s. Crown Ware was discontinued in 1930. The H prefix or the H^P symbol stands for Hotel Pattern. RWV stands for Royal Worcester Vitreous. B/735 was produced on RWV. B389 is the most common pattern number for Worcester Willow pattern with scroll and flower border in any color. B750 is the most common pattern number for Worcester Willow pattern with dagger border in any color.

Retailers/importers: R. J. Allen Son & Co., Philadelphia, * Bailey, Banks, and Biddle, Philadelphia*, Jones, McDuffey & Stratton, Boston*, H. G. Stephenson, Manchester*, and A. J. Wiley & Co., Montreal*.

The Legend of the Willow Pattern with drawing of a variation of the Standard Willow pattern from a leaflet produced by The Worcester Royal Porcelain Co. Ltd. The leaflet is displayed in the Museum of Worcester Porcelain with some Worcester Willow pattern pieces.

Pattern B/446 "Full Willow" light blue 5.25-inch saucer with Mark 1, dated 1880. Dark blue 5.25-inch saucer or sauce dish and 3.25-inch cup have B/446 with Mark 2. The cup is dated 1891, and the saucer is 1893. Note the pattern number is the same for both the light and dark blue pattern. All pieces are lined with gold. *Author's Collection.* $5 and $10-15.

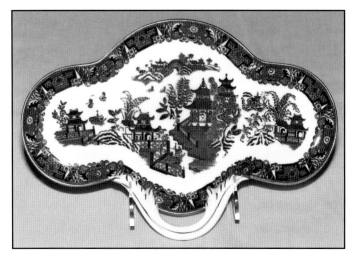

Worcester Willow pattern handled tray that is 11.25-inches long and 7.5-inches wide at the handle. There is no pattern number. Mark 2 dated 1915. It has gold outlining on the handle and around the edge. *Author's Collection.* $65-95.

Worcester Willow pattern wash set including large bowl and pitcher, chamber pot, sponge bowl with drain, and divided soap dish with two separate drainers. All pieces have gold trim. Mark 1 dated 1882. *Courtesy Ken Kowen.* $1,000+.

Worcester Willow pattern condiment set in a silver holder. Not only does this set include salt, pepper, and mustard, but it also has oil and vinegar containers. Pattern B/389 with Mark 1, dated 1880. *Courtesy Loren Zeller.* $400+.

Worcester Willow pattern spoon warmer that measures 6.5-by-4.5-inches and 3.25-inches high. Hot water is poured into the opening and spoons put inside to keep warm before using to stir tea in the cup. It is trimmed in gold, including the handles. Mark 1 dated 1880. *Courtesy Loren Zeller.* $250+.

Worcester Willow pattern Low Kettle No. 681, a teapot shape introduced in 1878. The molds were destroyed by 1927. The teapot is 6.75-inches tall to the top of the handle. It has lavish gold trim, including gold feet. This teapot was also made in pink. Mark 1 dated 1879. *Courtesy Loren Zeller.* $250+.

Worcester Willow pattern egg cup stand with center handle and 6 egg cups. It is unusual to find such a piece intact with no egg cups missing or damaged. All pieces are trimmed in gold. *Courtesy Paul Kirves and Zeke Jimenez.* $250+.

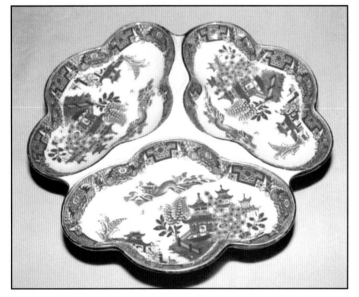

Worcester Willow pattern three part serving dish in light blue. Although there is no pattern number, it is B/389 (or B/446) as were all the dark blue pieces in the previous photos. The piece varies from 10- to 10.75-inches in diameter depending on where it is measured. It is standing on three feet curving downward from the points of a triangular-shaped support attached to the underside. The rims and feet are trimmed in gold. Mark 1 dated 1885. *Author's Collection.* $150-200.

Worcester Willow pattern four globular teapots illustrating different sizes as well as the two different borders: scroll and flower (B/389) and dagger border (B/750). The large dark blue teapot (B/750) on the right holds 36 oz. and has Mark 2 dated 1893. The light blue teapot (B/750) on the left holds 12 oz. and has Mark 3 dated 1926. The two B/389 teapots hold 24 oz. The dark blue one was made for Jones McDuffey & Stratton, Boston, with Mark 2 dated 1909. The light blue teapot in the back has Mark 1 and is dated 1886. *Author's Collection.* $75+ each.

Two Worcester Willow Tub Jugs, No. 4/105. These jugs were found in the Class 4 Shape Book and were made in at least 8 different sizes from 12s to 54s. The size numbers indicate how many of the item can be placed on a board carrying the ware through the pottery. The larger jugs bear smaller numbers. The Tub shape has a molded pattern around the circumference that resembles wood slats around a bucket or tub. The handles also have a more rustic appearance than one would expect with a gold-decorated pattern on porcelain. The 5.5-inch high jug (B/750) has Mark 1, dated 1885. The 3 1/8-inch jug (B389) has Mark 1, dated 1879. *Author's Collection.* $65-95 and $25-55.

Worcester Willow pattern 6.25-inch pink tub jug with gold trim. Evidently the pink jugs were made in several sizes also. A creamer and sugar have been seen in this shape in pink. The lid to the sugar has a rustic finial with two supports and a cross bar that overlaps the supports on both sides. The molded shape may be easier to see in this photo. This jug has the scroll and flower border and Mark 1 dated 1886. *Courtesy Charles and Zeta Hollingsworth.* $75-125.

Worcester Willow pattern B/750 pieces in dark blue. The tray is 17.25-inches measuring across the indentations and 19.5-inches at the widest part. It is intended to hold a teapot, cream, and sugar, and perhaps cups and saucers. Mark 1 dated 1890. The mug is 4-inches high and 3 5/8-inches wide. Mark 2 dated 1898. The fluted shape cup and saucer have Mark 1 dated 1887. *Author's Collection.* $150-225, $65-125, and $12-20.

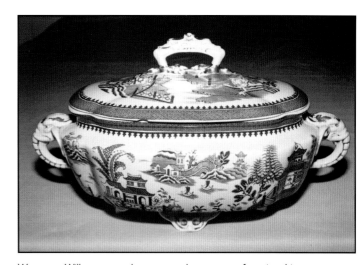

Worcester Willow pattern large covered tureen transfer-printed in brown underglaze with dagger border. The directions in the pattern book for this tureen would be "Elephant Claw". It is the same size with the same handles and finial and gold trim as the one in the previous photo; however, it is standing on four feet. Brown is not found often. Mark 1 dated 1880. *Courtesy Paul Kirves and Zeke Jimenez.* $500+.

Worcester Willow pattern jug group. Starting with the large B750 light blue jug, it stands 6.5-inches high and holds 21 oz. Mark 1 dated 1890. The dark blue B389 jug is 3.75-inches high and holds 7 oz. Mark 3 dated 1930. The B750 light blue jug is the same size with same capacity. Mark 1 dated 1881. The two-handled jug has two spouts. It may be a sauceboat. It stands 3.5-inches high and holds 8 oz. The gold finish is very dull. It is dated 1882. *Author's Collection.* $65+ apiece.

Worcester Willow central pattern 8-inch plate with no border. The light blue pattern extends up over the rim. It is unusual to find such a plate, and it has no pattern number. Mark 2 dated 1894. *Courtesy Paul Kirves and Zeke Jimenez.* $10-20.

Worcester Willow pattern large covered tureen with under tray. The tureen is ten-inches high and 15.5-inches long including the elephant head handles. The finial is made up of gold decorated chicken feet with duck heads meeting across the top. It has Mark 4 dated 1898. The directions in the pattern books for oval Crown Ware or Vitreous covered dishes such as this would be "Elephant Plain". This indicates the tureen has no feet. Worcester produced this same piece decorated with Grainger's Bamboo pattern. Mine is dated 1902. *Courtesy IWC Convention 2001.* $500+.

A photocopy from the Royal Worcester archives showing the Royal Worcester Willow Pattern on Crown Ware, the term used for earthenware. These pieces are Athens shape and usually carry the D33 pattern number. In the shape book, each piece is assigned a number: 10-inch plate – CW2, 31 oz. teapot – CW60, 25.5 oz. teapot – CW61, low tea cup and saucer – CW42, and covered dish, oval – CW35.

Worcester Willow pattern No. 422 Old Beer jugs in four sizes. The jugs were made in 7 sizes with shape numbers CW111-121. The 6-inch jug holds 48 oz. and has Mark 1 dated 1880. The 5-inch jug holds 28 oz. and has Mark 5 with a Rd No. dated 1923. The 4.75-inch jug holds 18 oz., and also has Mark 5 as well as pattern D/209. The 3-inch jug holds 6 oz., has Mark 6 dated 1924, and pattern D/209. *Author's Collection.* $125-175, $75-125, $55-95, and $35-65.

Worcester Willow pattern plate and pieces in Crown Ware not shown in the photocopy above. Oval dishes came in sizes 8, 9, 10, 12, 14, 16, and 18-inches with CW numbers 15-21. This one is 10-inches long and has the pattern on the rim and outside only. The gravy under plate is attached. It has Mark 5 dated 1923. *Author's Collection.* $10-20, $25-45, and $45-75.

Teapot, creamer, and open sugar with Worcester Willow pattern in gold over a rust-red ground The pieces all have sterling tops with inscriptions. The pieces were University of Oxford Sporting Awards and have the engraving "O.U.B.C. (Oxford University Boat Club) Swimming Races H. S. Salter." The teapot was given for First Prize in 1/2-mile race, 1883; cream jug was First Prize in 1/3-mile race, 1884; and the sugar was First Prize for 1/2-mile race, 1884. Henry Stuart Salter, the recipient of these awards received his BA Degree from Oxford University in 1886. Mark 1 dated 1882. *Courtesy Loren Zeller.* NP

Worcester Willow pattern (B389) 5.75-inch Old Beer jug transfer-printed in pink with gold trim. It has Mark 1 dated 1882. This size jug is shape CW116 in pink willow. It holds 30 oz. which is a "24" size. *Courtesy Charles and Zeta Hollingsworth.* $175-275.

Two Temples II pattern cup and saucer transfer-printed underglaze in gray-blue on cream-colored porcelain. The saucer is 5. 25-inches across. The cup is 3.25-inches wide and 2-inches high. The set has pattern C/160 and Mark 2 dated 1917. This may be a pattern carried over from the Grainger factory. It is not seen often with a Worcester mark. *Author's Collection*. $15-25.

Standard Willow variant pattern covered vegetable in underglaze blue. There is no gold used in this pattern. There are two versions of this New Gadroon oval shape: No. 45 was cast December 12, 1951, and No. 713 was cast November 11, 1952. Mark 4. *Courtesy Louise and Charles Loehr*. $165-200.

John Turner Willow pattern after dinner coffee set transfer-printed in blue underglaze on Crown Ware. The only evidence that this pattern was made at Worcester is the ware itself. The pattern has not been located in the Worcester pattern books. Biscuit jars are perhaps the form seen most often in this pattern. The pieces in this set bear Mark 6, many with a large letter H. Saucers are also impressed with 11, or 12 and a crown. The coffee pot has impressed 21. *Author's Collection*. $125-175.

This 10.5-inch plate has the Standard Willow central pattern in blue panels set in the pink diaper border. It is earthenware known as Crown Ware. The plate is marked with pattern W/1721 in addition to Mark 7 dated 1886. There are many different color schemes used on this pattern in the W pattern books. Each color variation has a different pattern number. Special orders would receive a different pattern number regardless of the colors used. Some versions do not have the central "star". The pattern is not often found. *Author's Collection*. $45-75.

Standard Willow variant pattern 10 3/8-inch soup plate transfer-printed in blue underglaze on RWV (Royal Worcester Vitreous). The border is the B/389 border; however, a bridge has been added to the central pattern with two figures on it. The third figure can be seen on the pathway in pursuit of the other two. The fence remains on the left hand side. A pair of birds has been added to the pattern. Mark 4 dated 1903. It has an impressed 17. *Author's Collection*. $35-65.

Wendy Cook, curator of the Museum of Worcester Porcelain, found this watercolor design in the archives that seems to have been painted in the 1870s. It is a very large scale for a large charger. She thinks this is possibly an inspiration for the Worcester Willow pattern first produced about 1875. There is no evidence that this particular design was ever produced.

Pattern B/446 "Full willow" designs for two different shape cups. This pattern is the same as B/389.

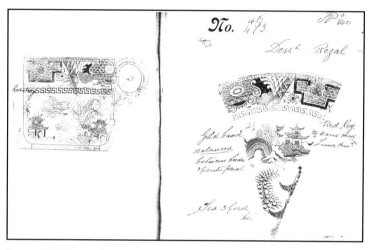

Pattern B/473 has a red key band between the border and center pattern. I have not seen an example of this pattern. The NPo. number at the top right indicates New Pattern No. This is a different numbering system from the series that began with a letter. Pattern B/473 was used on dessert services in Regal shape. There are directions for "balanced" gold band between border and center pattern. I don't know if "Copper 432" refers to a color or a copper plate.

A design for a Tea Tankard cup in B/389, the most commonly found pattern number on Worcester Willow with scroll and flower border.

Pattern B/735 has a dagger border and was evidently used on serving pieces in addition to other tableware. I have an oval covered vegetable in "Elephant Plain" shape with a foot like the drawing. Mark 4 and pattern number B/735.

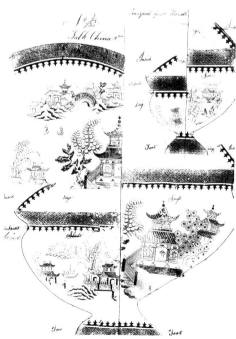

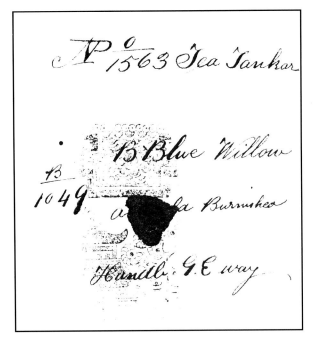

Pattern B/1049 has a faint pattern segment under the writing. It has New Pattern No. 1563 and Tea Tankard shape given. B Blue is Best Blue. Some part of it has Burnished Gold, and the handle has Gold Edge (GE).

Pattern W/738 has a dagger border. Just a small piece of the pattern is shown in the pattern book.

Pattern W/784 calls for Best Blue dagger border and Dove Willow. The illustration shows such a small part of a pattern that it may be a border-only pattern.

Pattern W/4885 is one of the many W patterns that are variations of W/1721 illustrated in the last photo above. This one is similar to W/1549 except for the Dogrose diaper in center in lieu of the Star. The Panels in the border are the Standard Willow pattern, and according to pattern W/4885, can be mulberry or other underglaze color.

NPo. 1564 has a small piece of the central pattern in the book. The cursive U/G stands for under glaze. There is no pattern number with a letter preceding the number. NPo. 1566 shows a bit of scroll and flower border pattern. It has pattern W/905. NPo.1568 has no illustration in the pattern book; however, it is also pattern W/903 that is probably also a willow-type pattern.

This is the pattern book illustration of pattern D/33 Table Athens in any color with Liquid Gold.

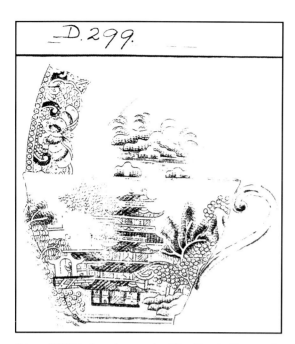

Pattern D/299 is the only example of Two Temples II pattern I found when looking through the pattern books. It may be one of the patterns carried over from Grainger & Co. as it was not made extensively by Worcester.

Wren Giftware

Location: King Street, Longton, Stoke-on-Trent, Staffordshire
Dates: c. 1991-98
Mark:

c. 1991-98

Brief History: Founded in 1990, Wren Giftware was purchased by the Denby Group in 1995. Wren was no longer in production in 1998. Mugs and other small items were decorated on bone china. Blue Willow was one of the patterns produced, a special back stamp was used to mark the ware.
Type of Willow Manufactured: Standard Willow pattern blue printed on bone china with gold trim.

Standard Willow pattern decorated 7-inch vase and 3-inch teapot. The outer border was used to decorate the top of the vase and the lid of the little teapot. *Author's Collection.* $15-20 each.

Yale & Barker

Location: Victoria Place Works, Longton, Staffordshire
Dates: c. 1841-42
Mark:

c. 1841-42

Brief History: George Yale and William Barker were in partnership for a short time succeeding the partnership of John Shaw and George Yale at Victoria Place Works. George Barker joined the firm in 1843, at which time it traded as Yale, Barker & Barker, and they moved to Anchor Lane where they produced china in addition to earthenware. The Victoria Place Works was a small factory with one or two kilns. Earthenware only was produced there.
Type of Willow Manufactured: Standard Willow pattern transfer-printed in blue on earthenware.

Worcester Willow pattern H/243 shows a Tea Tankard with filled in cup handle. It is a Hotel Pattern with Gold Edge that is the same pattern as B/389 with scroll and flower border.

Standard Willow pattern platter transfer-printed in blue underglaze on earthenware. The platter measures 14-by-17.75-inches and has a combed back. Three-point stilt marks on the back with double stilt marks on the front very close together. Extra scrolling leaves have been added to the outer border on the NE and SW corners. Cuts occur in the scrolling leaves in the SE and NW corners. *Author's Collection.* $125-175.

John Yates

Location: Broad Street (High St.) Shelton and Keelings Lane, Staffordshire
Dates: c. 1820-35
Mark:

c. 1820-35

Comments Concerning Mark: This is one of over fifty Pseudo Chinese Seal Marks documented by Margaret Ironside.
Brief History: There was a John Yates producing earthenware at Broad Street and at Keelings Lane as early as 1770. A Dissolution of partnership notice dated 1808, describes John and William Yates as manufacturing only earthenware; however, John Yates had been in partnership earlier with Shelley (and Shelleys) producing china. The main period of John Yates' production of fine quality bone china seems to have been c. 1820-35. Yates & May were in partnership after that time: c. 1835-43. Yates produced tea and dessert services in underglaze blue printed patterns as well as hand-painted floral patterns. Molded border designs can be found on dessert services, and pattern numbers were sometimes used.
Type of Willow Manufactured: Two Temples II pattern transfer-printed in pale blue underglaze on bone china with gold trim. These pieces are found with a Pseudo Chinese Seal Mark.

Two Temples II pattern cup and saucer transfer-printed in pale blue underglaze on bone china with gold trim. The saucer is 5.5-inches across with an indentation of 2.75-inches. The cup base is 1.75-inches. In addition to the Mark shown above, it has Pattern No. 1045 in red and the letter S. The cup is seen as fig. 1, p 25 in "The pseudo-Chinese Seal Marks", *Northern Ceramic Society Newsletter No. 89,* March 1993. *Courtesy Margaret Ironside.* $35-65.

Two Temples II pattern cup and saucer transfer-printed in pale blue underglaze on bone china with gold trim. The saucer is 6-inches across with an inner ring of 2 1/8-inches. The foot ring is 3.25-inches. Both the cup and saucer have the pseudo Chinese Seal Mark. *Courtesy Margaret Ironside.* $35-65.

Ynysmeudwy Pottery

Location: Nr. Swansea, Wales
Dates: c. 1845-75
Impressed Mark:

(GG4395)
c. 1850-70+

Brief History: The pottery at Ynysmeudwy was started as a brick works in 1845, by two brothers Michael Martyn Williams and William Williams. Within five years it was a typical Victorian pottery producing tablewares, jugs and child's plates. From 1860 to 1869, the factory was owned by Griffith Lewis and John Morgan. When Morgan died in 1869, Lewis sold the pottery to W. T. Holland, owner of Llanelly Pottery*. Holland removed what was of use to him to Llanelly and worked Ynysmeudwy Pottery as a brick works. It can be somewhat confusing because some Ynysmeudwy patterns were produced at Llanelly after 1869.

The transfer ware produced at Ynysmeudwy was of a very high quality, and many different patterns were made during the various partnerships. Flow blue patterns were also produced. Mocha ware for the pub trade was another staple of the factory. One of the specialties of the pottery was child's plates in many different interesting patterns. These patterns are recorded in the collection of the National Museum of Wales.
Type of Willow Manufactured: Standard Willow pattern transfer-printed in blue underglaze on earthenware.

Standard Willow pattern platter transfer-printed in blue underglaze on earthenware. The platter measures 12.5-by-15.75-inches and is a very nice quality. Three-point stilt marks on the front and single marks on the back. The white spot on the fence to the right of the path is a visible stilt mark. *Author's Collection.* $115-165.

II. RETAILERS and IMPORTERS

This section is devoted primarily to information found on impressed and printed marks. Location of the retailer/importer is given when known as well as occasional added bits of information. The marks are shown and photographs of the objects decorated in willow pattern. There are also some advertisements from trade journals illustrating willow pattern in the lines they carry. There has been no attempt to be all-inclusive; however, there are enough examples presented to demonstrate the widespread interest in the willow pattern by retailers and importers. I chose not to include these marks and photos in the main section of the book because not all of the marks include the name of the pottery that produced the ware.

Allan Line

Location: Montreal, Canada
Comments Concerning Company: The Allan Line was a Montreal-based trans-Atlantic steamship company founded in the nineteenth century. It was taken over by the Canadian Pacific Railway's steamship service in 1915.
Pottery: G. L. Ashworth & Bros. (Ltd.)
Mark:

c. 1862-80
(Ashworth)

Comment Concerning Mark: There is also an impressed ASHWORTH mark: (GG137)c. 1862-80.

Standard Willow pattern well and tree platter transfer-printed in blue underglaze on ironstone. The platter measures 10.5-by-12.75-inches. *Courtesy IWC Convention 2002.* $95-145.

R. J. Allen Son & Co.

Location: 309/311 Market St., Philadelphia, Pennsylvania
Pottery: Worcester Royal Porcelain Co. Ltd.
Mark:

(GG4354)
c. 1892

Worcester Willow pattern B/750 with dagger border 8-inch plate transfer-printed in dark blue underglaze on bone china. The rim is fluted shape, and the edge is trimmed in gold. *Author's Collection.* $12-20.

Bailey, Banks & Biddle

Location: Philadelphia, Pennsylvania
Pottery: Worcester Royal Porcelain Co. Ltd.
Mark:

(GG4354) c. 1910

Standard Willow pattern panels in green underglaze in the gray border pattern on a 9-inch plate. This color combination with no central pattern is Royal Worcester pattern # W/8465. The plate is non-translucent Crown Ware. Retailers often requested patterns with a specific color scheme that would result in the use of a new pattern number. *Courtesy Sandra and Terry Leonard.* $35-65.

L. Bamberger & Co.

Location: Newark, New Jersey
Comment Concerning Retailer: L. Bamberger & Co. is a department store chain.
Mark:

c. 1920+

Standard Willow pattern covered butter dish transfer-printed in blue underglaze on earthenware. The plate is 7.25-inches across. The maker is unknown. *Author's Collection.* $45-75.

Baur Au Lac

Location: Zurich
Additional Name: G. Kiefer & Gie Ltd., Sable – Zurich
Pottery: Dunn, Bennett & Co. Ltd.
Mark:

c. 1920+

Standard Willow pattern bottle holder transfer-printed in blue underglaze on earthenware. It is 4.25-inches across and the rim is one-inch high. It is a nice quality piece. *Author's Collection.* $15-22.

John Barker and Co. Ltd. (Barkers)

Location: Kensington, London
Pottery: Booths Ltd.

Pottery Gazette, May 1, 1924, p. 847, has an advertisement for The Barker Furnishing Services. At the top left are three pieces of "The Old Willow Pattern". It looks like Real Old Willow by Booths.

Henry Birks & Sons Ltd.

Location: Winnipeg, Canada
Pottery: Crown Staffordshire Porcelain Co. Ltd.
Marks:

Comment Concerning Marks: I am assuming that Hy Birks & Sons is the same firm as Henry Birks & Sons.

Mark 1 (GG1149)
c. 1906+

Mark 2
(GG1149) c.
1906+

Two Temples II 8-inch soup plate transfer-printed in blue underglaze on bone china. Two small birds have been added to the pattern at the top: just under the butterfly on the border. Mark 1. *Author's Collection.* $20-30.

Polychrome Chinese Willow pattern in linear form on a small compote. It stands 3.5-inches high and is 6.25-inches long. It has pattern #5256 and Mark 2. *Courtesy IWC Convention 2000.* $35-65.

Pottery: Grimwades Ltd.
Mark:

(GG1832) c. 1930+

Chinese Willow pattern cup and saucer printed in brown and filled in with a yellow-gold enamel. The set has added gilding. Mark 1. *Courtesy Geraldine Ewaniuk.* $25-45.

Pekin pattern compote with blue background and enameling overglaze. It has gold trim. The compote stands 5.25-inches tall and is 9.75-inches across. It is marked "Rideau Ware" and has pattern #1178. *Courtesy Loren Zeller.* $200+.

Burley & Co.

Location: Chicago, Illinois
Comments Concerning Retailer: Burley & Co. provided willow ware for the Old Faithful Inn at Yellowstone Park, Wyoming. The company published a pamphlet for the Inn with the Willow Legend. Grindley Hotel Ware Co. Ltd.* is another company that produced willow on vitrified ware for Burley & Co.
Pottery: John Maddock & Sons Ltd.
Mark:

c. 1896+

Standard Willow pattern jug transfer-printed in blue underglaze on vitrified ware. The jug is 4-inches to the top of the handle and holds 6 oz. *Courtesy IWC Convention 1995.* $15-25.

China Glass & Earthenware House

Location: No. 243, Pearl St., New York
Pottery: James and Ralph Clews
Marks:

(GG919) c.1818-34

Standard Willow pattern 5 5/8-inch plate transfer-printed in blue underglaze on pearlware. There is only one other impressed retailer mark documented, and it is for John Greenfield, an importer of china and earthenware at No. 77 Pearl St. That mark is also accompanied by GG919 impressed mark for James and Ralph Clews. It is recorded in the *FOB Bulletin* No. 94, Winter 1996-7, p. 8. *Courtesy Jeff Siptak.* $45-55.

Chinacraft Ltd.

Location: United Kingdom

Seven-inch plate with Standard Willow pattern borders. The central pattern was adapted to illustrate the caption: "My Goodness My Guinness!" The Guinness Collector's Club commissioned the plate in 1963 through Chinacraft Ltd.; however, the pottery that made it is unknown. This plate is very popular with willow collectors as are all parodies of the pattern. *Author's Collection.* $65-85.

Chinar Link Design for Great Eastern Life

Location: England
Mark:

c. 1990

This plate was designed to commemorate the 25th anniversary of Singapore in 1990. It is similar in concept to the plates designed at the Gladstone Pottery for several of the cities in England. The willow tree has been retained, but palm trees replace several of the others. The butterfly and orchids in the border speak to the Butterfly Park and Orchid Gardens in Singapore. The famous Raffles Hotel has replaced the teahouse. The plate is bone china and has a gold rim. *Author's Collection.* $25-45.

Gilman Collamore &Co.

Location: 5th Ave. & 30th Street, New York
Pottery: Booths
Mark:

(GG453) c. 1906+

Booths Willow variant pattern in gold over a black ground creamer and sugar with lid. Retailers often chose eye-catching color variations for the pieces that bore their name. *Courtesy IWC Convention 1997.* $75-125.

Pottery: Doulton
Mark:

(GG1333) c. 1930+

Cook's Restaurant Supplies

Location: U.S.A.
Pottery: Grindley Hotel Ware Co. Ltd.
Mark:

c. 1908+

An 8-inch vitrified plate with small green printed Two Temples II central pattern. The words SAVOY GARDEN appear under the pattern. Perhaps this is the name of the place where the plate would be used. The same pattern and color was also made for Cook's Restaurant Supplies by Jackson China, an American manufacturer. *Courtesy IWC Convention 1997.* $20-30.

This is a complete series of 6 Willow Pattern Story plates in polychrome with the Bird & Swirl border. The pattern number that appears on two of the plates is E7212. The plates are placed left to right: top row first. The captions on the back are as follows: 1. "Koongshee and Chang escape but are pursued by the Tipsy Mandarin who they elude." 2. "After living in the gardener's cottage where they had taken refuge from pursuit, they escape in a boat to avoid arrest by the Soldiers." 3. "After traveling many miles they moor their boat beside an island covered with reeds and there resolve to settle down and spend their days in peace." 4. "They purchased a free right to the little island and after having built a house, and from the sale of jewels, obtained all that was necessary. Chang brought the island into a high state of cultivation." 5. "Here they lived happily." 6. "Chang having achieved a competence by his cultivation of the land returned to his literary pursuits and wrote a book on agriculture which gained for him great reputation." *Courtesy IWC Convention 1998.* $1,500-3,000.

Crabtree & Evelyn

Location: London
Pottery: G. M. and C. J. Mason
Mark:

c. 1992

This blue printed mug is another example of how the Standard Willow pattern has been used as a starting point for re-interpretation with well-known substitutions. The first side is fairly uncluttered with Big Ben replacing the teahouse and the Eiffel Tower at the other end of the bridge. The other side is a hodge-podge including the Leaning Tower of Pisa, the Parthenon and a huge windmill in front with a willow tree and a boat stuck in amongst many other landmarks from around the world. *Author's Collection.* $25-50.

F. Crook

Location: Motcomb St., Belgrave Sq. S. W., London
Pottery: W. T. Copeland
Marks:

(GG1074) c. 1875-90

Two Temples I pattern 9.5-inch plate transfer-printed in dark blue underglaze on bone china trimmed in gold. This is a lovely example of the pattern where all the details can be seen. *Courtesy Tim and Kim Allen.* $55-75.

Pottery: Keeling & Co.
Marks:

c. 1892-1904

Comments Concerning Mark: The Semi China mark can be compared to the one on the copper plate engraving shown in the entry for Keeling & Co.

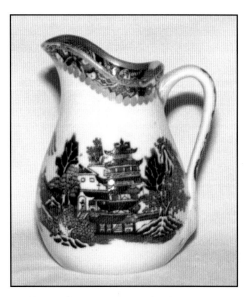

Two Temples II reversed pattern 4-inch jug transfer-printed in dark blue on semi china. It has a line of big gold dots on the inside edge of the border. The base of the handle is shaped like a leaf. *Author's Collection.* $45-65.

Dairy Outfit Co. Ltd.

Location: Office: Kings Cross, London
Pottery: attributed to Doulton
Comments Concerning Attribution: The CREAM jug was photographed next to an Arno shape jug by Doulton in order to compare the shapes of the two jugs. The Arno shape is documented by Louise Irvine in *Doulton Series Ware, Volume 1*, p. 105.
Mark:

c. 1882+

Standard Willow pattern jugs transfer-printed in blue underglaze on earthenware. The Doulton jug on the left is 7-inches high and trimmed in gold. It is marked with GG1332, c. 1891-1902. The CREAM jug is 8-inches high with no gold. The shape appears to be the same on the two jugs. *Author's Collection.* $100-175 and $265-300.

Standard Willow pattern large milk pail/dispenser transfer-printed in blue underglaze on earthenware and fitted with brass lid, plunger, and 1/2 pint measure. It stands 12.5-inches tall and is 16-inches across the top. It bears the Dairy Outfit Co. mark above. Similar milk pails without the handles and brass fittings have been seen marked Doulton. *Courtesy Loren Zeller.* $750+.

Daniell

Location: Wigmore St., London
Pottery: Mintons
Mark:

(GG2713)
c. 1873+

Standard Willow pattern 10-inch plate transfer-printed in blue underglaze on bone china. The inner border and the diamond pattern in the outer border have been gold encrusted. A fluted edge tops off this gorgeous plate. *Courtesy Charles and Zeta Hollingsworth.* $75-150.

Edward B. Dickinson, Inc.

Location: Fifth Avenue and 23rd Street, New York
Pottery: Booths Ltd.

The Pottery, Glass & Brass Salesman, 1921, p. 217, advertisement for "Real Old Willow" by Booths Ltd. by Edward B. Dickinson, Inc., Sole Agents for the pottery.

PLATE 54. Advertisement, 1921, of Booth's, Ltd., "Willow"; see No. 188.

Hugh C. Edmiston

Location: 129 Fifth Avenue, New York
Potteries: George L. Ashworth & Bros., Ltd. and Crown Staffordshire Porcelain Co., Ltd.

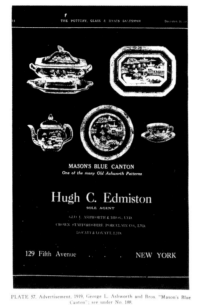

The Pottery, Glass & Brass Salesman, December 11, 1919, Plate 57, advertisement for Mason's Blue Canton produced by Geo. L. Ashworth &Bros., Ltd. Hugh C. Edmiston is also sole agent for Crown Staffordshire Porcelain Co. according to this ad; however, I do not know if Edmiston handled their willow patterns.

PLATE 57. Advertisement, 1919, George L. Ashworth and Bros. "Mason's Blue Canton"; see under No. 188.

Featherstone & Gray

Location: 9 Farringdon Ave., London E.C.
Pottery: Ridgways
Mark:

c. 1912+

Standard Willow pattern transfer-printed 7-inch plate in brown underglaze on earthenware and clobbered in shades of green, rust, and cobalt. This plate was made by Ridgways* as it has pattern number 3936: the same pattern number used on the clobbered pieces with Ridgways marks. The bottom of the plate also has two rings inside the main foot ring as do marked Ridgways plates. *Author's Collection.* $35-55.

Fisher, Bruce & Co.

Location: Philadelphia, Pennsylvania
Pottery: William Adams & Sons
Mark:

c. mid-twentieth century

Standard Willow pattern 10.5-inch plate transfer-printed in blue underglaze on heavy earthenware. *Author's Collection.* $20-30.

Fondeville & Co., Inc.

Location: 149 Fifth Avenue, New York
Pottery: Soho Pottery Ltd.
Mark:

c. 1930

Standard Willow pattern 10-inch plate transfer-printed in blue underglaze on earthenware. Under the mark are the words REG. U.S. PAT. OFF. Blue willow cups have been found with the mark in gold. *Author's Collection.* $15-18.

Pottery: Simpsons (Potters) Ltd.
Mark:

R°D. U.S. PAT. OFF.

c. 1944+

Comments Concerning Mark: This mark is accompanied by a Simpsons Solian Ware mark (seen earlier with the entry on Simpsons). This Ambassador Ware mark also appears as GG3615 with the words SOHO POTTERY replacing FONDEVILLE.

Gibson & Patterson Ltd.

Location: Wellington, New Zealand
Pottery: Grafton China
Comment Concerning Pottery: Duraline is evidently a name used for an earthenware body made by the firm.
Mark:

c. 1948

Comment Concerning Mark: The mark, printed in yellow, is difficult to read: Duraline, Grafton China, Made in England, Gibsons & Patterson Ltd., Wellington 1948.

Standard Willow pattern 8-inch plate transfer-printed in blue underglaze on earthenware. The plate has a beaded edge. *Author's Collection.* $10-15.

H. Friedman & Sons

Location: New York
Pottery: John Maddock & Sons Ltd.
Mark:

(GG2465)
c. 1896+

Standard Willow pattern 7-inch plate transfer-printed in blue underglaze on vitrified ware. This plate was probably used in a restaurant. *Author's Collection.* $10-15.

Booths Willow pattern 5-inch plate hand-painted in blue underglaze on earthenware. It is unusual to find a hand-painted plate produced by a large Staffordshire factory. *Courtesy Kathy and Hugh Sykes.* $10-20.

Thomas Goode & Co.

Location: South Dudley St., London W
Pottery: Booths Ltd.
Mark:

(GG453) c. 1906+

A gold variant pattern on a black background makes for a very striking coffee pot. It stands 7-inches high. *Courtesy IWC Convention 2000.* $95-150.

Pottery: W. T. Copeland
Mark:

(RC242)
c. 1904-54

Standard Willow pattern 8-inch plate transfer-printed in dark blue underglaze on bone china. There is a line of gold on the rim. It has a pattern number in red that is unreadable. *Author's Collection.* $10-18.

Pottery: Crown Staffordshire Porcelain Co. Ltd.
Mark:

(GG1149) c. 1906+

Gold variant willow pattern ink well on a tray. The pattern is done overglaze in gold over a blue ground. This is the same pattern as seen in gold over black in the last photo in the Crown Staffordshire Porcelain Co.* entry. Inkwells decorated with Standard Willow pattern are seldom seen, but many different variants have been found. The form is popular with collectors. *Courtesy Paul Kirves and Zeke Jimenez.* $125+.

Goodliffe Neale

Location: Alcester, England
Mark:

late twentieth century

Comments Concerning the Company:
Goodliffe Neale of Alcester (and Dublin) may have gone out of business recently. The company was a distributor of books and religious supplies as well as china souvenirs. "Fine China" is noted on the mark; however, the maker is unknown.

The Standard Willow pattern was the starting point for this interpretation that appears to be a train station. The track and train take the place of the water and boat. The bridge crosses over the tracks, and the willow tree is on the far side. The birds, orange tree, and fence are in place. The plate is 8 3/8-inches in diameter. *Courtesy Paul Kirves and Zeke Jimenez.* $10-20.

James Green & Nephew Ltd.

Location: London
Pottery: Grainger & Co.
Marks:

Comments Concerning Marks: A variation of Mark 1 has London & Hanley. Along with printed Mark 2, the piece has an impressed shield mark for Grainger & Co. Mark 3 is not often seen. The pottery is unknown.

Mark 1
c. twentieth
century

Mark 2 (GG1770)
c. 1870-89

Mark 3 c. twentieth
century

Standard Willow pattern 4-inch tip dish transfer-printed in blue underglaze on earthenware. These little dishes are advertising pieces for Schweppes. Various different beverages have been noted including Ginger Ale and Lemon Squash. Mark 1. *Courtesy Jeff Siptak.* $20-35.

Bamboo pattern crescent salad plate transfer-printed in red underglaze on bone china with gold trim. The plate is 10-inches long and 5.5-inches wide. Mark 2. *Courtesy Kathy and Hugh Sykes.* $30-45.

Standard Willow pattern 4-inch tip dish transfer-printed in blue underglaze on earthenware. The same style as the Schweppes dish above, this one advertises Tennent's Lager Beer. Mark 3 reads: James Green & Nephew, London, Designers & Manufacturers of Advertising Specialties. *Courtesy Jeff Siptak.* $20-35.

Harris & Marsh Pty. Ltd.

Location: 75-77 Liverpool St., Hobart
Mark:

OLD ENGLISH COTTAGE WILLOW
MANUFACTURED EXPRESSLY FOR
HARRIS & MARSH PTY. LD.
75-77 LIVERPOOL ST.,
HOBART
MADE IN ENGLAND

c. 1920+

Standard Willow pattern sauce dish transfer-printed in dark blue underglaze on earthenware. The pottery that made the dish is unknown. *Courtesy Charles and Zeta Hollingsworth.* $6-10.

Hartman

Location: Chicago
Mark:

c. 1920+

Standard Willow pattern 8-inch plate transfer-printed in blue underglaze on earthenware. There is very little white space in this version of the pattern. The outer border is too large for the piece. An entire section of two sets of scrolling leaves and Ju-Is with scroll cross was cut at 11 o'clock. The maker is unknown. *Courtesy IWC Convention 2000.* $5-8.

Hawkins

Location: Henley-on-Thames
Mark:

Twentieth century

Porcelain jug decorated in the polychrome lithograph based on the Two Temples II pattern. It has red line trim. The maker is unknown. *Author's Collection.* $25-35.

Charles Hawley

Location: Sheffield
Pottery: attributed to Sampson Bridgwood & Co.
Comment Concerning Attribution: The attribution to Sampson Bridgwood & Co. is based on the impressed P.G. in the mark. The initials were used by the firm to denote their Parisian Granite ware. It was given the name in the late 1880s to compete with French china imported into North America.
Mark:

c. 1880s+

Two Temples II pattern 6-inch plate transfer-printed in blue underglaze on earthenware. The blue has a slight flow blue effect. The cartouche in the center has the words: CONGREGATIONAL CHURCH BAKEWELL. The plates could have been put to use at the church or perhaps were commemorative souvenirs of the church. The pottery that supplied them to Charles Hawley the retailer in Sheffield may have been Sampson Bridgwood & Son. *Courtesy Jeff Siptak.* $15-25.

T. W. Heath

Location: Sydney or Melbourne
Pottery: Burgess & Leigh
Mark: (GG723) Burgess & Leigh. The retailer information is all on the front of the plate.

Burleigh willow pattern 5.5-inch dish transfer-printed in blue underglaze on earthenware. T. W. Heath evidently imported Burleigh willow pattern and used a number of retailers throughout the country for selling the goods. This little dish may have served as a business card. *Courtesy Kathy and Hugh Sykes.* $25-50.

Higgins & Leiter

Mark:

Twentieth century

Standard Willow pattern plate transfer-printed in blue underglaze on earthenware. The maker of the plate is unknown. *Author's Collection.* $8-10.

Jones, McDuffey & Stratton

Location: Boston, Massachusetts
Dates: c. 1871-1990s+
Brief History: Founded in 1871, the company's history goes back to 1810, when Otis Norcross founded his wholesaler/importer business on Fish Street, Boston. By 1900, it was one of the largest importers of pottery and glass in the U.S.A. The company was still in business in the mid-1990s.
Pottery: Worcester Royal Porcelain Co. Ltd.
Mark:

(GG4354) c. 1909

Worcester Willow pattern B389 24 oz. teapot transfer-printed underglaze on bone china. *Author's Collection.* $75-135.

Henry W. King & Co. Ltd.
(see R. Twining & Co. Ltd.)

Lawleys

Location: Stoke-on-Trent
Pottery: Burgess & Leigh
Mark:

1921+

Burleigh Willow pattern egg cup tray transfer-printed in blue underglaze on earthenware and trimmed in gold. There are indentations for 4 egg buckets and egg-shaped salt and pepper sitting at the ends. *Courtesy Nancee Rogers.* $150-250.

Lawleys Norfolk Pottery

Location: Stoke
Pottery: A. G. Harley Jones
Mark:

(GG2212)
c. 1923-34

Tobacco jar decorated with Worcester Willow pattern in gold and enameling overglaze. The background is black. The piece is 5.5-inches to the top of the lid. The gold foo dog finial adds another-inch. *Courtesy Tim and Kim Allen.* $125-250.

Pottery: Minton
Mark:

(GG2716)
c. 1912-50

Comment Concerning Mark: The piece shown is also impressed MINTONS..

Standard Willow pattern central pattern 3-part server with dagger border transfer-printed in dark blue underglaze on earthenware and trimmed in gold. This piece measures 10-inches across and has a handle across the top. *Courtesy IWC Convention 1993.* $135-200.

Lawleys Phillips

Location: Regent St., London
Pottery: Minton
Mark:

Comment Concerning Mark: The mark is difficult to read. In the space between the banners the words are: ESTD. PHILLIPS & S. 1760.

(GG2716)
c. 1912-50

Standard Willow pattern central pattern gravy boat with dagger border transfer-printed in dark blue underglaze on earthenware. *Author's Collection.* $45-75.

Pottery: attributed to Newport Pottery
Comments Concerning Attribution: In 1929, Clarice Cliff, at Newport Pottery, began designing new shapes. One technique used was to invert old shapes to make new ones. The "stepped" vase, shape 368 became candleholder shape 391.[1] The hollow vase side of the candleholders can be seen in the illustration of the mark.
Mark:

Comment Concerning Mark: The words Phillips and Lawley were applied in pale print at the base of the candle receptacle.

c. 1925-40

Standard Willow pattern pair of candle blocks. There is no border pattern used to decorate these pieces. The design originated with Clarice Cliff who turned a "stepped" vase upside down to form the candlesticks. *Courtesy IWC Convention 1993.* $100-200.

Maple

Location: London
Mark:

c. 1911+

Two Temples II pattern cup and saucer in gold and colored enamels over a blue ground on bone china. The decorative treatment is very similar to that seen by E. Hughes & Co.* It is possible that is the factory that produced the ware. *Courtesy IWC Convention 1995.* $35-55.

Hotel McAlpin

Location: New York
Pottery: Crown Staffordshire Porcelain Co. Ltd.
Mark:

(GG1149)
c. 1906+

Polychrome Willow variant pattern demitasse cup and saucer. The pattern is transfer-printed in black underglaze and finished with enameling overglaze. The pattern number is #6671 – a different number than on the same pattern shown previously in the entry under Crown Staffordshire Porcelain Co. Ltd.* A new pattern number is often assigned to special orders. The Rd. No. 589090 is the same. *Author's Collection.* $35-45.

1. Cunningham, Helen C., *Clarice Cliff & Her Contemporaries,* pp. 31-32.

Mermod & Jaccard Jewelry Co.

Location: St Louis, Missouri
Pottery: A. B. Jones
Comment Concerning Attribution to A. B. Jones: A collector has several cream soup bowls with the Mermod & Jaccard mark below in addition to GG2199.
Mark:

c. 1981+

Standard Willow pattern 7.75-inch plate transfer-printed in blue underglaze on bone china. It has a gold line at the rim and between the borders. *Courtesy IWC Convention 1999.* $8-12.

Mogridge & Underhay

Location: Stoke-on-Trent
Pottery: Davison & Son, Ltd.

Pottery Gazette, March 1, 1922, p. 383, "Buyers' Notes" discussion of the wares offered by Mogridge and Underhay included this picture of a toilet set by Davison & Son, Ltd.

Henry Morgan & Co., Ltd.

Location: Montreal
Pottery: Soho Pottery Ltd.
Mark:

c. 1930+

Standard Willow pattern 9-inch plate and cream soup transfer-printed in light blue underglaze on earthenware. Both pieces have a molded beaded edge. *Author's Collection.* $10-18 and $15-25.

Mortlock

Location: Oxford St./ Orchard St., London
Pottery: Minton
Mark:

Comment Concerning Mark: The piece shown is also marked with impressed MINTONS, (GG2711) c. 1873+

(GG2713) c. 1873+

Standard Willow pattern 10-inch plate transfer-printed in dark blue underglaze on bone china. The inner border is used, but the outer border has been replaced with a molded seed pattern on the rim that is 1.5-inches at the widest parts. There is a line of gold on either side of the molding. It is pattern no. 2652. *Author's Collection.* $55-85.

Pottery: Worcester Royal Porcelain Co. Ltd.
Mark:

(GG4350) c. 1880s

Worcester Willow pattern crescent salad transfer-printed in blue underglaze on bone china. It has a flow blue effect. The piece measures 5-by-9.5-inches and has a dagger border. *Courtesy IWC Convention 1995.* $75-110.

Pottery: Brown-Westhead, Moore & Co.
Mark:

Comments Concerning Mark: It is difficult to read the printed mark: John Mortlock Pottery Galleries, Oxford St./ Orchard St., London. In addition there is an impressed mark: BROWN-WESTHEAD, MOORE & CO. and impressed registration mark with the date May 17, 1881.

May 17, 1881

Standard Willow central pattern 10-inch plate transfer-printed in blue underglaze on pale blue earthenware plate. The words at the top are Esperance En Dieu. (Trust in God). Other than the motto, the plate has an undecorated rim with wavy edge. *Courtesy Jeff Siptak.* $35-65.

Mutual Store Ltd.

Location: Melbourne, Australia
Pottery: attributed to Burgess & Leigh
Comments Regarding Attribution: This pattern is the Burleigh willow central pattern and border pattern. No other company is known to have produced the central and border pattern although Palissy Pottery Ltd.* used a form of the central pattern.
Mark:

c. 1926+

Burleigh Willow pattern pudding bowl transfer-printed in blue underglaze on earthenware. The bowl is 3.5-inches high and 5.75-inches across the top. *Courtesy Kathy and Hugh Sykes.* $45-75.

A. S. Newman & Son

Location: 101/2 Hatton Garden, London
Pottery: Kensington Pottery Ltd.

Pottery Gazette, July 1, 1926, p.1032. One-half page advertisement for retailer A. S. Newman & Son. The plate and covered vegetable are the same pattern as seen in the Kensington Pottery Ltd. ad and identified as their pattern no. 863A. I have not seen it.

O'Neill-James Company

Location: England
Pottery: Stanley Pottery Co.
Marks:

Mark 1 twentieth century   Mark 2 c. 1928-31

Standard Willow pattern plates transfer-printed in blue underglaze on earthenware. The 7-inch plate on the left has Mark 1, and the 8.25-inch plate has Mark 2. The maker for the 7-inch plate is unknown. *Author's Collection.* $8-12 each.

Pottery: attributed to Wedgwood & Co.
Comments Concerning Attribution: The two jugs pictured together are the exact same size and shape. I assume both blanks were made by Wedgwood & Co. The one on the left with Standard Willow pattern has Mark 1. The jug on the right with Two Temples II pattern has Wedgwood & Co. Mark 3 (GG4059).

The Standard Willow pattern jug on the left has Mark 1. The Two Temples II jug on the right is marked Wedgwood & Co. (GG4059). The jugs are the same size and shape. Perhaps both were made by Wedgwood & Co. *Author's Collection.* $35-45 each.

This 10-inch plate is number 6 in the series of Doulton Willow Story plates. It has the very rare blue roses border. *Courtesy IWC Convention 1999.* $200+.

Ovington Bros.

Location: Brooklyn, New York
Pottery: Doulton
Marks:

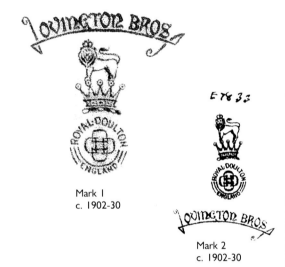

Mark 1
c. 1902-30

Mark 2
c. 1902-30

W. P. & G. Phillips

Location: Oxford St., New Bond St., London
Dates: c. 1858-97
Pottery: Minton
Mark:

(GG3006)
c. 1858-97

The center of this 10-inch plate is the 3rd in the series of 6 Doulton Willow Story plates. The daisy border is undocumented by Louise Irvine. The plate has pattern no.A22598. *Courtesy Loren Zeller.* $200+.

Demitasse cup and saucer decorated with Standard Willow pattern panel on brown ground and gold trim on bone china. It is not an especially appealing combination in my opinion. *Author's Collection.* $25-35.

Albert Pick & Co.

Location: Chicago, Illinois
Dates: c. 1915-27
Pottery: Cauldon Ltd.
Mark:

c. 1915-27 (Albert
Pick & Co.)

Standard Willow pattern 8.25-by-5.5-inch platter transfer-printed in blue underglaze on vitrified ware. This is a typical piece made for restaurant use. *Author's Collection.* $15-20.

Pottery: Wood & Sons
Mark:

c. 1915-27 (Albert
Pick & Co.)

Butter pats decorated with motifs from Standard Willow pattern. The butter pat on the right has the mark above. The one on the left has the standard Woods & Sons mark (GG4288). Note that the motif used is not the same on the two pieces. *Courtesy Dale S. Brouse.* $15-20 each.

Pitkin & Brooks

Location: Chicago, Illinois
Pottery: Hammersley & Co.
Mark:

c. 1912-39

Two Temples II pattern small cup and saucer transfer-printed in dark blue underglaze on bone china. The pattern (#6179) is very dense and crowded, but the shapes are interesting. Both pieces have a scalloped edge lined in gold. The saucer is 4.5-inches across with 1.5-inch recess for cup. The cup is 1.5-inches high and 3-inches across not measuring the ornate ring handle that extends up and out from the cup. *Author's Collection.* $25-40.

F. Primavesi & Son

Location: Cardiff & Swansea, Wales
Dates: c. 1860-1915
Marks:

Comments Concerning Marks: According to an article by Howard Mumford in FOB Bulletin 107, shards were found at Bovey Tracey* with Royal Arms marks with F. Primavesi & Son (c. 1863-71). Shards with the garter style mark (Mark 2 above) were found in excavations at Longton. These were similar to others found on the site made by Lowe and Deakin & Son who may have been producing wares for Primavesi & Son during the same time period. An article in FOB Bulletin 113 by Graham Aylett mentioned purchasing a brown printed plate in Annecy, Haute Savoie, France. It is the Wild Rose pattern and bears Mark 1 above. It may be a coincidence; however, the brown willow platter shown below also has Mark 1. Perhaps this mark was used on brown printed wares. Mark 3 is the only mark found that bears the name of the potter (Adams) in addition to Primavesi's name. The Adams mark is also seen in the entry under William Adams & Sons*.

Mark 1 c. 1860-1915

Mark 2 c. 1860-1915

Brief History: Fidele Primavesi was born in Italy as was his son Fidele. By 1851, the family was located in Cardiff. From 1855 the family worked as General Merchants dealing with shipping in the Bristol Channel. China and earthenware were among the goods they handled. From 1863-71, they traded as F. Primavesi & Son. In 1871, when Fidele Junior's sons came into the business, the trading style changed to F. Primavesi & Sons. Various backstamps were used on wares produced for the firm. It is possible that each pottery had a specific mark used even though the name of the pottery was not always included in the mark.

Mark 3
c. 1891-1915

Mark 4
c. 1860-1915

Standard Willow pattern 8.5-inch saucer transfer-printed in red underglaze on earthenware. It is interesting that these examples of willow pattern with Primavesi marks are in colors other than blue. Mark 3 includes the name of the pottery, William Adams & Sons*. *Courtesy Anna Morrison.* $5-12.

Standard Willow pattern platter transfer-printed in brown underglaze on earthenware. The platter measures 14.25-by-17.75-inches. It is unusual to find such a big nineteenth century platter in brown. Maker is unknown. Mark 1. *Author's Collection.* $150-200.

Standard Willow pattern sauce tureen with ladle transfer-printed in green underglaze on earthenware. Green is an uncommon color for the willow pattern, especially in this time period. Shards in the Longton area were found with this Mark 2. *Courtesy IWC Convention 1999.* $200+.

Standard Willow pattern 9 1/8-inch plate transfer-printed in blue underglaze on earthenware. The attribution of Mark 4 on this plate to F. Primavesi is due partly to a process of elimination. There are no known Staffordshire potters using the initials F. P. & S. Even though Primavesi & Son(s) was a retailer in Wales, it is known that the firm sold wares made in Staffordshire. This mark may be specific to one pottery. The plate has a concave rim and uneven edge. The single foot ring is 1/4-inch wide and low. Three-point stilt marks on the front of the well with single stilt marks on the back. The maker is unknown. *Author's Collection.* $25-35.

Regalcy

Pottery: Minton
Mark:

(GG2716)
c. 1912-50

Chinese Willow pattern covered tureen and 6-by-8.75-inch tray. The pattern is transfer-printed in black underglaze and clobbered in shades of red, green, yellow, and cobalt. It has gold trim. It is pattern #1242. Other tableware in this pattern has been found with the Rich & Fisher mark. *Courtesy Paul Kirves and Zeke Jimenez.* $150+.

Standard Willow pattern 4.75-inch dish transfer-printed in blue underglaze on earthenware. This seems to be an advertising piece, possibly for Star Beer, but I don't understand the significance of all of the words. *Courtesy IWC Convention 2002.* $35-55.

Ringtons Ltd.

Location: Newcastle upon Tyne
Pottery: James Broadhurst
Mark:

c. 1980-84

Rich & Fisher

Location: 467 Fifth Ave., New York
Pottery: John Aynsley & Sons
Mark:

(GG193) c. 1891+

Standard Willow pattern 7.75-inch soup bowl transfer-printed in blue underglaze on earthenware. This pattern and shape match the pieces shown in *Tableware International*, 1982. *Author's Collection.* $8-10.

Pottery: Hammersley & Co.
Mark:

c. 1974-82

Pottery: Palissy Pottery Ltd.
Mark:

c. 1976-82

Two Temples II pattern teapot transfer-printed in blue underglaze on earthenware. The teapot is rectangular in shape and holds about 4 cups. Mark 1 includes a picture of the headquarters building for the Ringtons Tea Co., Algernon Road, and it gives the name of the maker: "Maling Ware". *Courtesy Harry and Jessie Hall.* $75-150.

These two pieces are decorated with the same blue lithographic decal based on the Standard Willow pattern. The marks are very similar. The china mug is marked with Hammersley China and Royal Worcester Co. The little earthenware egg bucket has a Palissy mark with Royal Worcester Spode. Royal Worcester and Spode merged in 1976, so the mug may have been made shortly before the egg bucket. *Author's Collection.* $8-12 each.

Two Temples II pattern tea canisters transfer-printed in blue underglaze on earthenware. These are the two different shapes made. The one on the right is broader at the base and tapers upward. It has a lid that covers the top. The one on the left has a smaller base and widens toward the top. It has a small round lid. Both are 8-inches high. Mark 2 on the base and Mark 3 inside the lid. *Author's Collection.* $125-175 each.

Pottery: C. T. Maling & Sons
Marks:

Mark 1 c. late 1920s   Mark 2 c. late 1920s   Mark 3 c. late 1920s

Mark 4 c. 1828-29

Two Temples II pattern square teapot with handle and spout on opposite corners. The shape is similar to the tea canister on the right seen above. This teapot and square canister have been copied by the Japanese for at least 30 years. The copies don't have the slight flow blue effect or Mark 3 inside the lid of the canisters. This original teapot by Maling is rarely found. It has Mark 4 that includes the Reg. No. 740056 for 1928 the year Maling began producing ceramic wares for Ringtons. *Courtesy Joette Hightower.* $150-225.

Pottery: G. M. & C. J. Mason

Marks:

Mark 1 c. Twentieth century

Mark 2 c. 1982

Pottery: Wade Ceramics

Marks:

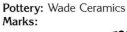

Mark 1 c. 1996

Mark 2 c. 1996

John Turner Willow pattern tea canister transfer-printed in blue underglaze on earthenware and named WILLOW in Mark 1. The lid is oversized and fits down over the top of the jar. *Author's Collection.* $25-40.

Three reproductions of Maling pieces using Two Temples II pattern transfer-printed in blue underglaze. All pieces are smaller than the originals. The rectangular teapot in front with Mark 1 is 4-inches high and holds just 2 cups. The square teapot in the back is dated 1997 and stands 6-inches high to the top of the finial. The covered jug with Mark 2 is an item not made by Maling. Beginning in 1994, each year in the 1990s a few other shapes were produced using the same pattern. *Author's Collection.* $40-60 each.

Rowland & Marsellus Co.

Location: New York
Dates: c. 1893-1920s
Client: A. S. Burbank, Plymouth, Mass.
Mark:

c. 1893-1920s

John Turner Willow pattern teapot with a new curlicue border. The teapot is dated 1982. Mark 2 also uses the name "WILLOW". *Courtesy Paul Kirves and Zeke Jimenez.* $25-50.

Standard Willow Pattern cup and saucer transfer-printed in light blue underglaze on bone china. The inside edge of the cup has the words "WELL TAK' A CVP O' KINDNESS YET FOR DAYS - O' AVLD LANG SYNE." Inside the cup at the bottom is a picture of Plymouth Rock, Massachusetts. Maker is unknown. *Courtesy Paul Kirves and Zeke Jimenez.* $25-30.

Sandbach & Co.

Location: King St., Manchester
Pottery: Davenport
Comment Concerning Attribution to Davenport: The pattern #3588 appears on the pieces with this retailer's mark as well as the teapots seen in the entry under Davenport. The pieces are also related by shape, style and decoration.
Mark:

c. 1870-86

J. J. Royle

Location: Manchester
Pottery: Doulton
Mark:

c. 1882+

Two Temples II pattern teapot, covered sugar and creamer, and cup and saucer transfer-printed in dark blue underglaze on bone china. The pieces have lavish gilding. The teapot is 5.75-inches high. The pattern number is 3588, the same as found on the two teapots shown in the Davenport entry above. *Courtesy Loren Zeller.* $350+.

Shorter Brothers

Location: Crispin Street, London

Standard Willow pattern pump teapot transfer-printed in light blue underglaze on earthenware. The pot has a chamber on the inside at the base with perforated holes for the tea. The metal lid is pumped which forces the hot water through the tea leaves and out through the spout. Doulton also made these pump teapots in dark blue willow pattern. *Courtesy Paul Kirves and Zeke Jimenez.* $300+.

Pottery Gazette, January 1, 1923, p. 48, carried an advertisement for Shorter Brothers, Wholesale and Export, London. Among the items in the inventory shown is a Worcester Shape "Willow" cup and saucer available in China and Semi-porcelain. The pottery that made the set is not mentioned. The same advertisement was seen in issues in 1922 as well.

A. Sneddon & Sons Ltd.

Location: Union Street, Glasgow
Mark:

c. 1897

Standard Willow pattern cup and saucer transfer-printed in blue underglaze on bone china. A gold line decorates both sides of the outer border on both pieces. From the mark, it appears the cup and saucer were made in England and sold through A. Sneddon & Sons Ltd., a large wholesale business in Glasgow. *Author's Collection.* $15-25.

Canton pattern 9-inch plate transfer-printed in blue underglaze on earthenware and clobbered in yellow, blue, and green. A few of these pieces have been found that have the retailer's mark. *Courtesy IWC Convention 1995.* $30-40.

H. G. Stephenson Ltd.,

Location: Manchester
Pottery: Worcester Royal Porcelain Co. Ltd.
Mark:

c. 1926

Soane & Smith Ltd.

Location: 462 Oxford St., London
Pottery: Wood & Sons
Mark:

(GG4288) c. 1917+

Worcester Willow pattern Athens Shape teapot transfer-printed in blue underglaze on earthenware called Crown Ware. Pattern number D/33 is on the teapot in addition to the retailer's mark. *Courtesy Charles and Zeta Hollingsworth.* $125-200.

Mark of Unknown Pottery:

c. 1909+

Comment Concerning Mark: "Barton Arcade" on the mark may be a location.

Standard Willow pattern teapot transfer-printed in blue underglaze on earthenware. These two teapots made for H. G. Stephenson appear to be at the low end of the price range. There is no decoration on the handle or finials of either one, and this teapot also has a plain spout. Incidentally, the bird on the left appears to be flying upside down. *Courtesy IWC Convention 1993.* $45-65.

L. Straus & Sons

Location: New York
Pottery: Dunn Bennett & Co.
Mark:

c. 1909+

Comments Concerning Mark: Dunn Bennett & Co. produced a vitrified clay body in 1909, that was virtually unchippable – hence the claim on the mark. The word PATENT is also impressed in the bottom of the piece.

Nathan Straus

Client: Los Angeles Athletic Club, Los Angeles, California
Mark:

c. 1926+

Comments Concerning Mark: The *Pottery Gazette*, September 1, 1926, p. 1405, has an illustration of the mark with these words: "New Trade mark: 468,847. Vitrified china and porcelain Class 16."

Standard Willow pattern 8-inch plate transfer-printed in blue underglaze on vitrified ware. *Courtesy IWC Convention 1997.* $8-12.

Thomas & Evans
Celebrated Tevna Tea

Mark:

Twentieth century

Standard Willow pattern 8.5-inch soup plate transfer-printed in dark blue underglaze on vitreous ware. In spite of the registered patent and claim on the mark, the piece has a chip on the underside. That is why I bought it! *Author's Collection.* $6-10.

Two Temples II pattern tea canister transfer-printed in blue underglaze on earthenware. The lid is missing from this rare tea canister. It is 6.75-inches high and 3.25-inches across. *Courtesy Bill and Joyce Keenan.* $75-150.

Tiffany & Co.

Location: New York
Pottery: Booths Ltd.
Mark:

(GG453) c. 1906+

Booths Real Old Willow pattern octagonal 3.5-inch jug transfer-printed in blue underglaze on Silicon China. The top edge and handle are decorated in gold. This is the same Mason's shape jug as seen in the entry under Booths Ltd. that had a polychrome decal pattern. *Courtesy Ohio Willow Society.* $75-125.

Pottery: W. T. Copeland & Sons
Mark:

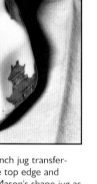

(RC241)
c. 1891-1920

Standard Willow pattern coffee pot transfer-printed in light blue underglaze on bone china. The pot is 10.25-inches high and 9.25-inches from handle to spout. It has the words around the shoulder: "WE'LL TAK' A CVP O' KINDNESS YET FOR DAYS – O' AVLD LANG SYNE". The coffee pot is lavishly trimmed in gold. *Courtesy Loren Zeller.* $250+.

Standard Willow pattern tea set on a tray transfer-printed in light blue underglaze on bone china. These pieces all have the same saying as the coffee pot seen above and are trimmed in gold. The teapot with gold foo dog finial is the Crichton shape with matching covered sugar and creamer. Pattern number 8669. *Courtesy IWC Convention 1995.* $500+.

Pottery: Crown Staffordshire Porcelain Co., Ltd.
Mark:

(GG1149) c. 1906+

Three Chinese Willow teapots decorated in the most common color combination. The globular shaped teapots are 6- and 4-cups. The small one is from a child's set. *Courtesy Michael Curtner.* $150-200, $100-150, and $75-125.

Three Chinese Willow pots decorated in pattern number 5356, as in the previous photo. The pots are for hot chocolate, hot water or what have you. The middle one is a most unique shape with a side handle. *Courtesy Michael Curtner.* $100-150 each.

R. Twining & Co., Ltd.

Location: London
Pottery: Burgess & Leigh
Mark:

"Willow"
Made especially for
R. Twining & Co Ltd
by
Burgess & Leigh Limited
Staffordshire England

Twentieth century

Comments Concerning Mark: The pottery doesn't always mark these tea canisters. The retailer (in this case Twinings) may prefer to put on a paper label. Fortnam and Mason, London, commissioned a run of tea canisters from Burgess, Dorling & Leigh for the Christmas season 2002. These were decorated with the Burleigh Willow pattern and were unmarked.

John Turner willow pattern covered tea canisters transfer-printed in blue underglaze on earthenware. It is only on this covered ginger jar shape that Burgess & Leigh used the John Turner willow pattern. The jar on the left has the underglaze mark shown for Twinings. The jar on the right has only a gold Twinings paper label and is still wrapped and full of tea. It was purchased at Williams Sonoma, c. 1995. *Courtesy Nancee Rogers.* $25-50. each.

Pottery: G. M. & C. J. Mason
Mark:

MASON'S
PATENT IRONSTONE
CHINA
ENGLAND
MADE FOR
TWININGS LTD
ENGLAND

Twentieth century

Two different shapes of covered tea canisters with John Turner willow pattern in green. The tea canister on the left has the Twinings mark shown above. The hexagonal shaped one is marked only with the Masons mark. *Author's Collection.* $35-55 each.

Pottery: Pountney & Co. Bristol Pottery
Mark:

Mark 1 c. 1965-69

Bristol Pottery Est. 1652
Made in England
R·TWINING & Co LTD
of
LONDON

Pottery: Pountney & Co. Royal Cauldon
Mark:

Mark 2 c. 1963-69

HENRY W·KING & CO·LTD • R·TWINING & CO·LTD·LONDON
K
MADE BY
ROYAL CAULDON
ENGLAND
FOR

Comments Concerning Pountney & Co. Marks: Royal Cauldon was acquired by the Bristol Pottery in 1962, and wares with Royal Cauldon mark were produced in Bristol until 1969. The Bristol Pottery mark was used 1965-69. Therefore the green ginger jar shown was made at the Bristol Pottery for R. Twining & Co. and issued with two different back stamps during the 1960s.

Simplified Standard Willow pattern covered tea canister decorated in a green decal. This is the only example I have seen of green Standard Willow pattern on this shape. Twinings evidently liked the ginger jar shape for storing tea. This tea canister was produced at the Bristol Pottery of Pountney & Co. after it acquired Cauldon Ltd.* late in 1962 and has been found with either Mark 1 or Mark 2. Henry W. King & Co. Ltd. may be a Canadian retailer for Twinings as this tea canister was purchased in Canada. *Courtesy Geraldine Ewaniuk.* The canister with Mark 1 was seen at the IWC Convention in 2002. A blue ginger jar was also made with the John Turner willow pattern marked: Royal Cauldon Bristol Ironstone, a mark used at the Cornwall factory, 1967-72. $45-75 each.

J. W. Co.

Possible Attributions: J. Waldonia Co., Canada or Jay Wilfred Co., New York. The J. Waldonia Co. bought the Pekin rights for Canada and introduced the pattern to Canada in 1951-52. More research is needed.
Pottery: Grimwades Ltd.
Mark:

c. 1951+

Pottery: Worcester Royal Porcelain Co. Ltd.
Mark:

(GG4354) c. 1906

Two tier server in Pekin polychrome pattern on hand-painted crimson background. This is a color that is hard to find. The bottom plate is 8-inches square, and the top one is 6-inches square. *Courtesy IWC Convention 1995.* $150+.

Worcester Willow pattern 8-inch plate transfer-printed in light gray-blue underglaze on bone china. This is an unusual shade of blue. *Author's Collection.* $15-25.

A. T. Wiley & Co.

Location: Montreal
Mark:

c. 1907+

Standard Willow pattern cup and saucer transfer-printed in dark blue underglaze on bone china with gold trim. The coffee can shape cup has a ring handle. Maker is unknown. *Courtesy Geraldine Ewaniuk.* $20-25.

Wilhelm & Graef

Location: New York
Pottery: Worcester Royal Porcelain Co. Ltd.
Mark:

(GG4350) c. 1883

Worcester Willow pattern 6.5-inch bowl transfer-printed in mulberry underglaze on bone china. It has been well used. The mark includes pattern #W/1085. *Courtesy IWC Convention 1999.* $10-15.

Wington Brothers

Pottery: Hammersley & Co.
Mark:

(GG1906)
c. 1912-39

Comment Concerning Mark: The mark is found on the base and inside the lid of the teapot shown with sugar and creamer in the entry under Hammersley & Co.

A. Yeates & Sons Ltd.

Pottery: Myott, Son & Co. Ltd.
Mark:

c. 1936+

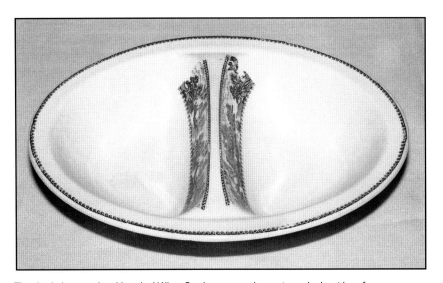

This divided serving bowl has the Willow Border pattern decorating only the sides of the divider. The rim has a simple blue line. *Courtesy IWC Convention 2001.* $10-18.

III. UNATTRIBUTED MARKS

PART 1: Initials and Words

B STAFFORDSHIRE STONE CHINA

Mark:

Comment Concerning Attribution: It is generally impossible to attribute a piece with just one initial in the mark.

Standard Willow pattern 8.25-inch plate transfer-printed in purple underglaze on stone china. The plate has a 12 panel rim and single flat foot ring. Three-point stilt marks on the back of the well and single stilt marks on the front. It has a pale blue glaze. The front gables of the building next to the teahouse are dark – a feature found primarily in Minton* Willow pattern. *Author's Collection.* $25-35.

B & B STONE WARE

Mark:

Comments Concerning Mark: B & B also appears on a Royal Arms Mark; however, it also cannot be attributed.

Partnerships Using B & B in the Third Quarter of the Nineteenth Century (from Geoffrey Godden):

1853-54 Beech & Brock
1854-58 Birks & Blood
1855 Bevington & Bourne
1855 Birks & Birks
1867-68 Bailey & Bevington
1868 Bevington & Bradley
1868-95 Bates & Bennett
1872-95 Brough & Blackhurst
1875-79 Bradshaw & Binns
1879 Beck & Blair
1880-92 Blackhurst & Bourne

Comments Concerning Attribution: The form of the Stoneware scroll mark was used by many different factories as already noted in this book. Except for Podmore, Walker & Co. and Wedgwood & Co., those partnerships were all in business primarily in the 3rd quarter of the nineteenth century. Here is a sampling:

Blackhurst & Tunnicliffe c. 1879
W. E. Emberton c. 1851-69
Eardley & Hammersley c. 1862-66
Ford & Challinor c. 1865-80
R. Hammersley c. 1860-83
Marple Turner & Co c. 1851-53

The potting characteristics of the plate relate to this period; therefore I eliminated the partnerships using B & B that began before 1850 as well as those that began after 1880, or there would easily have been twice as many to consider. Even so we can see that to attribute the B & B Stoneware mark to a specific partnership on the basis of initials alone cannot be done in this case.

Standard Willow pattern 8.75-inch plate transfer-printed in blue underglaze on stoneware. It has a slightly concave rim and single flat foot ring. There are single stilt marks in the well on the front among many imperfections and skips in the glaze. There are even more little bumps on the underside. The printing is good and clear. *Author's Collection.* $20-25.

B & H WARRANTED STAFFORDSHIRE

Mark:

Partnerships Using B & H:

1879-99 Bednall & Heath
1855-76 Beech & Hancock
1890-1932 Blackhurst & Hulme
1863-65 Bodley & Harrold.

Comments Concerning Attribution: Four possible partnerships in time frames that are feasible leaves this mark without attribution.

Standard Willow pattern plate transfer-printed in blue underglaze on heavy earthenware. The plate is round with a very white background. The outer border is pieced at 7 o'clock. *Author's Collection.* $25-35.

B. F. K.

Mark:

Comment Concerning Attribution: I find no partnerships with these initials. It is possible the piece is not English.

Standard Willow pattern saucer transfer-printed in blue underglaze on earthenware. The borders have been enlarged. The central pattern looks English, but the outer border is much like borders on Japanese willow pattern. The clay body also seems to be English, but perhaps it is not. *Author's Collection.* $3-5.

(ROYAL) BASSETT

Marks:

Comments Concerning Attribution: "Porcelon" may be the name used for earthenware. W. R. Midwinter used the term "Porcelon" in their mark for YANG pattern seen in the entry under Midwinter. The word "Royal" may pertain to Bassett or it could be the name for the vitrified ware: "Royal Hotel Ware". Perhaps Bassett is the name of a retailer or importer. The maker of these wares is unknown.

Mark I

Mark 2

Standard Willow pattern demitasse cup and saucer transfer-printed in dark blue underglaze on lightweight earthenware. There is no inner border on the 4.75-inch saucer. The outer border decorates the inside of the 2.5-inch cup. This set bears Mark I. The extra cup is vitrified ware. It has the border on the outside and inside of the 2.25-inch cup. It has Mark 2. *Author's Collection.* $10-15 and $6-8.

BEST ENGLISH MAKE

Mark:

Comment Concerning Attribution: Such a claim should include ownership; however, this small orange mark sits alone in the center of the back of the plate.

Standard Willow pattern 9-inch plate transfer-printed in light blue underglaze on bone china of average quality. There is a large white area between borders. It has a single foot ring. *Author's Collection.* $8-15.

D. & S. STONE CHINA STAFFORDSHIRE

Mark: No photo available.

Partnerships Using D. & S.:

c. 1833-62 Deakin & Son, Lane End
c. 1867-8 Dean & Stokes, Burslem
c. 1842-59 Dimmock & Smith, Hanley.

BROSELEY ENGLAND

Mark:

Comment Concerning Attribution: A mark with the name of the pattern and the name of the country in which it was made doesn't give us enough information to name the maker.

E. F. & Co.

Mark:

Comments Concerning Mark: The only company I can identify with these initials is Elsmore & Forster, Tunstall c. 1855-71. The style normally used in marks was E. & F. or the name in full. The company made stoneware and exported much of it to the USA – both transfer-printed and white ironstone. This is a possible attribution.

Two Temples II pattern 9.25 coupe shape plate transfer-printed in dark flow blue underglaze on earthenware. From the single foot ring outward the shape is swirled with a scalloped edge. With a chip and hairline, it was purchased for curiosity only. *Author's Collection.* $15-25 if mint.

Standard Willow pattern large platter transfer-printed in blue underglaze on earthenware. A good quality mid-nineteenth century platter with well balanced border patterns. *Courtesy Windwood Antiques.* $125-175.

E. H. & Co.

Mark:

Potters With the Initials E. H: These potters did not necessarily use & Co. in the mark. There are three potters with initials E. H.:

- c. 1851-54 E. Hallem, Burslem
- c. 1867-72 Elijah Hodgkinson, Hanley
- c. 1853-67 Elijah Hughes, Cobridge

According to one reference Elijah Hughes may have sometimes used E. H. & Co. This is a possible attribution.

Standard Willow pattern 5-inch plate transfer-printed in blue underglaze on thin earthenware. This plate has an impressed H that is 1/8-inch high. *Courtesy Harry and Jessie Hall.* $25-35.

Standard Willow pattern covered square serving dish transfer-printed in blue underglaze on earthenware. The dish has the full pattern inside the dish and strips of the pattern on each of the four sides. It has a lion finial on top of the domed lid. *Author's Collection.* $125-165.

Standard Willow pattern pickle dish transfer-printed in blue underglaze on heavy earthenware. It measures 5.25-by-6.25-inches and has a round foot ring that is 2.75-inches across. I call this a flounder shape dish that has a handle much like a tail with molded lines. The central pattern is pretty much complete except that there are just two figures on the bridge. *Author's Collection.* $55-85.

H impressed

Comments Concerning Mark: The impressed mark is 3/8 inch high. There is a strong possibility that the mark was used by one or more of the Hackwood potteries. Even the full name Hackwood doesn't necessarily define the specific potter. The consensus at this point; however, is that if it is a Hackwood mark, it was probably used by William Hackwood. Another possibility to consider: Pre-Dillwyn marks at the Cambrian Pottery include impressed H for George Haynes.

Some Possible Hackwood Attributions:

- c. 1827-43 William Hackwood, Eastwood, Hanley
- c. 1842-43 Josiah Hackwood, Upper High St., Hanley
- c. 1844-50 William & Thomas Hackwood, New Hall, Shelton
- c. 1850-55 Thomas Hackwood.

H STAFFORDSHIRE STONE CHINA

Mark:

Some Possible Attributions: In addition to any of the Hackwoods mentioned above, some single printed H marks have been attributed to Charles and William Kenwright Harvey & Sons, Longton, c. 1835-53. No photo available.

H & Co. WARRANTED

Mark:

Some Possible Attributions:

- c. 1807-27 Hackwood & Co.
- c. 1841-43 Hopkins & Co., Burslem
- c. 1845-48 Hallam & Co., Longton
- c. 1876-78 & 1889-93 Hobson & Co., Longton
- c. 1864 Hett & Co., Hanley
- c. 1865 Hampson & Co., Longton
- c. 1870-71 Holdcroft & Co., Burslem.

Standard Willow pattern 8.25-inch plate transfer-printed in blue underglaze on earthenware. There are 8 slight indentations on the edge of the concave rim. Three-point stilt marks on the back of the well with single stilt marks on the front. The single foot ring is low and flat. Because the outer border was too small, two extra sets of 3- and 4-spoke wheels were added at 10 o'clock. *Author's Collection.* $20-25.

I Impressed

Comment Concerning Mark: I don't know if this impressed mark is intended to be an initial or a number. In either case, the maker is unknown. It is an early nineteenth century plate, c. 1810.

Standard Willow pattern 9 5/8-inch plate transfer-printed in blue underglaze on lightweight earthenware. This plate has 8 indentations on the edge of a concave rim. The base is flat. The mark is a letter "I" impressed (or possibly number 1). *Courtesy Dennis Crosby.* $25-35.

IMPERIAL BONE CHINA ENGLAND

Mark:

Comments Concerning Attribution: Longton China Supplies Ltd., St. Louis Works, Edensor Road, Longton used the trade name IMPERIAL FINE BONE CHINA during the 1960s and 1970s. Perhaps the firm used this mark as well.

Standard Willow pattern tea set transfer-printed in dark blue underglaze on bone china. The pattern is in linear form, and all three pieces are trimmed in gold. *Courtesy Paul Kirves and Zeke Jimenez.* $75-150.

J. STAFFORDSHIRE STONE WARE

Mark:

Comment Concerning Attribution: It is not possible to attribute this platter to any specific firm with just the initial J.

Standard Willow pattern platter transfer-printed in blue underglaze on stoneware. The platter measures 12.25-by-15.75-inches and has a lightly combed back. *Author's Collection.* $100-155.

Jones & Middleton Ltd.

Mark:

Comments Concerning Attribution:
Jones & Middleton Ltd. is not a manufacturer. It is not known from what company the date of 1824 and claim "The Original Staffordshire Copperplate Etching" belong. Perhaps Jones & Middleton Ltd. is a distributor of some kind.

M & Co. STAFFORDSHIRE

Mark:

Some Possible Attributions:

Minton, Stoke c. 1841-73
Moore & Co., Hanley c. 1898-1903
Moore & Co., Fenton c. 1872-92
Meakin & Co., Hanley c. 1867-76

Standard Willow central pattern 7.75-inch plate with no outer border blue printed on earthenware. The plate appears to be of recent manufacture. *Author's Collection.* $8-10.

Standard Willow pattern 10 3/8-inch plate transfer-printed in blue underglaze on earthenware. There are 8 indentations on the edge of the flat rim with 3-point stilt marks on the back and single stilt marks on the top. The plate has a recessed foot ring and a pale blue glaze. *Author's Collection.* $30-40.

LINAN

Impressed Mark:

Comment Concerning Attribution: Linan may be the name of a pottery; however, it is unknown to me.

M over S

Mark:

Comment Concerning Mark: It is impossible to tell if the mark is M over S or S over M because the letters are on top of each other. The pottery is unknown.

Standard Willow pattern 9.75-inch soup plate transfer-printed in blue underglaze on earthenware. It has a recessed foot ring and 3-point stilt marks. The unknown mark is impressed. *Courtesy Renard Broughton.* $35-45.

Standard Willow pattern 9-inch plate transfer-printed in blue underglaze on earthenware. The plate has a low recessed foot ring. The printing is rather blotchy, and a bit of the roof is missing from the first story of the two-story building next to the teahouse. *Author's Collection.* $15-20.

N. S. STAFFORDSHIRE STONE CHINA

Mark:

Comment Concerning Mark: The first letter is definitely an N. The second could be a letter S. It is also possible that the first letter is N. and the second is 8, so that the mark says No. 8.

Standard Willow pattern 8.25-by-10.25-inch platter transfer-printed in blue underglaze on stone china. This little platter is discolored and actually burnt on the back from sitting too long on a hot stove. Three-point stilt marks on the back of the base with single stilt marks on the top. It has a concave rim and uneven edge. *Author's Collection.* $35-65.

OPAQUE CHINA WARRANTED

Mark:

Comments Concerning Mark: In *Encyclopedia of Marks* by the Kowalskys there are at least thirty-four potters who used the term Opaque China. Jacob Marsh is also known to have used the words Opaque China Warranted in connection with a Royal Arms mark; however, this mark remains unattributed.

Standard Willow pattern plate transfer-printed in blue underglaze on earthenware. There are 8 indentations on the edge of the concave rim. The outer border had to be extended with an extra piece of the geometric motif at 6 o'clock *Courtesy Frank Davenport.* $25-35.

PATENT IRONSTONE CHINA

Mark:

Comments Concerning Mark: Kowalskys list twelve firms using these words. The mark is similar to GG140 and may pertain to G. L. Ashworth.

Standard Willow pattern 8.5-inch rimmed soup plate transfer-printed in blue underglaze on ironstone. There are 12 sides to the faceted rim. *Courtesy Jeff Siptak.* $35-45.

R IRONSTONE CHINA

Mark:

Comment Concerning Mark: This mark has been found on two different Standard Willow pattern engravings.

Standard Willow pattern 10.5-inch plate transfer-printed in blue underglaze on ironstone. Under the last fence post on the right there is a tiny letter E pointing downward. The borders are well lined up on this plate. *Courtesy Dennis Crosby.* $35-45.

Standard Willow pattern 10.25-inch plate transfer-printed in blue underglaze on ironstone. A single flat foot ring and 3-point stilt marks on the back of the base. Single stilt marks on the front. There are many points at which this engraving is like the one in the previous photo including the path with narrow scalloped edges; however, the most notable difference is the willow tree itself. The tree on this plate looks as if it had lost its leaves. *Author's Collection.* $35-45.

ROYAL GRANITE

Impressed Mark:

Standard Willow pattern 10-inch plate transfer-printed in blue underglaze on thin heavy earthenware. The plate has a shiny pale blue glaze. There is a single foot ring and 3-point stilt marks on the back of the rim with single stilt marks on the top. While the border patterns are a little crowded, the printing is nice and clear. *Author's Collection.* $30-40.

SEMI CHINA in rectangle

Mark:

Reversed Two Temples II pattern frog mug transfer-printed in blue underglaze in earthenware with a green spotted frog attached to the inside. It looks like the frog is climbing out. The mug stands 3.5-inches high and 3-inches across. *Author's Collection.* $250+.

SEMI CHINA in ribbon with leaves

Mark:

Two Temples II covered bullion cup transfer-printed in blue underglaze on earthenware. The border pattern decorates the inside of the cup. It stands 2.5-inches high and is 4.5-inches across. The pieces have a pale blue glaze. The cup has been repaired with several staples. *Author's Collection.* $45-65 if mint.

SEMI CHINA in an oval rope

Mark:

Comments Concerning Mark: I sent this mark to Geoffrey Godden, and he replied March 21, 2002: " 'Semi China' mark – this is a standard device or wording used by many firms or independent engraving firms supplying sets of copper plates to the smaller potteries." The following double square Semi China marks have also been used by many firms – some of whom added initials or other symbols to identify the pottery; however, most did not.

Standard Willow pattern 10-inch plate transfer-printed in blue underglaze on earthenware. The border patterns are pretty well matched up on this plate. *Courtesy Dennis Crosby.* $35-45.

Semi China in Double Square

Marks:

Mark 1 Semi China

Two Temples II pattern 5 5/8-inch plate transfer-printed in pale blue underglaze on earthenware. The plate has a recessed foot ring and single stilt marks on the back of the base of the plate. It has a wavy edge. Mark 1 is so faint that if there are identifying symbols, they cannot be seen. *Author's Collection.* $10-15.

Mark 2 Semi China

Two Temples II pattern handle less cup and saucer transfer-printed in mulberry underglaze on earthenware. Mark 2. *Courtesy Joette Hightower.* $ 45-70.

 Mark 3 Semi China

Two Temples II pattern cup and saucer transfer-printed in red underglaze on earthenware. This is a standard size cup and saucer. Mark 5. *Author's Collection.* $25-35.

Two Temples II pattern cup and saucer transfer-printed in red underglaze on earthenware. This is a large set for breakfast. The saucer is 8-inches across and the cup is 4-inches. The cup is 3.75-inches high. Mark 3. *Courtesy IWC Convention 1995.* $45-60.

Mark 4 Semi China

Mark 6 Semi China

Two Temples II pattern child's tea set transfer-printed in blue underglaze on earthenware. A quarter was placed near the creamer to indicate the small size of the pieces. Mark 4 was taken off one of the cups in the set. It has a printed 8 in addition to the Semi China mark. *Courtesy Harry and Jessie Hall.* $200+ teapot, creamer, and sugar.

Mark 5 Semi China

Two Temples II coffee or teapot transfer-printed in dark blue underglaze on earthenware. Collectors often consider this large shape pot was intended for coffee, but it is probably a teapot. Mark 6. *Courtesy Joette Hightower.* $125-175.

Standard Willow pattern pancake plate with dome lid transfer-printed in blue underglaze on earthenware. The plate measures 10-inches. Mark 6. *Courtesy IWC Convention 1995.* $135-185.

STAFFORDSHIRE STONE CHINA

Mark:

Comments Concerning Mark: This is a standard mark that usually has the initials or names of the partners above the crown. It can be seen in entries above for Benjamin Floyd, Godwin, Rowley & Co., John Hulme, and Wathen & Hebb. In this case there are no initials or names to help with attribution.

Standard Willow pattern 9-inch plate transfer-printed in blue underglaze on stoneware. The plate has a single foot ring and 3-point stilt marks on the back of the base. There are 8 slight indentations on the edge of the concave rim. *Courtesy Dennis Crosby.* $35-45.

STONE CHINA

Mark:

Reversed Two Temples II pattern frog mug transfer-printed in blue underglaze on stoneware. The mug stands 5.25-inches high and is 5-inches across. It has a little yellow frog covered with many tiny black spots attached to the inside of the mug. *Courtesy IWC Convention 1999.* $300+.

Stone China

Mark:

Two Temples II large coffee or teapot transfer-printed in blue underglaze on stoneware. The pot is oval in shape and has an interesting handle. It has a pale blue glaze. *Courtesy IWC Convention 1995.* $350+.

STONE WARE

Standard Willow pattern platter transfer-printed in blue underglaze on stoneware. The platter measures 12.5-by-16-inches. The platter has indentations at the edge of the rim adding interest to the shape. *Author's Collection.* $125-175.

TUCKER'S PATENT

Comments Concerning the Mark: The words above are impressed in the base of the teapot. There is no other mark.

Reversed Two Temples II pattern 6-cup teapot transfer-printed in blue underglaze on earthenware. The central pattern was used on the lid as well as the body of the teapot. There is no border on the piece. The lid and handle are trimmed in gold. It is impressed TUCKER'S PATENT. *Courtesy IWC Convention 1995.* $55-75.

Stone Ware

Mark:

Comments Concerning Mark: This mark is similar to GG3257; however, that mark has the initials J.R. for John Ridgway. Other potters such as James Reed in Yorkshire used similar marks; therefore, it cannot be attributed as is.

Standard Willow pattern platter transfer-printed in blue underglaze on stoneware. The platter is 13.5-inches wide and 17.25-inches long. The print is good and clear on this platter. *Author's Collection.* $125-175.

W. & Co. SEMI CHINA

Mark:

Comments Concerning the Mark: In *Godden's Guide to Ironstone,* p. 350, the observation is noted that there were at least twelve pre-1900 firms that used W & Co. marks. This mark was obviously made for use on willow pattern; however, it is not possible to make an attribution.

Standard Willow pattern platter transfer-printed in blue underglaze on earthenware. It measures 10 7/8-by-13 5/8-inches. Three-point stilt marks on the base with single stilt marks on top. There is a large impressed number 11, and a small blue triangle printed underglaze in addition to the willow mark. *Author's Collection.* $75-150.

WARRANTED with Staffordshire Knot

Mark:

Standard Willow pattern 8 7/8-inch plate transfer-printed in blue underglaze on lightweight earthenware. There are 8 slight indentations on the edge of the rim that has 3-point stilt marks on the underside and single stilt marks on the top. It has a recessed foot ring and pale blue glaze with smudges on the back. There is a chip at 6 o'clock that is underglaze that didn't get any pattern to cover it. The small chip next to it is more recent. *Author's Collection.* $15-20.

WARRANTED in ribbon with animal head

Mark:

Standard Willow pattern 10-inch plate transfer-printed in blue underglaze on earthenware. The mark looks like it could be a boars head. *Courtesy Jeff Siptak.* $20-30.

WARRANTED STAFFORDSHIRE in ribbons with leaves

Mark:

Standard Willow pattern small tray transfer-printed in blue underglaze on earthenware. It measures 5.5-by-7.75-inches and was probably a stand for a small sauce tureen. *Courtesy IWC Convention 1999.* $35-55.

WARRANTED STAFFORDSHIRE with lioness

Mark:

Standard Willow pattern large platter transfer-printed in blue underglaze on earthenware. The photo was taken under artificial light at Alphies Antique Market in London with permission of the owner. $100-150.

WARWICK WARE

Marks:

Comments Concerning Marks: In addition to the printed mark, there is an impressed mark also shown that looks like two initials: B & K or B & A. B & K were used before 1898 by Barkers & Kent; however, that firm was in Fenton. Firms with initials B & A are unknown in Stoke.

Mark 1
twentieth
century

Information Regarding Possible Attribution: Warwick China was used as an "own label" for W. H. Smith & Son, a chain of newsagents and booksellers in the UK who sold crested china and miniatures in the early twentieth century. It's possible that other small items such as the little willow tile was part of their stock. Warwick China was made by Arcadian China or Arkinstall & Son. The company was in business c. 1908-31 and led by Harold J. Robinson. He may have gotten china from other companies such as Barkers & Kent. His company was based in Stoke-on-Trent; therefore, if the Warwick Ware mark was used by his company it would naturally have Stoke on the mark.

Mark 2 twentieth
century

Standard Willow pattern 9.75-inch soup plate transfer-printed in blue underglaze on thin earthenware. This is definitely a twentieth century piece. The outer border was too small, and an extra motif surrounded by scrolling leaves was added at 5 o'clock. *Author's Collection.* $15-20.

Standard Willow pattern 4.5-inch round tile transfer-printed in blue underglaze on earthenware trimmed in gold. This small tile is useful as a teapot stand for a small teapot. Warwick Ware appears to be a trade-mark used by the company. Marks 1 and 2. *Author's Collection.* $20-35.

WHITE BLOCK

Mark:

Standard Willow pattern sauce dish transfer-printed in blue underglaze on earthenware. The printing is rather splotchy on the dish. *Author's Collection.* $5-8.

WATKINS WILLOW

Mark:

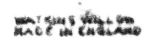

WILLOW

Mark:

Diamond in a box

Mark:

Standard Willow pattern 7.25-inch plate transfer-printed in green underglaze on earthenware. The plate has rust color clobbering and orange luster overglaze. The plate has quite a wide border (1.5-inches) in relation to the size of the central pattern of 2.75-inches diameter. In addition to the printed WILLOW mark, there is an impressed 7M. *Author's Collection.* $25-45.

Two Temples II pattern 7.75-inch plate transfer-printed in blue underglaze on porcelain. It has a single unglazed foot ring and a wavy edge. There are many imperfections in the clay body and glaze. The little line seen extending out from the tree opposite the willow tree looks and feels like a splinter of wood under the glaze. *Author's Collection.* $10-15.

Anchor with wreath and crown

Mark:

Standard Willow pattern 15-inch plate transfer-printed in brown underglaze on earthenware. The rim is 2-inches wide and is covered with the outer border. The well of the plate has the central pattern and two borders, probably using an engraving for a large dinner plate. *Courtesy IWC Convention 1999.* $65-100.

Eagle impressed

Mark:

Comments Concerning Mark: See Elkin Knight & Co.* for more information on the impressed eagle mark. It is a mark used with slight variations by different potteries. The printed mark was used by Goodwins & Harris. The

weight, color, glaze and over-all style of this plate is closely related to the platter with this printed mark and impressed GOODWINS & HARRIS. It is almost certain this plate was also made by that firm.

Standard Willow pattern 10-inch plate transfer-printed in blue underglaze on earthenware. There are 3 indentations on the edge of the concave rim. The plate has a recessed foot ring. The borders are well matched. *Author's Collection.* $30-40.

Royal Arms

Mark:

Comments Concerning Mark: It is rather difficult to see the details on this densely printed mark. The dating is after 1837 because the mark has a simple quartered shield. A large letter A is printed in blue underglaze elsewhere on the plate.

Standard Willow pattern 10.5-inch plate transfer-printed in blue underglaze on thick heavy earthenware. It has a pale blue glassy glaze giving a slightly blurred effect to the pattern. Two pieces of the border pattern were torn off. The plate has a wide, flat foot ring and 3-point stilt marks on the back of the rim with single stilt marks on the top. *Author's Collection.* $25-35.

Shell Ware

Mark:

Comments Concerning Mark: The words "Old English" do not appear on the tea set printed in light blue. Maker is unknown.

Standard Willow pattern tea set transfer-printed in dark blue underglaze on earthenware. The teapot is 4-inches high, and the creamer and open sugar are each 2.75-inches high. The saucers are 3.75-inches, and the plates are 4-inches across. *Courtesy Kathy and Hygh Sykes.* $150+.

Standard Willow pattern teapot, creamer, and open sugar transfer-printed in light blue underglaze on earthenware. The pieces are all trimmed in gold. The shape is different from the darker blue set, and the pieces are slightly larger. Many different variations of these sets were made including dinner sets. The light blue pieces do not have the words "Old English" on the mark. *Courtesy Joette Hightower.* $100+.

Staffordshire knot

Mark:

Comments Concerning Mark: A number of companies used the knot incorporated into their back stamp; however, there are usually initials to denote the name of the company. The mark generally has the word ENGLAND when it is used alone, dating it to after 1891.

Standard Willow pattern covered vegetable dish transfer-printed in blue underglaze on earthenware. The linear form of the pattern repeats three times on the lid. The bowl measures 9-inches in diameter, and it is 10-inches wide including the handles. *Courtesy IWC Convention.* $75-115.

Booths Willow pattern teapot transfer-printed in blue underglaze on earthenware. The pattern on this teapot looks like the Booth variant pieces made by Wood & Son*; however, it has a Staffordshire knot mark. *Courtesy Joette Hightower.* $65-100.

Tureen

Mark:

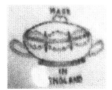

Comments Concerning Mark: This mark has been seen on open vegetable bowls in the Standard Willow pattern. No initials or name appear with the mark. No photo available.

Willow motif

Mark:

Comment Concerning Mark: This is a twentieth century mark found on a Standard Willow pattern plate. There is no maker's name on the piece, and I have been unable to find a similar mark with a name. *Courtesy Jeanne Smyers.* No photo available.

Key to Table
of Manufacturers and Patterns

Pattern
S – Standard
2T1 – Two Temples I
2T2 – Two Temples II
M – Mandarin
Bo – Booths
Bu – Burleigh
Tu – John Turner
W – Worcester
C – Canton
B – Border
Si – Simplified
V – Variant

Color
B – Blue
Bk – Black
Br – Brown
BD – Blue Decal
C – Clobbered
BC – Blue Clobbered
FB – Flow Blue
Gd – Gold
Gr – Green
Gy – Gray
GO – Gold Outlining
HP – Hand-painted
I – Ivory
L – Lavender
Ls – Luster
M – Mulberry
O – Orange (rust)
P – Purple
PC – Polychrome
PD – Polychrome Decal
Pl – Plum
R – Red (pink)
T – Turquoise
W – White
Y – Yellow

Variant
Bb – Bamboo
Ch – Chinese
CL – Chinese Legend
CW – Chinese Willow
D – Daisy
F – Figure
G – Gleneagle
HK – Hong Kong
L – Legend
M – Ming
Ma – Manchu
MS – Molded Shape
Pa – Pagoda
"RB" – "Red Bridge"
Re – Reversed
Sp – Spray
SW – Scale Willow
W&A – Willow & Aster
Y – Yang

In the table a comma (,) will separate entries in each column. Some symbols may be combined such as BC above – a combination of B for Blue and C for Clobbered. Seeing two entries together without a comma indicates they are to be considered together. Another examples is SReV (Standard Reversed Variant) Most entries are separate symbols. A more complete description, and usually a photograph will be found in the main section of the book under the name of the firm as listed here. This table is for reference and over-view.

Table of Manufacturers
and Willow Patterns

Pottery	S	2T1	2T2	M	Bo	Bu	Tu	W	C	B	Si	V
Adams & Co., Harvey	B											
Adams, William	B, BC, R		B, PD									
Adderley, William A.	B, Br, R		B, L									D: B, Bk, Br, R
Ainsworth, W.H.& J.H.	B		B									
Alcock, Henry				B								
Alcock, Samuel			B									
Allerton, Charles	B, BrC, R		B									
Allman, Broughton & Co.	B											
Amison, Charles				B								
Arklow	B											
Ashworth & Bros., G. L.	B, BrC		B				B, BC		B, FB			
Atlas China Co. Ltd.				B								
Aynsley & Co., H.	B			B								
Aynsley & Sons, John	B, Gd											CW: Gd, PC
Baker, Bevans & Irwin	B		B									
Baker & Chetwynd	B											
Baker& Co., W.	B		PD									
Bakewell Bros.	B										PD	
Barker												B
Barker Bros.	B											
Barker & Son	B											
Barker & Till	B											
Barker & Sons, Samuel	B											
Barkers & Kent Ltd.	B											
Barlow & Son Ltd., T. W.	B											
Barratt's of Staffordshire Ltd.	B											
Batkin, Walker & Broadhurst	B											
Beardmore & Birks	B											
Beardmore & Dawson	B											
Beardmore & Co., Frank	PC											
Bell, Isaac & Thomas	B											
Bell, Isaac and Galloway & Atkinson	B											
Bell & Co., J. & M.P.	B		B									
Belle-Vue Pottery	B-Gy											
Beswick												MS: B, PC
Bevington & Co.	B											
Biltons	B, R											
Birks, Rawlins & Co.	B											
Bishop & Stonier	B, Br											PC, "RB"

Pottery	S	2T1	2T2	M	Bo	Bu	Tu	W	C	B	Si	V
Blackhurst & Tunnicliffe	B											
Blairs	B											
Blyth Porcelain Co. Ltd.	B, B-Gy		PD									
Bodley, E. J. D.	B, Br.		B									
Bo'Ness Pottery	B											
Booths Ltd.	B, BC				B, Gd, Gr, PD, SW					B		
Bourne, Charles			B									
Bourne & Leigh	B, Br, R											
Bourne, William	B											
Bovey Tracey Pottery Co.	B											
Brain & Co., E.										PC		
Brameld	B											
Bridgwood & Son, Sampson	B		B							PC		
Bridgwood & Clarke			B									
Britannia Pottery Co.	B, M, R		R									
British Anchor Pottery	B, BrC, R		B, Br								PD	
British Art Pottery												PC
British Pottery Ltd.	B											
Broadhurst & Sons, James	B		B							B		
Brougham & Mayer	B											
Brown & Steventon	B		PD									
Brownfield, William	B, Br											
Brownhills Pottery Co.			B									
Brown-Westhead, Moore & Co.	B											
Burgess Bros.			PD		PD							PD
Burgess & Leigh	B		B, MC			B, BC, Gr, M, MC, R, RC						
Burn & Co., J.	B											
Burn & Woods	B											
Burslem Pottery Co. Ltd.	B											
Burton, Samuel & John	B											
Butterfield, W.& J.			R									
Callands Pottery	B											
Campbellfield Pottery	B		PC									
Cardew Designs	B											
Carr & Sons, John	B, Bk, Br											
Cartwright & Edwards Ltd.	B											
Caughley			B	B								
Cauldon Ltd.	B, Gr, PC			B								
Ceramic Art Co. Ltd.	B		PD									
Challinor	B											
Chambers Junior	B											

Pottery	S	2T1	2T2	M	Bo	Bu	Tu	W	C	B	Si	V
Chetham, Jonathan Lowe	B											
Chetham & Robinson & Son	B											
Churchill	B, R											
Clementson, Joseph	B, Br											
Clews, James & Ralph	B		B									
Clews & Co. Ltd.												Ch: HP
Clokie & Co. Ltd	B											
Clyde Pottery Co.	B											
Coalport Porcelain Works	B, Gr, O	B	B	B								B, CW
Cochran & Co., Robert	B											
Cochran & Fleming	B											
Cockson & Harding(s)			B									
Colcough, H.J.C.& Co. China Ltd.	B, BrC											
Collingwood Bros.	B		B									
Cone Ltd., Thomas	B			B, Gr, R								
Conway Pottery Co. Ltd.											B	
Co-operative Wholesale Society – Windsor China			B									
Co-operative Wholesale Society – Crown Clarence	B, Gr, R											
Copeland & Garrett	B	B										
Copeland, W. T.	B, Gd, R, T	B, Gd, GO	B, BC	B, Br, Gr, Gy, R								
Cork, Edge & Malkin	B											
Corn, W. & E.	B											
Cotton, Elijah	B										PD	
Couper & Son, James	B											
Crown Staffordshire Porcelain Co. Ltd.				B, BC								B, CW, PC, GO
Dale, Deakin & Bailey	B											
Davenport	B		B									
Davies & Co.	B											
Davies, Cookson & Wilson	B		B									
Davis	B											
Davison & Son Ltd.	B			B, PD								
Dawson & Co., John			B									
Deakin & Son	B											
Dillwyn & Co.	B											
Dimmock & Co., J	B, Br, R											
Dimmock, Thomas	B									FB		
Dixon & Co.	B											
Dixon, Austin & Co.	B		B									
Dixon, Phillips & Co.	B											
Don Pottery	B		B									

Pottery	S	2T1	2T2	M	Bo	Bu	Tu	W	C	B	Si	V
Doric China		PD										
Doulton & Co.	B, Bk, Br, R				B, O, PD							L, Sp, W&A
Dudson	B, Br, Gr, Gy, R		B									
Dudson Bros.	B, Gy, ReB											
Dudson, Wilcox & Till	B											
Dunn Bennett & Co.	B, R											
Eardley & Hammersley	B		B									
Edge, William & Samuel	B											
Edge, Barker & Co.	B											
Edge, Malkin & Co.	B, Br, Gr, R			B, R								
Edwards & Brown	B		B									
Elkin, Knight & Co.	B											
Elkins & Co.	B											
Elkin, Samuel	B											
Elkin & Newbon	B											
Ellgreave Pottery Co. Ltd.	B, Br											
Emberton, William	B, R											
Emberton, Thomas, Isaac & James	B											
Empire Porcelain Co.	B			B								"RB"
English Ironstone Pottery	B											
English Ironstone Tableware	B											
Evans & Glasson	B											
Evans, D. J.	B											
Fell & Co., Thomas	B											
Ferrybridge	B		B									
Fielding & Co., S.	B, BD, PCLs											PC
Finney & Sons, A. T.	B, BD											
Finsbury China	BD											
Flackett, Toft & Robinson	B											
Fleming	B											
Floyd, Benjamin	B											
Ford & Sons (Crownford)						Br						
Ford, Charles	B											
Ford & Challinor	B											
Forester & Son, Thomas	B	PD										
Forrester & Hulme	B											
Furnivals Ltd.	B, R		B									HK
Gater, Hall & Co.	B, BC, Bk, BrC, FB											
Gibson & Sons	B, Br, Gr, OC, RC			B, FB, Gd, PC								
Gill & Sons, William	B											

Pottery	S	2T1	2T2	M	Bo	Bu	Tu	W	C	B	Si	V
Gladstone Pottery Museum												B, Bk
Gladstone China	B											
Globe Pottery Co. Ltd.	B, R			B								
Godwin, John & Robert			R									
Godwin, T. & B.	B											
Godwin, Thomas	B											
Godwin, Rowley & Co.	B											
Goodwin Stoddard & Co., J.	B											
Goodwins & Harris	B											
Gordon's Pottery	B											
Goss, William Henry	B											
Grainger (& Co.), George			B, GO									Bb: B, Bk, Gy, O, PC
Green, T.G. & Co. Ltd.			B									M
Griffith, Beardmore & Birks	B											
Grimwades Ltd.	B		PD								PD	B, Bk, Gr, I, Pl, R, W, T
Grindley Hotel Ware Co. Ltd	B		Gr									
Hackwood, William	B											
Hackwood & Keeling	B		B									
Hall & Read	B											
Hamilton, Robert	B											
Hammersley, Ralph	B											
Hammersley & Co.			B									
Hampson	B											
Hancock & Sons, Sampson	B, FB											
Harding, Joseph	B											
Harley, Thomas	B											
Harley & Co.	B											
Harris & Goodwin			B									
Harrison, John	B											
Heath, Joseph	B											
Heath, Blackhurst & Co.	B											
Herculaneum	B		B									
Heron, Robert	B											
Heron Cross Pottery	BD											
Hicks & Meigh			B									
Hicks, Meigh & Johnson	B											
Hilditch & Son			B									
Hillchurch Pottery	B											
Hollins, T. & J.	B											
Hollinshead & Kirkham	B, Gd, PC		BrC									
Hoods Ltd.										PC		
Hope & Carter	B											
Howard Pottery Co. Ltd.	B											HP
Hudden, J.T.	B											
Hudson, William	B											
Hudson & Middleton	B											
Hughes & Co., E.			Gd, PC	B								

Pottery	S	2T1	2T2	M	Bo	Bu	Tu	W	C	B	Si	V
Hughes & Son, Thomas	B, Br											
Hulme, John	B											
Hulme, William	B, R											
Hulse & Adderley	B											
Hulse, Nixon & Adderley	B											
Industrial Pottery	B											
Jamieson & Co., James	B											
Johnson, H & R	BD											
Johnson Bros.	B, R											MS
Jones & Sons, A.B.	B				HP							
Jones, A. E.			PD									
Jones, A. G. Harley					B, BrC, PC			Gd, BC				
Jones, George	B											
Jones & Walley	B											
Keele St. Pottery Co.			PD									
Keeling & Co.			B, FB									B, BrC
Keeling & Co., Samuel	B											
Kensington Pottery											PD	
Kent, James	B											PD
Kent, William	BF											
Kidston & Co., Robert	B											
Kirkham Pottery & Co., Ltd.	BD											
Knapper & Blackhurst	B											
Knight, John King	B											
Lancaster & Sons Ltd.			PD									PC, "RB"
Lancaster & Sandland	PD											Pa: HPLs
Lawrence, Thomas												"RB"
Leighton Pottery	B											
Lingard Webster & Co.	BMS											
Lowe, William	B											
MacIntyre, James	B		B, FB									
McNay, Charles W.	B											
Machin, Joseph		B										
Machin & Co.		B										
Machin & Potts	B											
Machin & Thomas			B									
Maddock & Sons, John	B, BrC, PD											
Maling, C.T.	B, FB			B								
Maling & Sons (Ltd.), C.T.	B, FB		B, FB									
Malkin, Walker & Hulse	B											
Marple, Turner & Co.	B											
Marsh, Jacob	B											
Mason, Miles		B	B									
Mason, G.M.& C.J.		B					B, BC, Br, FB, GrC, R		B, FB			
Mayer & Sherratt	B										PD	

Pottery	S	2T1	2T2	M	Bo	Bu	Tu	W	C	B	Si	V
Meakin, Alfred	B, T Ma, R		PD							PC		
Meakin, J. & G.	B, Br										B, Gr, R	
Meir, John	B											
Meir & Son, John	B, Br, R		B									
Melba China Co. Ltd	B											
Methven & Sons, David	B		BGO									
Micklethwaite Tile	B											
Middlesbro' Pottery	B											
Midwinter, W.R.	B, Bn, Gr, R											Y: BkC, B
Minton	B, Bk, FB, O		B, BC, FB									
Minton Hollins	B, Br											
Montgomery, Robert	B											
Moore & Co., Samuel	B											
Morley Fox & Co., Inc.			PD									
Morris, Thomas	B											
Murray & Fullarton	B											
Myott Son & Co.	B		BD, PD							B		
Myott-Meakin Ltd.	B									B		
Newbon & Beardmore	B											
New Hall			B									
New Hall Pottery Co.,												PD
Newport Pottery Co. Ltd.	B, BrC, PD		PD									
Nicholls & Hallam	B											
North Staffordshire Pottery Co. Ltd.	B, Bk, R											
Old Hall Earthenware Co. Ltd.	B, Br			B								
Old Hall Porcelain Works Ltd.				B, Br								
Operatives Manufactory	B											
Palissy Pottery Ltd.						B, BrC						
Paragon China Ltd.												PC
Parrott & Co.			PD		B, PD							
Patterson, Thomas	B											
Pearl Pottery Co.	B											"RB"
Phillips, George	B											
Pilkington's Tile & Pottery Co. Ltd.	B											
Pinder, Bourne & Co.	B, Bk, Br											W&A
Plant, R.H.& S.L.	B			B								
Podmore Walker & Co.	B											
Pointon, William	B											
Pointon & Co.			B, BGO									
Poole, Thomas	B											
Pountney & Co. Ltd.	B, Gr, R							Gr, GrC, FB				

Pottery	S	2T1	2T2	M	Bo	Bu	Tu	W	C	B	Si	V
Pountney & Allies	B											
Price Brothers	B											
Price Kensington	BD											
Proctor (& Co.), J.& H.	B											
Radford, Samuel	B, Br, BrC		B, PD	B								
Ratcliffe & Co.	B											
Rathbone, Samuel & John			B									
Ravensdale Pottery Ltd.	B											
Read, Clementson & Anderson	Bk, Br, Gr											
Read & Clementson	P											
Redfern & Drakeford	B		PD									
Reed & Taylor	B											
Regal Pottery Co.	B											
Regal Pottery Ltd.	B, R											
Reid, William	B											
Ridgway, John			B									
Ridgway, W.R.	B											
Ridgway & Morley	B											
Ridgways	B, BrC		B									
Riley, John & Richard	B											
Robinson & Son				B								
Robinson, Kirkham & Co.	B											
Robinson, Wood & Brownfield	B											
Rogers, John & George	B		B									
Roslyn China										PC		
Royal Albion China Co.	B											
Rubian Art Pottery												"RB"
Sadler & Sons	B, Bk, Gd, Gr, R											
St. George Fine Bone China Ltd.	BD											
Salisbury Crown China Co.	B		PD									
Salt & Nixon	B											
Scott	B		B									
Sewell	B											
Sewell & Co.	B											
Sewell & Donkin	B											
Shaw, Anthony	B, Br, R											
Shelley Potteries Ltd.			BD, R									
Sheltonian China	BD											
Shirley & Co., Thomas			B									
Shore & Coggins	B			B								
Simpsons Ltd.	B											
Smith, G.F.	B											
Smith, Sampson	B, BF		B									
Smith & Co., William	B		B									
Soho Pottery Ltd.	B, Br, GdPC											

Pottery	S	2T1	2T2	M	Bo	Bu	Tu	W	C	B	Si	V
Spode, Josiah	B, Bk, Gr, L, R	B	B	B								
Staffordshire Fine Ceramics	BD											
Staffordshire Potteries Ltd.	BD											
Staffordshire Tableware Ltd.	B											
Stanley Pottery Co.	B											
Stanley & Lambert	B											
Star China Co.	B											PC
Stevenson, Andrew	B											
Stevenson, Alcock & Williams									B			
Stevenson & Co., Spencer	B, Br											
Steventon & Sons Ltd., John	B, Gr.R										PD	
Stubbs, Joseph	B											
Swansea Pottery (Cambrian)	B											B
Swillington Bridge	B											
Swinnertons Ltd.	B, R											"RB"
Tams & Son, John	B, BC, PC											
Tams & Lowe	B											
Taylor & Sons, Benjamin			B									
Taylor, G. & S.	B											
Taylor, John	B											
Taylor, William	B											
Taylor & Kent			PD									
Taylor, Tunnicliffe & Co.	B, Gr		B									
Thomson, John	B											
Till & Sons, Thomas	B		B									CW
Tomlinson & Co., William	B											
Townsend, George	B		B									
Turner, John				B			B					
Turpin & Co.	B		B									
Twigg (& Co.), J.	B											
Upper Hanley Pottery	B											
Vernon, James	B											
Victoria Porcelain	B, Gr											
Wain & Sons, H.A.	B											
Walker, Ambrose	B											
Walker, Thomas	B											
Walker, Thomas Henry	B											
Walker & Carter	B											
Wallace & Co.	B											
Walley, Edward	P											
Warren, James Thomas	B											
Washington Pottery Ltd.	B, R											

Pottery	S	2T1	2T2	M	Bo	Bu	Tu	W	C	B	Si	V
Wathen & Hebb	B											
Weatherby & Sons, J.H.	B, BrC											
Wedgwood & Co.	B, R		B									SreV, "RB"
Wedgwood, Josiah	B, BC, Bk, Br, BrC, CL, Gd, GO, Gr, Ls, O, R, Y		B, Bk, BnC, Gr									
Weston, George	B											
White & Co., I.			B									
Wild, Thomas C.	B			PD								
Wildblood, Heath & Sons	B											
Wileman, Henry	B											
Wileman, J.F.	B											
Wilkinson, A.J.	B, Br, BrC, PD								PD			
Wilkinson, John	B											
Williamson & Sons, H.M.	B											
Wiltshaw & Robinson	B, PC		B					GO, FB, PC,			Gd, PC	
Winkle & Co., F.	B											
Wolfe, Thomas	B											
Wolfe & Co., Thomas		B										
Wood, Arthur	B, Br, R											
Wood & Brownfield	B											
Wood, Challinor & Co.	B											
Wood, Enoch	B											
Wood & Sons	B, Br, BrC, R				FB, BrC, GrC, RC, TC				B, BC, R			G, PC
Wood, H.J.	B										Gd, Ls	
Woolf, Sydney	B											
Worcester Royal Porcelain Co. Ltd.	B, Gr, BV	B					B	B, Br, Gd, Gy, R				
Wren Fine Bone China	B											
Yale & Barker	B											
Yates, John			B									
Ynysmeudwy Pottery	B											

Pattern Names
for Willow Patterns

Pattern	Pottery	Source
Standard Willow		
Basaltine Willow	Frank Beardmore & Co.	Mark
Chinese Legend	Wedgwood (& Sons Ltd.)	Mark
Davenport Willow	Booths Ltd.	Mark
Manchu	Alfred Meakin	Mark
Nankin Willow	S. Hancock & Sons	*Pottery Gazette*, 12/23 p. 1943
Old Willow	W. A. Adderley	Mark
Old Willow	Cartwright & Edwards	Mark
Old Willow	Empire Porcelain Co.	Mark
Old Willow	English Ironstone Pottery	Mark
Old Willow	English Ironstone Tableware	Mark
Old Willow	Roy Kirkham & Co. Ltd.	Mark
Old Willow	Lingard, Webster & Co.	Mark
Old Willow	Alfred Meakin Ltd.	Mark
Old Willow	Swinnertons Ltd.	Mark
Old Willow	Washington Pottery Ltd.	Mark
Olde Willow	Alfred Meakin Ltd.	Mark
Old Chinese Willow	Simpsons Ltd.	Mark
Pagoda	Hollingshead & Kirkham	Mark
Royal Willow	John Maddock & Sons	Mark
Sing An	Cauldon	Mark
Ye Old Willow	John Maddock & Sons	Mark
Ye Olde Willow	T. W. Barlow & Son Ltd.	Mark
Ye Olde Willow	Gater, Hall & Co.	Mark
Ye Olde Willow	Grimwades Ltd.	Mark
Ye Olde Willow	James Kent (Ltd.)	Mark
Ye Olde Willow	Leighton Pottery Ltd.	Mark
Ye Olde Blue Willow	A. J. Wilkinson (Ltd.)	Mark
Two Temples I		
(Chinese)Temple	Minton	*Minton Printed Pottery 1796-1836*, p. 69
Pagoda	Miles Mason	*Mason's China and the Ironstone Wares*, Colour Pl. 1
Shuttered Window	Wolfe & Co.	*Made in Liverpool*, p. 35.
Temple	Caughley	*Minton Printed Pottery 1796-1836*, p. 69.
Temple	Spode	*Spode's Willow Pattern*, p. 53
Two Temples II		
Broseley	British Anchor Pottery	Mark
Broseley	Burgess & Leigh	Pattern book
Broseley	Caughley	*Minton Printed Pottery 1796-1836.* p. 3
Broseley	Furnivals Ltd.	*Pottery Gazette 1917*
Broseley	Grainger & Co.	*Grainger's Worcester Porcelain*, p. 174
Broseley	Keeling & Co.	Mark
Broseley	C. T. Maling & Sons	*Tyneside Pottery*, pp. 131-2
Broseley	Minton	*Minton Printed Pottery 1796-1836*, p. 29
Broseley	William Smith & Co.	"Stone China from the Stafford Pottery" NCS #102, p.20
Broseley	Spode	*Spode's Willow Pattern*, p. 53
Broseley-Willow	Miles Mason	*Mason's China and the Ironstone Wares*, p. 58

Pattern	Pottery	Source
Pagoda	Caughley	*Caughley & Worcester*, p. 18
Pagoda	Davison & Son Ltd.	Mark
Pagoda	Coalport	*Coalport 1795-1926*, pp. 91 & 405
Willow-type	Coalport	*Coalport & Coalbrookdale Porcelains*, p. 18 & pl. 70
Two Temples II Decal		
Ye Olde Willow	Myott, Son & Co.	Mark
Ye Olde Willow	Parrott & Co,	Mark
Mandarin		
British Nankin	Coalport	*Coalport & Coalbrookdale Porcelains*, pl. 12
Ching	Henry Alcock	Mark
Ching	Cauldon Ltd.	Mark
Ching	Globe Pottery Co. Ltd.	Mark
Persian Blue	C. T. Maling	*Tyneside Pottery*, p. 130
Willow-Nankin	Caughley	*Caughley & Worcester*, p. 16
Willow	Thomas Cone Ltd.	*Pottery Gazette 1952-53*
Willow No. 1	Edge Malkin & Co.	Mark
Booths Willow		
Willow (Georgian Shape)	Booths Ltd.	Mark
Old Willow	Unknown Pottery	Barker Furnishing Services, *Pottery Gazette*, May 1, 1924, p. 847
Real Old Willow	Booths Ltd.	Mark
Ye Old Chinese Willow	A. G. Harley Jones	Mark
Gleneagles	Wood & Son	Mark
Hankow	Wood & Son	Mark
Pekin	Wood & Son	Mark
Burleigh Willow		
Dillwyn Willow	Burgess & Leigh	*Pottery Gazette 1926*
Willow	Burgess & Leigh	Mark
Ye Olde Willow	Palissy Pottery Ltd.	Mark
John Turner		
Blue Chinese Landscape	G.M.& C.J. Mason	*Godden's Guide to Ironstone* p. 25
Chinese Landscape	Ashworth Bros.	*Historic Flow Blue*, pp. 124-5
Printed Willow	Ashworth Bros.	*Pottery Gazette, April 1920*
Two-man Willow Pattern	John Turner	*Blue & White Transfer Ware1780-1840*, p. 14-15
Willow	G.M.& C.J. Mason	Mark
Gold Willow	G.M.& C.J. Mason	Mark
Turners Willow	John Turner	*Northern Ceramic Society NL #101*, pp. 10-11
Worcester		
Full Willow	Royal Worcester	Pattern Books
Mandarin	Pountney & Co. Ltd	Mark
Ye Old Chinese Willow	A. G. Harley Jones	Mark

Pattern	Pottery	Source	Pattern	Pottery	Source
Canton			"Red Bridge"	Thomas Lawrence Ltd.	Author's name
Dagger Border	Thomas Dimmock	Mark	"Red Bridge"	William Lowe	Author's name
Real Old Canton	Ashworth Bros.	Mark	"Red Bridge"	Pearl Pottery Co. Ltd.	Author's name
Mason's Blue			"Red Bridge"	Rubian Art Pottery	Author's name
Canton #188	Ashworth Bros.	*Pottery Gazette, December 1919*	"Red Bridge"	Soho Pottery	Author's name
			"Red Bridge"	Swinnertons Ltd.	Author's name
Border			"Red Bridge"	Wedgwood & Co.	Author's name
Manchu	Alfred Meakin Ltd.	Mark	Willow & Aster	Doulton	Mark
Willowette	Alfred Meakin Ltd.	Mark	Willow & Aster	Pinder, Bourne & Co.	
Ye Olde Willow	Myott, Son & Co.	Mark			
Golden Willow	Roslyn China	Mark	**Variant names from one pottery only**		
			Bamboo	Grainger & Co.	*Grainger's Worcester Porcelain*
Variants					
Chinese Willow	John Aynsley & Sons		Chinese	George Clews	*Chameleon Ware Art Pottery*
Chinese Willow	Coalport	Mark			
Chinese Willow	Crown Staffordshire	Mark	Daisy	W. A. Adderley	Mark
Chinese Willow			Hong Kong	Furnivals	Mark
(Kang-He)	Thomas Till & Sons	*Pottery Gazette, March 1922*	Ming	T. G. Green	Mark
			Pagoda	Lancaster & Sandland	Mark
"Red Bridge"	Bishop & Stonier	Author's name	Spray	Doulton	Mark
"Red Bridge"	Empire Porcelain Co.	Author's name	Yang	W. R. Midwinter	Mark
"Red Bridge"	Lancaster & Sons Ltd.	Author's name			

Glossary

Armorial decoration: China bearing arms or crests of cities and towns, universities and colleges as well as families and other subjects. Also known as Heraldic or Crested China, W. H. Goss was the principal producer of these wares. Pieces ranged from little trinkets to lovely useful wares such as decorated jardinières.

Basalt: Black unglazed body. It was developed by Josiah Wedgwood in the late eighteenth century and copied by many other manufacturers into the early nineteenth century.

Biscuit (also known as Bisque): Clay that has been hardened through a first firing. It is unglazed.

Blank: A piece of ware that has not yet been decorated.

Body: The composition of a piece of pottery or porcelain. Different ingredients as well as ingredients in different proportions change the nature of the clay body. Color can be added to the body itself as well as on it in the form of glaze or decoration.

Bone China: A form of porcelain to which bone ash has been added to increase translucency and whiteness. It was developed by Josiah Spode I and II.

China: A general term referring to all ceramics, especially tableware. It is also more specifically a term that is synonymous with porcelain.

China Glaze: A term used in the late eighteenth century for the pale blue glaze used to make earthenware look whiter and more like porcelain. The term was replaced by the use of the word pearlware.

Chinaman: A dealer in china ware.

Chinoiserie: An imitation of an Oriental design by potteries in the Western world.

Clobbered ware: An underglaze design in one color to which enamel colors have been added. This term is used when the original design is considered complete without the overpainting. There are designs made up of printed outlines that have been filled in with printed or painted color as part of the original design; however, colors added to transfer-printed willow pattern can be considered as clobbered.

Cottage Ware: Tableware molded and decorated in the shape of a small cottage, often with a thatched roof.

Crazing: A network of fine cracks in the glaze results when there is unequal contraction of the body and the glaze after firing. Crazing is sometimes visible right after the firing, or it may occur after months or years. It can be caused from putting glazed ware in an oven over a period of time. If the glaze on a piece is crazed, the body can become discolored from the impurities reaching the body.

Creamware: A cream-colored earthenware which had its beginnings c. 1740 when a lead glaze was added to an earthenware body used with colored glazes. It was refined and improved by Josiah Wedgwood c. 1765. He gave his creamware the name Queen's Ware. Most of the potteries were producing a type of creamware from the 1770s on. In some listings of type of earthenware manufactured "cream color" refers to creamware.

Decal: The term Decalcomania is also used to describe a transfer decoration that is printed on special paper. Decals are placed on wares that have already been glazed and fired. Some decals are coated in plastic that is removed when they are placed on the ware. Other decals are wetted before application to the glazed ware. A low final firing causes the decal to "melt" onto the surface of the ware. Ware decorated with decal patterns applied overglaze are more subject to wear with use than underglaze decorated ware. Decal is a term used in the U.S.A. whereas the British use the term lithograph. I have used the words interchangeably throughout the book.

Dust pressed tile: A method of pressing finely ground and dampened clay dust into tiles was patented by Richard Prosser in 1840. A machine called a dust-tile press was used. It was possible to produce 1, 800 6-inch tiles per day using one of these powerful screw presses.

Earthenware: An opaque ceramic ware that is slightly porous and often has a transparent glaze. Widely used in the production of table and toilet wares.

Embossed: A raised decoration produced in the mold.

Engraving: The art of cutting lines and punching dots into a copper plate to form a pattern.

Fancies: Another term for ornamental ware. It covers almost anything that is not tableware.

Finial: The knob on top of a lid. The term is used especially when the knob is figural or fanciful.

Foot ring: I use this term rather than foot rim, saving the word "rim" for the section near the edge of a plate or platter. The various types of foot ring are illustrated here:

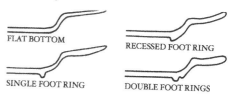

FLAT BOTTOM

RECESSED FOOT RING

SINGLE FOOT RING

DOUBLE FOOT RINGS

Flow Blue: A blurring of the printed pattern and coloring of the glaze caused by the addition of "Flow powder" into the saggar during firing. This powder is a mixture of salt, white lead, and calcium carbonate.

Frit: A glassy compound of silica and alkali used in some early porcelains.

Gadroon: A design of alternating ovals and lines on the rim of dinnerware items. It is an embossed design formed in the mold.

Gilding: The application of gold and/or platinum to the ware.

Glaze: A mixture of minerals in a liquid state into which the biscuit ware is dipped. When fired (glost firing) it will melt into a glassy surface on the ware. The glaze makes the body nonporous, more permanent, and adds beauty to the ware.

Greenware: Ware that has been formed but not fired.

Ground: A solid color underglaze decoration formed by dusting the powdered color onto an oil coating.

Holloware: Serving pieces of dinnerware such as bowls, pitchers, creamers, and sugars.

Impressed: Marked or stamped with pressure either by hand or in the mold.

Institutional Ware: Usually vitrified ware made for hotels, railroads, restaurants, and other public venues.

Ironstone: Patented by C. J. Mason in 1813, this strong, durable ware was developed to replace the demand for Chinese export porcelains by the British. The name was beneficial in projecting an image of strength. The shapes, patterns, and colors of the Ironstone wares produced by Mason were influenced by the Chinese. Stone China and Granite were two of the other terms used by British firms in the development of their competing wares. For many of the potteries, the actual wares were no more than ordinary earthenware with a stoneware name.

Kiln: An oven-like structure for the firing of greenware, glazes and decorations. Early kilns were also known as bottle ovens. In the twentieth century tunnel kilns were developed in which the ware is carried through on slow-moving flat cars.

Lead glaze: A shiny glaze containing lead oxide.

Lithograph: (see Decal)

Luster: A metallic glaze that gives ware an iridescent effect.

Matt Glaze (also **Matte** or **Mat**): A flat finish that is not reflective. It can also be rough.

Overglaze: Colors and decorations such as decals or lithographs are overglaze decorations added after the glost firing.

Parian: A creamy-white unglazed porcelain-type body that is smooth. It is an imitation of marble as it is used for figures and similar objects.

Pearlware: A light weight earthenware that was developed from creamware using a greater proportion of white clay to the body. The glaze has a slight blue tint to help give the ware a whiter appearance. Wedgwood's ware was called Pearl Glaze and later Pearl White. China Glaze is another term used to describe the ware that became popular in the late eighteenth century and into the nineteenth century.

Polychrome: A term used to indicate more than one color as opposed to monochrome meaning one color. Polychrome is often used to describe a decal or lithograph. The term multi-color can be used interchangeably; however, it is more often used to describe transfer printing underglaze in more than one color.

Porcelain: There are many different formulae for porcelain, resulting in descriptions such as soft-paste, hard-paste, or bone china: however, in general porcelain is a term that includes all translucent ware with a nonporous body.

Potbank or Potworks: Early terms used to describe a pottery. A potwork was usually established to produce useful wares from clay. Some of these works remained small, and others grew and developed into large ceramic manufacturing businesses.

Pottery: Another term for earthenware, referring to opaque, nonvitrified ware. Pottery is also a term used to describe the manufactory where ceramics are produced.

Registered Designs and Numbers: Thousands of designs and shapes were registered at the Patent Office to keep others from copying. From 1842 a diamond-shaped device was used with codes marking the months and years. The system was changed in 1884. Progressive numbers were used beginning with the abbreviation Rd. No.

Restaurant Ware: (see Institutional Ware).

Rim: The section of the plate or platter near the edge. These are either flat or concave as illustrated below:

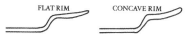

FLAT RIM   CONCAVE RIM

Saggar: A container made of high fired clay. Delicate wares were put inside to protect them during firings in the kiln.

Stilt Marks (also called **spur marks**): Small defects in the surface caused by the small supports that separated plates in the kiln. These can be three or four pointed or even single spurs. They are not present on porcelain with an unglazed foot ring.

Stone china: Another term for Ironstone.

Stoneware: Another term for Ironstone. Some of the printed marks have STONE WARE as two separate words; however, I have chosen to be consistent in spelling it as one word throughout the book.

Suiteware: Suite wares, "en suite" or "suited tablewares" are all terms that describe additional pieces that could be purchased in the same pattern as dinner, tea, and breakfast sets. Suiteware includes such things as fruit and dessert services, cruet sets, covered butter or marmalade dishes and sardine boxes.

Toilet Set or **Toilet Ware:** Also called Wash Set, these sets were in use before indoor plumbing was common in homes. The basic set is comprised of a wash basin and pitcher. Additional pieces include a second, smaller pitcher, soap dish, sponge bowl, toothbrush box, chamber pot (sometimes with a lid), and slop jar with lid.

Transfer printing: A design is engraved onto a copper plate. After the copper plate has been heated, colored ink is put on and rubbed well into the engraving. Surplus color is scraped off, leaving a thin film of color. A piece of special tissue paper that has been sized with soap and water is placed on the copper plate. The pattern is "transferred" to the tissue by means of a roller press going over it. The tissue is removed from the copper plate after it is softened by reheating. A cutter then snips apart the various elements of the pattern. The transferer places the different sections of the print in position on the ware, and gently rubs the back of the paper with a small piece of felt to allow the color to hold in position. The print is then rubbed vigorously with a stiff-bristled brush to ensure the color is thoroughly transferred to the porous biscuit earthenware. The paper is then washed off in cold water and the ware is fired in the kiln. The pieces are dipped in a glaze and refired in the glost kiln. This clear glaze allows the pattern to show through and yet be protected from the wear and tear of normal use.

Trinket Set: Also known as a dresser set. A set made up of a tray with ring stand, pin box, powder box, and a pair of small candlesticks. It was intended for a woman's dressing table.

Underglaze: Designs that are put on the biscuit ware before it is glazed are underglaze designs. Transfer-printed patterns are applied on the biscuit and are thus underglaze designs.

Useful ware: This is a general category including tea, dinner, and dessert wares as opposed to ornamental ware that is for display only.

Vitrified: Glass-like ware that has been fired at a higher temperature than earthenware. The clay formula includes silica, which makes the body nonporous and nonabsorbent.

White ware: Pottery or porcelain with a white body. This term is used to distinguish it from red ware and/or yellow ware. White ware also refers more specifically to the ware that replaced pearlware in the 1820s-30s. It has a whitened body and clear glaze.

White Granite: (see Ironstone).

Bibliography

Adams, Brian and Thomas, Anthony. *A Potwork in Devonshire*. Devon, UK: Sayce Publishing, 1996.

Anderson, Anne. *The Cube Teapot*. Somerset, England: Richard Dennis, 1999.

Atterbury, Paul. *Cornish Ware*. Somerset, England: Richard Dennis, 1996.

Atterbury, Paul, Denker, Ellen Paul & Batkin, Maureen. *Miller's Twentieth-Century Ceramics*. London: Octopus Publishing Group Ltd., 1999.

Atterbury, Paul. *The Story of Minton from 1793 to the present*. Stoke-on-Trent: Gordon Clark Limited, 1978.

Aylett, Graham. "Primavesi in France." *Friends of Blue Bulletin 113*, October 2001, p. 12.

Bailey, Syd (editor). *More Memories of Stoke-on-Trent*. Halifax, UK: True North Books Ltd., 2000.

Baker, John C. *Sunderland Pottery*. Tyne and Wear County Council Museums: Thomas Reed Industrial Press Limited, 1984.

Barker, Ray. *The Crown Devon Collectors Handbook*. London: Francis Joseph Publications, 1997.

Bartlett, John. *English Decorative Ceramics*. London: Kevin Francis Publishing Ltd., 1989.

Berthoud, Michael. *A Cabinet of British Creamers*. Bridgnorth, Shropshire: Micawber Publications, 1999.

Berthoud, Michael. *A Compendium of British Cups*. Bridgnorth, Shropshire: Micawber Publications, 1990.

Bell, R. C. *Tyneside Pottery*. London: Studio Vista, 1971.

Birks, Steve. www.thepotteries.org.

Branyan, Lawrence, French, Neal & Sandon, John. *Worcester Blue & White Porcelain 1751-1790 New Edition*. London: Barrie & Jenkins, 1990.

Broughton, Renard. " 'Old Blue' Revisited: Early Chinoiserie Printed Pottery Part II." *The Northern Ceramic Society Newsletter No. 101 (March 1996)*: 4-14.

Broughton, Renard. "Yorkshire Pottery: Identifying Early Blue Printed Patterns of the circa. 1785-1810 Period." *The Northern Ceramic Society Newsletter No. 109 (March 1998)*: 4-16.

Brown, E. Myra & Lockett, Terence A, editors. *Made in Liverpool, Liverpool Pottery & Porcelain 1700-1850*. Seventh Exhibition from the NCS Walker Art Gallery, Liverpool. Printed in Great Britain, 1993.

Burgess & Leigh Ltd. *A Century of Progress 1851-1951 Four Generations Continue the Story of Burleigh Ware*. Burslem, Stoke-on-Trent: Warwick Savage, 1951.

Burns, Peggy. *Memories of Stoke on-Trent*. Halifax, UK: True North Books, 1998.

Busby, Eileen Rose. *Royal Winton Porcelain Ceramics Fit for a King*. Marietta, Ohio: Antique Publications, 1998.

Callow, Diana and John. *Beswick Pottery*. Toronto: The Charlton Press, 1997.

Calvert, Hilary. *Chameleon Ware Art Pottery*. Atglen, Pennsylvania: Schiffer Publishing, 1998.

Casey, Andrew. *Susie Cooper Ceramics*. Stratford Upon Avon: Jazz Publications, 1992.

Cluett, Robert. *George Jones Ceramics 1861-1951*. Atglen, Pennsylvania: Schiffer Publishing, 1998.

Cockerill, John. "Stone China from the Stafford Pottery, South Stockton". *The Northern Ceramic Society Newsletter No. 102* (April 1996), 19-21.

Cockerill, John. "The North Shore Pottery. Stockton-on-Tees". *Northern Ceramic Society Journal Volume 17* (2000). 39-49.

Cockerill, John & Joyce. "Pattersons – Potters of Gateshead". *Northern Ceramic Society Newsletter No. 129* (March 2003), 13-15.

Collard, Elizabeth. *Nineteenth Century Pottery and Porcelain in Canada*. Montreal: McGill University Press, 1967.

Copeland, Robert. *Spode & Copeland Marks and other relevant intelligence, 2nd edition*. London: Studio Vista, 1997.

Copeland, Robert. *Spode's Willow Pattern and Other Designs After the Chinese*. London: Studio Vista, 1980, 1990, 1999.

Coysh, A. W. *Blue and White Transfer Ware 1780-1840*. Devon, UK: David & Charles (Publishers) Ltd., 1970, 1974.

Coysh, A. W. and Henrywood, R. K. *The Dictionary of Blue and White Printed Pottery 1780-1880 Vol. I*. Woodbridge, Suffolk: Baron Publishing, 1982

Coysh, A. W. and Henrywood, R. K. *The Dictionary of Blue and White Printed Pottery 1780-1880 Vol. II*. Woodbridge, Suffolk: Baron Publishing, 1989.

Cunningham, Helen C. *Clarice Cliff & Her Contemporaries: Susie Cooper, Keith Murray, Charlotte Rhead, and the Carlton Designers*. Atglen, Pennsylvania: Schiffer Publishing Ltd., 1999.

Dieringer, Ernie & Bev. *White Ironstone China Plate Identification Guice 1840-90*. Atglen, Pennsylvania: Schiffer Publishing Ltd., 2001.

Drakard, David and Holdway, Paul. *Spode Transfer-printed Ware 1784-1833*. Woodbridge, Suffolk: Antique Collector's Club, Inc., 2002.

Eberle, Linda and Scott, Susan. *The Charlton Standard Catalogue of CHINTZ, First Edition*. Birmingham, Michigan & Toronto, Ontario: The Charlgon Press, 1996.

Ewins, Neil. *"Supplying the Present Wants to our Yankee Cousins…": Staffordshire Ceramics and the American Market 1775-1880*. Stafford, England: George Street Press Ltd., 1997.

Eyles, Desmond. *The Story of Royal Doulton*. Stoke-on-Trent: Gordon Clark Publicity Ltd., 1983.

Finegan, Mary J. *Johnson Brothers Dinnerware Pattern Directory & Price Guide*. Statesville, N.C.: Signature Press, Inc., 1993.

Forbes, H. A. Crosby. *Hills and Streams: Landscape Decoration on Chinese Export Blue and White Porcelain*. Exhibition catalogue, China Trade Museum, Milton, Massachusetts. Baltimore: Garamond/Pridemark Press, Inc., 1982.

Frederick, Gale et al. *Flow Blue and Mulberry Teapot Body Styles*. The Flow Blue International Collectors' Club, Inc., 1993.

Fuller, L. G. "The Willow Pattern Plate." *Antique Collecting Volume 15, No. 2*. (June 1980), 27-29.

Furniss, David A., Wagner, J. Richard and Judith. *Adams Ceramics: Staffordshire Potters and Pots, 1779-1998*. Atglen, Pennsylvania: Schiffer Publishing Ltd., 1999.

Gaston, Mary Frank. *Blue Willow*. Paducah, Kentucky: Collector Books, 1983.

Gaston, Mary Frank. *Blue Willow Revised 2nd Edition*. Paducah, Kentucky: Collector Books, 1990.

Godden, Geoffrey A. *British Porcelain*. London: Barrie & Jenkins, 1974.

Godden, Geoffrey A. *Caughley & Worcester Porcelains 1775-1800*. New York, New York: Frederick A. Praeger Inc., 1969.

Godden, Geoffrey A. *Coalport & Coalbrookdale Porcelains*. New York: Praeger Publishers, 1970.

Godden, Geoffrey A. and Gibson, Michael. *Collecting Lustreware*. London: Barrie & Jenkins, 1991.

Godden, Geoffrey A. *Encyclopaedia of British Porcelain Manufacturers*. London: Barrie & Jenkins, 1988.

Godden, Geoffrey A. *Encyclopaedia of British Pottery and Porcelain*

Marks. New York, New York: Bonanza Books, 1964.

Godden, Geoffrey A. *Godden's Guide to Ironstone, Stone and Granite Wares*. Woodbridge, Suffolk: Antique Collector's Club, Inc., 1999.

Godden, Geoffrey A. *An Illustrated Encyclopedia of British Pottery and Porcelain*. New York: Bonanza Books, 1965.

Godden, Geoffrey A. *Jewitt's Ceramic Art of Great Britain 1800-1900*. London: Barrie & Jenkins, 1972.

Godden, Geoffrey A. *Mason's China and The Ironstone Wares*. Woodbridge, Suffolk: Baron Publishing, Reprinted, 1984.

Godden, Geoffrey A. *Minton Pottery & Porcelain of the First Period 1793-1850*. London: Herbert Jenkins, 1968.

Godden, Geoffrey A. *New Handbook of British Pottery & Porcelain Marks*. London: Barrie & Jenkins, 1999.

Godden, Geoffrey A. (editor and chief author). *Staffordshire Porcelains*. London: Granada, 1983.

Griffin, John D. *A Celebration of Yorkshire Pots*. Nottingham, England: Russell Press Ltd., 1997.

Griffin, John D. *The Don Pottery 1801-1893*. Doncaster: Doncaster Museum Service, 2001.

Gurnett, Robin. "The Bishop and Stonier Partnerships, 1851-1932. *The Northern Ceramic Society Newsletter No. 123* (September 2001): 15-16.

Haggar, Reginald. *English Country Pottery*. London: Phoenix House Ltd., 1950.

Haggarty, George. "Newbigging Pottery." *Scottish Pottery 18th Historical Review (1996)*: 15-38.

Halfpenny, Pat, editor. *Penny Plain Twopence Coloured Transfer-Printing on English Ceramics 1750-1850*. Stafford, UK: George Street Press, Ltd., 1994.

Hallesy, Helen L. *The Glamorgan Pottery Swansea 1814-38*. Llandysul, Dyfed, Wales: Gomer Press, 1995.

Hampson, Rodney. *Churchill China Great British Potters Since 1795*. Huddersfield, England: The Amadeus Press Ltd., 1994.

Hampson, Rodney. *Longton Potters 1700-1865, City Museum & Art Gallery, Stoke-on-Trent Journal of Ceramic History Volume 14*. Stafford: George Street Press, 1990.

Hampson, Rodney. *Pottery References in the Staffordshire Advertiser 1795-1865*. Hanley, Stoke on Trent: NCS Publications, 2000.

Hanning, Laurence. "Operatives Manufactory, High Street, Burslem." *Northern Ceramic Society Newsletter No. 118 (June 2000)*: 14-15.

Hawke-Smith, Cameron. *The Making of the Six Towns*. Stafford: George Street Press, 1985.

Hayden, Arthur. *English China*. London: The Gresham Press, 1904. New York: Special Silver Jubilee Edition: Ned J. Rube, 1977.

Heaivilin, Annise Doring. *Grandma's Tea Leaf Ironstone*. Lombard, Illinois: Wallace-Homestead, 1981.

Henrywood, R. K. "Staffordshire Potters Puzzles and Problems." *Antique Collecting, Volume 37 Number 9*, March 2003, 16-20.

Henrywood, R. K. *Staffordshire Potters 1781-1900*. Woodbridge, Suffolk: Antique Collectors Club, 2003.

Hill, Ellen R. *Mulberry Ironstone Flow Blue's Best Kept Little Secret*. Horsham, Pennsylvania: self-printed, 1993.

Holdaway, Minnie. *Hollins Blue & White Printed Earthenware*. London: Morley College Ceramic Circle, 2001.

Holdaway, Minnie. "The Wares of Ralph Wedgwood." *English Ceramic Circle Transactions Vol. 12 Part 3(1986)*: 255-264.

Hughes, G. Bernard. *English and Scottish Earthenware 1660-1860*. London: Abbey Fine Arts, 1970.

Ironside, Margaret. "The Pseudo-Chinese Seal Marks" *Northern Ceramic Society Newsletter No. 86* (1992): 27-30.

Ironside, Margaret. "The Pseudo-Chinese Seal Marks" *Northern Ceramic Society Newsletter No. 89* (1993): 25-29.

Ironside, Margaret, "The Pseudo Chinese Seal Marks (31-50)" *Northern Ceramic Society Newsletter No. 95* (1994): 35-38.

Irvine, Louise. *Royal Doulton Series Ware, Vol. 1*. London: Richard Dennis, 1980.

Jenkins, Steven. m*idwinter pottery a revolution in British tableware*. Somerset, England: Richard Dennis, 1997.

Jensen, Veryl M. *The First Book of International Willow Ware China*. Myrtle Creek, Oregon: The Mail Printers, 1975.

Jones, Joan. *Minton The First 200 Years of Design and Production*. Shrewsbury, England: Swan Hill Press, 1993.

Kelly, Henry E. *Scottish Ceramics*. Atglen, Pennsylvania: Schiffer Publishing Ltd., 1999.

Kelly, Henry E. "John Thomson of Annfield" *Scottish Pottery Society Bulletin No. 35* (September 2002). 1-5.

Kinchin, Perilla. *Taking Tea with Mackintosh: The Story of Miss Cranston's Tea Rooms*. Rohnert Park, California: Pomegranate Communications, Inc., 1998.

Kovel, Ralph & Terry. *Kovels' New Dictionary of Marks*. New York: Crown Publishers, Inc., 1986.

Kowalsky, Arnold A. & Dorothy E. *Encyclopedia of Marks On American, English, and European Earthenware, Ironstone, and Stoneware 1780-1980*. Atglen, Pennsylvania: Schiffer Publishing Ltd., 1999.

Kowalsky, Arnold A. "The Alcocks: Their Earthenware, Ironstone, Stoneware and Granite Production" *Northern Ceramic Society Journal 17* (2000): 23-38.

Kowalsky, Arnold A. "The Clementson Family – A Look into Successful Marketing 1833-1916." Copyright: New York, 1994.

Lawrence, Heather. *Yorkshire Pots and Potteries*. Newton Abbot: David & Charles Ltd., 1974.

Lechler, Doris Anderson. *English Toy China*. Marietta, Ohio: Antique Publications, 1989.

Leishman, Douglas. "The Industrial Pottery, Bo'ness" *Scottish Pottery Society Bulletin No.28*: 5-9.

Levitt, Sarah. *Pountneys The Bristol Pottery at Fishponds 1905-69*. Bristol: Red Cliff Press Ltd., 1990.

Lewis, Griselda. *A Collector's History of English Pottery*. Woodbridge, Suffolk Antique Collectors' Club Ltd., 5th edition, 1999.

Little, W. L. *Staffordshire Blue*. London: B. T. Batsford Ltd., 1969, 1987.

Lockett, Terence A. *Collecting Victorian Tiles*. Woodbridge, Suffolk: Antique Collectors' Club Ltd., Reprinted 1994.

Lockett, T. A. *Davenport Pottery and Porcelain 1794-1887*. Rutland, Vermont: Charles E. Tuttle Inc., 1972.

Martin, Trevor. "Thomas Wolfe's Pearlware and other Wares at Stoke Upon Trent." *The Northern Ceramic Society Newsletter No. 84* (December 1991) 29-37.

Miller, Philip and Berthoud, Michael. *An Anthology of British Teapots*. Wingham, Kent: Micawber Publications, 1985.

Nance, E. Morton. *The Pottery & Porcelain of Swansea & Nantgarw*. London: B. T. Batsford Ltd., 1942.

Niblett, Kathy. *Dynamic Design: The British Pottery Industry 1940-1990*. Stoke on Trent: City Museum and Art Gallery, 1990.

Macdonald, Irene. "List of Scottish Potters & China Merchants Insured by the Sun Life Insurance Co." *Scottish Pottery 16th Historical Review (1994)* 6-7.

Macdonald, Irene. "Diversification and the Potters of Prestonpans" *Scottish Pottery 16th Historical Review (1994)* 65-66.

McKeown, Julie. *Burleigh, the Story of a Pottery*. Somerset, England: Richard Dennis, 2003.

Messenger, Michael. *Coalport 1795-1926*. Woodbridge, Suffolk, 1995.

Miller, Muriel M. *Collecting Royal Winton CHINTZ*. London: Francis Joseph Publications, 1996.

Mumford, Howard. "Fidele Primavesi." *Friends of Blue Bulletin 107*, April 2000, p. 10.

Otto, Doreen. "John Meir of Tunstall and the Impressed Crown." *Friends of Blue Occasional Paper Number One*, Spring 1990.

Parkin, William M. *The Earthenwares of Booths 1864-1948*. Derbyshire, England: Higham Press Ltd., 1997.

Pigot and Co., J. *Commercial Directory: Merchants, Bankers, Professional Gentlemen, Manufacturers and Traders in Durham, Northumberland, and Yorkshire*. London, 1834. Facsimile Edition, 1994.

Piña, Leslie. *Pottery Modern Wares 1920-1960*. Atglen, Pennsylvania: Schiffer Publishing Ltd., 1994.

Pomfret, Roger. "The Bleak Hill Site Cobridge". *Northern Ceramic*

Society Journal, Vol. 19 (2002), 129-162.

Posgay, Mike and Warner, Ian. *Wade Price Trends, First Edition*. Marietta, Ohio: Antique Publications, 1996.

Pountney, W. J. *Old Bristol Potteries*. Bristol: J. W. Arrowsmith Ltd., 1920.

Priestman, Geoffrey H. *An Illustrated Guide to Minton Printed Pottery 1796-1836*. Sheffield, UK: Endcliffe Press, 2001.

Pugh, Robert. *Welsh Pottery: A Towy Guide*. Bath, England: Towy Publishing, 1995.

Quintner, David Richard. *Willow! Solving the Mystery of our 200-year Love Affair with the Willow Pattern*. Ontario, Canada: General Store Publishing House, 1997.

Reilly, Robin. *Wedgwood: The New Illustrated Dictionary*. Woodbridge, Suffolk: Antique Collectors' Club, 1995.

Rinker, Harry L. *Dinnerware of the twentieth century : The Top 500 Patterns*. New York: House of Collectibles, 1997.

Roberts, Gaye Blake (editor). *True Blue Transfer-printed Earthenware*. Over Whallop, Hampshire UK: B. A. S. Printers Ltd., 1998

Rogers, Connie and Berndt, Mary Lina. *International Willow Collectors' Convention Catalogs 1993-6*. Arlington, Texas: IWC.

Rogers, Connie. *International Willow Collectors' Convention Catalogs 1997-2001*. Cincinnati, Ohio: IWC.

Sandon, Henry. *An Illustrated Guide to Worcester Porcelain 1751-1793*. New York: Praeger Publishers, Inc., 1970.

Sandon, Henry. *British Pottery and Porcelain for pleasure and investment*. London: John Gifford, Revised edition 1980.

Sandon, Henry and John. *Grainger's Worcester Porcelain*. London: Barrie & Jenkins, 1989.

Sandon, Henry. *Royal Worcester Porcelain from 1862 to the Present Day*. New York: Clarkson N. Potter, Inc. Publisher, 1973.

Serpell, David. *Collecting Carlton Ware*. London: Francis Joseph Publications, 2nd edition 1999.

Shirley, Derek. *A Guide to the Dating of Royal Worcester Porcelain Marks from 1862*. Published by D. B. Shirley, May 1999.

Shuler, Vic. *Collecting British Toby Jugs Third Edition*. London: Francis Joseph Publications, 1999.

Skinner, Deborah S. and Young, Velma. *Miles Mason Porcelain A Guide to Patterns and Shapes*. Stoke-on-Trent, England: City Museum and Art Gallery, 1992.

Shaw, J. T.(editor).*Sunderland Ware Potteries of Wearside*. County Borough of Sunderland: Public Libraries Museum & Art Gallery. (no date)

Shaw, Simeon. *History of the Staffordshire Potteries*. New York, New York: Praeger Publishers, Inc., 1970. Originally published in Hanley, England in 1829.

Smith, Alan. *The Illustrated Guide to Liverpool Herculaneum Pottery*. New York: Praeger Publishers, 1970.

Snyder, Jeffrey B. *Flow Blue A Collector's Guide to Patterns, History, and Values*. Atglen, Pennsylvania: Schiffer Publishing Ltd., 1992.

Snyder, Jeffrey B. *Historic Flow Blue*. Atglen, Pennsylvania: Schiffer Publishing Ltd., 1994.

Snyder, Jeffrey B. *A Pocket Guide to Flow Blue*. Atglen, Pennsylvania: Schiffer Publishing Ltd., 1995.

Snyder, Jeffrey B. *Romantic Staffordshire Ceramics*. Atglen, Pennsylvania: Schiffer Publishing Ltd., 1997.

Stefano, Jr., Frank. *Pictorial Souvenirs &Commemoratives of North America*. New York: E. P. Dutton & Co., Inc., 1976.

Tanner, Arleen & Grahame, "Primavesi and Family Research." *Friends of Blue Bulletin 117,* October 2002, p. 12.

Taylor, Mervin and Susan. *The Wonderful World of Booths China. A Field Guide*. Canterbury: Prontaprint, 2003.

Towner, Donald. *The Leeds Pottery*. London: Cory, Adams & Mackay, 1963.

VanBuskirk, William H., *Late Victorian Flow Blue and Other Ceramic Wares*. Atglen, Pennsylvania: Schiffer Publishing Co., 2002.

Weatherbee, Jean. *A Second Look at White Ironstone*. Lombard, Illinois: Wallace-Homestead Book Co., 1985.

Weatherbee, Jean. *White Ironstone: A Collector's Guide*. Dubuque, Iowa: Antique Trader Books, 1996.

Williams, Petra. *Flow Blue China An Aid to Identification*. Jeffersontown, Kentucky: Fountain House East, Revised Edition, 1981.

Williams, Petra. *Flow Blue China II*. Jeffersontown, Kentucky: Fountain House East, Revised Edition, 1981.

Williams, Petra, *Flow Blue China and Mulberry Ware*. Jeffersontown, Kentucky: Fountain House East, Revised Edition, 1981.

"Wood & Sons Family Tree and History" provided by P. Farley, Secretary, January 30, 2002.

Appendices
Shape Index
(Index of objects)

Index of Retailers/Importers

Index of Potters'
Initials on Mark

Most marks are printed; however, some of them are impressed.